Maple
An Introduction and Reference

Michael Kofler

 **Addison-Wesley**

Harlow, England • Reading, Massachusetts • Menlo Park, California • New York
Don Mills, Ontario • Amsterdam • Bonn • Sydney • Singapore • Tokyo • Madrid
San Juan • Milan • Mexico City • Seoul • Taipei

Pearson Education Limited
Edinburgh Gate
Harlow
Essex CM20 2JE
England

and Associated Companies throughout the world

Visit us on the World Wide Web at:
http://www.pearsoneduc.com

Cover designed by Designers and Partners, Oxford
Translated and typeset in 10/12 Times by 46
Printed and bound by Bookcraft, Bath

First printed 1997

ISBN 0-201-17899-0

British Library Cataloguing-in-Publication Data
A catalogue record for this book is available from the British Library.

10 9 8 7 6 5 4 3 2
06 05 04 03 02

Maple

An Introduction and Reference

Contents

Preface

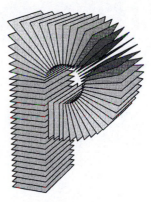

Maple is one of the most fully developed computer algebra programs currently on the market. Its correct application saves long manual calculations, which are obviously open to errors. This may well make a Maple-addict out of you, just like the author: you will end up not even dreaming of carrying out specific calculations manually. The aim of this book is to provide you with the required know-how, clearly and in a practice-oriented manner.

Maple has its own idiosyncrasies, ranging from a partly inconsistent syntax to actual errors. While working on this book, I constantly encountered examples in other books which worked correctly as shown, but which caused Maple insoluble problems as soon as the smallest detail was altered – true showcase examples. In this book, you will find no uncritical eulogies, but concrete advice as to where the limits of Maple lie and which calculations should be handled with care. I hope that this critical view of Maple, coupled with the author's enthusiasm, will help you to avoid unnecessary obstacles and frustration and thus generate the appreciation Maple fully deserves.

As a conclusion, a look into the future: in recent decades, the pocket calculator has completely transformed traditional scientific calculus. Slide rules have disappeared together with endless tables of elementary mathematical functions. Computer algebra systems, such as Maple, are now establishing themselves as tools whose use in high schools, universities and industry will shortly be as natural as today's use of pocket calculators. In this spirit, I wish you a lot of fun with this book about the 'pocket calculator of the future'!

Michael Kofler <kofler@ping.at>

April 1997

http://www.awl-he.com

XV

Structure of this book

This book is divided into three parts. Part I provides an introduction to Maple, Part II systematically describes all the main commands for standard use of Maple and Part III deals with various advanced topics.

Part I begins with an overview of what Maple can achieve. We only show that it works – not how it works. You will see that Chapter 1 does not go into details. Chapter 2 explains some important formalities in the usage of Maple and describes some elementary syntax conventions.

The titles of the next two chapters prove that the demands on the reader are not too high: *Using Maple as a pocket calculator* and *Graduating with Maple*. You may wish to use Maple in a different way. But do not be misled: easy examples will allow you to acquire a basic knowledge which you would otherwise have to learn in an abstract and theoretical way. Chapter 5 is a must for all readers, even for those who have already worked with Maple. In *Survival rules* we deal with the most frequent errors in the use of Maple.

With Part II the book becomes more systematic. In 15 relatively short chapters you learn the elementary Maple commands – from `sqrt` which calculates the square root to `plot3d` which draws three-dimensional graphics. Depending on your planned or current use of Maple, you may dispense with some of the chapters – but please note that most of the commands dealt with here belong to every Maple user's basic repertoire.

Part III is somewhat pompously called *Maple for advanced users* – but you do not have to be all that advanced to glance through any of the chapters in this part, something you should do in any case. Most chapters are completely self-contained and are based on the basic knowledge gathered in the second part. If you deal with vector analysis, if you want to use and extend Maple as a programming language, or if you want to exploit the graphical capabilities to their limits – this is where you find out how and why.

The book ends with two appendices. Appendix A briefly deals with the exchange of mathematical expressions between Maple and its competitor Mathematica. In this way, the results of mathematical transformations can be reliably proved. Appendix B provides the contents list of the enclosed CD-ROM.

Problems with Maple

Maple is often described as being an all-singing, all-dancing system, in that it is assumed to be able to solve any mathematical problems – no matter how complicated – quickly and without fuss. Many Maple books convey this impression, as they quote complex example after complex example which apparently function without a glitch. This book distances itself from such an uncritical view of Maple's capabilities. In order to use it successfully, it is very important to be aware not only of its positive features, but also of its current limitations.

The book therefore often refers to failed calculi and to the as yet insufficient development of Maple in some areas of mathematics (for example, integrals, differential equations), which means that, if the problem is not formulated absolutely correctly, the outcome will be wrong. Obviously, the majority of examples in this book are positive, for two reasons:

1. The task of a book is to describe what works and how it works, rather than whinge about what does not work.

2. Various questions arise within each problem: Is it an input error? An inadequate formulation, or a formulation which is unsuited to Maple? An error in the Windows version of Maple which might not occur at all on other computers? An error caused by insufficient memory (you do need 32 Mbytes of RAM, after all)? Lack of patience (because a calculation was aborted after 10 long minutes without results)? Or is it that Maple simply cannot solve the problem in this form?

It is easy to write about examples that work – because it is a fact that they work. But it is difficult to write about things that do not work, especially if the cause of the malfunction is not at all clear.

What you won't find in this book

- Maple exists in numerous versions for DOS, Windows, Macintosh and UNIX computers. The mathematical functions are the same in all versions, but details of usage depend on the type of computer and its operating system. For this reason, the book skims over Maple usage; the main emphasis is on mathematical commands. (An exception to this rule is Chapter 2, which provides basic information about the usage of Maple and its new worksheet concept. This chapter is based on the Windows version of Maple.)

- At present, Maple includes about 2500 commands. Many more commands can be found in various additional packages in the share library. For this reason, an exhaustive description of all commands is not provided – this would simply be impossible, for space reasons alone. This book cannot (and does not intend to) replace the original documentation and the online help.

- Finally, we have economized on longer examples. These are seldom necessary to explain the application of commands, would unnecessarily extend the book (and are of specific interest only to a restricted group of readers). If you wish to know how to apply Maple commands to the solution of more complex problems, you may consult the excellent book by Markus Hörhager (see References). The book contains a substantial collection of examples from the areas of differential and integral calculus, ordinary and partial differential equations, statistics, interpolation and equalization calculus.

Formalisms and notations

In Maple commands, most constants, such as I (imaginary unit), `exp(1)` (Euler's number) and `Pi` (cyclotomic number), are written with an initial upper case letter, others, such as `infinity`, with an initial lower case letter. The results use the common mathematical symbols and therefore we find I (upper case), π, e (lower case), and ∞.

Maple syntax sometimes differs slightly from standard mathematical conventions. Thus, `sin(x)^2` means the formula $(\sin x)^2$, whereas `sin(x^2)` stands for $\sin x^2$. Throughout this book, mathematical formulae are written in Maple syntax.

Commands and Maple inputs are set in the same typeface as this `command`. Maple output is set as mathematical formulae of the $\frac{\sin(\alpha)}{\pi}$ type. The Maple prompt > at the beginning of each command line is not shown. If space allows, the explanatory text is set in the left-hand text column, the corresponding command in the right-hand column. The example on the right-hand side shows a simple definite integral.

```
int(x^2+x^3,x=a..b);
```

$$\frac{b^4}{4} + \frac{b^3}{3} - \frac{a^4}{4} - \frac{a^3}{3}$$

Because of various internal processes in setting this book in LaTeX some formulae may not look the same as on your computer screen. For example, you may find that a fraction is displayed as such on your screen, whereas in this book the formula $(...)^{-1}$ is shown. Also, the denominator of a fraction may be written as a factor before or after the numerator, for example $\sqrt{x}\,1/2$ instead of $\frac{\sqrt{x}}{2}$. Mathematically, the results are obviously the same.

Problems with packages

Many examples in this book use commands from different packages. (You will find a short explanation of what a package is in Chapter 2.) These packages must be activated with `with(name)` before a command defined in them can be used. In the book, a `with` command is always specified with the first corresponding example (and, if needed, again in further sections), but not with *each* example. If an example does not work as expected or if it generates unexplained error messages, this may well be caused by the package not having been activated. Most frequently this problem will occur if you do not read linearly through a chapter, but enter an example from somewhere in the middle of it.

Remedy: check in the syntax summary at the end of each chapter whether one of the commands is contained in a package. Execute `with` and repeat the faulty command(s).

The same problem arises with commands that have to be activated with `readlib` (see Chapter 2) before being used. Again, refer to the syntax summary.

Part I

Getting to know Maple

The aim of the first part of this book is to facilitate your entry into the world of Maple. Unlike the other two, this part is not intended to present systematically ordered knowledge. You will find more than enough detailed information about individual commands from Part II onwards. The first five chapters, on the other hand, will simply give you a feeling for Maple, an overview of what is possible with Maple, some clarification of formal questions, hints and tips to avoid mistakes, and so on.

Chapter 1 demonstrates the capabilities of Maple, without going into too many details. Chapter 2 summarizes the most relevant formalities of Maple usage. In Chapters 3 and 4, we introduce some of the mathematical capabilities of Maple, using relatively simple calculi as examples.

A very important aspect in Chapter 4 is using several Maple commands to solve a problem. You will almost always need several commands to solve a real-life task. The main problem is how to use intermediate results as efficiently as possible (that is, without having to re-enter your data) in the subsequent calculation steps.

Chapter 5 summarizes some elementary (survival) rules for handling Maple. Even if you have already worked with Maple, you should at least glance through this chapter. Newcomers should invest more time – it is well worth it! You will find plenty of hints and tips that prevent you from committing those basic but frustrating beginners' errors.

Do not be turned off by the deceptive simplicity of the examples in Chapters 3 and 4! If you run Maple for the first time and immediately want to solve a problem with which you cannot get any further using manual calculus and traditional instruments, it is highly likely that you will fail. For such a high performance program, Maple is relatively easy to use, but such ease of use may prove insidious at first. For these reasons you should spend the first few hours (more realistically: the first two or three days) executing calculations for which you already possess indisputable results that you can use to cross-check the output from Maple.

Chapter 1

What is Maple?

A simplified answer to this question would be: a program for the execution of mathematical calculi. This minimalistic definition, however, does not do justice to Maple's actual capabilities. Maple is both a programming language (optimized for mathematical applications) and a very powerful graphical tool for the visualization of complex mathematical relations.

The following pages will provide some examples of what can be achieved with Maple. You will be able to understand these examples only to the extent of your knowledge of the underlying mathematics. The aim of this chapter is not to give you detailed knowledge, but to provide you with a general overview. For this very reason, the following pages do not include any explanation of 'how' and 'why' – be patient and wait for the following chapters, where you will find more text and fewer formulae.

Obviously, this chapter makes no claim to completeness. It simply presents the fundamental patterns of Maple application. Maple has such a large number of commands that a complete description within the framework of this book must be excluded *a priori*. The range of real-world applications of this program is even more far-reaching, since it stretches from business mathematics to physical calculi within the theory of relativity.

Calculating with Maple

Maple always tries to calculate exactly. For this reason, irreducible fractions stay as they are.

```
1/3 + 1/7;
```
$$\frac{10}{21}$$

Of course, a numerical evaluation is possible at any time and with arbitrary precision.

```
evalf(1/3 + 1/7);
```
$$0.4761904762$$

```
evalf(Pi, 50);
```
$$3.1415926535897932384626433832$$
$$7950288841971693993751$$

Maple usually makes no difference between real and complex numbers. All elementary functions are also defined for complex arguments. In Maple, the imaginary unit I is shown in upper case.

```
abs(2+3*I);
```
$$\sqrt{13}$$

```
(3+2*I)/(2-I);
```
$$4/5 + \frac{7\,I}{5}$$

Polynomials

Maple's true power lies in the fact that it can also calculate symbolically, that is, using variables such as x and y instead of concrete numerical values.

```
factor(x^4+2*x^3-12*x^2-40*x-32);
```
$$(x+2)^3\,(x-4)$$

```
expand((x-1)^4);
```
$$x^4 - 4\,x^3 + 6\,x^2 - 4\,x + 1$$

Maple is capable of performing very extensive simplifications.

```
simplify(exp(x*log(y)));
```
$$y^x$$

```
simplify(sin(x)^2+cos(x)^2);
```
$$1$$

Maple knows many rules for the simplification of trigonometrical expressions.

```
expand(cos(4*x)+4*cos(2*x)+3, trig);
```
$$8\,\cos(x)^4$$

```
combine(4*cos(x)^3, trig);
```
$$\cos(3\,x) + 3\,\cos(x)$$

Solution of equations

The solution of simple equations causes Maple no problems.

```
solve(x^2-x=5, x);
```
$$1/2 + \frac{\sqrt{21}}{2}, 1/2 - \frac{\sqrt{21}}{2}$$

Maple can also cope with equation systems.

```
glsys:={2*x + 3*y +   z = 1,
          x -   y -   z = 4,
        3*x        + 7*z = 5}:
solve(glsys);
```
$$\left\{ x = \frac{101}{41}, z = -\frac{14}{41}, y = -\frac{49}{41} \right\}$$

Complex equation systems for which no symbolic solution exists can always be solved numerically.

```
fsolve({x^2+y^2=10, x^y=2}, {x,y});
```
$$\{ x = 3.102449071, y = 0.6122170880 \}$$

Matrix calculus

Maple has many commands for the definition and manipulation of vectors and matrices. These commands are defined in a so-called
package and must be activated with `with` prior
to being used. In the example, the inverse matrix and the determinant of a are calculated.

```
with(linalg):
a:=matrix([[1,2],[3,4]]);
```

$$a := \begin{bmatrix} 1 & 2 \\ 3 & 4 \end{bmatrix}$$

```
inverse(a), det(a);
```

$$\begin{bmatrix} -2 & 1 \\ 3/2 & -1/2 \end{bmatrix}, -2$$

Calculi involving matrices are normally carried
out by means of the command `evalm`.

```
b:=matrix([[w,x],[y,z]]):
evalm(a + b);
```

$$\begin{bmatrix} 1+w & 2+x \\ 3+y & 4+z \end{bmatrix}$$

For the multiplication of matrices, the operator
`&*` has been defined.

```
evalm(a &* b);
```

$$\begin{bmatrix} w+2y & x+2z \\ 3w+4y & 3x+4z \end{bmatrix}$$

Limits, sums and products

The calculation of limits is also successful in
relatively complex cases, as shown in the second example.

```
limit((sqrt(1+x)-1)/x, x=0);
```

$$1/2$$

```
limit(x!/x^x, x=infinity);
```

$$0$$

Even when the symbolic calculation of sums or
products fails, a numerical evaluation is often
possible (second example).

```
sum(1/2^n, n=1..infinity);
```

$$1$$

```
evalf(product(1+1/x^2,
               x=1..infinity));
```

$$3.676077910$$

Differentiation and integration

The `diff` command is designed for differentiation. Often, the result can be further simplified with `simplify`. `diff` can also be used without problems for partial derivatives of multi-
variable functions.

```
simplify(diff((x-1)/(x^2+1), x));
```
$$-\frac{x^2 - 1 - 2\,x}{\left(x^2 + 1\right)^2}$$
```
diff(sin(x*y), x);
```
$$\cos(xy)y$$

With `integrate`, both general and definite integrals can be calculated (second example). For complex functions, the results become fairly long-winded.

```
integrate(1/(1+x^3), x);
```
$$\frac{\ln(x + 1)}{3} - \frac{\ln(x^2 - x + 1)}{6} + \frac{\sqrt{3}\ \arctan(\frac{(2\,x-1)\sqrt{3}}{3})}{3}$$
```
integrate(sin(x^2), x=a..b);
```
$$\sqrt{2}\ \sqrt{\pi}\ \mathrm{FresnelS}(\frac{\sqrt{2}\,b}{\sqrt{\pi}})1/2 - \sqrt{2}\ \sqrt{\pi}\ \mathrm{FresnelS}(\frac{\sqrt{2}\,a}{\sqrt{\pi}})1/2$$

Differential equations

The formulation of differential equations and side conditions is somewhat laborious. If the differential equation is not too complex, Maple rewards your efforts with the correct solution. If too few
secondary and boundary conditions are specified, Maple formulates the solution using the integration constants $\_Cn$.

```
deq:=diff(y(x),x) * y(x) * (1+x^2) = x;
```
$$deq := \left(\frac{d}{dx}y(x)\right)y(x)\left(1 + x^2\right) = x$$
```
dsolve({deq, y(0)=0}, y(x));
```
$$y(x) = -\sqrt{\ln(1 + x^2)}\,, y(x) = \sqrt{\ln(1 + x^2)}$$
```
dsolve((y(x)^2 - x)*D(y)(x) + x^2-y(x) = 0, y(x));
```
$$\frac{x^3}{3} - y(x)x + \frac{y(x)^3}{3} = \_C1$$

Series expansion

Where an exact solution of a mathematical problem is impossible, a series expansion using `series`
will often be of help.

```
series(sin(x), x=0, 10);
```

$$x - \frac{1}{6}x^3 + \frac{1}{120}x^5 - \frac{1}{5040}x^7 + \frac{1}{362880}x^9 + O\left(x^{10}\right)$$

The `dsolve` command is also capable of calculating solutions of differential equations in series form.

```
Order:=10:
deq:=diff(y(x), x$2) + diff(y(x), x) + y(x) = x+sin(x);
```

$$deq := \frac{d^2}{dx^2}y(x) + \frac{d}{dx}y(x) + y(x) = x + \sin(x)$$

```
sln1:=dsolve({deq, y(0)=0, D(y)(0)=0}, y(x), series);
```

$$sln1 := y(x) = \frac{1}{3}x^3 - \frac{1}{12}x^4 - \ldots + \frac{1}{181440}x^9 + O\left(x^{10}\right)$$

Laplace and Fourier transformations

The Laplace transformation is executed by means of the `laplace` command. `laplace` is part of the `inttrans` package. Prior to the use of `laplace`, the package must be activated with `with(inttrans)`. `invlaplace` is available for inverse transformation. After simplification with `combine`, the original function is recognizable again.

```
with(inttrans):
laplace(cos(t-a), t, s);
```

$$\frac{s\cos(a) + \sin(a)}{s^2 + 1}$$

```
invlaplace(", s, t);
```

$$\cos(a)\cos(t) + \sin(a)\sin(t)$$

```
combine(", trig);
```

$$\cos(-t + a)$$

In the example, first the rectangular impulse f is defined by the overlay of two (Heaviside) saltus functions. For $-1 < t < 1$, f yields 1, otherwise 0. At first sight, the Fourier transformation does not look like the expected result $\frac{2\sin(w)}{w}$, which Maple V Release 3 used to supply directly, but it can be suitably simplified (see Chapter 25).

```
alias(sigma=Heaviside):
f:=sigma(t+1)-sigma(t-1):
g:=simplify(fourier(f, t, w));
```

$$2\frac{I\left(\pi\operatorname{Dirac}(w)w - I\right)\sin(w)}{w}$$

Interpolation, approximation functions

The `interp` command calculates a polynomial of the order $n-1$, which leads exactly through n data points. In the following example, a curve is drawn through 10 random y values at the x positions between 1 and 10.

```
datax:=[seq(i,i=1..10)]:
datay:=[seq(rand(10)(), i=1..10)]:
dataxy:=zip((x,y)->[x,y], datax, datay):
```

$$dataxy := [[1,1],[2,0],[3,7],[4,3],[5,6],[6,8],[7,5],[8,8],[9,1],[10,9]]$$

```
f:=interp(datax, datay, x);
```

$$f := \frac{17\,x^9}{51840} - \frac{517\,x^8}{40320} + \frac{11699\,x^7}{60480} - \frac{3719\,x^6}{2880} + \frac{27323\,x^5}{17280} + \frac{176741\,x^4}{5760} - \frac{652577\,x^3}{3240} +$$

$$\frac{1816483\,x^2}{3360} - \frac{1669153\,x}{2520} + 293$$

Using a numerical procedure, `pade` calculates a rational approximation function to a given function. Apart from `pade`, various other commands are available for the numerical calculus of approximation functions.

```
with(numapprox):
x0:=solve(x^2=Pi/2)[1];
f:=pade(tan(x^2), x=x0, [3,3]):
evalf(normal(f));
```

$$\frac{-2719774873.0x^2 + 632510616.6x^3 - 675187878.0 + 3212301282.0x}{(2.0x - 2.506628274)\,(-109716870.0x^2 + 895824869.0x - 1356288866.0)}$$

Graphics

The two most versatile commands for the representation of two- and three-dimensional functions are `plot` and `plot3d`. The illustrations below give just a hint of the countless possibilities that Maple boasts for the graphical display of mathematical functions.

```
plot(sin(x)*exp(1)^(-x/5), x=0..4*Pi);
```
```
plot3d(sin(x)*exp(1)^y, x=0..2*Pi,
       y=0..Pi, axes=boxed);
```

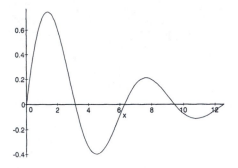

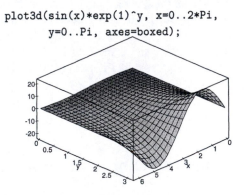

Programming

Maple is not only a system for the calculation of mathematical expressions, but a programming language in its own right. The example shows the recursive definition of the Fibonacci function.

```
f:=proc(x::nonnegint)
  option remember;
  if x=0 then 0
  elif x=1 then 1
  else f(x-1)+f(x-2) fi
end:

f(50);
```

    12586269025

Chapter 2

How to use Maple

This chapter presents a brief introduction to the practical usage of Maple. The emphasis lies less on the mathematical aspects than on details that are necessary for correct use. The chapter describes Maple's user interface (worksheet interface), the printing of documents and graphics, plus the most important syntactical conventions of Maple (special characters, handling of packages, and so on).

This chapter does not (or only marginally) deal with version-dependent peculiarities. From a mathematical/syntactical point of view, all Maple versions are equal, although there may be differences in special handling, menu structure, graphical potential, and so on. In the description of the worksheet interface, we use the keyboard shortcuts and menu commands of the Windows version of Maple V, Release 4. For different shortcuts and commands in other Maple versions, please consult the *Learning Guide* manual supplied with the Maple software.

The information contained in this chapter should be enough to start experimenting with Maple without major difficulties. Obviously, many subjects are only touched upon and will be dealt with in more depth in the following chapters:

Symbolical/numerical calculus   Chapter 3
Prevention of typical errors   Chapter 5
Variable management   Chapter 6
Elementary operators and functions   Chapter 7
User-defined functions   Chapter 8
Series, lists, sets   Chapter 11
Loading and saving of data   Chapter 29
Graphics   Chapters 19, 20, 31, 32
Hints and tips for Mathematica users Appendix A

The worksheet interface

The most important new feature of Release 4 is its totally revised user interface (worksheet interface). Maple now combines the capabilities of a simple text processing program with those of a computer algebra program. Freely definable character and paragraph formats are supported for text layout. Mathematical formulae can now also be used in normal flow text. Graphics generated with `plot` are linked directly into the Maple document and can be printed out in high definition.

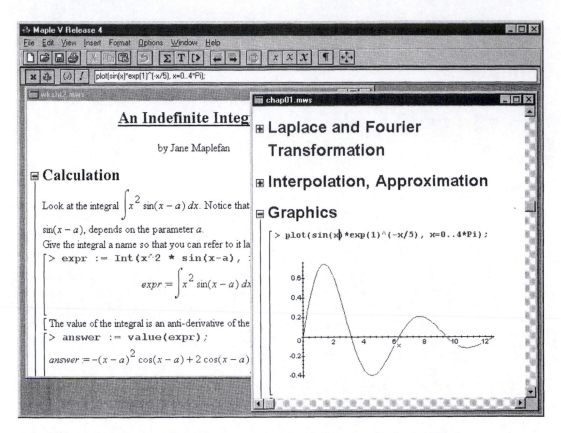

Note: The worksheet interface shows some occasional discrepancies in the Windows version we tested. On the one hand, the worksheet layout possibilities are impressive; on the other, the handling (especially via keyboard commands) still seems to be somewhat rudimentary.

The first Maple commands

After its startup, the Maple program shows the > prompt in the first line and waits for a command input. Commands must end with a semicolon and must be terminated with (←) (or with (Enter) or (Return), depending on the legend on your keyboard).

In this book, Maple commands and their results are represented in the following form:

```
2+3;
```

$$5$$

```
solve(x^2+x-1=0,x);
```

$$1/2\sqrt{5} - 1/2, -1/2 - 1/2\sqrt{5}$$

Within the worksheet (that is, the window that shows Maple commands and their results), you can move around both with the mouse and with the cursor keys. If you modify a command, you must trigger a new evaluation by pressing ⏎ – Maple does not carry out any calculations automatically by itself. If further instructions are affected by changes to a command (because they use its outcome as an intermediate result), these commands must be re-evaluated as well.

Interrupting calculations

If you want to interrupt Maple during a lengthy calculation, simply click on the STOP button in the symbol bar. (It may, however, be some time before Maple actually stops the calculation.) During a calculation, all menu commands remain available; thus, you might save the current workbook, switch to a different window, enter text, and so on.

Structuring Maple documents

A Maple command and its result constitute a group. Maple marks this group with a square bracket on the left-hand border. If several commands are present in the same group, all commands in this group are evaluated simultaneously with ⏎. (If an input is spread over several lines, Shift + ⏎ gets you onto a new line without triggering evaluation.)

Groups containing several commands can be divided into two groups with EDIT|SPLIT OR JOIN|SPLIT EXECUTION GROUP. Similarly, two groups can be joined together into a larger group with EDIT|SPLIT OR JOIN|JOIN EXECUTION GROUP.

Several groups can be joined into a section. To do this, first you mark the groups with the mouse or cursor keys, and then execute FORMAT|INDENT. Maple joins the groups with an additional square bracket. On the top of this bracket, a small button with a plus or minus sign is displayed. With this button, you can hide or show the whole section.

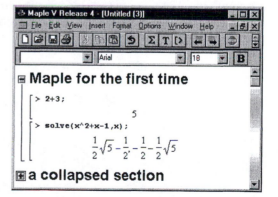

Sections can be embedded, that is, you can combine several sections into a further, higher-level section. As with groups, sections too can be split at the cursor position and joined together again, using the EDIT|SPLIT OR JOIN|SPLIT SECTION and ...|JOIN SECTION commands.

With VIEW|COLLAPSE ALL SECTIONS you can collapse all sections of a worksheet in a fairly compact and clear way. Similarly, you can expand all sections again using the VIEW|EXPAND ALL SECTIONS command.

Using text in Maple documents

Currently, worksheets only consist of Maple commands and their results. However, Maple also allows you to insert paragraphs of normal text into its documents. Thus, worksheets can contain not only mathematical formulae, but also freely formatted text. Although Maple does not offer the whole range of features of a text processing program (no footnotes, no automatic table of contents, no definable headers and footers, and so on), text can still be formatted surprisingly well.

Similarly to Word for Windows, Maple uses format templates. FORMAT|STYLES gives an overview of the predefined format templates. Each paragraph can be assigned one paragraph format. Furthermore, previously marked text passages can be highlighted with user-defined character formats. You can also modify format templates and even create new ones.

Before you can enter text (which should not be interpreted as Maple commands) you must create the space for a paragraph, using the commands INSERT|FORMAT|BEFORE or ...|AFTER. This inserts a new empty line before or after the command line of the current group. Now you can enter arbitrary text into this line. During text input, (↵) works in the same way as in a text processing program and starts a new paragraph. An evaluation of Maple commands is only possible if the line begins with >. (Text can be converted into a Maple command with FORMAT|CONVERT TO|MAPLE INPUT.)

You can also enter mathematical formulae into your text, using the normal Maple syntax for formulae. Subsequently, you mark the formula and execute FORMAT|CONVERT TO|MATH EXPRESSION. Instead of the Maple command, Maple now displays the corresponding formula. Further modification of the formula is only possible in the command input line, while the document shows the formula. (Direct editing of the formula itself is not possible.)

The illustration shows a heading (format template 'Heading 2') which contains a formula. The formula can only be edited in the command input line, where Maple syntax must be observed.

If you want formulae in the text to be evaluated by Maple (even this is possible) you must convert the formula into a Maple input. There is no menu command to do this; you have to click on the button with the green Maple symbol. This causes the formula to change colour. If you press (↵)

while the cursor is inside the formula, the corresponding Maple command is evaluated. (Like all Maple commands, it must obviously be terminated with a semicolon.)

Simultaneous processing of several Maple documents

In Maple, you can load several worksheets at a time. All worksheets are displayed in their own windows. Please note, however, that in the standard version of Maple all defined functions, variables, and so on are valid for all worksheets. If you define the variable x in one worksheet, that variable is defined for all other worksheets as well. This may have dreadful consequences. (Apart from the standard version, there are parallel versions of Maple on many computer platforms. In these versions, each worksheet is considered an independent unit. See page 29.)

When you start working on a new worksheet, it is usually a good idea to execute the `restart` command, which deletes all variable definitions and so on. Thus, Maple behaves as if it had just started up.

Cross-references to other documents

Maple documents can make use of cross-references. These may point to a different place in the same document or to another document. Cross-references are generally displayed underlined (just like they are in the online help or in World Wide Web documents).

Cross-references are entered via INSERT|HYPERLINK. In the corresponding dialog, you can specify the text of the cross-reference and its goal. Goals can be a bookmark in the current text, another Maple file or a help subject. Bookmarks must be previously defined with VIEW|BOOKMARK|EDIT.

Online help

For each command defined in Maple, there is a help text. Help can be called either via the HELP menu or the `?name` command or by pressing (F1). If the cursor is positioned inside a keyword, pressing (F1) automatically displays the corresponding help text. However, after clicking on several cross-references, the screen will be cluttered with open windows. This can be remedied by the WINDOWS|CLOSE ALL HELP command.

Some online help subjects are combinations of a main and several secondary subjects (for example, `plots,options`). In this case, the `?plot,options` or `?plot[options]` help calls must be used. Calling help via (F1) only works with the second, square bracket alternative.

When the option HELP|BALLOON HELP is ac-
tive, Maple displays speech bubbles with short
explanations for all options and menu commands. These speech bubbles are similar to
the Quickinfo texts of the Microsoft Office programs.

Internet: The Internet too is often a valuable source of information. Contributions to the discussion of problems with various computer algebra programs and their solution can be found in the
`sci.math.symbolic` newsgroup. The WWW server of Waterloo Software contains bug fixes, demo
versions and the latest updates of the `share` library (`www.maplesoft.com`), as well as their own ad-
vertising. Further cross-references can be found on the author's WWW page (for the address, see
the Preface).

Loading and saving

Maple worksheets are saved with FILE|SAVE and can be loaded again with FILE|OPEN. After
loading, Maple displays all results, so that the worksheet appears to be in the same state as when
it was saved. This appearance is deceptive! Maple has stored the worksheet as a text, and all the
variables used in the worksheet are still empty. (Unlike Release 3, Maple V Release 4 provides no
facilities for saving a worksheet together with the contents of its variables.)

In order to get the worksheet back into the state it was in before it was saved, all the
Maple commands have to be executed again. The easiest way to do this is to select
EDIT|EXECUTE|WORKSHEET.

With FILE|EXPORT|LaTeX, Maple worksheets can also be saved in LaTeX format. This allows
further processing of the worksheet with the LaTeX typesetting program. More about this later.

Printing Maple documents

Worksheet printouts are simply obtained via FILE|PRINT. With FILE|PRINT PREVIEW, you can
verify that Maple inserts page breaks at the correct points, before printing. Here are some hints and
tips on how you can improve the quality of your printouts:

- Use only black type. Blue headings, red Maple commands, and so on make working on screen
  with Maple much easier, but they are printed as shades of grey and give the impression that
  the printout is not crisp enough. (Colours are set with FORMAT|STYLES. With the MERGE
  EXISTING command, you can load the format template of another document, so that you need
  define a black-and-white template only once and can use it again any time you want.)

- In 2D graphics, use the `color=black` option. This causes all lines to be drawn in black.

- In 3D graphics, the `color=black` option only makes sense for graphics without shading. In graphics with shading, the `shading=zgreyscale` option yields the best results. (This option can be also set later via the graphics menu command COLOR|Z (GREYSHADE).)

- Before printing, turn the display of group and section brackets off (commands VIEW|SHOW GROUP RANGES and VIEW|SHOW SECTION RANGES).

- If you encounter problems with Maple's automatic page breaks, you may be annoyed by the fact that it offers no facilities for setting manual page breaks. However, this does not really matter: simply use FORMAT|STYLES to define a new paragraph format (for example, with the name *Newpage*) and select the START NEW PAGE option as its one and only format setting. Now you can simply insert a paragraph where you need a page break in your document and assign this paragraph the *Newpage* format.

Notes: Generally speaking, compared to Version 3, printing graphics directly from the worksheet interface now works correctly and produces good quality results. The only drawback is the print quality of shaded 3D graphics: the number of colours/shades is far too small to achieve a true 3D effect (comparable to the graphics in this book). High-quality printouts of 3D graphics are still only possible via PostScript files. (More about this subject on page 24.)

Unfortunately, it is still not possible to copy Maple graphics or formulae into text processing programs without great effort. Graphics are converted into bitmap format and this causes a severe loss of quality. Since Release 4, formulae can only be copied in ASCII format. In the case of graphics, the solution is to generate PostScript files within Maple and import these into text processing programs. Maple offers only one export filter for formulae, namely conversion into LaTeX format. The handling of LaTeX documents is briefly described on page 26.

Keyboard shortcuts (Windows version)

In your work with Maple, you will probably use keyboard shortcuts instead of the menu commands. The tables below summarize the most important shortcuts. These tables are valid for the Windows version of Maple, while other Maple versions may have different shortcuts.

Insertion and deletion

(↵)	execute command
(Shift)+(↵)	insert command line
(Tab)	cursor to next command
(Shift)+(Tab)	cursor to previous command

Ctrl + C	copy marked item to clipboard
Ctrl + V	paste clipboard
Ctrl + X	cut marked item and copy to clipboard
Shift + Del	cut marked item and copy to clipboard
Ctrl + Del	delete current paragraph
Ctrl + T	insert text into current line
Ctrl + M	insert Maple command or formula into current line
Ctrl + K	insert command line (new group) above
Ctrl + J	insert command line (new group) below
Shift + Ctrl + K	insert text paragraph above
Shift + Ctrl + J	insert text paragraph below

Processing groups and sections

Ctrl + .	combine several groups into a section (indent)
Ctrl + ,	dissolve section (outdent)
F3	split execution group
F4	join several marked groups
Shift + F3	split section
Shift + F4	join several sections

Miscellaneous

Ctrl + F4	close (Help) window
Shift + Ctrl + F6	switch active window
Ctrl + N	create new worksheet
Ctrl + O	open (load) worksheet
Ctrl + S	save worksheet
Ctrl + P	print worksheet
Ctrl + F	search for text within the worksheet

Syntax conventions

In order to make Maple execute a command (or a calculation), the command must be entered in a command line (recognizable by the > prompt at the beginning). The command must be terminated with a semicolon or a colon. If a colon is used, Maple executes the command, but does not display the result.

The names of functions, commands and operators are generally written in lower case, while constants are mostly in upper case. These rules obviously have their exceptions: some commands (for example, the integral command `int`) possess so-called inert versions which are written in upper case. These versions are not immediately evaluated and are often used for display purposes (the screen shows the integral sign) or for modulo calculations in which simplifications can be carried out due to the delayed evaluation. The most important exception with constants is the lower case keyword `infinity` for infinity (∞).

Arguments of commands and functions are enclosed in round brackets, such as `sin(x)` or `solve(gl,x)`. Several commands (for example `plot`) also allow options to be specified. The syntax for this is `optname=setting`. Normally, both the name of the option and the required setting have to be entered in lower case. Keywords for settings may also be written entirely in upper case; however, upper and lower case may not be mixed in the same word.

Wherever possible, Maple calculates symbolically. Thus, it does not evaluate terms such as $\sin(\pi/9)$ numerically, but lets them stand in this form. A numerical evaluation can be executed at any time by using the `evalf` function.

In the example, the square roots of 2 and 3 are evaluated numerically. However, only the square root of 2 is actually displayed.

```
evalf(sqrt(3)): evalf(sqrt(2));
```
$$1.414213562$$

Maple considers expressions separated by commas as series. For this reason, the instruction shown here is allowed. The result, however, represents one unit, not three individual results.

```
2+3,2*3,2^3;
```
$$5, 6, 8$$

The last result calculated can be accessed with `"`, the last but one with `""`, and the last but two with `"""`. Less recent results can only be used if they have been stored in variables. The `evalf` command in the example forces a numerical evaluation of the result.

```
sin(Pi/9);
```
$$\sin(\frac{\pi}{9})$$
```
evalf(");
```
$$0.3420201433$$

If a command yields several results as a series (simple enumeration), a list (ditto, but in square brackets) or a set (in braces), access to individual elements is carried out via a postfixed `[index]`. The first element has the index 1 (not 0).

```
solve(x+1/x=5,x);
```
$$5/2 + \frac{\sqrt{21}}{2}, 5/2 - \frac{\sqrt{21}}{2}$$
```
evalf("[2]);
```
$$0.208712152$$

Variables and functions

Basically, any symbol not yet in use can be used in a calculation as a variable in the sense of a placeholder for a still unknown result (see the `solve` example above).

Values or expressions can be stored in a variable by means of an assignment with := .

```
a:=3; b:=x^2;
```
$$a := 3$$
$$b := x^2$$

Please note that many commands presume that the variables used in them have not been assigned any value. The summation command can only be executed if x has no contents.

```
x:=2;
```
$$x := 2$$
```
sum(x^2, x=1..3);
     Error, (in sum) summation
     variable previously assigned,
     second argument evaluates to,
     2 = 1 .. 3
```

You can delete x by assigning the variable its own name. The name must be indicated with an acute apex '. In DOS and Windows versions, straight apices must be used instead of acutes.

```
x:='x';
```
$$x := x$$
```
sum(x^2,x=1..3);
```
$$14$$

In their simplest form, functions are defined in the same way as variables (see also Chapter 8). In the example, f is defined by a sine function. Subsequently, the integral over f from 0 to 2 is calculated.

```
f:=sin(x);
```
$$f := \sin(x)$$
```
int(f, x=0..2);
```
$$2$$

The above examples show that there is a fundamental difference between the operators := and = . := is used exclusively for assignments, that is, to store expressions or values in variables, while = is used for the formulation of equations, the specification of options and for temporary assignments within a command (such as x=1..3 in the last example).

Special characters in Maple

The following table summarizes the most important special characters used in Maple. A detailed description of the operators can be found in Chapter 7.

>	indicates a command line
;	terminates a command
:	as above, but without displaying the result
.	joining operator (a.b yields ab)
..	ranges operator (for example, for integrals and in the plot command)
!	factorial
?	calls online help
'	prevents the immediate evaluation of expressions
'	string delimiter (for example, 'filename.m')
"	accesses the last result

" "	accesses the last but one result
" " "	accesses the last but two result
:=	assignment operator (c:=3)
=	comparison operator (x^2+y^2=1)
\$	enumeration operator (x\$3 yields x, x, x)
@	concatenation operator ((a@b)(x) yields $a(b(x))$)
[ ]	identifies lists
{ }	identifies sets

Packages and libraries

In Maple, a very large number of commands are available automatically. Additionally, there are commands that must be activated by means of readlib or with, prior to being used. readlib refers to single commands (for example, poisson). with, on the other hand, activates a whole package of functions (for example, linalg which contains linear algebra functions).

As the following example shows, commands from packages can also be used without a previous with. However, for each function call, the complete function name (including the package name) must be specified – a rather time-consuming enterprise.

The array command is used to define a 2*2 matrix.

```
mat:=array([[1,2],[3,4]]);
```

$$mat := \begin{bmatrix} 1 & 2 \\ 3 & 4 \end{bmatrix}$$

As the det command for the calculation of the determinant is contained in the linalg package, the first attempt to call det is destined to fail. The calculation succeeds only after specifying the package.

```
det(mat);
```

$$\det([[1,2],[3,4]])$$

```
linalg[det](mat);
```

$$-2$$

It is easier to activate the functions of the currently needed package by means of with. While executing with, Maple issues warnings if already existing keywords are redefined. In addition, a list of all entirely new keywords is displayed. The list display can be avoided by terminating the with command with a colon instead of a semicolon.

```
with(linalg);
  Warning: new definition for norm
  Warning: new definition for trace
```

$$[BlockDiagonal, GramSchmidt, ...,$$

$$vectdim, vector]$$

det can now be used immediately.

```
det(mat);
```

$$-2$$

We will now conclude with some additional remarks: not all commands that can be used without readlib or with are contained in the Maple kernel. The names of many commands are predefined with `readlib` commands. When the command is executed for the first time, the corresponding code is loaded from the Maple library.

When you encounter problems while trying out examples from this book, one likely cause of errors may be the missing specification of the necessary `readlib` or `with` command. This can easily happen when you want to execute an example from the middle of a chapter: it may well be that the corresponding `with` command had been specified some pages earlier. The easiest way to determine whether a command is part of a package is to look at the syntax summary at the end of the chapter.

Maple provides a true programming language for the definition of commands and functions (see Chapters 28 to 30). For this reason, Maple's functionality can be simply increased by loading the program code for additional commands. In previous versions of Maple, packages existed as real files (for example, `plot.ms`). Since Release 2, all package files have been integrated into the library file `maple.lib`.

The share library

The `share` library stands for a series of additional commands, packages and sample files which are supplied together with Maple, but which are not officially part of the standard library and are not documented in the same way as other Maple commands.

The `share` library is activated by `with(share)`. Subsequently, new commands can be loaded using `readshare(name)` or `readshare(name, package)`. After loading the command(s), additional help subjects are available which contain information about the handling of the command(s).

```
with(share): readshare(Echelon, linalg);
```

See ?share and ?share, contents for information about the share library

See ?RowEchelon

This book does not contain a chapter dedicated to the `share` library. Instead, useful commands from the `share` library are described in those chapters into which they fit from a contents point of view. You will find a reference to all `share` library commands and packages dealt with in this book in the Index under `share`.

Remark: In `readshare`, correct upper and lower case spelling must be observed. Some names just begin with an upper case letter, others have to be written entirely in upper case. Chapter 30 shows how, with the additional program `march`, you can determine the entire contents of the `share` library together with the correct upper and lower case spelling of all names.

Graphics and animation

Nearly all graphics are drawn by means of the `plot` command or one of its numerous variations. Maple reacts to a `plot` command by displaying the graphics in the current window. The size of the graphics can be arbitrarily adjusted by changing the frame.

When graphics are clicked on with the mouse, both the menu and the symbol bar of Maple change: now a number of commands are available to process the graphics. In two-dimensional graphics, the position of coordinates and the line style (dotted, continuous) can be altered. Even more options are available for three-dimensional graphics: these can be rotated, recoloured, scaled, and so on. All settings can also be predefined via options in the `plot` command itself.

The illustration shows how three-dimensional graphics are displayed in a Maple worksheet. The representation of coordinates and the shading of the graphics do not correspond to the default setting, but have been chosen at a later stage by clicking on various buttons in the graphics symbol bar.

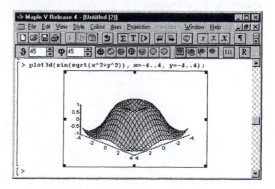

In this book, graphics are mostly represented as shown in this example, that is, with a short explanation on the left and the `plot` command and its result on the right. This example shows the use of options in the `plot` command: the sine curve is drawn as a dotted line (instead of the normal continuous line), and the legend is a rectangle (instead of the coordinate axes).

```
plot(sin(x), x=0..2*Pi, style=POINT,
     axes=BOXED);
```

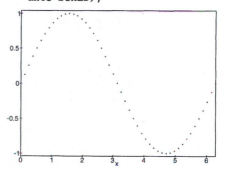

Animation

The `animate` command of the `plots` package calculates several two-dimensional graphics that differ only in one parameter. Maple provisionally displays only one of these graphics. As soon as it is clicked upon, its own menu and symbol bar appear, with which the animation can be started. Maple now projects the previously calculated images one after the other.

After starting the animation with the arrow button, the sine wave moves to the left. With the
other buttons on the animation symbol bar, projection direction and speed can be set. Also, it
is possible to toggle between a continuous and
a one-off projection of the previously calculated
animation.

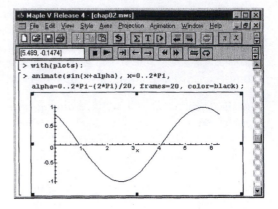

Printing graphics

Maple does not offer facilities for printing individual graphics directly. Graphics can only be printed
as components of a worksheet. (See above for information on how to print worksheets and improve
printing quality.) In some cases, this method of printing is not satisfactory: the quality of shaded
3D graphics is far from being perfect, and the export of graphics into text processing programs
is practically impossible. (In a data exchange via the clipboard, graphics are only transferred as
bitmaps.)

One way out of these problems is offered by the `plotsetup` command, which allows you to specify
that graphics are not to be displayed on screen, but stored in a file instead. (`plotsetup` is an easier-
to-handle variation of the `interface` command known from previous versions of Maple.)

By means of `plotsetup`, graphics files can be generated in different formats (such as PostScript,
HPGL, JPEG and so on). The `plot` command itself is not affected, but `plotsetup` must be executed
beforehand. The easiest way to generate a PostScript file is the following:

```
plotsetup(plotdevice=postscript, plotoutput='filename.eps'):
plot(sin(x),x=0..2*Pi);  #arbitrary graphics command
```

This causes the next `plot` command to write the drawing in PostScript format into the specified
file. When specifying the file name, please note the downward right pointing apex (graves). DOS
and Windows users must also remember to write the \ character twice when it is used to separate
directories in path names, for example `'c:\\maple\\test.eps'`. (By the way, in all versions – even
in the Windows version – the UNIX-specific / character can be used to separate directories.)

This PostScript file can now be imported into
a text processing program (Word for Windows
command INSERT|PICTURE) and printed out on
a PostScript printer. However, you will not be
very enthusiastic about the result: graphics are
rotated by 90 degrees (because Maple generates
EPS files in landscape format) and surrounded
by a relatively thick black frame. If you scale
the graphics down (as we have done with all
illustrations in this book), the legends on the
coordinate axes become illegibly small and the
graphics lines become so thin that they are practically invisible on a normal laser printer.

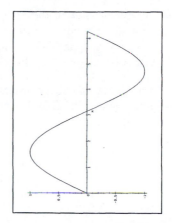

These problems can be remedied by certain options. The `portrait` option changes from landscape
to portrait format. `noborder` prevents a frame being drawn around the graphics. With `width` and
`height` graphics can be scaled to fit an arbitrary format. (In PostScript files, the unit for these
specifications is the point. 100 points correspond to about 3.5 centimetres. Although PostScript
graphics can be arbitrarily scaled, the size specification affects the final result: because text is
scaled down as well, alphabetic characters in a PostScript file that previously filled a page become
so small as to be illegible.)

```
plotsetup(plotdevice=postscript, plotoutput='filename.eps',
    plotoptions='portrait, noborder, width=350, height=260'):
plot(sin(x),x=0..2*Pi);
```

The illustration on the right shows the sine curve
after importing the generated PostScript file.
The result is still not perfect, as the bounding
box specified in the PostScript file does not exactly correspond to the actual size of the drawing.

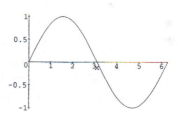

If you are not happy with the type and size of lettering in your graphics, you can specify characters
with the `font`, `axesfont` and `labelfont` options. Line details (width, dots and dashes, colour) can
also be specified with several options. These, however, must be given in the `plot` command (not in
`plotsetup`). A detailed description of these options can be found in Chapter 19.

The illustrations in this book have been generated with `plotdevice=postscript`, but without using any options. Subsequently, the illustrations have been modified using the additional program
`MaplePS`, written by the author of this book.

`MaplePS` modifies the PostScript code of `*.eps` files. Graphics are rotated from landscape to portrait
format, frames are removed, lettering types and line widths are changed, and so on. The main advan-

tage is that all the graphics in a worksheet file can easily be created using FILE|EXPORT|LaTeX. This command generates not only a LaTeX file of the current worksheet (see the following section), but also *.eps files of all graphics. The Windows version of MaplePS is included (together with its source code in Visual Basic) on the enclosed CD-ROM.

This is how the same drawing of the sine example above looks after the PostScript file has been processed by MaplePS.

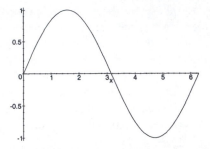

Using MaplePS is quite easy: first, you set the program options (in most cases, you can leave the default settings as they are), and then you select the required files with the TRANSFORM PLOT FILES button. You can choose more than one file at a time. As long as you have not activated the BUILD BACKUP FILES option, the program modifies the specified *.eps files without asking for further confirmation.

If you want to display your graphics again on screen, you must specify `plotdevice=inline`. However, this overwrites the last file selected (this is a bug in Maple). To prevent this from happening, you simply specify a valid file name which does not contain any data. During command execution, Maple creates an empty file with the specified name. (If this file contained data, it is deleted.)

```
plotsetup(plotdevice=inline, plotoutput='dummy.tmp'):
```

Maple and LaTeX

What is LaTeX?

LaTeX is a typesetting program (not a text processing program). It processes an ASCII text written with any text editor you like. This text contains all formatting instructions in the form of commands.

The above subheading, for example, was generated with \section{What is \LaTeX?}; the formula $\sqrt{\pi + x^2}$ is created by the character string $\sqrt{\pi+x^2}$.

LaTeX has become relatively popular for two reasons: for a long time, it was the only program that could handle mathematical formulae in a really efficient way and it is (still) available free of charge. LaTeX is widely used in the scientific world and on UNIX computers. There are also versions for DOS, Windows and the Macintosh.

Compared to modern text processing programs, the concept of LaTeX is Stone Age. Text input is carried out in an arbitrary text editor, in which you have no way of guessing what the text will look like when printed. Indeed, the text is continuously broken up by countless formatting commands and is hardly readable in this form. After the text has been input, it is processed with LaTeX. Generally, the result is a (more or less) long list of syntax errors. If after several attempts you succeed in eliminating all such errors, LaTeX produces a *.dvi file which describes the document in a printer-independent format. This file is subsequently translated into PostScript format by a conversion program and can at long last be printed.

So why use LaTeX when there are plenty of easy-to-handle sophisticated text processing programs around?

- There is no comparison between the quality of LaTeX documents and the results produced by the formula editors of Word for Windows, WordPerfect, Framemaker and so on. If you need formulae set to perfection, there is no alternative to LaTeX (other than systems such as Scientific Word, which are in fact based on LaTeX and can be considered as a type of user interface).

- Computer algebra programs such as Mathematica or Maple have one special feature: LaTeX is the only export format for formulae they support. Just try setting three or four complex formulae using a formula editor: you will immediately discover that learning LaTeX is probably the faster road to mathematical documents.

Printing worksheets as LaTeX text

The first step towards printing a worksheet as LaTeX text consists in saving the entire file as a *.tex file using FILE|EXPORT AS|LATEX. Since Release 4, Maple generates PostScript files of all graphics contained in the worksheet (landscape format, with frames). The corresponding file names consist of the name of the LaTeX file, plus a two-digit number, plus the extension .eps. The LaTeX file generated by Maple looks more or less like the following:

```
%% Created by Maple V Release 4 (IBM INTEL NT)
%% Source Worksheet: chap01.mws
%% Generated: Thu Feb 22 10:53:27 1996
\documentclass{article}
\usepackage{maple2e}
\DefineParaStyle{Heading 1}
\DefineParaStyle{Heading 2}
% and so on
```

```
\begin{document}
\begin{maplegroup}
\begin{Heading 1}
Chapter 1: Introduction
\end{Heading 1}
\end{maplegroup}
\section{Doing simple calculations}
\begin{maplegroup}
\begin{mapleinput}
\mapleinline{active}{1d}{1/3 + 1/7; }{}
\end{mapleinput}
\mapleresult
\begin{maplelatex}
\[{\displaystyle \frac {10}{21}} \]
\end{maplelatex}
\end{maplegroup}
\begin{maplegroup}
\begin{mapleinput}
\mapleinline{active}{1d}{evalf( 1/3 + 1/7); }{}
\end{mapleinput}
\mapleresult
\begin{maplelatex}
\[.4761904762\]
\end{maplelatex}
% and so on
```

As long as LaTeX is installed correctly and completely, the LaTeX file is translated into a DVI file with:

```
latex worksheetname
```

In order to carry out a successful translation, LaTeX must find the *.sty files contained in the Maple etc directory. The easiest thing to do is to copy these files into the directory in which you have saved your LaTeX file. (The *.sty files contain LaTeX macros needed for the formatting of Maple-generated text.) For correct handling of graphics, the LaTeX macro package epsfig is needed as well. This macro package is part of most LaTeX installations.

The result of the latex command is the file worksheetname.dvi. This file is now translated into PostScript format by means of a conversion program (the most popular one is dvips):

```
dvips worksheetname -o print.ps
```

Now the file print.ps can be displayed on screen using a PostScript viewer (for example, ghostview), and/or printed on any PostScript laser printer.

Note: This book has been produced using LaTeX under the Linux operating system. Linux has the advantage that not only LaTeX itself but also all necessary style files and additional programs, such as dvips and ghostview, are included in the distribution. Maple's LaTeX export mechanism has only been used for a quick conversion of the results of Maple commands into LaTeX code. LaTeX itself uses its own macros for the formatting of text (not those of the Maple `*.sty` files). All graphics PostScript files have been processed with `MaplePS` to achieve better results (see page 24). Subsequently, the `*.eps` files were imported into the LATEX text using `\epsfxsize=58mm\epsffile{name.eps}}`. Both `\epsfxxx` commands are defined in the LATEX `epsf` package.

Converting single formulae into LATEX format

If you do not want to save a whole document as a `*.tex` file, you can use the `latex` command to convert single Maple expressions. Until Release 2, this command was the only facility for converting Maple expressions and it was used several hundred times for typesetting the first (German) edition of this book.

Using this command is very simple: specify the expression to be converted as a parameter to `latex`. The example on the right shows both the character string generated by Maple and the corresponding formula generated by LATEX.

```
f:=Pi*sqrt(x+alpha/(1+x^2));
latex(");
    \pi \,\sqrt {x+{\frac {\alpha}
    {1+x^{2}}}}}
```

$$\pi \sqrt{x + \frac{\alpha}{1 + x^2}}$$

However, long-term use of `latex` has shown that the command contains several errors. The character strings generated by `latex` often do not match what is displayed on screen. For this reason, use of this command should be limited to simple formulae.

Information for advanced Maple users

Maple versions

Depending on the computer, Maple V Release 4 is available in up to three versions:

Standard version: Normally the description in this book refers to the standard version with its worksheet interface. Only *one* kernel is started for command evaluation. Therefore, variable definitions, packages, and so on are valid for *all* windows.

Parallel server version: This variation of Maple looks like the standard version. The only difference is that one kernel is started for each window. Thus, command evaluation can be carried out in parallel: while one command is executed in one window, you can switch to another window and start another command from there. On single processor computers this gives hardly any advantage, but on computers under UNIX or Windows NT which support several processors, true parallel processing can be achieved (at least theoretically).

In practice, the main difference from the standard version is that variables and functions defined in one window are completely independent of definitions in other windows. Consequently, this version uses slightly more memory than the standard version.

By the way, the parallel server version is not a program in its own right. Depending on the command option, Maple starts either in standard or in parallel mode (-km p option).

Command line version: This version of Maple has no graphical interface at all. There are no worksheets, and results (even graphics) are displayed as ASCII text. The advantage of this version is that the system requirements (available memory, speed) are much lower. Furthermore, this version can be used to execute Maple commands in batch mode (-f option). The Windows version, however, does not yet seem to be fully developed and presents substantial problems when you try to input special characters via the keyboard.

Additional information about Maple versions and command line options can be found in the cmdline.txt file in the Maple directory and in the online help text for maple.

Configuration and initialization

In the Windows version, information about the settings and options of the Maple user interface is stored in the MapleV4.ini file in the Windows directory. (For other Maple versions, please refer to the original documentation.)

During program startup, Maple reads a configuration file whose name, depending on the version, is src/init, mapleinit or something similar. On UNIX computers, the .mapleinit file of the current home directory is read as well. Under Windows, the maple.ini file is read from the current working directory. Directly after the installation of Maple, the Examples directory is considered as the working directory. If you change these settings (by changing the properties of the Maple icon in the Explorer or in the File Manager), you must also move maple.ini into the corresponding directory.

The configuration files can contain normal Maple commands which are executed when the files are read. This facility can be used to activate frequently used packages by means of with, to introduce abbreviations for frequently used commands with alias (see Chapter 6), or to preset options with interface or setoptions. Commands in the initialization file should be terminated with colons, otherwise their results are displayed in the first window opened by Maple. (A concrete application of the initialization file – changing global system variables – is shown in Chapter 30.)

File formats

Worksheets are stored in files with the extension *.mws. These files can be freely exchanged between different Maple versions (according to the online help). They contain only ASCII characters and can therefore be sent as e-mail without problems (and without previous encoding). *.mws files are incompatible with *.ms files (worksheet files from Release 3). In Release 4, *.ms files can be read. When saving, however, the new format is used automatically. Release 3 cannot read *.mws files.

Fields in which only mathematical information is stored (but no formatting data) mostly carry the *.m extension. Since Release 4, these files too are exclusively composed of ASCII characters; however, these are coded and can only be read by Maple. *.m files can be written with save and read with `read`. Although the file extension has not changed with respect to Release 3, `*.m` files in the two releases are completely incompatible with each other.

Since Release 4, files containing Maple program code carry the extension `*.mpl`. (In Release 3, no extension or `*.mp` used to be common practice.) These files are in ASCII format as well. Release 3 files can be adapted to the syntax conventions of Release 4 by running them through the additional program `Updtsrc`.

See also Chapters 28 to 30 about programming and the online help texts for `files`, `share`, `share[content]` and `share[contrib]`.

Chapter 3

Using Maple as a pocket calculator

Quite obviously, Maple is not a sensible replacement for your pocket calculator. If you simply need to add up some numbers, Maple is much too laborious. Thus, it is not our intention to get you to throw away your pocket calculator, but rather to give you a feeling for the way Maple deals with numbers/values. Several differences from the way your pocket calculator handles the same numbers will emerge. For example, Maple generally tries to avoid loss of precision by explicit calculations of mathematical terms. If you force Maple to calculate a concrete numerical value, you can specify a precision of any number of digits you wish (even 100 or 1000). In the end, though, your pocket calculator, however scientific it is, will have to give way when competing with Maple.

Fundamental operations

Maple obviously knows the fundamental operations, including factorial. Please note, however, that every input must be terminated with a semicolon and that multiplications have to be indicated explicitly with *. As the last example shows, you can also write several calculations on the same line.

```
2+3;
        5
2 3;
   syntax error:
   2 3;
     ^
2*3, 2^3, 5!;
      6, 8, 120
```

When the computer represents fractions as floating point numbers (for example, 0.83333333 instead of 5/6), a loss of precision occurs. 5/6 is 'infinitely' precise, 0.83333333 only in 8 digits after the decimal point. For this reason, Maple avoids calculating numerical results explicitly.

```
1/2;
      1/2
1/2+1/3;
      5/6
```

As you can see, this also applies to calculations with various functions.

```
sqrt(2), sin(Pi/4);
```
$$\sqrt{2}, \frac{\sqrt{2}}{2}$$

Obviously, you can always evaluate symbolic expressions such as `sqrt(2)` numerically. You can specify the desired number of digits in the second parameter of the `evalf` (evaluate floating point) function. If you do not specify this parameter, Maple calculates with a predefined precision (see below).

Please note the difference between symbolic and numeric calculations. In symbolic calculations, no rounding errors occur and Maple can employ mathematical procedures to simplify expressions.

```
evalf(sqrt(2));
```
$$1.414213562$$

```
evalf(sqrt(2), 50);
```
$$1.4142135623730950488016887242096980785696718753769$$

```
sqrt(2) * sqrt(8) - 4;
```
$$0$$

```
evalf(sqrt(2)) * evalf(sqrt(8)) -4;
```
$$-0.000000002$$

Precision

The precision of numeric calculations is determined by the system variable `Digits` and is generally 10 digits. By changing this variable, the precision can be adjusted. This influences the absolute error in numeric calculations, but not the fact that rounding errors will occur.

```
Digits;
```
$$10$$

```
Digits:=50;
```
$$Digits := 50$$

```
evalf(sqrt(2)) * evalf(sqrt(8)) -4;
```
$$-3.0 \times 10^{-49}$$

```
Digits:=10;
```
$$Digits := 10$$

`Digits` has no influence on the precision of symbolic calculations. The factorial of 100 is calculated with a precision of more than 150 digits, because Maple interprets the number 100 symbolically (that is, 'infinitely precise'). In spite of the size of this number, Maple has no reason to switch to numeric processing.

```
100!;
```
$$93326215443944152681699238856266700490715968264381621468592963895217599993229915608941463976156518286253697920827223758251185210916864000000000000000000000000$$

```
evalf(");
```
$$9.332621544 \times 10^{157}$$

The example on the right shows once again the difference between symbolic and numeric calculation. `log[2](256)` calculates the base 2 logarithm of 256. The result is, however, not simplified. If at this point you evaluate it numerically with `evalf`, a rounding error occurs. But if you ask Maple to simplify the result symbolically with `simplify`, the accurate final result is supplied.

```
lg2:=log[2](256);
```
$$lg2 := \frac{\ln(256)}{\ln(2)}$$
```
evalf(lg2);
```
$$7.999999999$$
```
simplify(lg2);
```
$$8$$

Please note that a later increase in the number of digits with `evalf(.., n)` only apparently increases the precision. Although the result of the calculation on the right has 50 digits, all figures after the tenth digit after the decimal point are wrong. The reason is that the value of the variable $sq2$ has only been calculated with 10-digit precision. Thus, no subsequent calculation involving $sq2$ can become more precise.

```
sq2:=evalf(sqrt(2));
```
$$sq2 := 1.414213562$$
```
evalf(1/sq2^2,50);
```
$$0.50000000026381803913919991547$$
$$705793946024635015556$$

Very large numbers can be written either as $n * 10^m$ or as nem. The second version has the advantage that you can sometimes save on parentheses. However, numbers in this format are mainly interpreted as floating point numbers, whereas for numbers in the $n * 10^m$ format exact (symbolic) calculation is attempted. In the examples, the time taken by a light beam to travel between the earth and the sun is calculated (in seconds).

```
149.6*10^9 / (3*10^8);
```
$$498.6666666$$
```
149.6e9 / 3e8;
```
$$498.6666667$$

Complex numbers, matrices, statistical functions

Maple does not differentiate between calculating with complex numbers and calculating with normal numbers (this only applies since Release 2; before that, `evalc` had to be called).

```
-20 * I + 200 * I / (20 + 10 * I);
```
$$4 - 12\,I$$
```
abs(4-12*I); evalf(");
```
$$4\sqrt{10}$$
$$12.64911064$$

Matrices are normally defined with the `array` command. If more than one line needs to be entered, you must press (Shift)+(↵) to advance to the next line. If an input is terminated with a colon (for example, the definition of *mat2*), Maple suppresses the display on your screen, which would otherwise be automatic.

```
mat1:=array([[1, 2, 3],
             [7,11,-3]]);
```

$$mat1 := \begin{bmatrix} 1 & 2 & 3 \\ 7 & 11 & -3 \end{bmatrix}$$

```
mat2:=array([[0,7], [-3,17],
             [5,-1]]):
```

The `evalm` command is used to calculate with matrices. In addition, there is a special operator `&*` for non-commutative matrix multiplication.

```
mat3:=evalm(mat2 &* mat1 +
       [[1,0,0],[0,1,0],[0,0,1]]);
```

$$mat3 := \begin{bmatrix} 50 & 77 & -21 \\ 116 & 182 & -60 \\ -2 & -1 & 19 \end{bmatrix}$$

Additional commands for matrix calculus can be found in the `linalg` package. This must be activated by means of `with` prior to using the functions. Two warnings indicate that the Maple commands `norm` and `trace` are redefined in `linalg`. Subsequently, the determinant and the inverse matrix can be calculated without difficulties.

```
with(linalg):
  Warning: new definition for norm
  Warning: new definition for trace
det(mat3);
```

4224

```
inverse(mat3);
```

$$\begin{bmatrix} \frac{1699}{2112} & -\frac{721}{2112} & -\frac{133}{704} \\ -\frac{521}{1056} & \frac{227}{1056} & \frac{47}{352} \\ \frac{31}{528} & -\frac{13}{528} & \frac{7}{176} \end{bmatrix}$$

Statistical functions have their own package, too. In the example below, the mean value, variance and standard deviation are calculated for a sequence of numbers.

```
with(stats): with(describe):
data:=[10.2, 9.9, 10, 9.95, 10, 10.1, 10.4, 9.3, 9.85, 10.05, 10.1];
```

$$data := [10.2, 9.9, 10, 9.95, 10, 10.1, 10.4, 9.3, 9.85, 10.05, 10.1]$$

```
mean(data);
```

9.986363636

```
variance(data);
```

.06776859503

```
sqrt(");
```

.2603240193

Chapter 4

Graduating with Maple

Simple examples are the best way to familiarize yourself with the use of Maple. Such examples have several advantages: it is relatively easy to calculate the solution manually or with a pocket calculator, so that the solution found by Maple can be checked, and most solution methods are so easy that there is no substantial time lag. (With more complex tasks, Maple may take a few minutes to complete calculating.) Also, as a rule, several solution methods are possible – thus, experimenting is well worth your while.

Obviously, the tasks in this chapter are trivial compared to the problems for which Maple is commonly employed. Nevertheless, in the next few pages you will encounter many elementary Maple commands, which you will be able to apply later to more complex problems in much the same way. Furthermore, the following examples show one particular aspect of Maple usage better than most of the later chapters concerning 'higher' mathematics: they show how several commands interact with one another. It is often not too easy to use intermediate results of one command in the next command, carry out additional corrections at a later stage, and so forth. In this chapter, you will find some hints and tips.

Explanations of Maple commands are kept as brief as possible, because all commands will be described in detail in the second part of this book.

Damped oscillation

Given:

$$f(x) := 5e^{-0.1x} sin(x)$$

Required:

- Value table and graph for $0 <= x <= 3\pi$.
- From which multiple k of π onwards is the absolute value of the amplitude y less than 0.1?

To begin with, the given function must be defined in a form that Maple can understand. Please note that the form `f(x):=..` cannot readily be used like this. (See also the notes at the end of the next example.)

```
f:=5*exp(-0.1*x)*sin(x);
```

$$f := 5\,e^{-0.1x}\,\sin(x)$$

A first visual impression of this function can be easily obtained through the `plot` command. In the first parameter of this command, you specify the function to be drawn. The second parameter contains the variable and the value range. This function is to be drawn for values of x between 0 and 3π.

`plot(f, x=0..3*Pi);`

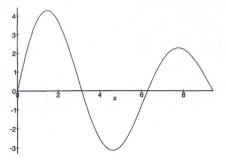

Now we want to find out from which value of x onwards (expressed as a multiple of π) the absolute value of the function becomes less than 0.1. As the sine function supplies values in the range ± 1, an analysis of the exponential function is sufficient.

The standard command for such cases is `solve`. This solves all kinds of equations and equation systems. As the following examples will show, problems can occur, but in the present case Maple immediately supplies the correct solution.

`sln:=solve(5*exp(-0.1 * x)=0.1, x);`

$$sln := 39.12023005$$

As k is required to be a multiple of π, the solution must be divided by π. However, the first attempt fails – Maple does not evaluate the division. Therefore, the `evalf` command must be employed.

`k:=sln/Pi;`

$$k := \frac{39.12023005}{\pi}$$

`k:=evalf(sln/Pi);`

$$k := 12.45235597$$

There are two ways of checking the result. One is to put the solution value in the function f. This is done by means of the `subs` command, which carries out a temporary substitution $x = sln$ without changing x permanently.

`evalf(subs(x=sln,f));`

$$0.09888191285$$

The other is to draw the function in the solution range by means of `plot`, with a vertical line drawn at $y = 0.1$ as an additional visual aid.

`plot({abs(f),0.1}, x=10*Pi..15*Pi);`

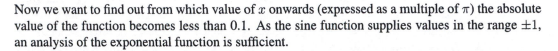

Obtaining a visually clear and structured value table is more difficult. The following four commands are a very compact introduction to the subject of sequences, lists, fields, and so on (which, initially, may be difficult to understand). These data types are used by Maple to manage and process larger amounts of data. Systematic information on this subject can be found in Chapters 11 and 12.

The function f is to be calculated for the values 0, $\pi/8$, $2\pi/8$, $3\pi/8$, and so on in the range between 0 and 3π. The first step is to generate a list with these x values. A good choice could be the seq command which puts a sequence of numbers (for example, from 0 to 24) in a function. n is used as a control variable for the sequence.

The seq instruction must be enclosed in square brackets in order to have the result returned as a list. Without these, Maple supplies the result as a sequence. However, a list is better suited for further processing.

```
data:=[seq(n*Pi/8, n=0..24)];
```

$$data := [0, \frac{\pi}{8}, \frac{\pi}{4}, \frac{3\pi}{8}, \frac{\pi}{2}, \frac{5\pi}{8}, \frac{3\pi}{4}, \frac{7\pi}{8}, \pi, \frac{9\pi}{8}, \frac{5\pi}{4}, \frac{11\pi}{8}, \frac{3\pi}{2}, \frac{13\pi}{8}, \frac{7\pi}{4}, \ldots, \frac{23\pi}{8}, 3\pi]$$

In the second step, these values are to be put in the function f. The instruction is rather complex. The subs command carries out a substitution $x = n$. The value of n is only put temporarily in x. evalf ensures that the function is evaluated into a floating point number. In seq, the range for n this time is not specified by a range in the form of start..end, but by the list just calculated above.

```
fdata:=[evalf(seq(subs(x=n,f), n=data))];
```

$$fdata := [0, 1.839733687, 3.268478238, 4.106021670, 4.273179996, \ldots, 0.7754458273, 0]$$

All numerical values required have now been calculated – now the task is to present the result in a more attractive way. For this reason, the number sequences are changed to a two-dimensional field which Maple automatically displays as a matrix. First, the two lists $[x1, x2, x3, ..]$ and $[f1, f2, f3, ..]$ must be converted into the form $[[x1, f1], [x2, f2], ..]$. This is done by means of the zip command, which applies a function to the contents of the two lists. In this case, the function is (x,y)->[x,y], whereby the required grouping into pairs of numbers is achieved.

```
zip((x,y)->[x,y], data, fdata);
```

$$[[0, 0], [\frac{\pi}{8}, 1.839733687], [\frac{\pi}{4}, 3.268478238], \ldots, [\frac{23\pi}{8}, 0.7754458273], [3\pi, 0]]$$

This interleaved list can now be converted into the required matrix notation by means of a simple `array` command.

```
array(");
```

$$\begin{bmatrix} 0 & 0 \\ \frac{\pi}{8} & 1.839733687 \\ \frac{\pi}{4} & 3.268478238 \\ \frac{3\pi}{8} & 4.106021670 \\ \vdots & \vdots \\ \frac{23\pi}{8} & 0.7754458273 \\ 3\pi & 0 \end{bmatrix}$$

Curve discussion

Given:

$$f(x) = \frac{x^2}{x^2 - 4}$$

Task:

Discuss the function f (definition range, symmetry, asymptotes, zero points, extreme values, monotony and curvature behaviour) and draw the graph for $-5 \le x \le 5$.

If you want to try out this example directly after the previous one, you should delete the definitions made up to this point. In a Maple version with a worksheet interface, this can be done by calling the menu command NEW. In all Maple versions, the `restart` command can be used.

While in the previous section the function was defined in the form `f:=..`, a different system will be used here. 'True' functions, in which an arbitrary parameter is specified postfixed in parentheses, are defined in Maple by means of the arrow operator. The parameter list (in this case, only x) is shown on the left of the arrow operator, while the function specification is placed on the right.

With `f(x)`, the function f can be used for calculations. `f(3)` calculates the function at the point $x = 3$; `f(sin(y))` would substitute the parameter x of the function specification with $\sin(y)$.

```
restart;
f:=x->x^2/(x^2-4);
```

$$f := x \mapsto \frac{x^2}{x^2 - 4}$$

```
f(3);
```

$$9/5$$

In order to get an overview of the function to be analyzed, the function is defined in the variable f and drawn by means of plot. The third parameter, -10..10, ensures that the diagram is limited to the y range ± 10. Unintentionally, Maple also draws the vertical asymptotes at the points $x = \pm 2$.

```
plot(f(x), x=-5..5,-10..10);
```

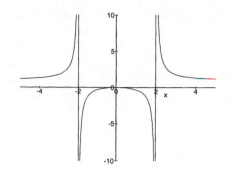

The place of the vertical asymptotes can be easily recognized from the function specification and the above diagram. However, we want to show how the asymptotes can be determined by way of calculation. The most obvious way would be the solution of the equation $f = \infty$ for the variable x. This attempt, however, fails miserably: Maple comes up with two erroneous results! (It had better not happen in your finals!)

```
s:=solve(f(x)=infinity, x);
```

$$1, -1$$

In order to avoid this problem, we choose a more convoluted solution method. The equation $f = inf$ is solved for the unknown x, where for the moment inf is a still undefined variable. For both solutions of these equations a limit value transition $inf \to \infty$ is carried out, which leads to the expected solutions $x = \pm 2$.

```
s:=solve(f(x)=inf, x);
```

$$s := \frac{2\sqrt{-\inf + \inf^2}}{1 - \inf},$$

$$-\frac{2\sqrt{-\inf + \inf^2}}{1 - \inf}$$

```
limit(s[1],inf=infinity);
```

$$-2$$

```
limit(s[2],inf=infinity);
```

$$2$$

The horizontal asymptote at $y = 1$ can be obtained either through a polynomial division by means of the quo command or through the limit value transition $x \to \infty$.

```
quo(x^2, x^2-4, x);
```

$$1$$

```
limit(f(x), x=infinity);
```

$$1$$

The evident symmetry of the curve resulting from the above diagram can be proven with solve. The equation $f(x) = f(-x)$ holds for all x.

```
solve(f(x) = f(-x));
```

$$x$$

The first derivative of the function is calculated by means of the `diff` command and stored in *f1*. In this process, the `unapply` command is worth noting. Maple needs such a command to transform the derivative $f'(x)$ calculated by `diff` into a function specification with the arrow operator. (See also the notes at the end of this section.)

```
f1:=unapply(diff(f(x),x), x);
```

$$f1 := x \mapsto \frac{2x}{x^2 - 4} - \frac{2x^3}{(x^2 - 4)^2}$$

Subsequently, the first derivative of f is drawn with `plot`. The diagram shows that f is monotonously falling for all $x < 0$.

```
plot(f1(x),x=-5..5,-10..10);
```

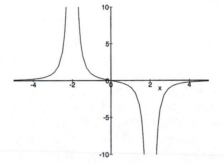

By setting the first derivative to zero, the only extreme value of f at $x = 0$ is determined by way of calculation.

```
solve(f1(x)=0, x);
```

$$0$$

The diagram of the second derivative shows that the curvature of f in the range $-2 < x < 2$ is convex (thus, $f2(x) < 0$).

```
f2:=unapply(simplify(diff(f1(x),x)),x);
```

$$f2 := x \mapsto \frac{24x^2 + 32}{(x^2 - 4)^3}$$

```
plot(f2(x),x=-5..5, -10..10);
```

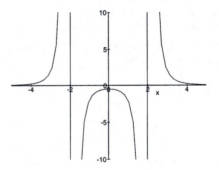

The search for inflection points only yields complex solutions, thus f has no inflection points.

```
solve(f2(x)=0,x);
```

$$\frac{2I\sqrt{3}}{3}, -\frac{2I\sqrt{3}}{3}$$

Problems with user-defined functions

The first attempt to define one's own function will probably look more or less like the one on the right.

```
f(x):=x^2/(x^2-4);
```

$$f(x) := \frac{x^2}{x^2 - 4}$$

At first sight, everything seems to work. But the attempt to use the function with parameters other than (x) is destined to fail.

```
f(x), f(0), f(y);
```

$$\frac{x^2}{x^2-4}, f(0), f(y)$$

The reason is that with the assignment `f(x):=..` Maple has stored the function specification only for the special case of 'x'. (A detailed description of what really happens here follows in Chapter 8. Please note that you can execute `f(x):=..` only if f is empty. Otherwise, you must first delete f with the assignment `f:='f';`.)

As could well be expected, Maple handbooks show a more elegant way of defining functions. A general parameter is joined to a function specification by means of the arrow operator. Through this assignment, the function rule is stored in f (and this time, as a one-parameter function, independently of 'x').

The first experiments with the function defined via the arrow operator look promising:

```
f:=x -> x^2/(x^2-4);
```

$$f := x \mapsto \frac{x^2}{x^2-4}$$

```
f(x), f(0), f(y);
```

$$\frac{x^2}{x^2-4}, 0, \frac{y^2}{y^2-4}$$

Problems occur once you actually try to calculate with f. Thus, the attempt fails to define $f1$ in the same way as f through the derivative $f'(x)$.

```
f1:=x->diff(f(x), x);
```

$$f1 := x \mapsto diff(f(x), x)$$

```
f1(0);
        Error, (in f1) wrong number
        (or type) of parameters in
        function diff
```

What went wrong? The arrow operator `->` does not evaluate the right part (that is, the function specification). The attempt to display $f1(0)$ fails because Maple first puts 0 into the term `diff(f(x), x)` and only subsequently tries to differentiate (which at this point is mathematically meaningless).

Remedy is found in the unapply command. This command converts a function of the form `f(x)` into a function specification in arrow notation: `x->f`.

```
f1:=unapply(diff(f(x),x), x);
```

$$f1 := x \mapsto \frac{2x}{x^2-4} - \frac{2x^3}{(x^2-4)^2}$$

As an alternative to true functions, you can also employ pseudo-functions as described in the first section of this chapter. Such functions are defined in the form `f:=x^2+..`, without an arrow operator. In this way, however, f is not a true function in the sense that its parameter cannot simply be specified in round parentheses.

There are two ways of putting the value 0 in the parameter x. Either x is really set to 0 by an assignment (which makes no sense, because x will remain a variable and will not become a constant) or, within f, x is substituted by 0. The command which carries out such substitutions is `subs`.

The commands on the right illustrate the rather
laborious handling of the function f. By means
of the subs command, $f(y)$ is obtained.

```
f:=x^2/(x^2-4);
```

$$f := \frac{x^2}{x^2 - 4}$$

```
subs(x=y,f);
```

$$\frac{y^2}{y^2 - 4}$$

Both kinds of functions have advantages and disadvantages and are employed depending on the
application area. True functions have the advantage that numerical values or other mathematical
expressions can be put in without the circumstantial subs command. The disadvantage is that
functions which are results of calculations can only be stored and processed further with unapply,
which can be rather annoying.

The handling of user-defined functions and the commands subs and unapply are described in detail
in Chapter 8.

Extreme value calculus 1

Given for $x > 0$:

$$f(x) := \frac{x}{8} + \frac{2}{x}$$

Task:

Draw the graph of the curve. In the area between the curve and the x axis, a width 3 strip parallel
to the y axis is to be inserted in such a way that its surface is as limited as possible. Calculate the
location of the two parallels and the resulting minimum area.

In order to solve this problem, the best thing to
do is to get a visual idea of the curve, once again
by using the plot command.

```
f:=x/8+2/x;
```

$$f := \frac{x}{8} + \frac{2}{x}$$

```
plot(f,x=0..50,0..10);
```

Now, the result of a surface integral is to be minimized, that is, the start and end points of the
integral are required. Thus, the surface is defined in a general form, that is, as an integral starting
with $x = start$ and ending with $x = start + 3$.

The use of the `int` command is nearly self-explanatory: in the first parameter, the function to be integrated is specified, in the second parameter, the integration range.

```
surface:=int(f, x=start..start+3);
```

$$surface := \frac{3\,start}{8} + \frac{9}{16} +$$
$$2\,\ln(start + 3) - 2\,\ln(start)$$

In order to determine the extremes of the surface, the function is differentiated with regard to the variable *start*.

```
dfl:=diff(surface,start);
```

$$dfl := 3/8 + \frac{2}{start + 3} - \frac{2}{start}$$

`solve` determines the solutions to $dfl = 0$. The command supplies two solutions, one of which is negative and therefore not usable.

```
sln:=solve(dfl);
```

$$sln := -3/2 + \frac{\sqrt{73}}{2}, -3/2 - \frac{\sqrt{73}}{2}$$

```
evalf(sln);
```

$$2.772001873, -5.772001873$$

Thus, the parallels required in the task run through $x = 2.77$ and $x = 5.77$. The surface can now be determined by simple substitution with the first two solution values.

```
evalf(subs(start=sln[1], surface));
```

$$3.068899118$$

Extreme value calculus 2, volume integral

Given:

A rectangle is to be drawn into the ellipse $9x^2 + 16y^2 = 144$. The surface of the rectangle is as large as possible and its sides are parallel to the coordinate axes.

Required:

a) Dimensions of the rectangle and
b) Volume of the ellipsoid and the cylinder for rotation around the x axis.

The first step towards the solution of this task is to define the equations *ellipse* and *surface*. *surface* expresses the surface of the rectangle to be maximized. The commands on the right show that variables can even store entire equations. Please note the difference between the assignment operator `:=` and the comparison operator `=`.

```
ellipse:=9*x^2+16*y^2=144;
```

$$ellipse := 9\,x^2 + 16\,y^2 = 144$$

```
surface:=a=4*x*y;
```

$$surface := a = 4\,xy$$

The next step is to represent the surface a as a function of one variable (that is, x). Thus, the common variable y must be eliminated from the two equations *ellipse* and *surface*. As no dedicated Maple command exists for this purpose, some manual work is required:

First, by means of `solve`, y is isolated in *surface*. The result is put in the ellipse equation with `subs`. The feature used for this purpose (and further purposes in the course of this task) is the command `"` which allows access to the last result calculated. The resulting equation is stored in *eqn*.

```
solve(surface, y);
```

$$\frac{a}{4\,x}$$

```
eqn:=subs(y=", ellipse);
```

$$eqn := 9\,x^2 + \frac{a^2}{x^2} = 144$$

By means of `solve`, a can now be isolated without problems. Then, the first of the two solutions of the quadratic equation is assigned to a.

```
solve(eqn,a);
```

$$3\,x\sqrt{-x^2+16}\,, -3\,x\sqrt{-x^2+16}$$

```
a:="[1];
```

$$a := 3\,x\sqrt{-x^2+16}$$

a now contains the formula for the surface depending on x. In order to maximize the surface, the derivative with respect to x must be generated and set to 0.

```
a0:=diff(a,x);
```

$$a0 := 3\,\sqrt{-x^2+16} - \frac{3\,x^2}{\sqrt{-x^2+16}}$$

`solve` supplies both possible solutions. For the remaining calculation, only the positive alternative is of interest.

```
solve(a0);
```

$$\sqrt{8}\,, -\sqrt{8}$$

Please note the formulation `max(")` in the assignment to x. `"` accesses the previous result. As this result is a sequence (that is, several expressions separated by commas), which of these results is required must be specified. `max` ensures that the greatest result is used.

```
x0:=max(");
```

$$x0 := \sqrt{8}$$

```
ellipse;
```

$$72 + 16\,y^2 = 144$$

The y value corresponding to the x coordinate can easily be determined through the ellipse equation.

```
subs(x=x0,ellipse);
solve(ellipse);
```

$$\frac{3\,\sqrt{2}}{2}\,, -\frac{3\,\sqrt{2}}{2}$$

```
y0:=max(");
```

$$y0 := \frac{3\,\sqrt{2}}{2}$$

The maximum surface of the rectangle is also already known.

```
subs(x=x0, y=y0, a);
simplify(");
```

$$6\,\sqrt{8}\,\sqrt{2}$$

$$24$$

This first part of the task could have been solved even more easily and quickly by means of the special command `extrema`. This command must first be loaded with `readlib(extrema)`. Subsequently, the command is passed the function to be optimized (in the first parameter), the limit(s) (in the second parameter), a list of variables (in the third parameter), and the name of a variable (in the fourth parameter). `extrema` then optimizes the function and writes the solution points into the specified variable. `allvalues` simplifies the mathematical description of the solution points obtained internally by Maple (see Chapter 11). As in the example above, here again negative solutions for x and y occur, which leads to four pairs of solutions.

```
readlib(extrema):
extrema(4*x*y, {9*x^2+16*y^2=144}, {x,y}, 'sln');
```

$$\{-24, 24\}$$

```
allvalues(sln,dependent);
```

$$\left\{\left\{x = 2\sqrt{2}, y = \frac{3\sqrt{2}}{2}\right\}, \left\{y = -\frac{3\sqrt{2}}{2}, x = -2\sqrt{2}\right\},\right.$$

$$\left.\left\{x = 2\sqrt{2}, y = -\frac{3\sqrt{2}}{2}\right\}, \left\{x = -2\sqrt{2}, y = \frac{3\sqrt{2}}{2}\right\}\right\}$$

As a next step, in the second part of the task the volume generated by rotation of the ellipse and the rectangle around the y axis is to be calculated. In order to get a better idea of the task and to determine the integral boundaries, the ellipse is drawn.

Implicit functions are drawn with the `implicitplot` command. This command must first be made available by activating the `plots` package by means of `with`.

```
with(plots):
implicitplot(ellipse, x=-5..5,y=-5..5);
```

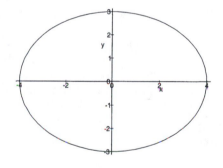

We need the y function of the ellipse in order to calculate the integral. This is again determined with `solve` and stored in f. `"[1]` accesses the first partial result of the solution set.

```
solve(ellipse,y);
```

$$\frac{3\sqrt{-x^2+16}}{4}, -\frac{3\sqrt{-x^2+16}}{4}$$

```
f:="[1];
```

$$f := \frac{3\sqrt{-x^2+16}}{4}$$

Now, the calculation of the volume integral of the ellipse causes no problems. The calculation of the cylinder volume is even easier by means of the formula $y0^2\pi 2x0$, where we use the values determined above.

```
ellvol:=Pi * int(y^2,x=-4..4);
```

$$ellvol := 48\pi$$

```
zylvol:=y0^2* Pi *2*x0
```

$$zylvol := 18\sqrt{2}\pi$$

Calculating with complex numbers

Task:

Find the solution in **C** (the set of complex numbers) and show the solution graphically:

a) $z^3 = \frac{(3+4I)^5}{(4-3I)^2}$

b) $z^2 + 4z + 13 = 0$

c) $z^2 + (5+5i)z - 24 + 40i = 0$

Such equations are no problem for Maple and can be solved immediately by means of `solve`. With `evalf`, the symbolic solution can be evaluated numerically. The second parameter of this function specifies the required number of digits (in this case, only five digits, in order to keep the result easy to read).

```
solve(z^3=(3+4*I)^5/(4-3*I)^2);
```

$$3/2 + 2I + \frac{\sqrt{3}\sqrt{7-24I}}{2}, 3/2 + 2I - \frac{\sqrt{3}\sqrt{7-24I}}{2}, -3-4I$$

```
sol:=evalf(",5);
```

$$sol := 4.9642 - 0.5982I, -1.9642 + 4.5982I, -3.0 - 4.0I$$

Since Release 4, the graphical representation of the solution points is no longer a problem. The new command `complexplot` from the `plots` package is capable of outputting the solution directly in graphical form.

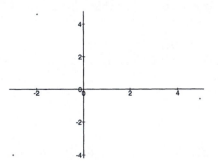

```
with(plots):
complexplot([sol], style=point);
```

Subtasks b) and c) can be solved as easily; no graphical representation needs to be shown.

```
sln:=evalf(solve(z^2+4*z+13=0),5);
```

$$sln := -2.0 + 3.0I, -2.0 - 3.0I$$

```
sln:=evalf(solve(z^2+(5+5*I)*z-24+40*I), 5);
```

$$sln := 3.0 - 5.0I, -8.0$$

Converting parametric equations into explicit form

Task:

Convert the function $x = 2\cos(t)$, $y = \cos(3t)$ into explicit form and draw the graph. Determine the area of the surfaces enclosed between the curve and the x axis.

The function can be drawn immediately (that is, without previously converting it into explicit form). The `plot` command must simply be formulated differently. Instead of the usual form `plot(f,x=..)`, parametric functions must be specified as a list (enclosed in square brackets): `[x, y, t=..]`. For unknown functions, the value range for t will possibly have to be determined by trial and error.

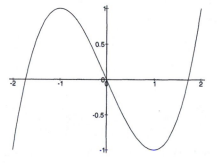

```
plot([2 * cos(t), cos(3*t),
      t=0..Pi]);
```

In order to convert the function into explicit form, the variable t must be eliminated from both equations for x and y. Unfortunately, `solve` is not suited for this purpose: if the equation system is specified in the first parameter and the two variables x and y in the second parameter (as unknowns to be determined), Maple sees no reason to process the equations any further, because solutions already exist both for x and for y. Please note that equation systems and variable lists must be passed to `solve` as sets (enclosed in braces).

```
solve({x=2*cos(t), y=cos(3*t)}, {x, y});
```

$$\{x = 2\cos(t), y = \cos(3\,t)\}$$

If, on the other hand, only one variable is specified, Maple answers with the empty set, which means that it is overstretched (or that no solution exists).

```
solve({x=2*cos(t), y=cos(3*t)}, x);
```

The command with the promising name `eliminate`, which prior to being used must be activated with `readlib(eliminate)`, is also a disappointment.

In this situation, only manual calculation with some Maple support will help. With `expand`, $y = \cos(3t)$ is converted into a simpler form. `expand` is normally used to multiply out products and transform them into sums with simpler terms. In trigonometrical functions, `expand` tries to simplify the function arguments (here, $3t$).

```
y:=cos(3*t);
```

$$y := \cos(3\,t)$$

```
expand(y);
```

$$4\cos(t)^3 - 3\cos(t)$$

With the `subs` command already known from the previous examples, $\cos(t)$ is substituted with $x/2$ – this relation is given by the first parametric equation of the task. Once again, " is used to access the result of the last calculation.

```
y:=subs(cos(t)=x/2, ");
```

$$y := \frac{x^3}{2} - \frac{3x}{2}$$

Now, y is present as a function of x. The result is checked via a `plot` command.

```
plot(y,x=-2..2);
```

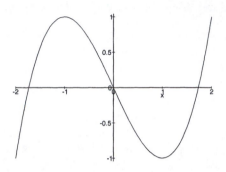

In order to calculate the surface integral of the function, we must first determine the integration boundaries, that is, the intersection points of the function with the x axis.

```
solve(y);
```

$$0, \sqrt{3}, -\sqrt{3}$$

Subsequently, the integration is carried out with the `int` command. As an integration between $-\sqrt{3}$ and $\sqrt{3}$ would yield 0, the integration is only carried out over one half. Then, the result is multiplied by 2.

```
2*int(y,x=-sqrt(3)..0);
```

$$9/4$$

Numeric solution of a transcendental equation

Task:

How deeply will a cylindrical aluminium tube (wall thickness $d = 1$ cm, external radius $2R = 60$ cm, $\rho = 2.7$ g/cm³) immerse into water?

Hint: After geometrical determination of the first approximation value, the resulting transcendental equation is solved with five-digit precision by using a pocket calculator.

The idea for the solution looks like this: the weight of the tube must be equated to the weight of the displaced water. The calculation is carried out for a tube length of 1 cm, so that the tube length is cancelled out. (It has, indeed, no influence on the result – the longer the tube, the more water is displaced.)

In order to calculate the weight of the displaced water (the specific weight of water being approximately 1), *water_weight* uses the circular equation $y = \sqrt{30^2 - x^2}$. The factor 2 in front of the integral is necessary because the integral is calculated only from 0 to the positive root, whereas it should actually reach from the negative root to the positive one.

```
tube_weight:=(30^2-29^2)*Pi*2.7; evalf(");
```

$$tube\_weight := 159.3\pi$$

$$500.4557098$$

```
water_weight:=2*int(sqrt(30^2-x^2), x=-30..-30+depth);
```

$$water\_weight := -30\sqrt{-depth^2 + 60\,depth} + \sqrt{-depth^2 + 60\,depth}\,depth +$$

$$900\,\arcsin(-1 + \frac{depth}{30}) + 450\,\pi$$

The illustration on the right shows the weight of the displaced water over the immersion depth of the tube. The weight of the tube is approximately 500 g/cm, so that the resulting immersion depth will be somewhere around 15 cm.

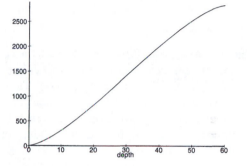

```
plot(water_weight, depth=0..60);
```

In the first attempt, `solve` is used to calculate the exact depth. As the task itself suggests that there is no exact (symbolic) solution, it is not very surprising that `solve` does not find a solution.

```
solve(water_weight=tube_weight);
```

A second attempt to calculate the immersion depth is now carried out with `fsolve`. This variation of `solve` is specially optimized for numerical solution methods and supplies the correct result.

```
fsolve(water_weight=tube_weight);
```

$$13.98139860$$

```
evalf(subs(depth=", water_weight));
```

$$500.3847589$$

Rectangular intersection between circle and quadratic curve

Task:

The circle $x^2 + y^2 + 6y - 91 = 0$ and the curve $y = ax^2 + b$ intersect in $P(6, y > 0)$ under an angle of 90 degrees. Calculate a and b.

To begin with, a brief description of the solution method: in order to determine the two unknowns a and b, two equations are required. One equation immediately results from inserting the coordinates of the intersection point (which is determined by the circular equation). The second equation is arranged over the slope. In order to achieve a rectangular intersection, the slopes of both curves must be negatively reciprocal to each other at the point of intersection.

The example shows that Maple itself has no problems with the underlying mathematics, whereas the user has some difficulties in formulating the problem in a way which is suitable for Maple.

As a first step, the intersection point of the two curves is to be determined. $x = 6$ is known from the specification of the task, thus y can be immediately calculated by means of the circular equation. However, the first attempt with `solve` fails. The command does not seem to be able to calculate the solution.

```
circle:=x^2+y^2+6*y-91=0:
curve:= y=a*x^2+b:
solve({circle, x=6}, y);
```

After some experimenting, the reason for the erroneous behaviour will emerge. $x = 6$ has been specified in `solve` as a second equation. Thus, from Maple's viewpoint, we have two equations with two unknowns. `solve`, however, can only determine a solution for both unknowns, but not an isolated solution for y.

```
slncir:=solve({circle, x=6},{x,y});
```
$$slncir := \{x = 6, y = -11\},$$
$$\{x = 6, y = 5\}$$

The problem would not have occurred, if in `solve` we had specified no second parameter at all (then `solve` would have automatically solved the equation system for all unknowns), or if instead of specifying the second equation, we had substituted $x = 6$ directly in the circular equation. Both alternatives are shown on the right.

```
solve({circle, x=6});
```
$$\{x = 6, y = -11\}, \{x = 6, y = 5\}$$
```
solve(subs(x=6, circle), y);
```
$$5, -11$$

The next surprising result emerges when trying to differentiate the circular equation partially with respect to x. As Maple is not in a position to know that y is dependent on x, it simplifies $\frac{dy}{dx}$ to 0.

```
dcircle:=diff(circle,x);
```
$$dcircle := 2\,x = 0$$

In this case too the remedy will be found by experimenting. If, instead of y, the expression $y(x)$ is written in the circular equation, Maple recognizes the dependence on x and differentiates as required. (Since Release 4, the new `implicitdiff` command can be used as an alternative – see Chapter 16.)

Since the continuous spelling out of $y(x)$ in the course of this calculation would become too laborious, we use `alias` to define y as an abbreviation of $y(x)$. Subsequently, the two equations *circle* and *curve* must be entered again, as they are still stored with the old definition of y.

```
alias(y=y(x)):
circle:=x^2+y^2+6*y-91=0:
curve:=y=a*x^2+b:
dcircle:=diff(circle,x);
```
$$dcircle := 2\,x + 2\,y\frac{d}{dx}y + 6\,\frac{d}{dx}y = 0$$

The above equation expresses the relation between $\frac{dy}{dx}$ (that is, the slope of the circular curve) and x. The equation is resolved with respect to $\frac{dy}{dx}$ by means of `solve`. Subsequently, an attempt is made to insert the intersection point $(6, 5)$ calculated above, using `subs`. The result, however, looks unusual.

The reason is that *slncir* was still calculated with y, whereas in *dcircle* the `alias` definition $y(x)$ was used. It is therefore necessary to recalculate *slncir*. Subsequently, the slope of the circle at point $(6, 5)$ can be calculated without further problems.

In the next step, the derivation of *curve* is generated. By equating the right side of the equation *dcurve* with the negative reciprocal value of the slope calculated above, an equation can be arranged for the unknown a. By inserting $x = 6$, the value of a can be calculated as 1/9.

Now, only b remains to be calculated. The point of departure is the equation of *curve*, in which the known values for a, x and y are inserted with `subs`. Once again, the first attempt fails:

The reason for the strange result: `subs` carries out the substitutions one after the other. Therefore, $y(x) \rightarrow y(6)$, but subsequently Maple no longer recognizes the substitution of $y(x)$ with 5. The remedy is to enclose the substitution rules in square brackets or in braces – then Maple carries out all three substitutions simultaneously. Thus, $b = 1$ is calculated too.

The values of the calculated solutions are stored in a and b in order to be able to draw the required curve.

```
slndy:=solve(dcircle, diff(y,x));
```
$$slndy := -\frac{2\,x}{2\,y + 6}$$
```
slope:=subs(slncir[2], slndy);
```
$$-\frac{12}{2\,5(6) + 6}$$
```
slncir:=solve({circle, x=6});
```
$$slncir := \{y = -11, x = 6\},$$
$$\{y = 5, x = 6\}$$
```
slope:=subs(slncir[2], slndy);
```
$$slope := -3/4$$
```
dcurve:=diff(curve,x);
```
$$dcurve := \frac{d}{dx}y = 2\,ax$$
```
eqa:=-1/slope=rhs(dcurve);
```
$$eqa := 4/3 = 2\,ax$$
```
solve(subs(x=6, eqa), a);
```
$$1/9$$

```
curve;
```
$$y = ax^2 + b$$
```
solve(subs(a=1/9, x=6, y=5,
          curve), b);
```
$$y(6) - 4$$
```
solve(subs({a=1/9, x=6, y=5},
          curve), b);
```
$$1$$

```
a:=1/9: b:=1: curve;
```
$$y = \frac{x^2}{9} + 1$$

The `plot` command is well suited for drawing curves whose functions are known explicitly, but not for the graphical representation of implicit equations. For this special case, the `plots` package contains the special command `implicitplot`. The package is activated by means of `with`. In its first parameter, the command is passed the equations to be drawn as a set, in the two following parameters the required x and y range. The attempt to draw the two curves, however, results in an error message.

```
with(plots):
implicitplot({circle,curve}, x=-10..10,y=-15..10);
    Error, (in plot/iplot2d) bad range arguments, x = -10 .. 10, y = -15 .. 10
```

The reason is the `alias` instruction above, with which y was defined as a function of x. In its second parameter, `implicitplot` seems to accept only true variables. Here, a further `alias` command helps, which converts y back into its original state. The option `scaling=constrained` ensures that Maple does not distort the drawing as usual (in order to fill the maximum available space), but that the circle really appears as a circle and not as an ellipse.

```
alias(y=y):
implicitplot({circle,curve}, x=-10..10,
    y=-15..10, scaling=constrained);
```

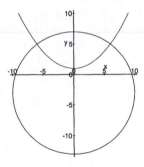

Vector calculus, circumcircle to a triangle

Task:

Given the triangle ABC with $A(-8,0)$, $B(2,2)$ and $C(2,-10)$, determine the equation of the circle Ci through the corner points.

The three points A, B and C are defined as lists (square brackets) under the names $p1$, $p2$ and $p3$.

```
p1:=[-8, 0]:  p2:=[2, 2]:  p3:= [2,-10]: p1,p2,p3;
```

$$[-8,0],[2,2],[2,-10]$$

The circular equation with the required centre point coordinates cx and cy and the also unknown radius rad are given as follows:

```
circle:=(x-cx)^2 + (y-cy)^2 = rad^2;
```

$$circle := (x - cx)^2 + (y - cy)^2 = rad^2$$

In order to determine the three unknowns cx, cy and rad, three equations are required. These result from inserting $p1$ to $p3$ in the circular equation. The substitution command for $p1$ is easily understandable:

```
subs(x=p1[1], y=p1[2], circle);
```

$$(-8 - cx)^2 + cy^2 = rad^2$$

x is substituted by the first list element in $p1$, y by the second list element. Obviously, the above instruction could also be typed in for $p2$ and $p3$ analogously; however, the following command is much more elegant:

```
seq(subs(x=p.i[1], y=p.i[2], circle), i=1..3);
```

$$(-8 - cx)^2 + cy^2 = rad^2, \ (2 - cx)^2 + (2 - cy)^2 = rad^2,$$
$$(2 - cx)^2 + (-10 - cy)^2 = rad^2$$

This executes the substitution three times in a row. A new feature is the notation `p.i`. Maple substitutes i with the values 1 to 3 and subsequently joins p and the figures into the variable names $p1$ to $p3$. Thus, the point operator serves to join compound variable names. Now, the three equations above are still to be solved – no problem for `solve`:

```
solve({"});
```

$$\{cx = -2, \ cy = -4, \ rad = 2\,\mathrm{RootOf}(\_Z^2 - 13)\}$$

```
allvalues(");
```

$$\{cx = -2, \ cy = -4, \ rad = 2\sqrt{13}\}, \ \{cx = -2, \ cy = -4, \ rad = -2\sqrt{13}\}$$

Alternative solution using the geometry package

The above example can be solved much more efficiently (although didactically less clearly) with the aid of the `geometry` package. This package contains a number of commands for two-dimensional vector calculus, such as `point` for defining coordinate points, `triangle` for defining triangles and `circle` for defining circles. Since `circle` can automatically form the circular equation from the positions of the three points, the example is reduced to a few instructions:

```
restart: with(geometry):
point(A, -8,0), point(B, 2,2), point(C, 2,-10):
triangle(Tr, [A,B,C]):
circle(Ci, [A, B, C]):
coordinates(center(Ci));
```

$$[2, -4]$$

```
radius(Ci);
```

$$\sqrt{52}$$

What makes the `geometry` package particularly
attractive is the possibility of drawing the previously defined graphical objects without much
effort:

```
draw([Tr, Ci], scaling=constrained,
  axes=normal);
```

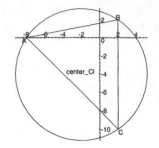

Vector calculus, sphere–straight line intersection

Given:

– Sphere $k : x^2 + y^2 + z^2 = 45$ and
– Straight line g through the points $P1(9, -15, 18)$ and $P2(-3, 15, -6)$.

Required:

– Intersection points of the straight line g with the sphere k,
– Equation of the two tangent planes on the sphere in the intersection points and
– Equation of the line of section of the two tangent planes.

To start with, we again try to arrange the problem into some easy-to-handle equations. The
equation of the sphere is given anyway, and the equations of the straight lines in the form
point + directionvector can also be easily arranged for the three components x, y and z. The
sets of equations are united by means of `union`.

```
sphere:=x^2+y^2+z^2=45;
```

$$sphere := x^2 + y^2 + z^2 = 45$$

```
straight_line:={x=9-12*t, y=-15+30*t, z=18-24*t};
```

$$straight\_line := \{z = 18 - 24\,t, y = -15 + 30\,t, x = 9 - 12\,t\}$$

```
eqsys:=straight_line union {sphere};
```

$$eqsys := \left\{ z = 18 - 24\,t, y = -15 + 30\,t, x^2 + y^2 + z^2 = 45, x = 9 - 12\,t \right\}$$

`solve` solves the equation system at the first attempt, so the two intersection points of the straight
line with the sphere are known. Next, the tangent planes are to be determined. The most suitable
formulation is the Hesse normal form (HNF), that is, using the normal vectors of the tangent planes.
As the sphere lies in the coordinate origin, the normal vectors are identical to the vectors to both
intersection points. With `subs`, the vectors can be formulated with minimum typing effort.

```
sln:=solve(eqsys);
```

$$sln := \left\{z = 6, y = 0, x = 3, t = 1/2\right\}, \left\{z = 2/3, y = \frac{20}{3}, x = 1/3, t = \frac{13}{18}\right\}$$

```
n1:=subs(sln[1], [x,y,z]);
```

$$n1 := [3, 0, 6]$$

```
n2:=subs(sln[2], [x,y,z]);
```

$$n2 := [1/3, \frac{20}{3}, 2/3]$$

To continue the calculation, we need some commands from the `linalg` package which must be activated by means of `with`. The package contains many functions for vector and matrix calculus. During the loading of the function definitions of this package, some warning messages are displayed, but these are of no consequence in the present context.

```
with(linalg):
    Warning: new definition for    norm
    Warning: new definition for    trace
```

The following two commands, which set up the equations for the tangent planes, are not very easy to understand. The description is given from the inside outwards: `normalize` forms a vector normalized to length 1 out of *n1*. With `dotprod` this is multiplied by the vector $[xyz] - n1$ (scalar product). The result is set to 0 and simplified by means of `simplify`. It corresponds to the HNF $\frac{\vec{n}\cdot(\vec{x}-\vec{n})}{|\vec{n}|} = 0$. Please note that Maple can execute more complex vector calculations only with the `evalm` command (see Chapter 14).

```
plane1:=simplify(dotprod(normalize(n1) , [x,y,z]-n1)=0);
```

$$plane1 := \frac{\sqrt{5}\,(x - 15 + 2\,z)}{5} = 0$$

```
plane2:=simplify(dotprod(normalize(n2) , [x,y,z]-n2)=0);
```

$$plane2 := \frac{\sqrt{5}\,(x - 135 + 20\,y + 2\,z)}{45} = 0$$

In order to establish the intersection line of the two planes, first one intersection point is calculated, with its z coordinate arbitrarily set to 0. (There are infinitely many intersection points and the solution becomes unique only by choosing $z = 0$.) Via `subs`, the solution is stored as a vector in p.

```
solve({plane1,plane2,z=0});
```

$$\{z = 0, x = 15, y = 6\}$$

```
p:=subs(", [x,y,z]);
```

$$p := [15, 6, 0]$$

Now, one point of the intersection line is known, that is, $(15, 6, 0)$. The direction of the line can be determined very simply: it must be at right angles to both *n1* and *n2* (otherwise it would not run on the corresponding tangent planes). Thus, the directional vector can be uniquely determined by the cross product of *n1* and *n2*.

```
direc:=crossprod(n1,n2);
```

$$direc := [-40, 0, 20]$$

The only problem that remains is to formulate the intersection line equation in a mathematically usable form. One possibility would be a vector notation, but this is difficult to use in further calculations.

```
intersec_line:=evalm([x,y,z] = p + r * direc);
```

$$intersec\_line := [x, y, z] = [15 - 40\,r, 6, 20\,r]$$

The `equate` command from the `student` package allows easy formulation of a set of equations (in the same form used for the above line).

```
with(student):
intersec_line:=equate([x,y,z], evalm(p+r*direc));
```

$$intersec\_line := \{x = 15 - 40\,r, z = 20\,r, y = 6\}$$

Simulation

Task:

The cars C1 and C2 are each travelling at a speed of 126 km/h, with a distance of 12 m between them. After 3 seconds C1 brakes with a deceleration of 6 m/s^2; after a further second, C2 too brakes with a deceleration of 8 m/s^2. Determine the equations of the movements and generate a graphical representation. Interpret the mathematical analysis of the outcome.

In order to formulate the speed progression of the two cars mathematically, the sigma function is required (unit step function). This function yields 0 for x values less than 0 and 1 for x values greater equal 0. In Maple, this function is available under the name `Heaviside`. Since typing this name over and over again can be tiresome, we use `alias` to define an abbreviation – the function can now be called under the shorter name of `sigma`.

The illustration on the right shows the progression of the sigma function. The option `axes=frame` prevents the coordinates from being drawn through (0,0) – otherwise, you would not see much of the step function.

```
alias(sigma=Heaviside):
plot(sigma(x), x=-1..1, axes=frame);
```

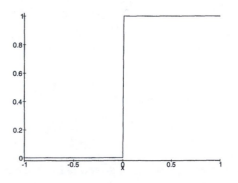

Now, the speed functions can be defined and drawn without problems:

```
v0:=126*1000/3600:
v1:=v0-6*(t-3)*sigma(t-3);
v2:=v0-8*(t-4)*sigma(t-4);
```

$$v1 := 35 - 6\,(t-3)\,\sigma(t-3)$$

$$v2 := 35 - 8\,(t-4)\,\sigma(t-4)$$

```
plot({v1,v2}, t=0..10,0..40);
```

Obviously, the functions $v1$ and $v2$ do not exactly reproduce a real-life situation. For a very large t, the speed becomes negative, which you would hardly expect when actually braking. However, for an analysis of this near accident (as will shortly become evident), the definition of $v1$ and $v2$ is sufficient.

The location of both cars can be determined by the integral over the speed. (The simple formula $s = v\,t$ is not admissible here, as v is not constant.) In the integral command, the upper integration boundary is set to $t1$. Thus, the result is a function of this variable and specifies the distance covered up to this point in time. In $s1$, the initial distance between the two cars is taken into account.

```
s1:=12+int(v1,t=0..t1);
```

$$s1 := -3/2 + 44\,t1 + 9\,t1\,\mathrm{signum}(t1-3) - \frac{27\,\mathrm{signum}(t1-3)}{2} - \frac{3\,t1^2\mathrm{signum}(t1-3)}{2} - \frac{3\,t1^2}{2}$$

```
s2:=int(v2,t=0..t1);
```

$$s2 := 51\,t1 + 16\,t1\,\mathrm{signum}(t1-4) - 32\,\mathrm{signum}(t1-4) - 32 - 2\,t1^2\mathrm{signum}(t1-4) - 2\,t1^2$$

A first impression of the course of the accident is given by the illustration on the right which shows the location of both cars at each point in time. The illustration suggests that car 2 managed to avoid 'crashing' because of its superior braking power.

```
plot({s1,s2}, t1=0..8);
```

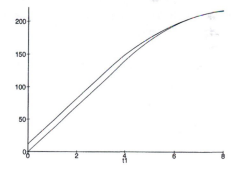

As the illustrations do not allow an accurate analysis of the 'accident', we need to do some more calculations. First, we want to determine the moments in time where the two cars come to a standstill. As could be expected, solve is overstretched with the signum functions. At the first attempt, however, even fsolve fails. The manual will show that, in an additional parameter, the command can be provided with the range of the expected solution.

```
solve(v1=0, t);
fsolve(v1=0, t);
t11:=fsolve(v1=0,t, {t=5..10});
```

$$t11 := 8.833333333$$

```
t12:=fsolve(v2=0,t, {t=5..10});
```

$$t12 := 8.375000000$$

Next, we determine the position for each car at each specific moment in time $t11$ and $t12$. The result tells us that there is a distance of two and a half metres between them.

```
subs(t1=t11,s1);
```

$$270.1250 - 51.04167\mathrm{signum}(5.833333)$$

```
eval(");
```

$$219.0833333$$

```
eval(subs(t1=t12,s2));
```

$$216.5625000$$

It would still be interesting to find out what happened before. Did the two cars come into contact while braking? For this, fsolve determined the point of 7.0 seconds after the start of the braking process. An insertion of the result in $v1$ and $v2$ reveals that at this point in time, both cars were travelling at exactly the same speed. As the second car enjoys superior braking power, from this point onwards, the distance between the cars increases again.

```
fsolve(s1=s2,t1,{t1=6..10});
```

$$7.0$$

```
eval(subs(t=7, v1));
```

$$11$$

```
eval(subs(t=7, v2));
```

$$11$$

Finally, we want to generate a table with the entries *Time* and *distance between the cars* for the critical lapse of time $6 \leq t \leq 8$.

```
s:=seq([t1,s1-s2],
       t1 = seq(i/10.,i=60..80));
```

$$s := [6.0, 1.0], [6.100000000, 0.8100000],$$

$$..., [8.0, 1.0]$$

```
s:=evalf(s, 5);
```

$$s := [6.0, 1.0], [6.1000, 0.81000],$$

$$..., [8.0, 1.0]$$

```
array([s]);
```

$$\begin{bmatrix}
6.0 & 1.0 \\
6.1000 & 0.81000 \\
6.2000 & 0.64000 \\
6.3000 & 0.49000 \\
6.4000 & 0.36000 \\
6.5000 & 0.25000 \\
6.6000 & 0.16000 \\
6.7000 & 0.090000 \\
6.8000 & 0.040000 \\
6.9000 & 0.010000 \\
7.0 & 0 \\
7.1000 & 0.010000 \\
7.2000 & 0.040000 \\
7.3000 & 0.090000 \\
7.4000 & 0.16000 \\
7.5000 & 0.25000 \\
7.6000 & 0.36000 \\
7.7000 & 0.49000 \\
7.8000 & 0.64000 \\
7.9000 & 0.81000 \\
8.0 & 1.0
\end{bmatrix}$$

Chapter 5

Survival rules for handling Maple

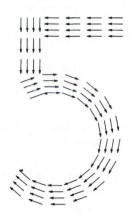

This chapter offers some basic hints and tips about how to avoid typical mistakes (especially while you are getting acquainted with Maple). Even if you have already been working with Maple for a while, reading this chapter will be useful.

This chapter may be perceived as being almost redundant: on the one hand, some of the problems described here have already been dealt with in previous chapters. On the other hand, most of the subjects mentioned here are picked up again later in the book and explained with more comprehensive background information. It should therefore come as no surprise if in some examples you encounter new commands you have not met yet.

The aim of this chapter is not to impart detailed knowledge, but rather to point out frequently occurring problems, possible misunderstandings and syntactical subtleties. This chapter should therefore be seen as a compact summary of information which will be found again, scattered throughout the entire book.

How to employ the symbols , ; : correctly

Maple input is normally terminated by a semicolon and ⟨Return⟩. Maple then evaluates the input, carries out the calculation(s) and displays the result(s).

Instead of the semicolon, you may also put a colon at the end of a command. In this case, the calculation is carried out as above, but the result is not displayed on screen. Use of the colon prevents commands which are only executed as intermediate steps from producing page after page of formulae which (at an intermediate stage) are of no interest at all. However, the undisplayed result can still be accessed as normal, using " (see the next section).

You may formulate several commands on one line. These commands can be separated either by semicolons or by colons. The results are displayed on different lines for each command (but, obviously, only for commands terminated with a semicolon).

In principle, it is also possible to separate several calculations (but not variable assignments) with commas. Maple executes these calculations one after the other, but supplies the result as a unit (that is, a sequence). For short results, this method has the advantage that it saves space and allows direct comparison of the results (on one line).

In this context, the opposite situation should be mentioned as well, that is, when a command goes over several lines. In this case, you advance to the next line with (Shift)+(Return), without starting the calculation.

To conclude, some examples: first, a normal calculation whose result is displayed (;). Subsequently, two variable assignments are carried out and the display of their new values on screen is suppressed (:).

```
2+3;
    5
a:=3: b:=5:
```

The three calculations $ab, a + b$ and a^b are first formulated as a sequence (,); the result is a unit and is displayed on one line. For comparison, the same calculations are separated with ; into three independent commands.

```
a*b, a+b, a^b;
    15, 8, 243
a*b; a+b; a^b;
    15

    8

    243
```

How to access partial results correctly

The results of the three previous calculations (no matter whether these results are displayed on screen or suppressed with :) can be accessed by means of the symbols ", "" and """ . Please note that where you input a new command does not impact on the " symbols. " refers to the result calculated most recently in time. If, after the last calculation, you move the cursor to a different location in your worksheet, " will not correspond to the result of the command above the cursor position.

The example on the right shows an elegant formulation of a transformation, that is, visually clear and not involving much typing: the expression to be simplified is first formulated as an expression using :. In the second command, the (invisible) result is accessed twice, once with a transformation command and once without.

```
(a+b)^3: " = expand(");
    (a + b)^3 = a^3 + 3 a^2 b + 3 ab^2 + b^3
```

You have to be careful when using the " symbols. If, in two commands, you want to access the last result, you must refer to it with " in the first command and with "" in the second command. If, during input of a command, you make a logical (not a syntactical) error and you want to execute the command again (in its modified version), you must change " into "" as well. On the whole, there is a substantial risk of errors in the use of " symbols. It is much more sensible to store intermediate results in variables which can be accessed as often as you like (not only three times).

In the example on the right, both solutions of a second degree equation are calculated with `solve`. In order to allow easy access to the result in the subsequent examples, it is stored in the variable *sln*.

```
solve(x^2+x-1,x);
```
$$1/2\sqrt{5} - 1/2, -1/2 - 1/2\sqrt{5}$$

```
sln:=";
```
$$sln := 1/2\sqrt{5} - 1/2, -1/2 - 1/2\sqrt{5}$$

Things become slightly more fraught if you only want to process a part of the result. This occurs quite frequently with commands such as `solve`, which supplies more than one result as a solution. Mostly, only one result (often the positive one) is of interest.

There are several ways of accessing the positive solution: `sln[1]` accesses the first element of the sequence of results. In principle, this works fine, but problems may arise if the worksheet is evaluated again later: the sequence of results of `solve` is not fixed and the second time `solve` may well first return the smaller solution, then the greater one. For this reason, `max(sln)` (which determines the solution with the greater value) is a safer alternative. However, `max` only functions if the sequence of results can be determined, that is, if the solution contains no variables.

```
x1:=sln[1];
```
$$x1 := 1/2\sqrt{5} - 1/2$$

```
x1:=max(sln);
```
$$x1 := 1/2\sqrt{5} - 1/2$$

Occasionally, Maple may supply a rather long formula as a result, but you may wish to process only part of this formula. Access via " does not help, as " always refers to the whole expression. Since Release 4, the easiest solution to this problem is to highlight the relevant part of the formula with the mouse, copy it with CTRL+C, and insert it into the input line for the new command with CTRL+V. Maple automatically converts the formula into command syntax.

The disadvantage of this method is that it cannot be reconstructed. If at a later stage you change an initial variable of your calculation, re-evaluation will lead to a different intermediate result. Copying and inserting a part of the formula would again have to be carried out manually. For this reason, Maple offers several commands which allow you to determine single components of more complex expressions – for example, `op`, `remove` or `select`. Commands for the elaboration of complex expressions are described in Chapters 10, 12 and 28.

Another example: the formula on the right contains a sin term which we want to remove because it becomes negligible for large values of x. To achieve this, `remove` is used. (Please note, however, that `remove` often fails with more complex expressions and manual re-editing becomes unavoidable.)

```
expr:=1+diff(sin(x)/x^2, x);
```
$$expr := 1 + \frac{\cos(x)}{x^2} - \frac{2\sin(x)}{x^3}$$

```
remove(has, expr, sin);
(1+cos(x)/x^2)^(1/2);
```
$$1 + \frac{\cos(x)}{x^2}$$

How to distinguish between different types of quote

Maple has two types of quote: left quotes ' (acute) and right quotes ' (grave). Left quotes (which in this book are generally just called quotes) occur relatively often. They delay the evaluation of a mathematical expression. Right quotes are used to identify strings of characters. They are most frequently employed in file name specifications and when quoting variable or procedure names that contain Maple-specific special characters.

The application of quotes is one of the most bewildering syntactic peculiarities of Maple. Especially in complex compound instructions, correctly placed quotes are often the key determinant between syntactically correct and erroneous or non-executable expressions. Thus, it is essential that you become fully acquainted with the use of quotes. You will find several examples in the following two survival rules and in the next chapter, which deals extensively with the peculiarities of variable management.

Delaying evaluation using left quotes ' (acutes)

Normally, Maple evaluates mathematical expressions immediately. If x contains the symbol π and you enter $\mathtt{sin(x/2)}$, Maple immediately replaces the variable x with π, that is, immediately evaluates the expression x. In some situations, this is not desirable.

Typical applications of left quotes are delayed assignments, the specification of a return parameter into which a command should store a result and the formulation of embedded expressions which are syntactically correct only if given variables are initialized with numerical values before the expression is evaluated. Two simple examples will illustrate this:

In Maple, a variable is deleted by assigning it its own name. Thus, immediate evaluation of this name must be prevented and this is achieved through the use of left quotes.

```
x:=3: x;
```
$$x := 3$$
```
x:='x': x;
```
$$x := x$$

Through the use of left quotes, the function f is defined independently of the current value of x. Only when f is actually called is x replaced by its current value.

```
f:='x^2-7';
```
$$f := x^2 - 7$$

Warning: In the Windows version, you must enter straight quotes instead of left quotes. (Unlike most other operating systems, Windows knows three kinds of quote: straight, left and right quotes.)

Identification of character strings through right quotes ' (grave)

At first sight, it looks as though right quotes have the same effect as left quotes:

```
x:=3:
'x+1';
```

$$x + 1$$

```
'x+1';
```

$$'x+1'$$

Only when you force evaluation of the resulting expressions with `eval` does the difference become evident.

```
eval('x+1');
```

$$4$$

```
eval('x+1');
```

$$x+1$$

For Maple, the characters enclosed in right quotes are no longer mathematical expressions, but strings of characters. Evaluation is not delayed, but has become completely impossible. Therefore, character strings are never used to specify or store mathematical expressions, but only file or variable names.

In the example on the right, the variable *test/option* is assigned the value 3. *test/option* contains a fraction stroke and can therefore be used as a variable name only if the whole expression is identified as a character string.

```
'test/option':=3;
```

$$test/option := 3$$

In the second example, all variables defined in the Maple session up to this point are stored in the file `session.tst`. In Maple, the dot is interpreted as a special character for joining symbols, which accounts for the need to enclose the file name in right quotes in order to define it as one character string.

```
save 'session.tst';
```

How to account for the global validity of variables

In Maple, problems frequently occur because already initialized variables are used in places where empty symbols are needed as placeholders for unknown or variable expressions.

In the course of a calculation, x has been assigned $\sqrt{3}$. For this reason, the attempt to solve an equation in x later on fails. Before attempting to solve the equation, Maple substitutes x with $\sqrt{3}$; after this, there is no unknown quantity left in the equation. The problem can easily be solved by deleting x – subsequently, `solve` will work again.

```
x:=sqrt(3);
```
$$x := \sqrt{3}$$
```
solve(x^2+3*x+6, x);
    Error (in solve) a constant is
    invalid as a variable, 3^(1/2)
x:='x';
```
$$x := x$$

Often enough, value assignments of the `x:=`... kind are only carried out in order to evaluate a function. For this purpose, however, Maple offers substitution mechanisms which prevent permanent assignment: for example, `subs` temporarily substitutes a variable with a value (see right). x, however, still remains a variable. Function specifications are further useful features (see further below).

```
f:=x^2+5*x;
```
$$f := x^2 + 5\,x$$
```
subs(x=sqrt(3), f);
```
$$3 + 5\,\sqrt{3}$$
```
x;
```
$$x$$

How to distinguish between direct and delayed assignments

In Maple, variable assignments are usually executed immediately. As a consequence, modifications do not affect other variables retroactively. An example:

The variable x stores the value 4. y is assigned the contents of x, z the contents of y.

```
x:=4; y:=x; z:=y;
```
$$x := 4$$
$$y := 4$$
$$z := 4$$

If x now gets modified, this no longer affects y and z at all!

```
x:=3;
```
$$x := 3$$
```
z;
```
$$4$$

Such a procedure can easily be followed and is, in most cases, also the most efficient solution, but it may occasionally be useful to carry out delayed assignments which are only evaluated when the variables are actually needed. In order to achieve this in Maple, you must enclose the right-hand side of an assignment in left quotes. These quotes delay evaluation. When you enter `y:='x'`, Maple stores the symbol x in y. The quotes are removed, but x is not evaluated, unlike a normal assignment. Thus, y points to x (as opposed to the above example, where y simply had the contents 4).

The commands on the right show delayed assignments involving the variables x, y and z.

```
x:=5; y:='x'; z:='y';
```

$$x := 5$$

$$y := x$$

$$z := y$$

Only when z is actually needed (for example, to output its contents, as in the command on the right), is an evaluation performed: z points to y, thus y is evaluated too. y points to x, and x has the value 5.

```
z;
```

$$5$$

Now, the modification of x retroactively affects z as well!

```
x:=6;
```

$$x := 6$$

```
z;
```

$$6$$

How to get the syntax right when defining functions

Maple has quite an unusual syntax for the definition of user-defined functions:

```
name:=(var)->function specification;
```

If you want to define the function $f(x)$ as $x^2 + 3x + 5$, you must enter the command shown on the right.

```
f:=(x)->x^2+3*x+5;
```

$$f := x \mapsto x^2 + 3x + 5$$

By entering f(expression) you substitute x with the expression:

```
f(sin(y));
```

$$\sin(y)^2 + 3\sin(y) + 5$$

Another way of defining functions is the immediate assignment of the function specification, that is, f:=func or f:='func'. Both variations have the disadvantage that the variables occurring in the functions cannot be specified as function parameters, but can only be set through direct assignment or through subs.

The obvious formulation f(x):=func for a function definition does not lead to an error message, but, on the other hand, does not have the intended effect either. On the contrary, the function is stored as the result of f which applies every time $f(x)$ is used. This function, however, cannot be accessed via $f(y)$, $f(1)$, $f(\sin(z))$, and so on.

Further information about user-defined functions can be found in Chapter 8, which also describes how to define recursive functions.

How to distinguish between sequences, lists and sets

In Maple, three data types occur frequently which look very similar to each other, but which actually enjoy entirely different properties: sequences, lists and sets.

All expressions that are simply separated by commas are considered *sequences*. The example on the right shows the use of a sequence in both input and output (in the result of `solve`).

```
sin(Pi/3), sin(Pi/2);
```

$$\frac{\sqrt{3}}{2}, 1$$

```
solve(x^2+x=1, x);
```

$$-1/2 + \frac{\sqrt{5}}{2}, -1/2 - \frac{\sqrt{5}}{2}$$

Sets look like sequences enclosed in braces. Actually, the differences go deeper: in sets, elements that occur more than once are automatically eliminated and, furthermore, Maple seems to change the sequence of elements arbitrarily. For this reason, sets can only be used where the sequence of elements plays no role.

In practice, sets are mostly used when several expressions have to be passed to a command – for example, several equations to `solve`, in order to solve the resulting equation system, or several functions to `plot`, in order to draw the relevant graphs. Maple too sometimes returns results as sets.

```
solve({x^2+y^2=13,x^2-y^2=5},
        {x,y});
```

$$\{y = 2, x = 3\},$$

$$\{y = 2, x = -3\},$$

$$\{y = -2, x = 3\},$$

$$\{y = -2, x = -3\}$$

Lists look like sequences in square brackets. The difference from sets is that the sequence of elements is not changed and elements are not removed. The difference from sequences is that lists can be embedded (that is, an element can contain a sublist) and that a certain number of commands can handle lists, but not sequences.

In the example on the right, a list of four elements is defined. Subsequently, the root is extracted for each element in the list and the mean value of the roots is calculated.

```
l1:=[1, 2, 3, 4];
```

$$l1 := [1, 2, 3, 4]$$

```
l2:=map(sqrt, l1);
```

$$l2 := [1, \sqrt{2}, \sqrt{3}, 2]$$

```
sum(l2[i], i=1..4) / nops(l2);
```

$$3/4 + \frac{\sqrt{2}}{4} + \frac{\sqrt{3}}{4}$$

The handling of sequences, lists and sets is described in detail in Chapter 12. All Maple users who also work with Mathematica should remember that lists and sets must not be confused. (In Mathematica, lists are formulated with {}; sets in the sense of Maple do not exist.) The example below shows where confusion between [] and {} can lead.

The intention was to construct a table in which the numbers from 1 to 4 are stored together with their square roots. The first command uses sets, which made $\{1, 1\}$ become $\{1\}$ and $\{4, 2\}$ become $\{2, 4\}$. Only a formulation using lists leads to the desired result.

```
seq({i, sqrt(i)}, i=1..4);
```

$$\{1\}, \left\{2, \sqrt{2}\right\}, \left\{3, \sqrt{3}\right\}, \{2, 4\}$$

```
seq([i, sqrt(i)], i=1..5);
```

$$[1, 1], \left[2, \sqrt{2}\right], \left[3, \sqrt{3}\right], [4, 2]$$

How to distinguish between symbolic and numeric calculations

Maple clearly distinguishes between symbolic and numeric calculations. Normally, Maple tries to calculate symbolically: this is why expressions such as π, $\sqrt{2}$ or $\tan(1)$ simply remain in this form. Symbolic calculations are 'infinitely' exact; no rounding errors can occur.

Maple calculates numerically when it is explicitly asked for a floating point evaluation with `evalf`, `fsolve`, and so on, or if a floating point number occurs in an expression $(1.5, 1e-5)$. This second point can become critical, because Maple distinguishes between 1.5 and $3/2$ or between $1e-5$ and 10^{-5}, although – from a mathematical point of view – the terms are equivalent. The precision of numerical calculations does not depend on how many digits you type in, but on the system variable `Digits` which sets the number of digits.

Obviously, there are also situations in which a numerical calculation is required. For example, the inversion of a large matrix can be calculated much faster numerically than symbolically.

Some commands, such as `limit` for calculation of limits or `int` for integration, exist in two versions, a symbolic one and a numeric one. If you want to calculate purely numerically, the correct way is to write `evalf(Int(..))`, that is, with an upper case initial in `Int`, `Limit`, and so on. Through these upper case initials, you use the so-called inert versions of the commands whose evaluation is delayed in the same way as with quotes. If you use `evalf(int(..))` instead, Maple first calculates the integral as far as possible and then evaluates the result numerically.

Chapter 3 contains a number of examples that show the difference between numeric and symbolic calculations.

And, finally, do not take Maple results on trust

Maple is often seen as a universal program that solves all mathematical problems – no matter how complicated – quickly and without problems. This is an illusion, for several reasons:

- In the first instance, because of its very general approach, Maple is a relatively slow program. It is therefore not suitable for specific problems for which dedicated, specially optimized programs have been developed. Such applications range from the calculation of Mandelbrot and fractal graphics to signal processing and the execution of finite element analyses.

- Secondly, the mathematical possibilities of Maple are limited. When you ask Maple to solve an equation system with `solve` and Maple does not return a solution, there are three possibilities: either you have formulated the equation system incorrectly (or in a manner not suited to Maple's requirements), or the equation system actually defies solution, or – for whatever reasons – Maple is unable to find an existing solution.

- Thirdly, just like any other program, Maple is not fault free. Errors in Maple results can be due to a variety of causes: actual programming errors in the Maple code, mathematical special cases and exceptions not yet dealt with, a simplification prohibited under unfavourable conditions, unsolved ambiguities (for example, both signs of a root, periodicity of trigonometric functions, and so on).

Therefore you should always look at Maple results with a certain degree of scepticism. The better your knowledge of the underlying mathematics, the higher the probability of detecting such errors and possibly finding an alternative formulation for which Maple supplies the correct result. Plausibility checks, attempting to calculate results in a different way and numerical control of symbolic results should become second nature when executing critical calculations!

The following examples are not intended to scare you off calculating with Maple, but rather to shed some light on the actual limitations of Maple (other computer algebra programs generate the same or different errors). They are, however, meant to warn you to be cautious. Though Maple may generate 99 correct results, you cannot be absolutely sure that the hundredth result will be correct as well!

In the example on the right, Maple is asked to calculate the integral over $1/x^2$ for $x = 0$ to infinity numerically. The result Maple supplies is 2, although this integral yields ∞. As the second example shows, when calculating symbolically, Maple arrives at the correct result.

```
evalf(Limit(Int(1/x^2,
  x=n..infinity), n=0)); #incorrect
```

$$2.0$$

```
int(1/x^2, x=0..infinity); #correct
```

$$\infty$$

The second example too shows weaknesses in the `int` command: the integral along the circle with radius 1 over the complex function $1/z$ incorrectly yields the value 0. The integrand could, however, be simplified without problems; if this simplification is forced with `simplify`, the result is correct.

```
z:=cos(t) + I*sin(t): dz:=diff(z,t):
f:=1/z: f*dz;
```

$$\frac{-\sin(t) + \sqrt{-1}\cos(t)}{\cos(t) + \sqrt{-1}\sin(t)}$$

```
int(f * dz, t=0..2*Pi); #incorrect
```

$$0$$

```
simplify(f*dz); #correct
```

$$I$$

```
int(simplify(f * dz), t=0..2*Pi);
```

$$2I\pi$$

Integration problems are also caused by the following function:

```
f:=1/(1-x+x^4);
```

$$f := \frac{1}{1 - x + x^4}$$

```
plot(f,x=-5..5);
```

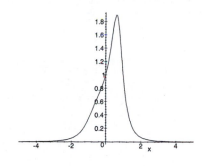

Maple yields an incorrect result for the symbolic integral from $-\infty$ to ∞. A symbolic result can be calculated (which is not listed here) through a modification of the integration limits. The numerical evaluation then yields the correct result, as would a purely numerical calculation or an evaluation of the integral for the range between -100 and 100.

```
int(f,x=-infinity..infinity);
```

$$0$$

```
int(f,x=-infinity..0)+
  int(f,x=0..infinity): evalf(");
```

$$2.683548244$$

```
evalf(Int(f,x=-infinity..infinity));
```

$$2.683548244$$

```
evalf(int(f,x=-100..100));
```

$$2.683547578$$

The last example shows that even `solve` can produce incorrect results when the problem is formulated in a unsuitable manner: the intention was to find those values for x for which f tends to ∞. An immediate evaluation with `solve` leads to two incorrect results. If, however, the equation is first solved for a temporary variable and then a limit value transition is carried out, the solution is correct.

```
f:=x^2/(x^2-4);
```

$$f := \frac{x^2}{x^2 - 4}$$

```
solve(f=infinity,x); #incorrect
```

$$1, -1$$

```
s:=solve(f=inf, x);
```

$$s := \frac{2\sqrt{-\inf + \inf^2}}{1 - \inf},$$

$$-\frac{2\sqrt{-\inf + \inf^2}}{1 - \inf}$$

```
limit(s[1],inf=infinity),
limit(s[2],inf=infinity);
```

$$2, -2$$

Part II

Maple in practice

This part of the book represents a systematic introduction to working with Maple. The first four chapters (*Variable management*, *Constants, operators and functions*, *User-defined functions*, *Complex numbers*) do not entirely fulfil the claim to illustrate practical Maple applications, but the fundamental knowledge you will acquire will prove essential for any further use of Maple. The same applies to Chapters 12 and 13 (lists, arrays, tables).

The remaining chapters are more practice-oriented. Chapter 10 describes processing and simplification of mathematical expressions. Computer algebra programs – and Maple is no exception – tend to present their results as endless mathematical formulae. Thus, the simplification of such expressions is one of the most important (and probably most difficult) tasks the program has to solve, with intensive aid from the user.

Chapter 11 deals with symbolic and numeric solutions of equations and systems of equations. From Chapter 14 onward, things become more specific: you learn commands for vector and matrix calculus, for the calculation of sums, products and limits, for differentiation and integration and for the solution of differential equations. Chapters 19 and 20 contain a comprehensive introduction to the handling of Maple's graphics commands.

In all chapters we have tried to accommodate as many examples as possible, as well as making them as practical as possible. Apart from detailed information on the syntax of each command, you will also find hints and tips on how to avoid typical mistakes. Most chapters conclude with a syntax summary, so that you do not have to leaf through the whole chapter if you simply need to look up some details (such as order of parameters or names of options).

Chapter 6

Variable management

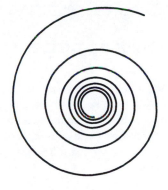

This chapter covers all the subtle points concerning the handling of variables: assignment (direct or delayed), substitution, deletion, specification of additional features, and so on. The following are some of the operators and commands dealt with in the course of the chapter:

`:=`   `:=',..'`

is used to assign variables. Delayed assignment can be achieved by enclosing the assigned expression in quotes.

`assign`

is an occasionally needed variation of the `:=` operator.

`subs`

carries out a temporary variable substitution. This allows evaluation of mathematical expressions without permanently changing the variables used in them.

`assume`

stores additional features of a variable, for example, `assume(a>0)`. Some Maple commands use this additional information (for example, for integrating).

`alias` and `macro`

represent two ways of defining abbreviations.

`restart`

deletes all defined variables, functions, packages, macros, abbreviations, and so on. Thus, Maple behaves as though it had a new startup.

`.` or `cat`

concatenates two or more characters (and/or strings) into a variable name.

Reference: You will find a list of predefined system constants together with hints and tips about how to define your own variables in the next chapter. The advantage of constants as opposed to variables is that involuntary assignments of new values are impossible.

Handling variables

Variables, in the sense of mathematical placeholders for still unknown expressions, are symbols which have not yet been assigned a value (expression, meaning). Usually, however, we still talk about variables (in the sense of a programming language) when symbols have been assigned a fixed expression. For example, even after the assignment x:=5, x is still considered a variable. However, once an assignment has been made, many commands can no longer be executed (see the example below).

The contents of a not yet assigned variable ('empty symbol') are taken to be the name of that variable. Thus, the contents of the above variable x would be 5, whereas the contents of the not yet used variable y would be the character string 'y'. Not only can variables store numerical values, but also arbitrary mathematical expressions, functions, whole programs, lists, matrices, equation systems, and so on.

Variable names are arbitrary character strings which begin with a letter. In principle, the underscore character is allowed as a first character too, but since Maple uses such variables internally as global variables for a variety of purposes, it is better not to use them. The subsequent characters may also include digits and the underscore _ (but not foreign language special characters, such as umlauts, accented letters, and so on, mathematical operators and the dot). If you want to construct variable names including special characters, you must enclose the whole variable name in right quotes – then all characters are allowed. Maple distinguishes between upper and lower case! Since Release 3, predefined keywords are protected against accidental assignment.

After all this theory, we continue with some examples. Our departure point is a freshly started Maple session, that is, the symbols x, sln, and so on, are not yet defined.

```
sln:=solve(x^2-5*x+6=0, x);
```

$$sln := 3, 2$$

The above command was used to determine the solution of the quadratic equation $x^2 - 5x + 6 = 0$. The two values 2 and 3 were stored in the variable sln. x is a not yet occupied symbol (a free variable) and has not been modified by solve.

Please note the difference between := for the assignment of the result in sln and = for the formulation of the equation! The following assignment stores the first result of the solution in x.

```
x:=sln[1];
```

$$x := 3$$

Now, x is no longer a free variable and cannot be used as a placeholder any more. The attempt to solve the same equation system again is destined to fail. The reason: first, Maple evaluates the expression $x^2 - 5 * x + 6 = 0$ to $9 - 15 + 6 = 0$, that is, to $0 = 0$. Only then is solve applied. However, the first parameter of the command no longer contains an equation system, which leads to the error message.

```
solve(x^2-5*x+6=0, x);
    Error, (in solve)
    a constant is invalid
    as a variable, 3
```

This can be remedied by deleting the variable x. To do this, the variable is assigned its own name (enclosed in left quotes). The quotes prevent the evaluation of x to 3. Variables that contain their own name are considered empty (free).

```
x:='x';
```
$$x := x$$
```
solve(x^2-5*x+6=0, x);
```
$$3, 2$$

When you start a new sample calculation, it is best to delete all symbols occupied up to that point. This can be achieved by means of the `restart` command.

Warning: The worksheet menu command FILE|NEW does not cause any variables to be deleted!

Internals of variable management

This section contains some further information on variable management and describes additional commands for variable administration. If you are not currently interested in this subject, it is perfectly safe to skip this section – the information given here will only become necessary at a fairly advanced stage of Maple usage (programming, and so on).

You can use the `assigned` function to check whether a symbol is already occupied (if it has contents).

```
x:=3:
assigned(x), assigned(a);
```
$$true, false$$

Since the deletion of occupied variables by means of `x:='x'` assignments is rather laborious, Maple provides the `unassign` command which can be passed a whole list of variables to be deleted. The variables must be enclosed in quotes to prevent them from being evaluated beforehand.

```
a:=1: b:=2: c:=3:
unassign('a,b,c');
a,b,c;
```
$$a, b, c$$

As we have already mentioned in the previous section, variables can be used to store the most varied kinds of data: numbers, lists, formulae, and so on. The `whattype` command gives preliminary information about the stored data.

```
w:=1: x:=a^2+b^2: y:={a+b=5, a-b=1}:
z:=array([[1,2],[3,4]]):
whattype(w), whattype(x),
whattype(y), whattype(z);
```
$$integer, +, set, string$$

While `whattype` only knows the basic data types and only supplies the very general information *string* for z, the `type` command is suitable for a more detailed analysis of the data. However, `type` does not determine the data type on its own, but checks out your assumption. This means that you must already know with some degree of accuracy which of the many data types might be eligible.

```
type(y,set)
```
$$true$$
```
type(z,array), type(z,matrix);
```
$$true, false$$

You can find a complete list of Maple data types in the help subjects whattype and, in more detail, type.

Information about symbols in use is given by the commands anames (assigned names, that is, occupied variables) and unames (unassigned names, that is, symbols used but still free). Since in both cases all symbols used up to that point are displayed (even those defined by loading packages or special functions), the output normally extends over several pages and, in this form, is of little use for practical application.

Things become more interesting when you sort the information with sort and/or select it with select. (Both commands will be described in Chapter 10.) In the example below, all occupied variables with names of less than 8 characters are displayed. Amongst the variables listed, we find the most recently defined w, x, y and z.

```
sort(select(x->length(x)<8, [anames()]));
```

$$[fed, fred, latex/@, latex/D, w, x, xed, y, z]$$

The output can be restricted to symbols of a specific data type, using an optional parameter to anames. anames(string), for example, only displays variables that contain character strings.

Protection of variables

Variables can be protected against further assignments with protect. Any attempt to assign new contents to a protected variable will lead to an error message. unprotect deactivates this protection. Inside Maple, nearly all commands are protected against erroneous overwriting by protect.

Like most other programming languages, Maple understands local variables whose existence is restricted to one procedure. Local variables will be dealt with in Chapter 29 about programming.

Immediate and delayed variable assignment

When processing commands, Maple first tries to evaluate all symbols and substitute them with their contents. In assignments with :=, this evaluation is restricted to the right-hand side. Also, there are some data types which are not evaluated directly (arrays, tables, functions). Evaluation of these data types must be explicitly forced by means of the eval command.

In the assignment x:=y, Maple first substitutes y with its contents and then stores them in x. If y is not yet occupied, Maple stores the name of the symbol y in x.

Sometimes it would be useful if a later change in one variable affected the contents of another variable. In this case, we have to work with delayed assignments. For this purpose, the expression to be assigned must be enclosed in left quotes '. Thus, Maple refrains from immediately evaluating the quoted expression and stores it in the variable in its quoted form.

```
x:=2;
```
$$x := 2$$

```
y:='x'; z:='y';
```
$$y := x$$
$$z := y$$

The variable is actually evaluated only when it is used. Thus, a later change in x affects z. The reason: during evaluation of z, Maple encounters the symbol y, and during evaluation of y, it finds x whose evaluation in turn leads to the current contents of x.

```
z;
```
$$2$$

```
x:=3; z;
```
$$x := 3$$
$$3$$

If, in the above example, the second command had been y:=x; z:=y;, z would have been assigned the original contents of x, that is, the value 2. This value would not have changed even after a new assignment to x.

The meaning of quotes has been slightly simplified in the above example. Actually, quotes do not prevent evaluation, but delay it. The evaluation of 'x' leads to x (without quotes), but this expression is not evaluated any further. x has been changed to its current contents 3 only during a second evaluation step.

Quotes can also be used on several levels. Each evaluation removes one pair of quotes. '''x''' becomes ''x'', then 'x', x and finally 3.

A special case of delayed assignments is the deletion of variables: by means of x:='x', the unevaluated symbol x is stored in the variable x – thus x is considered to be empty.

For many applications, quotes are not flexible enough, because they completely block the evaluation of an expression. For indexed variables f[x] (these are arrays, see Chapter 13) or compound variable names v.i (see the section on the concatenation operator below), it would be useful if x were evaluated (and its current contents substituted), but not the resulting variable name $f[3]$ or $v3$. In such situations, the command evaln (evaluate to name) proves useful, which carries out an evaluation up to the variable name.

The following example shows an application of evaln: in a seq loop, the elements $a[0]$ to $a[5]$ of the vector a are to be assigned 2^n. The first attempt goes well even without using evaln. The assignment is carried out by means of the assign command, since inside seq, the operator := cannot be employed (see next section). The second seq command merely displays the contents of the elements $a[0]$ to $a[5]$.

```
a:=array(0..5);
```
$$a := \mathrm{array}(0..5, [])$$

```
seq(assign(a[i],2^i), i=0..5);
seq(a[i], i=0..5);
```
$$1, 2, 4, 8, 16, 32$$

The attempt to change the variables in the same way and to assign them 3^n, however, fails. The reason: in `assign`, for $i = 0$, `a[i]` is evaluated to `a[0]` and thus to 1. However, `assign` cannot store a new value in the value $1 -$ it needs a variable. The variable name is now determined with `evaln`. The previous example only worked because the array elements $a[i]$ were still free at that moment in time.

```
seq(assign(a[i],3^i), i=0..5);
    Error, (in assign) invalid
    arguments
seq(assign(evaln(a[i]),3^i),
    i=0..5);
seq(a[i], i=0..5);

    1, 3, 9, 27, 81, 243
```

Variable assignment with assign

In the previous examples, we mostly used the `:=` operator for variable assignments. Alternatively, Maple has the command `assign(var,expression)`, which stores the specified expression in the variable. This command is only rarely needed – for example, when several variables are to be assigned in a `seq` loop (see the example above).

However, the possibilities of `assign` do not end here. In contrast to variable assignment with `:=`, `assign` also evaluates the left-hand side (details of how Maple expressions are evaluated follow in the next section). If the variable x contains a pointer to the variable y, `assign(x,3)` also modifies the variable y! The `restart` command at the beginning of the example serves to delete all variables used up to this point.

```
restart;
x:=y;

    x := y

assign(x, 3); x,y;

    3, 3
```

At first sight, the above result may seem a bit surprising. Through the `assign` command, the value 3 was stored in the variable y (!). In the output of x and y, the value 3 is output twice – once because x points to y, and the second time because y effectively contains the value 3.

`assign` can also be passed a list or a set of equations of the form `var=expression`. Then, `assign` carries out the assignments expressed with `=` (not `:=`). This variation of `assign` is particularly useful to convert the solutions of equation systems determined by `solve`.

```
restart; solve({x+y=3, x-y=2});

    {y = 1/2, x = 5/2}

assign("); x,y;

    5/2, 1/2
```

Variable substitution

In the last few pages, we have more than once mentioned the problems which occur when naming already assigned variables in various commands. For this reason, it is often useful to do without direct assignment of variables.

An alternative is represented by the `subs` command, which *temporarily* substitutes variables with values (or arbitrary expressions). The command syntax becomes clear through the example on the right. Please note that assignments in `subs` are formulated with = and not with :=.

Care must be taken when several substitutions are to be carried out simultaneously. `subs` usually executes the substitutions one after the other. If simultaneous execution is required (for example, if the substitution instruction leads to an exchange of variables as in the examples below), the substitution rules must be written as a set enclosed in braces.

The last command also shows a further application of `subs`: the solutions found by `solve` can be easily inserted into mathematical expressions.

In principle, `subs` is also capable of substituting whole expressions (and not just single variables) with new data. However, this works only if the expression to be substituted represents a unit. This is the case in the first of the two examples on the right, but not in the second one (because $x + y$ is a part of the sum $x + y + z$).

The `algsubs` command (new in Release 4) has been specifically designed to cope with such cases. It does not perform the substitution by purely mechanical pattern matching, but by using a mathematical transformation.

```
restart; # delete all variables
subs(x=2, y=3, x^2 + 2*x*y + y^2);
```
$$25$$

```
subs(x=y^2, y=x^2, sin(x)+cos(y));
```
$$\sin(x^4) + \cos(x^2)$$

```
subs(y=x^2, x=y^2, sin(x)+cos(y));
```
$$\sin(y^2) + \cos(y^4)$$

```
subs({x=y^2, y=x^2}, sin(x)+cos(y));
```
$$\sin(y^2) + \cos(x^2)$$

```
solve({x^2+y^2=10, x+y=4});
```
$$\{y = 1, x = 3\}, \{y = 3, x = 1\}$$

```
subs("[1], x^2 + 2*x*y + y^2);
```
$$16$$

```
subs(x+y=3, sin(x+y));
```
$$\sin(3)$$

```
subs(x+y=3, x+y+z);
```
$$x + y + z$$

```
algsubs(x+y=3, x+y+z);
```
$$3 + z$$

```
algsubs(x^2=a, x^5);
```
$$a^2 x$$

```
algsubs(s/t=v, s/t^2);
```
$$v/t$$

Depending on each individual case, optional parameters must be used to specify exactly how algsubs is to behave. In the first example (default), the first substitution variable is eliminated; in the second example, y is specified as the primary substitution variable. In example three, algsubs is instructed to perform the substitution only if the mathematical expression appears in exactly the same form – in this case, Maple does not carry out any substitution at all.

```
algsubs(x+y=3, 2*x+y+z);
```
$$-y + 6 + z$$
```
algsubs(x+y=3, 2*x+y+z, [y]);
```
$$x + 3 + z$$
```
algsubs(x+y=3, 2*x+y+z, exact);
```
$$2x + y + z$$

In complex cases, both subs and algsubs are problematic: in the example here, both roots in the function f are to be substituted with the abbreviations A and B. The first attempt with subs fails, and Maple returns f unchanged.

```
f:=x/sqrt(10+2*sqrt(5))+
   y/sqrt(10-2*sqrt(5)):
a:=sqrt(10-2*sqrt(5)):
b:=sqrt(10+2*sqrt(5)):
subs(a=A, b=B, f);
```
$$\frac{x}{\sqrt{10 + 2\sqrt{5}}} + \frac{y}{\sqrt{10 - 2\sqrt{5}}}$$

Maple does not recognize the substitution because both roots are in the denominator. However, with a reformulation of the command, which may at first sight not seem very straightforward, but which comes much closer to Maple's internal representation of the expression, the task finally succeeds.

```
f1:=subs(1/a=1/A, 1/b=1/B, f);
```
$$f1 := \frac{x}{a} + \frac{y}{b}$$

algsubs completely fails with this example. Firstly, it can only carry out one substitution (and not two at a time), and secondly, it can only substitute variables (not numerical expressions). But even an example designed to fit algsubs still fails.

```
restart; # delete a and b
f:=x/sqrt(a+b*sqrt(c));
```
$$f := \frac{x}{\sqrt{a + b\sqrt{c}}}$$
```
algsubs(sqrt(a+b*sqrt(c))=A, f);
   Error, (in algsubs) no variables
   in pattern
```

The example shows that the substitution of expressions can be a difficult business. In very pertinacious cases, select, remove (Chapter 10) and subsop (Chapter 12) can be used. It is also useful to know how Maple represents mathematical expressions internally. More information on this subject can be found in Chapter 28.

Defining properties of variables with assume

When you use a still unassigned variable in an equation, Maple knows nothing about the properties of this variable. You yourself, however, may well know from the formulation of the problem that the variable must be greater than 0 or that only real (but not complex) numbers are allowed.

With `assume`, you can tell Maple about such properties. Some Maple commands make use of this additional information and are thus capable of carrying out simplifications in the calculating process or of making it possible at all. In the results, Maple marks all variables for which properties have been defined with a postfixed ˜ character. The following examples illustrate the use of `assume`.

The commands on the right are to be used to calculate the real component of $(a + Ib)^2$. The task suggests that a and b are real numbers, but Maple does not know this. For this reason, the result turns out to be more complicated than is really necessary.

```
Re(expand((a+I*b)^2));
```
$$\Re(a^2 + 2\,I\,a\,b - b^2)$$
```
assume(a,real, b,real);
Re(expand((a+I*b)^2));
```
$$a^{˜2} - b^{˜2}$$

The simplification of $\sqrt{n^2}$ to n only applies under the condition that $n >= 0$. For this reason, Maple only carries out the simplification when the properties of n are specified with `assume`. (Alternatively, you can also use `simplify(..,symbolic)` – see Chapter 10.)

```
sqrt(n^2);
```
$$\sqrt{n^2}$$
```
assume(n>0);
sqrt(n^2);
```
$$n^˜$$

When Maple has information about variables in trigonometric functions, very extensive simplifications may succeed. In the example on the right, `n:='n'` is first used to delete all former properties of n.

```
n:='n': cos(n*Pi);
```
$$\cos(n\,\pi)$$
```
assume(n,integer): cos(n*Pi);
```
$$(-1)^{n^˜}$$
```
assume(n,odd): cos(n*Pi);
```
$$-1$$

`assume` information is also evaluated by many commands for the execution of symbolic and numeric calculations. The following example shows an integral which can be solved after the property $a >= 0$ has been defined. ($a >= 0$ simultaneously defines a as a real (not complex) number.)

```
restart; int(exp(-a*x^2), x=0..infinity);
   Definite integration: Can't determine if the integral is convergent.
   Need to know the sign of --> a
   Will now try indefinite integration and then take limits.
```

$$\lim_{x \to \infty} \frac{1}{2} \frac{\sqrt{\pi} \operatorname{erf}(\sqrt{a}\, x)}{\sqrt{a}}$$

```
assume(a>=0): int(exp(-a*x^2), x=0..infinity);
```

$$\frac{1}{2} \frac{\sqrt{\pi}}{\sqrt{a^{\sim}}}$$

This has been just a small taste of the applications of `assume`. For the actual use of `assume`, countless attributes have been defined (see `?property`), of which we list the most important.

Integer numbers: `integer, posint, odd, even`
Fractions and real numbers: `fraction, rational, real, negative, positive, nonneg`
Complex numbers: `imaginary, complex, NumeralNonZero, GaussianInteger` ...
Function properties: `commutative, continuous, differentiable, monotonic` ...
Matrix properties: `antisymmetric, diagonal, tridiagonal, Hermitian` ...

Several attributes can be logically combined with `AndProp` or `OrProp`. Furthermore, number ranges can be specified in the form `RealRange(a,b)` where, apart from numbers, `infinity` and `Open(x0)` can be specified as well. `Open` is needed for $\leq$ or $\geq$. Usually, number ranges can also be indicated in the short notation `assume(x>0)`.

`assume` assumptions can be deleted together with the contents of the variable by means of the `var:='var'` assignment.

Further assume commands

`assume` is a member of a whole family of commands. The following paragraphs briefly describe the most important commands of this family:

`additionally`
works like `assume`, with the exception that the properties defined in this way apply in addition to the already existing properties (whereas `assume` deletes all previous properties). When a variable is deleted with `var:='var'`, all its properties are deleted too.

`is`
checks whether an object satisfies a specific assumption (see the example below), on the basis of the properties defined up to this point. Results can be: `true` (if the assumption is always satisfied), `false` (if the assumption is not satisfied for at least one case) or `FAIL` (if Maple does not have sufficient information for decision making).

`about`
displays all known information about a symbol.

`addproperty`

allows an extension of the properties supported by `assume`. However, the possibilities this offers will not be dealt with at this point.

The following examples illustrate the application of these commands. The hypothesis $x0 > -1$ is definitely true, because $x0 > 0$ was defined beforehand. $x0 > 1$ may apply in some cases, but does not apply to all permitted values of $x0$ – thus, the result is $false$. $x0$ is considered by Maple to be a real number (because the property $x0 > 0$ would make no sense for complex numbers). The hypothesis $x0 > x1$ cannot be evaluated by `is`, because information is lacking about $x1$.

```
assume(x0>0);
is(x0>-1), is(x0>1),
is(x0,real), is(x0>x1);
```
$$true, false, true, FAIL$$
```
about(x0);
    Originally x0, renamed x0~:
    is assumed to be:
        RealRange (Open(0),infinity)
```

When you need multiple stage conclusions, you must employ the commands of the `totorder` package. The `tassume` command defined there has a similar meaning to `assume`, and `tis` corresponds to `is`. (Internally, however, these commands work differently and are not compatible with each other.)

```
restart: with(totorder):
tassume(a>b, b>c, c>d);
```
$$assumed, b < a, c < b, d < c$$
```
tis(a>d);
```
$$true$$

As fascinating as the above examples may be, the power of the `assume` command should not be overestimated. Many Maple commands do not consider `assume` properties at all. `solve`, for example, ignores the information stored by `assume` and in spite of `assume(x>0)` still supplies negative solutions. Furthermore, `assume` is unable to define dependents. Especially in the case of differentiation of functions with several variables, there is no easy-to-handle mechanism to tell Maple that x depends on y. Yet another irritating fact is that there is no help text to document which commands support `assume` and which do not. Thus, every command must be checked individually to establish whether and to what extent it takes `assume` properties into account.

Abbreviations via macro and alias

Both `macro` and `alias` may be used to define abbreviations. At first sight, the only difference between the two commands is that `macro` abbreviations only apply to the input of Maple commands, whereas `alias` abbreviations also affect the output of results. In practice, however, the differences between the two commands go deeper, as shown by the following examples, first for `macro`, and then for `alias`.

`macro(x=expression)` assigns the symbol x an expression. Neither x nor the specified expression is evaluated by `macro`. Thus, the character string 'x' is merely assigned the new meaning 'expression'.

`macro(s=solve): s(x^2-2);`

$$\sqrt{2}, -\sqrt{2}$$

`macro(s=sin): s(x^2-2);`

$$\sin(x^2 - 2)$$

Not only variables, but also mathematical expressions are allowed for x, for example `macro(sin(x)=0)`. The `macro` instruction has no influence on the homonymous variable. The new meaning of $\sin(x)$ only shows when inputting Maple commands: when you enter `sin(x)+1`, Maple converts it into `0+1`, evaluates this expression and subsequently supplies the result 1. When you input `diff(cos(x),x)`, Maple arrives at the result $-\sin(x)$ and outputs it. Thus, the macro for $\sin(x)$ affects neither the output nor the true value of $\sin(x)$.

`macro` is specially useful for the definition of constants. Any attempt to modify or delete s by a subsequent normal assignment fails because of the protection afforded by `macro`. If you really want to delete s, you must once again use `macro`.

`macro(s=1.2345);`

  1.52399025

`s:=3;`

  Error, Illegal use
  of an object as a name

`macro(s=s);  # deletes the macro for s`

The command `macro(a=b)` differs from the assignment `a:='b'` in three respects: firstly, the `macro` abbreviation only applies to the input (whereas the assignment applies in general). Secondly, a can also be a generic mathematical expression (for example, x^2+y^2). Thirdly, a can only be modified or deleted by a further `macro` instruction; erroneous assignments are excluded. Please note, however, that abbreviations can be defined directly by variable assignments of the `s:=solve` kind, although this is unusual.

Now to `alias`: the command has the same syntax as `macro`, but outputs a list of all abbreviations defined up to that point. The example on the right shows the most important difference from `macro`: `alias` abbreviations also apply to the output.

`restart;`
`alias(s=sin);`

  I, s

`sin(x);`

  $s(x)$

Maybe the most important application of `alias` is the definition of the imaginary unit I. This has simply been created by the instruction `alias(I=sqrt(-1))`. Each time the symbol I occurs in the input, Maple substitutes it with $\sqrt{-1}$. Vice versa, in the output $\sqrt{-1}$ is substituted with I.

Another hint concerning `alias`: you cannot use `alias` to define abbreviations which refer back to `alias` abbreviations. In particular, you must write $\sqrt{-1}$ instead of I if you want to use the imaginary unit inside an `alias` instruction.

A further, very useful application consists in storing dependences. The derivative $\frac{df}{dx}$ obtained by `diff(f,x)` normally yields 0. Through the command `alias(f=f(x))` Maple recognizes that f is a function of x, without requiring any additional typing effort during further calculations:

```
alias(f=f(x)):
diff(f^2,x);
```

$$2 f \frac{d}{dx} f$$

A further example of this application of `alias` can be found in Chapter 4 in the section on rectangular intersection.

In contrast to `macro`, `alias` has the following peculiarities: `alias` also affects the output, expressions specified in `alias` are evaluated before the abbreviation is stored, and `alias` is not capable of defining constants.

Thus, the following guidelines apply to the use of the two commands: `macro` is suitable for (formal) input facilitation, that is, for abbreviating long function or command names or for defining constants, whereas `alias` is a mathematical tool for the simplification of expressions in both input and output.

The concatenation operator .

The concatenation operator . is used to combine several expressions into character strings. The main application is the management of numbered variables ($x1$, $x2$, $x3$).

In the processing of `a.b.c`, a remains unevaluated, whereas b and c are substituted by their current contents. Subsequently, all three character strings are combined into one string and can then be used as a variable name. The examples on the right illustrate this mechanism.

```
a.b.c;
```

$$abc$$

```
b:=1: c:=2: a.b.c;
```

$$a12$$

```
a:=x: a.b.c;
```

$$a := a12$$

The last command was intended to produce $x12$. However, this could not work, since Maple leaves the first symbol of a . string unevaluated. This restriction (which makes sense for most applications) can be circumvented by specifying an empty string ` `` ` as the first symbol, or by using the `cat` command.

```
``.a.b.c;
```

$$x12$$

```
cat(a,b,c);
```

$$x12$$

The command on the right calculates the sum of $x0$ to $x5$. Here, `x.i` must be enclosed in quotes to prevent an evaluation prior to the substitution of i.

```
sum('x.i', i=0..5);
```

$$x0 + x1 + x2 + x3 + x4 + x5$$

A further example of how to handle the concatenation operator, which illustrates the assignment of several variables within `seq`, can be found above in the section on the `assign` command.

System variables

Maple has several system variables which influence its behaviour in different situations. System variables can be divided into two groups: *environment* and *interface* variables.

Environment variables are `Digits` and `Order`, amongst others. `Digits` specifies the number of digits used for numerical calculations, `Order` the order of magnitude up to which sequences are to be developed. `infolevel` and `printlevel` determine how much information is to be displayed during the processing of Maple commands (see Chapter 28).

Further *environment* variables are those whose names begin with _. The typical feature of *environment* variables is that their assignment in a procedure only applies inside that procedure, without causing any permanent change.

```
Digits:=20: evalf(1/3);
```

$$Digits := 0.33333333333333333333$$

```
series(sin(x)/(x+1), x);
```

$$\left(x - x^2 + \frac{5}{6}x^3 - \frac{5}{6}x^4 + \frac{101}{120}x^5 + O\left(x^6\right)\right)$$

```
Order:=10: series(sin(x)/(x+1), x);
```

$$\left(x - x^2 + \frac{5}{6}x^3 - \frac{5}{6}x^4 + \frac{101}{120}x^5 - \frac{101}{120}x^6 + \frac{4241}{5040}x^7 - \frac{4241}{5040}x^8 + \frac{305353}{362880}x^9 + O\left(x^{10}\right)\right)$$

`interface` variables control the connection between Maple and the user interface. Some background information: Maple consists of three parts, the kernel (command interpreter, memory management), the library (definition of all functions, partly in external packages) and the user interface. The first two components are responsible for the mathematical part (and are largely identical in all Maple versions), whereas the third component is responsible for communication with the user and is computer-dependent.

The command `interface(var=value)` is used to set some predefined `interface` variables. The most important of these concern the output of graphics (`plotdevice`, `plotoutput`). A complete description of all `interface` variables is contained in the online help subject `?interface`.

In the example on the right, the `interface` variable `showassumed` is set to 2. Now, variables with `assume` properties are no longer marked with the ~ character; instead, at the end of each command, a list of all `assume` variables is displayed.

```
interface(showassumed=2);
assume(n,odd); sin(n*x);
```

$$\sin(n^\sim x)$$

with assumptions on n

Syntax summary

`var:=expression;    var:='expression';    var:='var';`

carries out a variable assignment. The expression on the right-hand side is evaluated prior to the assignment. Immediate evaluation is prevented by inserting quotes, so that the assignment is only carried out when the variable is actually used. This feature can be used for the deletion of variables (third syntax variation).

`assign(var=expression);    assign(var, expression);    assign({v1=a,v2=b,..});`

constitutes an alternative to variable assignment with `:=`. `assign` differs from the assignment operator insofar as the left-hand side is evaluated as well, prior to the assignment. Furthermore, `assign` is allowed in places where `:=` would cause a syntax error (for example, inside `seq`). The last syntax variation allows simultaneous assignment of a whole list of variables.

`evaln(expression);`

evaluates the expression until variable names are present, but does not substitute them with their contents. For `i=3`, `evaln(x[i])` produces the variable name `x[3]`.

`subs(v1=a1, v2=a2,.., expression);`

carries out a temporary variable substitution for $v1$, $v2$ ..., thus evaluating the expression specified in the last parameter.

`macro(var=expression);`

defines an abbreviation for var. Neither 'var' nor 'expression' is evaluated prior to the assignment. The abbreviation only applies to command input. var cannot be modified through a normal assignment with `:=` and, if necessary, must be deleted with `macro(var=var)` beforehand.

`alias(var=expression);`

defines an abbreviation for var. Both 'var' and 'expression' are evaluated prior to assignment. Assignment of constants is not allowed. The abbreviation applies to both commands input and results output.

`x.i.j;    ''.x.i.j;    cat(x.i.j);`

concatenates the specified symbols to a character string (a variable name). In the first variation, x remains unevaluated, and i and j are substituted with their current contents ($i = 1$ and $j = 2$ result in $x12$). In the other two variations, x is substituted with its contents as well.

Internals of variable management

`restart;`
   deletes all variables, loaded packages, and so on.

`unassign('var1,v2,..');`
   deletes the list of variables specified inside the quotes.

`assigned(var);`
   checks whether a variable is already occupied. Returns *true* or *false*.

`anames();       unames();`
   displays an unsorted sequence of all occupied or free variables, respectively.

`whattype(var);`
   determines the data type of a variable (`string`, `integer`, and so on). However, it will only
   differentiate between approximately 25 basic types.

`type(var,type);`
   checks whether the variable is of the specified type. Returns *true* or *false*. `type` knows more
   than 80 predefined data types.

`protect(name);       unprotect(name);`
   `protect` protects the variable against erroneous assignments. `unprotect` deactivates this protection.

assume and related commands

`assume(var op expression);       assume(var, property);`
   stores a property of the specified variable, for example that it can only assume values greater
   than 0 (`assume(x>0)`) or that it represents a real (but not complex) number (`assume(x,real)`).
   A list of all currently permitted `assume` attributes can be obtained through `?assume`. The
   property specified with `assume` replaces all previously specified properties of this variable.
   `var:='var'` deletes all properties.

`additionally(var ..);`
   as `assume`, but the property is stored in addition to all other properties already defined for the
   variable in question.

`is(expression);       is(expression, property);`
   checks whether, on the basis of the properties stored up to this point, the assumption formulated
   in `is` applies to all possible contents of the specified variable. Possible results are *true*, *false*
   or *FAIL* (if the information needed to formulate a conclusion is insufficient).

`about(var);`
   displays all existing information about *var*.

Chapter 7

Constants, operators and functions

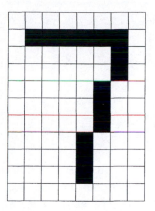

This chapter gives an overview of the most important predefined constants, operators and functions. In contrast to the other chapters, the syntax summary has been placed at the beginning of each section, rather than collected at the end.

The most important functions defined in Maple include root, logarithmic and exponential functions, trigonometric functions, Bessel functions and sphere surface functions. Obviously, this overview is far from being complete: specifically, it does not contain functions for processing complex numbers (see next chapter), functions for vector and matrix calculus (Chapters 13 and 14), probability distribution (Chapter 21), and a large number of additional special functions which are either not dealt with at all in this book or dealt with in the chapters concerning related subjects.

In this context it should also be mentioned that the distinction made in this book between function and command is purely linguistic. For Maple, this distinction does not exist; sin is considered a function (or a command, as you prefer) in exactly the same way as subs. The distinction between functions (where functions are taken in the mathematical sense of the term) and commands (denoting Maple functions which evaluate expressions, execute calculations, and so on) is only meant to facilitate understanding.

Reference: User-defined functions and operators will be discussed in the next chapter.

Constants

Pi   the cyclotomic number $\pi = 3.141592654$.

I   the imaginary unit $\sqrt{-1}$.

exp(1)   Euler's number 2.718281828. *Warning:* Since Release 4, E must no longer be used as an abbreviation for exp(1) in commands! When $\exp(1)$ occurs in results, however, it is still displayed as e.

Gamma   Euler's constant $\gamma = 0.577216$. *Warning:* There is also the function GAMMA, which is described further below.

catalan   the Catalan constant 0.915966.

infinity	the value infinity. `infinity` can occur as a result (for example, in a division by 0), or it can be used as a parameter (for example, as an integration limit). `infinity` is written in lower case – the same as `catalan`!
true false	the truth values *true* and *false*. Neither constant is assigned a value.

A list of all constants defined in Maple can be obtained through `constants`. You will note that the imaginary unit I is missing. The reason for this is that I is simply defined as an abbreviation for `sqrt(-1)` by means of the `alias` command.

`constants;`

$$false, \gamma, \infty, true, Catalan, FAIL, \pi$$

The list of constants can be extended by the user. Unlike variables, constants have the advantage that their value cannot be erroneously changed by a simple assignment – Maple reacts with an error message. Constants are assigned their values by means of the `macro` command. In the example below, the constant E is defined to denote Euler's number. E must not have been previously occupied.

`constants:=constants,E: macro(E=exp(1)): constants;`

$$false, \gamma, \infty, true, Catalan, FAIL, \pi, E$$

`E, evalf(E), ln(E);`

$$e, 2.718281828, 1$$

Elementary calculating operators

+ - * /	fundamental operations (addition, subtraction, multiplication, division). Please note that a specific operator `&*` is defined for matrix multiplication (see also Chapter 14).
mod	modulo operator. `mod` is only suitable for calculations with integer numbers (including fractions, powers and even polynomials). `mod` issues an error message if either of the operands is a floating point number. The modulo operator is usually defined by the function `modp` which only yields positive results. Alternatively, the operator can be redefined by means of the instruction `'mod':=mods`. The function `mods` yields negative values if the amount is less than the corresponding positive modulo result. For example, `mods(5,7)` yields the result -2.
^ **	^ and ** represent two equivalent power operators.
!	factorial. 5! yields 120.

Assignment, comparison and other operators

`:=`	operator for variable assignments, for example, `x:=3`. The right-hand side of the assignment is evaluated immediately. A delayed assignment (where the variable is only evaluated when it is actually used) can be achieved by using left quotes, that is, by `x:='y'` (see previous chapter).
`=`	equality operator for checking equality, formulating equations and carrying out temporary assignments inside a command (for example, `subs(x=3, sin(x))`) or in options (`plot(sin(x), x=1..3, axes=none)`).
`->`	function operator for the definition of function specifications (for example, `f:=x->sin(x)`, see Chapter 8).
`<>`	inequality operator.
`>    >=    <    <=`	greater than, greater equal, less than and less equal operators.
`.`	concatenation operator, corresponds to the `cat` command. The expression `a.1` produces $a1$ (see previous chapter).
`..`	range operator, used in a large number of Maple commands to formulate ranges in the form `from..to`.
`$`	sequence operator. In `a$n`, a is repeated n times. `x$3` results in x, x, x. `diff(f,x$3)` constructs f'''.
`f @ g` `f @@ n`	composition operator. `(sin@sqrt)(x)` constructs $\sin(\sqrt{x})$, `(exp@@2)(x)` results in $\left(\exp^{(2)}\right)(x)$.
`not    and    or`	logical negation, AND and OR combination.

`union`
`intersect`
`minus`
	union, intersection and difference of sets. The three operators are exclusively defined to process sets (see Chapter 12).

Maple offers the possibility of creating user-defined operators by means of the `define` command. Such operators generally begin with the `&` character. Many packages offer their own operators; for example, `linalg` offers the operator `&*` for non-commutative matrix multiplication, or `logic` the operators `&and`, `&nand`, and so on, for the formulation of Boolean expressions.

Numeric functions

`abs(z);`	calculates the amount of the number.

`sign(x);`	yields -1 for negative numbers, $+1$ for positive numbers and 0 (!). With complex numbers, the evaluation of sign leads to an error. `sign` can also be applied to polynomials, in which case the sign of the highest priority coefficient is taken.

`signum(z);`
`signum(1,z);`
`signum(0,z,z0);`
	is, unlike `sign`, suited for complex numbers as well and yields $\frac{z}{\|z\|}$, that is, a complex pointer of length 1. `signum(1,z)` represents the first derivation of `signum(z)`. The derivation is 0 for all real z not equal to 0. The derivation is not defined for any other values. `signum(0,z,z0)` again means the normal `signum` function, but in addition gives a value for $z = 0$. Alternatively, this 0 value can also be set through the system variable `_Envsignum0`. `_Envsignum0` has an influence on whether and how expressions can be simplified with the `signum` function.

`csgn(z);`	represents the third signum variation. The function determines in which half-plane z is located. The function returns $+1$ for $z = 0$, for $\Re(z) > 0$ and for $\Re(z) = 0$, if $\Im(z) > 0$. All other situations result in -1.
`max(x1,x2,..);` `min(x1,x2,..);`	determine the greatest or smallest of the specified numbers, respectively. Complex numbers are not allowed.
`round(x);`	rounds up or down to the next integer number. 0.5 is rounded up to 1, -0.5 down to -1. In complex numbers, real and imaginary parts are rounded independently of each other. *Warning:* In Maple V Release 4, Windows 95/NT version, `round` contains a serious error: for example, `evalf(round(10.^11))` results in 0.110^{20}! It is not known whether other Maple versions are affected by the same error.
`floor(x);`	rounds down to the next smaller integer number.
`ceil(x);`	rounds up to the next higher integer number.
`trunc(x);`	rounds in the 0 direction (that is, positive numbers are rounded down, negative numbers are rounded up).
`frac(x);`	determines the part following the decimal point (signed, that is, frac(-5.7) yields -0.7).

Please note that Maple always tries to calculate symbolically. Expressions such as $\sqrt{2}$ or $\pi/2$ are only evaluated numerically when the `evalf` command is employed! `evalf` belongs to a whole group of `eval` commands, only two of which are of interest in this context:

`evalf(expr);` `evalf(expr, digits);`	numeric evaluation of symbolic expressions (evaluate floating point). The first variation calculates with the precision preset with `Digits`, the second variation allows the required number of digits to be specified explicitly. Please note, however, that the result can never become more precise than the most inexact value that is used in the calculation (for example, a physical constant with 8 digits). If required, Maple shows an arbitrary number of digits, but these will be of no relevance.
`evalhf(expr);`	numeric evaluation using the floating point arithmetic of the computer (evaluate hardware floating point). For complex calculations, this command can lead to a significant increase in speed, because the computer's floating point unit (FPU) is accessed if present. On the other hand, this means that precision is determined by the hardware. Furthermore, `evalhf` is only suitable for some of Maple's functions and commands.

Random numbers

`rand();`
`rand(x);`
`rand(y..z);`
	supplies a 12-digit integer number between 0 and 10^{12}.
	returns a procedure whose evaluation yields an integer number between 0 and $x - 1$ or between y and z (inclusive), respectively. In order to calculate the procedure, a pair of parentheses must be appended, for example `x:=rand(3); x();` or directly `rand(3)();`.

Generally, the `rand` command only supports integer random numbers with a maximum of 12 digits. Larger random numbers can be put together with multiple calls to `rand`.

`rand(), rand()+10^12*rand();`

> 427419669081, 3916959416003916959416160

If the number range is to be restricted, `rand(x)` or `rand(x..y)` can be used. Please note that neither formulation supplies random numbers, but functions to create them. A pair of parentheses must be appended for actual evaluation.

`rand(1..5)();`

> 2

If you need floating point numbers, you must calculate them yourself (using the `rand` function). `rand()/1e12` supplies random numbers between 0 (inclusive) and 1 (exclusive). A higher number of digits can only be achieved by changing `Digits` (the number of digits for numeric calculations).

`rand()/1e12;`

> 0.088430571674

`Digits:=24: rand()/1e12+rand()/1e24;`

> 0.960498834085960498834085

Apart from `rand`, there are various functions derived from it: the `stats` package contains several commands which calculate random numbers according to different probability distributions (see the section on special functions later in the chapter). `randpoly` determines polynomials with random coefficients; `randmatrix` in the `linalg` package constructs random matrices (see Chapter 14).

Square root, generic powers, logarithms and exponential function

`sqrt(x)`	calculates the square root.
`x^y`	calculates x^y. Instead of `^`, you can also use `**`.
`log(z)`; `ln(z)`;	calculates the natural logarithm to the base of E=2.7182818.
`log10(z)`;	calculates the logarithm to base 10.
`log[base](z)`;	calculates the logarithm to the specified base.
`exp(z)`	calculates e^z.

The following examples show that the square root is defined for both real and complex numbers. Information about the `evalc` command can be found in the next chapter. An alternative notation for `sqrt(x)` is `x^(1/2)`.

`sqrt(2), evalf(sqrt(2));`

$$\sqrt{2}, 1.414213562$$

`sqrt(a + I*b);`

$$\sqrt{a + I\,b}$$

`evalc( " );`

$$\sqrt{\frac{\sqrt{a^2 + b^2}}{2} + \frac{a}{2}} + I\,csgn(b - I\,a)\sqrt{\frac{\sqrt{a^2 + b^2}}{2} - \frac{a}{2}}$$

The functions `ln` and `log` can be used synonymously for the calculation of the natural logarithm.

`log(exp(1)), ln(exp(1)^2);`

$$1, 2$$

The logarithm to base 10 has its own calculation function which works only numerically. For symbolic calculus, the general logarithm function `log[b](x)` to the base of b is much better suited.

```
log10(100), simplify(log10(100)), evalf(log10(100));
```

$$\log_{10}(100), \log_{10}(100), 2.0$$

```
log[10](100), simplify(log[10](100));
```

$$\frac{\ln(100)}{\ln(10)}, 2$$

Trigonometric and hyperbolic functions

`Pi`	the constant 3.141592654.

`sin(x);`   `sinh(x);`
 `cos(x);`   `cosh(x);`
 `tan(x);`   `tanh(x);`
	the trigonometric functions sine, cosine and tangent, and the corresponding hyperbolic functions. All trigonometric functions expect their arguments and supply their results in radians (not in degrees).

`csc(x);`   `csch(x);`
 `sec(x);`   `sech(x);`
 `cot(x);`   `coth(x);`
	the reciprocal values of the trigonometric and hyperbolic functions.

`arcsin(z);`
 `arc...(z);`
 `arctan(x,y);`
	the inverse functions of the 12 functions mentioned above. The only syntactic peculiarity is presented by the `arctan` function, which can also be passed two arguments: `arctan(x,y)` calculates the arc tangent of x/y.

Maple obviously knows all trigonometric standard functions and their inverse functions. All these functions (like most of Maple's functions) are also defined for complex arguments. Usually, the functions do not supply numeric results, so that numeric values must be determined with `evalf`. Processing and simplification of expressions containing trigonometric functions are discussed in Chapter 10.

```
sin(Pi/4), evalf(sin(Pi/15));
```

$$\frac{\sqrt{2}}{2}, 0.2079116909$$

```
evalf(sin(1 + I))
```

$$1.298457581 + 0.6349639148I$$

There are two definitions for the `arctan` function: if only one parameter is specified, Maple calculates the corresponding function value. If two parameters are specified with `arctan(x,y)`, Maple calculates the arc tangent of x/y. This variation of `arctan` has the advantage that the signs of both parameters can be considered separately, which makes the result lie in the range between $-\pi$ and π (instead of $-\pi/2$ to $\pi/2$). Furthermore, $y = 0$ does not cause an error message.

```
evalf([arctan(1/3), arctan(1,3), arctan(-1,-3)]);
```

$$[0.3217505544, 0.3217505544, -2.819842100]$$

Special functions (gamma, Bessel, sphere functions)

`binomial(n,m);`	calculates the binomial coefficient $\binom{n}{m}$. If no positive integers are used for n or m, `binomial` resorts to the GAMMA function: $\frac{\Gamma(n+1)}{\Gamma(m+1)\Gamma(n-m+1)}$.
`GAMMA(z);`	calculates the gamma function, which is defined as follows: $\Gamma(z) = \int_0^\infty e^{-t} t^{z-1} dt$.
`GAMMA(z,a)`	calculates the incomplete gamma function: $\Gamma(z,a) = \int_z^\infty e^{-t} t^{a-1} dt$.
`Psi(z);`	calculates the digamma function: $\Psi(x) = \frac{\frac{d}{dx}\Gamma(x)}{\Gamma(x)}$.
`Psi(n,z);`	calculates the nth polygamma function (that is, the nth derivative of the digamma function): $\Psi(n,x) = \frac{d^n}{dx^n}\Psi(x)$.
`Beta(x,y);`	calculates the beta function: $\beta(x,y) = \frac{\Gamma(x)\Gamma(y)}{\Gamma(x+y)}$.
`Zeta(x);` `Zeta(n, x);`	calculates the Riemann zeta function or its nth derivative: $\zeta(x) = \sum_{i=1}^\infty 1/i^s$, $\zeta(n,x) = \frac{d^n \zeta(x)}{dx^n}$.

`BesselJ(n,z);`
`BesselI(n,z);`
`BesselY(n,z);`
`BesselK(n,z);`
	`BesselJ` calculates the first class Bessel function of nth order (cylinder function). `BesselI` calculates the modified first class Bessel function. `BesselY` stands for the second class Bessel function (Weber function), `BesselK` for the modified second class Bessel function (Macdonald function).

`LegendreF(x,k);`
`LegendreE(x,k);`
`LegendreKc(k);`
`LegendreEc(k);`
	`LegendreF` and `LegendreE` represent the first and second class elliptic integrals. `LegendreKc` and `LegendreEc` stand for the complete first and second class elliptic integrals.

`Si(z);  Ci(z);` `Ei(z);  Li(z);`	calculate the integral sine $\int_0^z \frac{\sin(t)}{t} dt$, integral cosine $\gamma + \ln(Iz) - \frac{I\pi}{2} + \int_0^z \frac{\cos(t)-1}{t} dt$, integral exponential function $\int_{-\infty}^z \frac{e^t}{t} dt$ and integral logarithm $Ei(\ln(z))$.
`FresnelS(z);` `FresnelC(z);`	calculate the Fresnel sine integral function $\int_0^z \sin(\frac{\pi t^2}{2})dt$ and the Fresnel cosine integral function $\int_0^z \cos(\frac{\pi t^2}{2})dt$. *Warning*: In Maple, the functions are defined differently from Bronstein and Semendjajew (1989). See the example below!
`with(orthopoly);` `P(n,x);`	constructs the Legendre polynomial (the sphere (surface) function) of nth order for the variable x.

The above syntax overview of special functions from different areas of mathematics is obviously far from complete. A good overview of all functions predefined in Maple can be obtained by means of the help command `?inifcns`. Special functions concerning various subjects are contained in the packages `orthopoly` (orthogonal polynomials), `numtheory` (number theory), `combinat` (combinatorics) and `stats` (statistics), amongst others.

When using these functions, care must be taken to check whether their definition matches the conventions used by yourself. Depending on the literature, several mathematical functions present different formulae or different conventions for the order and/or the meaning of their parameters. For example, the Fresnel sine integral function is defined as follows in Bronstein and Semendjajew (1989): $\frac{1}{\sqrt{2\pi}} \int_0^z \frac{sin(t)}{t} dt$.

To make the results of `Fresnel` match those in Bronstein and Semendjajew (1989), $\sqrt{2z\,\pi}$ must be inserted as an argument.

```
evalf(FresnelS(sqrt(2/Pi*0.1)));
```

$$0.008404436193$$

The function `P` from the `orthopoly` package does not really fit into the above list of functions. Generally, `P` supplies a polynomial (and not a numeric value or a simple function) as a result.

```
with(orthopoly);  P(7,x);
```

$$\frac{429\,x^7}{16} - \frac{693\,x^5}{16} + \frac{315\,x^3}{16} - \frac{35\,x}{16}$$

```
P(7,0.05);
```

$$-0.1069275767$$

As a conclusion, we present two illustrations which are intended as templates to help you view the behaviour of all functions listed above without too much effort.

```
plot(GAMMA(x), x=-5..5, -5..5);
```

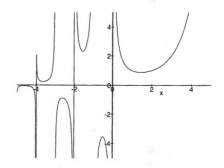

If a whole family of curves is to be drawn, the set of functions put together with `seq` must be enclosed in braces. The third parameter limits the y drawing range. The illustration shows the modified first class Bessel functions of orders 1 to 4.

```
plot({seq(BesselY(n,x), n=1..4)},
     x=0..12, -1..0.5);
```

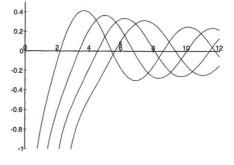

Chapter 8

User-defined functions

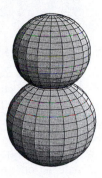

After the discussion of predefined Maple functions in the previous chapter, we are now going to deal with user-defined functions. Maple provides various mechanisms which, depending on the area of application, are more or less suited to defining such functions. A warning to start with: the obvious formulation, that is, `f(x):=..`, does not lead to the desired result.

At this point, we should also clarify the terminological conventions generally used in Maple: `sin(x)` is considered a function, whereas `sin` without a parameter is considered an operator! In order to ensure terminological differentiation between this and other operators, such as + or `mod`, Maple differentiates between functional operators (such as `sin` or `x->x^2`), unary operators (such as the + and - signs and `not`) and binary operators (such as all calculation and comparison operators). However, not even the original Maple manuals get the exact distinction between operators and functions correct.

In this book, the term operator, without any further explanation, means the usual (unary or binary) operator. Functional operators are either clearly named as such, or more briefly as functions or function specifications. Thus, the section about user-defined functions actually talks about functional operators.

```
f := (x,y,z) -> expression(x,y,z);
```
shows the definition of a three-parameter function specification by means of the arrow operator.

```
unapply(func(x,y,z), x,y,z);
```
converts the function $func(x, y, z)$ into the function specification in arrow notation. This command is indispensable for any further processing of functions.

```
piecewise(cond1, f1, cond2, f2, ... , other);
```
defines a function put together piece by piece.

Handling apparent functions

The term apparent function means a function of the kind `f:=x^2-3*x`. This is an apparent function (and not a true function), because the parameter x is fixed. The advantage of apparent functions is that their handling (definition, execution of calculations) is very easy. The disadvantage is that `subs` must be used to insert values (or mathematical expressions), that is, `f(y)` or `f(2)` is not allowed.

```
f:=x^2-3*x;
```
$$f := x^2 - 3x$$
```
f1:=2*diff(f,x);
```
$$f1 := 4x - 6$$
```
subs(x=3,f1);
```
$$6$$

The obvious solution of defining functions by means of `f(x):=..` does not lead to the desired result because Maple misinterprets the instruction (from the user's point of view). When it sees `f(x):=sin(x)` Maple stores in a table the information that f, in the special case when the argument is x, leads to the result $sin(x)$. Now, if you enter `f(y)` or `f(2)`, Maple has no information at its disposal about what it should do with the argument, so it returns the function unevaluated in the form $f(y)$ or $f(2)$, respectively.

```
restart:
f(x):=sin(x);
```
$$f(x) := \sin(x)$$
```
f(x), f(y), f(2);
```
$$\sin(x), f(y), f(2)$$

Such apparent misbehaviour by Maple is, in reality, a mechanism which allows fast access to already calculated function values; this can significantly accelerate the calculation of recursive functions. This mechanism (the `remember` option) is briefly introduced in this chapter in the section on the definition of recursive functions, and described in detail in Chapter 28 on programming.

Defining user functions

The formulation of true functions is carried out by means of a so-called functional operator. This is how Maple calls the function specification. Functional operators can be indicated in two syntactically different but semantically equivalent notations. Usually, the definition of functional operators looks like this:

```
func := (variable list) -> function specification;
```

This scheme is illustrated by the examples on the right. The function specification f has one parameter which can be arbitrarily specified, enclosed in a postfixed pair of parentheses.

```
f:=x->x^2-3*x;
```
$$f := x \mapsto x^2 - 3x$$

```
f(x), f(sin(y)), f(25.77);
```
$$x^2 - 3x, \sin(y)^2 - 3\sin(y), 586.7829$$

```
diff(f(x),x);
```
$$2x - 3$$

g has three parameters, so the entire parameter list must be enclosed in parentheses.

```
g:=(x,y,z)->(x^y)^z;
```
$$g := (x, y, z) \mapsto x^{y^z}$$

```
g(a,b,c), g(2,3,4);
```
$$a^{b^c}, 4096$$

The examples on the right show that the functions – which become proper functions only after inserting the parameters – can be used for normal calculations. However, it is also possible to combine function specifications.

```
f:=x->x^2: g:=y->y^3:
(f+2*g)(z), (f*g)(z), (f@g)(z);
```
$$z^2 + 2z^3, z^5, z^6$$

Please note that whether a function is defined with x or with y plays no role – these symbols only represent placeholders for the function parameters. (f@g)(z) is equivalent to $f(g(z))$. When embedding functions, care must be taken to use the correct number of parameters – if f only yields scalar results, but g expects two parameters, the combination results in an error message.

Functions can also be defined in such a way that they supply several results as a sequence. In the last example, f is inserted into g. This insertion would not work the other way round, because f expects only one parameter, whereas g supplies a sequence of two parameters.

```
f:=x->(x,1+1/x);
```
$$f := x \mapsto x, 1 + x^{-1}$$

```
g:=(x,y)->(x^2/y, y^2/x);
```
$$g := (x, y) \mapsto \frac{x^2}{y}, \frac{y^2}{x}$$

```
f(3), (g@f)(3);
```
$$3, 4/3, \frac{27}{4}, \frac{16}{27}$$

If, after the arrow operator ->, square brackets or braces are used instead of the round parentheses, the function supplies its results as a list or a set, but these results cannot be inserted into another function.

To conclude, a practical example: the newly defined command chop rounds numerical values with a precision that is two digits less than Maple's predefined global precision. The number of digits used for numerical calculations is taken from the global variable Digits.

```
chop:=x->round(x*10^(Digits-2)) / 10^(Digits-2);
```
$$chop := x \mapsto \text{round}(x * 10^{(Digits-2)}) / 10^{(Digits-2)}$$

The following examples illustrate the application of chop: single numbers can be directly specified as the function value. If a whole list of values is to be processed (for example, the numerical solution of an equation), the function specification must be applied to all elements of the list by means of map.

```
chop(0.999999999+1.00000000001 *I);
```

$$1 + I$$

```
f:=expand((x+100)*(x-3)*(x-I)*(x-2+I)^2): sln:=fsolve(f,x);
```

$$sln := -100.0 - 8.939053788 \times 10^{-17} I, 1.0I, 3.0 - 3.233523490 \times 10^{-18} I, 2.0 - 1.0I,$$

$$2.0 - 1.0I$$

```
map(chop,[sln]);
```

$$[-100, I, 3, 2 - I, 2 - I]$$

Warning: In Maple V, Release 4 there is a serious error in the round function. For very large numbers, round supplies results that are wrong by several powers of 10. Thus, evalf(round(10.^11)) yields the result 0.110^{20}. This error obviously affects chop as well; chop(1000) yields 1000 (symbolic calculation), chop(1000.) instead yields 100000000000 (numeric calculation). This error occurs in the Windows version of Maple. It is not known whether other versions are affected as well.

Bracket notation for functional operators

In previous versions of Maple, functions could also be defined in bracket notation. Since Release 4, this possibility no longer exists. You must use either the arrow operator or a function definition with proc (see the section below on defining functions via procedures).

```
Release 3                          since Release 4
f:=<x^2|x>;                        f:=x->x^2;
f:= < (y*z,x*z,x*y) | x,y,z >;     f:=(x,y,z)->(y*z, x*z, x*y);
f:= < seq(x^i,i=1..n) | x,n | i >; f:=proc(x,n) local i:
                                         seq(x^i, i=1..n);
                                       end:
```

The unapply command

Problems occur when the results of one calculation are to be stored in a new function specification. A direct assignment fails because Maple does not evaluate the expression specified after the arrow operator, but stores it unchanged.

```
f:=x->1/(1+x^2):
f1:=x->diff(f(x),x);
```

$$f1 := x \mapsto diff(f(x), x)$$

```
f1(1);
     Error, (in f1) wrong number
     (or type) of parameters in
     function diff;
```

Maple first substitutes *f1*, that is, the expression `diff(f(x), x)`, with $x = 1$ and subsequently fails during differentiation. To ensure that *f1* contains the result of $\frac{df}{dx}$, the `unapply` command must be used. This command converts a function of the form $f(x)$ into a function specification $x \mapsto f$.

```
f1:=unapply(diff(f(x),x) ,x);
```

$$f1 := x \mapsto -\frac{2x}{(1+x^2)^2}$$

```
f1(1);
```

$$-1/2$$

`unapply` can also be used for multi-parameter functions. However, the function is only generalized for those parameters that are actually specified in `unapply` (thus, in the first example on the right, only for x, y and z, not for a and b).

```
unapply(a*x^2+b*y^2+c*z^2,x,y,z);
```

$$(x, y, z) \mapsto ax^2 + by^2 + cz^2$$

```
unapply([1/x,1/(x+y),1/y], x,y);
```

$$(x, y) \mapsto [x^{-1}, (x+y)^{-1}, y^{-1}]$$

Anonymous functions

In the above examples, the function specifications were principally stored by means of assignment to a variable which was then used as a function by appending a parameter. In many Maple commands, the parameter must be a function specification. In this case, it is possible and sensible to use the bare function specification (without parameters). Such function specifications are known as anonymous.

In the example on the right, the list in *data2* is generated from the data contained in *data1* by using the `map` command to apply the function specification square, that is, $x \mapsto x^2$, to *data1*.

```
data1:=[1,2,3,4,5]:
data2:=map(x->x^2, data1);
```

$$data2 := [1, 4, 9, 16, 25]$$

Now, `zip` is used to generate a further embedded list by applying the function specification $(x, y) \mapsto [x, y]$. (Further information about `map` and `zip` can be found in Chapter 12.)

```
data3:=zip((x,y)->[x,y],
           data1, data2);
```

$$data3 := [[1, 1], [2, 4], [3, 9], [4, 16], [5, 25]]$$

The two commands on the right first generate a list of ten random numbers; subsequently, all values less than 50 are filtered out. The anonymous function used is $x \mapsto (x < 50)$. Depending on the contents of x, this function supplies the truth value *true* or *false*, which serves as the basis on which the `select` function selects the required list elements.

```
data:=[seq(rand(100)(),i=1..10)];
```

$$data := [60, 82, 92, 13, 77, 49, 35, 61, 48, 3]$$

```
select(x->(x<50), data);
```

$$[13, 49, 35, 48, 3]$$

Defining functions via procedures

Even though Maple normally hides this fact beneath the surface, Maple's function specifications are represented as procedures in the syntax of Maple's internal programming language. The same syntax is used to realize the majority of Maple commands.

```
f:=x->x^2;
```
$$f := x \mapsto x^2$$

```
lprint(");
    proc (x) options operator, arrow;
    x^2 end
```

The above example shows the general syntax of procedures. The procedure begins with the keyword proc, followed by a list of parameters. Subsequently, various options can be named and local variables can be defined with local. Here, the main part of the procedure simply consists of x^2, but it can be much more extensive and contain branching conditions with if ... then ... fi and loops with for ... od. The procedure terminates with the keyword end.

Now, apart from the arrow and bracket notations, you have a third variation for formulating functions at your disposal. The definition of functions with proc, however, only makes sense when you use the additional possibilities it offers, such as the automatic data type checking of parameters or the remember option, which causes the function to store all calculated results in a table so that when it is called later with the same parameters, the results can be accessed immediately without recalculation.

When inputting the function, you must separate the lines with (Shift)+ (←) and terminate the input with (←) only after the last line. The sample function diffn produces the first n derivatives of the passed function.

```
diffn:=proc(f,n)
  local i:
  seq(diff(f,x$i), i=1..n);
end:
diffn(arctan(x), 4);
```
$$\frac{1}{(1+x^2)}, -\frac{2\,x}{(1+x^2)^2}, \frac{8\,x^2}{(1+x^2)^3} - \frac{2}{(1+x^2)^2}, -\frac{48\,x^3}{(1+x^2)^4} + \frac{24\,x}{(1+x^2)^3}$$

Defining recursive functions

In practice, you particularly need procedures for the definition of mathematical functions when you want to work with recursive functions. Let us take the well-known Fibonacci function as an example. This recursive function is defined as follows:

$$f(0) = 0, f(1) = 1, f(n) = f(n-1)+f(n-2)$$

```
f:=x->if x=0 then 0
    elif x=1 then 1
    else f(x-1)+f(x-2) fi:
f(5), f(25);
```
$$5, 75025$$

This definition uses the syntax elements `if`, `elif`, and so on, which are also allowed for use with the arrow operator. However, the definition has two disadvantages: firstly, it is rather slow. (The calculation of $f(25)$ takes several seconds and for higher Fibonacci numbers the calculation time rises exponentially.) And secondly, the protection against errors is completely insufficient.

```
f(-4); f(3.5); f(x);
  Error, too many levels of recursion
  Error, too many levels of recursion
  Error, too many levels of recursion
```

The following redefinition as a procedure represents a twofold improvement: firstly, an automatic type check is carried out for the x parameter (only non-negative integer numbers are allowed), and secondly the `remember` option ensures that the function internally stores all Fibonacci numbers calculated at any time (even as intermediate results). This accelerates the recursive calculation by several orders of magnitude.

```
f:=proc(x::nonnegint)
  option remember;
  if x=0 then 0
  elif x=1 then 1
  else f(x-1)+f(x-2) fi
end:
```

Even $f(50)$ is now calculated without a noticeable delay.

```
f(50);
      12586269025
```

If the function is passed an illegal parameter, it now reacts with an understandable error message.

```
f(1.5);
      Error, f expects its 1st argument,
      x, to be of type nonnegint, but
      received 1.5
```

Note: Both the possibilities of defining functions with `proc` and the background to the `remember` option have only been lightly touched upon in this section. More in-depth information, for example on the commands `profile` (time and memory analysis) and `forget` (processing of the `remember` table), can be found in the chapters about programming in Maple, from Chapter 28 onward.

Piecewise assembled functions

With the `piecewise` command you can assemble functions piece by piece. The function expects its parameters as pairs, with the first parameter being a condition and the second parameter a function which applies if the condition is satisfied. An additional optional parameter can be used to specify a default value which applies if none of the conditions is satisfied.

Warning: `piecewise` has been thoroughly revised in Release 4. There is only one detail in which the new syntax is incompatible with the one used in Release 3: here, the first parameter of `piecewise` used to specify how many times the function could be differentiated. In the new version of `piecewise`, this parameter no longer exists.

The handling of `piecewise` is best shown with the aid of an example: the function f is defined as 0 for values of x less than 0, as the function x for values of x between 0 and 1, as 1 for values of x between 1 and 2, as the function $3 - x$ for values of x between 2 and 3, and again as 0 for all other values of x.

The example also shows the application of the function (numeric evaluation for a given value, integration, differentiation). At some points (points of discontinuity), the derivative is not defined.

```
f:=x->piecewise(x<0,0, x<1,x, x<2,1,
                x<3,3-x,0): f(x);
```

$$\begin{cases} 0 & x < 0 \\ x & x < 1 \\ 1 & x < 2 \\ 3 - x & x < 3 \\ 0 & \textit{otherwise} \end{cases}$$

```
f(2.6);
```

$.4$

```
int(f(x), x=0..3);
```

2

```
fin:=unapply(int(f(x),x), x): fin(x);
```

$$\begin{cases} 0 & x \le 0 \\ \dfrac{1}{2}x^2 & x \le 1 \\ -\dfrac{1}{2} + x & x \le 2 \\ -\dfrac{1}{2}x^2 - \dfrac{5}{2} + 3x & x \le 3 \\ 2 & 3 < x \end{cases}$$

```
f1:=unapply(diff(f(x),x), x): f1(x);
```

$$\begin{cases} 0 & x < 0 \\ \textit{undefined} & x = 0 \\ 1 & x < 1 \\ \textit{undefined} & x = 1 \\ 0 & x < 2 \\ \textit{undefined} & x = 2 \\ -1 & x < 3 \\ \textit{undefined} & x = 3 \\ 0 & 3 < x \end{cases}$$

The illustration on the right shows the function f (at the top) and its derivative $f1$, which has been decreased by 2 for visual reasons.

```
plot({f,f1-2}, x=-1..4, axes=boxed);
```

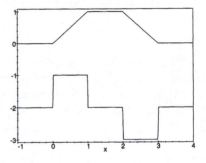

When attempting to produce the second derivative of f, `diff` supplies an incomplete definition: only the points of discontinuity are indicated, but not the function value proper. `convert(.., piecewise)` completes the definition.

```
f2a:=unapply(
  convert(f2(x),piecewise), x):
f2a(x);
```

$$\begin{cases} 0 & x < 0 \\ \textit{undefined} & x = 0 \\ 0 & x < 1 \\ \textit{undefined} & x = 1 \\ 0 & x < 2 \\ \textit{undefined} & x = 2 \\ 0 & x < 3 \\ \textit{undefined} & x = 3 \\ 0 & 3 < x \end{cases}$$

convert(..,piecewise) can also cope with much more complex cases: in the example on the right, the case conditions derive from the points of discontinuity of the abs and signum functions.

```
convert(-signum(x)*abs(1-abs(x)),
        piecewise);
```

$$\begin{cases} -1-x & x \leq -1 \\ 1+x & x < 0 \\ 0 & x = 0 \\ -1+x & x < 1 \\ 1-x & 1 \leq x \end{cases}$$

The following commands present a final example of the versatility of piecewise: a function is defined which describes an arc of a circle. convert(,..piecewise) substitutes the condition $x^2 \leq r^2$ with conditions into which x enters as a simple variable. The assume property for r is a precondition for this conversion.

```
assume(r>0); f:=unapply(piecewise(x^2<=r^2, sqrt(r^2-x^2),0), x): f(x);
```

$$f := \begin{cases} \sqrt{r^{\sim 2} - x^2} & x^2 \leq r^{\sim 2} \\ 0 & \text{otherwise} \end{cases}$$

```
convert(f(x),piecewise,x);
```

$$\begin{cases} 0 & x \leq -r^{\sim} \\ \sqrt{r^{\sim 2} - x^2} & x \leq r^{\sim} \\ 0 & r^{\sim} < x \end{cases}$$

A piecewise function can be transformed into an expression with the Heaviside unit-step function with convert(..,Heaviside). Mathematically, the representations are equivalent. For the function used at the beginning of this section, this looks as follows:

```
f:=x->piecewise(x<0,0, x<1,x, x<2,1, x<3,3-x, 0):
convert(f(x),Heaviside);
```

$$x\,\text{Heaviside}(x) - x\,\text{Heaviside}(x-1) + \text{Heaviside}(x-1) + 2\,\text{Heaviside}(x-2) -$$

$$3\,\text{Heaviside}(x-3) - x\,\text{Heaviside}(x-2) + x\,\text{Heaviside}(x-3)$$

Syntax summary

```
f:=x -> expression(x);
f:=(x,y,..) -> expression(x,y,..);
```
    defines a one- or multi-parameter function by means of the arrow operator.

```
f:=proc(x::typ1, y::typ2, ..)
   local l1,l2,..;  options ..;
   expression(x,y,..);
end:
```
    defines a multi-parameter function by means of a procedure. A permitted option is, for example, remember. An automatic data type check is carried out for all parameters. A detailed description of Maple's language elements can be found in Chapter 12.

`f:=unapply(expression(x,y,..), x,y,..);`

transforms the specified expression of the variables $x, y, ..$ into a functional operator in arrow notation. `unapply(sin(x*y), x, y)` becomes $(x, y) \mapsto sin(x, y)$. `unapply` is needed to define new functions.

`f:=piecewise(cond1, f1, cond2, f2, ..., condn, fn, fdefault);`

defines the function f. For all values of x which satisfy the condition *cond1*, f is defined by $f1$, for all values of x which satisfy the condition *cond2*, by $f2$, and so on. For values of x which satisfy none of the specified conditions, the optional default function *fdefault* applies.

`convert(f, piecewise, x);`

converts f into a piecewise defined function. This conversion makes sense when f contains discontinuous functions, such as `abs`, `signum` or `Heaviside`.

`convert(f, Heaviside);`

converts f into a function, in which `Heaviside` is used to bridge points of discontinuity. This conversion is particularly useful for piecewise defined functions (`piecewise`).

Chapter 9

Complex numbers

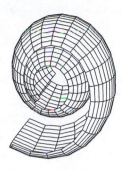

Maple essentially does not differentiate between real and complex numbers. Nearly all Maple functions (for example, `sin`, `cos`, `sqrt` or `abs`) can be applied to complex numbers as well as real numbers. True differences in the treatment of real and complex numbers only occur when real and imaginary parts are stored in two different variables (which can often be useful). In this case, complex expressions can be simplified with the aid of `evalc`. The most important functions and commands discussed in this chapter are:

`I`
the imaginary unit $\sqrt{-1}$.

`Re, Im`
determine the real and imaginary parts of complex numbers or expressions.

`abs, argument`
determine amount and phase angle.

`polar`
calculates a complex number from amount and phase angle.

`evalc`
simplifies expressions under the assumption that the variables used in it are real. The result is split into real and imaginary parts (if possible).

`assume`
defines individual variables as real or complex and thus allows simplifications without having to use `evalc`.

Elementary functions for the processing of complex numbers

The functions `Re` and `Im` are used to determine the real and imaginary parts of a complex expression. Please note that in contrast to most other Maple functions, these functions must be spelt with upper case initials.

```
z:=1 + 3*I;
```
$$z := 1 + 3\,I$$
```
Re(z), Im(z);
```
$$1, 3$$

abs calculates the amount of a complex number, argument the phase angle. conjugate returns the conjugate-complex number (that is, the sign of the imaginary part is changed).

```
abs(z), argument(z);
```
$$\sqrt{10}, \arctan(3)$$
```
conjugate(z);
```
$$1 - 3I$$

There are two different signum functions for complex numbers. signum(z) normalizes a complex number to length 1, that is, $\frac{z}{|z|}$ is calculated. signum(0) returns the result 1.

```
signum(2+3*I);
```
$$\left(2/13 + \frac{3I}{13}\right)\sqrt{13}$$

Alternatively, the csgn can be used. This function returns 1 for complex numbers in the right half-plane (that is, $\Re(z) > 0$) and -1 for numbers in the left half-plane ($\Re(z) < 0$). If $\Re(z) = 0$ applies, the result depends on the sign of the imaginary part.

```
csgn(1+I), csgn(1-I), csgn(-1+I);
```
$$1, 1, -1$$
```
csgn(2), csgn(2*I), csgn(-I), csgn(0);
```
$$1, 1, -1, 1$$

Maple usually displays complex numbers in the form $a + Ib$. With convert(z, polar) you can force a notation of the polar(r,phi) form. You can also use the polar function when you want to write complex numbers in polar form yourself.

```
convert(z,polar);
```
$$polar(\sqrt{10}, \arctan(3))$$
```
z1:=polar(1,Pi/3);
```
$$z1 := polar(1, \frac{\pi}{3})$$
```
abs(z1);
```
$$1$$

Complex numbers with separate real and imaginary parts

Complex numbers are normally stored in a complex variable. If the components are to be assigned to two real variables for further processing, then, in most cases, the evalc command must be used. evalc processes expressions under the assumption that all variables are real. Thus, Maple can carry out various simplifications which would otherwise not be possible.

```
evalc(Re((a + I*b)^3));
```
$$a^3 - 3ab^2$$
```
evalc(polar(a, b));
```
$$a\cos(b) + I a\sin(b)$$
```
evalc(Re(sqrt(a+I*b)));
```
$$\sqrt{\frac{\sqrt{a^2+b^2}}{2} + \frac{a}{2}}$$

The above results are only valid under the assumption that a and b are real numbers! If you substitute a with an arbitrary complex number with an imaginary part $\neq 0$, the results are wrong! For this reason, Maple normally does not carry out this kind of simplification and must be explicitly told to do so with evalc.

evalc is also capable of transforming complex E powers into sine and cosine terms.

```
f:=(3-I)* exp((3-I)*t)
 + (3+I)* exp((3+I)*t);
```

$$f := (3 - I)\, e^{(3-I)t} + (3 + I)\, e^{(3+I)t}$$

```
evalc(f);
```

$$6\, e^{3t} \cos(t) - 2\, e^{3t} \sin(t)$$

Apart from evalc, there is a second, more elegant way of simplifying complex expressions with real variables: the assume command already introduced in Chapter 6. This can be used to provide Maple with information about the contents of a variable – for example, that the variable is real. Maple will then automatically recognize possibilities for simplification (without using evalc).

```
assume(a1, real);
assume(b1, real); Re(a1);
```

$$a1^{\sim}$$

```
Re((a1+I*b1)^3);
```

$$\Re((a1^{\sim} + I\, b1^{\sim})^3)$$

```
Re(expand((a1+I*b1)^3));
```

$$a1^{\sim 3} - 3\, a1^{\sim} b1^{\sim 2}$$

Maple marks all variables for which additional information is available via assume with a postfixed ~ character. In the second example, the simplification does not seem to work. This is due to the fact that Maple does not calculate the term (a1+I*b1)^3 and cannot therefore simplify it. We need to apply the expand command (see next chapter).

In some cases, assume is also the more efficient way to reach results. In particular, the combination of evalc and polar does not always work satisfactorily, although with assume (thus, with the variables *a1* and *b1*), Maple is perfectly capable of providing clearer results:

```
convert(evalc(sin(a+I*b)), polar);
```

$$polar(|\sin(a) \cosh(b) + I\, \cos(a) \sinh(b)|, \, argument(\sin(a) \cosh(b) + I\, \cos(a) \sinh(b)))$$

```
convert(sin(a1+I*b1), polar);
```

$$polar(\sqrt{\sin(a1^{\sim})^2 \cosh(b1^{\sim})^2 + \cos(a1^{\sim})^2 \sinh(b1^{\sim})^2}, \,$$

$$\arctan(\cos(a1^{\sim}) \sinh(b1^{\sim}), \sin(a1^{\sim}) \cosh(b1^{\sim})))$$

Syntax summary

I
   imaginary unit I, abbreviation for $\sqrt{-1}$.

Re(z);   Im(z);
   determine real and imaginary parts of a complex number.

abs(z);   argument(z);
   determine amount and phase angle of a complex number.

`conjugate(z);`

calculates the conjugate-complex number for z, thus, modifies the sign of the imaginary part.

`signum(z);`

yields $\frac{z}{|z|}$, that is, a complex pointer of length 1.

`csgn(z);`

determines in which half-plane z is located. The function returns +1 for $z = 0$, for $\Re(z) > 0$ and for $\Re(z) = 0$, if at the same time $\Im(z) > 0$. All other situations lead to the result -1.

`polar(amount, angle);`

converts the complex number $amount * E^{I*angle}$ into the form $a + Ib$ normally used in Maple.

`convert(z, polar);`

converts the complex expression z into the form `polar(amount, angle)`.

`evalc(expression);`

simplifies the complex expression under the assumption that all variables occurring in it are real (and not complex).

`assume(x, real);`

defines the variable x as real (and not complex). Maple then recognizes various simplifications when calculating with x, for example $\Re(x) = x$ and $\Im(x) = 0$.

Chapter 10

Processing and simplification
of mathematical expressions

Although the title of this chapter may sound rather abstract, the chapter deals with one of the most important subjects of this practice-oriented book: simplification of mathematical expressions. This is of utmost importance, because computer algebra systems such as Maple tend to produce endless formulae (often several pages long). These formulae are mathematically correct, but in this form they neither lend themselves to further processing nor allow the user to understand the result.

The main part of this chapter discusses a series of commands which (may) help with the simplification of mathematical expressions:

`simplify`
tries to simplify a mathematical expression.

`expand`, `factor` and `combine`
are mutually complementary commands. `expand` multiplies out all open products. `factor` and `combine` try to combine the sum of single terms back into the underlying terms.

`normal`
transforms rational functions into their normal form.

`sprint`
formats very complex expressions in a space-saving manner.

In addition, some commands will be introduced which are suitable to further processing in a mathematical sense: for example, `quo` to divide polynomials or `convert(..., apart)` to carry out expansions into partial fractions.

Maple's simplification effort: simplify

It cannot always be clearly decided which is the simplest form of a mathematical expression. A definition which comes close to human thinking may be that an expression is simple when it is made up of as few single terms as possible. However, this certainly does not mean that this form is also mathematically suitable (for example, if the expression is to be integrated later on).

Even less obvious is the means of achieving a simpler form of a mathematical expression. When $(x-2)(x+2)(x^2-4)$ is multiplied out, the result x^4-16 is shorter, but multiplying out $(x-1)^{10}+1$ would be the wrong approach – it leads to a sum of 10 terms.

The `simplify` command tries to simplify a given mathematical expression by applying various transformation rules. The emphasis is on 'tries', since fairly often the result of `simplify` is more complicated than the original expression. Thus, you should not expect miracles from this command! When you have the result of a calculation and you do not know which of the commands listed in the next sections will help, then `simplify` is at least worth a try – as the old saying goes: It may not help, but at least it doesn't hurt. (Care must be taken with very complex expressions: the calculation time may tend to rise astronomically.)

The following examples show some applications of `simplify`. First, the third derivative of $\frac{x}{1-x^2}$ is to be simplified and this is successfully achieved. `simplify` transforms rational functions into their normal form (see also `normal` some sections further down).

```
diff(x/(1-x^2), x$3);
```
$$\frac{48\,x^2}{(1-x^2)^3} + \frac{6}{(1-x^2)^2} + \frac{48\,x^4}{(1-x^2)^4}$$

```
simplify(");
```
$$\frac{36\,x^2 + 6\,x^4 + 6}{(-1+x^2)^4}$$

Nor do simple expressions with trigonometrical expressions, powers, logarithms, and so on cause insurmountable difficulties.

```
simplify(sin(x)^2+cos(x)^2);
```
$$1$$

```
simplify(exp(a*ln(b)));
```
$$b^a$$

While the above examples give the impression that `simplify` works rather well, it is very easy to find examples to the contrary which raise doubts about the practicability of `simplify` (see also the second paragraph of this section).

```
simplify((x-2)*(x+2)*(x^2+4));
```
$$(x-2)(x+2)\left(x^2+4\right)$$

```
simplify((x-1)^10+1);
```
$$x^{10} - 10\,x^9 + 45\,x^8 - 120\,x^7 + 210\,x^6 -$$
$$252\,x^5 + 210\,x^4 - 120\,x^3 + 45\,x^2 -$$
$$10\,x + 2$$

Also, as soon as the argument x is modified, Maple no longer recognizes the already known relation $\sin(x)^2 + \cos(x)^2 = 1$. However, if the whole expression is processed beforehand with `expand` (see next but one section), the simplification will eventually succeed.

```
f:=sin(a^2-b^2)^2 + cos((a-b)*(a+b))^2; simplify(f);
```
$$f := \sin(-a^2 + b^2)^2 + \cos((a-b)(a+b))^2$$
$$1 - \cos(-a^2+b^2)^2 + \cos((-a+b)(a+b))^2$$

```
expand(f); simplify(");
```
$$\sin(a^2)^2\cos(b^2)^2 + \cos(a^2)^2\sin(b^2)^2 + \cos(a^2)^2\cos(b^2)^2 + \sin(a^2)^2\sin(b^2)^2$$
$$1$$

Maple is also overstretched by the task of determining common factors (here: $\frac{1}{(1-\sin(x))^n}$). Neither simplify nor any other Maple command succeeds in unifying terms 1 and 4 and terms 2 and 5. We will show in other sections, further down, how this task can be solved with the use of select, at least for this example.

```
diff(x/(1-sin(x)),x$3);
```

$$\frac{6\,\cos(x)^2}{(1-\sin(x))^3} - \frac{3\,\sin(x)}{(1-\sin(x))^2} + \frac{6\,\cos(x)^3 x}{(1-\sin(x))^4} - \frac{6\,\cos(x)\sin(x)x}{(1-\sin(x))^3} - \frac{\cos(x)x}{(1-\sin(x))^2}$$

```
simplify(");
```

$$\frac{-3\,\sin(x)\cos(x)^2 - 6\,\sin(x) + \cos(x)^3 x - 4\,\cos(x)\sin(x)x + 4\,\cos(x)x + 6}{8 - 8\,\sin(x) + 4\,\sin(x)\cos(x)^2 - 8\,\cos(x)^2 + \cos(x)^4}$$

For expressions in the form a^b simplify carries out only those simplifications that are mathematically permitted for every possible value of a and b. Further simplifications, which only apply under conditions such as $a > 0$, can be obtained by using the optional keyword symbolic or by specifying further properties with assume.

```
simplify(sqrt(Pi^2 * n^2)), simplify(sqrt(Pi^2 * n^2), symbolic);
```

$$\pi\,\text{csgn}(\,n\,)\,n,\,\pi\,n$$

```
assume(n>=0): simplify(sqrt(Pi ^2 * n^2));
```

$$\pi\,n^\sim$$

```
simplify((a*b)^c), simplify((a*b)^c, symbolic);
```

$$(\,a\,b\,)^c,\,a^c\,b^c$$

```
simplify(sqrt(1/x)), simplify(sqrt(1/x), symbolic);
```

$$\sqrt{\frac{1}{x}},\,\frac{1}{\sqrt{x}}$$

Restricting the effect of simplify

simplify applies a variety of simplification rules in turn to the expressions passed to it. If you want to restrict the effects of simplify to a particular area, you can specify one of the keywords listed below as a second parameter. This kind of restriction has two advantages: simplify works significantly faster with large expressions, and you can avoid simplifications which are not actually required.

atsign	operators, inverse functions, such as $\arcsin @ \sin \to 1$
Ei	integral functions
exp	exponential functions
GAMMA	gamma functions
hypergeom	hypergeometric functions
ln	logarithmic functions

polar	complex expressions in polar notation, such as $\mathrm{polar}(a, b)^c \to \mathrm{polar}(a^c, b * c)$
power	powers
radical	generic expressions with roots, such as $\frac{(a^2 - b^2)^{3/5}}{(a-b)^{2/5}} \to \sqrt[5]{a-b}\,(a+b)^{3/5}$
sqrt	square roots, such as $\sqrt{32^3} \to 128\sqrt{2}$
trig	trigonometric functions

Please note that in this instance the syntax of `simplify` differs from that of many other Maple commands. The specification of one of the above keywords in `simplify` leads to a restriction of the simplification. In most other commands (for example, `combine`) it is only the specification of additional keywords that actually activates additional mechanisms which would otherwise not be taken into consideration at all!

The following examples demonstrate the restriction of `simplify`. The function f is first simplified only with respect to trigonometric functions.

```
f:=exp(b*ln(a))-
   (a*sin(x)^2+a*cos(x)^2)^b;
```

$$f := e^{b\ln(a)} - \left(a\sin(x)^2 + a\cos(x)^2\right)^b$$

```
simplify(f,trig);
```

$$e^{b\ln(a)} - a^b$$

The second `simplify` command simplifies with regard to the exponential function only.

```
simplify(f,exp);
```

$$a^b - \left(a\sin(x)^2 + a\cos(x)^2\right)^b$$

`simplify` carries out its entire spectrum of activity only at the third call.

```
simplify(f);
```

$$0$$

Eliminating variables (simplify with end conditions)

If one or more equations are given in a list (square brackets) or a set (braces) in the second parameter of `simplify`, Maple uses this additional information in the simplification of polynomials. The most impressive example comes from Heck (1993) and was the task of the 1991 Dutch Mathematical Olympics:

How big is $a^4 + b^4 + c^4$, if a, b and c are real numbers and the following assumptions apply: $a+b+c = 3$, $a^2+b^2+c^2 = 9$ and $a^3+b^3+c^3 = 24$? `simplify` reaches this non-trivial solution at the first try (and in a very short time).

```
eqn1:=a+b+c = 3:
eqn2:=a^2+b^2+c^2 = 9:
eqn3:=a^3+b^3+c^3 = 24:
simplify(a^4+b^4+c^4, {eqn1,eqn2,eqn3});
```

$$69$$

The mathematical background for this simplification is represented by a Gröbner basis, which Maple constructs from the three equations. Further information on this subject can be found in Heck (1993) and by calling help about `?simplify,siderels`.

In the third parameter of `simplify`, the variables for which the Gröbner basis is constructed can be specified. This specification is only important if the number of variables that occur is higher than the number of equations. If this specification is omitted, Maple itself selects the variables for the Gröbner basis.

```
simplify((a-b+c)^2, {a+b=1});
```
$$c^2 - 2c + 1 + (4c - 4)a + 4a^2$$
```
simplify((a-b+c)^2, {a+b=1},{a});
```
$$4b^2 - 4bc + c^2 - 4b + 2c + 1$$

Thus, `simplify` can be used to eliminate specific variables from equation systems with several variables. In the example on the right, first x and then y is eliminated from the equation system $\{eqn1, eqn2\}$. Thus, the result is presented in the form of an equation with one variable.

```
eqn1:=x^2+3*x+4*x*y=7;
```
$$eqn1 := x^2 + 3x + 4xy = 7$$
```
eqn2:=y^2-6*x*y+x=0;
```
$$eqn2 := y^2 - 6xy + x = 0$$
```
simplify(eqn1,{eqn2},{x});
```
$$\frac{\left(14y + 25y^2 - 3\right)y^2}{(6y - 1)^2} = 7$$
```
simplify(eqn2,{eqn1},{y});
```
$$\frac{94x^3 + 25x^4 - 173x^2 - 42x + 49}{16x^2} = 0$$

In the example on the right, the three equations for variables a, b and c are reduced to two equations for variables b and c.

```
eqn1:=a+b+c = 7:
eqn2:=a-b+3*c = 8:
eqn3:=a-2*b+5*c = 9:
simplify({eqn1,eqn2}, {eqn3}, {a});
```
$$\{b - 2c + 9 = 8, 3b - 4c + 9 = 7\}$$

Expanding products (expand)

Maple usually leaves products as they are, without multiplying them out. `expand` carries out the multiplications.

```
x*(x-a)^2*(x-b)^3;
```
$$x(x - a)^2(x - b)^3$$
```
expand(");
```
$$x^6 - 3x^5b + 3x^4b^2 - x^3b^3 - 2x^5a +$$
$$6x^4ab - 6x^3ab^2 + 2x^2ab^3 + a^2x^4 -$$
$$3a^2x^3b + 3a^2x^2b^2 - xa^2b^3$$

`expand` has a similar effect on powers. Please note the unusual way in which the first example has been formulated: the formula to be expanded is given as a Maple command, which is subsequently referred to twice with ".

```
a^(b+c^(d+e*f)): " = expand( " );
```
$$a^{b+c^{d+ef}} = a^b a^{c^d c^{ef}}$$
```
expand(log(a*b)), expand(log(a^b));
```
$$\ln(a) + \ln(b), b\ln(a)$$

In trigonometric and logarithmic functions, expand tries to simplify the arguments, whereby single terms are often converted into sums.

```
expand(sin(4*x));
```

$$8 \sin(x) \cos(x)^3 - 4 \sin(x) \cos(x)$$

```
expand(sin(a+b));
```

$$\sin(a) \cos(b) + \cos(a) \sin(b)$$

In rational functions, expand only affects the numerator.

```
f:=(x-a)^2/(x+b)^3: expand(f);
```

$$\frac{x^2}{(x+b)^3} - \frac{2\,xa}{(x+b)^3} + \frac{a^2}{(x+b)^3}$$

If the denominator is to be multiplied out as well, the function can be split into numerator and denominator with numer and denom and subsequently processed separately. You can arrive at the same result with normal(..., expanded) – see the section about processing rational functions in this chapter.

```
expand(numer(f))/expand(denom(f));
```

$$\frac{x^2 - 2\,xa + a^2}{x^3 + 3\,x^2 b + 3\,xb^2 + b^3}$$

Factorizing sums (factor)

factor is the counterpart to expand, insofar as the multiplying out of products is concerned. factor tries to convert a sum of single terms back into product form.

```
factor(x^4-4*x^3*b+4*x^2*b^2+x^3*a-
    4*x^2*a*b+4*x*a*b^2);
```

$$x\,(x - 2\,b)^2\,(x + a)$$

```
factor(x^4-y^4);
```

$$(x - y)\,(x + y)\,(y^2 + x^2)$$

Rational functions are first converted into their normal form (see next but one section), then numerator and denominator are factorized.

```
factor((x^2+x-6)/(x^2-1));
```

$$\frac{(x - 2)\,(x + 3)}{(x - 1)\,(x + 1)}$$

When factor does not find integer roots, it leaves the expression in its original form. However, an additional argument can help Maple with the task of factorizing.

```
factor(1+x^2);
```

$$1 + x^2$$

```
factor(1+x^2,I);
```

$$(x + I)\,(x - I)$$

Since Release 4, factor is rather pernickety over the notation for roots: these must be written in the form $-x^{n/m}$. The usual Maple notation with the imaginary unit I is no longer allowed.

```
factor(x^2+3,I*sqrt(3));
   Error, (in factor) 2nd argument is
   not a valid algebraic extension
factor(x^2+3,sqrt(-3));
   Error, (in factor) 2nd argument ...
factor(x^2+3,(-3)^(1/2));
```

$$(x + I\,\sqrt{3})(x - I\,\sqrt{3})$$

Combining similar terms (combine)

combine represents a second counterpart to expand. Whereas factor combines multiplied-out terms into factors, combine is responsible for the combination of more generic functions and commands.

combine combines the exponents of a product into a sum.

```
combine(x^a*x^b,power);
```
$$x^{a+b}$$

combine combines several roots into a common root.

```
combine(sqrt(3)*sqrt(5));
```
$$\sqrt{15}$$

```
combine(sqrt(a)*sqrt(b));
```
$$\sqrt{a\,b}$$

With radnormal, expressions containing roots can often be simplified to a higher degree than with combine.

```
f:=(sqrt(2)-sqrt(3)) /
   (sqrt(2)*sqrt(3));
```
$$f := \frac{1}{6}\left(\sqrt{2}-\sqrt{3}\right)\sqrt{2}\,\sqrt{3}$$

```
combine(f);
```
$$\sqrt{6}\left(1/6\,\sqrt{2}-1/6\,\sqrt{3}\right)$$

```
radnormal(f);
```
$$\frac{1}{3}\,\sqrt{3}-\frac{1}{2}\,\sqrt{2}$$

combine carries out most simplifications only if the required type of simplification is specified in the second parameter. At present, the following keywords are allowed: abs, atatsign, conjugate, exp, ln, plus, power, product, Psi, range, trig and signum. The examples on the right show some trigonometric simplifications.

```
combine(4*cos(x)^3 ,trig);
```
$$\cos(3\,x)+3\,\cos(x)$$

```
combine(sin(x+y)*sin(x-y), trig);
```
$$\frac{\cos(2\,y)}{2}-\frac{\cos(2\,x)}{2}$$

```
combine(cos(x)^2, trig);
```
$$\frac{\cos(2\,x)}{2}+1/2$$

In general, ln and exp must be used as keywords with logarithms and powers of e, respectively.

```
combine(exp(sin(x)^2)*exp(cos(x)^2));
```
$$e$$

```
combine(-ln(a)+2*ln(b),ln);
```
$$\ln(\frac{b^2}{a})$$

combine is capable of combining integrals with common integration limits, sums with corresponding indices, and the sums of two limiting values.

```
combine(int(f(x), x=a..b) +
        int(g(x), x=a..b));
```
$$\int_a^b f(x)+g(x)dx$$

Although `combine` produces an effect which is complementary to that of `expand`, it is not always capable of reconstructing the original expression. In this example `expand` produces a sum of 28 terms, which is not shown.

```
expand((sin(5*x)-cos(5*x))^3):
combine(",trig);
```

$$\frac{3\,\sin(5\,x)}{2} - \frac{3\,\cos(5\,x)}{2} + \frac{\sin(15\,x)}{2} + \frac{\cos(15\,x)}{2}$$

Although the name of the command suggests the contrary, `combine` is not capable of combining common terms in a sum (in the example on the right, the first and the third term). At present, there exists no Maple command at all to fulfil such a task (at first sight trivial).

```
diff(x/(1-a^x), x$2);
```

$$\frac{2\,a^x\,\ln(a)}{(1-a^x)^2} + \frac{2\,xa^{x^2}\,\ln(a)^2}{(1-a^x)^3} + \frac{xa^x\,\ln(a)^2}{(1-a^x)^2}$$

```
combine(",power);
```

$$\frac{2\,a^x\,\ln(a)}{(1-a^x)^2} + \frac{2\,xa^{x^2}\,\ln(a)^2}{(1-a^x)^3} + \frac{xa^x\,\ln(a)^2}{(1-a^x)^2}$$

Conversion into different notations (convert)

The `convert` command plays an important role in Maple in two respects: firstly, it is used for conversions between different data types (for example, between matrices and lists), and secondly, it is used to convert mathematical expressions into different notations. At this point, only the second aspect is of interest.

The general syntax of the command is `convert(expression, type)`. The conversion type can be specified by means of various keywords, some of which are described in the following table:

`exp`	write trigonometric functions as powers of E
`expln`	write all elementary functions as powers of E and logarithms
`expsincos`	write trigonometric functions as sin and cos functions, hyperbolic functions as powers of E
`ln`	write inverse trigonometric functions (`arc...`) in logarithmic form
`sincos`	write trigonometric functions as sin and cos terms, hyperbolic functions as sinh and cosh terms
`tan`	represent trigonometric functions as tan functions
`trig`	replace complex powers of E with trigonometric functions
`radical`	represent `RootOf` terms as complex roots
`RootOf`	write complex roots as `RootOf` terms
`factorial`	represent binomial and gamma functions as factorials
`GAMMA`	represent factorials as gamma functions

Reference: A few more `convert` variations are discussed in the section about processing polynomials and rational functions. For example, it is shown that `convert(..., parfrac)` is responsible for expansion into partial fractions and `convert(..., confrac)` for conversion into continued fractions. `convert(..., piecewise)` and `convert(..., Heaviside)` for handling discontinuous functions have already been introduced in Chapter 8.

The examples on the right show various applications of `convert`.

```
convert(sin(x), exp);
```

$$-I \left(e^{I\,x} - e^{I\,x^{-1}} \right) 1/2$$

```
convert(sin(2*x)^2, tan);
```

$$\frac{4 \tan(x)^2}{\left(1 + \tan(x)^2\right)^2}$$

Some care must be taken with the `convert-trig` variation: powers of E must be written using the `exp` function; `E^x` is not accepted.

```
convert(exp(I*x), trig);
```

$$\cos(x) + I \sin(x)$$

```
convert(arctan(x), ln);
```

$$\frac{I \left(\ln(1 - I\,x) - \ln(1 + I\,x) \right)}{2}$$

Maple is not capable of simplifying the `arctan(tan(t))` function into t by means of commands such as `simplify` or `combine`. This only succeeds if the `arctan` term is first converted into powers of e with `convert`. A subsequent `simplify` leads to the desired result.

```
f:=arctan(tan(t));
```

$$f := \arctan(\tan(t))$$

```
convert(f, exp);
```

$$-I\,arctanh(\frac{\left(e^{I\,t}\right)^2 - 1}{\left(e^{I\,t}\right)^2 + 1})$$

```
simplify(");
```

$$t$$

A conversion between the gamma function (see also Chapter 7) and factorial will probably be needed somewhat less frequently.

```
convert((n+m)!, GAMMA);
```

$$\Gamma(n + m + 1)$$

```
convert(GAMMA(n+m), factorial);
```

$$\frac{(n + m)!}{n + m}$$

The `share` library contains the definition of the `convert` variation `arctanh` which can be used to convert logarithmic functions into `arctanh` functions.

```
with(share):
readshare(arctanh, convert):
convert(ln(x), arctanh);
```

$$2 \operatorname{arctanh} \left(\frac{x - 1}{x + 1} \right)$$

Processing polynomials and rational functions

The emphasis in the preceding pages was on the simplification of generic mathematical expressions; this section, on the other hand, deals with the further processing of (possibly previously simplified) terms.

Two useful functions for handling rational functions are `numer` for the determination of the numerator and `denom` for the determination of the denominator. As the second example shows, for the determination of the numerator or denominator rational functions are first reduced to a common denominator.

```
sin(x)/x^2: numer("), denom(");
```
$$sin(x), x^2$$

```
a*x/(1-x^2)+b/x;
```
$$\frac{ax}{1-x^2} + \frac{b}{x}$$

```
numer(")/denom(");
```
$$\frac{-ax^2 - b + bx^2}{(-1+x^2)\,x}$$

For the division of polynomials, the `quo` and `rem` commands can be used. `quo` determines the quotient, `rem` the remainder. Please note that in both commands a division variable must be specified as a third parameter. In the second example, a check is carried out: quotient times divisor plus remainder must produce the dividend (which is indeed the case).

```
quo(x^2-3,x+1,x);
```
$$x - 1$$

```
p1:=a*x^2+b*x+c: p2:=d*x+e:
quo(p1,p2, x);
```
$$\frac{ax}{d} - \frac{-db + ea}{d^2}$$

```
rem(p1, p2, x);
```
$$\frac{d^2c - edb + e^2a}{d^2}$$

```
simplify("" * p2 + ");
```
$$ax^2 + bx + c$$

The command `normal` converts rational functions into their normal form. The whole expression is reduced to a common denominator; terms that can possibly be reduced are in fact reduced. The keyword `expanded` in the second parameter causes the factors in numerator and denominator to be multiplied out.

```
diff(x^n/(a+x),x);
```
$$\frac{x^n n}{x\,(a+x)} - \frac{x^n}{(a+x)^2}$$

```
normal(");
```
$$\frac{x^n\,(na + nx - x)}{x\,(a+x)^2}$$

```
normal(",expanded);
```
$$\frac{x^n na + x^n nx - x^n x}{xa^2 + 2\,ax^2 + x^3}$$

There is no special command for expansion into partial fractions; instead, the already known `convert` command is used with the keyword `parfrac`.

```
convert(x/(x^4-1),parfrac,x);
```
$$\frac{1}{4x-4} + \frac{1}{4x+4} - \frac{x}{2x^2+2}$$

As a third parameter, the variable over which the expansion is carried out must be specified. The example on the right shows the meaning of this variable.

```
convert(x*y/(x-y)^2,parfrac,x);
```

$$\frac{y^2}{(x-y)^2} + \frac{y}{x-y}$$

```
convert(x*y/(x-y)^2,parfrac,y);
```

$$\frac{x^2}{(x-y)^2} - \frac{x}{x-y}$$

parfrac only processes pure rational functions. For this reason, Maple refuses to carry out the expansion shown on the right.

```
f:=-(-exp(-s)/s+exp(-2*s)/s)/(s+1);
```

$$f := -\left(-\frac{e^{-s}}{s} + \frac{e^{-2s}}{s}\right)(s+1)^{-1}$$

```
convert(f, parfrac, s);
    Error, (in convert/parfrac)
    argument not a rational function
```

To ensure that expansion into partial fractions can be carried out in spite of this, the non-rational parts of the function are substituted with the new variables $e1$ and $e2$.

```
subs(exp(-s)=e1, exp(-2*s)=e2, f);
```

$$-\left(-\frac{e1}{s} + \frac{e2}{s}\right)(s+1)^{-1}$$

```
convert(", parfrac, s);
```

$$-\frac{-e1+e2}{s} + \frac{-e1+e2}{s+1}$$

After expansion into partial fractions has succeeded, the substitution can be undone.

```
subs(e1=exp(-s), e2=exp(-2*s), ");
```

$$-\frac{-e^{-s}+e^{-2s}}{s} + \frac{-e^{-s}+e^{-2s}}{s+1}$$

For rational functions with complex roots, a complete expansion can be achieved by using the keyword fullparfrac:

```
convert((x^2+1)/(x^2+x+1), parfrac, x);
```

$$1 - \frac{x}{x^2+x+1}$$

```
convert(", fullparfrac, x);
```

$$1 + \left(\sum_{\_\alpha=\%1} \frac{-\frac{1}{3}\_\alpha - \frac{2}{3}}{x - \_\alpha}\right)$$

$$\%1 := RootOf(\_Z^2 + \_Z + 1)$$

Conversions into continued fractions too are carried out by convert, this time with the keyword confrac.

```
convert((x^4-2)/x^6,confrac,x);
```

$$\frac{1}{x^2 + 2\frac{1}{x^2 - 2\frac{1}{x^2}}}$$

Polynomials can also be arranged following Horner's method. For multi-variable terms, the third parameter can be used to specify a single variable or a list of variables by which the polynomial is split.

```
f:=expand((x-y)^3*x^2*y^2+y^3+y^2+y);
```

$$f := x^5 y^2 - 3\,x^4 y^3 + 3\,x^3 y^4 - x^2 y^5 + y^3 + y^2 + y$$

```
convert(f,horner,x);
```

$$y^3 + y^2 + y + \left(-y^5 + \left(3\,y^4 + \left(-3\,y^3 + xy^2\right)x\right)x\right)x^2$$

```
convert(f,horner,[x,y]);
```

$$(1 + (1 + y)\,y)\,y + \left(-y^5 + \left(3\,y^4 + \left(-3\,y^3 + xy^2\right)x\right)x\right)x^2$$

`compoly` is a kind of inverse command to `subs` for polynomials: `compoly` tries to filter common terms out of an expression. This is best shown with an example. Like most other commands in this section, `compoly` is not suited for trigonometric, logarithmic and other special functions.

```
f:=expand(subs(a=x^2+x, (a^2-a+1)^2));
```

$$f := x^8 + 4\,x^7 - 2\,x^5 - 2\,x^4 + 4\,x^6 + 4\,x^3 + x^2 - 2\,x + 1$$

```
compoly(f);
```

$$x^4 + 1 - 2\,x + 3\,x^2 - 2\,x^3, \ x = x^2 + x$$

```
f:=subs(a=x+y+z, sin(a)^2-cos(a)+a^2);
```

$$f := \sin(x + y + z)^2 - \cos(x + y + z) + (x + y + z)^2$$

```
compoly(f);
```

```
  Error, (in compoly) invalid arguments
```

Additional help with trigonometric simplifications

Some of the commands described up to now are capable of carrying out trigonometric simplifications, in particular `simplify`, `expand`, `combine` and `convert`. In situations where none of these commands gets any further, `trigsubs` may occasionally help. This command does not carry out any simplifications itself, but it can supply a whole series of possible substitution terms.

Prior to being used, the command must be activated with `readlib`. Subsequently, `trigsubs(x)` supplies all trigonometric expressions known in Maple that match x. For x, only elementary trigonometric functions are allowed (such as $\sin(x)$, $\sin(2x)$, $\sin(x^2)$ or $\sin(x)^2$), not compound expressions (such as $\sin(x) + \cos(x)$). You will certainly notice that in the example below x itself occurs several times in the list of equivalent functions.

```
readlib(trigsubs):
trigsubs(sin(x)^2);
```

$$\left[\sin(x)^2, 1 - \cos(x)^2, 1/2 - \frac{\cos(2\,x)}{2}, \sin(x)^2, \sin(x)^2, 4\,\sin(\tfrac{x}{2})^2 \cos(\tfrac{x}{2})^2, \csc(x)^{-2},\right.$$

$$\left.\csc(x)^{-2}, \frac{4\,\tan(\tfrac{x}{2})^2}{\left(1 + \tan(\tfrac{x}{2})^2\right)^2}, -\frac{\left(e^{I\,x} - e^{-I\,x}\right)^2}{4}\right]$$

Analogously to `subs`, `trigsubs` can be used to carry out substitutions in trigonometric expressions. The peculiarity of `trigsubs` is that the command carries out only those substitutions which it can prove are correct on the basis of its built-in knowledge base. The advantage of greater security against errors is, however, counteracted by a disadvantage: sometimes `trigsubs` refuses to carry out a substitution which should actually be possible without problems (as you can see in the following example).

```
trigsubs(sin(x)=sqrt(1-cos(x)^2), (sin(x)^2-cos(x)^2)^2);
      Error, (in trigsubs) not found in table - use subs to override
trigsubs(sin(x)^2=1-cos(x)^2, (sin(x)^2-cos(x)^2)^2);
```

$$\left(1 - 2\,\cos(x)^2\right)^2$$

`trigsubs` can also be used simply to check whether two trigonometric expressions match or not (with the same restrictions as above!).

```
trigsubs(sin(x+y)=2*sin((x+y)/2)*cos((x+y)/2));
```

   `found`

Processing voluminous or multi-variable expressions (sort, select, remove, collect)

The commands described in this section are specifically of interest for very voluminous or for multi-variable expressions.

`sort` sorts the expression by decreasing powers. Please note that `sort` permanently changes the expression itself and does not – unlike nearly all other Maple commands – supply its own, independent result.

```
f:=expand((a*x^2*y+b*y)^2+(x-2*y+c*y^2)^2+x^3+x^4*y^2);
```

$$f := a^2 y^2 x^4 + 2\,aby^2 x^2 + b^2 y^2 + x^2 - 4\,yx + 2\,cy^2 x + 4\,y^2 - 4\,cy^3 + c^2 y^4 + x^3 + x^4 y^2$$

```
sort(f);
```

$$a^2 y^2 x^4 + 2\,aby^2 x^2 + y^4 c^2 + y^2 x^4 + b^2 y^2 - 4\,y^3 c + 2\,y^2 cx + x^3 + 4\,y^2 - 4\,yx + x^2$$

The above example shows that without the specification of additional parameters, `sort` simply sorts by the sum of the powers of the individual variables. In practice, however, it is usually more useful to sort by the powers of one given variable:

```
sort(f,x);
```

$$a^2 y^2 x^4 + y^2 x^4 + x^3 + 2\,aby^2 x^2 + x^2 - 4\,yx + 2\,y^2 cx + b^2 y^2 + 4\,y^2 - 4\,y^3 c + y^4 c^2$$

The command is also capable of sorting by several variables. When two variables are specified in a list (square brackets), Maple sorts first by the powers of the first variable, and then by the powers of the second variable (in the remaining expressions).

```
sort(f,[x,y]);
```

$$a^2x^4y^2 + x^4y^2 + 2\,abx^2y^2 + c^2y^4 + x^3 + 2\,cxy^2 - 4\,cy^3 + x^2 - 4\,xy + b^2y^2 + 4\,y^2$$

A certain affinity to the `sort` command is shown by `collect`. This command combines terms that share the factor specified in the second parameter.

```
collect(f,x);
```

$$\left(a^2y^2 + y^2\right)x^4 + x^3 + \left(1 + 2\,aby^2\right)x^2 + \left(2\,cy^2 - 4\,y\right)x + c^2y^4 + b^2y^2 - 4\,cy^3 + 4\,y^2$$

In this command too, combinations can be carried out over several variables at the same time. In the default setting, groups are formed first by the powers of the first variable; subsequently these are resolved by the powers of the second variable. If the keyword `distributed` is specified as a third parameter, `collect` sorts by the common powers of both variables (and therefore combines the two terms with the common factor x^4y^2).

```
collect(f,[x,y]);
```

$$\left(a^2 + 1\right)y^2x^4 + x^3 + \left(1 + 2\,aby^2\right)x^2 + \left(2\,cy^2 - 4\,y\right)x + c^2y^4 - 4\,cy^3 + \left(b^2 + 4\right)y^2$$

```
collect(f,[x,y],distributed);
```

$$2\,cy^2x + \left(a^2 + 1\right)y^2x^4 + 2\,aby^2x^2 + c^2y^4 + x^3 - 4\,cy^3 + \left(b^2 + 4\right)y^2 + x^2 - 4\,yx$$

Both `sort` and `collect` can sort/group by functions, for example by $\sin(x)$. However, more complex expressions, such as $1/x$ or $x + y$, are not allowed.

```
f:=expand((sin(x)-cos(x)^2)^2+(a-cos(x))^2);
```

$$f := \sin(x)^2 - 2\,\sin(x)\cos(x)^2 + \cos(x)^4 + a^2 - 2\,\cos(x)a + \cos(x)^2$$

```
sort(f,cos(x));
```

$$\cos(x)^4 - 2\,\sin(x)\cos(x)^2 + \cos(x)^2 - 2\,a\cos(x) + a^2 + \sin(x)^2$$

```
collect(f,cos(x));
```

$$\cos(x)^4 + \left(1 - 2\,\sin(x)\right)\cos(x)^2 - 2\,a\cos(x) + a^2 + \sin(x)^2$$

Since Release 4, `collect` can also group by partial derivatives (keywords `diff` or `D`).

```
f:=(y*diff(f1(x),x$2) + x*diff(f1(x),x$2));
```

$$f := y\,(\frac{\partial^2}{\partial x^2}\,\text{f1}(x)) + x\,(\frac{\partial^2}{\partial x^2}\,\text{f1}(x))$$

```
collect(f,diff);
```

$$(y + x)\,(\frac{\partial^2}{\partial x^2}\,\text{f1}(x))$$

While `sort` and `collect` change the order, but not the (mathematical) contents of the expression as a whole, `select` shows a completely different behaviour: it selects single terms of an expression which satisfy a certain selection criterion. The simplest way to formulate such a criterion is by means of `select(has,f,property)`. `has` checks which parts of f satisfy the specified property (or contain the specified function). Both examples still refer to the function f defined above.

```
select(has,f,a);
```

$$-2\,a\cos(x)+a^2$$

```
select(has,f,cos(x)^2);
```

$$-2\,\sin(x)\cos(x)^2+\cos(x)^2$$

```
select(has,f,{cos(x)^2,sin(x)^2});
```

$$-2\,\sin(x)\cos(x)^2+\cos(x)^2+\sin(x)^2$$

The selection criterion can also be formulated by means of an anonymous function in arrow notation. In the example below, degree is substituted in the anonymous function. degree determines the rank (order, power) of an expression, either with regard to all unknown items occurring in it or with regard to single variables. Thus, degree(x^2*y) yields 3, degree(x^2*y,x) yields 2 and degree(x^2*y,y) yields 1.

```
f:=expand((x-y)^8);
```

$$f := x^8 - 8\,x^7 y + 28\,x^6 y^2 - 56\,x^5 y^3 + 70\,x^4 y^4 - 56\,x^3 y^5 + 28\,x^2 y^6 - 8\,xy^7 + y^8$$

```
select(p->degree(p,x)>4,f);
```

$$x^8 - 8\,x^7 y + 28\,x^6 y^2 - 56\,x^5 y^3$$

The complementary function to select is remove, which has the same syntax as select, but removes the selected expressions.

```
remove(p->degree(p,x)>4,f);
```

$$70\,x^4\,y^4 - 56\,x^3\,y^5 + 28\,x^2\,y^6 - 8\,x\,y^7 + y^8$$

```
simplify("+""-f);
```

$$0$$

select and remove only work if the expressions to be processed are not embedded.

```
select(has,sin(x)+cos(x),sin);
```

$$\sin(x)$$

```
select(has,sqrt(sin(x)+cos(x)),sin);
  Error, non algebraic expressions in power should be of the same type
```

Grouping by powers of x with series

In rare cases – that is, if the task is exclusively to form groups of common powers of x – the series command can be misused for this purpose. In reality, this command has been designed to carry out the development of series. A detailed description can be found in Chapter 24.

In the following example, $(x^{1/2} + a)^3 + (x^{3/2} + b)^3$ is to be grouped by powers of x. The only command capable of doing this is series. The third parameter specifies up to which order the series development is to be carried out (in this case, the grouping of coefficients of x^n). You had better specify a sufficiently large value, otherwise `series` eliminates the terms with high powers and supplies an ordering term $O(x^n)$ as a result.

```
expand((x^(1/2)+a)^3+(x^(3/2)+b)^3);
```

$$x^{3/2} + 3\,xa + 3\,\sqrt{x}\,a^2 + a^3 + x^{9/2} + 3\,x^3b + 3\,x^{3/2}b^2 + b^3$$

```
series(",x, 20);
```

$$a^3 + b^3 + 3\,\sqrt{x}\,a^2 + 3\,xa + \left(1 + 3\,b^2\right)x^{3/2} + 3\,x^3b + x^{9/2}$$

If the polynomial exclusively contains integer powers (and not $x^{n/2}$, as in the above example), `series` does not produce a true polynomial, but the data type `series` (visually not recognizable). In this case, the entire expression must be subsequently converted back into a polynomial by means of `convert(",polynom)`.

Advanced examples

The three advanced examples presented in this section show the simplification of complex mathematical expressions. The first two examples concern a problem which has already been mentioned several times in this chapter: Maple is not capable of extracting the common factors out of several related terms. The two examples show different (and in all cases rather long-winded) ways of solving this problem. A third example illustrates how Maple can help with the simplification of formulae by approximation. Finding approximate solutions is particularly important in real-life technical calculations.

Example 1: simplifying a derivative with select

This example shows once more the wide range of applications of `select`. The third derivative of $\frac{x}{1-\sin(x)}$ is to be simplified:

```
f:=diff(x/(1-sin(x)), x$3);
```

$$f := \frac{6\,\cos(x)^2}{(1-\sin(x))^3} - \frac{3\,\sin(x)}{(1-\sin(x))^2} + \frac{6\,x\cos(x)^3}{(1-\sin(x))^4} - \frac{6\,\cos(x)x\sin(x)}{(1-\sin(x))^3} - \frac{\cos(x)x}{(1-\sin(x))^2}$$

`select` is used to form three groups which are combined by the rank of the denominator term. The command below shows that `has` can also be used directly to formulate the anonymous selection function.

```
f1:=seq(select(p->has(p,1/(1-sin(x))^n), f), n=2..4);
```

$$f1 := -\frac{3\,\sin(x)}{(1-\sin(x))^2} - \frac{\cos(x)x}{(1-\sin(x))^2}, \frac{6\,\cos(x)^2}{(1-\sin(x))^3} - \frac{6\,\cos(x)x\sin(x)}{(1-\sin(x))^3}, \frac{6\,x\cos(x)^3}{(1-\sin(x))^4}$$

By means of the `seq` command, the three groups are reduced to one common denominator each with `normal`. Since the groups are already combined by equal denominators, this is not difficult at all – only the two numerators have to be added up. The `normal` command has been described further above in the section on processing polynomials. Here, it is better suited than `simplify`, because `simplify` carries out additional 'simplifications' which only make the result more complicated.

The square brackets before and after `seq` convert the resulting sequence into a list which is in turn converted into a sum by means of `convert`.

```
convert([seq(normal(p), p=[f1])], '+');
```

$$-\frac{3\,\sin(x)+\cos(x)x}{(-1+\sin(x))^2}+\frac{6\,\cos(x)\,(-\cos(x)+x\sin(x))}{(-1+\sin(x))^3}+\frac{6\,x\cos(x)^3}{(-1+\sin(x))^4}$$

A subsequent proof checks that there is nothing untoward about this simplification. In particular, the application of `select` as shown here can relatively easily lead to single terms of the original expression being either forgotten or entered twice. This time, however, everything has gone all right.

```
simplify("-f);
```

$$0$$

Example 2: simplifying an integral with op

In the second example, the integral $\int\left(1+x^5\right)^{-1}dx$ is to be reduced to a simpler form. Maple supplies the result of this integral in a fairly long formula in which several terms could be combined together without excessive effort.

```
f:=int(1/(1+x^5),x);
```

$$f := \frac{\ln(x+1)}{5}-\frac{\ln(2\,x^2-x-\sqrt{5}\,x+2)\sqrt{5}}{20}-\frac{\ln(2\,x^2-x-\sqrt{5}\,x+2)}{20}+$$

$$\mathrm{arctan}(\frac{4\,x-1-\sqrt{5}}{\sqrt{10-2\,\sqrt{5}}})\frac{1}{\sqrt{10-2\,\sqrt{5}}}-\mathrm{arctan}(\frac{4\,x-1-\sqrt{5}}{\sqrt{10-2\,\sqrt{5}}})\sqrt{5}\,1/5\frac{1}{\sqrt{10-2\,\sqrt{5}}}+$$

$$\frac{\ln(2\,x^2-x+\sqrt{5}\,x+2)\sqrt{5}}{20}-\frac{\ln(2\,x^2-x+\sqrt{5}\,x+2)}{20}+$$

$$\mathrm{arctan}(\frac{4\,x-1+\sqrt{5}}{\sqrt{10+2\,\sqrt{5}}})\frac{1}{\sqrt{10+2\,\sqrt{5}}}+\mathrm{arctan}(\frac{4\,x-1+\sqrt{5}}{\sqrt{10+2\,\sqrt{5}}})\sqrt{5}\,1/5\frac{1}{\sqrt{10+2\,\sqrt{5}}}$$

In the first step the roots $\sqrt{10+2\,\sqrt{5}}$ and $\sqrt{10-2\,\sqrt{5}}$ are to be substituted with the abbreviations A and B. (A comparable substitution which is limited to the on-screen display is carried out in most Maple versions with the abbreviations %1 and %2.)

First, a and b are defined for the substitution. In the substitution rules, however, $1/a$ and $1/b$ are used, because otherwise Maple would not recognize the roots in the denominator (see also Chapter 6).

```
a:=sqrt(10-2*sqrt(5)): b:=sqrt(10+2*sqrt(5)):
f1:=subs(1/a=1/A, 1/b=1/B, f);
```

$$f1 := \frac{\ln(x+1)}{5} - \frac{\ln(2\,x^2 - x - \sqrt{5}\,x + 2)\sqrt{5}}{20} - \frac{\ln(2\,x^2 - x - \sqrt{5}\,x + 2)}{20} +$$

$$\arctan(\frac{4x-1-\sqrt{5}}{A})A^{-1} - \arctan(\frac{4x-1-\sqrt{5}}{A})\sqrt{5}1/5A^{-1} +$$

$$\frac{\ln(2\,x^2 - x + \sqrt{5}\,x + 2)\sqrt{5}}{20} - \frac{\ln(2\,x^2 - x + \sqrt{5}\,x + 2)}{20} + \arctan(\frac{4x-1+\sqrt{5}}{B})B^{-1} +$$

$$\arctan(\frac{4x-1+\sqrt{5}}{B})\sqrt{5}1/5B^{-1}$$

As a next step, the obviously matching terms are to be reduced to a common denominator. Using `select`, as in the previous example, is too complicated in this case; here, the `op` command is a faster solution. With this command you can access single terms in the sum $sln1$. Two similar terms at a time are combined with `collect` or `normal` (depending on which of the two commands supplies the more advantageous result in each case).

```
part1:=op(1,f1);
```

$$part1 := \frac{\ln(x+1)}{5}$$

```
part2:=collect(op(2,f1)+op(3,f1), ln);
```

$$part2 := -\frac{\ln(2\,x^2 - x - \sqrt{5}\,x + 2)\left(\sqrt{5}+1\right)}{20}$$

```
part3:=collect(op(6,f1)+op(7,f1), ln);
```

$$part3 := \frac{\ln(2\,x^2 - x + \sqrt{5}\,x + 2)\left(-1+\sqrt{5}\right)}{20}$$

```
part4:=normal(op(4,f1)+op(5,f1));
```

$$part4 := \arctan(\frac{-4x+1+\sqrt{5}}{A})\left(-5+\sqrt{5}\right)1/5A^{-1}$$

```
part5:=normal(op(8,f1)+op(9,f1));
```

$$part5 := \arctan(\frac{4x-1+\sqrt{5}}{B})\left(5+\sqrt{5}\right)1/5B^{-1}$$

Now, the five partial results must be combined into the new and simplified overall result.

```
f2:=sum('part.i', i=1..5);
```

$$f2 := \frac{\ln(x+1)}{5} -$$

$$\frac{\ln(2\,x^2 - x - \sqrt{5}\,x + 2)\left(\sqrt{5}+1\right)}{20} + \frac{\ln(2\,x^2 - x + \sqrt{5}\,x + 2)\left(-1+\sqrt{5}\right)}{20} +$$

$$\arctan(\frac{-4x+1+\sqrt{5}}{A})\frac{-5+\sqrt{5}}{5A} + \arctan(\frac{4x-1+\sqrt{5}}{B})\frac{5+\sqrt{5}}{5B}$$

For the final proof, the substitutions for A and B must be undone:

```
simplify(f-subs(A=a, B=b,f2));
```

$$0$$

Doing the example this way has a serious disadvantage: it depends on the order of the summands and is not predictable. In a different version of Maple the nine summands of the above integral might be arranged in a different order. In this case, the indices in the `op` command would have to be changed. In comparison, using `select` has a more general validity.

A final note: Chapter 28 contains detailed information about the way Maple stores mathematical expressions internally and how you can read parts of these expressions. This information is extremely useful in case you want to write your own commands for processing or simplifying Maple expressions.

Example 3: eliminating negligible terms

A favourite sport in the engineering sciences is to eliminate mathematically insignificant (because negligibly small) terms from more complex formulae and to continue calculating with a now somewhat easier to handle result. It is quite clear that Maple is overstretched by such a task. The elimination of single terms presumes a very precise idea of the (real-world) problem and can therefore only be carried out manually. The aim of this section is to show once more how the `select` command can be applied. The command requires that you tell Maple very precisely what to do, but at least it saves you the laborious and error-prone task of rewriting formulae.

Let us take an example from the field of electrotechnics: E_r describes the r component (spherical coordinate) of the field intensity of an idealized dipole antenna. Since the upper case letter I is used in electrotechnics to represent electric currents, the symbol j is commonly used to denote the imaginary unit. Two `alias` commands are used to substitute the present abbreviation for $\sqrt{-1}$ with a new one.

```
restart; alias(I=I): alias(j=sqrt(-1));
```

$$j$$

```
Z:=beta/omega/epsilon;
```

$$Z := \frac{\beta}{\omega \epsilon}$$

```
Er:=Z*I*dl/(2*Pi*r^2)*(1+1/(j*beta*r))*exp(-j*beta*r)*cos(theta);
```

$$Er := \beta\, I\, dl \left(1 - \frac{j}{\beta r}\right) e^{-j \beta r} \cos(\theta) \frac{1}{2\omega\epsilon\pi r^2}$$

In the following, approximations of this field intensity are to be calculated for the near field and the far field (Fraunhofer region) of the antenna. The near field is characterized by a very small r (thus, a very small distance to the antenna). Therefore, the expression $e^{-j\beta r}$ verges towards 1 and can be cancelled from the product. Now, `select` is used to select all terms of E_r which do not contain the term $-j\beta r$:

```
Er1:=select(x->not has(x,-j*beta*r),Er);
```

$$Er1 := \beta\,I\,dl\,\left(1 - \frac{j}{\beta\,r}\right)\cos(\theta)\frac{1}{2\omega\epsilon\pi r^2}$$

The intermediate result $Er1$ is now split into two components with expand. Since r is very small, the term containing $1/r^2$ is negligible compared with the one containing $1/r^3$. A second select command leads to the formula for the near field.

```
Er2:=expand(Er1);
```

$$Er2 := \frac{\beta\,I\,dl\,\cos(\theta)}{2\,\omega\,\epsilon\,\pi\,r^2} - \frac{j\,I\,dl\,\cos(\theta)}{2\,\omega\,\epsilon\,\pi\,r^3}$$

```
E_near:=select(has, Er2,r^(-3));
```

$$E_{near} := -\frac{j\,I\,dl\,\cos(\theta)}{2\,\omega\,\epsilon\,\pi\,r^3}$$

The far field is characterized by the assumption that r is very large. In this case, $1/r^3$ becomes negligibly small and can be eliminated. Further simplifications are not possible.

```
Er3:=expand(Er);
```

$$Er3 := \frac{\beta\,I\,dl\,\cos(\theta)}{2\,\omega\,\epsilon\,\pi\,r^2 e^{j\,\beta\,r}} - \frac{j\,I\,dl\,\cos(\theta)}{2\,\omega\,\epsilon\,\pi\,r^3 e^{j\,\beta\,r}}$$

```
E_far:=select(has, Er3,r^(-2));
```

$$E_{far} := \frac{\beta\,I\,dl\,\cos(\theta)}{2\,\omega\,\epsilon\,\pi\,r^2 e^{j\,\beta\,r}}$$

In view of the palaver involved in this kind of transformation, the question arises (once again) whether it would not be more reasonable to calculate with pen and paper ...

Compact output of voluminous expressions (sprint)

Sometimes Maple supplies a result in the form of a formula that spreads over several pages. In such cases, it is often difficult even to get an overall impression of the principal components of the result. The sprint command from the share library offers some help. It tries to represent the expression in a more compact way by shortening long chains of operands into the form <<+10>> (for a sum of 10 terms).

The use of sprint is simple: the only parameter is used to specify the expression to be shortened. The result can be influenced via the system variable _EnvSprint. The smaller this value (default value 100), the more compact the result.

```
with(share): readshare(sprint, system):
test:=int(1/(a+b*x^5), x): sprint(test);
```

$$<<*4>> + <<*5>> + <<*6>> + <<*6>> + <<*6>> + <<*6>> + <<*7>>+$$

$$<<*7>> + <<*7>> + <<*5>> + <<*5>> + <<*6>> + <<*5>>$$

```
_EnvSprint:=200: sprint(test);
```

$$\frac{\ln(<<+2>>)}{5\,a^{4/5}\sqrt[5]{b}} + \frac{\ln(<<+14>>)}{4\,a^{4/5}\left(\sqrt{5}-5\right)\sqrt[5]{b}} + \frac{I\,\arctan(<<+37>>\ )}{2\,a^{4/5}\left(\sqrt{5}-5\right)\sqrt[5]{b}} + \frac{I\,\arctan(<<+51>>)}{2\,a^{4/5}\left(\sqrt{5}-5\right)\sqrt[5]{b}} +$$

$$\frac{I\,\arctan(<<*4>>\ )}{2\,a^{4/5}\left(\sqrt{5}-5\right)\sqrt[5]{b}} - \frac{3\,\sqrt{5}\,\ln(<<+14>>)}{20\,a^{4/5}\left(\sqrt{5}-5\right)\sqrt[5]{b}} - \frac{3\,I\,\sqrt{5}\,\arctan(\ <<+37>>)}{10\,a^{4/5}\left(\sqrt{5}-5\right)\sqrt[5]{b}} -$$

$$\frac{3\,I\,\sqrt{5}\,\arctan(<<+51>>)}{10\,a^{4/5}\left(\sqrt{5}-5\right)\sqrt[5]{b}} - \frac{3\,I\,\sqrt{5}\,\arctan(<<*4>>)}{10\,a^{4/5}\left(\sqrt{5}-5\right)\sqrt[5]{b}} - \frac{4\,\arctan(<<*2>>)}{a^{3/5}\left(\sqrt{5}-5\right)\sqrt{<<+2>>}} -$$

$$\frac{\ln(<<+4>>)}{2\,a^{4/5}\left(\sqrt{5}+5\right)\sqrt[5]{b}} - \frac{3\,\sqrt{5}\,\ln(<<+4>>)}{10\,a^{4/5}\left(\sqrt{5}+5\right)\sqrt[5]{b}} + \frac{4\,\arctan(<<*2>>)}{a^{3/5}\left(\sqrt{5}+5\right)\sqrt{<<+2>>}}$$

```
test:=simplify(diff(1/(x+sin(x)), x$10)*diff(1/(x^2+cos(x)^2), x$10)):
sprint(test);
```

$$\frac{512\,<<+420>>}{<<+172>>}$$

Syntax summary

```
simplify(expression);    simplify(expression, type);
```
    simplify tries to simplify the specified expression. By specifying a simplification type in the second parameter, the effect of simplify can be restricted to a particular area. Permitted keywords are: atsign, Ei, exp, GAMMA, hypergeom, ln, polar, power, radical, RootOf, sqrt and trig.

```
simplify(expression, symbolic);
```
    In contrast to the above keywords, symbolic does not restrict the effect of simplify, but extends it. simplify now also executes those simplifications that are mathematically critical and apply only under certain conditions (thus, $\sqrt{x^2} \mapsto x$ only applies for $x > 0$).

```
simplify(expression, {equations}, {var});
```
    The third variation of simplify uses the equations specified in the second parameter to simplify the expression. For this purpose, a Gröbner basis is constructed for the variables (optionally) specified in the third parameter.

```
expand(expression);
```
    multiplies out the factors contained in the expression. With trigonometric and some other functions, expand tries to simplify their arguments, which generally leads to sums and/or products of several functions. With rational functions, expand only concerns the denominator. When numerator and denominator are multiplied out, normal(f,var,expanded) leads to the result.

```
factor(expression);  factor(expression, {x0,x1,x2...});
```
    tries to split the polynomial into its underlying factors. If the polynomial shows non-integer zero points, these must be specified as a set or a list in the second parameter.

`combine(expression, type);`

    tries to combine the functions contained in the expression. Without the (optional) specification of the simplification type, `combine` only carries out some rather basic simplifications. The following keywords are defined for the simplification type: `abs`, `atatsign`, `conjugate`, `exp`, `ln`, `plus`, `power`, `product`, `Psi`, `range`, `trig` and `signum`.

`radnormal(expression);`

    tries to combine or transform the (square) roots contained in the expression into a simpler form.

`convert(expression, type);`

    transforms the expression into a new notation. The following types can be specified for generic mathematical transformations: `exp`, `expln`, `expsincos`, `factorial`, `GAMMA`, `ln`, `radical`, `RootOf`, `sincos`, `tan` and `trig`. For the transformation of polynomials and rational functions, the keywords `confrac`, `horner`, `parfrac` and `fullparfrac` are defined (see below). Furthermore, `convert` has a large number of additional keywords but these are of no interest in the present context and will be described in other chapters of this book.

Processing polynomials and rational functions

`numer(ratfunc);`   `denom(ratfunc);`

    determine the numerator and denominator of a fraction. Rational functions are previously reduced to a common denominator by means of `normal`.

`normal(ratfunc);`   `normal(ratfunc, expanded);`

    reduces the rational function to a common denominator and cancels factors occurring more than once. By additionally specifying the keyword `expanded`, the numerator and denominator are subsequently multiplied out.

`quo(poly1, poly2, var);`   `quo(poly1, poly2, var, 'remainder');`
`rem(poly1, poly2, var);`

    carries out a polynomial division of the two polynomials over the specified variable. `quo` determines the result, `rem` the remainder. In the second syntax variation of `quo`, the remainder is stored in the variable *remainder*. In this way, quotient and remainder can be determined in a single calculation.

`convert(ratfunc, confrac, var);`
`convert(ratfunc, parfrac, var);`
`convert(poly, horner, var);`

    carries out a continued fraction, partial fraction or Horner expansion. Instead of a variable, it is also possible to specify an elementary function (for example, for an expansion into partial fractions over $\sin(x)$).

`compoly(f,x);`

    searches for common terms in f and isolates them as a substitution expression. For simple expressions, this command represents an inverse function to `subs`.

Special functions

```
trigsubs(trigfunc);
trigsubs(trigfunc1=trigfunc2);
trigsubs(trig1a=trig1b, trig2a=trig2b,... expression);
```
helps with the simplification of trigonometric expressions. The first syntax variation leads to a set of all functions known to Maple, equivalent to *trigfunc*. In the second variation, the identity of both functions is checked. The third variation carries out the specified substitutions (same as `subs`), if the identity of the substitution rules can be determined. *Warning*: `trigsubs` recognizes many, but by no means all identities!

```
sort(expression);
sort(expression, varlist);
```
sorts the expression by decreasing powers. When variables are specified in a list or a set, only the powers of those variables are considered.

```
collect(expression, varlist);
```
groups the common factors specified in a list or a set. However, only variables or elementary functions are allowed as factors, not compound expressions.

```
select(has, expression, property);     select(boolfunc, expression);
remove(has, expression, property);     remove(boolfunc, expression);
```
selects or removes those terms of the expression which satisfy the selection criterion. The criterion can be formulated by specifying a property with `has` or by an anonymous function with Boolean result.

```
degree(expression, varlist);
has(expression, property);
```
are often useful for the formulation of selection criteria for `select`. `degree` determines the rank of an expression (`degree(x^2*x,x)` yields 2). `has` checks whether the expression has the specified 'property'. A property could, for example, be the existence of a sine function: `has(..., sin(x))`.

```
series(polynomial, x, 100);
```
groups the polynomial by increasing powers of x. If only integer powers of x occur, the result must be subsequently converted from the data type `series` back into a polynomial by means of `convert(",polynom)`. `series` normally carries out series developments and will be described in that context in Chapter 24.

```
op(n, expression);
```
reads the nth term of the expression. `op` is suitable for reading single summands or factors of a sum or a product.

```
subs(sub1a=sub1b, sub2a=sub2b,..., expression);
```
substitutes the a terms with the b terms. subs only recognizes uniquely connected terms, but not $x + y$ inside $x + y + z$.

```
with(share):     readshare(sprint, system):
_EnvSprint:=n:   sprint(expression);
```
represents the expression in a compact notation. n affects the length of the result (default setting 100).

Chapter 11

Solving equations analytically and numerically

This chapter summarizes the most important commands for the solution of single equations or whole equation systems, describing both analytic and numeric solution methods.

`solve`
represents the standard command for the analytic (symbolic) solution of equations.

`fsolve`
uses various numeric methods to determine the location of single solution points.

`subs` and `assign`
are used to assign identified solutions to variables on a temporary or permanent basis.

`isolve` and `rsolve`
are two variations of `solve`. `isolve` only determines integer solutions, `rsolve` tries to derive the general function specification from the recursive definition of a function.

Reference: Apart from the `solve` variations mentioned above, Maple has a large number of additional commands that can, in a wider sense, also be used for solving equation systems: `simplify` is capable of eliminating single variables from an equation system with several variables (Chapter 10). `linsolve` solves equation systems written in matrix form (Chapter 14), `dsolve` solves differential equations (Chapter 18), `extrema` solves boundary value problems with end conditions and, finally, `minimize` and `maximize`, included in the `simplex` package, carry out linear optimizations (Chapter 23). Further information on the application of the `solve` commands can be found in the Maple file `Examples\Solve.mws`.

Solving equations analytically (solve)

The standard command for the solution of equations is `solve`. The first parameter specifies the equation to be solved, the second parameter specifies the variable.

```
solve(x^2+3*x+2=0, x);
```

$$-1, -2$$

If a function is specified instead of an equation, Maple automatically sets it to 0. If no variables are specified, Maple solves the equation for one of the unknown symbols occurring in it.

```
solve(x^2+3*x+2);
```
$$-1, -2$$

The specification of a variable for which the equation is to be resolved is compulsory when more than one unknown occurs in an equation. In such cases, Maple cannot recognize which symbols are variables and which are parameters of the equation to be substituted at a later stage.

```
solve(a*x^2+b*x+c);
```
$$\left\{ c = -ax^2 - bx, x = x, a = a, b = b \right\}$$

```
solve(a*x^2+b*x+c,x);
```
$$\frac{-b + \sqrt{b^2 - 4ac}}{2a}, \frac{-b - \sqrt{b^2 - 4ac}}{2a}$$

solve tries to determine all solutions. Multiple solutions (as in the example on the right, where 1 occurs twice) occur several times in the solution sequence as well.

```
f:=expand((x-1)^2*(x+Pi)*(3*x-1/x));
```
$$f := 3x^4 + 2x^2 + 3x^3\pi + 2x\pi - 6x^3 +$$
$$2x - 6x^2\pi + 2\pi - 1 - \frac{\pi}{x}$$

```
solve(f);
```
$$\frac{\sqrt{3}}{3}, -\frac{\sqrt{3}}{3}, 1, 1, -\pi$$

Solutions with floating point numbers

solve tries to determine the solution of equations symbolically. If numerical values occur in the equation (thus, 1.5 instead of $3/2$), these values are first approximated by fractions in order to continue the calculation symbolically. Subsequently, the solution is converted back into floating point numbers.

```
solve(x^3=8);
```
$$2, -1 + I\sqrt{3}, -1 - I\sqrt{3}$$

```
solve(x^3=8.0);
```
$$2.0, -1.0 - 1.732050808\,I,$$
$$-1.0 + 1.732050808\,I$$

solve in combination with numerical values is not equivalent to the fsolve command which will be described later. For example, as a standard, fsolve supplies only one solution (not several).

```
fsolve(x^3=8);
```
$$2$$

```
fsolve(x^3=8, x, complex);
```
$$-1.0 - 1.732050808\,I,$$
$$-1.0 + 1.732050808\,I, 2.0$$

Furthermore, fsolve is not capable of solving equations with symbolic parameters, whereas solve arrives at usable results.

```
solve(x^2=1.5+a,x);
```
$$1/2\sqrt{6 + 4a}, -1/2\sqrt{6 + 4a}$$

```
fsolve(x^2=1.5+a,x);
    Error, (in fsolve) should use
    exactly all the indeterminates
```

Solution manifolds of trigonometric equations

solve can also cope with trigonometric equations.

```
solve(sin(x)=cos(x));
```
$$\frac{\pi}{4}$$

Since Release 4, Maple can even cope with solution manifolds (of the kind $x = \pi/4 + n\pi$). For this purpose, prior to calling solve, the environment variable _EnvAllSolutions must be set to true. Maple then formulates the solution with the variables $\_Z$ for integer numbers, $\_N$ for non-negative integer numbers or $\_B$ for binary values (0/1).

```
_EnvAllSolutions:=true:
solve(sin(x)=cos(x));
```
$$1/4\,\pi + \pi\,{}^{`}\_Z\,{}^{`}$$

```
s:=solve(sin(x^2)=1/2);
```
$$s := \frac{1}{6}\sqrt{6\pi + 24\pi\,\_B1\tilde{} + 72\pi\,\_Z1\tilde{}},$$
$$-\frac{1}{6}\sqrt{6\pi + 24\pi\,\_B1\tilde{} + 72\pi\,\_Z1\tilde{}}$$

The possibilities for processing these expressions further are just as ill-devised as the above results are fascinating: the attempt to substitute the first of the two solutions in the original equation and to simplify it to 0 fails miserably.

```
test:=subs(x=s[1], sin(x^2)):
simplify(test);
```
$$\sin(\frac{1}{6}\pi + \frac{2}{3}\pi\,\_B1\tilde{} + 2\pi\,\_Z1\tilde{})$$

Although $\_Z1$ is marked with the assume tilde ˜, there seems to be no internal information about $\_Z1$:

```
about(_Z1);
 _Z1:
 nothing known about this object
```

But even after the attempt to set the properties of $\_Z1$ and $\_B1$ manually, simplification still fails.

```
assume(_Z1,integer,_B1,boolean);
simplify(test);
```
$$\sin(\frac{1}{6}\pi + \frac{2}{3}\pi\,\_B1\tilde{} + 2\pi\,\_Z1\tilde{})$$

It is not even possible to substitute the variables with other values! In view of so many restrictions – which are fairly unusual in Maple – enthusiasm for solution manifolds is somewhat dimmed.

```
subs(_Z1=0, test);
```
$$\sin(\frac{1}{6}\pi + \frac{2}{3}\pi\,\_B1\tilde{} + 2\pi\,\_Z1\tilde{})$$

Equation systems

When solve is to solve entire equation systems, both the equations and the variables occurring in them must be written as sets (in braces). If no other symbols occur in the equation system apart from the variables, the set of variables may be left unspecified. solve groups the solution units in sets.

```
solve({5*x^2 - 5*y^2 - 3*x + 9*y=0, 5*x^3+5*y^3-15*x^2-13*x*y-y^2=0}, {x,y});
```
$$\{y = 0, x = 0\}, \{y = -1, x = 2\}, \{y = 2, x = 1\}, \left\{x = \frac{42}{25}, y = \frac{63}{25}\right\}$$

In the solution of equation systems the number of equations and the number of variables must be matched. In a system of three equations in three variables, it is not possible to determine the solution for one variable only or, even worse, convert the system into an equation system with two variables.

```
eq:={x+y+z-4, x-3*y+z, 2*x-y+z}:
solve(eq, x);
solve(eq, {x,y,z});
```

$$\{y = 1, z = 5, x = -2\}$$

Maple can also cope with many non-linear equation systems: in the following example, trigonometric functions and e terms occur as well. The result is evaluated numerically with `allvalues` (see the following subsection). For a subsequent countercheck, the result is substituted in the original equations.

```
eq:={exp(x)+exp(y)+exp(z)=1, sin(x)+sin(y)=1, y+z=1}:
solve(eq, {x,y,z});
```

$$\{y = -\arcsin(-1 + \sin(\%2)), x = \%2, z = \arcsin(-1 + \sin(\%2)) + 1\}$$

$$\%1 := e^{\arcsin(-1+\sin(\_Z))}$$

$$\%2 := \mathrm{RootOf}(\_Z - \ln(-1 - e^{(\arcsin(-1+\sin(\_Z))+1)}\%1 + \%1) + \arcsin(-1 + \sin(\_Z)))$$

```
evalf(allvalues("));
```

$$\{x = 1.926433253 - 1.711725280\,I, y = -1.000578839 - 1.314917616\,I,$$

$$z = 2.000578839 + 1.314917616\,I\}$$

```
evalf(subs(",eq));
```

$$\{1.000000005 - .21\,10^{-8}\,I = 1., 1.000000000 = 1., 1.000000001 - .2\,10^{-9}\,I = 1.\}$$

Reference: The handling of inequation systems is described at the end of this chapter. For the elimination of one variable from several equations, `simplify` with the specification of side conditions is better suited than `solve` (see previous chapter). In some cases, transformations can also be carried out with `algsubs` (see Chapter 6). Finally, information about the handling of equation systems can also be found in Chapter 14, which deals with equation systems which can be formulated by means of matrices (linear algebra).

The commands RootOf and allvalues

When `solve` is not capable of indicating solutions explicitly, although it recognizes that solutions do exist, it uses the `RootOf` command to formulate the solution. In `RootOf`, the characteristic equation of a polynomial is used to represent the resulting zero points. Expressions with `RootOf` can be further processed in the same way as other results. `allvalues` determines all solutions of the `RootOf` terms. If a symbolic evaluation is impossible, `allvalues` automatically works numerically.

```
s:=solve(x^6+x+1,x);
```

$$s := RootOf(\_Z^6 + \_Z + 1)$$

```
allvalues(s);
```

$$-0.7906671888 - 0.3005069203I \,, ..., 0.9454023333 + 0.6118366938I$$

If the same `RootOf` expression occurs more than once in a result, it is usually requested that the roots of these expressions are used together and not independently of each other. Until Release 3, the option 'd' had to be used with `allvalues` to obtain an evaluation in this form. Since Release 4, this behaviour is the standard setting. An independent resolution of the `RootOf` expressions can now be obtained with the `independent` option.

The example below shows the importance of this option: with `allvalues` all solutions are determined once with the correct default setting and once with the (in this case unsuitable) `independent` option. For a countercheck, the solutions are subsequently substituted in the original equations with subs and evaluated numerically. In the `independent` variation, two invalid solutions are found.

```
eq:={x+y=5, x*y=7}: s:=solve(eq, {x,y});
```

$$s := \left\{ y = RootOf(\_Z^2 - 5\_Z + 7), x = -RootOf(\_Z^2 - 5\_Z + 7) + 5 \right\}$$

```
dep:=allvalues(s);
```

$$dep := \{x = \frac{5}{2} - \frac{1}{2}I\sqrt{3}, y = \frac{5}{2} + \frac{1}{2}I\sqrt{3}\}, \{x = \frac{5}{2} + \frac{1}{2}I\sqrt{3}, y = \frac{5}{2} - \frac{1}{2}I\sqrt{3}\}$$

```
seq(evalf((subs(i, eq))), i=dep);
```

$$\{7.000000000 = 7., 5. = 5.\}, \{7.000000000 = 7., 5. = 5.\}$$

```
ind:=allvalues(s,independent);
```

$$ind := \{x = \%1, y = \%2\}, \{x = \%2, y = \%2\}, \{x = \%1, y = \%1\}, \{x = \%2, y = \%1\}$$

$$\%1 := \frac{5}{2} - \frac{1}{2}I\sqrt{3}$$

$$\%2 := \frac{5}{2} + \frac{1}{2}I\sqrt{3}$$

```
seq(evalf((subs(i, eq))), i=ind);
```

$$\{7.000000000 = 7., 5. = 5.\},$$

$$\{5.500000000 + 4.330127020\,I = 7., 5. + 1.732050808\,I = 5.\},$$

$$\{5. - 1.732050808\,I = 5., 5.500000000 - 4.330127020\,I = 7.\},$$

$$\{7.000000000 = 7., 5. = 5.\}$$

Solving equations numerically (fsolve)

The `fsolve` command has the same syntax as `solve`, but the search for solutions is carried out numerically. The essential difference from `solve` is that `fsolve` normally determines only one solution, even though `solve` recognizes several without effort. For this reason, `fsolve` should be employed only when an exact (symbolic) solution does not exist or when the underlying equations contain numeric coefficients in the first place.

The logarithmic equation on the right does not cause `fsolve` any problems.

```
fsolve(ln(1+x)+ln(3+x)+x=5);
```
$$2.192154954$$

In other equations, the search for solutions only succeeds when the solution range is very tightly restricted by the indication of `x=x1..x2`.

```
f:=2*x + cos(x) - 2*sin(2*x):
fsolve(f);
```
$$\text{fsolve}(\,2\,x + \cos(\,x\,) - 2\sin(\,2\,x\,), x\,)$$

```
fsolve(f, x=-2..2);
```
$$\text{fsolve}(\,2\,x + \cos(\,x\,) - 2\sin(\,2\,x\,), x, -2..2\,)$$

```
fsolve(f, x=-2..-1);
```
$$-1.074907239$$

For polynomials, `fsolve` normally only determines real solutions. When the `complex` option is set, complex solutions are calculated as well. Please note that `fsolve` determines several solutions for polynomials only.

```
fsolve(x^3+2*x-1);
```
$$0.4533976515$$

```
fsolve(x^3+2*x-1, x,complex);
```
$$-0.2266988258 - 1.467711509I\,,$$
$$-0.2266988258 + 1.467711509I\,,$$
$$0.4533976515$$

If `solve` is capable of finding a solution, numerical values should not be calculated with `fsolve`, but via a numerical evaluation of the symbolic solution with `evalf`. The advantage is that then all solutions are calculated (and not just one).

```
fsolve({x+y=9/2, x*y=5}, {x,y});
```
$$\{x = 2.500000000, y = 2.0\}$$

```
solve({x+y=9/2, x*y=5}, {x,y}):
evalf(");
```
$$\{x = 2.500000000, y = 2.0\}\,,$$
$$\{y = 2.500000000, x = 2.0\}$$

There are cases in which `fsolve` does not supply a solution, although the equation appears quite simple. In such cases, the additional keyword `complex` is often missing, as this would ask `fsolve` to take complex solutions into consideration as well.

```
fsolve(x^2+5);
fsolve(x^2+5,x, complex);
```
$$-2.236067978I\,, 2.236067978I$$

Quite often, `fsolve` finds no or only a single solution, although several solutions exist. In the present example, the zero points of the function $\cos(x^2) - x/3$ are to be determined. A quick plot of the function helps enormously with the search for solutions.

```
f:=cos(x^2)-x/3:
plot(f,x=0..4);
```

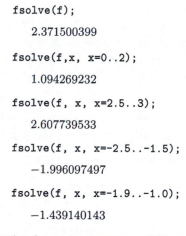

`fsolve` supplies the middle one of the five zero points straight away.

```
fsolve(f);
```

$$2.371500399$$

For the remaining zero points, it is necessary to give Maple a hint about the range in which a solution value may be expected. These hints are formulated in the form of `x=from..to`.

```
fsolve(f,x, x=0..2);
```

$$1.094269232$$

```
fsolve(f, x, x=2.5..3);
```

$$2.607739533$$

```
fsolve(f, x, x=-2.5..-1.5);
```

$$-1.996097497$$

```
fsolve(f, x, x=-1.9..-1.0);
```

$$-1.439140143$$

For high precision calculation, the `fulldigits` option becomes necessary. This option prevents Maple from temporarily reducing the calculating precision while searching for a solution in order to achieve a higher speed. In the following example, the specification of `fulldigits` changes several decimal digits of the result. However, Maple is overstretched with the numeric solution of this example anyway.

```
Digits:=40:        f:=sinh(x)-cosh(x):
sln1:=fsolve(f); sln2:=fsolve(f, x,fulldigits);
```

$sln1 := 57.31137182831180864568963072827875470550$

$sln2 := 57.31148716486415372856890701142667105759$

With the equation $\sinh(x) - \cosh(x)$, increasing the calculating precision only leads to another erroneous result. The two hyperbolic functions approach each other asymptotically and are only identical for $x \to \infty$.

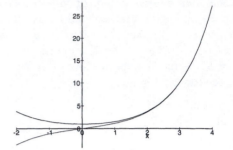

```
plot({sinh(x), cosh(x)}, x=-2..4);
```

Maple has great difficulties with this equation, since both $\sinh(x)$ and $\cosh(x)$ assume very high values. Because of the limited calculating precision, the calculation of the difference of the two values inevitably leads to 0 from a determined x value onward. Therefore, the `evalf` proof with a preset calculating precision of 70 digits seems to come out even. If, however, `evalf` is asked to calculate more precisely, the tiny difference between $\sinh(x)$ and $\cosh(x)$ comes to light again.

```
Digits:=70:
sln1:=fsolve(f); sln2:=fsolve(f, x,fulldigits);
```

$sln1 := 96.13985348413628296484194453246246062243703986285240659174081209680638$

$sln2 := 96.13997599857237960796748095199162328890106768607565127372111894709221$

```
evalf(subs(x=sln2, sinh(x)-cosh(x)));
```

0

```
evalf(subs(x=sln2, sinh(x)-cosh(x)), 120);
```

$-1.76578951416721039125247540106943064 1 \times 10^{-42}$

Further processing of solutions of equations (subs, assign)

In principle, there are two possibilities for further processing the results supplied by `solve` or `fsolve`: either the results are temporarily substituted in variables by means of the already described `subs` command, or `assign` is used to store the values permanently in variables. As a rule, the first variation is more practical and flexible.

In the present example, the first solution of the quadratic equation (that is, $x = 3$) is substituted in the expression $\sin(\frac{1}{1+x^2})$. Please note the use of the square brackets to access the first partial result of the solution sequence.

```
s:=solve(x^2-x-6);
```

$s := 3, -2$

```
subs(x=s[1], sin(1/(1+x^2)));
```

$\sin(1/10)$

Slightly less typing effort is required with equation systems with several variables. There, the variable names are already contained in the solution.

```
s:=solve({x^2+y^2=5, x+y=3});
```

$$s := \{y = 1, x = 2\}, \{x = 1, y = 2\}$$

```
subs(s[2], 3*x^2+5*y-x*y);
```

$$11$$

The loop command seq can be used for processing all solutions (and not just one). In the example on the right, the solutions are assigned to the loop variable i one after the other and further processed with subs.

```
seq(subs(i,3*x^2+5*y-x*y), i=s);
```

$$15, 11$$

With assign, a whole list of equations of the kind var=.. can be converted into assignments. The example on the right refers once more to the above result. x and y now contain the values 2 and 3 and can no longer be used as unknown variables in equations.

```
assign(sln[2]);
x,y;
```

$$1, 2$$

The following example shows how the simplify function is applied to several solutions by means of map. map is easier to handle than seq (no loop variable), but it is not that flexible. The attempt to process the solution s directly with simplify fails for the reason that simplify can only simplify one expression at a time (and not a whole set of expressions simultaneously).

```
_EnvAllSolutions:=true:
s:=solve(sin(x)+cos(x)=1/sqrt(2));
```

$$s := \arctan\left(\frac{\frac{1}{4}\sqrt{2} - \frac{1}{4}\sqrt{6}}{\frac{1}{4}\sqrt{2} + \frac{1}{4}\sqrt{6}}\right) + 2\pi\,\_Z\tilde{}, \ \arctan\left(\frac{\frac{1}{4}\sqrt{2} + \frac{1}{4}\sqrt{6}}{\frac{1}{4}\sqrt{2} - \frac{1}{4}\sqrt{6}}\right) + \pi + 2\pi\,\_Z\tilde{}$$

```
simplify(s);
  Error, (in simplify) invalid simplification command
map(simplify,["]);
```

$$\left[-\arctan(\frac{-1+\sqrt{3}}{1+\sqrt{3}}) + 2\pi\,\_Z\tilde{}, \ -\arctan(\frac{1+\sqrt{3}}{-1+\sqrt{3}}) + \pi + 2\pi\,\_Z\tilde{}\right]$$

The following example shows how the solutions of a trigonometric equation can be checked. For this purpose, the solutions are substituted in turn in the original equations and simplified with simplify. If simplify does not function straight away as in the present example, a numeric evaluation with evalf can often save much time.

```
_EnvAllSolutions:=false:
eq:=sin(x)^2+cos(x)=1/2: s:=solve(eq, x);
```

$$s := \arctan\left(\frac{1}{2}\frac{\sqrt{2}\,3^{1/4}}{-\frac{1}{2}\sqrt{3}+\frac{1}{2}}\right) + \pi, \; -\arctan\left(\frac{1}{2}\frac{\sqrt{2}\,3^{1/4}}{-\frac{1}{2}\sqrt{3}+\frac{1}{2}}\right) - \pi,$$

$$\arctan(\frac{1}{2}\sqrt{-2\sqrt{3}},\, \frac{1}{2}\sqrt{3}+\frac{1}{2}), \; \arctan(-\frac{1}{2}\sqrt{-2\sqrt{3}},\, \frac{1}{2}\sqrt{3}+\frac{1}{2})$$

```
seq(simplify(subs(x=i, eq)), i=s);
```

$$\frac{1}{2} = \frac{1}{2}, \; \frac{1}{2} = \frac{1}{2}, \; \frac{1}{2} = \frac{1}{2}, \; \frac{1}{2} = \frac{1}{2}$$

```
seq(evalf(subs(x=i, eq)), i=s);
```

$$.4999999992 = .5000000000, \; .4999999992 = .5000000000, \; .5000000000 = .5000000000,$$

$$.5000000000 = .5000000000$$

Sometimes, the (complex) solution points of an equation are to be displayed graphically. For this purpose, not only must the solution be evaluated numerically, but a new list must be produced as well in which real and imaginary parts are separated from each other. Here again, the loop command seq is of great help.

```
s:=solve(sin(x)^2+cos(x)+3);
```

$$s := \arctan(\frac{1}{2}\sqrt{-14+2\sqrt{17}},\, \frac{1}{2}-\frac{1}{2}\sqrt{17}), \; \arctan(-\frac{1}{2}\sqrt{-14+2\sqrt{17}},\, \frac{1}{2}-\frac{1}{2}\sqrt{17}),$$

$$\arctan(\frac{1}{2}\sqrt{-14-2\sqrt{17}},\, \frac{1}{2}+\frac{1}{2}\sqrt{17}), \; \arctan(-\frac{1}{2}\sqrt{-14-2\sqrt{17}},\, \frac{1}{2}+\frac{1}{2}\sqrt{17})$$

```
sf:=map(evalf,[s]);
```

$$sf := [3.141592654 - 1.015558753\,I, \; 3.141592654 + 1.015558753\,I, \; 1.593277489\,I,$$

$$-1.593277489\,I]$$

```
pts:=[seq([Re(i),Im(i)], i=sf)];
```

$$pts := [[3.141592654, -1.015558753], [3.141592654, 1.015558753], [0, 1.593277489],$$

$$[0, -1.593277489]]$$

```
plot(pts, style=point, symbol=circle);
```

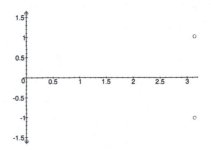

Since Release 4, the `plots` package provides the `complexplot` command. This command can represent complex points immediately, so the manual separation of real and imaginary parts is no longer needed. The solution must simply be enclosed in square brackets and numerically evaluated with `evalf`.

```
with(plots);
complexplot([evalf(s)],
            style=point, symbol=circle);
```

Solution of recursive equations

The `rsolve` command is suited for the extraction of general function specifications from functions that are given in recursive form. Our example is (yet again) the well-known Fibonacci formula:

```
sln:=rsolve({f(n)=f(n-1)+f(n-2), f(0)=0, f(1)=1}, f(n));
```

$$sln := \sqrt{5}\left(\frac{2}{-1+\sqrt{5}}\right)^{n} 1/5 - \sqrt{5}\left(-\frac{2}{1+\sqrt{5}}\right)^{n} 1/5$$

```
fib:=unapply(simplify(sln), n);
```

$$fib := n \mapsto -\frac{\left(-\left(-1/2+\frac{\sqrt{5}}{2}\right)^{-n} + \left(-1/2-\frac{\sqrt{5}}{2}\right)^{-n}\right)\sqrt{5}}{5}$$

This formula does not look very elegant, but apart from some small rounding errors, it does work (here, in comparison with the Fibonacci function of the `combinat` package):

```
evalf(fib(5)), combinat[fibonacci](5);
```

$4.999999988, 5$

```
evalf(fib(50)), combinat[fibonacci](50);
```

$12586268740.0, 12586269025$

Coefficient comparison (solve/identity, match)

The command `match(eqn1=eqn2, x, 'sln')` carries out a coefficient comparison, that is, it tries to obtain a match (identity) of the two equations by transforming the equations and determining the unknowns contained in them (with the exception of the variable x). If this is successful, `match` supplies the result *true*, otherwise *false*. The equations for the coefficients are written into the variable *sln* which must be specified enclosed in quotes in the third parameter of `match`.

```
match(x^2-1= (x-a)*(x-b), x, 'sln');
```

true

```
sln;
```

$$\{a = 1, b = -1\}$$

The identity variation of `solve` works in a very similar way to `match`. Its syntax is `solve(identity(eqn1=eqn2, x), {a,b,..})`.

```
solve(identity(x^2-1=(x-a)*(x-b), x), {a,b});
```

$$\{a = -1, b = 1\}, \{a = 1, b = -1\}$$

Unfortunately, the difference between the two commands (apart from the syntax) is not described anywhere. Sometimes, `solve` produces several results when `match` produces only one. Then again, `solve` may not find a result at all, whereas `match` does.

```
match(2*sin(3*x^4)= a*sin(n*x^k), x, 'sln'); sln;
```

true

$$\{a = 2, k = 4, n = 3\}$$

```
solve(identity(2*sin(3*x^4)= a*sin(n*x^k), x), {a,n,k});
```

`match` is not deterred by complicated polynomial transformations and partly supplies the result for the coefficients in the `RootOf` form described earlier:

```
match(x^2+3*x+5= a*(x+b)^2+c*x, x, 'sln'); sln;
```

true

$$\left\{a = 1, b = RootOf(-5 + \_Z^2), c = -2\,RootOf(-5 + \_Z^2) + 3\right\}$$

```
allvalues(");
```

$$\left\{a = 1, c = -2\sqrt{5} + 3, b = \sqrt{5}\right\}, \left\{a = 1, c = 2\sqrt{5} + 3, b = -\sqrt{5}\right\}$$

```
subs("[1], a*(x+b)^2+c*x);
```

$$\left(x + \sqrt{5}\right)^2 + \left(-2\sqrt{5} + 3\right)x$$

Vice versa, both `solve` and `match` may well fail with comparatively simple transformations. In the example below, it is clear at first sight that c must be equal to $\pi/2$ in order to make the two equations match.

```
solve(identity(sin(2*x)+sin(x) = cos(x+c)+cos(2*x+c),x), {c});
match(sin(2*x)+sin(x) = cos(x+c)+cos(2*x+c), x, 'sln');
```

false

Special commands (solve/functions, solve/ineqs, isolve)

Determining solution functions

Normally, `solve` determines only one or several isolated values of solutions. However, when the unknown in an equation is formulated as a function in the form $f(x)$, `solve` tries to generate the program code for a corresponding function as a solution. The following example shows such an application of `solve`:

```
sln:=solve(f(x)+f(x)^2=1+x^3, f);
    sln:=proc(x) -1/2+1/2*(5+4*x^3)^(1/2) end,
        proc(x) -1/2-1/2*(5+4*x^3)^(1/2) end
```

`solve` actually supplies two alternative functions as the solution for the equation $f(x) + f(x)^2 = 1 + x^3$. The functions are written in Maple's programming language with `proc` and `end`. In spite of this unusual notation, these functions can be used in the same way as any true function (see also Chapters 8 and 29).

In the following example, the first of the two solution functions is stored in *test*. In order to demonstrate that the function really can be used in a completely normal way, *test*(x) is converted into arrow notation by means of `unapply` (see Chapter 8). Subsequently, `test(x)^3+test(x)` is simplified. As requested, the result is $1 + x^3$.

```
test:=sln[1];
    test:=proc(x) -1/2+1/2*(5+4*x^3)^(1/2) end
unapply(test(x), x);
```
$$x \mapsto -1/2 + \frac{\sqrt{5 + 4\,x^3}}{2}$$
```
simplify(test(x)+test(x)^2);
```
$$1 + x^3$$

Handling inequations

When an inequation is specified in `solve`, Maple tries to find the ranges of the variable x to which the inequation applies. The solution is formulated with the `RealRange` term. Only when the variables are enclosed with braces does Maple use a clearer notation.

```
solve(abs(x)<1);
```
$$\text{RealRange}(\text{Open}(-1), \text{Open}(1))$$
```
solve(abs(x)<1, {x});
```
$$\{-1 < x, x < 1\}$$

The syntax of the results needs explanation: two results indicated in separate pairs of braces mean 'or', that is, $x^2 + x > 2$ applies if $x < -2$ or $x > 1$ applies. Several inequations within one level of braces are to be joined with 'and', that is, $x^2 + x < 2$ applies if both $x > -2$ and $x < 1$ apply.

```
solve(x^2+x>2, {x});
```
$$\{x < -2\}, \{1 < x\}$$
```
solve(x^2+x<2, {x});
```
$$\{-2 < x, x < 1\}$$

Analogously, this scheme also applies to the `RealRange` expressions. Here, `Open` corresponds to the less-equal or greater-equal operators, respectively. Conversion functions between the two notations are not documented. Some brief information about the keywords `RealRange` and `Open` can be found with `?property`.

```
solve(x^2+x>2);
```
$$\text{RealRange}(-\infty, \text{Open}(-2)),$$
$$\text{RealRange}(\text{Open}(1), \infty)$$
```
solve(x^2+x<2);
```
$$\text{RealRange}(\text{Open}(-2), \text{Open}(1))$$

solve can also cope with simple inequation systems with several variables.

```
eq:={x+y>=5, x-y>=1, y-x/2<=1/2}:
solve(eq, {x, y});
```
$$\{5 - x - y <= 0, 1 - x + y <= 0,$$
$$y - 1/2x - 1/2 <= 0, 3 <= x\}$$

In complex cases, solve refuses to answer.

```
solve(a*x^2+b*x+c>0,x);
solve(sin(x)>1/2);
```

Integer solutions of equations

isolve is not simply a variation of solve that restricts the results to integer numbers. On the contrary, isolve determines entire solution families depending on the variables specified in the second parameter.

```
isolve(x+2*y+3*z=10, {k,l});
```
$$\{y = k, z = l, x = 10 - 2k - 3l\}$$

Syntax summary

```
solve({eqnn}, {var});
```
solves the equations specified in the first set for the variables specified in the second set. When functions are specified instead of equations, solve automatically sets them to 0. If no variables are specified, solve solves the equation system for all unknown symbols occurring in it.

```
fsolve({eqnn}, {var}, options);
```
in the main works in the same way as `solve`, but carries out a numeric solution search. When `fsolve` does not find a solution, the range for the solution can be restricted by a third parameter in the form `x=start..end`. Amongst others, `fsolve` has the following options: `complex` (consider complex solutions) and `fulldigits` (calculate with maximum precision (although it is slower)).

```
match(eqn1=eqn2, var, 'sln');
solve(identity( eqn1=eqn2, var), {coeffa, b, c...});
```
carry out a coefficient comparison. Both commands try to transform the equations in such a way that the coefficients contained in them can be determined. `match` writes the solution into the quoted variable *sln*. `solve` returns the solution directly; however, the coefficients to be determined must be explicitly specified.

```
solve(equation(f(x)), f);
```
determines the solution function $f(x)$ which satisfies the specified equation. The solution is formulated as program code in the form `proc ... end`.

```
solve(inequation, var);
```
tries to resolve the specified inequation and to determine those ranges of the variable x for which the inequation is satisfied.

```
isolve({eqnn}, {k,l,..});
```
solves the equations and formulates the result as a function of the integer variables $k, l, \ldots$.

Chapter 12

Sequences, lists and sets

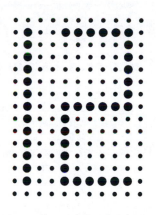

Maple currently has five different ways of combining several expressions in an ordered manner. Although the five variations look very similar at first sight, they differ fundamentally in their internal representation and must be processed with completely different methods.

```
sq    := a,b,c;              sequence
lst   := [a,b,c];            list
st    := {a,b,c};            set
tb[3] := c;                  table
fld   := array( [a,b,c] );   array
```

This chapter deals with the first three data types and describes the most important commands for their administration. The next chapter describes the remaining two data types (tables and arrays) and summarizes the possible conversions between all five data types. Another point of interest in connection with data sets is the dot operator and the corresponding `cat` command. These can be used for easy construction of variable lists (for example, $x1, x2, x3, ..$). The dot operator is described in Chapter 6.

Now to the most important commands of this chapter:

`seq`
generates a sequence. When the entire instruction is enclosed in square brackets or in braces, it is immediately converted into a list or a set.

`op`
returns the elements of an arbitrary expression as a sequence. `op` can be used to convert lists and sets into sequences.

`subsop`
changes an element inside an expression. Not suitable for sequences.

`map, zip`
successively applies the elements of a set or a list to a function (to an expression). Only for sets and lists.

Sequences, lists and sets in the day-to-day use of Maple

Sequences, lists and sets are omnipresent elements of Maple which occur with practically every command (both in its formulation and in its result).

The function min determines the smallest value of a series of numbers given in a *sequence*.

```
min(1, sqrt(2), sqrt(2)/2);
```

$$\frac{\sqrt{2}}{2}$$

The root command determines a *list* of all zero points of a polynomial. The zero points are displayed in the form $[x0, n]$, meaning zero points of the $(x - x0)^n$ kind.

```
f:=expand((x-2)^3 * (x-3) * (x-1));
```

$$f := x^5 - 10\,x^4 + 39\,x^3 -$$

$$74\,x^2 + 68\,x - 24$$

```
roots(f);
```

$$[[1, 1], [2, 3], [3, 1]]$$

solve supplies several solutions of an equation as a *sequence*.

```
solve(x^4-10*x^3+35*x^2-50*x+24,x);
```

$$1, 2, 3, 4$$

As far as the command is concerned, it can be passed an entire equation system and the list of variables contained in it as a *set* (enclosed in braces). The solution (which is now grouped into several single solutions for all variables concerned) is again displayed as a *set*.

```
solve({x^2+y^2=13,x^2-y^2=5},{x,y});
```

$$\{y = 2, x = 3\},$$

$$\{y = 2, x = -3\},$$

$$\{y = -2, x = 3\},$$

$$\{y = -2, x = -3\}$$

When plot is used to draw several curves at a time, the function equations are again passed as a *set*:

```
plot({sin(x), sin(3*x)/3, sin(5*x)/5},
     x=0..Pi);
```

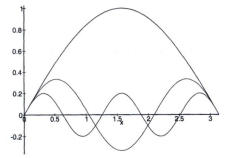

Sequences

Sequences represent the most elementary data type for the administration of several units of information. At each call of a function with more than one argument, you enter the arguments as a sequence (separated by commas). Maple, in turn, prefers to return the results as sequences. Unlike lists and sets, sequences cannot be embedded – thus, an element of a sequence cannot itself be a sequence.

Sequences can be constructed by simple enumeration.

```
sq:=a,b,c;
```
$$sq := a, b, c$$

More frequently, however, the `seq` command is used. The first parameter of this command contains a function specification, the second parameter the permitted value range. Maple varies the specified variable between both limit values, using a step width of $+1$ on principle.

```
sq:=seq(2^n-2*n, n=0..3);
```
$$sq := 1, 0, 0, 2$$

```
seq(i^2,i=1.5..3);
```
$$2.25, 6.25$$

`seq` can be used in a second variation. Here, the number values to be substituted are taken from a sequence, a list or a set.

```
seq(i^2, i=[1.5, 2, 2.5, 3]);
```
$$2.25, 4, 6.25, 9$$

This second sequence can also be generated with `seq`. Thus, sequences with a different step width than $+1$ can be generated in a fairly clear manner. In Chapter 30, which is dedicated to the subject of programming, we will present the `seqn` command which is suited for the formulation of sequences with arbitrary step widths.

```
seq(i^2, i=seq(j*0.5, j=3..6));
```
$$2.25, 4.0, 6.25, 9.0$$

Sequences can be extended without problems by adding elements at the beginning or at the end of the sequence.

```
sq1:=sq,8;
```
$$sq1 := 1, 0, 0, 2, 8$$

Elements of a sequence are accessed through the specification of an index in square brackets. Please note that the first element has the index 1 (and not 0, as in some programming languages). Instead of a single index, you can also specify a range in the form `n..m`.

```
sq[4];
```
$$2$$

```
sq[2..4];
```
$$0, 0, 2$$

Since Release 4, negative indices allow access to the end of a sequence.

```
sq[-1];
```
$$8$$

Things become more difficult when elements of a sequence are to be modified. The most obvious solution would be an assignment of the form `sq[n]:=m`. This is exactly what you must not do – because you would create a table (see next chapter) and simultaneously delete all elements of the sequence!

On the contrary, you must bring into play the `subsop` command whose idiosyncratic syntax makes every mathematician's hair stand on end.

```
sq1:=op(subsop(4=3,[sq1]));
```
$$sq1 := 1, 0, 0, 3, 8$$

The above command is not very easy to understand: with [sq] the sequence is converted into a list (because subsop can only process lists). Subsequently, subsop substitutes the fourth element of the list with the value 3. Thus, the first parameter of subsop specifies the substitution instruction (element number=new value), the second parameter the expression to be processed.

Finally op is used to convert the modified list back into a sequence. Conversion between different data types is the subject of a dedicated section in the next chapter.

subsop can also be used to delete single elements of a sequence. You simply substitute the element to be deleted with NULL.

```
sq1:=op(subsop(4=NULL,[sq1]));
```
$$sq1 := 1, 0, 0, 8$$

Lists

Lists differ visually from sequences by their enclosing square brackets. Lists are more difficult to extend than sequences, but more powerful. In particular, lists can be embedded.

Basically, lists are created in the same way as sequences – but the square brackets must be included.

```
lst:=[1,2,3];
```
$$lst := [1, 2, 3]$$

```
lst:=[seq(2^n-2*n,n=0..3)];
```
$$lst := [1, 0, 0, 2]$$

List elements are accessed in the same way as elements of sequences. For modifications, you must again call the subsop command.

```
lst[2];
```
$$0$$

```
st:=subsop(2=3,lst);
```
$$st := [1, 3, 0, 2]$$

When lists are to be extended, they must first be reduced to sequences by means of op.

```
lst:=[a,b,op(lst),c,d,x,x^2,x^3];
```
$$lst := [a, b, 1, 3, 0, 2, c, d, x, x^2, x^3]$$

The sort command is available for sorting lists.

```
sort(lst);
```
$$[x^3, a, b, d, 3, 0, 1, 2, c, x, x^2]$$

However, this command needs some explanation: numbers are, as expected, sorted by their values (if the list is exclusively composed of numbers). Character strings (unassigned variables) and mathematical expressions, in contrast, are sorted by the address in which they were stored in memory. This sorting order may be acceptable for a computer, but it is completely useless for any practical work. Since the user has no influence whatsoever on where and how Maple stores its objects, the order is unpredictable and can differ between two practically identical Maple sessions. This slightly idiosyncratic ordering of elements also applies for sets, which are discussed in the next section.

In the second argument of `sort`, `lexorder` can be specified as the sorting order, in which case the command sorts character strings by their internal code (that is, upper case letters before lower case letters).

```
sort([e,E,Z,b,a], lexorder);
```
$$[E, Z, a, b, e]$$

Now, however, `sort` comes up with an error message when the list also contains mathematical expressions, such as x^2.

```
sort([e,E,Z,b,a,x,x^2,x^3],
        lexorder);
```
```
Error, invalid arguments to sort
```

This means that `sort` can only reasonably be used for lists that contain either numbers or character strings exclusively. The command can also be used to sort terms within mathematical expressions (for example, the terms of a polynomial). In this application area, the command works significantly better.

Sets

At first sight, lists (square brackets) and sets (braces) seem to be the same.

```
st:={0,1,2};
```
$$st := \{0, 1, 2\}$$

However, this is not the case: in sets, duplicate elements are automatically eliminated. Furthermore, the order of elements is determined by Maple in a seemingly arbitrary way and is not predictable (see the next example below). Thus, sets are only suited to problems where the order of elements is of no significance (for example, in the specification of several equations of an equation system).

Individual elements of a set are accessed in the same way as elements of lists. Please note, however, that you can never predict the position of an element within the set beforehand!

In addition to the commands introduced above for handling lists, there are three operators which are specially designed for processing sets: `union` produces the union of two sets, `intersect` the intersection, and `minus` removes subsets.

```
{1,2,3} union {3,4,5};
```
$$\{3, 4, 5, 1, 2\}$$
```
{1,2,3,4,5} intersect {4,5,6};
```
$$\{4, 5\}$$
```
{1,2,3,4} minus {1,2};
```
$$\{3, 4\}$$

Embedded lists and sets

Embedding lists and sets means that individual elements of a list/set can themselves be lists/sets. In practice, embedding occurs when, for example, `solve` finds several solutions for an equation system with several variables. Each of these solutions is formulated as a set, and all the sets are returned as a sequence (see the example in the introduction to this chapter).

In principle, matrices could also be represented by embedded lists. In Maple, however, this makes no sense, as the `linalg` package for matrix calculation only accepts arrays. More information about this data type will be given in the next chapter.

The command on the right defines a list whose first element is a set, whose second element is a list and whose third element is a simple variable.

```
lst:=[{1,2,3},[a,b,c,d,e],x];
```
$$lst := [\{3,1,2\},[a,b,c,d,e],x]$$

Individual elements are again accessed by specifying indices in square brackets. In order to access elements in the sublists, the indices must be specified in separate pairs of brackets.

```
lst[2];
```
$$[a,b,c,d,e]$$
```
lst[2][3];
```
$$c$$

The example on the right shows that it is also possible to read a range from within a sublist.

```
lst[2][2..4];
```
$$b,c,d$$

In contrast, it is not possible to read each of the first elements in the first two sublists, as the command on the right was planned to do. `lst[1..2]` leads to a sequence of the first two elements of the list. The postfixed characters `[1]` access the first element of this sequence.

```
lst[1..2][1];
```
$$\{3,1,2\}$$

Things become complicated when you want to modify individual elements in sublists: here you must employ the already mentioned `subsop` command in an embedded way. As a rule, it is better in such cases to use arrays where it is much easier to modify individual elements.

In the example on the right, the third element of the sublist of *lst* is replaced by the variable x.

```
lst:=subsop(2=subsop(3=x, lst[2]), lst);
```
$$lst := [\{3,1,2\},[a,b,x,d,e],x]$$

Processing lists and sets (member and select)

The `member` command can be used to check whether a specific element is part of a list or set. When the name of a variable is specified as an optional third parameter, Maple assigns this variable the position of the element sought within the list.

```
member(2, [1,2,3]);
```
$$true$$
```
member(x^3, [x, x^2, x^3], 'pos'):
pos;
```
$$3$$

Please note that in the second command the variable *pos* is enclosed in quotes. This call of `member` would also work without quotes, since *pos* is not yet occupied at that point in time. In a subsequent call, *pos* already contains a value which Maple substitutes as third parameter. This substitution of the variable name with its value is prevented by `'pos'`. See also the fifth survival rule in Chapter 5.

Another useful command for processing lists and sets is `select`. It selects the elements of a list (or sequence or set) that satisfy a given criterion.

The command has three different syntax variations. In the example on the right, the selection criterion is specified by means of a Boolean function which returns *true* or *false*. The selection criterion is formulated as an anonymous function (see Chapter 8).

```
data:=seq(rand(1..20)(),i=1..10);
```
$$data := 12, 14, 1, 12, 19, 14, 1, 5, 6, 12$$
```
select(x->x>=10, [data]);
```
$$[12, 14, 12, 19, 14, 12]$$

In the remaining two variations, the criterion is specified either in the form `type, ...,` `data_type` or by means of `has, ..., property`. In the second command on the right, several 'properties' (that is, the occurrence of the numbers 12, 13 or 14) are formulated in a set.

```
select(type,[data],odd);
```
$$[1, 19, 1, 5]$$
```
select(has,[data],{12,13,14});
```
$$[12, 14, 12, 14, 12]$$

Reference: The `select` command is also very well suited to processing mathematical expressions. Some further examples can be found in Chapter 10.

Calculating with lists and sets (map and zip)

Since Release 4, Maple can carry out addition, subtraction and scalar multiplication of lists without having to resort to special commands.

```
[1,2,3] + [4,5,6];
```
$$[5, 7, 9]$$
```
[1,2,3] - 2*[4,5,6];
```
$$[-7, -8, -9]$$

Any other form of processing, however, needs special commands, such as `map` and `zip`. The main application of `map` is to apply a command to several elements of a single list.

```
lst:=[1,2,3]: sqrt(lst);
```
$$lst := \sqrt{[1, 2, 3]}$$
```
map(sqrt, lst);
```
$$[1, \sqrt{2}, \sqrt{3}]$$

In its first argument, which usually contains only a single function, `map` can also accept a whole list of functions.

```
map([sin,cos],1);
```
$$[\sin(1), \cos(1)]$$
```
map([sin,cos], [1,2]);
```
$$[[\sin(1), \cos(1)], [\sin(2), \cos(2)]]$$

For functions with several arguments, `map` allows specification of additional parameters.

```
map(arctan, x,y);
```
$$\arctan(x, y)$$

The following two examples show that the flexibility of map has its limits. Thus, map cannot cope with embedded lists.

```
map(sqrt, [1,2,[3,4]]);
```
$$[1, \sqrt{2}, \sqrt{[3,4]}\,]$$

It is also impossible to insert several pairs of variables of the form $(x1, y1), (x2, y2), \ldots$ into arctan.

```
map(arctan, [x1,x2], [y1,y2]);
```
$$[\mathrm{arctan}(x1, [y1, y2]),$$
$$\mathrm{arctan}(x2, [y1, y2])]$$

zip is used to join two lists: the elements of both lists are inserted pairwise into the two-parameter function.

```
zip(arctan, [x1,x2], [y1,y2]);
```
$$[\mathrm{arctan}(x1, y1), \mathrm{arctan}(x2, y2)]$$

zip cannot simply be passed an operator. In order to add the elements of two lists, a matching two-parameter function has to be created. Maple normally uses the arrow notation described in Chapter 8 for these so-called anonymous functions.

```
zip((x,y)->x+y, [1,2,3], [a,b,c]);
```
$$[1 + a, 2 + b, 3 + c]$$

Quite often, two simple lists have to be combined into one pairwise embedded list. This too can be achieved with zip.

```
zip((x,y)->[x,y], [x1,x2,x3],
    [y1,y2,y3]);
```
$$[[x1, y1], [x2, y2], [x3, y3]]$$

A final remark: map can also be applied to sets, but zip is limited to lists and vectors (see next chapter).

map and zip allow you to carry out relatively complex operations, but in most cases it is better to switch from lists or sets to arrays. Then you can use the linalg package to carry out most arithmetic operations. The commands of this package, which are primarily designed for vector and matrix calculus, will be described in Chapter 14.

Syntax summary

```
a,b,c;      [a,b,c];      {a,b,c};
```
The above line shows once again the syntax of a sequence, a list and a set. The order of the elements in a set is determined by Maple and is not predictable. Duplicate elements are eliminated.

```
list[n];      list[n..m];      list[n][m];
```
reads individual list elements. The first element of a list has the index 1. With [n..m], several elements can be read simultaneously. [n][m] accesses the mth element of the nth sublist. The elements can only be modified with subsop, not with an assignment – otherwise, a table would be created.

`op(expression);     op(n, expression);`

 converts the list or set specified in the first parameter into a sequence. In embedded lists/sets only the outermost level of brackets is removed. By specifying an index as the second parameter, a single element can be read from a list or a set. `op` can also be applied to generic mathematical terms. `op(x+y+z,2)` returns y as a result.

`nops(expression);`

 determines the number of elements in a list or a set. In embedded lists or sets, only the number of elements in the outermost level is counted. Like `nops`, `op` too can be used for generic expressions.

`subsop(n1=new1, n2=new2,.., expression);`

 substitutes the nth element of a list, set or generic expression with a new one. Please note the order of parameters: first, (any number of) substitution instructions with =, then the expression to be modified.

`seq(fnx, x=start..end);     seq(fnx, x=[a,b,c,..]);`

 inserts the values specified in the second parameter into *fnx*. In the first syntax variation, a loop with a step width of $+1$ is created; in the second variation, the specified list elements are simply inserted one after the other. As a result, `seq` returns a sequence which can be immediately converted into a list or set by enclosing the whole command in square brackets or braces.

`sort(list);`

 sorts the specified list, taking the internal position of the elements in memory as a sorting criterion. The additional specification of `lexorder` allows alphabetical sorting of character strings or sorting of numbers in ascending order, but there must be no generic mathematical terms in the list. `sort` changes the order of elements in the list, even when no assignment is carried out!

`set1 union set2;     set1 intersect set2;     set1 minus set2;`

 `union` produces the union of both sets, `intersect` the intersection, and `minus` removes the elements specified in the second set from the first set.

`member(element, list);     member(element, list, 'position');`

 `member` checks whether the element specified in the first parameter is present in the list or set and returns *true* or *false* as a result. When a variable name enclosed in quotes is specified in the third parameter, Maple assigns it the position of the element.

`select(boolfunc, list);`
`select(has, list, property);`
`select(type, list, data_type);`

 selects single elements of a list or set and returns these elements as a reduced list/set. The selection criterion can be formulated as an anonymous Boolean function (for example, `x->x<5`) or by specifying a property with `has` or a data type with `type`. `select` can also be used for processing mathematical expressions (see Chapter 10).

```
map(fnx, list);     map([fnx1, fnx2,..], list);
```
map applies all one-parameter functions specified in the first parameter to the elements enumerated in the second parameter in the form of a list or a set. Depending on the type of the second parameter, map returns a list or a set.

```
zip(fnxy, list1, list2);
```
zip works similarly to map, but is designed for two-parameter functions. Elements from both lists are inserted pairwise into the function specified in the first parameter. This function can be formulated in arrow notation ((x,y)->...).

Chapter 13

Tables and arrays

Maple has five data types for combining several expressions in an ordered manner. Three of these, namely sequences, lists and sets, were the subject of Chapter 12. Tables and arrays differ from these three data types insofar as the enumeration characteristic is of less importance. Reading and changing individual elements is possible without problems (even with multi-dimensional sets of data).

The peculiarity of tables is that not only numbers, but arbitrary character strings and even mathematical expressions are allowed as indices to access individual elements. Data can be added and modified without restrictions.

In comparison, arrays are organized more rigidly: they must be dimensioned in advance, and only integer numbers are allowed as indices. In Maple, arrays are used particularly to store vectors and matrices (see also Chapter 14 on matrix calculus).

To begin with, here is a brief overview of the most important commands for handling tables and arrays and for converting them from/to other data types:

`table`
defines a table and fills it with data.

`array`
defines an array and fills it with data.

`eval`
evaluates the table or array structure. With this command, all the data in a table or array can be displayed.

`convert`
converts from one data type to another. However, conversion is not possible for all possible combinations of the five data types described in this and the previous chapter.

Tables

Tables represent a universally valid data type. Their special feature, as opposed to sequences, lists and sets, is that elements of a table are not accessed according to their memory position but via a unique index. This index must be specified together with the definition of the table itself. Indices can be arbitrary expressions: integer numbers, floating point numbers, character strings, equations, formulae, and so on.

Thus, tables can be used for the administration of data which would otherwise be difficult to structure with enumeration indices. Their main application is in combining several related functions or commands into a group. This is widely used for Maple commands included in packages (see the `plots` example below).

The definition of a table is carried out by a simple assignment, with the index specified in square brackets. In the two examples on the right, the character strings 'one' and 'two' are used as indices.

```
tab[one]:=x1+y1;
```
$$tab[one] := x1 + y1$$
```
tab[two]:=x2+y2;
```
$$tab[two] := x2 + y2$$

Individual elements are accessed simply by specifying the index. Changes too are possible without problems (unlike lists and sets – see previous chapter).

```
tab[one];
```
$$x1 + y1$$
```
tab[one]:=x1+y1+z1;
```
$$tab[one] := x1 + y1 + z1$$

When you want to display the table as a whole, merely specifying the table name is not sufficient. Unlike most other data types, Maple does not carry out automatic evaluation of tables and arrays. This must be forced with `eval`.

```
tab;
```
$$tab$$
```
eval(tab);
```
$$\text{table}([$$
$$(two) = x2 + y2$$
$$(one) = x1 + y1 + z1$$
$$])$$

The following examples show that nearly every kind of expression is allowed as an index: a floating point number, a sequence of the numbers 1 and 2, and a mathematical formula.

```
tab[0.3]:=f(x):
tab[1,2]:=anOtherEntry:
tab[x^2+y^2]:=1:
```

When multiple indices are specified in pairs of [] brackets, Maple creates a subtable within the table. In the current example, element 1 contains a table which in turn contains two elements with the indices 1 and 2. This can be better shown by an evaluation of the entire table.

```
tab[1][1]:=y: tab[1][2]:=y:
eval(tab);
```

$$
\begin{aligned}
&\text{table(symmetric, [} \\
&\quad (two) = x2 + y2 \\
&\quad (one) = x1 + y1 + z1 \\
&\quad (1, 2) = anOtherEntry \\
&\quad (x^2 + y^2) = 1 \\
&\quad (1) = \text{table([} \\
&\quad\quad (1) = y \\
&\quad\quad (2) = y \\
&\quad\quad]) \\
&\quad (.3) = f(x) \\
&\quad])
\end{aligned}
$$

Tables can also be created with the `table` command. In the second argument, a list giving the initial data can be specified. When no index is specified, Maple automatically uses 1, 2 ... .

```
table([x,y]);
```

$$
\begin{aligned}
&\text{table([} \\
&\quad (1) = x \\
&\quad (2) = y \\
&\quad])
\end{aligned}
$$

Optionally, an indexing function can be specified in the first parameter of `table`. This subject will be discussed in more detail in the next but one section.

```
tab:=table(symmetric,
    [(1,1)=1, (1,2)=2, (2,2)=3]):
tab[2,1];
```

$$2$$

In practice, tables are often used to combine several related functions or commands.

```
func:=table([sin2=sin^2,
                cos2=cos^2]):
func[sin2](x);
```

$$\sin(x)^2$$

Maple employs this mechanism in the administration of library functions in packages. For example, you can access the `polarplot` command of the `plots` package with the instruction `plots[polarplot]` without previously loading the package with `with`. The following command shows the reason: `plots` contains a table whose indices are the names of the `plots` commands and whose elements are `readlib` commands.

```
eval(plots);
```

$$
\begin{aligned}
&\text{table([} \\
&\quad (odeplot) = \text{readlib}('plots/odeplot') \\
&\quad (densityplot) = \text{readlib}('plots/densityplot') \\
&\quad \dots \\
&\quad (animate3d) = \text{readlib}('plots/animate3d') \\
&\quad])
\end{aligned}
$$

Arrays

Arrays are a special case of tables. Unlike tables, the following two restrictions apply to arrays: firstly, the size of arrays is not variable and must be determined beforehand by calling the `array` command. Secondly, only integer numbers are allowed as indices. These restrictions almost inevitably lead to the main application of arrays: the storage of vectors and matrices. All matrix commands in the `linalg` package assume that the matrices are passed as arrays. (Obviously, arrays can also be defined in three or more dimensions.)

On screen, arrays are displayed in different ways, depending on their contents: after the execution of `array`, `eval` or `print` commands, one- and two-dimensional arrays whose indices both start with 1 are displayed in matrix form. Multi-dimensional arrays and arrays in which individual index ranges do not start with 1 are displayed in the `table` structure shown in the previous section. In this book, one- and two-dimensional arrays that do not satisfy this condition are nevertheless displayed in matrix form, with the index ranges additionally displayed in the lower right corner (see the last example in this section).

Arrays must be created with `array`. The command can be passed an (embedded) list of the elements and/or the range limits for the indices. When, as in the example on the right, no range limits are specified, Maple assumes that each lowest index value is 1.

```
ar:=array([[a,b],[c,d]]);
```

$$ar := \begin{bmatrix} a & b \\ c & d \end{bmatrix}$$

Elements are accessed by specifying all indices in one set of square brackets (unlike embedded lists and sets where each index must be enclosed in its own brackets!). As with tables, the contents of arrays are only displayed when `eval` or `print` is explicitly specified.

```
ar[1,1]:=a^2;
```

$$ar[1,1] := a^2$$

```
eval(ar);
```

$$\begin{bmatrix} a^2 & b \\ c & d \end{bmatrix}$$

As a rule, vectors are displayed as one-dimensional arrays. Column vectors which necessitate a two-dimensional array are a special case.

```
array(1..3,[1,2,3]);
```

$$[1,2,3]$$

```
array(1..3,1..1,[[1],[2],[3]]);
```

$$\begin{bmatrix} 1 \\ 2 \\ 3 \end{bmatrix}$$

With `map`, a function can be applied to all elements of an array. Otherwise, calculations involving arrays are carried out with the commands of the `linalg` package. This package also contains commands for initializing vectors and matrices, reading partial matrices, and so on (see next chapter).

```
map(sin,ar);
```

$$\begin{bmatrix} \sin(a^2) & \sin(b) \\ \sin(c) & \sin(d) \end{bmatrix}$$

Arrays can be defined with arbitrary dimensions and with arbitrary integer range limits. When the index function `sparse` is specified, all elements which are not explicitly otherwise assigned are set to 0. Further information about index functions can be found in the next section.

```
ar:=array(sparse,-1..1,-1..1);
```

$$ar := \mathrm{array}(sparse, -1..1, -1..1, [])$$

```
eval(ar);
```

$$\mathrm{array}(sparse, -1..1, -1..1, [$$
$$(-1, -1) = 0$$
$$(-1, 0) = 0$$
$$...$$
$$(1, 1) = 0])$$

Index functions for tables and arrays

Maple has five predefined index functions whose names can be specified as an additional argument in `table` or `array`. This gives Maple additional information about how the data is organized. Especially for large matrices, the index functions allow more economical memory administration, in terms of space. In symmetric matrices, for example, only half the number of array elements must be stored. Furthermore, various simplifications are possible in symbolic calculations. Before we illustrate this feature with some examples, here is a brief description of the five index functions:

`identity`
Elements for which all indices are identical have the value 1, all others the value 0. Since with `identity` all elements are predefined, assignments of individual elements are no longer possible!

`diagonal`
Like `identity`, but the elements of the main diagonal can be assigned arbitrary values.

`sparse`
All elements that have not been explicitly assigned are set to 0. Much memory and computing time can be saved in matrices where most elements are 0.

`symmetric`
The best-known (and most easily understandable) symmetry is that of quadratic matrices: all elements mirrored at the main diagonal are identical. For multi-dimensional arrays the symmetry is defined in such a way that elements are considered symmetric if their indices can be put into the same order by arbitrary shifting. Thus, in a 3*3*3 array the following array elements match: $x_{1,2,3}$,

$x_{1,3,2}$, $x_{2,1,3}$, $x_{2,3,1}$, $x_{3,1,2}$ and $x_{3,2,1}$. In symmetric arrays only one of these six elements has to be initialized. Subsequently, all six elements can be accessed.

`antisymmetric`

The definition of antisymmetry is slightly more complicated: elements for which more than two indices match are defined as 0 (for example, $x_{1,1,1}$ or $x_{1,2,2}$). Elements whose indices can be made to match by an even number of shifts are identical (for example, $x_{1,2,3} = x_{2,3,1}$). Elements whose indices can be made to match by an odd number of shifts differ in their sign (for example, $x_{1,2,3} = -x_{1,3,2}$).

In the example on the right, an antisymmetric 3*3 matrix is defined. The example shows that Maple exploits the symmetry rules and knows $ar_{2,3,1}$ although only $ar_{1,2,3}$ has been initialized.

```
ar:=array(antisymmetric,
            1..3,1..3):
ar[1,2,3]:=1:
ar[2,3,1];

    1
```

Although only three elements are assigned, Maple knows all nine elements because of the antisymmetry rules.

```
ar:=array(antisymmetric,1..3,1..3):
ar[1,2]:=4: ar[1,3]:=5: ar[2,3]:=6:
eval(ar);
```

$$\begin{bmatrix} 0 & 4 & 5 \\ -4 & 0 & 6 \\ -5 & -6 & 0 \end{bmatrix}$$

Assignment and copying of tables and arrays

Normally, in an assignment of the form x:=y, the expression in y is evaluated and subsequently stored in x. Thus, x has the same contents as y. However, x and y are obviously independent of each other. When one variable is modified, this has no influence at all on the other variable.

This applies to most Maple data types, except for tables and arrays. When y contains a table, then, after assignment, x points to the same table. Thus, a change in the first variable affects the second variable as well.

```
a:=array([[1,2],[3,4]]):
b:=a: b[2,2]:=5:
eval(a),eval(b);
```

$$\begin{bmatrix} 1 & 2 \\ 3 & 5 \end{bmatrix}, \begin{bmatrix} 1 & 2 \\ 3 & 5 \end{bmatrix}$$

If this dependence is to be avoided, the copy command must be used.

```
a:=array([[1,2],[3,4]]):
b:=copy(a): b[2,2]:=5:
eval(a),eval(b);
```

$$\begin{bmatrix} 1 & 2 \\ 3 & 4 \end{bmatrix}, \begin{bmatrix} 1 & 2 \\ 3 & 5 \end{bmatrix}$$

Please note that copy is unable to cope with embedded (recursive) array or table structures. When an element of a table is itself a table, copy makes a copy only of the outer table, not the inner one.

Conversion between sequences, lists, sets, tables and arrays

Conversion between the five data types mentioned above is carried out by various commands. With sequences, lists and sets, the op command and bracketing with [] or {} are often sufficient.

When sets or tables come into play, the convert command must be used quite frequently. The syntax of this command is convert(expression,type), where about 50 different keywords can be specified for the requested data type. In this section, however, only a few of these are mentioned.

In principle, conversion is possible only for non-embedded data types. The only exception to this rule is conversion between lists and arrays, which can be carried out to any depth of embedding (conversion type listlist).

Conversion is carried out in two steps: first, the data is reduced to a sequence or a list which is then further processed in the second step.

Conversion into sequences	Conversion into lists	Conversion into sets
op(list);	[sequence];	{sequence};
op(set);	[op(set)];	{op(list)};
op(convert(table, list));	convert(set, list);	convert(list, set);
op(convert(array, list));	convert(table, list);	convert(table, set);
	convert(array, list);	convert(array, set);
	convert(array, listlist);	

Conversion into tables	Conversion into arrays
table([sequence]);	convert([sequence], array);
table(list);	convert(list, array);
table(set);	convert(set, array);
table(convert(array,list));	convert(table, array);

The above table is obviously only a guideline for typical conversion cases. With a modicum of skill, special cases can always be handled by means of a step-by-step conversion. In the example below, the elements of an array (a 3*3 matrix) are converted into a sequence. Such a conversion may, for example, become necessary when the biggest element of a matrix is to be found with max.

The test matrix is given as an array and is converted into an embedded list with convert.

```
test:=array([[1,2,3],[4,5,6],
                    [7,8,9]]):
data:=convert(test,listlist);
```

$$data := [[1,2,3],[4,5,6],[7,8,9]]$$

Subsequently, the sublists in *data* are converted into sequences with op. op(data[1]) produces [1, 2, 3]. With seq, the sequences of the rows of the matrix are joined together into one long sequence.

```
seq(op(data[i]), i=1..3);
```
$$1, 2, 3, 4, 5, 6, 7, 8, 9$$
```
max(");
```
$$9$$

Syntax summary

```
table();
table([element1, element2,,]);
table([(index1)=element1, (index2)=el2,...]);
```
creates a table and, if specified, fills in some data. When no indices are specified, Maple uses 1,2,3.... The table can be arbitrarily extended by means of tab[index]:=element.

```
array(s1..e1, s2..e2,...);
array(data);
array(index_range, data);
```
creates an array. In the first syntax variation, only the size of the array is specified, while the elements remain unassigned. The index limits must be integer numbers. In the second variation, the size of the array is determined by the data passed as an (embedded) list, for example, 2*2 for the data $[[a, b], [c, d]]$. In this case, the lowest index is always 1.

```
sparse    diagonal    identity    symmetric    antisymmetric
```
selects one of the five predefined index functions as an additional parameter in table or array. Maple uses this information for a more efficient administration and processing of the data.
A brief explanation of the keywords:
sparse: All data not explicitly assigned is set to 0.
diagonal: All data outside the main diagonal is set to 0.
identity: Identity matrix, elements with identical indices are set to 1, all others to 0.
symmetric: Elements whose indices can be made to match by shifting are considered identical.
antisymmetric: As symmetric, but negative sign with an odd number of shifts; elements with several identical indices are considered to be 0.

```
map(func, x);
```
applies the function specified in the first parameter to all elements of the table or array.

```
eval(x);      print(x);
```
displays the entire contents of a table or an array on screen. A simple specification of the variable name is not sufficient, as Maple carries out no automatic evaluation of tables and arrays.

```
x:=copy(y);
```
copies the data of table or array y to x. A simple assignment would lead to x and y pointing to the same data. When x and y are to be independent of each other, copy is needed (only for tables and arrays).

```
convert(data, type);
```
converts the data into the required data type (if possible). In connection with tables, arrays, and so on, the following data types make sense: list (simple lists), listlist (embedded lists), set (simple sets), array (arrays).

Chapter 14

Vector and matrix calculus

In the course of this chapter, we will be dealing with two packages that contain commands for vector, matrix and tensor calculus:

`geometry`
contains commands for vector calculus in a two-dimensional coordinate system. These commands can be used to define and process geometrical objects (such as points, lines, triangles, circles).

`linalg`
provides a number of commands for the definition, administration and processing of matrices (linear algebra). Some examples are `matrix` for the definition of a matrix, `evalm` for the execution of arithmetic matrix commands, `det` for the calculation of the determinant, `inverse` for the calculation of the inverse matrix, and so on. In Maple, vectors and matrices are represented by means of arrays. Thus, knowledge of the array processing commands described in the previous chapter is a necessary precondition for the understanding of the present chapter.

Reference: Vector analysis, that is, the calculation of divergence, rotation, gradient, and so on, of vector or scalar functions will be described in Chapter 27.

Vector calculus with the geometry package

In this section, the term vector calculus is used in the sense of school mathematics and means the application of vector calculus to calculations in analytical geometry. The aim is to define and process geometrical objects (such as points, lines, triangles, circles).

For this purpose, Maple provides the commands of the `geometry` package for calculations in two-dimensional space. With Release 4, this package has been completely revised. Although the re-design of the package offers many advantages, it is quite irritating that many commands are incompatible with those of the previous versions. It is also rather intriguing that the packages `geom3d` for calculations in three-dimensional space and `projgeom` for calculations with homogeneous (instead of Cartesian) coordinates have been eliminated without replacement.

For reasons of space, this section cannot give a complete description of the `geometry` package. The following paragraphs just demonstrate the general usage of the commands. A further example can be found in Chapter 4 (graduation examples).

Two-dimensional geometry with the geometry package

A special feature of the commands of the `geometry` package is that the result of the calculations is stored in a variable which has to be specified as a parameter. Thus, a point is not defined by means of `p1:=point(...)`, but by `point(p1,...)`.

After loading the `geometry` package, `point` is used to define three coordinate points and `line` to define a (straight) line. Please note that the symbol D cannot be used to store points, since `D` is already occupied by Maple's differentiation operator.

```
with(geometry):
point(A,1,1), point(B,3,5),
point(C,6,3);
```
$$A, B, C$$
```
line(g, [A,B]);
```
$$g$$

`detail` displays information about the internal representation of a line in the geometry package.

```
detail(g);
  name of the object: g
  form of the object: line2d
  assume that the name of the horizontal
     and vertical axis are _x and _y
  equation of the line: 2-4*_x+2*_y=0
```

After the definition of an additional line h which leads through the points C and (0,0), `intersection` can be used to find the point of intersection of the two lines. As a result, the command supplies the point IP, whose coordinates are determined with `coordinates`.

```
line(h, [C, point('',0,0)]);
```
$$h$$
```
intersection(IP,g,h);
```
$$IP$$
```
coordinates(IP);
```
$$\left[\frac{2}{3}, \frac{1}{3}\right]$$

`circle` is used to define the circle c. As parameters, you can specify either three points or one point and the radius. `intersection` calculates the two points of intersection between c and h. Their coordinates can be displayed with `coordinates`.

```
circle(c, [A,B,C]):
intersection(IP,h,c);
```
$$h\_intersect1\_c, h\_intersect2\_c$$
```
map(coordinates, IP);
```
$$\left[[6,3], \left[\frac{5}{4}, \frac{5}{8}\right]\right]$$

The geometry commands can also be used to check hypotheses. In the example on the right, the point P is defined with the coordinates $(7, py)$. `AreCollinear` checks whether the three points A, B and P lie on one line. As a result, the command supplies a condition for py.

```
point(P, [7,py]):
AreCollinear(A,B,P);
  AreCollinear:   hint: could not
  determine if -26+2*py is zero
```
$$FAIL$$

One of the most essential new features in Release 4 is the `draw` command which allows you to draw the `geometry` objects.

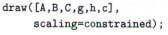

```
draw([A,B,C,g,h,c],
     scaling=constrained);
```

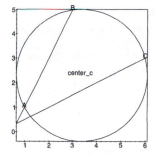

The linalg package

In the remainder of this chapter, it is assumed that the `linalg` package has been activated. This is achieved by the following instruction:

```
with(linalg);
```
        Warning: new definition for   norm
        Warning: new definition for   trace

[*BlockDiagonal, GramSchmidt, JordanBlock, Wronskian, add, addcol, addrow, adj, adjoint, angle, augment, backsub, band, basis, bezout, blockmatrix, charmat, charpoly, col, coldim, colspace, colspan, companion, concat, cond, copyinto, crossprod, curl, definite, delcols, delrows, det, diag, diverge, dotprod, eigenvals, eigenvects, entermatrix, equal, exponential, extend, ffgausselim, fibonacci, frobenius, gausselim, gaussjord, genmatrix, grad, hadamard, hermite, hessian, hilbrt, htranspose, ihermite, indexfunc, innerprod, intbasis, inverse, ismith, iszero, jacobian, jordan, kernel, laplacian, leastsqrs, linsolve, matrix, minor, minpoly, mulcol, mulrow, multiply, norm, normalize, nullspace, orthog, permanent, pivot, potential, randmatrix, randvector, range, rank, ratform, row, rowdim, rowspace, rowspan, rref, scalarmul, singularvals, smith, stack, submatrix, subvector, sumbasis, swapcol, swaprow, sylvester, toeplitz, trace, transpose, vandermonde, vecpotent, vectdim, vector*]

Maple reacts to this command in two ways: firstly, it warns you that the already existing commands `norm` and `trace` have been redefined by the `linalg` package. `norm` originally calculates the norm of a polynomial, whereas after the `with` command it calculates the norm of a matrix. `trace` is originally used to search for errors in Maple procedures, whereas after `with` it calculates the trace of a matrix (that is, the sum of its diagonal elements).

If you need `norm` or `trace` in their original meaning, you can reactivate the two commands with `readlib(norm) readlib(trace)`. This causes Maple to reload the code of these commands from the standard library, which obviously deletes the homonymous `linalg` commands.

Secondly, Maple displays a long list of all newly defined commands. You can suppress the display by terminating the `with` command with a colon (instead of the semicolon).

Creating and processing vectors

Maple distinguishes between row and column vectors; however, nearly all commands expect row vectors as arguments and supply row vectors as results.

Row vectors can be easily created by means of `vector`. Please note how, in the second example, an anonymous function is used to calculate the individual elements of the vector.

```
v1:=vector([a,b,c]);
```

$$[a, b, c]$$

```
v2:=vector(3, n->x^n);
```

$$[x, x^2, x^3]$$

Elementary arithmetic operations with vectors are carried out (as with matrices) via the `evalm` command. The required operation is formulated in the first parameter of `evalm`, with the possibility of using the common Maple operators.

```
evalm(v1 + 1);
```

$$[a + 1, b + 1, c + 1]$$

```
evalm(v1 * 2);
```

$$[2\,a, 2\,b, 2\,c]$$

```
evalm(v1 + v2);
```

$$[a + x, b + x^2, c + x^3]$$

Multiplication of two vectors with `evalm` is not possible – neither with the normal multiplication operator nor with the `&*` operator for matrix multiplication. Two special commands exist for this purpose: `dotprod` for calculating the scalar product and `crossprod` for the cross product. Both commands only process row vectors (not column vectors).

When the second vector contains complex values, then, prior to the multiplication, `dotprod` automatically constructs the conjugate-complex values (Hermitian metrics). This is useful when the length of a vector is to be determined with `sqrt(dotprod(v, v))`. With the orthogonal option, the construction of conjugate-complex values can be prevented. Please note that `dotprod` – as well as a series of other commands for handling vectors – can also handle ordinary lists.

```
dotprod(v1,v2);
```

$$ax + bx^2 + cx^3$$

```
dotprod([1, I], [1,I]);
```

$$2$$

```
dotprod([1, I], [1,I], orthogonal);
```

$$0$$

`crossprod` calculates the cross product of two vectors with a maximum of three elements each.

```
crossprod(v1,v2);
```

$$[bx^3 - cx^2, cx - ax^3, ax^2 - bx]$$

The horizontal notation of the result of a cross product is somewhat unusual and visually not very clear. Thus, if, for clarity, you want to represent a row vector vertically, you can simply convert it into a 3*1 matrix.

```
convert(",matrix);
```

$$\begin{bmatrix} bx^3 - cx^2 \\ cx - ax^3 \\ ax^2 - bx \end{bmatrix}$$

Column vectors are actually needed only for visual reasons (see above). The above example already suggests how Maple represents column vectors: as a special case of a matrix with n rows and one column. Usually, column vectors are defined with `matrix`.

```
v3:=matrix(3,1,[d,e,f]);
```

$$v3 := \begin{bmatrix} d \\ e \\ f \end{bmatrix}$$

An alternative notation for the definition of the same vector could look as shown on the right.

```
v3:=matrix([[d], [e], [f]]);
```

$$v3 := \begin{bmatrix} d \\ e \\ f \end{bmatrix}$$

Since commands such as `dotprod` and `crossprod` presume row vectors, it is sometimes necessary to convert column vectors into row vectors. Here again, the `convert` command can be applied, this time with the keyword `vector`.

```
convert(v3, vector);
```

$$[d, e, f]$$

Norm of a vector, angle between two vectors

`norm` calculates the norm of a vector. The second parameter can be used to specify the calculation method. The default setting is `infinity`, that is, the norm is determined by the greatest value of a vector element. If an integer number n is specified, the values of the elements are raised to the nth power and added together, and subsequently the nth root is extracted.

```
norm([a,b,c]);
```

$$\max(|a|, |b|, |c|)$$

```
norm([a,b,c], 1);
```

$$|a| + |b| + |c|$$

```
norm([a,b,c], 2);
```

$$\sqrt{|a|^2 + |b|^2 + |c|^2}$$

A variation of `norm` is the `normalize` command which normalizes the vector to length 1 (measured against the above norm of 2).

```
normalize([1,2,3]);
```

$$[\frac{\sqrt{14}}{14}, \frac{\sqrt{14}}{7}, \frac{3\sqrt{14}}{14}]$$

`angle` calculates the angle between two vectors using the formula $\cos(\theta) = \frac{u.v}{|u||v|}$.

```
angle([1,0,0],[1,1,1]);
```

$$\arccos(\frac{\sqrt{3}}{3})$$

```
evalf("*180/Pi);
```

$$54.73561030$$

Creating matrices

The standard command for the definition of matrices is `matrix`. In addition to the required dimensions of the matrix, the command can also be passed a one- or two-dimensional list containing the matrix elements.

```
with(linalg): matrix(2,2,[a,b,c,d]);
```

$$\begin{bmatrix} a & b \\ c & d \end{bmatrix}$$

When the matrix elements are passed in the form of an embedded list, Maple can determine the dimensions of the matrix for itself.

```
matrix([[a,b,c], [d,e,f], [g,h,i]]);
```

$$\begin{bmatrix} a & b & c \\ d & e & f \\ g & h & i \end{bmatrix}$$

The matrix elements can also be initialized via an anonymous function. The first parameter of this function contains the row index (beginning with 1), the second parameter the column index.

```
matrix(3,3, (n,m)->n*x^m);
```

$$\begin{bmatrix} x & x^2 & x^3 \\ 2\,x & 2\,x^2 & 2\,x^3 \\ 3\,x & 3\,x^2 & 3\,x^3 \end{bmatrix}$$

For special matrices, the combination of the `array` command – introduced in the previous chapter – and an index function is often more practical than `matrix`. In the example on the right, a 0 matrix is created. Even less typing effort would be required by `matrix(n,m,0)`. The advantage of a `sparse` matrix is that it can be internally managed more efficiently (only useful with large matrices with a substantial number of 0 elements).

```
array(sparse, 1..3, 1..3);
```

$$\begin{bmatrix} 0 & 0 & 0 \\ 0 & 0 & 0 \\ 0 & 0 & 0 \end{bmatrix}$$

The command on the right creates a 3*3 identity matrix. Inside `evalm` the identity matrix can also be abbreviated with `&*()`.

```
array(identity, 1..3,1..3);
```

$$\begin{bmatrix} 1 & 0 & 0 \\ 0 & 1 & 0 \\ 0 & 0 & 1 \end{bmatrix}$$

The `linalg` package also provides a large number of commands for the creation of mathematically (or physically) significant matrices. `diag` creates a diagonal matrix. Instead of $a, b, c...$, you could also specify square matrices.

```
diag(a,b,c);
```

$$\begin{bmatrix} a & 0 & 0 \\ 0 & b & 0 \\ 0 & 0 & c \end{bmatrix}$$

band creates a band matrix in which only the elements of the main diagonal and their neighbours are occupied.

```
band([1,x,-1], 4);
```

$$\begin{bmatrix} x & -1 & 0 & 0 \\ 1 & x & -1 & 0 \\ 0 & 1 & x & -1 \\ 0 & 0 & 1 & x \end{bmatrix}$$

In Toeplitz matrices, the elements of one row are circulated.

```
toeplitz([a,b,c,d]);
```

$$\begin{bmatrix} a & b & c & d \\ b & a & b & c \\ c & b & a & b \\ d & c & b & a \end{bmatrix}$$

jacobian creates the Jacobian matrix. The example on the right clearly shows how the elements are calculated. alias has been used to express the dependence of the three generic functions f, g and h upon the variables x, y and z.

```
alias(f=f(x,y,z), g=g(x,y,z),
     h=h(x,y,z));
```

$$I, f, g, h$$

```
jacobian([f,g,h], [x,y,z]);
```

$$\begin{bmatrix} \frac{\partial}{\partial x}f & \frac{\partial}{\partial y}f & \frac{\partial}{\partial z}f \\ \frac{\partial}{\partial x}g & \frac{\partial}{\partial y}g & \frac{\partial}{\partial z}g \\ \frac{\partial}{\partial x}h & \frac{\partial}{\partial y}h & \frac{\partial}{\partial z}h \end{bmatrix}$$

For test purposes, it is often very useful to have matrices with random numbers. An optional third parameter of randmatrix can be used to influence the contents of the matrix: sparse for mostly empty matrices, symmetric for symmetric matrices and unimodular for matrices in which the elements on the main diagonal are 1 and all elements below the diagonal 0.

```
randmatrix(3,3);
```

$$\begin{bmatrix} 22 & -8 & 53 \\ 84 & -98 & -5 \\ 20 & -72 & 10 \end{bmatrix}$$

With entries=rand(a..b), a different random function can be chosen (instead of the default setting rand(-99..99)).

```
randmatrix(2,2,entries=rand(0..10));
```

$$\begin{bmatrix} 10 & 8 \\ 8 & 10 \end{bmatrix}$$

Some additional commands for the creation of matrices are briefly described in the syntax summary at the end of this chapter; these include blockmatrix, vandermonde, sylvester, hilbert, and so on.

Accessing matrix components

A single matrix element is simply accessed by specifying its indices (row first, then column, each beginning with 1). Index ranges of the a..b form are not possible; partial matrices must be accessed by means of submatrix (see next example).

```
m1:=matrix([[1,2,3,4],[a,b,c,d],
            [e,f,g,h],[w,x,y,z]]);
```

$$m1 := \begin{bmatrix} 1 & 2 & 3 & 4 \\ a & b & c & d \\ e & f & g & h \\ w & x & y & z \end{bmatrix}$$

```
m1[2,3];
```

$$c$$

submatrix reads a partial matrix and returns the result as a matrix (even if this partial matrix consists of only one element, one row or one column). The area to be read is specified either by a..b or as a list. In the second example, the four elements at the intersection points of the first and third rows with the second and fourth columns are combined into a new matrix.

```
submatrix(m1,1..2,3..4);
```

$$\begin{bmatrix} 3 & 4 \\ c & d \end{bmatrix}$$

```
submatrix(m1,[1,3],[2,4]);
```

$$\begin{bmatrix} 2 & 4 \\ f & h \end{bmatrix}$$

The subvector command works similarly to submatrix: it reads part of a row or column of a matrix and returns the elements as a (row) vector. Either the row or the column must be uniquely specified, while in the other parameter a range or a list is allowed. In the first example, the entire first row is read, in the second example the fourth, third and first elements of the third column (in that order).

```
subvector(m1, 2, 1..4);
```

$$[a, b, c, d]$$

```
subvector(m1, [4,3,1], 3);
```

$$[y, g, 3]$$

For reading whole rows or columns, the commands row and col are more suitable. Please note that even though col reads a column of the matrix, it still returns the elements as a row vector.

```
row(m1,4);
```

$$[w, x, y, z]$$

```
col(m1,2);
```

$$[2, b, f, x]$$

Thus, there are various possibilities for reading matrix elements. There are, however, only two ways to modify them: the assignment mat[r,c]:=.. modifies a single element of a matrix, and the command copyinto copies a partial matrix from one matrix to another. Often it is even easier to program a small loop. Even if you have had no previous programming experience in Maple, you will immediately understand the following example.

In the example on the right, the elements of *v1* are to be written into the third row of *m1*. In the `for` loop, the variable i cycles through the values 1 to 4. The body of the loop is enclosed by the keywords `do` and `od`. The line feeds have been inserted for better readability; they are not necessary, and simple spaces would be sufficient. The `eval` command displays the modified matrix.

```
v1:=vector(4,n->x^n);
```

$$v1 := [x, x^2, x^3, x^4]$$

```
for i from 1 to 4 do
  m1[i,3]:=v1[i]
od:
eval(m1);
```

$$\begin{bmatrix} 1 & 2 & x & 4 \\ a & b & x^2 & d \\ e & f & x^3 & h \\ w & x & x^4 & z \end{bmatrix}$$

The command `copyinto(m1,m2,r,c)` copies from the first specified matrix into the second one, with $m1[1,1]$ being copied to $m2[r,c]$ – thus, c and r specify the target offset. As a result, `copyinto` returns the matrix $m2$, as shown on the right.

```
m2:=matrix(4,4,0):
copyinto(m1,m2,2,2);
```

$$\begin{bmatrix} 0 & 0 & 0 & 0 \\ 0 & 1 & 2 & x \\ 0 & a & b & x^2 \\ 0 & e & f & x^3 \end{bmatrix}$$

Elementary arithmetic operations with matrices

Arithmetic operations with matrices usually assume the `evalm` command. In this command, arithmetic operations with scalars, vectors and matrices can be formulated with the usual operators. In some special cases, either `map` or other special commands such as `innerprod` must be applied. The following examples are based on the two matrices *m1* and *m2*.

```
m1:=matrix([[a,b],[c,d],[e,f]]);
```

$$m1 := \begin{bmatrix} a & b \\ c & d \\ e & f \end{bmatrix}$$

```
m2:=matrix([[r,s,t],[u,v,w]]);
```

$$m2 := \begin{bmatrix} r & s & t \\ u & v & w \end{bmatrix}$$

`transpose` transposes the matrix, that is, the elements are exchanged along the main diagonal; rectangular matrices change their form from $n*m$ to $m*n$. A variation of this is `htranspose` where the conjugate-complex values are constructed simultaneously with the exchange (Hermitian metrics).

```
transpose(m2);
```

$$\begin{bmatrix} r & u \\ s & v \\ t & w \end{bmatrix}$$

In scalar multiplication, each element is multiplied by the scalar. Scalar addition leads to the addition of the identity matrix multiplied by the scalar.

```
evalm(m2 * 3);
```

$$\begin{bmatrix} 3\,r & 3\,s & 3\,t \\ 3\,u & 3\,v & 3\,w \end{bmatrix}$$

```
evalm(m2 + 3);
```

$$\begin{bmatrix} r+3 & s & t \\ u & v+3 & w \end{bmatrix}$$

When a function is to be applied to all elements of a matrix, it is best to use map.

```
map(sqrt, m2);
```

$$\begin{bmatrix} \sqrt{r} & \sqrt{s} & \sqrt{t} \\ \sqrt{u} & \sqrt{v} & \sqrt{w} \end{bmatrix}$$

The addition of two matrices assumes that both matrices have the same dimensions. For this purpose, in the example on the right, the 3*2 matrix $m2$ is transposed into a 2*3 matrix.

```
evalm(m1 + transpose(m2));
```

$$\begin{bmatrix} a+r & b+u \\ c+s & d+v \\ e+t & f+w \end{bmatrix}$$

For non-commutative matrix multiplication, the &* operator must be used. Once more, the example emphasizes that in matrix multiplication the order of elements is not arbitrary. If, inadvertently, you use the * operator instead of &*, Maple may well change the order of multiplication or completely cancel certain operations (for example, $v*M*v \to v^2 * M$).

```
evalm(m1 &* m2);
```

$$\begin{bmatrix} ar+bu & as+bv & at+bw \\ cr+du & cs+dv & ct+dw \\ er+fu & es+fv & et+fw \end{bmatrix}$$

```
evalm(m2 &* m1);
```

$$\begin{bmatrix} ar+cs+et & rb+sd+tf \\ ua+vc+we & bu+dv+fw \end{bmatrix}$$

Division by a matrix is reduced to multiplication by the inverse matrix. Thus, both evalm(1/m3) and inverse(m3) lead to the same result.

```
m3:=matrix([[1,2],[3,4]]):
evalm(1/m3);
```

$$\begin{bmatrix} -2 & 1 \\ 3/2 & -1/2 \end{bmatrix}$$

Exponentiation of matrices corresponds to a repeated matrix multiplication.

```
evalm(m3^3), evalm(m3 &* m3 &* m3);
```

$$\begin{bmatrix} 37 & 54 \\ 81 & 118 \end{bmatrix}, \begin{bmatrix} 37 & 54 \\ 81 & 118 \end{bmatrix}$$

Multiplying matrices by vectors

There are a relatively large number of possibilities for multiplying matrices and vectors, all of which can be mathematically sensible, depending on the application. Therefore, some care must be taken when formulating multiplications.

The following examples make use of a 3*3 matrix, plus one row vector and one column vector containing the same elements u, v and w.

```
m1:=matrix([[a,b,c],[d,e,f],[g,h,i]]):
v1:=vector([u,v,w]);
```

$$v1 := [u, v, w]$$

```
v2:=matrix([[u],[v],[w]]);
```

$$v2 := \begin{bmatrix} u \\ v \\ w \end{bmatrix}$$

The multiplication of the matrix by one of the two vectors results in a 1*3 or a 3*1 matrix, depending on whether the row or the column vector is used.

```
evalm(m1 &* v1);
```

$$[au + bv + cw, du + ev + fw,$$
$$gu + hv + iw]$$

```
evalm(m1 &* v2);
```

$$\begin{bmatrix} au + bv + cw \\ du + ev + fw \\ gu + hv + iw \end{bmatrix}$$

In `evalm`, the multiplication of a vector by a matrix is (for whatever reasons) not possible. `innerprod` can only handle row vectors. However, `innerprod` at least allows a continued multiplication of the kind $v*M*v$.

```
innerprod(v1,m1);
```

$$[au + vd + wg, ub + ev + wh,$$
$$uc + vf + iw]$$

```
innerprod(v1,m1,v1);
```

$$au^2 + uvd + uwg + vub + ev^2 + vwh+$$
$$wuc + wvf + iw^2$$

Determinant, inverse matrix, trace, norm and rank of a matrix

The determinant of a matrix is calculated with `det`.

```
m1:=matrix([[1, 2, 3],
            [4,-5, 6],
            [9, 8, 7]]);
det(m1);
```

200

The inverse matrix is constructed with `inverse` or `evalm(1/m)`.

`m2:=inverse(m1);`

$$m2 := \begin{bmatrix} -\frac{83}{200} & 1/20 & \frac{27}{200} \\ \frac{13}{100} & -1/10 & \frac{3}{100} \\ \frac{77}{200} & 1/20 & -\frac{13}{200} \end{bmatrix}$$

The inverse matrix can be used to solve the equation system $m1x = b$. See also the next section about solving linear equation systems.

`b:=vector([14,12,46]);`

$$b := [14, 12, 46]$$

`evalm(m2 &* b);`

$$[1, 2, 3]$$

As a countercheck, the result vector is multiplied by $m1$ – as expected, the result is again b.

`evalm(m1 &* ");`

$$[14, 12, 46]$$

The trace of a matrix is defined as the sum of the diagonal elements and is calculated with `trace`.

`trace(m1);`

$$3$$

The norm of a matrix can be calculated in various ways which are specified in the second parameter of `norm`. The default setting is `infinity`. This means that the norm is determined by the maximum of the sum over the values of the elements in one row. The keyword `frobenius` simply calculates the root of the sum over the squared values of *all* elements. The first norm (1 in the second parameter of `norm`) is calculated as with `infinity`, but with sums over columns. The second norm is extremely expensive in calculating time and power: here, the root of the maximum eigenvalue of the matrix $A * A^T$ is the norm. For a 3*3 matrix with nine symbols, the attempt at symbolic calculation had to be aborted with a system reboot. The following examples will illustrate the calculation specifications better than the above explanations:

`norm([[a,b,c],[d,e,f],[g,h,i]]);`

$$\max(|a| + |b| + |c|, |g| + |h| + |i|, |d| + |e| + |f|)$$

`norm([[a,b,c],[d,e,f],[g,h,i]], frobenius);`

$$\sqrt{|a|^2 + |b|^2 + |c|^2 + |d|^2 + |e|^2 + |f|^2 + |g|^2 + |h|^2 + |i|^2}$$

`norm([[a,b,c],[d,e,f],[g,h,i]], 1);`

$$\max(|a| + |d| + |g|, |b| + |e| + |h|, |c| + |f| + |i|)$$

`norm([[1,2],[3,x]],2);`

$$\sqrt{\max\left(\left|7 + \frac{x^2}{2} - \frac{\sqrt{52 + 24 x^2 + x^4 + 48 x}}{2}\right|, \left|7 + \frac{x^2}{2} + \frac{\sqrt{52 + 24 x^2 + x^4 + 48 x}}{2}\right|\right)}$$

The calculation of the rank of a matrix (that is, the calculation of the number of independent rows/columns) is much easier.

```
rank([[1,2],[3,4]]);

       2

rank([[1,2],[3,6]]);

       1
```

Solving matrix equation systems

linsolve solves the equation system $A * x = b$ and supplies the result vector x.

```
A:=matrix([[1,  2,  3],
           [4,-5,  6],
           [9,  8,  7]]):
b:=vector([14,12,46]):
linsolve(A,b);
```

$$[1, 2, 3]$$

When the equation system cannot be solved (for example, because A contains dependent rows), linsolve yields a 0 result. In this case, kernel or the synonymous ?nullspace command can be used to determine the solution of the equation system $A * x = 0$. Subsequently, the result can be multiplied by an arbitrary scalar. In the example on the right, a check is carried out as well.

```
A:=matrix([[1,  2,  3],
           [4,  8,12],
           [1,-1,  0]]):
linsolve(A,b);
kernel(A);
```

$$\{[-1, -1, 1]\}$$

```
evalm(A &* "[1]);
```

$$[0, 0, 0]$$

Vice versa, a whole multitude of solutions may occur. This is displayed with the independent variables v_i. When no variable name is specified in the fourth parameter of linsolve, Maple automatically uses the variable name _t. The rank of the matrix is stored in the variable specified in the third parameter.

```
A:=matrix([[1,2,3],[4,5,6],[0,0,0]]):
b:=vector([1,2,0]):
sln:=linsolve(A,b,'rank','v');
```

$$sln := [v_1 - 1/3, -2 v_1 + 2/3, v_1]$$

```
evalm(A &* sln);
```

$$[1, 2, 0]$$

A variation of linsolve is the command leastsqrs which chooses the solution vector in such a way that the second norm of $A * x - b$ becomes minimal.

When your equation system does not yet exist in matrix notation, you can create A and b relatively easily by means of the genmatrix command.

```
eqnsys:={x+2*y+3*z=14,
         4*x-5*y+6*z=12,
         9*x+8*y+7*z=46}:
```

genmatrix is passed the set (or list) of equations. In the second parameter, the variables must be specified in list form (square brackets!). If you use the curly set braces in this parameter, genmatrix may arbitrarily change the order of the variables!

```
eqnmat:=genmatrix(eqnsys, [x,y,z]);
```

$$eqnmat := \begin{bmatrix} 1 & 2 & 3 \\ 4 & -5 & 6 \\ 9 & 8 & 7 \end{bmatrix}$$

Without the specification of an arbitrary third parameter, genmatrix only produces the coefficient matrix (see above). If, in contrast, an arbitrary expression is specified in the third parameter, genmatrix adds a further column with the negative (!) values of the right-hand side of the equations.

```
eqnmat:=genmatrix(eqnsys, [x,y,z], flag);
```

$$eqnmat := \begin{bmatrix} 1 & 2 & 3 & -14 \\ 4 & -5 & 6 & -12 \\ 9 & 8 & 7 & -46 \end{bmatrix}$$

With submatrix and col, you can extract A and b from the newly created matrix.

```
A:=submatrix(eqnmat,1..3,1..3);
```

$$A := \begin{bmatrix} 1 & 2 & 3 \\ 4 & -5 & 6 \\ 9 & 8 & 7 \end{bmatrix}$$

```
b:=col(eqnmat,4);
```

$$[-14, -12, -46]$$

When calling linsolve, you must take care to specify a negative sign for b!

```
linsolve(A,-b);
```

$$[1, 2, 3]$$

Matrix transformations

Maple has a large number of commands for the execution of various matrix transformations. The two most important commands are gausselim and ffgauselim. These commands carry out the Gaussian elimination process and transform a given matrix into a triangular matrix with which the equation system $A * x = b$ can be solved immediately. ffgausselim supplies results without fractions.

An overview of the most important transformation commands of the linalg package and the share library can be found in the syntax summary at the end of this chapter. More detailed information about the commands can be found in the online help and the Maple manuals.

`ffgausselim` transforms the 4*4 random matrix m into an integer diagonal matrix.

```
restart: with(linalg):
m:=randmatrix(4,4):
ffgausselim(m);
```

$$\begin{bmatrix} -85 & -55 & -37 & -35 \\ 0 & 1085 & -3126 & -1365 \\ 0 & 0 & 136528 & -43190 \\ 0 & 0 & 0 & -5825992 \end{bmatrix}$$

The `RowEchelon` command of the `share` library performs an Echelon factorization of the given matrix. For the four result matrices P, L, U and R, the relation $P * L * U * R = m$ applies.

```
with(share): readshare(Echelon, linalg):
R := RowEchelon(m,'dt','rank','P','L','U'): print(P,L,U,R);
```

$$\begin{bmatrix} 1 & 0 & 0 & 0 \\ 0 & 1 & 0 & 0 \\ 0 & 0 & 1 & 0 \\ 0 & 0 & 0 & 1 \end{bmatrix}, \begin{bmatrix} 1 & 0 & 0 & 0 \\ \frac{-97}{85} & 1 & 0 & 0 \\ \frac{-49}{85} & \frac{-76}{31} & 1 & 0 \\ \frac{-9}{17} & \frac{631}{217} & \frac{-2589}{1484} & 1 \end{bmatrix}, \begin{bmatrix} -85 & -55 & -37 & -35 \\ 0 & \frac{-217}{17} & \frac{3126}{85} & \frac{273}{17} \\ 0 & 0 & \frac{19504}{155} & \frac{-1234}{31} \\ 0 & 0 & 0 & \frac{-31663}{742} \end{bmatrix},$$

$$\begin{bmatrix} 1 & 0 & 0 & 0 \\ 0 & 1 & 0 & 0 \\ 0 & 0 & 1 & 0 \\ 0 & 0 & 0 & 1 \end{bmatrix}$$

`evalm` can be used to check whether the product of the four matrices P, L, U and R effectively yields m.

```
evalm(P &* L &* U &* R - m);
```

$$\begin{bmatrix} 0 & 0 & 0 & 0 \\ 0 & 0 & 0 & 0 \\ 0 & 0 & 0 & 0 \\ 0 & 0 & 0 & 0 \end{bmatrix}$$

Eigenvalues and eigenvectors

The eigenvalues of a matrix M are defined as those λ values for which the equation system $M * x = \lambda x$ can be solved. Eigenvectors are the corresponding solution vectors x.

Since the symbolic calculation of eigenvectors leads to rather voluminous expressions, `evalf(map,..)` is used to substitute the integer and therefore symbolically exact values with floating point values in the sample matrix $m1$. The calculation of the eigenvalues is carried out with `eigenvals`:

```
m1:=matrix([[1, 2, 3], [4, 5, 6], [1,-1, 0]]): m1:=map(evalf, m1);
```

$$m1 := \begin{bmatrix} 1.0 & 2.0 & 3.0 \\ 4.0 & 5.0 & 6.0 \\ 1.0 & -1.0 & 0 \end{bmatrix}$$

```
ew:=eigenvals(m1);
```

$$ew := 5.725448748, -1.123983181, 1.398534444$$

A more bulky solution is supplied by `eigenvects`: the command formulates the result as a sequence, in which each element is in turn formulated as a list consisting of eigenvalue, multiplicity and eigenvector.

```
ev:=eigenvects(m1);
```

$$ev := [1.398534444, 1, \{[-0.1409415877, -1.696481953, 1.112264614]\}],$$

$$[5.725448739, 1, \{[-0.3135448945, -0.8924994103, 0.1011195011]\}],$$

$$[-1.123983181, 1, \{[0.9080616118, 0.1060124826, -0.7135775189]\}]$$

Accessing individual elements of this solution is not a trivial task: `ev[i][1]` means the first list element of the ith expression of the solution sequence and corresponds to `op(1, op(i, [ev]))`. Access to the eigenvalue is embedded one level further with `ev[i][3][1]`.

In the first two `seq` loops, the eigenvalues are stored in the variables $ew1$, $ew2$ and $ew3$, the eigenvectors in $ev1$ to $ev3$. Inside `seq`, `assign` must be used for variable assignments. In order to make the assignment work even when ewi is already occupied, `evaln` must be used to restrict the evaluation to the formulation of the variable name. Both commands are described in Chapter 6.

The third `seq` loop displays the results. Since the eigenvectors are internally represented as arrays and not as lists, they can only be displayed with `eval`. (As we all know by now, Maple does not automatically evaluate tables and arrays – see also the previous chapter.)

```
seq(assign(evaln(ew.i), ev[i][1]), i=1..3);
seq(assign(evaln(ev.i), ev[i][3][1]), i=1..3);
seq([ew.i, eval(ev.i)], i=1..3);
```

$$[1.398534444, [-0.1409415877, -1.696481953, 1.112264614]],$$

$$[5.725448739, [-0.3135448945, -0.8924994103, 0.1011195011]],$$

$$[-1.123983181, [0.9080616118, 0.1060124826, -0.7135775189]]$$

The eigenvalues and eigenvectors, which are now stored in handy variables, are used for proofing purposes according to the above definition of eigenvalues. Apart from relatively large rounding errors, the expression results in the expected 0 vector.

```
evalm(m1 &* ev1 - ew1 * ev1);
```

$$[0.0000000130, 0.000000013, -0.000000009]$$

`charpoly` can be used to determine the typical equation for calculating eigenvalues. The same result can be achieved by subtracting the identity matrix multiplied by x from the matrix and subsequently calculating the determinant. As expected, `fsolve` again supplies the three eigenvalues.

```
charpoly(m1, 'x');
```
$$x^3 - 6.0x^2 + 9.0$$

```
det(evalm(m1 - x));
```
$$6.0x^2 - 9.0 - x^3$$

```
fsolve(");
```
$$-1.123983180, 1.398534444, 5.725448735$$

Calculating the orthonormal basis

The command `GramSchmidt` constructs the orthonormal basis for a given list of vectors. The special feature of a normal basis is that the basis vectors stand normally on each other. `GramSchmidt` does not carry out an automatic normalization of the vector to length 1. In the example below, this normalization is performed by the first `seq` command. Since the result contains a lot of unresolved products with roots, it is simplified in a second step with `combine`. The two `dotprod` commands check the result.

```
v1:=vector([-1,2,3,0]): v2:=vector([0,1,2,1]): v3:=vector([2,-1,-1,1]):
GramSchmidt([v1,v2,v3]);
```
$$[[\frac{7}{10}, 1/5, 1/10, -2/5], [4/7, -1/7, 2/7, 1], [-1, 2, 3, 0]]$$

```
seq(normalize(i), i="):
on:=seq(map(combine, i,power), i=");
```
$$on := [\frac{\sqrt{70}}{10}, \frac{\sqrt{70}}{35}, \frac{\sqrt{70}}{70}, -\frac{2\sqrt{70}}{35}], [\frac{2\sqrt{70}}{35}, -\frac{\sqrt{70}}{70}, \frac{\sqrt{70}}{35}, \frac{\sqrt{70}}{10}], [-\frac{\sqrt{14}}{14}, \frac{\sqrt{14}}{7}, \frac{3\sqrt{14}}{14}, 0]]$$

```
dotprod(on[1], on[2]), dotprod(on[1], on[1]);
```
$$0, 1$$

Tensor calculus

Maple has a number of commands for the tensor calculus, which must be activated with `with(ten-sor)` prior to being used. The package has been completely revised in Release 4, and this has also led to a change in the internal storing of tensors. Now the package also contains commands which were previously defined in the `debever`, `cartan` and `petrov` packages.

Syntax summary

Two-dimensional vector calculus with the geometry package

```
with(geometry);
```
activates the commands of the geometry package. Only a few of the most important commands will be listed in this summary.

```
point(p, [x,y]);
```
defines the point p with the coordinates x and y.

```
line(1, [p1,p2]);      line(1, [eqn]);
```
defines the straight line l which leads through the points $p1$ and $p2$ or which is defined by the line equation $a * x + b * y + c = 0$.

```
circle(c1, [p1,p2,p3]);      circle(c2, [m,r]);
```
defines the circle $c1$ which leads through the points $p1$ to $p3$ or the circle $c2$ with the centre point m and the radius r.

```
triangle(t, [p1,p2,p3]);      triangle(t, [11,12,13]);
triangle(t, [s1,s2,s3]);      triangle(t, [s1,angle=a,s2]);
```
defines the triangle t by means of three corner points, three sides, three side lengths or two side lengths and one angle. In the last two variations, only the size is defined, but not the position of the triangle.

```
intersection(11,12);      intersection(c1,c2);      intersection(1,c);
```
calculates the point(s) of intersection between two straight lines, two circles, or a circle and a line.

```
reflect(r, object, 1);      reflect(r, object, p);
```
mirrors *object* with respect to the line l or the point p and stores the mirrored image in r.

```
rotation(r, object, angle, clockwise, p);
rotation(r, object, angle, counterclockwise, p);
```
rotates *object* around the rotation centre p and stores the result in r. The third and fourth parameters specify rotation angle and direction.

Linear algebra with the linalg package

```
with(linalg);
```
activates the linalg package. This command must be executed prior to any calculation which makes use of one of the commands described in the following paragraphs.

Creating and processing vectors

`vector(n);     vector(n,i->f(i));     vector([a,b,c...]);`
   defines a vector. The first variation creates an empty vector for n elements; in the second variation, the elements are assigned according to the function specification; the third variation takes its vector elements from a list.

`matrix(n,1);     matrix(n,1,i->f(i));     matrix([[a],[b],...]);`
   creates a column vector, otherwise as above.

`convert(vec, matrix);     convert(mat, vector);`
   converts a row vector into a column vector and vice versa. `convert` can also be employed instead of `vector` or `matrix` to convert (embedded) lists into vectors or matrices.

`dotprod(v1, v2);`
   supplies the inner product (scalar product) of two vectors or lists. In the standard variation, the elements of $v2$ are used in conjugate-complex form. The keyword `orthogonal` in the optional third parameter prevents this behaviour.

`crossprod(v1, v2);`
   supplies the cross product of two vectors with 2 or 3 elements each.

`norm(v, mode);`
   calculates the norm of v. The following modes are allowed: `infinity` (default setting, maximum amount), `frobenius` (root of the sum of squares) or an arbitrary integer number ($\sqrt[n]{a^n + b^n + c^n...}$).

`normalize(v);`
   determines the normalized vector of v. This causes the vector to be normalized to length 1 (measured against the above norm 2).

`angle(v1, v2);`
   calculates the angle between the two vectors.

Creating matrices

`matrix(r,c);     matrix(r,c,(n,m)->f);     matrix([[...],...]);`
   defines a matrix with r rows and c columns. The contents of the matrix can be specified by a two-parameter anonymous function or by an embedded list.

`array(sparse, 1..r, 1..c);`
   creates a matrix, in which all unassigned elements are set to 0.

`array(identity, 1..r, 1..c);`
   creates an identity matrix of the specified size.

```
band([a,b,c...]);
```
creates a band matrix in which the specified elements are arranged around the diagonal element.

```
diag([a,b,c...]);
```
creates a diagonal matrix with the specified diagonal elements.

```
hessian(f, [x,y...]);
```
creates the Hessian matrix. The element of row r and column c is determined by the partial derivative of f using the rth and cth variable of the variable list.

```
hilbert(n,x);
```
creates the Hilbert matrix of nth order. The element of row r and column c is determined by $\frac{1}{c+r-x}$.

```
jacobian([f,g,...], [x,y,...]);
```
creates a Jacobian matrix whose elements are specified by the partial derivatives of the functions using the variables.

```
randmatrix(r, c); randmatrix(r, c, opt);
```
creates a matrix filled with random numbers. Permitted options are the keywords sparse, symmetric and unimodular. In addition, entries=... can be used to specify a user-defined random function for the calculation of the matrix elements.

```
sylvester(p1, p2, x);
```
creates the Sylvester matrix for two polynomials.

```
toeplitz([a,b,...]);
```
creates a Toeplitz matrix. The elements specified for the first row are circulated through the subsequent rows.

```
vandermonde(a,b,...);
```
creates a Vandermonde matrix whose first column is $1, 1, ...$, the second $a, b...$, the third $a^2, b^2...$, and so on.

Processing matrices

```
mat[r,c];
```
reads (or modifies) the element of row r and column c.

```
submatrix(mat, r, c);
```
reads the partial matrix of specified rows and columns. The specification can be either a range of the a..b form or a list.

```
subvector(mat, r, c);
```
reads several elements of the specified row or column and returns the result as a row vector.

```
row(mat,r); col(mat,c);
```
   reads the specified row or column and returns the result as a row vector.

```
copyinto(sourcem, targetm, roff, coff);
```
   copies data from the source matrix into the target matrix. *roff* and *coff* specify the offset inside the target matrix, that is, $sourcem[1, 1]$ is copied to $targetm[roff, coff]$.

```
blockmatrix(n, m, A, B, ...);
```
   combines a new matrix from $n * m$ matrices A, B, and so on.

Calculating with vectors and matrices

```
evalm(expression);
```
   carries out the matrix calculation specified in the expression. For matrix multiplication, the `&*` operator must be used; the identity matrix can be abbreviated as `&*()`.

```
map(func, mat);
```
   applies the function to all elements of the matrix.

```
transpose(mat);      htranspose(mat);
```
   transposes the matrix. `htranspose` simultaneously produces conjugate-complex values.

```
innerprod(v1,m);       innerprod(v1,m,v2);
```
   multiplies the specified vectors and matrices.

```
inverse(mat);
```
   constructs the inverse matrix.

```
det(mat);
```
   calculates the determinant of the matrix.

```
trace(mat);
```
   calculates the trace of a matrix (sum of diagonal elements).

```
norm(mat, mode);
```
   calculates the norm of a matrix. Modes can be: `infinity` (default setting, maximum root of the squares of one row), `frobenius` (root of the sum of squares of all elements), 1 (maximum root of the squares of one column) and 2 (root of the greatest eigenvalues of $mat * mat^T$).

```
rank(mat);
```
   calculates the rank of a matrix (number of independent columns/rows).

```
linsolve(A, b);
```
   solves the equation system $A * x = b$.

```
leastsqrs(A, b);
```
   as above, but simultaneous minimization of the second norm of $A * x - b$.

genmatrix({eqn1, eqn2,...}, [x,y,...]);
>   constructs the coefficient matrix for the specified equation system. With the additional speci-
>   fication of a third parameter, the right-hand side of the equations is included in an additional
>   column of the coefficient matrix.

eigenvals(mat);
>   calculates the eigenvalues of the matrix.

eigenvects(mat);
>   calculates eigenvalues, multiplicities and eigenvectors of the matrix.

charpoly(mat);
>   constructs the characteristic polynomial of a matrix for the calculation of the eigenvalues.

GramSchmidt([v1,v2,...]);
>   constructs the orthonormal basis for the specified vectors.

Matrix transformations

with(share):
readshare(pffge, linalg);   readshare(sffge, linalg);
readshare(transform, linalg); readshare(class, linalg);
readshare(Echelon, linalg);
>   activate the various packages of the share library. Please note the upper case initial of Echelon!

gausselim(m);   ffgausselim(m);   pffge(m);   sffge(m);
>   carry out a Gaussian elimination. In ffgausselim, the result does not contain fractions
>   (ff stands for fraction free). For some matrices, pffge and sffge are more efficient than
>   ffgauselim.

smith(m,x);   ismith(m);   hermite(m,x);
smithex(m,x);   ismithex(m);   frobenius(m);
ratjordan(m);   jordan(m);   jordansymbolic(m);
classical(m,'P');
>   calculate various matrix normal forms.

RowEchelon(m,'dt','rank','P','L','U'):
>   determines the row-echelon matrix R for a given matrix m. For the further matrices $P * L *$
> $U * R = m$ applies.

Chapter 15

Limits, sums and products

This chapter deals with two subjects which are only indirectly related: the calculation of limits or asymptotic approximations with the commands `limit` and `asympt`, and the construction of sums and products with the commands `sum` and `product`. The calculation of infinite sums or products especially often necessitates a combined application of `limit` and `sum` or `product`. `sum` and `product` can also be used for the construction of large formulae or the development of sequences and series.

`limit`
carries out a limit transition.

`sum`
supplies the finite or infinite sum of an expression.

`eulermac`
carries out a series development for a generic summation formula.

`product`
supplies the finite or infinite product of an expression.

`evalf`
carries out a purely numerical calculation in connection with the three commands above.

References: The `sumtools` package contains some special commands for the calculation of sums which are not described in this book. Chapter 24 deals with the development and processing of series (Taylor series, Laurent series, and so on).

Limit calculations

The command `limit(f(x),x=x0)` calculates the limit transition for $x \to x0$. This allows the calculation of expressions which, with direct insertion of a critical value, would yield an undefined result (for example, $\frac{\infty}{\infty}$).

```
limit((sqrt(1+x)-1)/x, x=0);

    1/2

limit(tan(Pi/4+x)^cot(2*x), x=0);

    e

limit(x!/x^x, x=infinity);

    0
```

`limit` always tries to evaluate the result symbolically, even when the expression contains unknown variables.

```
f:=(-x^(-a)+x^a) / (x-1/x);
```

$$f := \left(-x^{-a} + x^a\right)\left(x - x^{-1}\right)^{-1}$$

```
limit(f, x=1);
```

$$a$$

In the example on the right, Maple recognizes that a has no influence on the result and solves the example. However, the result is only correct under the assumption that a does not verge towards infinity itself!

```
limit(cos(a/x)^x, x=infinity);
```

$$1$$

When you want to check the result of a limit transition, you can use `subs` to insert a value near the critical point $x0$ and evaluate the expression numerically.

```
limit(sin(3*x)/tan(5*x),x=Pi);
```

$$-3/5$$

```
evalf(subs(x=Pi+1e-10,
            sin(3*x)/tan(5*x)));
```

$$-0.6000000001$$

In complex cases, Maple is not capable of finding a symbolic solution (for the sum shown on the right, this would be $1/9$).

```
limit(
    sum((1+k^2/n^3)^(1/3)-1, k=1..n),
    n=infinity);
```

$$\lim_{n\to\infty}\sum_{k=1}^{n}\sqrt[3]{1+\frac{k^2}{n^3}} - n$$

In some cases, only a numerical evaluation of the entire expression with `evalf` will help. In the present case, however, even `evalf` does not succeed.

```
evalf(");
```

$$\lim_{n\to\infty}\sum_{k=1}^{n}\sqrt[3]{1+\frac{k^2}{n^3}} - n$$

With the following command, the sum for the first 10, 100 or 1000 summands is calculated explicitly. This reveals why Maple has such difficulties with numerical approximation solutions: the convergence of the sum is very poor; even after 1000 terms, the result is only exact for three digits.

```
seq(evalf(subs(n=i, sum((1+k^2/n^3)^(1/3) - 1, k=1..i))), i=[10,100,1000]);
```

$$0.125634199, 0.112556350, 0.111255322$$

In some cases, `limit` supplies a result in the form $a \ldots b$ instead of an explicit limit. This suggests that, even though no limit exists, the expression for $x \to x0$ stays within the specified range.

```
limit(sin(1/x), x=0);
```

$$-1\ldots1$$

`limit` can also be misused for symbolic differentiation.

```
limit((sin(x+dx) -sin(x)) / dx, dx=0);
```

$$\cos(x)$$

Multi-variable limits

limit is also capable of calculating limits for multi-variable functions. Then, $x0$ must be specified in the form {x=x0, y=y0,..}.

```
limit((x+y)/x + (x+y)/y,
      {x=0, y=1});
```
$$\infty$$

When the multi-variable variation of limit fails, you can try a conversion into a one-dimensional function (see the second command). The keyword complex is described further below.

```
limit((x+3*y)/sqrt(x^2+y^2),
      {x=0, y=0}, complex);
```
$$\lim_{\{x=0,y=0\}} \frac{x+3\,y}{\sqrt{x^2+y^2}}$$

```
limit((x+3*x)/sqrt(x^2+x^2), x=0,
      right);
```
$$2\sqrt{2}$$

Limits of discontinuity points

limit calculates the limit of $1/x^2$ for $x \to 0$ without problems as ∞, but then, somehow surprisingly, supplies the result *undefined* for the same limit of $1/x$. The reason is that Maple recognizes that the limit $\lim_{x\to 0} 1/x$ depends on the direction of the approximation.

```
limit(1/x^2, x=0);
```
$$\infty$$

```
limit(1/x, x=0);
```
$$undefined$$

The options left or right allow you to calculate the left-hand or right-hand limit.

```
limit(1/x, x=0, left);
```
$$-\infty$$

```
limit(1/x, x=0, right);
```
$$\infty$$

The left and right options should also be used in functions when discontinuity points (jumps) are not infinite. (In such a case, limit sometimes supplies a result even without the specification of an option, but it is not predictable whether it will be the left-hand or the right-hand limit).

```
f:=cos(x)/sqrt(1-sin(x));
```
$$f := \frac{\cos(x)}{\sqrt{1-\sin(x)}}$$

```
limit(f, x=Pi/2, left);
```
$$\sqrt{2}$$

```
limit(f, x=Pi/2, right);
```
$$-\sqrt{2}$$

The illustration on the right shows the curve of the function f defined above with a jump at the point $x = \pi/2$.

```
plot(f, x=0..2*Pi);
```

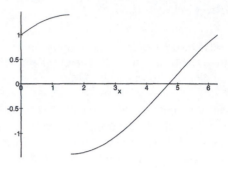

Complex limits

A similar problem to that encountered with (real) discontinuity points arises with complex limits. Without the specification of an additional option, `limit` supplies the result *undefined*.

```
f:=z->z^2/(z-2-I);
```

$$f := z \mapsto \frac{z^2}{z - 2 - I}$$

```
limit(f(z), z=2+I);
```

   undefined

When the option `complex` is used, Maple calculates the multi-directional limit, that is, without considering the complex direction.

```
limit(f(z), z=2+I, complex);
```

   ∞

Up to Release 3, for complex limits approaching infinity, `limit` used to supply not simply ∞ but, depending on the approximation towards the discontinuity point, also the direction on the complex number plane in which the limit converges (for example $(3/5 + \frac{4I}{5})\infty$). Since Release 4, you must either do without this additional information or carry out a numerical evaluation.

```
limit(f(z), z=2+I, right);
```

   ∞

```
evalf(subs(z=2+I+1e-9, f(z)));
```

   $3000000004.0 + 4000000002.0\,I$

```
signum(");
```

   $0.6000000002 + 0.7999999996\,I$

Sums

The usage of the `sum` command is extremely simple: the first parameter specifies the function to be summarized, the second the summation variable and limits in the form `var=a..b`. If *var* is already occupied, this variable and the entire first parameter must be enclosed in quotes.

```
sum(1/x^n, n=1..5);
```

$$x^{-1} + x^{-2} + x^{-3} + x^{-4} + x^{-5}$$

```
sum(1/x^3, x=1..5);
```

$$\frac{256103}{216000}$$

Maple tries to evaluate and simplify the sum symbolically. This may cause functions such as Ψ or ζ to appear in the result. The digamma and zeta functions are briefly mentioned in Chapter 7. With `evalf`, a numerical evaluation can be forced.

```
sum(1/x^3, x=1..1000);
```
$$\frac{\Psi(2, 1001)}{2} + \zeta(3)$$
```
evalf(");
```
$$1.202056403$$

Since Release 4, the `add` command is available in addition to `sum`. `add` allows an efficient numerical calculation of a finite number of summands. Unlike `sum`, neither a symbolic evaluation nor a limit transition is attempted.

The command on the right produces a fraction with about 1300 digits in the numerator and denominator!

```
add(1/x^3, x=1..1000);
```
$$\frac{17350...9343}{14434...0000}$$
```
evalf(");
```
$$1.202056403$$

When you want to calculate infinite sums, you can simply specify `infinity` as a summation limit in `sum`.

```
sum(1/2^n, n=1..infinity);
```
$$1$$
```
sum((1+2*I)^n / n!, n=0..infinity);
```
$$e^{1+2I}$$

Where more complex functions are concerned, Maple often fails to find a symbolic solution. In many cases, however, the entire expression can be successfully evaluated with `evalf`.

```
sum(1/(x^4+1), x=1..infinity);
```
$$\sum_{x=1}^{\infty} \left(x^4 + 1\right)^{-1}$$
```
evalf(sum(1/(x^4+1), x=1..infinity));
```
$$0.5784775797$$

Alternatively, you can also try to calculate sums via the detour of a limit transition, which in many cases leads to a symbolic (and thus exact) solution. Quite often, however, terms of the $O(..)$ kind will appear in the result. Such terms specify the order of the residual term and suggest that the limit transition was calculated via a series development. The order of the residual term can be set by changing the value of the global variable `Order` (default value 6). In the example below, the sum over $\frac{1}{1+x^4}$ is calculated once again. The reliability of the result is checked by means of an approximation solution (sum of the first hundred terms).

```
limit(sum(1/(x^4+1), x=1..n), n=infinity);
```

$$-\left(\sum_{\_\alpha=\%1} \left(-\frac{1}{4}\,\_\alpha\,\Psi(1-\_\alpha)\right)\right)$$

$$\%1 := \mathrm{RootOf}(\_Z^4+1)$$

```
evalf(");
```

0.5784775797

```
evalf(sum(1/(x^4+1), x=1..100));
```

0.5784772513

Where sums over terms with alternating signs are concerned, Maple often fails even where a symbolic solution would be possible. In such cases, you can try to split the sum into two partial sums yourself and then calculate these separately. In the example below, this leads to the desired result. For safety, the result is checked by means of an approximation solution for the first hundred terms.

```
sum(1/(x^2+1)*(-1)^x, x=1..infinity);
```

$$\sum_{x=1}^{\infty} \frac{(-1)^x}{x^2+1}$$

```
sum(1/((2*x)^2+1), x=1..infinity);
```

$$-\frac{I\,\Psi(1+\frac{I}{2})}{4} + \frac{I\,\Psi(1-\frac{I}{2})}{4}$$

```
sum(1/((2*x-1)^2+1), x=1..infinity);
```

$$-\frac{I\,\Psi(1/2+\frac{I}{2})}{4} + \frac{I\,\Psi(1/2-\frac{I}{2})}{4}$$

```
s:=simplify(""-");
```

$$s := -\frac{I\,\left(\Psi(1+\frac{I}{2}) - \Psi(1-\frac{I}{2}) - \Psi(1/2+\frac{I}{2}) + \Psi(1/2-\frac{I}{2})\right)}{4}$$

```
evalf(s), evalf(sum(1/(x^2+1)*(-1)^x, x=1..100));
```

$-0.3639854725, -0.3639359774$

If you want to construct sums over several variables, you must employ several embedded sum commands. If the expression to be summed contains variables that are already occupied, it must be enclosed in several pairs of quotes (as many as there are summation levels). The example below shows how sum is used to construct a formula which uses elements of an array (a matrix) as coefficients.

```
k:=array(1..3, 1..3):
sum(sum(k[i,j]*x^(i+j), i=1..3), j=1..3);
```

$$k_{1,1}x^2 + k_{2,1}x^3 + k_{3,1}x^4 + k_{1,2}x^3 + k_{2,2}x^4 + k_{3,2}x^5 + k_{1,3}x^4 + k_{2,3}x^5 + k_{3,3}x^6$$

Series development with sum

You can also employ sum to create series developments. In the following example, the series development is shown for the sine function around the point $x = 0$:

```
f:=unapply(sum((-1)^n * x^(2*n+1) / (2*n+1)!, n=0..6), x);
```

$$f := x \mapsto x - \frac{x^3}{6} + \frac{x^5}{120} - \frac{x^7}{5040} + \frac{x^9}{362880} - \frac{x^{11}}{39916800} + \frac{x^{13}}{6227020800}$$

The illustration on the right shows that up to $x = 3\pi/2$ the series development largely coincides with the sine function.

```
plot({sin(x), f(x)},
     x=0..3*Pi, -1..4);
```

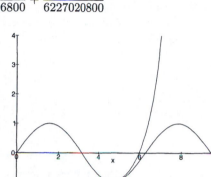

In the second example, $\sin(x)^2 + \frac{1}{x-1}$ around the point $x0 = \pi/2$ is developed into a Taylor series. The derivatives after x^i are produced with diff. Since this command cannot cope with the special case $i = 0$, the first element of the sum must be specified explicitly.

```
f:=x->sin(x)^2+1/(x-1);
```

$$f := x \mapsto \sin(x)^2 + (x-1)^{-1}$$

```
g:=(x-x0)^0 * f(x0) /0! + sum((x-x0)^i * diff(f(x0),x0$i) / i!, i=1..9):
g:=unapply(evalf(subs(x0=-Pi/2, g)),x);
```

$$g := x \mapsto 0.3733399057 - 0.1513089639x - 1.058856847\,(x + 1.570796327)^2 -$$

$$0.02289440294\,(x + 1.570796327)^3 + \ldots - 0.00007930914916\,(x + 1.570796327)^9$$

Once again, plot is used to check the coincidence between approximation and original function.

```
plot({f(x), g(x)},
     x=-2*Pi..Pi, -2..2);
```

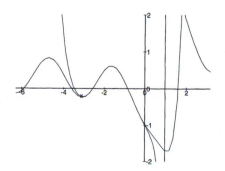

Note: In most cases, the `series` command can produce Taylor and Laurent series for a given function immediately – that is, without the detour via `sum` (see Chapter 24).

Generic summation formula for the first n terms

When `sum` is used in the form `sum(f,x)`, that is, without the specification of summation limits, it develops the function f into a new function g so that $g(n+1) - g(n) = f(n)$ applies.

```
f:=x->x/(1-x^2);
```

$$f := x \mapsto \frac{x}{1 - x^2}$$

```
g:=sum(f(x), x);
```

$$g := x^{-1} + \frac{1}{2\,x\,(x-1)} - \Psi(x+1)$$

```
g:=unapply(g,x);
```

$$g := x \mapsto x^{-1} + \frac{1}{2\,x\,(x-1)} - \Psi(x+1)$$

The function g can now be used to calculate the sum over f for an arbitrary range, as shown by the examples on the right.

```
g(3)-g(2), f(2);
```

$$-2/3, -2/3$$

```
g(4)-g(2), f(2)+f(3);
```

$$-\frac{25}{24}, -\frac{25}{24}$$

```
sum(f(x), x=2..8), g(9)-g(2);
```

$$-\frac{9883}{5040}, -\frac{9883}{5040}$$

Euler–Maclaurin's series development for the generic summation formula

The `eulermac` command carries out an Euler–Maclaurin's series development for the generic summation formula. Prior to being used, the command must be read with `readlib`. The first parameter specifies the function to be summed, the second parameter the variable and the third parameter the required order of the series development. When the third parameter is not specified, the order is given by the global variable `Order`.

Usually, this command is only employed when a symbolic calculation of the sum is impossible due to the complexity of the function to be summed. The example below shows that the precision of the series development (especially for small values of x) is not too high.

In the following example, an Euler–Maclaurin's series of fourth order is developed for the function $x/(1 + x^2)$. Subsequently, several variations are shown to calculate the sum of this function for $x = 1$ to $x = 100$.

```
readlib(eulermac):
fa:=eulermac(x/(1+x^2), x, 4);
```

$$fa := \frac{\ln(1+x^2)}{2} - \frac{x}{2+2x^2} + \frac{1}{12+12x^2} - \frac{x^2}{6(1+x^2)^2} - \frac{x^2}{15(1+x^2)^3} +$$

$$\frac{1}{120(1+x^2)^2} + \frac{x^4}{15(1+x^2)^4} + O(\frac{5760x^4}{(1+x^2)^5} - \frac{2160x^2}{(1+x^2)^4} + \frac{120}{(1+x^2)^3} - \frac{3840x^6}{(1+x^2)^6})$$

The series has only been developed up to the fourth order so that the formula does not become too bulky. The `eulermac` command supplies the result together with the order term O which specifies at which point the series development was aborted. To make the result usable for further calculations, the order term must be eliminated. The easiest way to do this is to call `eval(subs(O=0, fa))`:

```
fa:=eval(subs(O=0, fa));
```

$$fa := \frac{\ln(1+x^2)}{2} - \frac{x}{2+2x^2} + \frac{1}{12+12x^2} - \frac{x^2}{6(1+x^2)^2} - \frac{x^2}{15(1+x^2)^3} +$$

$$\frac{1}{120(1+x^2)^2} + \frac{x^4}{15(1+x^2)^4}$$

Now to the different variations to calculate the sum of $x/(1+x^2)$ for $x = 1$ to 100: the reference value is constituted by the symbolic calculation of the sum of all 100 terms. For this purpose, `seq` was used to produce a set containing the 100 single terms. Subsequently, this set was converted into a sum with `convert` and numerically evaluated with `evalf` to a precision of 20 digits. This calculation variation is expensive, but exact. Since `seq` assigns the value 101 to the variable x, x must subsequently be deleted.

```
evalf(convert({seq(x/(1+x^2), x=1..100)}, '+'), 20);
```

> 4.5155610321652721734

```
x:='x':
```

The normal symbolic and numerical calculation with `evalf(sum(..))` and `evalf(Sum(..))` supplies exact results for the given function:

```
evalf(sum(x/(1+x^2), x=1..100), 20);
```

> 4.5155610321652721734

```
evalf(Sum(x/(1+x^2), x=1..100), 20);
```

> 4.5155610321652721734

Now to the application of the Euler–Maclaurin's series. In order to calculate the new sum from $x = 1$ to 100, the difference of this series must be calculated for $x = 101$ (!) and $x = 1$. The result is, however, only exact up to the third digit after the decimal point. An increase in the order of series development improves the result only marginally. When a higher order than 100 is specified, the convergence becomes even worse again.

```
evalf(subs(x=101,fa)-subs(x=1,fa), 20);
```

   4.5157210958411135595

```
fa:=eulermac(x/(1+x^2), x, 10): fa:=fa-select(has, fa, 0):
evalf(subs(x=101,fa)-subs(x=1,fa), 20);
```

   4.5154606791744431626

Finally, the generic summation formula was directly produced with sum. The result corresponds (as expected) to the one calculated with evalf(sum(..)).

```
fb:=sum(x/(1+x^2), x);
```

$$fb := \frac{\Psi(x+I)}{2} + \frac{\Psi(x-I)}{2}$$

```
evalf(subs(x=101, fb)-subs(x=1, fb), 20);
```

   $4.5155610321652721736 + 2.6 \times 10^{-21} I$

Products

The same syntax as sum is also used in the product command. It calculates the product of the expression specified in the first parameter.

```
product(x,x=1..5);
```

   120

```
evalf(product(1+1/x^2, x=1..100));
```

   3.639682295

product can also calculate infinite products.

```
product(1+1/x^2, x=1..infinity);
```

   $\dfrac{\sinh(\pi)}{\pi}$

```
evalf(");
```

   3.676077910

The same result can also be achieved by calculating the product by means of a limit transition.

```
limit(product(1+1/x^2, x=1..n),
       n=infinity);
```

   $$\frac{1}{\Gamma(1-I)\Gamma(1+I)}$$

```
evalf(");
```

   3.676077912

Analogously to add, the mul command is available for the efficient multiplication of a finite number of factors.

```
mul(1+1/x^2, x=1..20);
```

   $$\frac{1060759394707991417279425}{302973535625290620862464}$$

```
evalf(");
```

   3.501161884

Numerical calculations

In the previous pages, `evalf` has been used several times to calculate limits, sums or products numerically, when these could not be calculated symbolically. Sometimes (for example, for control purposes) it makes sense to work numerically even in cases where `limit`, `sum` or `product` produces a symbolic result. When you simply write `evalf(sum(..))`, Maple first calculates the symbolic solution and then evaluates it numerically. If you want to work numerically right from the beginning, you must use the inert variations of the three commands, that is, `Limit`, `Sum` and `Product`.

The following example shows the difference between a mixed symbolic–numerical calculation and a purely numerical calculation. The sum of the first 2000 terms $\frac{(-1)^x}{x^2}$ is first calculated normally, that is, with `sum`, and subsequently evaluated numerically. In the second `evalf` command, a purely numerical calculation is forced through using `Sum`, which can be executed much faster and with much less memory consumption. (The reason: in the first variation, the symbolic result – a sum of 2000 terms – must be stored prior to evaluation with `evalf`.)

Time and memory consumption were measured by means of the `showtime` command. Once activated, after the end of each calculation, this command automatically displays the CPU time used (in seconds) and the memory consumption. `off` deactivates the automatic timing. The measurement of the CPU time depends on the operating system.

```
readlib(showtime):
showtime();
evalf(sum((-1)^x/x^2, x=1..2000), 40);
```

$$-0.8224669084866132026112193020564110699511$$

```
    time = 8.87, bytes = 6 918 902
evalf(Sum((-1)^x/x^2, x=1..2000), 40);
```

$$-0.8224669084866132026112193020564110699511$$

```
    time = 1.11, bytes = 1 030 858
off;
```

The second example shows the calculation of a limit, first symbolic, then purely numerical. Here, the numerical evaluation fails and supplies the result with an incorrect sign.

```
f:=sinh(x)^2-sinh(x^2);
```

$$f := \sinh(x)^2 - \sinh(x^2)$$

```
limit(f, x=infinity);
```

$$-\infty$$

```
evalf(Limit(f, x=infinity));
```

$$\infty$$

```
evalf(subs(x=10^2, f));
```

$$-4.403409113 \times 10^{4342}$$

Syntax summary

```
limit(f, x=x0);
limit(f, x=x0, option);
limit(f, {x=x0, y=y0,..}, option);
```
calculates the limit of f for $x \rightarrow x0$. The following options can be specified: `left` (approximation from the left), `right` (approximation from the right), `real` (approximation from both sides) or `complex` (multi-directional approximation, result without complex direction). The third syntax variation calculates the limit of a multi-variable function.

```
sum(f, x=start..end);
sum(sum(f, x=sx..ex), y=sy..ey);
```
calculates the sum over f, where x cycles through the integer range from *start* to *end*. `infinity` (∞) too is allowed as a range limit. The second syntax variation shows the calculation of a multi-variable sum.

```
sum(f, x);
```
calculates a generic summation formula g for the first n terms of f so that $g(n+1) - g(n) = f(n)$ applies.

```
add(f, x=start..end);
```
numerically sums the function values f, with x cycling through the integer range from *start* to *end*.

```
product(f, x=start..end);
product(product(f, x=sx..ex), y=sy..ey);
product(f, x);
```
calculates products, otherwise as above.

```
mul(f, x=start..end);
```
numerically multiplies the function values f, with x cycling through the integer range from *start* to *end*.

```
limit(sum(f, x=start..n), n=end);
limit(product(f, x=start..n), n=end);
```
reduces the calculation of a sum or a product to a limit calculation.

```
evalf(Limit(f, x=xd));
evalf(Sum(f, x=start..end));
evalf(Product(f, x=start..end));
```
carries out a purely numerical calculation of the limit, the sum or the product.

`convert({x1,x2,x3..}, '+');`   `convert({x1,x2,x3..}, '*');`

converts the set or list in the first parameter into the sum $x1 + x2 + x3 + ..$ or the product $x1 * x2 * x3 * ...$.

`readlib(eulermac);`   `eulermac(f, x, n);`

carries out an Euler–Maclaurin's series development of nth order for the generic summation formula (that is, for `sum(f,x)`).

Chapter 16

Differentiation

This chapter deals with the generation of derivatives. The standard command for this purpose is `diff`. Since Release 4, functions which are defined through equations (for example $x^2 + y^2 = 1$) can be very easily derived with `implicitdiff`. Functional operators (that is, function specifications of the form `(x)->f(x)`) can be derived with `D`. It is essential for the generation of derivatives that you tell Maple which symbols depend on what.

`diff`
generates the derivative of a function.

`implicitdiff`
generates the implicit derivative of a function which is defined through an equation.

`D`
generates the derivative of a function specification or a procedure.

Reference: Chapter 18 deals with the solution of differential equations, frequently resorting to `D` for the formulation of differential equations. Chapter 27 describes commands for vector analysis which are used to calculate the divergence, gradient and rotor of vector or scalar functions, amongst other things. These commands represent an extension to the usual differentiation commands for scalar functions.

Derivatives of functions

diff generates the derivative of the function specified in the first parameter using the variables specified in the later parameters.

```
diff(x^3+x^2+x,x);
```
$$3x^2 + 2x + 1$$

```
diff(x^3+x^2+x,x,x);
```
$$6x + 2$$

For multiple derivatives, the short notation `x$n` can be used, which Maple converts to $x, x, ..., x$. Please note that only integer numbers greater than 0 are allowed for n. `diff(f,x$0)` leads to an error message (which is sometimes irritating in loops for the development of series).

```
diff(x^3+x^2+x,x$3);
```
$$6$$

Obviously, Maple knows all the rules of differentiation, such as product rule, inner derivative, and so on.

```
diff(sin(cos(x)), x);
```
$$-\cos(\cos(x))\sin(x)$$

For embedded functions, Maple uses the differentiation operator D to formulate the result (see below).

```
diff(f(g(x)), x);
```
$$\mathrm{D}(f)(g(x))\frac{d}{dx}g(x)$$

In principle, in a derivative Maple assumes that symbols which are not further defined are constant (and independent of the derivative variable). When a and b are to represent functions of x, (x) must be postponed.

```
diff(a*x+b, x);
```
$$a$$

```
diff(a(x)*x+b(x), x);
```
$$\left(\frac{d}{dx}a(x)\right)x + a(x) + \frac{d}{dx}b(x)$$

Derivative of multi-variable functions

Several variables can be specified in the parameters to `diff`. In this case, the command first generates the derivative using the first variable, then the derivative using the second one, and so on.

```
diff((x^2+y^3)^4, x, y);
```
$$72\left(x^2 + y^3\right)^2 xy^2$$

In a derivative of functions with several variables, `diff` usually assumes that no dependences exist between the variables. $\frac{d}{dx}y$ is thus simplified to 0. When y depends on x, you must tell Maple that this is the case – the simplest way is to postpone (x). This causes y to be considered a generic (but still unknown) function of x.

```
diff((x^2+y^3)^4, x);
```
$$8\left(x^2 + y^3\right)^3 x$$

```
diff((x^2+y(x)^3)^4, x);
```
$$4\left(x^2 + y(x)^3\right)^3 \left(2x + 3y(x)^2\frac{d}{dx}y(x)\right)$$

Both input and output become clearer when you use `alias` to define y as an abbreviation for $y(x)$.

```
alias(y=y(x)):
diff((x^2+y^3)^4, x);
```
$$4\left(x^2 + y^3\right)^3 \left(2x + 3y^2\frac{d}{dx}y\right)$$

When a function depends on several variables, you must specify all of them. Prior to this, in the example on the right, the `alias` abbreviation for y is deleted.

```
alias(y=y):
diff(f(x,y,z), x$2,y,z$2);
```

$$\frac{\partial^5}{\partial z^2 \partial y \partial x^2} f(x, y, z)$$

Determining your own differentiation rules for user-defined functions

With `alias`, you can also define an abbreviation for the result of a derivative. This abbreviation has no influence on the result, but it can lead to a clearer notation.

```
alias(fd(x)=diff(f(x),x)):
diff(f(x), x), diff(f(x), x$2);
```

$$fd(x), \frac{d}{dx} fd(x)$$

You can obtain a farther-reaching effect by defining your own differentiation specification `'diff/f'` for a generic function f. When differentiating, Maple automatically checks whether any functions are associated with their own differentiation rules under the name `'diff/fnname'`, and if so uses these instead of the 'normal' differentiation rules.

For two reasons, the following example begins with `restart`: firstly, any still existing `alias` abbreviations (for instance, those of the previous example) are to be deleted. Secondly, Maple is forced to recalculate the derivative $\frac{d}{dx} f(x)$. Maple normally stores already calculated results and, if needed, accesses them again. Under unfavourable conditions (as in the following example), however, this generally useful feature may cause Maple not to carry out a recalculation even if the preconditions for the calculation have changed.

In the example on the right, $f(x)$ is to be differentiated to $-f(2x)x$. The corresponding differentiation rule is stored under the name `'diff/f'` (note carefully the right quotes!).

```
restart;
'diff/f':=proc(x,dx)
   -f(2*x) * dx;
end:
```

The commands on the right show that the new differentiation rule is applied for both single and multiple derivatives. Furthermore, Maple recognizes that the derivative after a variable which does not occur at all in the function is 0 (see the second command). In contrast, the name of the variable (x or n) does not impact on the result, as intended.

```
diff(f(x), x);
```
$$-f(2x)x$$
```
diff(f(x), y);
```
$$0$$
```
diff(f(n), n$3);
```
$$-f(8n)n^3 + 3 f(4n)n$$

Further information about programming in Maple, about the keywords `proc` and `end`, and so on, can be found from Chapter 28 onward.

Implicit differentiation of function equations

`implicitdiff` is better suited than `diff` for the differentiation of functions which are defined through an equation. In most cases, `implicitdiff` automatically considers the dependences between the functions. The syntax of the command can best be shown by means of some examples.

In the example on the right, the function $y(x)$ is defined through the circular equation $x^2 + y^2 = 1$. From this, `implicitdiff(f,y,x)` derives $\frac{\partial}{\partial x} y$.

```
implicitdiff(x^2+y^2=1,y,x);
```
$$-\frac{x}{y}$$

In the above example, `implicitdiff` recognizes that y is a function of x. In complex cases, the dependences must be specified explicitly. In the first parameter, `implicitdiff` expects a set of function equations, in the second parameter the definition of the dependences in the form $y(x)$, in the third parameter the functions from which derivatives are to be generated, and in the fourth parameter the variables to be used in the derivatives.

```
implicitdiff({f},{y(x)},{y},x);
```
$$\{\frac{\partial}{\partial x} y = -\frac{x}{y}\}$$

The option `notation=Diff` supplies the result in a clearer notation.

```
implicitdiff({f},{y(x)},{y},x,
             notation=Diff);
```
$$2x + 2y(x)\,(\frac{\partial}{\partial x} y(x)) = 0$$

The example on the right again generates $\frac{\partial}{\partial x} y$ for a circular equation. This example is already known from Chapter 4 (graduation examples, see page 52).

```
implicitdiff(x^2+y^2+6*y-91=0,y,x);
```
$$-\frac{x}{y+3}$$

In the example on the right, z is defined through the equation $x^2\,y^2\,z^2 = 1$. `implicitdiff` generates the derivative $\frac{\partial^2}{\partial x \partial y} z$ twice, once in the short notation and once in the longer version. As with `diff`, several differentiation variables must be specified for the generation of multiple derivatives.

```
f:=x^2*y^2*z^2=1:
implicitdiff(f,z,x,y);
```
$$\frac{z}{x\,y}$$

```
implicitdiff({f}, {z(x,y)}, {z},
             x,y, notation=Diff);
```
$$\frac{\partial^2}{\partial x \partial y} z = \frac{z}{x\,y}$$

The differentiation operator D for functional operators

The `diff` command differentiates normal functions, such as $x^2 + 3x$ or $\sin(x)$, whereas D is used for the differentiation of functional operators, for example $x \mapsto x^2 + 3x$ or sin. (The difference between functions and functional operators (function specifications) is discussed in Chapter 8.)

Without additional parameters, D is only suitable for differentiating function specifications with only one parameter. The function specification of the second example corresponds to the function $\sin(\cos(x))$.

```
D(sin);
```
$$\cos$$

```
D(sin@cos);
```
$$-\cos^{(2)} \sin$$

For functions with several parameters, the parameter for which the differentiation is to be carried out must be specified in square brackets. For the following examples, a function specification with two parameters is defined. `D[1](f)` differentiates the function using the first of these parameters (that is, x).

```
f:=(x,y)->sin(x)+cos(y)+sin(x*y);
```
$$f := (x, y) \mapsto \sin(x) + \cos(y) + \sin(xy)$$

```
D[1](f);
```
$$(x, y) \mapsto \cos(x) + \cos(xy)y$$

When an additional pair of brackets enclosing parameters is appended to the term `D[n](f)`, these parameters are inserted into the function specification after the differentiation.

```
D[2](f);
```
$$(x, y) \mapsto -\sin(y) + \cos(xy)x$$

```
D[2](f)(alpha,beta);
```
$$-\sin(\beta) + \cos(\alpha\,\beta)\alpha$$

The most elegant way to formulate multiple derivatives is `D[n1$m1, n2$m2,...](f)`. Here, f is differentiated $m1$ times using the parameter $n1$, $m2$ times using the parameter $n2$, and so on.

```
D[2$2](f);
```
$$(x, y) \mapsto -\cos(y) - \sin(xy)x^2$$

Alternative notations for the generation of the double derivative using the second parameter could be `D[2](D[2](f))` or the corresponding but almost unreadable abbreviation `(D[2]@@2)(f)`.

The two examples below show two alternative notations for the formulation of the same task: f is to be differentiated three times using x (the first parameter) and four times using y. If needed, the result of the second command could be converted into operator notation by means of `unapply`.

```
D[1$3,2$4](f);
```
$$(x, y) \mapsto -\cos(xy)y^3x^4 - 12\,\sin(xy)y^2x^3 + 36\,\cos(xy)yx^2 + 24\,\sin(xy)x$$

```
diff(f(x,y), x$3, y$4);
```

$$-\cos(xy)x^4y^3 - 12\sin(xy)x^3y^2 + 36\cos(xy)x^2y + 24\sin(xy)x$$

Conversion between diff and D notation

Expressions in which D or diff occur to represent the differentiation of generic functions can be converted into the opposite notation with convert.

```
restart:
diff(f(x,y,z), x,y,z$2);
```

$$\frac{\partial^4}{\partial y \partial z^2 \partial x} f(x, y, z)$$

```
convert(", D);
```

$$(D_{1,2,3,3})(f)(x, y, z)$$

lprint can be used to display the internal structure of the expression.

```
lprint(");
    ((D[1,2,3,3])(f))(x,y,z)
```

This can be used to prevent the otherwise automatic representation as a mathematical formula.

```
convert(", diff);
```

$$\frac{\partial^4}{\partial y \partial z^2 \partial x} f(x, y, z)$$

```
lprint(");
    diff(diff(diff(diff(f(x,y,z),
        z),z),y),x)
```

Differentiation of procedures

The differentiation operator D can also be used for the differentiation of procedures. The result of the differentiation is a new procedure. When the procedure uses local variables, the derivative of a procedure can turn out to be significantly more compact than the direct derivative of an equivalent function. Even a subsequent numeric evaluation will be more efficient, because terms that occur several times need be calculated only once. Maple even allows the differentiation of procedures containing conditions or loops.

```
f:=proc(x) local t0,t1,t2;
  t0:=sin(x): t1:=cos(x):
  t2:=(t0^2+t1+3)/(t1^3-t0);
  sin(t2^2+1)*cos(t2^2-1);
end:
```

```
f(x);
```

$$\sin\left(\frac{\left(\sin(x)^2 + \cos(x) + 3\right)^2}{(\cos(x)^3 - \sin(x))^2} + 1\right) \cos\left(\frac{\left(\sin(x)^2 + \cos(x) + 3\right)^2}{(\cos(x)^3 - \sin(x))^2} - 1\right)$$

```
fd1:=diff(f(x), x);   #direct differentiation of the function
```

$$fd1 := \cos(\%2 + 1)$$

$$\left(2\frac{\%1\,(2\sin(x)\cos(x) - \sin(x))}{(\cos(x)^3 - \sin(x))^2} - 2\frac{\%1^2\left(-3\cos(x)^2\sin(x) - \cos(x)\right)}{(\cos(x)^3 - \sin(x))^3}\right)$$

$$\cos(\%2 - 1) - \sin(\%2 + 1)\sin(\%2 - 1)$$

$$\left(2\frac{\%1\,(2\sin(x)\cos(x) - \sin(x))}{(\cos(x)^3 - \sin(x))^2} - 2\frac{\%1^2\left(-3\cos(x)^2\sin(x) - \cos(x)\right)}{(\cos(x)^3 - \sin(x))^3}\right)$$

$$\%1 := \sin(x)^2 + \cos(x) + 3$$

$$\%2 := \frac{\%1^2}{(\cos(x)^3 - \sin(x))^2}$$

```
fd2:=D(f);   #differentiation of the equivalent procedure

fd2:=proc(x)
    local t1x,t2x,t0x,t2,t1,t0;
        t0x:=cos(x);
        t0:=sin(x);
        t1x:=-sin(x);
        t1:=cos(x);
        t2x:=(2*t0*t0x+t1x) / (t1^3-t0) -
            (t0^2+t1+3) / (t1^3-t0)^2 * (3*t1^2*t1x-t0x);
        t2:=(t0^2+t1+3)/(t1^3-t0);

2*cos(t2^2+1)*t2*t2x*cos(t2^2-1)-2*sin(t2^2+1)*sin(t2^2-1)*t2*t2x
    end

simplify(fd1-fd2(x));   # check

    0
```

Reference: The above example shows the difference between the differentiation of a procedure and that of an equivalent function. If you are not sure about the meaning of 'procedure' and 'local variable', please read Chapter 29.

Syntax summary

`diff(f,x);      diff(f, x$n, y$m,...);`
> generates the derivative of the function f using x. In the second syntax variation, f is differentiated n times using x and m times using y.

`implicitdiff(eq,y,x);`
`implicitdiff({eq}, {y(x1,x2)}, {y}, x1,x2,...);`
`implicitdiff({eq}, {y(x1,x2)}, {y}, x1,x2,..., notation=Diff);`
> generates the derivative $\frac{\partial}{\partial x}y$ or $\frac{\partial^n}{\partial x1 \partial x2 \cdots}y$. y is implicitly defined through the equation eq. The option `notation=Diff` can be used to obtain a clearer representation of the result. Many more syntax variations (in particular for the simultaneous generation of several derivatives to y_n which are defined through several equations eq_n) can be obtained with `?implicitdiff`.

`D(f);         D[n1$m1, n2$m2](f);`
> generates the derivative of the functional operator (the function specification) f. In the second syntax variation, the differentiation is carried out $m1$ times using the parameter $n1$, $m2$ times using the parameter $n2$, and so on.

`convert(x, diff);     convert(x, D);`
> converts the expression x (if possible) into a notation with `diff` or `D`, respectively.

Chapter 17

Integration

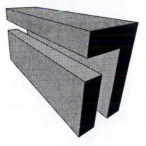

While construction of derivatives is relatively simple (from a mathematical point of view), the reverse process often represents an unsolvable problem. There is no single method of processing that achieves the same goal for all integrals. For manual integration (without Maple) entire books with tables of known integrals are used. When the integral cannot be reduced to known elements, various integration rules are applied which in very special cases achieve the goal. And often an integral cannot be solved at all mathematically.

How does integration look in Maple? The program handles a large number of integrals, but certainly not all the ones that are known to have been solved in mathematics. In some special cases Maple simply supplies erroneous results.

The present chapter mainly describes one command, namely `int`. The chapter introduces various forms of application of this command, for example for numeric integration, execution of double and multiple integrals, integration of complex functions, and so on.

`int`
integrates the specified function and if needed inserts the integration limits.

`evalf(Int(..))`
uses a purely numeric integration process.

`residue`
calculates residues (for integration of complex functions).

Symbolic integration

The examples on the right show the general application of int: the command can be used to calculate both general integrals (first example) and determined integrals with given integration limits (second and third examples).

```
int(x^2+x^3,x);
```
$$\frac{x^3}{3} + \frac{x^4}{4}$$

```
int(x^2+x^3,x=2..3);
```
$$\frac{271}{12}$$

```
int(x^2+x^3,x=a..b);
```
$$\frac{b^4}{4} + \frac{b^3}{3} - \frac{a^4}{4} - \frac{a^3}{3}$$

With evalf you can evaluate the result of an integration numerically.

```
evalf(int(x^2+x^3,x=2..3));
```
$$22.58333333$$

Maple can cope with many improper integrals. Additional examples of such integrals can be found in the following sections.

```
int(1/x^2, x=1..infinity);
```
$$1$$

Maple also integrates correctly over the points of discontinuity in f for $x = \pi/2$.

```
f:=cos(x)/sqrt(1-sin(x));
```
$$f := \frac{\cos(x)}{\sqrt{1 - \sin(x)}}$$

```
int(f, x=0..2*Pi);
```
$$0$$

The illustration on the right shows the course of f in the integration range.

```
plot(f, x=0..Pi);
```

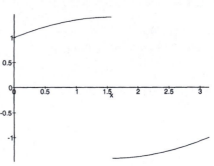

Maple can also cope with the Dirac impulse and the unit-step function. The unit step is defined in Maple under the name of Heaviside.

```
int(f(x)*Heaviside(x-2), x=0..5);
```
$$\int_2^5 f(x)dx$$

The unit step yields 0 for $x < 0$ and 1 for $x > 0$. By multiplying a function by the unit step, the integration range can be restricted.

```
int(sin(x)*Heaviside(x-Pi/2),
    x=0..Pi);
```
$$1$$

The result of the last command corresponds to the integral $\int_{x=\pi/2}^{x=\pi} sin(x)\,dx$. The illustration on the right shows the influence of the step function on the function $sin(x)$.

```
plot(sin(x)*Heaviside(x-Pi/2), x=0..Pi);
```

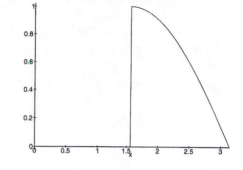

The Dirac impulse represents the derivative of the unit step and yields the value 0 for all $x \neq 0$. At the point $x = 0$ the size of the Dirac impulse is defined in such a way that the integral over it yields 1. Integration over the function $f(x)\,\text{Dirac}(x - x0)$ therefore yields $f(x0)$ (thus, $sin(\pi/4)$ in the example on the right).

```
diff(Heaviside(x), x);
```
$$Dirac(x)$$

```
int(sin(x) * Dirac(x-Pi/4),
    x=-infinity..infinity);
```
$$\frac{\sqrt{2}}{2}$$

Multiple integrals

Multiple integrals are constructed in Maple by embedding several `int` commands. The examples show two trivial surface integrals, one over a rectangle, the other over a quarter circle. Please note that Maple evaluates the integration commands from the inside out.

```
int(int(1, x=0..2), y=0..3);
```
$$6$$

```
int(int(1, y=0..sqrt(1-x^2)), x=0..1);
```
$$\frac{\pi}{4}$$

In multiple integrals, you must pay special attention to the correct order of integration ranges. The first command on the right calculates:

$$\int_{x=1}^{2} \int_{y=1}^{x^2} x^2 + y^2 \, dy \, dx$$

```
int(int(x^2+y^2, y=1..x^2), x=1..2);
```
$$\frac{1006}{105}$$

The second command, conversely, calculates the following integral:

$$\int_{y=1}^{x^2} \int_{x=1}^{2} x^2 + y^2 \, dx \, dy$$

```
int(int(x^2+y^2, x=1..2), y=1..x^2);
```
$$\frac{7\,x^2}{3} + \frac{x^6}{3} - 8/3$$

With the first integration command of the above example, the function $x^2 + y^2$ is integrated over the range shown on the right. The integration surface is limited by the curves $x = 2$, $y = 1$ and $y = x^2$.

For a graphic representation, the first curve is represented by a vertical line between (2,0) and (2,5), and the other two curves are drawn with the `plot` command. `plots` from the `display` package combines the two drawings into one.

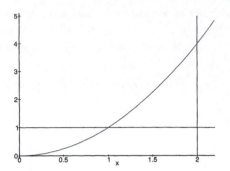

```
p1:=plot([[2,0],[2,5]]):
p2:=plot({x^2, 1}, x=0..2.2):
with(plots): display({p1,p2});
```

The last example is taken from the file `science\quantopt.ms` of the `share` library. It shows the solution of a triple integral from quantum physics. Please note that Maple uses the symbol ~ to mark the `assume` variables. Because of the smaller letter size, it can easily be confused with a negative sign for exponents.

```
assume(P>0): assume(S>0): inf:=infinity:
p1:=(x^2+y^2+z^2)/P^2:
p2:=subs(x=x-a,y=y-b,z=z-c,P=S,p1):
f:=(2*x^2-P^2)*exp(-p1-p2);
```

$$f := (2\,x^2 - P^{\sim 2})\,e^{\left(-\frac{x^2+y^2+z^2}{P^{\sim 2}} - \frac{(x-a)^2+(y-b)^2+(z-c)^2}{S^{\sim 2}}\right)}$$

```
int(int(int(f, x=-inf..inf), y=-inf..inf), z=-inf..inf):
factor(");
```

$$\frac{e^{\left(-\frac{c^2+a^2+b^2}{S^{\sim 2}+P^{\sim 2}}\right)}\,S^{\sim 3}\,P^{\sim 7}\,\pi^{3/2}\,(-S^{\sim 2} + 2\,a^2 - P^{\sim 2})}{(S^{\sim 2} + P^{\sim 2})^{7/2}}$$

Numeric integration

With the `evalf` command, you can obtain a numeric evaluation of the integral. Two variations must be distinguished: with `evalf(int(..))`, the integral is first calculated symbolically (as far as possible); only then is the result evaluated numerically. With the inert variation of the integration command, that is, with `evalf(Int(..))`, Maple uses a purely numerical integration process. In most cases, both variations arrive at the same result (sometimes with small rounding errors), but one or the other may lead to an erroneous result. The combination of both types of calculation – provided both can be executed – is quite useful for checking the result.

In this context, a note on the difference between `int` and `Int` is needed: the commands `Int`, `Diff`, `Sum` and `Product` are called inert commands, because they block evaluation of the mathematical instruction. They only come into effect in cooperation with other commands, for example with `evalf` for numeric evaluation of the entire expression. See also Chapter 28, Section 'The structure of Maple'.

Frequently, numeric integration is the only way to arrive at a result.

```
int(sin(1/x^3), x=1..2);
```

$$\int_1^2 \sin(x^{-3})dx$$

```
evalf(");
```

0.3548334332

Depending on the structure of the mathematical function, Maple uses one of three integration methods for numerical integration which can be selected by specifying an option in the fourth parameter: you can choose between _CCquad (Clenshaw–Curtis quadrature method, default setting), _Dexp (double-exponential method) or _NCrule (Newton–Cote method). Generally, it makes no sense to apply a different method than the one Maple chooses – usually, the only thing you obtain is a (significantly) longer computing time.

```
evalf(Int(sin(x)/x, x=1..100, 15, _NCrule));
```

0.616142396521873

The following example shows both integration variations: the function $\frac{1}{1+x^7}$ is to be integrated for the range between 1 and 2. The first (symbolic) attempt fails (for reasons that are logically not very clear). Then, the integration is carried out for the two unknown integration limits a and b. Subsequently, subs is used to insert the values 1 and 2 into the resulting formula.

```
f:=1/(1+x^7);
```

$$f := \left(1 + x^7\right)^{-1}$$

```
int(f, x=1..2);
```

$$\int_1^2 \frac{1}{1+x^7}\, dx$$

```
int(f, x=a..b);
```

$$\frac{\ln(b+1)}{7} + \sum_{\_R=\%1} \_R \ln(b+7\_R) - \frac{\ln(a+1)}{7} - \sum_{\_R=\%1} \_R \ln(a+7\_R)$$

$$\%1 := RootOf\left(117649\_Z^6 + 16807\_Z^5 + 2401\_Z^4 + 343\_Z^3 + 49\_Z^2 + 7\_Z + 1\right)$$

```
evalf(subs(a=1, b=2, "), 20);
```

0.11630170437709733349

The purely numerical calculation requires even less typing effort. In contrast to the above result, no imaginary rounding error (originating in the resolution of the RootOf term) gets into the result.

```
evalf(Int(f, x=1..2), 20);
```

0.11630170437709733349

The following example shows that the numeric calculation can also be treacherous. Here, the symbolic calculation of $\int_0^\infty 1/x^2\, dx$ works immediately. The attempt to solve the same integral numerically results in an error message. Then, the integral is converted into a limit calculation (purely numerically too) and now yields the erroneous (!) result 2.

```
int(1/x^2, x=0..infinity);
```

$$\infty$$

```
evalf(Int(1/x^2, x=0..infinity));
   Error, (in evalf/int) integrand has a pole in the interval
evalf(Limit(Int(1/x^2, x=n..infinity), n=0));
```

2.0

Improper integrals

There are two types of improper integrals: those in which the integration limits are infinite, and those in which the function value infinity occurs in the integration range. Integrals belonging to the first type are often calculated without problems using int – some examples can be found on the previous pages.

The result of improper integrals belonging to the second type is mathematically not defined; instead, the so-called Cauchy principal value exists. In order to calculate this principal value, the option CauchyPrincipalValue must be specified in the third parameter of int.

In the present example, $1/x^3$ is to be integrated in the range between -3 and 2. int returns the integral unevaluated. When CauchyPrincipal-Value is specified as the option, Maple returns the result $-5/72$, which corresponds to $\int_{-3}^{-2} 1/x^3 \, dx$. The rest of the integral has practically cancelled itself out – thus, Maple has made use of the point symmetry of the function $1/x^3$ left and right of the discontinuity point $x = 0$.

```
int(1/x^3, x=-3..2);
```

$$\int_{-3}^{2} x^{-3} dx$$

```
int(1/x^3, x=-3..2,
    CauchyPrincipalValue);
```

$$-\frac{5}{72}$$

Maple can also cope with the case where several discontinuity points lie in the integration range of the Cauchy principal value (in the example on the right, in the points $x = -1$ and $x = 0$).

```
int(1/(x^2+x), x=-2..1,
    CauchyPrincipalValue);
```

$$-2\ln(2)$$

```
evalf(");
```

$$-1.386294361$$

The illustration on the right shows the course of the function of the above example.

```
plot(1/(x^2+x), x=-2..1, -20..20);
```

Integration in polar coordinates

In the following example, the volume of the solid is to be calculated which is enclosed by the cylinder surface $x^2 + y^2 = 1$, the base $z = 0$ and the 'lid' $z = e^{-(x^2+y^2)}$.

The first attempt to solve the integral symbolically fails. But at least Maple arrives at a numeric solution.

```
macro(E=exp(1)):
4*int(int(E^(-x^2-y^2),
            y=0..sqrt(1-x^2)), x=0..1);
```

$$4 \int_0^1 \frac{\sqrt{\pi}\, erf(\sqrt{1-x^2})}{2\, e^{x^2}}\, dx$$

```
evalf(");
```

1.985865304

The integral poses fewer problems when it is transformed into polar coordinates: $x = r\cos(\phi), y = r\sin(\phi), x^2 + y^2 = r^2, dx\, dy = r\, dr\, d\phi$. Maple is (at least in its present version) not capable of recognizing such transformations on its own.

```
4*int(int(E^(-r^2) * r, r=0..1),
        phi=0..Pi/2);
```

$$-\pi\, e^{-1} + \pi$$

```
evalf(");
```

1.985865304

For a graphic representation of this solid, we need r as a function of z. Subsequently, the 'lid' and the cylinder wall can be drawn with `cylinderplot` and combined into one illustration with `display`.

```
solve(z=E^(-r^2), r);
```

$$\sqrt{-\ln(z)}, -\sqrt{-\ln(z)}$$

```
with(plots):
p1:=cylinderplot("[1], phi=0..2*Pi,
                z=1/E..1):
p2:=cylinderplot(1, phi=0..2*Pi,
                z=0..1/E):
display([p1,p2]);
```

Integration of complex functions, residues

Path integrals between two points of the complex number plane without singularities pose no problems.

```
int(z^2, z=0..1+I);
```

$$-2/3 + \frac{2I}{3}$$

```
int(z*cos(z^2), z=0..Pi*I);
```

$$-\frac{\sin(\pi^2)}{2}$$

Quite often, close path integrals around singularity points are needed (for example, around the point $z = 0$ for the complex function $1/z$). The usual integration method is to substitute z with $z0 + r*(\sin(t) + I\cos(t))$ and subsequently integrate it over the real variable t along the circle (that is, from 0 to 2π). Care must be taken not to forget the derivative from z to t. The sign of the result depends on the direction of integration; in the following examples, integration is always carried out counterclockwise.

$$\oint_C f(z)\,dz = \int_0^{2\pi} f(z(t))\,\frac{d\,z(t)}{dt}\,dt \qquad \text{with} \qquad z(t) = z0 + r\,(\cos(t) + I\,sin(t))$$

Example 1: path integral around 1/z

In Maple, the above formula for the sample function $1/z$ is transformed as follows:

```
z:=cos(t) + I*sin(t); dz:=diff(z,t);
f:=1/z;
```

$$z := \cos(t) + I\,\sin(t)$$

$$dz := -\sin(t) + I\,\cos(t)$$

$$f := \frac{1}{\cos(t) + I\,\sin(t)}$$

The attempt to integrate $f\,dz$ over t leads to an erroneous result.

```
int(f * dz, t=0..2*Pi);
```

$$0$$

Then, $f\,dz$ is simplified with simplify, and the result (the imaginary unit I) is integrated again. Now Maple supplies the correct result.

```
simplify(f*dz);
```

$$I$$

```
int(", t=0..2*Pi);
```

$$2\,I\,\pi$$

You also arrive at the correct result when you integrate from $-\pi$ to π instead of 0 to 2π.

```
int(f * dz, t=-Pi..Pi);
```

$$2\,I\,\pi$$

Purely numeric integration too leads to the required results in this and the following examples.

```
evalf(Int(f * dz, t=0..2*Pi));
```

$$-1.897322754 \times 10^{-14} + 6.283185307I$$

An analysis of why the symbolic integration attempt has failed leads to the following result: Maple has integrated $f\,dz$ to $\ln(\cos(t) + I\sin(t))$. Because of the periodicity of the trigonometric functions, the results for $t = 0$ and $t = 2\pi$ yield the same value.

```
i1:=int(f * dz, t);
```

$$i1 := \ln(\cos(t) + I\sin(t))$$

Through a conversion of the trigonometric terms into powers of e, the result can be simplified in such a way that the periodicity falls out. Inserting the integration limits now leads to the correct solution.

```
convert(i1, exp);
```

$$\ln(e^{I\,t})$$

```
i2:=simplify(");
```

$$i2 := I\,t$$

```
subs(t=2*Pi, i2) - subs(t=0, i2);
```

$$2\,I\,\pi$$

The illustration on the right shows the imaginary parts of the function ($f\,dz = I$) to be integrated, the result of symbolic integration ($i1$ with a step at π) and the simplified solution ($i2 = I\,t$).

```
plot({Im(f*dz), Im(i1), Im(i2)},
     t=0..2*Pi);
```

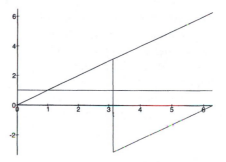

Example 2: path integral around $\frac{\sin(z)}{z^4}$, residue rule

A second example, this time for the function $\frac{\sin(z)}{z^4}$, confirms the first impression that extreme care must be taken with complex path integrals. Once again, Maple supplies the erroneous result 0.

```
f:=sin(z)/z^4;
```

$$f := \frac{\sin(\cos(t) + I\sin(t))}{(\cos(t) + I\sin(t))^4}$$

```
int(f *dz, t=0..2*Pi);
```

$$0$$

The correct result can again be obtained by modifying the integration limits.

```
int(f *dz, t=-Pi..Pi);
```

$$-\frac{I\,\pi}{3}$$

Apart from small rounding errors, the numeric variation of the integration command also supplies the correct result.

```
evalf(Int(f * dz, t=0..2*Pi));
```

$$-5.0 \times 10^{-13} - 1.0471975511I$$

In order to track down the symbolic integration error, $f\,dz$ is integrated generally (that is, without inserting the integration limits).

```
i1:=int((f*dz), t);
```

$$i1 := -\frac{\sin(\%1)}{3\,(\%1)^3} - \frac{\cos(\%1)}{6\,(\%1)^2} +$$

$$\frac{\sin(\%1)}{6\,\%1} - \frac{Ci(\%1)}{6}$$

$$\%1 := \cos(t) + I\,\sin(t)$$

The illustration on the right shows the imaginary part of $f\,dz$ and the imaginary part of the integral over this function, both in the range between $-\pi$ and 2π. At the point π, a step occurs which results from the cosine integral function.

```
p1:=plot(Im(f * dz), t=-Pi..2*Pi):
p2:=plot(Im(i1), t=-Pi..2*Pi):
with(plots): display([p1,p2]);
```

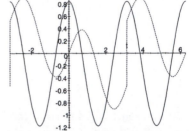

Unfortunately, there is no successful simplification of the result to eliminate this step as in the previous example. The basic problem is that we are faced with a closed path integral, that is, a path integral that starts in a point P and ends in the same point. Normally, such an integral obviously yields the value 0. The peculiarity of the integrals in this section, however, lies in the fact that there is a singularity point inside the integration path. In the present version, Maple is overstretched by the task of recognizing this fact. With an unfortunate choice of integration limits Maple may simply supply erroneous results without any warning.

The safest way out of this problem is to use a different method to determine path integrals. Following the residue rule

$$\oint_C f(z)\,dz = 2\pi I \sum_{j=1}^{k} \operatorname*{Res}_{z=z_j} f(z)$$

closed path integrals around singularity points can also be calculated out of the sum of the residues of the enclosed singularity points. With these signs, the residue rule applies to counterclockwise path integrals. In manual calculations too, this is often to be preferred to the direct determination of path integrals, because the resulting formulae are easier to handle.

The residue of a function is defined by the coefficient preceding $1/z$ or $1/(z - z0)$ of a **Laurent** series around the singularity point. For calculation of residues, the `residue` command can be used.

Before calculating the path integral around $\frac{\sin(z)}{z^4}$ after the residue rule, the above definition of z must be deleted and f must be redefined. Usage of `residue` is simple – in the first parameter, the complex function is specified, in the second parameter, the location of the singularity point. At this point Maple immediately supplies the correct solution.

```
readlib(residue):
z:='z': f:=sin(z)/z^4:
2*Pi*I*residue(f, z=0);
```

$$-\frac{I\,\pi}{3}$$

Example 3: path integral around $\frac{8-22z-z^2}{4z-5z^2+z^3}$

To conclude, here is an example of the application of the residue rule: a complex path integral is to be calculated on the circle around the centre point 0 and with the radius $3/2$.

```
z:='z':
f:=(-z^2-22*z+8)/(z^3-5*z^2+4*z);
```

$$f := \frac{8 - 22z - z^2}{4z - 5z^2 + z^3}$$

The first solution step is to determine the singularity points that lie inside the integration range. Here, `solve` is used to calculate the zero points of the denominator.

```
solve(denom(f));
```

$$0, 4, 1$$

Now, the integral can be calculated without problems over the two residues at the locations $z = 0$ and $z = 1$.

```
2*Pi*I*(residue(f, z=0) +
        residue(f, z=1));
```

$$14\,I\,\pi$$

```
evalf(");
```

$$43.98229716 I$$

The result is confirmed by the numeric integration, although – surprisingly – even the symbolic integration immediately supplies the correct result.

```
z:=1.5*(cos(t)+ I*sin(t)):
dz:=diff(z,t):
evalf(Int(f*dz, t=0..2*Pi));
```

$$2.0 \times 10^{-12} + 43.98229715 I$$

```
int(f*dz, t=0..2*Pi);
```

$$14\,I\,\pi$$

Integration control

The examples on the previous pages have shown that when integrating under unfavourable circumstances, Maple supplies erroneous results. The likely reasons for this could be either errors or not yet implemented case distinctions in Maple and an incorrect (or, as in the above examples, at least mathematically dangerous) formulation of the integral. It would be too much to ask Maple to recognize from the passed parameters alone that a given integral is a closed path integral around a

singularity point and that therefore special integration methods must be applied. This also applies
to other mathematical special cases.

The most effective control mechanism is to calculate the integral in different ways. For complex
integrals, for example, an alternative calculation with the residue rule suggests itself. Often a purely
numerical integration is possible for certain integrals, which is internally carried out following a
completely self-contained algorithm (remember the upper case spelling of the initial letter in Int!).

Furthermore, for determined integrals it can be useful to calculate the corresponding general integral and draw it with plot (separately for the real and the imaginary parts). If a step occurs, the
probability is extremely high that the determined integral is incorrect. An attempt might be made
to eliminate the point of discontinuity through left and right limit values, which also is not always
successful. All variations mentioned here have been introduced through practical examples in the
course of the last section.

The easiest way of checking general integrals is to differentiate them again and compare them with
the original function. Construction of the derivative is a relatively easy process mathematically,
so that at least here it can be assumed that Maple works correctly. But even this seemingly elegant
solution can be treacherous. First, the points of discontinuity in the integral can be cancelled through
the differentiation. Second, computing time can become an obstacle with complicated integrals.
And third, the original function and the derivative of the integral may well look completely different,
although mathematically they have the same meaning.

The following example shows this problem: simplify is not capable of simplifying the difference
between f and the derived integral to 0. (In the present example, simplification would be possible
with expand. However, the problem is not to find the most suitable command for a simplification
but rather the basic issue that under certain circumstances Maple cannot simplify an expression
although it is mathematically 0.)

```
f:=sin(a+1/x);
```

$$f := \sin(a + x^{-1})$$

```
int(f,x);
```

$$\sin(a + x^{-1})x + Si(x^{-1})\sin(a) - Ci(x^{-1})\cos(a)$$

```
diff(",x);
```

$$-\frac{\cos(a + x^{-1})}{x} + \sin(a + x^{-1}) - \frac{\sin(x^{-1})\sin(a)}{x} + \frac{\cos(x^{-1})\cos(a)}{x}$$

```
testexpr:=simplify("-f);
```

$$testexpr := -\left(\cos(\frac{ax + 1}{x}) + \sin(x^{-1})\sin(a) - \cos(x^{-1})\cos(a)\right)x^{-1}$$

If a simplification does not succeed, you can check the identity of two expressions by inserting
random numbers. Obviously, this method is not completely reliable. However, the probability that
two expressions are mathematically equivalent when they match for a series of 10 random numbers
is quite high. An important factor is that the random numbers correspond to your problem, that is,
in the most general case they should be complex floating point numbers from all four quadrants of

the complex number plane. Sometimes, however, it may be reasonable to insert integer numbers or fractions and then carry out a symbolic simplification.

The example below is a continuation of the example above. In *testexpr*, several floating point random numbers in the range ± 5000 are inserted for x and a. The two concluding commands calculate the greatest absolute deviation from 0. This method of working can be particularly useful for voluminous test series.

```
test:='5000-rand()/1e8';
```

$$5000 - 0.00000001\,rand()$$

```
seq(evalf(subs(x=test, a=test, testexpr)), i=1..5);
```

$$-2.97 \times 10^{-11}, -0.0000000001010, -2.4 \times 10^{-11}, 2.82 \times 10^{-11}, 1.82 \times 10^{-11}$$

```
map(abs, [']);
```

$$[2.97 \times 10^{-11}, 0.0000000001010, 2.4 \times 10^{-11}, 2.82 \times 10^{-11}, 1.82 \times 10^{-11}]$$

```
max(op("));
```

$$0.0000000001010$$

Watching Maple integrate

If you want to know how Maple arrives at its results, you can watch it integrate. For this purpose, you must set the system variable `infolevel` for `int` to a value between 2 and 5 (the higher the value, the more detailed the information). The first example shows Maple's (unsuccessful) attempt to integrate $\frac{1}{1+\ln(x)}$.

```
infolevel[int]:=3:
int(1/(1+ln(x)), x);
```

```
int/indef:    first-stage indefinite integration
int/indef2:   second-stage indefinite integration
int/ln:    case of integrand containing ln
int/rischnorm:    enter Risch-Norman integrator
int/risch:    enter Risch integration
int/risch/algebraic1:    RootOfs should be algebraic numbers and functions
int/risch:    the field extensions are
```

$$[\_X, \ln(\_X)]$$

```
int/risch:    Introduce the namings:
```

$$\{\_th_1 = \ln(\_X)\}$$

```
unknown:    integrand is
```

$$(1 + \_th_1)^{-1}$$

```
int/risch/ratpart:    integrating
```

$$(1 + \_th_1)^{-1}$$

```
int/risch/ratpart:    Hermite reduction yields
```

$$\int (1 + \_th_1)^{-1} \, d\_X$$

```
int/risch/ratpart:    Rothstein's method - resultant is
```

$$\_X - z$$

```
          nonconstant coefficients; integral is not elementary
int/risch:    exit Risch integration
```

$$\int (1 + \ln(x))^{-1} \, dx$$

In the second example, the function $\frac{sin(x)}{x}$ is numerically integrated in the range between 1 and 2. In this case, `infolevel` must be increased for the `'evalf/int'` command.

```
infolevel['evalf/int']:=2:
evalf(Int(sin(x)/x, x=1..2));

  evalf/int:    entering
  evalf/int/control:    integrating on   1   ..   2   the integrand
```

$$\frac{\sin(x)}{x}$$

```
  evalf/int/control:    procedure for evaluation is
  proc (x) evalf(sin(x)/x) end
  evalf/int/control:  from ccquad, error =    9168221737354543.0E-28
                      error tolerance =    3296649532178.0E-22
                      integrand evals =   19
                              result =   .6593299064355
  evalf/int:    exiting

  .6593299064
```

Syntax summary

```
int(f,x);       int(f,x=a..b);       int(f,x=a..b,opt);
```
   calculates the general or the determined integral of the function f. When integration is to be carried out over points of infinity, the option `CauchyPrincipalValue` must be used – then int supplies the Cauchy principal value.

```
evalf(Int(f,x=a..b));
```
   carries out a purely numerical integration.

```
readlib(residue);        residue(f,x=x0);
```
   calculates the residue of f at the point $x0$.

```
with(share):  readshare(hint, calculus):
hint(h,x);      hyperint(p,q,f,x);
```
   hint solves the undetermined hyperelliptic integral specified by h. hyperint solves the integral $\int p(x)/(q(x)\,y)dx$, where the hyperelliptic curve is determined by $y^2 = f$. See ?hint and ?hyperint.

Chapter 18

Differential equations

Solving differential equations has the same problems as integrating functions: there are a large number of mathematical methods which lead to the required result only in specific cases. For most possible differential equations (that is, those equations that can be mathematically formulated) there are no symbolic solutions at all.

This introductory remark is meant to warn you not to expect too much from the dsolve command. The command for symbolic solution of differential equations or of systems of differential equations can only cope with a very restricted selection of differential equation types. The numeric variation of dsolve (option numerical) is slightly more flexible.

dsolve
tries to solve a differential equation. Either a Laplace transformation or a series development is carried out, or a numeric method is used, depending on the option.

pdesolve
tries to solve a partial differential equation symbolically. However, this is only successful for a few types of first-order differential equations.

odeplot
from the plots package, represents numeric solutions of differential equations graphically.

DEtools
is a package containing various commands for graphic representation of (still unsolved) differential equations.

Reference: Other methods of solving differential equations are described in Chapters 24 to 26 (series development, Fourier and Laplace transformations).

Symbolic solution of differential equations

Differential equations can be formulated either with diff or with the differential operator D (see also Chapter 16) – the notation is unclear in any case. The two equivalent commands below both mean the differential equation $y' + y = 1$. The second parameter of dsolve contains the target function. Several freely selectable integration constants $\_Cn$ may occur in the result, which can be determined by means of end conditions.

```
dsolve(D(y)(x) + y(x) = 1, y(x));
```

$$y(x) = 1 + e^{-x}\_C1$$

```
dsolve(diff(y(x), x) + y(x) = 1, y(x));
```

$$y(x) = 1 + e^{-x}\_C1$$

In the next example, the initial condition $y(0) = 0$ is specified.

```
de:=diff(y(x),x) * y(x) * (1+x^2) = x;
```

$$de := \left(\frac{d}{dx}y(x)\right) y(x) \left(1 + x^2\right) = x$$

```
dsolve({de, y(0)=0}, y(x));
```

$$y(x) = -\sqrt{\ln(1 + x^2)}, y(x) = \sqrt{\ln(1 + x^2)}$$

For a countercheck, subs is used to insert the first of the two possible solutions into the original equation.

```
subs("[1], de);
```

$$-\left(\frac{d}{dx}\left(-\sqrt{\ln(1 + x^2)}\right)\right)\sqrt{\ln(1 + x^2)}\left(1 + x^2\right) = x$$

```
simplify(");
```

$$x = x$$

When initial or boundary conditions for derivatives are to be specified, the notation D(y)(x0)=y0 must be used. Higher derivatives are written in the form D(D(D(y)))(x0)=y0 or in the even more unclear notation (D@@3)(y)(x0)=y0. The boundary conditions are enclosed in curly brackets together with the differential equation.

```
dsolve({de, D(y)(1)=1}, y(x));
```

$$y(x) = -\sqrt{\ln(1 + x^2) - \ln(2) + 1/4}, y(x) = \sqrt{\ln(1 + x^2) - \ln(2) + 1/4}$$

For some differential equations, Maple formulates the solution in implicit form. If this is not required, the option explicit can be specified in the third parameter.

```
dsolve((y(x)^2 - x)*D(y)(x) + x^2-y(x) = 0, y(x));
```

$$\frac{x^3}{3} - y(x)x + \frac{y(x)^3}{3} = \_C1$$

```
dsolve((y(x)^2 - x)*D(y)(x) + x^2-y(x)=0, y(x), explicit);
```

$$y(x) = -\frac{\sqrt[3]{\%1}}{2} - \frac{x}{2\sqrt[3]{\%1}} - I\sqrt{3}\left(\sqrt[3]{\%1} - \frac{x}{\sqrt[3]{\%1}}\right)1/2,$$

$$y(x) = -\frac{\sqrt[3]{\%1}}{2} - \frac{x}{2\sqrt[3]{\%1}} + I\sqrt{3}\left(\sqrt[3]{\%1} - \frac{x}{\sqrt[3]{\%1}}\right)1/2,$$

$$y(x) = \sqrt[3]{\%1} + \frac{x}{\sqrt[3]{\%1}}$$

$$\%1 = -\frac{x^3}{2} + \frac{3\_C1}{2} + \frac{\sqrt{-4x^3 + x^6 - 6x^3\_C1 + 9\_C1^2}}{2}$$

With the option `output=basis`, `dsolve` supplies a list of general and special solutions of the differential equation.

```
de:=diff(y(x), x$4) + 5*diff(y(x),x$2) - 36*y(x)=sin(x);
```

$$de := \left(\frac{\partial^4}{\partial x^4}y(x)\right) + 5\left(\frac{\partial^2}{\partial x^2}y(x)\right) - 36y(x) = \sin(x)$$

```
dsolve(de, y(x));
```

$$y(x) = -\frac{1}{65}\sin(x) + \frac{1}{156}\cos(3x)\sin(2x) - \frac{1}{312}\cos(3x)\sin(4x) + \frac{1}{312}\sin(3x)\cos(4x)$$
$$-\frac{1}{156}\sin(3x)\cos(2x) + \_C1\,e^{(2x)} + \_C2\,e^{(-2x)} + \_C3\cos(3x) + \_C4\sin(3x)$$

```
dsolve(de, y(x), output=basis);
```

$$\left[[\cos(3x),\sin(3x),e^{(2x)},e^{(-2x)}], -\frac{1}{65}\sin(x) + \frac{1}{156}\cos(3x)\sin(2x)\right.$$
$$\left. -\frac{1}{312}\cos(3x)\sin(4x) + \frac{1}{312}\sin(3x)\cos(4x) - \frac{1}{156}\sin(3x)\cos(2x)\right]$$

Further processing of solutions to differential equations

Normally, differential equations are not solved simply to see whether Maple can cope with that particular type of differential equation. Rather, the resulting solutions are to be used in further calculations and frequently also represented graphically. Maple supplies the solutions as equations which in this form are well suited to be substituted into the differential equation. In this way, it is relatively easy to check whether the solution is correct – see the example at the beginning of the previous section. To obtain generally usable functions from the solution equations, we need detours via `rhs` and `unapply` which are presented in the following examples. Examples of processing solutions to systems of differential equations and of numeric solutions can be found in the following sections.

In the example on the right, the differential equation for free fall without air resistance is solved. A solid begins to fall at a height of 10 metres with a starting speed of 0.

```
dsolve({m*D(D(z))(t) = -m*g,
         z(0)=10, D(z)(0)=0}, z(t));
```

$$z(t) = -\frac{gt^2}{2} + 10$$

Maple supplies the result in the form of an equation $z(t) = \dots$. In order to convert this into a true function, the right-hand side of the equation is isolated with `rhs` (right side), converted into a function specification with `unapply` and stored in *funcz*.

```
funcz:=unapply(rhs("), t);
```

$$funcz := t \mapsto -\frac{gt^2}{2} + 10$$

In order to determine when the solid reaches the ground, the gravitational constant g is set to 9.81. Please note that this step is only allowed after the differential equation has been solved. No floating point numbers are allowed in the differential equation if `dsolve` is to supply a symbolic result.

```
g:=9.81;
```

$$g := 9.81$$

```
solve(funcz(t)=0, t);
```

$$-1.427843124, 1.427843124$$

```
t0:=max(");
```

$$t0 := 1.427843124$$

Now we can draw the height of the solid and its speed. The speed (derivation of the height) is negative, since the z axis points upwards, whereas the solid falls downwards.

```
plot({funcz(t), diff(funcz(t),t)},
     t=0..t0);
```

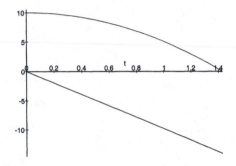

The second example calculates the damped oscillation of a solid on a spring where the solid is released at time $t = 0$ outside the position of rest ($y(0) = 1$). The solution of the differential equation is again isolated with `rhs` and immediately (without `unapply`) stored in *funcy*.

```
restart: m:=1: c:=1: k:=1:
dsolve({m*D(D(y))(t) + c*D(y)(t) + k*y(t)=0, y(0)=1, D(y)(0)=0}, y(t));
```

$$y(t) = \frac{\sqrt{3}\,e^{-\frac{t}{2}}\sin(\frac{\sqrt{3}\,t}{2})}{3} + e^{-\frac{t}{2}}\cos(\frac{\sqrt{3}\,t}{2})$$

With `rhs`, the right-hand side of the equation is extracted.

```
funcy:=rhs("): funcy;
```

$$\frac{e^{-\frac{t}{2}}\left(\sqrt{3}\,\sin(\frac{\sqrt{3}\,t}{2}) + 3\cos(\frac{\sqrt{3}\,t}{2})\right)}{3}$$

The illustration shows the oscillation during the first 10 seconds.

```
plot(funcy, t=0..10, -0.2..0.35);
```

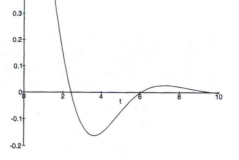

Differential equations in DESol

Since Release 3, Maple occasionally supplies partial solutions of unsolvable differential equations in form of DESol terms. The DESol function is comparable with RootOf and represents the non-calculable solution of a differential equation. The practical gain is, however, rather small since it is nearly impossible to extract the DESol part from the total solution and process it further.

The order of parameters in DESol differs from that in DSolve: the first parameter contains a sequence of the differential equations, the second parameter a sequence of the variables occurring in them and the third parameter a sequence of boundary conditions. (In dsolve, differential equations and boundary conditions are written as one common sequence.) There are also differences in the contents of parameters: while in dsolve the notation D(y)(x) is allowed, in DESol it must be either diff(y(x),x) or abbreviated to D(y). This second variation is new and not allowed in dsolve.

Simple DESol expressions can be derived with diff, integrated with int and converted into a series of powers with series.

```
desol:=DESol(diff(y(x), x) + y(x) = 1, y(x), y(0)=0);
```

$$desol := \mathrm{DESol}\left(\left\{\left(\frac{\partial}{\partial x}\,\mathrm{y}(\,x\,)\right)+\mathrm{y}(\,x\,)-1\right\},\{\,\mathrm{y}(\,x\,)\,\},\{\,\mathrm{y}(\,0\,)=0\,\}\right)$$

```
int(desol, x);
```

$$-\mathrm{DESol}\left(\left\{\left(\frac{\partial}{\partial x}\,\mathrm{y}(\,x\,)\right)+\mathrm{y}(\,x\,)-1\right\},\{\,\mathrm{y}(\,x\,)\,\},\{\,\mathrm{y}(\,0\,)=0\,\}\right)$$
$$-\ln\left(\mathrm{DESol}\left(\left\{\left(\frac{\partial}{\partial x}\,\mathrm{y}(\,x\,)\right)+\mathrm{y}(\,x\,)-1\right\},\{\,\mathrm{y}(\,x\,)\,\},\{\,\mathrm{y}(\,0\,)=0\,\}\right)-1\right)$$

```
simplify(diff(", x));
```

$$\mathrm{DESol}\left(\left\{\left(\frac{\partial}{\partial x}\,\mathrm{y}(\,x\,)\right)+\mathrm{y}(\,x\,)-1\right\},\{\,\mathrm{y}(\,x\,)\,\},\{\,\mathrm{y}(\,0\,)=0\,\}\right)$$

```
series(desol, x);
```

$$x-\frac{1}{2}\,x^2+\frac{1}{6}\,x^3-\frac{1}{24}\,x^4+\frac{1}{120}\,x^5+\mathrm{O}(\,x^6\,)$$

Systems of differential equations

dsolve is also capable of solving (relatively simple) systems of differential equations. All differential equations must be specified in a set (curly brackets) in the first parameter of dsolve. In the first example, an attempt is made to determine a general solution for a second-order linear system with constant coefficients.

```
dsolve({D(x)(t)=a11*x(t)+a12*y(t),D(y)(t)=a21*x(t)+a22*y(t)},
       {x(t), y(t)});
```

$$\{y(t) = \_C1 \, e^{\frac{(a22+a11+\%1)t}{2}} + \_C2 \, e^{-\frac{(-a22-a11+\%1)t}{2}},$$

$$x(t) = \frac{\_C1 \, (-a22 + a11 + \%1) \, e^{\frac{(a22+a11+\%1)t}{2}}}{2 \, a21} -$$

$$\frac{\_C2 \, (a22 - a11 + \%1) \, e^{-\frac{(-a22-a11+\%1)t}{2}}}{2 \, a21} \}$$

$$\%1 = \sqrt{a22^2 - 2 \, a11 \, a22 + a11^2 + 4 \, a12 \, a21}$$

The second example represents a special case of the above system of differential equations ($a11 = 0, a12 = 1, a21 = -1, a22 = 0$); in addition, two boundary conditions are formulated.

```
sol:=dsolve({D(x)(t)=y(t), D(y)(t)=-x(t), x(0)=1, D(y)(1)=2},
       {x(t), y(t)});
```

$$sol := \left\{ y(t) = -\sin(t) - \frac{(\cos(1) + 2)\cos(t)}{\sin(1)}, x(t) = -\frac{(\cos(1) + 2)\sin(t)}{\sin(1)} + \cos(t) \right\}$$

In order to be able to use both solution functions x and y, the whole solution is substituted with subs in $x(t)$ and $y(t)$ and stored in *funcx* and *funcy*.

```
funcx:=subs(sol, x(t));
```

$$funcx := -\frac{(\cos(1) + 2)\sin(t)}{\sin(1)} + \cos(t)$$

```
funcy:=subs(sol, y(t));
```

$$funcy := -\frac{(\cos(1) + 2)\cos(t)}{\sin(1)} - \sin(t)$$

The solution curve (a circle) can now be drawn as a parametric function of t.

```
plot([funcx, funcy, t=0..2*Pi],
     scaling=constrained);
```

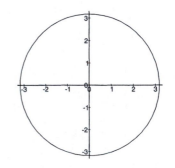

Solution via Laplace transformation

In order to solve a differential equation via a Laplace transformation, you must specify the option `laplace` in the third parameter. `laplace` must in particular be used when the differential equation contains the unit-step function `Heaviside` or the Dirac impulse `Dirac`.

Often Maple itself recognizes the Laplace transformation as a suitable solution method and uses it even if this option is not specified. In other cases, specifying `laplace` can save an enormous amount of time, for example in the differential equation for an RLC resonant circuit shown in Chapter 25 in the section on solving differential equations with Fourier series.

In order to save typing and to be able to represent results in a clearer way, the `Heaviside` unit-step function is abbreviated to σ. Subsequently, the function u is defined, which yields the value 1 for $1 \le t \le 5$, otherwise the value 0. The differential equation to be solved is $y' + y = u$. As expected, attempting the solution without `laplace` does not lead to a usable solution. With the `laplace` option, on the other hand, `dsolve` supplies the correct result.

```
alias(sigma=Heaviside):
u:=sigma(t-1)- sigma(t-5):
de:=diff(y(t), t) + y(t) = u:
dsolve({de, y(0)=0}, y(t));
```

$$y(t) = e^{(-t)} \int_0^t e^u \, \sigma(u-1) \, du - e^{(-t)} \int_0^t e^u \, \sigma(u-5) \, du + e^{(-t)} \left(e - e^5\right)$$

```
dsolve({de, y(0)=0}, y(t), laplace);
```

$$y(t) = \sigma(t-1)\left(1 - e^{(-t+1)}\right) - \sigma(t-5)\left(1 - e^{(-t+5)}\right)$$

Inserting the solution into the differential equation shows that the solution is correct. (`simplify` does not recognize that this equation corresponds to $0 = 0$. `lhs(")- rhs(")` would supply the required result.)

```
sol1:=rhs("):
simplify(subs(y(t)=sol1, de));
```

$$\sigma(t-1) - \sigma(t-5) = \sigma(t-1) - \sigma(t-5)$$

The illustration on the right shows the input function u and the solution function $sol1$, which follows the input function (exponentially delayed).

```
plot({u, sol1}, t=0..10);
```

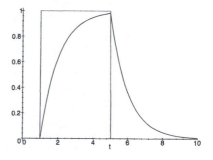

Approximation solution via series development

A further possible option of `dsolve` is `series`. Maple carries out a series development for all functions involved and also supplies the solution to the differential equation as a series. The advantage of this process is that a symbolic solution might be found even when the normal `dsolve` variation would be overstretched because of the complexity of the input functions. The disadvantage of the `series` option is that the resulting solution is only an approximation which is valid for a (in most cases rather small) range of numbers. Since Release 3, boundary conditions may also be specified for $t0 \neq 0$.

The number of terms in a series development is specified by means of the global variable `Order` which is usually preset to the value 6. In order to make the resulting series, whose term $O(x^{10})$ specifies the rank of the remaining terms, usable as a normal function, it must be converted with `convert/polynom` into a polynomial without $O(x^{10})$.

```
Order:=10:
de:=diff(y(x), x$2) + diff(y(x),x) + y(x) = x+sin(x);
```

$$de := \frac{d^2}{dx^2}y(x) + \frac{d}{dx}y(x) + y(x) = x + \sin(x)$$

```
sol1:=dsolve({de, y(0)=0, D(y)(0)=0}, y(x), series);
```

$$sol1 := y(x) = (\frac{1}{3}x^3 - \frac{1}{12}x^4 - \ldots + \frac{1}{181440}x^9 + O\left(x^{10}\right))$$

```
f1:=convert(rhs(sol1), polynom);
```

$$f1 := \frac{x^3}{3} - \frac{x^4}{12} - \frac{x^5}{120} + \frac{x^6}{240} - \frac{x^7}{5040} - \frac{x^8}{20160} + \frac{x^9}{181440}$$

Maple is also capable of solving this differential equation symbolically. The result is rather long-winded and is not shown here.

```
sol2:=dsolve({de, y(0)=0, D(y)(0)=0}, y(x)):
f2:=rhs(sol2):
```

The illustration on the right shows the actual solution (*sol2*, which is the flatter of the two curves) and the approximation solution *sol1* determined by series development. In the range $0 \leq t \leq \pi$ both curves match quite nicely.

```
plot({f1,f2}, x=0..2*Pi, 0..8);
```

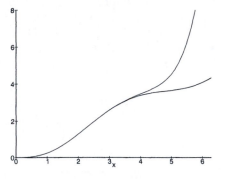

Additional information on solution finding

If you want to know how Maple arrives at its results, you can watch it solving the differential equation. You simply set the system variable `infolevel` for `dsolve` to a value between 2 and 5 (the higher the value, the more detailed the information). With the following differential equation, Maple fails.

```
infolevel[dsolve]:=3:
dsolve(3*D(y)(x) + y(x)* (1 + (2*x-1)*y(x)^3) = 0, y(x));
```

```
    dsolve/diffeq/dsol1:    -> first order, first degree methods :
    dsolve/diffeq/dsol1:    trying linear bernoulli
    dsolve/diffeq/dsol1:    trying separable
    dsolve/diffeq/dsol1:    trying exact
    dsolve/diffeq/dsol1:    trying general homogeneous
    dsolve/diffeq/dsol1:    trying Riccati
    dsolve/diffeq/linsubs:    trying linear substitution
    dsolve:    Warning: no solutions found
```

With `alias`, you can save on typing and define y as $y(x)$. This makes the formulation of a differential equation somewhat clearer. However, it is no longer possible to write a boundary condition in the form y(x0)=y0, since Maple immediately substitutes y with $y(x)$ and then complains about the resulting expression $y(x)(x0) = ...$. The following example shows that in some cases Maple can also handle higher-order differential equations.

```
alias(y=y(x)):
dsolve(diff(y, x$4) + 5*diff(y,x$2) - 36*y=0, y);
```

```
    dsolve/diffeq/polylinearODE:    trying linear constant coefficient
    dsolve/diffeq/polylinearODE:    linear constant coefficient successful
```

$$y(x) = \_C1\, e^{2\,x} + \_C2\, e^{-2\,x} + \_C3\, \sin(3\,x) + \_C4\, \cos(3\,x)$$

As a conclusion, here is an overview of the types of differential equations with which `dsolve` can usually cope.

- first-order: linear, exact, homogeneous, with separate variables, Bernoulli, Riccati, Clairaut
- second-order: linear, Euler, Bessel, Bernoulli's
- higher-order: linear with constant coefficients
- linear systems

In some cases, `dsolve` succeeds in transforming differential equations into one of the above forms by substitution. With partial differential equations, `dsolve` is generally overstretched, although the `liesymm` and `difforms` packages contain commands with which some very special forms of partial differential equations can be processed (although not solved) – more about this in one of the following sections in this chapter.

Numeric solution of differential equations

When dsolve is not capable of solving your differential equation symbolically, you can always hope that the numeric variation of dsolve can handle the equation. The precondition for using the numeric option is, however, that you can formulate enough end and boundary conditions to make a unique solution possible. Furthermore, the differential equation must not contain any symbolic constants.

The result of the numeric variation of dsolve is an interpolation function which behaves like a black box. The function is defined externally as a procedure. You can calculate individual values and represent the curve graphically, but you cannot obtain any information about the internal composition of the function or its validity range, although the latter in particular would be very useful for practical application. There is no possibility of deriving the solution function. Therefore, it is practically impossible to countercheck the correctness of the solution by substituting it into the differential equation and checking the evaluation for different values of t. Although dsolve often finds usable numeric solutions, the lack of any control mechanism whatsoever means that the whole affair is really a game of chance.

For graphic representation of numeric solutions, the plots package provides the odeplot command. This command is described in the following section.

The first example (a damped oscillation) is already known from above. We have chosen on purpose an example that Maple can also solve symbolically. Thus, a comparison between the symbolic and numeric solutions is possible. In the commands below, the differential equation $my'' + cy' + ky = 0$ is defined, where m is the mass, k the spring constant and c the damping coefficient. The symbolic solution of the differential equation is stored in *funcy1* as a function specification (unapply). Subsequently, the location of the oscillating solid is calculated for $t = 3$.

```
restart:
de:=m*diff(y(t), t$2) +c*diff(y(t),t)+k*y(t)=0;
```

$$de := \frac{d^2}{dt^2}y(t) + \frac{d}{dt}y(t) + y(t) = 0$$

```
sol1:=dsolve({de, y(0)=1, D(y)(0)=0}, y(t)):
funcy1:=unapply(rhs(sol1),t):
m:=1: c:=1: k:=1:
evalf(funcy1(3));
```

$$-0.1243547675$$

The numeric solution of the same differential equation is supplied by Maple as a procedure which is subsequently stored in *funcy2*.

```
sol2:=dsolve({de, y(0)=1, D(y)(0)=0}, y(t), numeric);
    sol2:=proc(rkf45_x) ... end

funcy2:=":
```

The evaluation of this function does not simply supply a solution value, but also a sequence of equations for t and $y(t)$. subs must be employed to isolate $y(t)$.

```
funcy2(3);
```

$$[y(t) = -0.1243547644, t = 3.0]$$

```
subs(funcy2(3), y(t));
```

$$-0.1243547644$$

With the complicated-looking seq command, a table is generated which contains the t values $0, 0.2, ..., 2$ and their corresponding y values. Formulation as a list ensures that the order of t and y cannot be arbitrarily confused by Maple, as would be the case if the result of *funcy2* (a sequence!) was used directly.

```
seq([t=n*0.2,
    y=subs(funcy2(n*0.2), y(t))],
    n=0..10):
```

With the array command, the result of seq is transformed into a matrix and clearly displayed.

```
array(["]);
```

$$\begin{bmatrix} t = 0 & y = 1.0 \\ t = 0.2 & y = 0.9813307545 \\ t = 0.4 & y = 0.9305870049 \\ t = 0.6 & y = 0.8554164086 \\ t = 0.8 & y = 0.7629629594 \\ t = 1.0 & y = 0.6597001501 \\ t = 1.2 & y = 0.5513186057 \\ t = 1.4 & y = 0.4426623722 \\ t = 1.6 & y = 0.3377073448 \\ t = 1.8 & y = 0.2395749741 \\ t = 2.0 & y = 0.1505743634 \end{bmatrix}$$

The easiest way of representing the solution graphically is provided by the odeplot command, which will be presented in more detail in the next section.

```
with(plots):
odeplot(funcy2, [t,y(t)], 0..10);
```

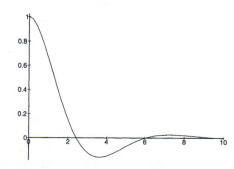

Things become more difficult when the deviation between the numeric and symbolic solutions is to be drawn, as in the following illustration. The subs term for isolation of the y solution value is already known from the last but one command for generating the table. The quotes are used to prevent Maple from carrying out this substitution before the different t values are inserted, which would lead to an error message.

The illustration on the right shows the minimal deviation between the symbolic and numeric solutions. (Do not be frightened by the form of the curve. Look at the scale of the y axis!)

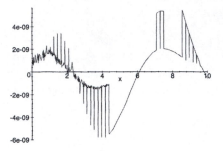

```
plot(funcy1(x)-
     'subs(funcy2(x),y(t))',
     x=0..10);
```

The second example is more complex. The equation system describes a moving proton in a magnetic field (for example, in a particle accelerator). The system of differential equations has been formulated in vector notation in order to save on typing. Maple is capable of solving this equation system both symbolically and numerically; in this example, however, we are only interested in the numeric result.

```
with(linalg):

m:=1.6e-27:                    # mass of a proton [kg]
q:=1.6e-19:                    # charge [Coulomb]
bz:=1:                         # magnetic field in z-direction [Tesla]
r:=vector([x(t), y(t), z(t)]): # position of the proton
v:=map(diff, r, t):            # speed
a:=map(diff, v, t):            # acceleration
b:=vector([0,0,bz]):           # magnetic field

sys:=evalm(m*a - q*crossprod(v,b)):
de:=seq(sys[i]=0, i=1..3);
```

$$de := 1.6 \times 10^{-27} \frac{d^2}{dt^2} x(t) - 1.6 \times 10^{-19} \frac{d}{dt} y(t) = 0,$$

$$1.6 \times 10^{-27} \frac{d^2}{dt^2} y(t) + 1.6 \times 10^{-19} \frac{d}{dt} x(t) = 0,$$

$$1.6 \times 10^{-27} \frac{d^2}{dt^2} z(t) = 0$$

```
conditions:=x(0)=0, y(0)=0, z(0)=0, D(x)(0)=1e8, D(y)(0)=0, D(z)(0)=1e6:
sol:=dsolve({de, conditions}, convert(r,set), numeric);
     sol:=proc(rkf45_x) end
```

As the solution for a given t value, Maple now supplies a set of four equations. What surprisingly causes many problems is the graphic representation of this solution. The `odeplot` command which is specially designed for drawing numeric solutions of differential equations is hopelessly overstretched by this solution. It can draw three-dimensional curves of the form $[x(t), y(t), t]$, but not curves of the form $[x(t), y(t), z(t)]$. Even the attempt to represent these equations in space via spacecurve fails. spacecurve is obviously not capable of calculating the values of x, y and z correctly.

```
sol(1e-8);
```

$$\left[t = .1\,10^{-7}, x(t) = .8414709861286803, \frac{\partial}{\partial t}\,x(t) = .5403023068318053\,10^8, \right.$$

$$y(t) = -.4596976931681948, \frac{\partial}{\partial t}\,y(t) = -.8414709861286806\,10^8,$$

$$\left. z(t) = .01000000000000000, \frac{\partial}{\partial t}\,z(t) = .1000000\,10^7 \right]$$

```
with(plots):
spacecurve(['subs(sol(t), x(t))', 'subs(sol(t), y(t))', 'subs(sol(t), z(t))'],
        t=0..1e-7);
```

In order to obtain a drawing in spite of all this, seq is used to generate an embedded list of 100 coordinate points of the curve in the range $t = 0$ to $t = 10^{-7}$. By using the internal graphics structures of Maple directly, it is possible to represent these data points as a three-dimensional continuous line. (See also Chapter 32 where the internal representation of graphics is discussed.)

```
data:=[seq(
        [subs(sol(n*1e-9), x(t)),
        subs(sol(n*1e-9), y(t)),
        subs(sol(n*1e-9), z(t))],
        n=0..100)]:

PLOT3D(CURVES(data), AXESSTYLE(BOX),
        COLOR(RGB,0,0,0));
```

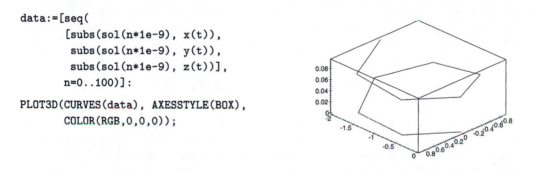

The drawing looks surprisingly angular. Although Maple displays the results with 16 digits (Digits has been left unchanged at 10), it supplies the same results for $t = 25 * 10^{-9}$ and $t = 26 * 10^{-9}$ (two arbitrary test values).

```
subs(sol(25e-9), x(t)), subs(sol(26e-9), x(t));
```

$$0.5984721468178301, 0.5984721468178301$$

Increasing the calculation precision to 16 digits does not change the number of digits in the result, but changes the actual precision. At the same time, calculation time increases many times over.

```
Digits:=16: sol:=dsolve({de, conditions}, convert(r,set), numeric):
subs(sol(25e-9), x(t)), subs(sol(26e-9), x(t));
```

$$0.5984721441039560, 0.5155013718214638$$

When the `data=...` and `PLOT3D(...)` commands shown above are repeated, Maple supplies the drawing on the right (after several minutes).

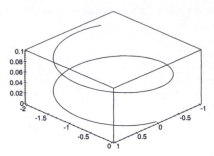

Graphic representation of differential equations

In principle, Maple handles two different types of graphics commands for representation of differential equations. `odeplot` from the `plots` package tries to represent the numeric solution of a
differential equation. In contrast to this, the commands from the `DEtools` package can draw phase
plane and individual phase curves of differential equations *without* solving the differential equation
first. All the graphics commands presented here have one irritating feature in common: their computing times are very high. You should not therefore be unduly surprised when you have to wait for
a minute and more for simple-looking drawings even on a powerful computer.

Graphic representation of numeric solutions of differential equations

The two examples in the last section have shown that graphic representation of numeric solutions
is more difficult than it would appear at first sight. In many cases, the `odeplot` command can
facilitate this task. The solution function is specified in the first parameter of this command. The
second parameter contains a list of variables to be drawn, for example $[t, y(t)]$. The third parameter
contains the drawing range for the control variable (here, t), where only the form `a..b` is allowed,
not `t=a..b`.

In the first example, the differential equation
$y' + 3y = \sin(t^2)$ is solved numerically. The
graphic representation of the solution does not
cause problems.

```
sol:=dsolve(
  {diff(y(t),t)+3*y(t)=sin(t)^2,
   y(0)=0}, y(t), numeric):

with(plots):
odeplot(sol, [t, y(t)], 0..3);
```

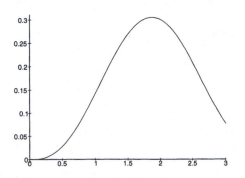

The second example which deals with the differential equation system $x' = -y, y' = x + sin(t)$ is more interesting:

```
sol:=dsolve(
  {diff(y(t),t)=x(t)+sin(t), diff(x(t),t)=-y(t),  x(0)=0, y(0)=0},
  {x(t), y(t)}, numeric);
  sol:=proc (rkf45_x) ... end
```

The first illustration represents x over t.

```
odeplot(sol, [t, x(t)], 0..20);
```

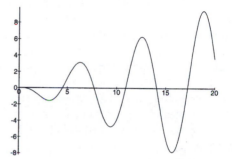

The second illustration shows the same solution, but in the view y over x, with t cycling through the values from 0 to 20. In order to make this drawing look reasonable, some additional options had to be employed (see Chapter 19). In particular, view causes the left part of the drawing ($x < 0$) to be shown as well.

```
odeplot(sol, [x(t), y(t)], 0..20,
   view=[-10..10, -10..10],
   numpoints=500,
   scaling=constrained);
```

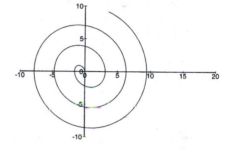

In the third illustration, the result is finally displayed in three dimensions.

```
odeplot(sol, [t, x(t), y(t)],
  0..20, shading=none, axes=boxed);
```

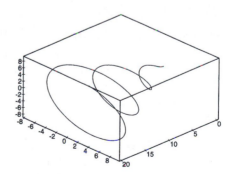

Drawing phase plane and phase curves of differential equations

The DEtools package contains several commands which can be used to represent differential equations graphically (without determining their solution). These commands also function for a vast number of differential equations which cannot be solved with dsolve. The following commands can be used:

dfieldplot	draws a phase plane in arrow representation.
phaseportrait	draws the phase plane plus individual phase curves.
DEplot	graphically represents a common DEQ.
DEplot3d	represents the DEQ in three dimensions.
PDEplot	draws a quasi-linear partial first-order DEQ.

Note: The commands have been completely revised in Release 4, but it is difficult to understand why the names of many commands and most of the options had to be changed as well. Practically all the commands that worked in Release 3 provoke various error messages from the new version of the DEtools package. Specifically, the short notations used in Release 3 are no longer accepted as correct input.

All commands are passed the differential equation (or the system of differential equations) in the first parameter, the variable list in the second parameter, and the independent variable (mostly t) in the third parameter. Any further parameters depend on the command.

The commands can handle individual differential equations of the form $y' = f(y, t)$ (with $y = y(t)$) and differential equation systems of the form $x' = f1(x, y, t), y' = f2(x, y, t)$ (with $x = x(t)$ and $y = y(t)$). DEplot and PDEplot also support even more complex differential equations – see the examples below.

In most commands, starting conditions can or must be specified. Two notations are possible: the extended variation is $\{y(t0) = y0, y(t1) = y1, ...\}$ or $\{[x(t0) = x0, y(t0) = y0], [...], ...\}$ for a system of two differential equations. The short notation is $\{[t0, y0], [t1, y1], ...\}$ or $\{[t0, x0, y0], [...], ...\}$.

Important options for the commands are color for setting the colours of arrows (for example color= sin(y)), linecolor for setting the colour of phase curves, arrow for setting the arrowhead shape (SMALL, MEDIUM, LARGE, LINE or NONE), dirgrid for setting the number of arrows (the default setting is dirgrid=[20,20]) plus stepsize for changing the step width for the numeric calculation methods. Furthermore, all options described in the two following chapters for finishing 2D and 3D graphics can be used.

Hint 1: The commands fieldplot and gradientplot from the plots package represent vector and gradient fields in a similar way to the commands discussed here (again with arrows). The commands are described in Chapter 27 on vector analysis.

Hint 2: A large number of sample applications of the commands and in particular of the meaning of the numerous options can be found in the files Deplot.mws, Deplot3d.mws and Pdeplot.mws in the Examples directory of Maple.

The illustration on the right shows the phase plane for the differential equation $y' = \sin(y)$.

```
restart: with(DEtools):
dfieldplot(diff(y(t),t)=sin(y(t)),
   [y(t)], t=-1..5, y=-1..4);
```

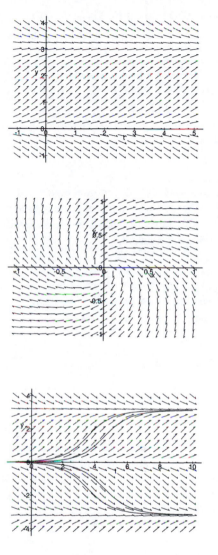

In the second example of `dfieldplot`, the differential equation system $x' = \sin(x) + y, y' = \sin(y) - x$ is shown. When no drawing range is specified for x and y, Maple automatically shows the phase plane for the range between $(-1, -1)$ and $(1, 1)$.

```
dfieldplot(
   [diff(x(t),t)=sin(x(t))+y(t),
    diff(y(t),t)=sin(y(t))-x(t)],
   [x(t),y(t)],
   t=0..1, x=-1..1, y=-1..1);
```

`phaseportrait` draws individual curves of the phase plane. The differential equation is specified as in `dfieldplot`. In addition, at least one starting condition for the starting point of a phase curve must be specified in a set.

```
phaseportrait(diff(y(t),t)=sin(y(t)),
   [y(t)], t=-1..10, [[y(4)=1],
   [y(4)=2], [y(4)=-1], [y(4)=-2]]);
```

The second example of `phaseportrait` below shows some solution curves of the differential equation system $x' = \sin(x) + y, y' = \sin(y) - x$. With `seq`, several starting conditions have been formulated in the short notation $[t0, x0, y0]$. The `stepsize` option is needed in order to prevent the phase curves from becoming angular. The `arrows` option ensures that no arrows are drawn for the phase plane apart from the phase curves. The `linecolor` option forces a black representation of the phase curves (which is particularly sensible for printing out the graphics). For technical reasons, the phase curves appear much thicker on screen than they will actually be in print.

```
start:=seq([0,0,n*0.1], n=0..10);
```

$$start := [0,0,0],[0,0,0.1],\ldots,[0,0,1.0]$$

```
phaseportrait(
  [diff(x(t),t)=sin(x(t))+y(t),
  diff(y(t),t)=sin(y(t))-x(t)],
  [x(t),y(t)], t=0..10, {start},
  stepsize=0.1, arrows=NONE,
  linecolor=black);
```

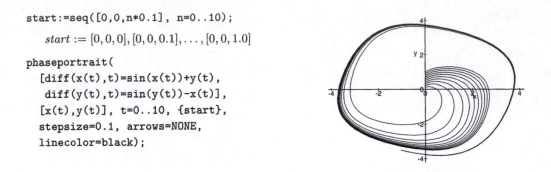

DEplot represents differential equations, resorting to phaseportrait and dfieldplot. The illustration below shows the phase plane plus some curves for the differential equation $x' = 1 + x - x^2$ for $x = x(t)$. With the alias abbreviations for x and y, typing effort for formulating the differential equations is reduced.

```
alias(x=x(t), y=y(t)):
DEplot(diff(x,t)=1+x-x^2, [x],
  t=0..3, {seq([0,n/2], n=-3..5)},
  x=-1..3, dirgrid=[10,10],
  arrows=THICK);
```

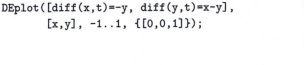

DEplot is also suitable for systems of two first-order differential equations. In the example, the differential equation system $x' = -y, y' = x - y$ is specified by an array. The illustration below shows the phase plane and a phase curve for $x(0) = 0, y(0) = 1$.

```
DEplot([diff(x,t)=-y, diff(y,t)=x-y],
      [x,y], -1..1, {[0,0,1]});
```

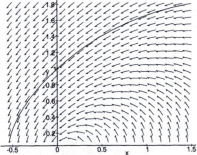

DEplot3d represents differential equation systems in three dimensions. The following illustration shows the differential equation system $x' = \sin(y) - x/10, y' = x$. The above alias abbreviations still apply to x and y.

```
DEplot3d(
  [diff(x,t)=sin(y)-x/10, diff(y,t)=x],
  [x,y], 0..40, {[0,1,1]},
  stepsize=0.1, linecolor=black);
```

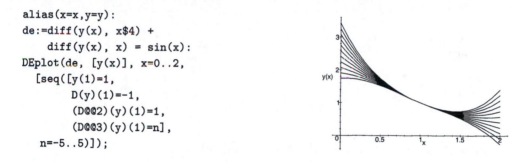

The illustration below shows a family of curves for the differential equation $y'''' + y' = sin(x)$ for $y = y(x)$. With seq, an embedded list is created that contains the starting parameters $y(1) = 1, y'(1) = 1, y''(1) = -1$ and $y'''(1) = n$ for n between -5 and 5.

```
alias(x=x,y=y):
de:=diff(y(x), x$4) +
    diff(y(x), x) = sin(x):
DEplot(de, [y(x)], x=0..2,
  [seq([y(1)=1,
        D(y)(1)=-1,
        (D@@2)(y)(1)=1,
        (D@@3)(y)(1)=n],
  n=-5..5)]);
```

Partial differential equations

Since Release 4, the pdesolve command can be used to solve partial differential equations. However, you should not (yet) have too many expectations for the command: it can only cope with very few types of equation. Differential equations from second order onward overstretch pdesolve almost without exception; even types of equation that occur quite frequently or whose solution is known, such as the wave equation or the Laplace equation, remain unsolved. We can certainly look forward to improvements in future versions. Unlike dsolve, pdesolve does not have a numeric variation; thus, the search for a solution can only be carried out symbolically.

In order to facilitate writing partial differential equations, the abbreviation f is introduced for the function $f(x, y)$. pde contains the equation $x f_x + y f_y = f$.

```
restart: alias(f=f(x,y)):
pde:=x*diff(f,x) + y*diff(f,y)=f;
```

$$pde := x\left(\frac{\partial}{\partial x} f\right) + y\left(\frac{\partial}{\partial y} f\right) = f$$

```
sol:=pdesolve(pde, f);
```

$$sol := f = \_F1\left(\frac{y}{x}\right) x$$

The solution of the differential equation succeeds at the first attempt. Also, a subsequent countercheck by way of insertion into the original equation and simplification leads to the required result 0.

```
subs(sol, pde);
```

$$x\,(\frac{\partial}{\partial x}\,\_F1(\frac{y}{x})\,x) + y\,(\frac{\partial}{\partial y}\,\_F1(\frac{y}{x})\,x) =$$

$$\_F1(\frac{y}{x})\,x$$

```
simplify(lhs(")-rhs("));
```

$$0$$

There are also no problems with the one-dimensional wave equation $u_{tt} = a^2\,u_{xx}$, where we have additionally inserted the noise function $\sin(t)$. The two-dimensional wave equation $u_{tt} = a^2\,(u_{xx} + u_{yy})$ with $u = u(x, y, t)$, however, can no longer be solved.

```
alias(u=u(t,x)):
pde:=diff(u,t$2)=
a^2*diff(u,x$2)+sin(t):
sol:=pdesolve(pde,u);
```

$$sol := u = t - \sin(t) + \_F1(x + a\,t) +$$

$$\_F2(x - a\,t)$$

```
subs(sol,pde):
simplify(lhs(")-rhs("));
```

$$0$$

Reference: Further examples of the application of `pdesolve` are contained in the file `part2\chap18.mws` (on the enclosed CD-ROM) and the Maple file `examples\pdesolve.mws`.

Graphic representation of partial differential equations

The `PDEplot` command from the `DEtools` package is capable of graphically representing quasi-linear partial differential equations of the form $Pz_x + Qz_y = R$. Here, z is a function of x and y; P, Q and R are functions of x, y and z.

In the first parameter, the command is passed a list of the three functions P, Q and R, in the second parameter a list of the three variables (for example, $[x, y, z]$). The third parameter again contains a list of three functions which specify a parametric curve in space. In the last parameter, the required range of the control variable of the space curve is specified. Maple now draws a solution surface for this curve.

In the example below, a solution surface is drawn for the differential equation $2 * z_x - z * z_y = 1/10$. The solution surface is determined by the space curve $[1 + s, s^2, s]$, where s is cycled through from -2 to 2. The option `numsteps` specifies the number of surface points to be calculated (like `grid` in other `plot` commands). The options `style` and `shading` ensure that the surface is drawn in one colour and with a visibility check (see also Chapter 20).

```
PDEplot([2,-z,1/10], [x,y,z],
        [1+s,s^2,s], s=-2..2,
     numsteps=[20,20], style=HIDDEN,
     shading=NONE, axes=BOXED);
```

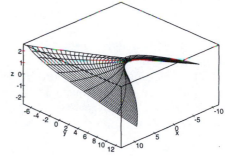

The liesymm and difforms packages

When pdesolve cannot cope with the solution of a differential equation, you can at least use Maple as an aid to the manual processing of the equation. The packages difforms and liesymm provide several commands to support this.

difforms helps with the calculation of differential forms. With the difforms command, individual variables can be defined as constants, scalars, and so on. Subsequently, d constructs the outer derivative of multi-variable functions that contain these variables. The &^ operator is used to write the alternating hook product. Expressions containing this operator can subsequently be simplified with difforms.

A wider application area is covered by the liesymm package whose function range includes difforms in many points. This package allows processing of differential forms and handles the same operator for constructing the hook product as difforms. Construction of differential forms for a given partial differential equation is largely automated with makeforms. determine calculates the characteristic system of a partial differential equation. This system can then be simplified with autosimp. In the most favourable case (which unfortunately only occurs very rarely), autosimp supplies the solution to the differential equation. Otherwise, the resulting equation system must be further processed manually.

Reference: Additional information on both packages is contained in the online help. A true example, namely the solution to the differential equation $u_t + u * u_x + u_{xxx} = 0$ for $u = u(x, t)$ by means of the commands of the liesymm package, can be found in the Maple book by André Heck (see References at the end of this book).

Syntax summary

`dsolve({de}, {var}, options);`
  tries to solve the specified differential equation. If a whole system of differential equations or additional starting conditions are specified, *de* must be written as a set. The variables (functions) of the differential equation must be recognizable as functions, that is, must be written in the form `x(t)`. Derivatives can be formed either with `diff` or with `D`. Initial conditions are formulated in the form `x(t0)=x0, D(x)(t0)=dx0, D(D(x))(t0)=ddx0`, and so on.

  The command supports the following options:
  `explicit`: write the result explicitly
  `output=basis`: write the result as a list of general and special solutions
  `serial`: formulate the solution via a series development
  `laplace`: determine the solution via a Laplace transformation
  `numeric`: numeric solution attempts

  When the `numeric` option is specified, numerous other options for setting the approximation method are allowed: `method=rkf45` or `=dverk78` for selection of the approximation method, `aerr`, `rerr` and `minr` for controlling the minimal absolute and relative error, and so on. See online help `?dsolve,numeric`.

`DESol({de}, {var}, {randbed});`
  represents the (non-calculable) solution to a differential equation. `DESol` terms can be differentiated, integrated or converted into series.

`pdesolve(de, var);`
  tries to solve the specified partial differential equation. For the solution function, the dependent variables must be specified, for example $u(x, t)$. `pdesolve` does not handle any option for numeric search of solutions; boundary and starting conditions cannot be formulated.

Graphic representation of differential equations

`with(plots):`
`odeplot(sol, {vars}, t=start..end);`
  represents the numeric solution to a differential equation in two dimensions (`vars=t, x(t)` or `x(t),y(t)`) or in three dimensions (`vars=t,x(t),y(t)`). `sol` must be the result of a `dsolve` command with the `numeric` option.

`with(DEtools):`
`DEplot(de, [var(t)], trange, init);`
  represents a first-order differential equation in graphic format. The differential equation must be indicated as with `dsolve`. *trange* specifies the drawing range for the dependent variable (mostly t). `init` specifies starting conditions for individual phase curves in the form $\{[t0, y0], [t1, x1], ...\}$.

```
DEplot([de1,de2], [var1(t), var2(t)], trange, init);
```
   draws a system of two first-order differential equations.

```
DEplot3d([des], [var1(t), var2(t)], trange, init);
DEplot3d([des], [var1(t), var2(t), var3(t)], trange, init);
```
   graphically represents a system of differential equations in three dimensions. (In the first syntax variation, t represents the third coordinate.)

```
PDEplot(pde, vars, param, prange);
```
   represents the quasi-linear partial differential equation $Pz_x + Qz_y = R$ in graphic format. The differential equation is written in the form $[P, Q, R]$, that is, the syntax of this command is fundamentally different from all other `DEtools` commands. *param* contains the list of three functions which describe a parametric curve through space. In *prange*, the range of the control variable of this curve is specified. `PDEplot` draws the solution surface for this curve.

```
dfieldplot(de, [var], trange);
```
   draws the phase plane of the differential equation in arrow representation.

```
phaseportrait(de, [var], trange, init);
```
   draws one or more phase curves of the differential equation that are determined by the starting conditions in *init*.

Chapter 19

Graphics I: 2D graphics

Graphics is such a wide field that the description of commands and options had to be spread across several chapters. This chapter and the next deal with basic commands for the representation of function curves and point sets. This chapter introduces the commands for two-dimensional graphics, the next chapter those for three-dimensional graphics.

Chapter 31 describes several special commands (representation of complex functions, graphics in different coordinate systems) and discusses the subject of animation. Chapter 32 deals with the internal structure of graphics and the possibility of programming your own graphics commands.

Furthermore, special forms of graphics are dealt with in the corresponding chapters, such as the representation of differential equations in the previous chapter, the representation of statistical data in Chapter 21, vector fields in Chapter 27, and so on. Information on how to print graphics can be found in Chapter 2.

Setting options

The first step towards obtaining an impressive illustration is normally the input of a (in most cases quite simple) plot command. However, the result of this command will often not be satisfactory. For this reason, Maple provides countless options which allow illustration details to be adjusted.

There are two ways of setting the options: the first and easier variation is to select the options in a graphics window by means of various menu items. This procedure is very user-friendly, but it has two disadvantages: first, not all options provided by Maple can be set in this way; second, the outcome cannot be reproduced. When the graphics command is to be executed again at a later stage, all the options must be set again in the graphics window.

For this reason, the options can also be specified directly during input of the command. This assumes, however, that you know the most important options and settings. The syntax summaries of this and the next chapter give a very compact and clearly structured overview of all important options and settings.

A final remark: when you do not specify any options, how graphics are displayed on screen and in print depends on your version of Maple. The reason for this is that the default settings of several options vary with the various versions of Maple (as well as the graphics capabilities of the computer on which that version is running).

Overview of this chapter

The central point of this chapter is the universal command `plot` which can be controlled with a large number of options. Many of these options can also be used in other graphics commands. While `plot` is available immediately after starting Maple, some other commands (such as `implicitplot` or `display`) are located in the `plots` package which must be activated with the `with(plots)` command.

```
plot(func, x=x0..x1);
```
draws a function curve.

```
plot([fx, fy, t=t0..t1]);
```
draws a parametric function.

```
implicitplot(...);
```
draws a function defined implicitly (through an equation).

```
plot(..., style=point);
```
draws a point set.

```
textplot([x,y,'text']);
```
outputs a line of text at an arbitrary position.

```
display(...);
```
combines several graphics into one illustration.

Drawing function curves with plot

The `plot` command has already been used many times without further explanation. It is an easy to handle universal command whose main application is to draw simple curves.

The following commands are equivalent and show the flexible syntax of `plot`. The command can handle both function specifications and normal functions. When no drawing range is specified in the second parameter, Maple automatically draws the range between -10 and 10.

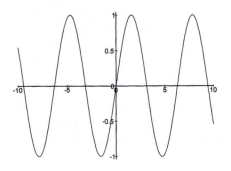

```
plot(sin);
plot(sin, -10..10);
plot(sin(x), x=-10..10);
```

If you want to draw several curves at the same time, you must write these as a set (curly brackets) or as a list (square brackets).

```
plot({sin(x), x^2/20}, x=0..2*Pi);
```

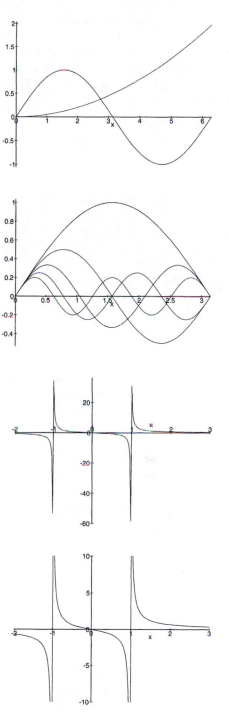

The illustration on the right shows the curves $\sin(n * x)/n$ for n between 1 and 5. In order to save on typing, the functions are generated with seq.

```
plot({seq(sin(n*x)/n, n=1..5)},
    x=0..Pi);
```

When the curve to be drawn contains discontinuity points, Maple often has difficulties finding a reasonable range for the y axis.

```
plot(x/(x^2-1), x=-2..3);
```

With the third parameter, you can limit the drawing range. If the vertical lines at the discontinuity points ($x = -1, x = 1$) bother you, you must specify the option discont=true.

```
plot(x/(x^2-1), x=-2..3, -10..10);
```

plot is even capable of drawing functions in an infinite (!) x axis range. Internally, this is achieved through a transformation similar to the arctan function. Obviously, this leads to distortions, but a rough estimate of the function course is still possible.

```
plot({x,1+x^2,2+x^x},
    x=0..infinity, 0..infinity);
```

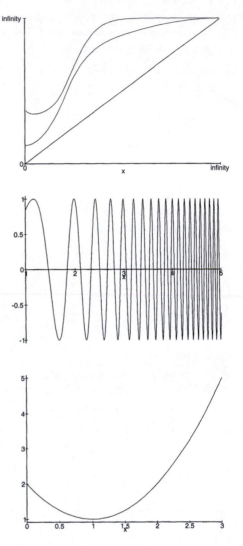

With very complicated curves, the number of data points to be calculated may have to be increased by means of the numpoints option or by setting resolution=n − otherwise, the curve will look too angular.

```
plot(sin(x^3), x=1..5,
    numpoints=1500);
```

plot can only be used when a numeric calculation of the function values is possible. In the example below, the coefficients a, b and c have been temporarily set through subs.

```
plot(subs(a=1, b=-2, c=2,
        a*x^2+b*x+c),
    x=0..3);
```

plot first evaluates the function specified in the first parameter and then inserts numerical values. In some cases, this process leads to errors, when evaluation only makes sense after inserting the values. In such situations, the function to be drawn must be enclosed in quotes or bracketed with evaln.

For positive values of x, f is defined as $\sin(x)$, and for negative values of x as x. Which of the two function specifications applies only becomes clear when inserting the actual values.

```
f:=proc(x)
    if x>0 then sin(x) else x fi
end:
```

```
plot(f(x), x=-2..5);
    Error, (in f) cannot evaluate
    boolean
```

```
plot('f(x)', x=-2..5);
```

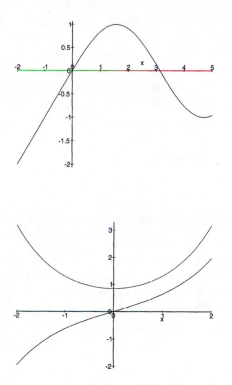

plot is not capable of drawing complex functions. You must specify explicitly whether you want to see the real or the imaginary part, the value of the function, and so on.

```
plot(sin(I*x), x=-1..1);
    Warning in iris-plot: empty plot
```

```
plot({Re(sin(1+I*x)),
    Im(sin(1+I*x))}, x=-2..2);
```

Parametric functions

In order to draw parametric functions in which the x and y coordinates are defined by two separate functions of a third variable, a special variation of plot must be used: in the first parameter, a list (square brackets!) of the two functions and the drawing range is passed. When several parametric functions are to be drawn at the same time, the first parameter is $\{[fx1, fy1, t = ...], [fx2, fy2, t = ...], ...\}$.

The illustration on the right shows the parametric curve $(x, y) = (t\cos(t), t\sin(t))$ for $0 \le t \le 6\pi$. The scaling option in the command below prevents the drawing from being distorted.

```
plot([t*cos(t), t*sin(t),
    t=0..6*Pi],
    scaling=constrained);
```

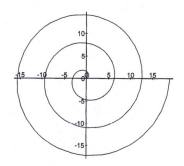

By means of the option `coords=polar`, parametric functions are drawn in polar coordinates. In this case, the first parameter of `plot`
is $[fr, fphi, phi = ...]$. (More information on
the use of different coordinate systems can be
found in Chapter 31.)

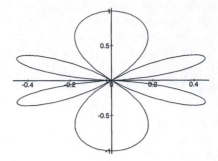

```
plot([sin(phi)*sin(3*phi), phi,
     phi=0..2*Pi],
   coords=polar);
```

Implicitly defined functions

In the previous examples, the functions to be drawn were explicitly known in the form $y = y(x)$ or
$x = x(t), y = y(t)$. In contrast, implicit functions are defined by way of an equation, for example
$x^2 + y^2 = 1$ for a circle. In order to represent such equations graphically, the `plots` package
provides the `implicitplot` command. In the first parameter of `implicitplot`, the equation to be
drawn is specified. You can also specify a function or function specification which is then set to 0.
In the next two parameters, the drawing range for the x and y coordinates must be specified.

The two commands below are equivalent. In the
first case, the implicit equation is specified directly; in the second case it is specified through
a function specification which Maple sets to 0.

```
with(plots):
implicitplot(x^2-x=y^3-3*y,
             x=-3..3, y=-2..3);
implicitplot((x,y)-> x^2-x-y^3+3*y,
             -3..3, -2..3);
```

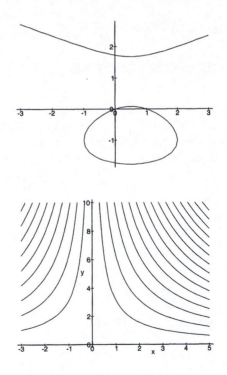

In complicated functions, the curve may become very angular. In this case, the number of points to be calculated can be increased
either with the option `numpoints=n` or with
`grid=[nx,ny]`.

```
implicitplot(sin(x*y),
    x=-3..5, y=0..10, grid=[80,80]);
```

Representation of point sets and continuous lines

Instead of a function, `plot` can also be passed a points set in the form $[[x1, y1], [x2, y2]...]$. `plot` then joins these points with a continuous line. This variation of `plot` is particularly suitable for inserting single lines (asymptotes, tangents, and so on) into existing drawings. An example can be found in the next section, on 'Overlaying several drawings'.

The illustration on the right shows a line through the points $(1, 1), (2, 2), (3, 2)$ and $(4, 1)$. When closed lines are to be drawn, the first and last points must be the same.

```
plot([[1,1], [2,2],
      [3,2], [4,1]]);
```

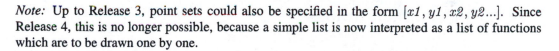

Note: Up to Release 3, point sets could also be specified in the form $[x1, y1, x2, y2...]$. Since Release 4, this is no longer possible, because a simple list is now interpreted as a list of functions which are to be drawn one by one.

When `plot` is used with the option `style=point`, points are drawn instead of lines. This option applies both when drawing normal functions and when generating representations of explicitly enumerated point sets. An essential disadvantage of representing point sets with `plot` is that you cannot influence the point size. When only a few data points are to be shown, these are much too small and barely perceptible. In Chapter 32 we therefore show how an improved command for representation of points can be programmed.

With the option `style=point`, the curve $\sin(x)$ is represented by way of numerous minute points.

```
plot(sin(x),x=0..2*Pi, style=point);
```

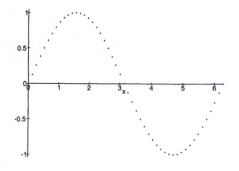

In the following example, `seq` is used to create a list of 100 randomly determined data points.

```
data:=seq([rand(100)(),
          rand(100)()], n=1..100):
```

$$data := [93, 44], [42, 8], \ldots, [28, 44]$$

```
plot([data], style=point);
```

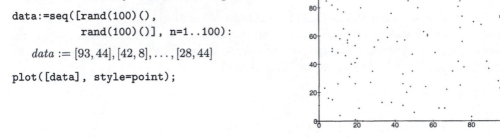

Besides `plot`, you can also use the commands `listplot` and `pointplot` from the `plots` package to draw point lists. Neither of the two commands, however, has any advantage over `plot`, apart from the fact that coordinate lists can also be specified in the form $[x1, y1, x2, y2...]$. `listplot` differs from `pointplot` only in that the points are joined by a line as standard: the option `style=point` eliminates even this difference.

Overlaying several drawings

Frequently one needs to combine several drawings by laying them on top of each other. For this purpose, Maple provides the `display` command from the `plots` package. In order to use this command, the individual drawings are first stored in variables. Subsequently, these variables are passed to `display` in a list. Although the application of `display` looks very easy, frequent difficulties arise in practice, since `display` inexplicably changes individual options or other formal details of the individual drawings (see the third example).

In the following illustration, a tangent of gradient 1 is to be overlaid against the function $x + \sin(x)$. With the first commands, the function is defined and the contact point of the tangent is calculated. Subsequently, the function is drawn for the range in question and stored in $p1$. The tangent is drawn with a further `plot` command and stored in $p2$. `display` then shows the two drawings together; the `constrained` option ensures that the tangent is actually drawn with a 45 degree gradient.

```
with(plots);
f:=x+sin(x): df:=diff(f,x):
x0:=evalf(solve(df=1));
```

$$x0 := 1.570796327$$

```
y0:=evalf(subs(x=x0, f));
```

$$y0 := 2.570796327$$

```
p1:=plot(x+sin(x), x=0..4):
p2:=plot([[x0-0.5, y0-0.5],
          [x0+0.5, y0+0.5]]):
display([p1, p2],
        scaling=constrained);
```

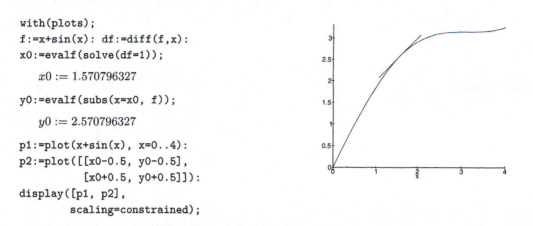

The second example is slightly more extensive. It shows a point set which represents a sine curve, together with a third-order approximation polynomial constructed with the `fit` command. This command is part of the `share` library and is explained in Chapter 22. The `zip` command takes the separate lists for the x and y coordinates and combines them into a common list of the form $[[x1, y1], [x2, y2], ...]$, as required for the `plot` command.

```
datax:=[seq(i*0.3,i=1..20)]:
datay:=map(sin, datax):
data:=zip((x,y)->[x,y], datax,
                        datay):
with(share): readshare(fit,numerics):
f:=fit(datax, datay,
       [1,x,x^2, x^3], x);
```

$$f := -0.317 + 2.07x - 0.938^2 + 0.0995x^3$$

```
p1:=plot(data, style=point):
p2:=plot(f, x=0..6):
display([p1,p2]);
```

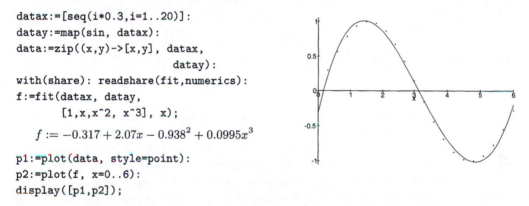

Since Release 4, `display` can not only overlay several drawings, but also place illustrations in a raster side by side or below each other. The individual drawings must be passed to `display` in an array structure. The strange legend on the y axis of the first drawing in the following illustration is caused by a bug in `display`. When $p1$ is drawn without `display`, the axis is labelled properly.

```
p1:=plot(sin(x),x=-Pi..Pi):
p2:=plot(cos(x),x=-Pi..Pi):
p3:=plot(sinh(x),x=-Pi..Pi):
p4:=plot(cosh(x),x=-Pi..Pi):
display(array(1..2,1..2,
        [[p1,p2],[p3,p4]]));
```

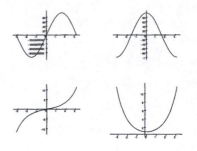

Labelling of graphics

The simplest form of labelling is the `title` option. The character string specified in this option is displayed at the top of the drawing. Similarly, the `labels` option is used for labelling the two coordinate axes.

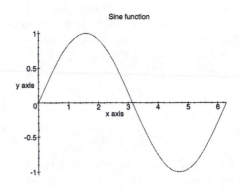

```
plot(sin(x), x=0..2*Pi,
     title='Sine function',
     labels=['x axis', 'y axis');
```

Many more layout possibilities are provided by the `textplot` command from the `plots` package. With this command, text can be output at an arbitrary position. The text is specified in the form `[x,y,'text']` and is centred both vertically and horizontally relative to the coordinate point. The option `align=...` can be used to obtain a different alignment. Possible settings are ABOVE, BELOW, LEFT and RIGHT. When horizontal and vertical alignments are to be combined, the settings must be specified in a sequence (not in a list, as wrongly stated in the online help): `align = {LEFT, BELOW}`.

Labelling generated with `textplot` must be combined with the illustration proper by means of `display`.

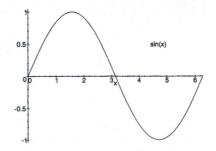

```
p1:=plot(sin(x), x=0..2*Pi):
p2:=textplot([3*Pi/2, 0.5,'sin(x)']):
display([p1, p2]);
```

The four options `font`, `titlefont`, `axesfont` and `labelfont` are used to set the fonts for texts occurring in a drawing. `font` only applies to texts generated with `textplot`, `titlefont` for the title, `axesfont` for the figures at the coordinate axes and `labelfont` for labelling the coordinate axes.

Fonts are specified in a syntax whose inconsistency is hard to match. In general, the three principal syntax variations are [font] or [font, size] or [font, style, size]. Four fonts are available, namely COURIER, HELVETICA, TIMES and SYMBOL.

No style can be specified for SYMBOL. COURIER and HELVETICA allow the application of BOLD, OBLIQUE (italic) or BOLDOBLIQUE (bold and italic) style. TIMES, in principle, has the same styles, except that they are called BOLD, ITALIC and BOLDITALIC. As a particular speciality, now you have to specify ROMAN when the style is to remain unchanged but the size is to be altered. In total, the following possibilities exist:

```
font=[COURIER or HELVETICA or TIMES or SYMBOL]
font=[COURIER or HELVETICA or SYMBOL, size]
font=[TIMES, ROMAN or BOLD or ITALIC or BOLDITALIC, size]
font=[COURIER or HELVETICA, BOLD or OBLIQUE or BOLDOBLIQUE, size]
```

Font size is specified in points. The specification, however, refers to a printout in A4 format. When the drawing is written to a PostScript file and the file is reduced during embedding in the text (as in this book), the labelling becomes smaller too! Therefore, you must specify proportionally higher values for the font size in order to obtain the required effect.

The illustration on the right again resorts to the two plots *p1* and *p2* of the previous example, but changes the labelling size.

```
display([p1, p2],
        font=[TIMES, ITALIC, 50],
        axesfont=[TIMES,ROMAN,30]);
```

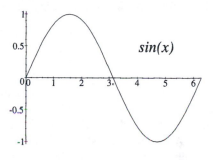

Representation options

Some options have already been introduced in the previous sections. With numpoints=n, resolution=n and grid=[nx,ny], the drawing precision for complex graphics can be increased. numpoints specifies the minimum number of data points to be calculated. resolution specifies the resolution of the output medium (normally, the screen). Default is 200; higher values improve quality. grid is suitable for two-dimensional data sets (as occur, for example, in the implicitplot command) and specifies the number of data points in two directions, such as [80, 80] for 6400 points. style specifies how the points of a drawing are to be linked. The standard setting is line; with style=point you can draw point graphics.

A new feature in Release 4 is the availability of plot for drawing several graphics at the same time and differentiating them by way of different line styles. In order to do this, you must specify the

functions to be drawn and the settings for thickness, linestyle, symbolstyle or color as a list.
(Up to Release 3, this could only be done by combining several individual graphics with display.)

With the thickness option, the line thickness in
a drawing can be set to a value between 1 and
3. *Caution*: the default setting is 1 for screen
display, but 2 for printing.

```
plot([seq(sin(x+n*Pi/8),n=1..3)],
    x=0..2*Pi, thickness=[1,2,3]);
```

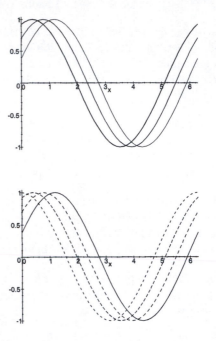

The linestyle option controls the line pattern.
The illustration on the right shows the four possible patterns for printing. For screen display,
there are five different patterns.

```
plot([seq(sin(x+n*Pi/8),n=1..4)],
    x=0..2*Pi, linestyle=[1,2,3,4]);
```

The symbolstyle option determines how the points will look. Besides the standard symbol (a
minute cross), five further symbols are defined for screen display: a square, a bigger cross, a circle,
a lozenge and a minute point. Unfortunately, even in Release 4 it is still not possible to control the
point size. As standard, the symbols are drawn rather small, therefore they are barely distinguishable
(see the following illustration). Chapter 32 on graphics programming will show how to program a
new command, dotplot, which remedies this fault.

```
plot([seq(sin(x+n*Pi/4),n=1..5)],
    x=0..2*Pi, style=point,
    symbol=[BOX, CROSS, CIRCLE,
            DIAMOND, POINT],\\
    numpoints=100);
```

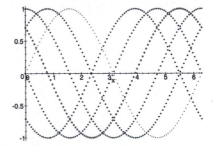

With the color option the colour of the drawing can be set. Predefined colours are black, red,
green, blue, and so on (see online help on ?plot,color). In addition, you can specify colours
using COLOR(RGB,r,g,b) or COLOR(HUE,h). For r, g, b and h, floating point numbers between 0 and
1 must be specified.

When `plot` is used to draw several curves at the same time, the `color` setting applies to all curves. If several curves are to be drawn in colours specified by yourself, the colours must be indicated in a list, as shown in the above examples. Farther-reaching setting possibilities are provided by the `color` option for three-dimensional graphics – this subject will be discussed again in the next chapter.

Two settings exist for the `scaling` option. The default setting unconstrained uses the whole available space for the representation of the drawing. If `constrained` is used, Maple uses the same scaling for the x and y axes. This avoids distortion: circles really look like circles and not like ellipses.

```
implicitplot(x^2+y^2=1, x=-1..1,
    y=-1..1);
```

```
implicitplot(x^2+y^2=1, x=-1..1,
    y=-1..1, scaling=constrained);
```

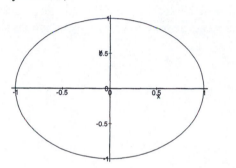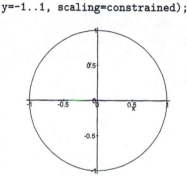

The `axes` option determines the look of the coordinate axes. Normally, these are drawn through the zero points of the coordinate field. The `frame` setting shifts the coordinate axes into the lower left corner. `boxed` frames the drawing on all four sides. With `none`, no coordinate axes are drawn at all.

```
plot([sin(3*t), cos(5*t),
    t=0..2*Pi], axes=boxed);
```

```
plot([sin(3*t), cos(5*t),
    t=0..2*Pi], axes=frame);
```

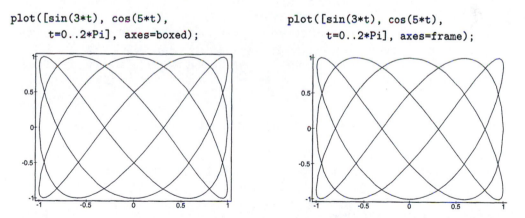

The options `xtickmarks` and `ytickmarks` specify the required number of labelling points on the coordinate axes. Maple only approximately follows your requests since it always tries to label axes at multiples of 1, 2 or 5.

When you repeatedly need certain options, you can set them permanently with the `setoptions` command from the `plots` package. After executing the following command, all further 2D diagrams are framed with a coordinate box.

```
with(plots): setoptions(boxes=boxed):
```

Syntax summary

```
plot(f, x=a..b);
plot({f1, f2...}, x=a..b, c..d, options);
plot([f1, f2...], x=a..b, c..d, options);
```
  draws the function f or the functions $f1$, $f2$... indicated in a set or a list. With $c..d$, the drawing range of the y axis can be limited. From the fourth parameter onward, a number of options can be specified which are described further below.

```
plot([fx, fy, t=a..b], options);
```
  draws the parametric function $(fx(t), fy(t))$ for the specified t range.

```
plot([x0,y0,x1,y1...], options);
plot([[x0,y0],[x1,y1]...], options);
```
  joins the specified coordinate points with a continuous line. When the option `style=points` is specified, `plots` draws points.

```
with(plots):
```
  activates the commands of the `plots` package. This command must be executed prior to using `textplot`, `implicitplot`, `setoptions` and `display`.

```
textplot([x,y,'text']);      textplot([x,y,'text'], align=...);
```
  outputs the specified text centred with regard to the position (x, y). With the `align` option, alignment of the text can be changed. Possible settings are ABOVE, BELOW, LEFT and RIGHT. When the alignment is to be changed both horizontally and vertically, a sequence must be specified.

```
implicitplot(eqn, x=a..b, y=a..b, options);
```
  draws the implicit function of x and y defined by the equation.

```
display([p1, p2, p3 ...], options);
```
  combines the drawings pn into a new drawing, changing the specified options.

```
display(array(1..n, 1..m, [[p11, p12, ...], [p21, p22, ...]], options);
```
  displays the drawings pn in a raster.

Options (alphabetical)

`coords=polar`
> represents the drawing in polar coordinates. This option is only suited for the `plot` variation for drawing parametric functions. The function is then written in the form $[r, \phi, t = ...]$. Further coordinate systems are described in Chapter 31.

`discont=true`
> prevents vertical lines from being drawn at discontinuity points of the function to be output.

`grid=[nx,ny]`
> specifies the number of data points to be calculated for a two-dimensional data set in the x and y directions. Of the commands described in this chapter, it can be used only for `implicitplot`.

`labels=[zx,zy]`
> specifies the labelling of the coordinate axes with a character string each.

`numpoints=n`
> specifies the *minimum* number of data points to be calculated for drawing a function.

`resolution=n`
> specifies the resolution of the drawing medium (default setting 200). With this indication, Maple is usually capable of determining the number of necessary data points.

`title=z`
> specifies the title of the drawing (as a character string).

Representation options (alphabetical)

`axes=...`
> determines the look of the coordinate axes:
> `normal`: the axes go through the 0 point.
> `frame`: the axes are located in the lower left hand corner of the diagram.
> `boxed`: the diagram is completely framed.
> `none`: no coordinate axes are drawn at all.

`axesfont=...`
> changes the fonts of the figures alongside the coordinate axes. See `font`.

`font=...`

    changes the font of texts generated with `textplot`. The upper case letters for the setting of `font` are compulsory! Possible settings are:

    `font=[COURIER or HELVETICA or TIMES or SYMBOL]`

    `font=[COURIER or HELVETICA or SYMBOL, size]`

    `font=[TIMES, ROMAN or BOLD or ITALIC or BOLDITALIC, size]`

    `font=[COURIER or HELVETICA, BOLD or OBLIQUE or BOLDOBLIQUE, size]`

`labelfont=...`

    changes the font for labelling the coordinate axes. See `font`.

`linestyle=n`

    controls the line pattern. n must be assigned a value between 1 and 5.

`scaling=...`

    specifies how the diagram is to be scaled:

    `unconstrained`: uses the entire available space, but leads to distortions (default).

    `constrained`: x and y axes are represented in the same scale.

`style=...`

    specifies how the data is to be represented. Possible settings:

    `line`: representation as continuous line, default.

    `point`: representation as points.

`symbolstyle=...`

    determines the look of symbols in point diagrams. Possible settings are `BOX`, `CROSS`, `CIRCLE`, `DIAMOND` and `POINT`.

`thickness=n`

    controls the line thickness. n must be assigned a value between 1 (thin) and 3 (thick).

`titlefont=...`

    changes the font of the title of the drawing. See `font`.

`xtickmarks=n`
`ytickmarks=n`

    specifies the minimum number of points on the x and y axes Maple is to label.

Note: The names of the options (for example, `scaling`) must be written in lower case letters. Most keywords for setting options, such as `CONSTRAINED`, can be written either in lower case or in upper case letters. Exception: the parameters for setting `font` *must* be written in upper case.

Chapter 20

Graphics II: 3D graphics

This chapter is a continuation of the previous chapter which described two-dimensional graphics commands. Here we will deal with commands for three-dimensional representation of data. The commands are similar to their two-dimensional counterparts, and a large number of options have the same or at least a similar meaning.

A general overview of the subject of graphics and an overview of where the various aspects of this subject are discussed in this book can be found in the introduction to the previous chapter. Now, let us look at the most important commands of this chapter.

`plot3d`
represents functions of the $f(x, y)$ kind by way of three-dimensional surfaces.

`coords=spherical` and `coords=cylindrical`
are two options which allow representation of graphics in sphere or cylinder coordinates.

`spacecurve` and `tubeplot`
draw parametric space curves in the three-dimensional space. In `tubeplot`, the radius of this curve can be varied, whereas in `spacecurve` it is 0 (only one line is drawn).

`surfdata`
draws an arbitrary three-dimensional surface whose coordinate points are specified in a list.

`pointplot`
represents a coordinate list as a three-dimensional curve of points.

For the rest, the emphasis is on the numerous options for controlling the above-mentioned commands. By means of such options, you can influence the surface design of three-dimensional surfaces (that is, shading, colours, visibility checks, and so on).

Three-dimensional representation of surfaces

`plot3d` is an extension of the `plot` command which was the central theme of the previous chapter. Now, instead of a two-dimensional curve $y = f(x)$, a three-dimensional surface $z = f(x, y)$ is drawn.

As could be expected, usage of the command is similar to plot: in the first parameter, the function is specified (which is now dependent on two variables); in the two following parameters, the number ranges of these variables are specified. Additional parameters can be used for specifying options. The two following illustrations show two typical examples for plot3d.

```
with(plots): setoptions3d(style=patch):        plot3d(Im(sin(x+I*y)), x=0..2*Pi,
plot3d(x^2-y^2, x=-1..1, y=-1..1);                 y=-Pi/2..Pi/2, axes=boxed);
```

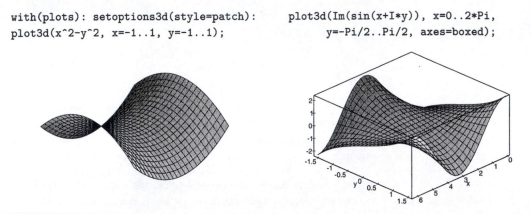

Note: In Release 3, style=patch was the default setting, that is, surfaces were as standard represented as filled polygons. Since Release 4, the default setting is style=hidden, that is, the surface is represented as a line pattern (which has a poor contrast). In order to obtain illustrations like the ones in this chapter, you must either specify style=patch with each command or use setoptions3d to define a new default setting for style.

The following two illustrations show the grid option which can be used to set the number of points to be calculated (default: [15, 15]) for both control variables. An increase in the number of points is necessary for graphics with quickly varying z values.

There is also a further option: orientation defines the viewing direction from which the surface is looked at. The direction is specified by way of two space angles measured in degrees (not in radians!). Setting the viewing direction is most easily carried out in the graphics window, where the box enveloping the surface can be easily rotated with the cursor keys or the mouse. The first angle specifies the horizontal viewing angle (0, 90, 180 or 270 degrees for a view from front, right, behind or left).

With the default setting of [45, 45] you look at the surface diagonally from above; the x axis points to front left (for increasing values of x), the y axis to front right. A more widely used view is $[-45, 60]$: the view is no longer so steep from above, the x axis points to front left, and the y axis to back left. This achieves an approximation to the usual view of two-dimensional graphics where the x axis points to the left and the y axis points upwards.

```
plot3d(sin(x*y), x=0..7, y=0..7,
  axes=framed, scaling=constrained);
```

```
plot3d(sin(x*y), x=0..7, y=0..7,
  axes=framed, grid=[50,50],
  scaling=constrained,
  orientation=[-45,60]);
```

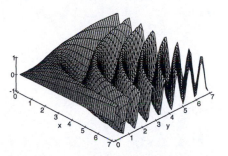

In combination with `orientation`, the `projection` option is also of interest. This option defines the perspective distortion. The range of values goes from 0 (strong distortion) to 1 (no distortion). In Release 4, this option is unfortunately ignored by the `plot3d` command. Here, perspective distortion can only be set via the graphics menu PROJECTION.

```
plot3d(sin(6*sqrt(x^2+y^2)),
  y=-2..2, x=-2..2,
  grid=[40,40], scaling=constrained,
  orientation=[7,45],
  projection=1);
```

```
plot3d(sin(6*sqrt(x^2+y^2)),
  y=-2..2, x=-2..2, grid=[40,40],
  scaling=constrained,
  orientation=[7,45],
  projection=0.02);
```

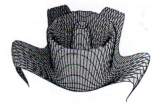

Some three-dimensional graphics need a limitation of the x range in the same way that the drawing range of the y axis frequently had to be limited through an additional parameter $y1..y2$. This can be achieved by using the option `view=z1..z2`. The following two illustrations show the outcome of this option.

```
plot3d(Re(tan(x+I*y)),
   x=0.05-Pi/2..0.05+Pi,
   y=-Pi/2..Pi/2,
   orientation=[-126,55],
   scaling=unconstrained,
   axes=boxed,
   grid=[40,40]);
```

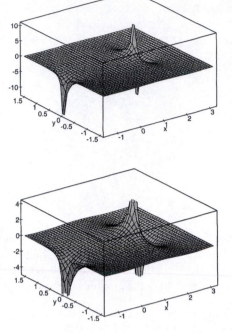

```
plot3d(Re(tan(x+I*y)),
   x=0.05-Pi/2..0.05+Pi,
   y=-Pi/2..Pi/2,
   orientation=[-126,55],
   scaling=unconstrained,
   axes=boxed,
   grid=[40,40], view=-5..4.5);
```

Parametric 3D graphics

There are several possibilities for drawing three-dimensional parametric functions: the representation of parametric surfaces is carried out by means of plot3d, where the first parameter must be formulated as a list $[x(s,t), y(s,t), z(s,t)]$. The spacecurve command from the package plots draws a thin (radius 0) curve $[x(t), y(t), z(t)]$ through the three-dimensional space. More variations are offered by the tubeplot command from the same package. Here, the radius of this curve too can be varied according to the control variable t.

The parametric variation of plot3d is used to draw a spherical surface defined by three functions.

```
plot3d([sin(s)*cos(t),
        cos(s)*cos(t),
        sin(t)],
        s=0..Pi, t=0..2*Pi,
        scaling=constrained);
```

The `spacecurve` command draws three-dimensional parametric curves which are dependent on one parameter only.

```
with(plots):
spacecurve(
  [t/10,
    (1+t/10)*sin(t),
    (1+t/10)*cos(t)], t=0..30*Pi,
  numpoints=500, axes=framed,
  shading=none,
  orientation=[25,62]);
```

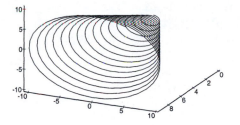

In its simplest variation, the `tubeplot` command works in a very similar way to `spacecurve`: instead of a line in space, the command draws a tube with radius 1.

```
tubeplot([2*sin(t), 2*cos(t), t/3],
         t=-1.5*Pi..2*Pi,
         orientation=[45,68]);
```

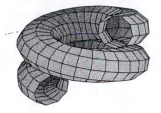

More interesting graphics can be obtained when the radius is also varied.

```
tubeplot(
  [-t^1.5/5, 3*cos(t), 3*sin(t)],
  t=0..8*Pi, radius=t/8,
  scaling=constrained,
  orientation=[107,56],
  grid=[60,15]);
```

Three-dimensional surfaces defined through lists

In the commands discussed up to now, the surfaces to be represented are described with one or more functions. The calculation proper of the coordinate points is subsequently carried out by the command itself, where in some cases a conversion can even be made from an arbitrary coordinate system into Cartesian coordinates (see Chapter 31).

If you want to calculate the z coordinates of the points yourself, and Maple is only to draw the corresponding surface, you can use the `listplot3d` command from the `plots` package instead of

plot3d. It expects a list of the z coordinates as the first parameter, structured in the following way:
$[[z11, z12, z13, ...], [z21, z22, z23, ...], [...], ...]$.

```
restart: with(plots):
listplot3d([[0,0,0,0,0],
            [0,0,1,2,2],
            [0,1,2,1,0],
            [0,2,3,2,0]],
    axes=frame, style=hidden,
    color=black, orientation=[45,11]);
```

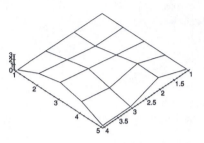

Much more flexibility (at the price of slightly more complicated handling) is offered by the surfdata command. This command is passed an embedded list of coordinate points. Each point consists of the specification $[x, y, z]$. The sum of all points forms a net that is stretched over the surface. For this purpose, the coordinate points are joined into sublists in rows. Thus, the whole surface is described through a list of the following structure:

$$[[p_{11}, p_{12}, p_{13}, ...], [p_{21}, p_{22}, p_{23}, ...], [p_{31}, p_{32}, p_{33}, ...], [...], ...]$$

In this list, p_{nm} is used as an abbreviation for $[x_{nm}, y_{nm}, z_{nm}]$.

The real problem with surfdata is the construction of this triply embedded list which leads to rather complicated seq constructions.

```
setoptions3d(style=hidden,color=black):
data:=[seq([seq([i,j,
    evalf(cos(sqrt(i^2+j^2)/2))],
    i=-5..5)], j=-5..5)]:
surfdata(data, axes=frame,
         labels=[x,y,z]);
```

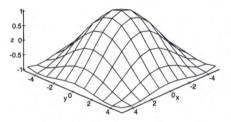

As the above example shows, seq is suitable for the construction of coordinate lists but only to a limited extent. Since seq always uses 1 as the step width, the structure of the formula is often hardly recognizable. In Chapter 30, a new command, seqn, is introduced which constructs arbitrarily embedded lists, and where any step width can be used for the control variables. In anticipation of that chapter, the program code of the seq2 command for doubly embedded lists is shown without further explanation.

```
seq2:=proc(f, l1::list, l2::list)
  local i,j, data1, data2, range1, range2;
  range1:=evalf(l1): range2:=evalf(l2):
  data1:=[];
  for i from op(1,op(2,range1[1])) to op(2,op(2,range1[1])) by range1[2] do
    data2:=[];
```

```
    for j from op(1,op(2,range2[1])) to op(2,op(2,range2[1])) by range2[2] do
      data2:=[op(data2), eval(subs(op(1,range2[1])=j, op(1,range1[1])=i, f))];
    od;
    data1:=[op(data1), data2];
  od;
  RETURN(data1);
end:
```

Handling the command is easy: in the first parameter, the function to be calculated (or a list of functions) is specified, depending on two control variables. The value ranges of the control variables are written as lists in the form $[x = start..end, step]$.

```
seq2([x,y,x+y], [x=1..3,1], [y=0.1..0.3, 0.1]);
```

$$[[[1.0, 0.1, 1.1], [1.0, 0.2, 1.2], [1.0, 0.3, 1.3]], [[2.0, 0.1, 2.1], [2.0, 0.2, 2.2], [2.0, 0.3, 2.3]],$$

$$[[3.0, 0.1, 3.1], [3.0, 0.2, 3.2], [3.0, 0.3, 3.3]]]$$

With the new command, the calculation of the data for a three-dimensional chute becomes a pleasure:

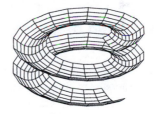

```
data:=seq2([r*sin(phi),
            r*cos(phi),
            1.5*phi+3*sin(r)],
         [r=Pi..2*Pi, Pi/9],
         [phi=0..4*Pi, Pi/10]):
surfdata(data);
```

Three-dimensional point diagrams

In all commands discussed up to now, the option `style=point` causes the data to be displayed in the form of points. However, in order to keep the resulting graphics still recognizable, we often need an asymmetric setting of the `grid` option, so that the points move relatively close to each other in one direction and show significant distances in the other.

Here, `plot3d` is used in its parametric variation. With `shading=none`, colouring of the points is prevented. Please note the `grid` setting of $[80, 20]$!

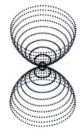

```
plot3d(
  [sin(s)*cos(t), cos(s)*cos(t), t],
  s=0..2*Pi, t=0..Pi, grid=[80,20],
  shading=none, scaling=constrained,
  style=point);
```

If you do not want to specify the point set through a function, but want to specify a list of coordinate points, you must use the `pointplot3d` command for drawing. Similarly to `surfplot`, the command is passed a list of coordinate points. The form of this list is $[[x1, y1, z1], [x2, y2, z2], ...]$. When you specify the additional option `style=line`, the command draws a continuous line instead of individual points.

The `seq` command is used to calculate a list of 1000 coordinate points of a spiral in space. `pointplot` represents this curve in three dimensions.

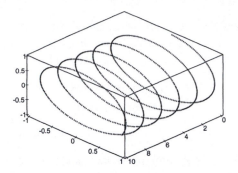

```
with(plots):
data:=[seq(evalf(
    [t/100, sin(t/30), cos(t/30)]),
    t=0..1000)]:
pointplot3d(data, axes=boxed);
```

Surface design options

Normally (the default setting may vary depending on the Maple version), three-dimensional surfaces are combined on screen from coloured pieces of surface (rectangles) which are each surrounded by a thin black frame. The `style` option, however, also allows other variations in representation. You already know the standard variation `style=patch` from a large number of illustrations in this chapter; an illustration of `style=point` can be found in the previous section. The following four illustrations show the remaining four settings: `hidden`, `wireframe`, `patchnogrid` and `patchcontour`.

In order to avoid recalculation of the graphics, the diagram is first stored in p and subsequently displayed by means of `display` (from the `plots` package) with additional specification of further options.

```
with(plots):

p:=plot3d(-5*cos(sqrt(x^2+y^2))*exp(-0.1*sqrt(x^2+y^2)),
          x=-2*Pi..7*Pi, y=-2*Pi..4*Pi, grid=[45,35], axes=framed,
          scaling=constrained, orientation=[-157,62]):
```

In the following two illustrations, the diagram is exclusively represented through lines – on the left with a visibility check, on the right without it. With the option `shading=none` all lines are drawn in black.

```
display(p, shading=none,          display(p, shading=none,
        style=hidden);                    style=wireframe);
```

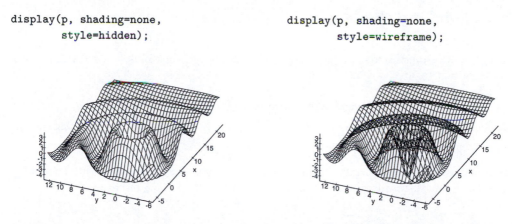

With the setting `patchnogrid` the diagram is displayed with shading, but without the usual line raster. With `patchcontour`, the line raster is substituted by contour lines (as on a geographical map). Furthermore, you can use the setting `contour` which causes the diagram to be represented exclusively through contour lines (but without shading and, in particular, without a visibility check).

```
display(p, style=patchnogrid);        display(p, style=patchcontour);
```

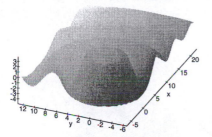

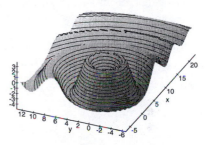

In combination with `style=patchcontour`, you can use the option `contours`. This option specifies how many contour lines are to be drawn (`contours = n`) or at which heights the contour lines are to be drawn (`contours = [z1, z2, z3 ...]`).

```
display(p, style=patchcontour,
        contours=[-2,-1,0,1,2]);
```

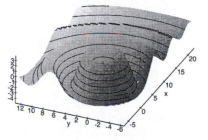

Colour, light and shadow

Colouring of three-dimensional graphics is controlled through four options: `shading`, `color`, `ambientlight` and `light`.

- `shading` selects one out of several default algorithms for colouring the graphics.

- `color` defines a function which calculates the colour according to the x and y coordinates. `shading` and `color` cannot be used in combination, but only as alternatives.

- `light` and `ambientlight` specify one or more directed light sources together with the ambient light. The light sources illuminate the surfaces coloured with `shading` or `color`.

Standard colour distribution with the shading option

The `shading` option controls the algorithm which controls the shading (colour distribution) across the surface. The default setting is version-dependent, but usually `xyz`. In this case, the colour depends on all three coordinate components. Which formula is actually used to calculate the colour is not specified in the Maple documentation. With the setting `xy` the colour is only dependent on the x and y coordinates (but not on z). The settings `z` and `zhue` cause the colour to depend purely on the height. `zhue` generates more colourful pictures. A very similar effect is caused by `zgreyscale`, but the z values are now transformed into different shades of grey (which is more suitable for printing).

The illustration on the right still refers to the diagram stored in p in the previous section.

```
display(p, style=patchnogrid,
        shading=zhue);
```

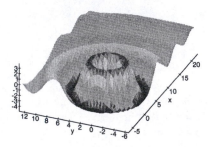

The last possible setting is `none`: this completely avoids colouring the graphics; lines and points appear in black, surfaces in white. This setting is particularly used in combination with `style=point` or `=hidden`, when the diagram is represented only through points and lines (see the examples in the previous section).

When a colour function (option `color`) or light sources (option `light`) are explicitly used for colouring the graphics, colour distribution is no longer influenced by `shading`!

Controlling colour distribution through a user-defined function

If you are not happy with the colours used by Maple as standard, you can use the `color` option to set your own colours. Usually, a two-parameter function is used with `color` which controls the colour distribution across the surface. In special cases (such as the following illustration) it may be sensible to keep the whole graphics in one single colour.

On screen, the higher of the two diagrams which penetrate each other is drawn in blue, the lower one in red.

```
p1:=plot3d(1.5*cos(x^2+y^2),
          x=-2..2, y=-2..2,
      style=hidden, color=red):
p2:=plot3d(2*sin(sqrt(x^2+y^2)),
          x=-2..2, y=-2..2,
      style=hidden, color=blue):
display([p1, p2]);
```

Let us now look at the specification of a colour function which is dependent on the x and y coordinates of the diagram. Two syntax variations exist:

`color=f(x,y)`
defines the tint (passing from red over blue, green, yellow back to red).

`color=COLOR(RGB, r(x,y), g(x,y), b(x,y))`
defines the colour through the additive mixture of the red, green and blue components.

A further peculiarity of Maple applies to both variations: the colour components can be specified in an arbitrary range of values (the usual restriction to values between 0 and 1 does not apply). Before Maple displays the graphics, it determines the smallest and the greatest value (separately for each component) and subsequently scales the values into the range between 0 and 1. On the one hand, this behaviour is quite useful, since you do not have to do a lot of thinking when formulating the colour function. On the other hand, you lose an important control mechanism for precise setting of colours: for example, it is not possible to colour two surfaces where one shows z values between 0 and 3 and the other z values between 0 and 4 in such a way that points with $z = 2$ have the same colour on both surfaces! (But this can nevertheless be done and the process is shown in Chapter 32 on graphics programming.)

An example to make this clearer: the diagram `plot(sin(x*y),x=0..2, y=0..2)` is identically (!) coloured through the following three `color` options.

```
color=COLOR(RGB, x, y, 0)
color=COLOR(RGB, x/2, y, 0)
color=COLOR(RGB, x/2, 0.5+y/4, 0)
```

```
greyscale:=x->COLOR(RGB,x,x,x):          greyscale:=x->COLOR(RGB,x,x,x):
plot3d(Re(sin(x+I*y)),                   plot3d(abs(sin(x+I*y)),
   x=0..2*Pi, y=-1..1, axes=framed,         x=0..2*Pi, y=-1..1, axes=framed,
   orientation=[-103,26],                   orientation=[-103,26],
   style=patch,                             style=patch,
   color=greyscale(Im(sin(x+I*y)))));       color=greyscale(
                                               Pi+argument(sin(x+I*y))));
```

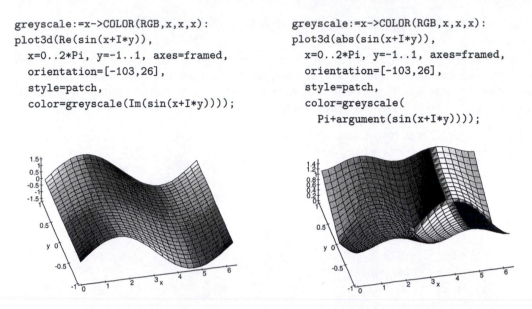

The most important application of the `color` option (apart from the creation of 'pretty' graphics) is to accommodate four-dimensional data in a three-dimensional diagram. This occurs most often in complex functions where four parameters (x and y parameters, value and phase or real and imaginary part) occur. (See also the `complexplot3d` command described in Chapter 31.)

In the two illustrations above, the complex function $\sin(x + I * y)$ is drawn. On the left, the z coordinate is defined through the real part, the colour through the imaginary part. On the right, the height (z coordinate) is defined through the value of the function, the colour through the phase angle. In order to ensure an optimal representation in black-and-white printing, the *greyscale* function was defined which allows you to create grey shades easily.

A last remark to conclude: the `color` option cannot be used in `display` to change the colour distribution of an already calculated diagram. If you want to represent a drawing in different colours, you must calculate it again.

Illumination

In addition to colouring with `shading` or `color`, graphics can also be illuminated by several light sources. While colours without illumination are exclusively defined by means of `shading` or `color`, the specification of light sources also takes into account the angle under which the light beams hit the solid. Maple has two light sources:

`ambientlight=[r,g,b]`
describes the ambient light in its red, green and blue components (each between 0 and 1) which equally illuminates all partial surfaces independently from any direction.

```
light=[phi, theta, r, g, b]
```
describes a light source which illuminates the solid under the angles ϕ and θ. The ϕ angle describes the vertical location of the light source (0, 90, 180, 270 degrees for illumination from top, front, bottom, back), whereas θ defines the horizontal location of the light source (0, 90, 180, 270 degrees for illumination from front, right, back, left). The option may be used several times in sequence in order to define several directed light sources.

It is essential for the definition of directed light sources that the specified angles have nothing (!) to do with the angles used for viewing (orientation option). orientation specifies from which angle the graphics is to be viewed. The point of departure for this is the coordinate system of the graphics. The angles in light, on the other hand, refer to the already rotated solid (which means to the screen coordinate system). When you change your viewing direction, the light sources do *not* move with you.

Please also note that the order of angles is different for orientation and light. In orientation, first the horizontal, then the vertical view angle is specified; in light, the specification occurs in reverse order.

You can create very colourful illumination models by specifying several differently coloured light sources from different directions. In Maple's graphics editor, you can choose between four predefined illumination models.

The following examples have been kept somewhat simpler. They refer to a sphere whose surfaces have explicitly been coloured white. Thus, the shading effects in the following illustrations exclusively originate from the different illumination models.

The drawing on the right shows the white sphere without any use of an illumination model.

```
p:=plot3d([sin(s)*cos(t),
           cos(s)*cos(t),
           sin(t)],
   s=0..Pi, t=0..2*Pi,
   scaling=constrained, color=white,
   orientation=[38,75], style=patch):

with(plots):
display(p);
```

On the right, the sphere is illuminated by a
white light source from top right. As soon as a
light source is defined, all non-illuminated partial surfaces of the sphere appear black.

```
display(p,
  light=[60,45,1,1,1]);
```

Here, in addition to the directed light source of
the previous illustration, a not too strong ambient light is used.

```
display(p,
  light=[60,45,1,1,1],
  ambientlight=[0.3,0.3,0.3]);
```

In the last illustration of this series, the sphere
is illuminated from top right with a red light,
from top left with a green light, and from the
bottom with a blue light. On a colour monitor,
the sphere shines in all colours that result from
an additive mixture of colours.

```
display(p,
  light=[60,45,1,0,0],
  light=[60,-45,0,1,0],
  light=[135,0,0,0,1]);
```

Syntax summary

```
plot3d(f, x=x0..x1, y=y0..y1, options);
```
   represents the surface $z = f(x, y)$ in three dimensions. Instead of f, a set of several functions
   can be specified. The possible options are described further below.

```
plot3d([fx,fy,fz], s=s0..s1, t=t0..t1, options);
```
   draws the parametric surface defined through the functions $[fx, fy, fz]$. fx, fy and fz are dependent on s and t.

```
with(plots);
```
    activates the commands of the `plots` package. This command must be executed prior to using `spacecurve`, `tubeplot`, `surfdata`, `pointplot`, `textplot3d`, `setoptions3d` and `display`.

```
spacecurve([fx, fy, fz], t=t0..t1, options);
```
    draws the curve in a space defined by the parameter t.

```
tubeplot([fx, fy, fz], t=t0..t1, options);
tubeplot([fx, fy, fz], t=t0..t1, radius=fr, options);
```
    as `spacecurve`, except that the space curve is represented by a tube of radius 1. In the second syntax variation, the radius of the tube is defined with the function $fr(t)$.

```
listplot3d([[z11,z12,...], [z21,z22,...], [...], ...]);
```
    draws the surface defined by the z coordinates. x and y coordinates are chosen directly by `listplot3d`.

```
surfdata(data, options);
```
    represents a surface defined through *data* in three dimensions. *data* is composed of a doubly embedded list of the form $[[p11, p12, p13...], [p21, p22, p23...], ...]$, where each coordinate point is specified in the form $p = [x, y, z]$.

```
pointplot3d(data, options);
```
    draws the points defined by their coordinates in space. *data* is formed by a simple list of coordinate points, that is, $[[x0, y0, z0], [x1, y1, z1], ...]$.

```
textplot3d([x,y,z,'text'], color=black);
```
    outputs the text at the specified coordinate position. The labelling can subsequently be combined with another three-dimensional graphics by means of `display`.

```
setoptions3d(option=setting);
```
    sets the specified option for all further `plot3d` commands.

```
display(p, options);
display([p1, p2,...], options);
```
    displays one or more 3D graphics with the use of new options. The `color` option cannot be used in combination with `display`. `orientation` must be newly set in any case, even if it has already been used in p.

Surface design options

`style=`...
    specifies the representation of data:
    `point`: in the form of points.
    `wireframe`: in the form of lines without visibility check.
    `hidden`: in the form of lines with visibility check.
    `patch`: in the form of shaded patches with line raster.
    `patchnogrid`: in the form of shaded patches without line raster.
    `patchcontour`: in the form of shaded patches with contour lines.

`contours=n`
`contours=[z0,z1...]`
    defines the number or height of contour lines. This option only makes sense in combination
    with `style=patchcontour`.

`shading=`...
    chooses one of the standard algorithms for colouring the graphics. Possible settings are:
    `xyz`: the colour depends on all three coordinate components.
    `xy`: the colour only depends on the x and y coordinates.
    `z`: the z coordinate determines the tint.
    `zhue`: the z coordinate determines the colour.
    `zgreyscale`: the z coordinate determines the grey shades.
    `none`: no colours (lines and points are black, surfaces white).

`color=`...
    specifies a colour function which defines the colour according to the two control variables
    x and y. The colour function can either be formulated directly and then defines the tint, or
    it is indicated with the aid of `COLOR(RGB,r,g,b)` and defines the colour with an additive or
    subtractive mixture of colours.

`light=`...
    defines a directed light source in the form $[\phi, \theta, r, g, b]$. The first angle determines the ver-
    tical direction of illumination, the second angle the horizontal direction. Through multiple
    specification of this option, several light sources can be defined.

`ambientlight=`...
    defines an undirected ambient light in the form $[r, g, b]$.

General options

`axes=...`
> determines the look of the coordinate axes:
> `normal`: the axes go through the 0 point.
> `frame`: the axes cross in the lower left-hand corner of the diagram.
> `boxed`: the diagram is framed with a box.
> `none`: no coordinate axes are shown at all (default).

`tickmarks=[nx,ny,nz]`
> specifies the minimum number of points on the x, y and z axes that Maple is required to label.

`grid=[nx,ny]`
> specifies the number of points to be calculated in the x and y directions. Default setting is [15, 15].

`orientation=[theta,phi]`
> specifies the viewing direction from which the graphics is looked at. θ defines the horizontal angle, ϕ the vertical angle.

`projection=n`
> specifies the amount of perspective distortion. The value range reaches from 0 (strong distortion) to 1 (no distortion, default).

`view=...`
> specifies the visible part of the graphics. Normally, this range is only limited for the z axis ($z0..z1$), but it is also possible to limit all three coordinates in the form [$x0..x1$, $y0..y1$, $z0..z1$].

Note: Many options shown in the syntax summary of the previous chapter on 2D graphics can be applied to 3D graphics in the same way: `axesfont`, `font`, `labels`, `labelfont`, `linestyle`, `scaling`, `symbol`, `thickness`, `title` and `titlefont`.

Part III

Maple for advanced users

The third and last part of this book deals with problems which seldom occur in day-to-day use of Maple. For many readers, only one of the subjects may be of interest or importance; the others may not be relevant. For this reason, the chapters are largely independent of each other. They do, however, assume some basic knowledge from Part II of this book (for example, handling lists).

The following chapters can be divided into three groups:

- Chapters 21 to 27 discuss advanced mathematical subjects: statistics and probability calculus, construction of regression and interpolation functions, solution of optimization problems, constructing and calculating with series, handling commands for Laplace and Fourier transformations and finally calculating with vectorial functions (vector analysis).

- Chapters 28 to 30 provide an introduction to Maple programming. The emphasis is on basic knowledge of Maple internal data structures (for example, the structure of a mathematical expression), on procedural elements of Maple's language (conditions, loops, and so on) and finally on programming your own packages. Some practical examples round off this introduction.

- Chapters 31 and 32 again deal with the subject of graphics which has been extensively discussed in Chapters 19 and 20. Chapter 31 introduces various special commands, while Chapter 32 gives an introduction to graphics programming. Together with the knowledge from the three chapters on programming, this will allow you to program your own graphics commands.

Chapter 21

Combinatorics, statistics, probability calculus

This chapter begins with a section on combinatorics which introduces some functions from the combinat package. The remainder of the chapter is dedicated to the functions contained in the statistics package. This package is divided into several subpackages:

`transform`
contains commands for execution of elementary processing steps (such as `statsort` for sorting statistical data or `split` and `tallyinto` for dividing data into groups).

`statevalf`
defines the command `statevalf` for numeric evaluation of a number of continuous and discrete probability distributions. For all distributions, it is possible to calculate values of density function, cumulative density function (distribution function) and the corresponding inverse function.

`random`
contains commands for the generation of random numbers distributed according to different probability functions.

`statsplot`
defines several commands for drawing statistical diagrams (`scatter1d`, `scatter2d`, `boxplot`, `histogram`, and so on).

Reference: While this chapter briefly touches upon statistical functions, Hörhager (1996) dedicates more than 50 pages to statistics and quality assurance, and shows the application of many commands in practical examples. Generation of regression functions through given data points is discussed in the next chapter on regression and interpolation functions.

Combinatorics

The ! operator for calculating the factorial and the `binomial` command for determining the binomial coefficient belong to the basic functions of Maple. `binomial` can also be used for symbolic calculus; however, the result must be further processed with `expand`.

```
5!;
```
$$120$$

```
binomial(12,10);
```
$$66$$

```
binomial(a+3,a);
```
$$\text{binomial}(\,a+3,a\,)$$

```
expand(");
```
$$\frac{1}{6}\,(\,a+1\,)\,(\,a+2\,)\,(\,a+3\,)$$

Farther-reaching commands concerning the subject of combinatorics are defined in the `combinat` package. These commands can be employed not only to calculate the possible number of combinations, permutations, and so on, but also actually to carry out permutations with given list elements. The following examples introduce the most important commands.

`multinomial` is an extension of `binomial`. The command divides the factorial of the first parameter by the product of the factorials of all further parameters. The first parameter and the sum of all further parameters must be identical.

```
with(combinat):
multinomial(12,5,5,2);
```
$$16632$$

```
12! / (5! * 5! *2!);
```
$$16632$$

`choose` generates all possible combinations of the elements of a list. Instead of a list, an integer number n may be passed. In this case, Maple interprets n as the list $[1, 2, ..., n]$. In combinations, the order of the elements plays no role. An optional second parameter can be used to specify that only combinations with a given number of elements are to be generated.

`numbcomb` determines the number of combinations without actually generating them and is therefore significantly faster than the equivalent command `nops(choose(m,n))`. `randcomb` determines a random combination with a given number of elements. With this command, the second parameter is therefore not optional.

```
choose([a,b,b,c]), numbcomb([a,b,b,c]);
```
$$[[\ ], [b], [c], [b, c], [b, b], [b, b, c], [a], [a, b], [a, c], [a, b, c], [a, b, b], [a, b, b, c]], 12$$

```
choose([a,b,b,c],2), numbcomb([a,b,b,c],2);
```
$$[[a, b], [a, c], [b, b], [b, c]], 4$$

```
randcomb([a,b,b,c],2);
```
$$[b, b]$$

The `permutation` command is very similar to `choose` and it determines all possible permutations of the list elements. `numbperm` calculates the number of possible permutations; `randperm` determines a random permutation (where the number of elements cannot be specified).

```
permute([a,b,b,c]), numbperm([a,b,b,c]);
```

$$[[a,b,b,c],[a,b,c,b],[a,c,b,b],[b,a,b,c],[b,a,c,b],[b,b,a,c],[b,b,c,a],[b,c,a,b],$$
$$[b,c,b,a],[c,a,b,b],[c,b,a,b],[c,b,b,a]],12$$

```
permute([a,b,b,c],2), numbperm([a,b,b,c],2);
```

$$[[a,b],[a,c],[b,a],[b,b],[b,c],[c,a],[c,b]],7$$

```
randperm([a,b,b,c]);
```

$$[b,a,b,c]$$

`cartprod` is used to generate all possible combinations of elements from several lists. When the command is passed three lists, it generates lists whose first element is taken from the first list, the second element from the second list and the third element from the third list.

Handling this command is, however, slightly more long-winded than handling `choose` and `permute`. This is because `cartprod` does not directly generate a list, but a procedure which must subsequently be called in order to determine the individual lists. Prior to each call, `proc[finished]` must be used to check whether there are any list elements left to be processed. If so, the next element can be read with `proc[nextvalue]`.

The example below shows a small loop which supplies the required list in the variable l. Information on loop commands can be found in Chapter 29.

```
cproc:=cartprod([[a,b,c],[x,y],[1,2]]):
l:=[]: while not cproc[finished] do l:=[op(l),cproc[nextvalue]()]: od: l;
```

$$[[a,x,1],[a,x,2],[a,y,1],[a,y,2],[b,x,1],[b,x,2],[b,y,1],[b,y,2],[c,x,1],[c,x,2],$$
$$[c,y,1],[c,y,2]]$$

`partition` supplies a list of all possible values that yield a given integer sum. `numbpart` calculates the number of possibilities for calculating this sum. `composition` and `numbcomp` are variations of the above commands: here, the number of summands must be specified; unlike `partition`, the order of summands is taken into account.

```
partition(6), numbpart(6);
```

$$[[1,1,1,1,1,1],[1,1,1,1,2],[1,1,2,2],[2,2,2],[1,1,1,3],[1,2,3],[3,3],[1,1,4],[2,4],$$
$$[1,5],[6]],11$$

```
composition(6,2), numbcomp(6,2);
```

$$\{[3,3],[2,4],[1,5],[5,1],[4,2]\},5$$

Processing of statistical data

The statistics package contains commands for carrying out statistical analyses, drawing statistical diagrams and calculating probability distributions. The `stats` package is divided into subpackages. Before any statistics command can be executed, you must first execute `with(stats)` and subsequently `with(subname)`. Most subpackages are described in the course of this chapter, with the exception of the subpackage `fit` which is discussed in Chapter 22 on regression and interpolation functions.

A common peculiarity of all statistics commands is that individual parameters must often be specified in square brackets (such as `split[2](list)` instead of `split(2,list)`).

Reference: Examples of the application of the `stats` package can also be found in the subdirectories of `\share\stats`.

Representation of statistical data

The precondition for understanding the statistics commands is a knowledge of how statistical data can be represented. Statistical data is generally stored in lists. Within lists, the `stats` package provides the following data types:

`x`	data point x.
`x1..x2`	data range $x1..x2$. A data range means an arbitrary point which lies between $x1$ (inclusive) and $x2$ (exclusive).
`missing`	missing data point. Most statistics commands can also cope with data sets that are incomplete. In practice, this happens very often, for example during evaluation of questionnaires when some questions simply have not been answered. Non-existing data points must be marked with the keyword `missing`.
`Weight(x,w)`	weighted data points. Any of the above three data types can be used for x. w indicates the weight. `Weight(2, 3)` is equivalent to three data points of weight 2. `Weight(1..5, 4)` indicates that four data points lie between 1 and 5. `Weight` itself does not fulfil any function and can therefore not be evaluated. `Weight` is only used for internal representation of weighted data.

The following example is intended to clarify the use of these data types. *data* shows a typical statistical list, consisting of three normal data points 2, 3 and 4, data point 5 which occurs four times, one missing data point and the data range 1..4, in which three additional data points are located. `mean` calculates the mean value of this list. The instruction also shows how `mean` arrives at its result.

```
with(stats): with(describe):
data:=[2,3,4,Weight(5,4),missing,Weight(1..4,3)];
```

$$data := [2, 3, 4, \text{Weight}(5, 4), missing, \text{Weight}(1..4, 3)]$$

```
mean(data), (2+3+4+5*4+(1+4)/2*3)/10;
```

$$\frac{73}{20}, \frac{73}{20}$$

Reading statistical data from a file

Maple provides the `importdata` command to allow easy reading of data from a text file into Maple lists. This command is directly contained in the `stats` package; no subpackage need be loaded. The text file must contain only numbers and the * sign for missing data points. The data points must be separated from each other by spaces or tabs or line feeds.

The following example assumes that the file `statdata.dat` contains the four lines of text shown on the right.

```
1 2 3.5
1 * 4
2 7 3
9 8 7
```

When `importdata` is called without further parameters, it supplies the data in one single sequence of numbers. The data can be arranged columnwise into sublists through specification of an optional second parameter.

```
importdata('statdata.dat');
```

$$1., 2., 3.5, 1., missing, 4., 2., 7., 3., 9., 8., 7.$$

```
importdata('statdata.dat',3);
```

$$[1., 1., 2., 9.], [2., missing, 7., 8.],$$

$$[3.5, 4., 3., 7.]$$

Note: `importdata` finds the required file only in the current directory. However, the current directory is not the directory that also contains the worksheet file, but normally `maple\example`! Unfortunately, in Maple there is no possibility of accessing files that are located in the same directory as the current worksheet (except by specifying the complete path – but this is obviously not portable when you want to use your worksheet on a different computer later on). When specifying file names, please note that the name must be enclosed in right quotes. In the DOS and Windows versions, the backslash must be indicated twice, thus, for example, `c:\\mapleV4\\'file.dat'`.

For data which is not present in the format required by `importdata`, a special procedure must be programmed for reading the data (see `readdata`, `readline` and `sscanf` in Chapter 29).

Transforming statistical data

Lists containing statistical data can in principle be processed with all commands designed for the manipulation of lists (`map`, `zip`, `op`, and so on: see Chapter 12). However, the advantage of the special commands defined in the subpackage `transform` is that they take the peculiarities of statistical data into account and can cope with data ranges, missing data points and weighted data. The point of departure for the following examples is the sample data contained in the variable *tst*.

```
with(stats): with(transform):
tst:=[Weight(1..3,4), 3..4, Weight(4..7,4), 8];
```

$$tst := [\text{Weight}(1..3, 4), 3..4, \text{Weight}(4..7, 4), 8]$$

statvalue determines the values or value ranges of a statistical list and removes weights by means of Weight. With classmark, all ranges can be substituted with their mean values. frequency supplies a list of all weighting factors. cumulativefrequency has a similar function, but sums the factors in succession.

```
statvalue(tst);
```

$$[1..3, 3..4, 4..7, 8]$$

```
classmark(tst), statvalue(classmark(tst));
```

$$\left[\text{Weight}(2, 4), \frac{7}{2}, \text{Weight}\left(\frac{11}{2}, 4\right), 8\right], \left[2, \frac{7}{2}, \frac{11}{2}, 8\right]$$

```
frequency(tst), cumulativefrequency(tst);
```

$$[4, 1, 4, 1], [4, 5, 9, 10]$$

In its functioning, apply corresponds to map and applies the function specified in the first parameter to all list elements. In ranges, both range limits are modified. Weighting factors remain unchanged. multiapply is comparable to zip and generates a new list where one element of each list passed is inserted into the multi-parameter function. Please note that in both commands the processing functions are specified in square brackets.

```
apply[sin](tst);
```

$$[\text{Weight}(\sin(1)..\sin(3), 4), \sin(3)..\sin(4), \text{Weight}(\sin(4)..\sin(7), 4), \sin(8)]$$

```
multiapply[(x,y)->x*y]([[1,2,3], [4,5,6]]);
```

$$[4, 10, 18]$$

scaleweight multiplies all weighting factors by the factor specified in square brackets. In the example below, the function count from the describe subpackage is used to divide the weights by the number of data points. Afterwards, the sum of all weights is 1.

```
with(describe):
scaleweight[1/count(tst)](tst);
```

$$\left[\text{Weight}\left(1..3, \frac{2}{5}\right), \text{Weight}\left(3..4, \frac{1}{10}\right), \text{Weight}\left(4..7, \frac{2}{5}\right), \text{Weight}\left(8, \frac{1}{10}\right)\right]$$

statsort sorts the specified data points. When data ranges overlap or when individual data points lie within data ranges, statsort reacts with an error message. A remedy is offered by classmark which converts data ranges into mean values.

```
statsort([6,missing,3,Weight(4..5,2)]);
```

$$[3, \text{Weight}(4..5, 2), 6, missing]$$

`split` splits a list into n partial lists of equal length. The order of the elements is not changed, that is, the list must be sorted *beforehand*, if necessary. When the number of data points is not a multiple of n, individual data points are split as well and inserted proportionally (with weighting factors) into both partial lists.

`split[3]([1,2,3,4,5,6]);`

$$[[1,2],[3,4],[5,6]]$$

`split[4]([1,2,3,4,5,6]);`

$$\left[\left[1, \text{Weight}\left(2, \frac{1}{2}\right)\right], \left[\text{Weight}\left(2, \frac{1}{2}\right), 3\right], \left[4, \text{Weight}\left(5, \frac{1}{2}\right)\right], \left[\text{Weight}\left(5, \frac{1}{2}\right), 6\right]\right]$$

`tallyinto` is suited to carrying out class divisions. The command generates a list of weighted ranges where given ranges (lower limit inclusive, upper limit exclusive) must be observed. The data need not be previously sorted.

`tallyinto([1,2,2,2,3,4,5,6,6], [1..3,3..4,4..7]);`

$$\text{Weight}(1..3, 4), 3..4, \text{Weight}(4..7, 4)]$$

The following example shows a further application of `tallyinto`, this time for a class division of 100 random numbers. Particularly worth noting is how `seq` is used to generate the range limits and store them in the variable *bins* with minimum typing effort.

`tst:=[seq(rand(100)(), n=1..100)];`

$$tst := [33, 83, 16, 98, 8, 38, 16, 21, 54, 53, 22, 92, 57, 95, 30, 16, 53, 67, 31, 8, 1, 29, 79, ...,$$
$$34, 0, 88, 73, 37, 54, 58, 85, 86, 97, 47, 14, 39, 75, 27, 81, 75, 35, 81, 81, 36, 73, 8, 2, 34]$$

`bins:=[seq(10*n..10*n+10, n=0..9)];`

$$bins := [0..10, 10..20, 20..30, 30..40, 40..50, 50..60, 60..70, 70..80, 80..90, 90..100]$$

`tallyinto(tst,bins);`

$$[\text{Weight}(10..20, 8), \text{Weight}(20..30, 11), \text{Weight}(30..40, 15), \text{Weight}(40..50, 6), ...,$$
$$\text{Weight}(90..100, 7), \text{Weight}(0..10, 11)]$$

`frequency(");`

$$[8, 11, 15, 6, 16, 3, 8, 15, 7, 11]$$

Basic statistical numbers (descriptive statistics)

The `stats` subpackage `describe` contains a large number of commands for calculating elementary statistical numbers (mean value, standard deviation, and so on). The application of these commands is in most cases so easy that examples are given only for the most important functions.

```
with(stats): with(describe):
```

$[coefficientofvariation, count, countmissing, covariance, decile, geometricmean, harmonicmean,$
$\quad kurtosis, linearcorrelation, mean, meandeviation, median, mode, moment, percentile,$
$\quad quadraticmean, quantile, quartile, range, skewness, standarddeviation, variance]$

The test data for the following examples is the number sequence in *tst*: three data points, one doubly weighted number range between 4 and 6 plus two missing data points. `count` determines the number of valid data, `countmissing` the number of missing data points. `range` supplies the range embraced by the test data.

```
tst:=[1,2,3,Weight(4..6,2),
        Weight(missing,2)]:
count(tst), countmissing(tst);
```

$\quad 5,2$

```
range(tst);
```

$\quad 1..6$

`mean` calculates the mean value of the data. Besides `mean`, there are several other mean value commands, such as `quadraticmean`, `harmonicmean` or `geometricmean`.

```
mean(tst);
```

$\quad \dfrac{16}{5}$

```
quadraticmean(tst);
```

$\quad \dfrac{3}{10}$

The standard deviation and the variance are calculated with `standarddeviation` and `variance`. Here too, some variations exist, for example `coefficientofvariation` or `meandeviation`.

```
standarddeviation(tst),
  variance(tst);
```

$\quad \dfrac{8}{5}, \dfrac{64}{25}$

`median`, `quartile`, `decile`, `percentile` and `quantile` determine the (in most cases interpolated) data point at which data can be split into two parts. The example on the right shows three equivalent possibilities of determining the splitting point between the lower three quartiles and the upper quartile.

```
quantile[3/4](tst), quartile[3](tst),
  percentile[75](tst);
```

$\quad \dfrac{39}{8}, \dfrac{39}{8}, \dfrac{39}{8}$

Currently, Maple lacks commands for carrying out meaningful analyses of several data series. The only two commands are `linearcorrelation` and `covariance` which determine the correlation coefficient and covariance of two data series.

```
tst:=[1,2,3,4],[2,4,5,6]:
linearcorrelation(tst); evalf(");
```

$\quad \dfrac{13}{35} \sqrt{7}, .9827076297$

```
covariance(tst); evalf(");
```

$\quad \dfrac{13}{8}, 1.625000000$

Statistical diagrams

The `statplots` subpackage provides several commands for graphic representation of statistical data. The commands are useful, but are not fully developed and their handling is cumbersome. It is particularly irritating that these commands can be passed none of the usual options for 2D diagrams. These limitations can be circumvented partly by using `display` directly and partly by defining new commands.

Histograms

Histograms (bar charts) are the best known and simplest form of statistical diagrams. The `histogram` command expects a list of `Weight` functions as the parameters, which can be easily generated through `tallyinto`. In the example below, normally distributed random numbers are divided into classes with `tallyinto`. The resulting list of `Weight` functions is scaled to the sum of 1 by means of `scaleweight`.

```
with(stats): with(statplots): with(transform):
with(random): with(describe): with(plots):
f:=normald[5,1]: data:=[f(100)]:
tallyinto(data, [seq(n*0.5..(n+1)*0.5,n=1..20)]):
histdata:=scaleweight[1./count(")](");
```

$$histdata := [\text{Weight}(\,0.5..1, 0\,), ..., \text{Weight}(\,4..4.5, 0.18\,), ..., \text{Weight}(\,10..10.5, 0\,)]$$

Through the following commands, the histogram of the above class distribution and the corresponding distribution curve are overlaid in one diagram:

```
p1:=histogram(histdata):
fpdf:=statevalf[pdf,f]:
p2:=plot(fpdf(x), x=0.5..10):
display([p1,p2]);
```

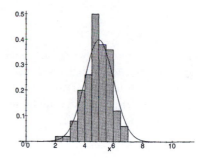

Maple also provides a command for three-dimensional representation of column charts: the `matrixplot` command is hidden in the `plots` package. The options of the following example are chosen in such a way that the shading of the columns is as neutral as possible. (The default setting supplies a chaotic jumble of colours.)

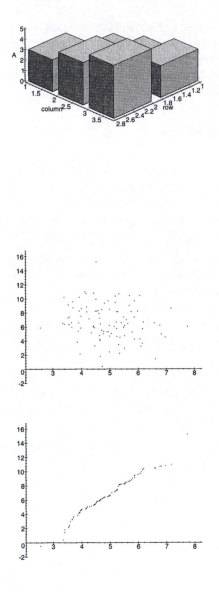

```
matrixplot([[1,2,3], [3,4,5]],
  heights=histogram, axes=framed,
  gap=0.2, ambientlight=[0.5,0.5,0.5],
  shading=none, style=patch,
  light=[45,45,0.5,0.5,0.5]);
```

Two-dimensional scatter plots

`scatter2d` draws a point diagram. The coordinates of the points are taken from the elements of two lists. The order of the list elements is not changed.

```
datax:=[normald[5,1](100)]:
datay:=[normald[7,3](100)]:
scatter2d(datax,datay);
```

The `quantile2` command works in much the same way as `scatter2d`, with the difference that the two lists are previously sorted. The smallest value in each list defines the coordinates of the first point, and so on.

```
quantile2(datax,datay);
```

Supplementary commands for two-dimensional scatter plots

With the commands `scatter1d`, `boxplot` and `notchedbox`, the distribution of one-dimensional data can be graphically represented. The resulting graphics, however, are seldom displayed on their own, but are in most cases used as a supplement for a scatter plot. The problem of combining these diagrams is that the partial drawings must be correctly repositioned and in part rotated. For this purpose, the `statplots` package provides the commands `xscale`, `xshift` and `xyexchange`.

For each data point, `scatterplot` draws one point on the axis $y = 1$. The point density is a good visual measure of the distribution of the data. The data in *datax* is still the same as in the previous example.

```
scatter1d(datax);
```

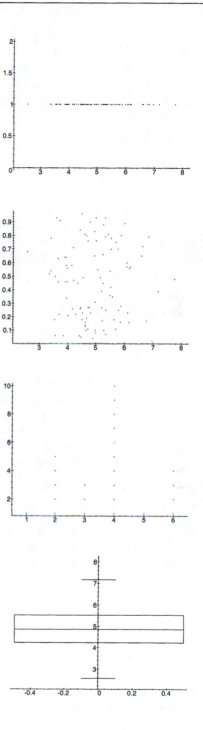

When the `jittered` option (indicated in square brackets) is used, `scatter1d` randomly varies the y coordinate of the points between 1 and 0.

```
scatter1d[jittered](datax);
```

The `stacked` option causes several points with the same value to be drawn one above the other. As a rule, this option only makes sense for integer values. The short notation 2\$5 with the enumeration operator \$ means $2, 2, 2, 2, 2$.

```
scatter1d[stacked]([1, 2$5, 3$3,
                    4$10, 5, 6$4]);
```

`boxplot` draws a vertical bar that gives information about the value range of the data, the location of the first and third quartile and the location of the median.

```
boxplot(datax);
```

notchedbox is a variation of boxplot. The bar between the first and the third quartile is notched, thus giving additional information on how the data is distributed. The location and width of the bar can be specified in brackets (this also applies to boxplot).

```
notchedbox[5,2](datax);
```

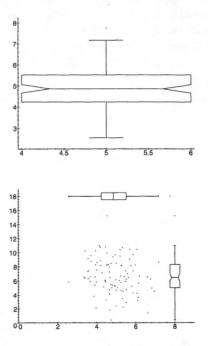

The diagram on the right shows a combination of a scatter plot with a box plot (on top) and a notch plot (on the right). Please note the positioning of *p2* and *p3* and the rotation of *p2* by means of xyexchange.

```
p1:=scatter2d(datax, datay):
p2:=xyexchange(boxplot[18,1](datax)):
p3:=notchedbox[8,0.5](datay):
display([p1,p2,p3], view=[0..9,0..19]);
```

The statplots package provides the commands xshift and xscale for horizontal shifting and scaling of 2D diagrams, but there are no equivalent commands for the y direction. When you want to shift a scatter1d diagram upwards, you must first rotate it by 90 degrees with xyexchange, then shift it with xshift and finally rotate it back with xyexchange. This process becomes considerably easier when you define two new procedures, yshift and yscale, which take on this task. (The proc command is described in more detail in Chapter 29.)

```
yshift:=proc(x) xyexchange(xshift[op(procname)](xyexchange(x))); end:
yscale:=proc(x) xyexchange(xscale[op(procname)](xyexchange(x))); end:
```

With this, you can now generate the last illustration of this section: a histogram with a class division of the data in *datay* and a one-dimensional scatter plot placed over it. This scatter plot is transformed with yscale and yshift from a y range between 0 and 1 into a range between 0.2 and 0.23.

```
tallyinto(datay,
          [seq(n..n+1, n=-2..18)]):
histdata:=scaleweight[1./count(")]("):
p1:=greyhist(histdata):
p2:=scatter1d[jittered](datay):
p2:=yshift[0.2](yscale[0.03](p2)):
display([p1,p2], axes=boxed);
```

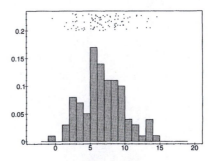

Continuous and discrete probability distributions

In the **stats** package, a large number of continuous and discrete probability distributions are defined. In order to allow numeric evaluation of these distribution functions, the **statevalf** subpackage must be activated. Subsequently, the density function, the cumulative density function (distribution function) and the corresponding inverse function can be calculated for all defined probability distributions. The following examples show the application of **statevalf** for several distribution functions. The only problem lies in the equally uncommon and unclear syntax of this command with its doubly embedded square brackets.

Reference: The syntax summary at the end of this chapter lists all available distribution functions (13 continuous and six discrete functions) together with their parameters. A detailed description of the functions can be obtained with **?stats, distributions**.

Continuous probability distributions

In the example on the right, the functions $f1$ to $f3$ are defined with the three distribution functions of a normal distribution with mean value 0 and standard deviation 1, where **pdf** stands for probability density function, **cdf** for cumulative density function and **icdf** for inverse cumulative density function. Thus, $f2$ and $f3$ are mutually inverse (see second example). The two illustrations below show the course of the three functions.

```
with(stats): with(statevalf):
f1:=statevalf[pdf,normald[0,1]]:
f2:=statevalf[cdf,normald[0,1]]:
f3:=statevalf[icdf,normald[0,1]]:
f1(1), f2(1), f3(0.841);
```
      .39894228, .841344746, .998576271

```
f3(f2(3));
```
      3.000000007

```
plot({f1(x), f2(x)}, x=-4..4);
```

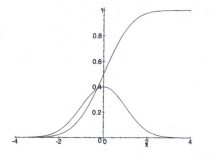

```
plot(f3(x),x=0..1, -3..3);
```

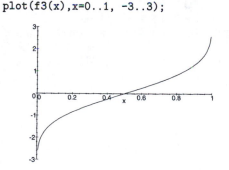

With **fsolve**, you can also numerically solve equations containing probability distributions. With the following **fsolve** command you can answer the question: How long must the average life span of an engine be when the standard deviation is 20 000 km and at least 80 per cent of all engines are supposed to run 90 000 km?

```
f:=1-statevalf[cdf,normald[x,20000]](90000): fsolve(f(x)=0.8, x);
```

    106832.4247

The illustration on the right shows the density
function of an exponential distribution with $\lambda =$
1.

```
f1:=statevalf[pdf,exponential[1]]:
plot(f1(x), x=0..4);
```

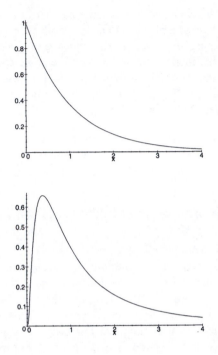

The illustration on the right shows a logarithmic
normal distribution. The two parameters μ and
σ are not specified; thus, Maple automatically
uses 0 and 1.

```
f1:=statevalf[pdf,lognormal]:
plot(f1(x), x=0..4);
```

Discrete probability distributions

For discrete probability distributions, `statevalf` requires the keywords `pf` for probability function,
`dcdf` for discrete cumulative density function and `idcdf` for inverse discrete cumulative density
function. The example below shows the course of a Poisson distribution with $\mu = 5$.

```
f1:=statevalf[pf,poisson[5]]:
seq(f1(n), n=1..10);
```

    .03368973500, .08422433749, .1403738958,

    .1754673698, .1754673698, .1462228081,

    .1044448629, .06527803935, .03626557742,

    .01813278870

```
plot(f1(floor(x)), x=1..10,
    numpoints=1000);
```

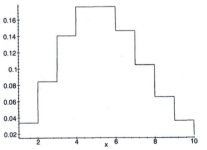

Probability-distributed random numbers

After activation of the `random` subpackage, random numbers can be calculated for all probability distributions. In the simplest case, the syntax is that the name of the distribution and the number of required random numbers are specified as the parameters. Instead of the number, you can also specify the keyword `generator` – in this case, Maple returns a procedure which can be used for the calculation of random numbers. Optionally, you can specify in square brackets the number of digits for the random numbers.

```
with(stats): with(random):
normald[10,1](3);
```

> 11.17583957, 9.436635869, 10.23539400

```
f:=normald[10,1](generator[20]):
f(), f(), f();
```

> 9.5091101253731983605, 9.3614149769836458270, 10.764824589892271837

```
with(statplots): with(plots):
yshift:=proc(x) xyexchange(xshift[op(procname)](xyexchange(x))); end:
yscale:=proc(x) xyexchange(xscale[op(procname)](xyexchange(x))); end:
f:=normald[5,2]:
p1:=plot(statevalf[pdf,f](x), x=-2..12):
p2:=yshift[0.2](yscale[0.03](scatter1d[jittered]([f(300)]))):
display([p1,p2]);
```

The illustration on the right shows the normal distribution f for $\mu = 5$ and $\sigma = 2$ together with the corresponding distribution of random numbers. Information about the rather complicated `plot` commands can be found in previous pages.

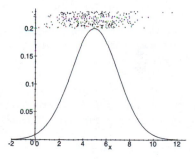

The routines for generating random numbers leave a fairly immature impression. The optional parameter `inverse` described in `?random` is not taken into account in several functions. In some functions, the distribution of random numbers does not match the density function.

The illustration on the right shows the discrepancy between supposedly beta-distributed random numbers and the actual course of the beta distribution.

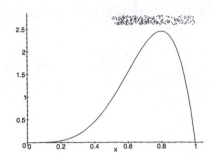

```
f:=beta[5,2]:
p1:=plot(statevalf[pdf,f](x), x=0..1):
p2:=yshift[2.6](yscale[0.2](
    scatter1d[jittered]([f(300)]))):
display([p1,p2]);
```

Syntax summary

Combinatorics

```
!n;      binomial(n,m);
```
calculate the factorial of n and the binomial coefficient of n over m, respectively

```
with(combinat);
```
activates the commands of the `combinat` package.

```
multinomial(n,m1,m2,m3,...,mk);
```
calculates the multinomial coefficient $n!/(m1! * m2! * ... * mk!)$.

```
choose([a,b,c]);        choose([a,b,c], n);     randcomb([a,b,c]);
numbcomb([a,b,c]);      numbcomb([a,b,c], n);
```
`choose` determines a list of all combinations (with n elements) of the specified list elements, `randcomb` a random combination. `numbcomb` calculates the number of possible combinations.

```
permute([a,b,c]);       permute([a,b,c],n);     randperm([a,b,c]);
numbperm([a,b,c]);      numbperm([a,b,c], n);
```
as above, but for permutations instead of combinations.

```
proc:=cartprod([list1,list2,list3,...]);
```
defines a new procedure with which all element combinations from the specified lists can be determined. `proc[finished]` checks whether there are any combinations left to be processed. `proc[nextvalue]` supplies the next combination.

```
partition(n);           numbpart(n);
composition(n,m);       numbcomp(n,m);
```
determine lists whose elements yield the sum n. In `composition`, the number of elements is limited to m.

Processing of statistical data

`with(stats):` `with(transform):`
    activates the commands of the `transform` subpackage of the `stats` package.

`importdata('file_name');` `importdata('file_name',n);`
    reads statistical data from the specified file and returns the result as a simple sequence of numbers or as a sequence of n columnwise ordered lists.

`statvalue(lst);` `classmark(lst);`
    determines the values or mean values of a statistical list, respectively.

`frequency(lst);` `cumulativefrequency(lst);`
    determines the weighting factors or the summed weighting factors of a statistical list, respectively.

`apply[fn](lst);` `multiapply[fn]([lst1,lst2,...]);`
    applies the function fn to the list elements.

`scaleweight[f](lst);`
    scales the weighting factors by a factor of f.

`statsort(lst);`
    sorts the list by data values. Weights are not taken into account. Ranges must not overlap.

`split[n](lst);`
    splits the list into n partial lists of equal length. If the number of list elements is not a multiple of n, individual data points (with weighting factors < 1) are split as well.

`tallyinto(lst, [b1..b2,b2..b3,b3..b4,...]);`
    assigns the list elements to the specified ranges. The result is a list of `Weight` functions.

Basic statistical numbers (descriptive statistics)

`with(stats):` `with(describe):`
    activates the commands of the `describe` subpackage.

`count(lst);` `countmissing(lst);`
    determines the number of valid or missing data points, respectively.

`range(lst);`
    determines the range in which the elements of the list lie.

```
mean(lst);     quadraticmean(lst);     geometricmean(lst);     harmonicmean(lst);
```
   calculates various mean values of the list.

```
variance(lst);     standarddeviation(lst);     meandeviation(lst);
```
   calculates variance and standard deviation.

```
median(lst);              quartile[n](lst);              decile[n](lst);
percentile[n](lst);     quantile[n1/n1](lst);
```
   determines the splitting point of a list. In quartile, n specifies the quartile where the list is
   to be split (1 to 3), in decile the decile (1 to 9), in percentile the percentile (1 to 99). In
   quantile, an arbitrary fraction (for example, $1/3$) may be specified.

```
linearcorrelation(lst1,lst2);     covariance(lst1,lst2);
```
   calculate the correlation coefficients and the covariance of two data series, respectively.

Statistical diagrams

```
with(stats):  with(statplots):  with(plots):
```
   activates the commands of the statplots subpackage and of the plot package.

```
histogram(data);
```
   draws a histogram. In *data*, a list of Weight functions must be passed.

```
matrixplot(data, height=histogram, gap=0.2);
```
   draws a three-dimensional column diagram.

```
scatter2d(datax, datay);     quantile2(datax,datay);
```
   draws a two-dimensional scatter diagram, where quantile2 first sorts the data (independently
   of each other).

```
scatter1d(data);     scatter1d[jittered](data);     scatter1d[stacked](data);
```
   draws a one-dimensional horizontal scatter diagram. The jittered option causes a random
   vertical distribution of the points between 0 and 1. With stacked identical points are arranged
   one above the other.

```
boxplot(data);         boxplot[x,width](data);
notchedbox(data);     notchedbox[x,width](data);
```
   each draw a vertical bar which indicates the distribution of the data. With the optional parameters x and *width*, the x position and the width of the bar can be specified.

```
yshift:=proc(x) xyexchange(xshift[op(procname)](xyexchange(x))); end:
yscale:=proc(x) xyexchange(xscale[op(procname)](xyexchange(x))); end:
xscale[f](diag);     xshift[dx](diag);     xyexchange(diag);
yscale[f](diag);     yshift[dy](diag);
```
   scale, shift and rotate a 2D diagram. xscale, xshift and xyexchange are predefined; yshift
   and yscale must be defined by the user if needed.

Continuous and discrete probability distributions

```
with(stats):  with(statevalf):
    activates the commands of the statevalf subpackage.
```

```
statevalf[pdf, cont_dist](x):
statevalf[cdf, cont_dist](x):
statevalf[icdf, cont_dist](x):
```
calculate density function, cumulative density function and the corresponding inverse function of a continuous probability distribution. Example: `statevalf[pdf, beta[3,2]](0.3)`:

```
beta[nu1, nu2]        cauchy[a, b]      chisquare[nu]     exponential[alpha, a]
fratio[nu1, nu2]      gamma[a, b]       laplaced[a, b]    logistic[a, b]
lognormal[mu, sigma]  normald[mu, sigma] students[nu]     uniform[a, b]
weibull[a, b]
```
are the available continuous distribution functions. More detailed information about the meaning of the parameters can be obtained with `?stats, distribution`.

```
statevalf[pf, discrete_dist](x):
statevalf[dcdf, discrete_dist](x):
statevalf[idcdf, discrete_dist](x):
```
calculate density function, cumulative density function and the corresponding inverse function of a discrete probability distribution.

```
binomiald[n,p]         discreteuniform[a,b]
empirical[listprob]    hypergeometric[N1, N2, n]
negativebinomial[n,p]  poisson[mu]
```
are the available discrete distribution functions.

Probability-distributed random numbers

```
with(stats):      with(random):
    activates the commands of the random subpackage.
```

```
dist(n);
```
supplies a sequence of n random numbers in the specified distribution. Any of the continuous and discrete distributions listed above can be used as the distribution. Thus, `normald[5, 2](3)` generates three normally distributed random numbers.

```
f:=dist(generator);     f();
```
returns a procedure f for calculating random numbers. In the procedure call, a pair of parentheses must be specified.

Chapter 22

Regression and interpolation functions

This chapter deals with the task of drawing a curve through several given data points. The function of this curve can be used for further calculations, for example to calculate approximation values for unknown points of the curve. The four most important commands are:

`interp`
calculates an interpolation polynomial which leads exactly through the specified data points.

`spline`
constructs an interpolation function piecewise assembled through polynomials which leads exactly through the specified data points.

`leastsqr`
from the subpackage `fit` of the `stats` package calculates a linear combination of the specified functions, so that the curve passes as near as possible to the data points.

`fit`
from the `share` library essentially fulfils the same task as `leastsqr`, but has a slightly different syntax. `fit` is particularly suitable for multi-dimensional approximation functions.

Reference: Commands for the calculation of an approximation function to a given, mathematically more complicated function are discussed in Chapters 24 (Series expansion) and 25 (Fourier transformation).

Exact interpolation through given points

The `interp` command calculates a polynomial of order $n-1$ which leads through n data points. Data is passed to the command in the form $[x0, x1, x2, ...], [y0, y1, y2, ...]$. In the following example, a curve is drawn through 10 random y values at the x positions between 1 and 10.

```
datax:=[seq(i,i=1..10)];
```

$$datax := [1, 2, 3, 4, 5, 6, 7, 8, 9, 10]$$

```
datay:=[seq(rand(10)(), i=1..10)];
```

$$datay := [1, 0, 7, 3, 6, 8, 5, 8, 1, 9]$$

```
dataxy:=zip((x,y)->[x,y], datax, datay);
```

$$dataxy := [[1, 1], [2, 0], [3, 7], [4, 3], [5, 6], [6, 8], [7, 5], [8, 8], [9, 1], [10, 9]]$$

```
f:=interp(datax, datay, x);
```

$$f := \frac{17\,x^9}{51840} - \frac{517\,x^8}{40320} + \frac{11699\,x^7}{60480} - \frac{3719\,x^6}{2880} + \frac{27323\,x^5}{17280} + \frac{176741\,x^4}{5760} - \frac{652577\,x^3}{3240} +$$

$$\frac{1816483\,x^2}{3360} - \frac{1669153\,x}{2520} + 293$$

The biggest disadvantage of `interp` is that the curve strongly tends to overswing because of the high order of the polynomial. An interpolation over the data range of the given points is practically impossible. The function f calculated above already reaches the value 293 for $x = 0$; for $x = 11$ it goes up to 755!

For the graphical representation of the 10 data points, the specially developed `dotplot` command was used, whose code can be found in Chapter 32 (Graphics programming). If you do not feel like entering the required 15 lines of program code, you can always use the `plot(dataxy, style=list)` command instead. In this case, however, the 10 points will be output in such a small size that they can barely be recognized beneath the line.

The illustration on the right shows 10 data points and the curve together with the corresponding interpolation function.

```
p1:=plot(f, x=0.9..10.1):
p2:=dotplot(dataxy, 0.1, 50/10):
with(plots):
display([p1,p2]);
```

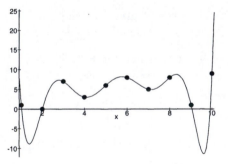

Piecewise interpolation with spline

As already mentioned, the biggest disadvantage of `interp` is that the curve strongly tends to overswing. This disadvantage is overcome with the `spline` command which assembles the curve piecewise through several polynomials of a lesser order (usually, through third-order polynomials). The curve is smooth even at the points of intersection. As the example will show, even the first derivative is still smooth, that is, without sudden changes in gradient.

Obviously, this method too has its disadvantage – because of the piecewise assembly, there is no longer a traditional function. It must be converted into a procedure if you want to represent the curve graphically or use it in any other way.

The following example starts with the same 10 data points as the example in the previous section.

```
datax:=[seq(i,i=1..10)];
```
$$datax := [1, 2, 3, 4, 5, 6, 7, 8, 9, 10]$$

```
datay:=[seq(rand(10)(), i=1..10)];
```
$$datay := [1, 0, 7, 3, 6, 8, 5, 8, 1, 9]$$

```
dataxy:=zip((x,y)->[x,y], datax, datay):
```

In the first two parameters, spline is passed the data lists for the x and y coordinates. The third parameter contains the required variable name of the function, the fourth parameter the order of the curve; 2 or 3 are reasonable values.

```
readlib(spline):
f:=unapply(spline(datax, datay, x, 3),x): f(x);
```

$$\begin{cases} 7 - \dfrac{14392}{4505} x + \dfrac{21588}{4505} x^2 - \dfrac{7196}{4505} x^3 & x < 2 \\[2ex] -\dfrac{205753}{4505} + \dfrac{68308}{901} x - \dfrac{156378}{4505} x^2 + \dfrac{4493}{901} x^3 & x < 3 \\[2ex] \cdots & \\[2ex] -\dfrac{4742291}{4505} + \dfrac{1549106}{4505} x - \dfrac{166308}{4505} x^2 + \dfrac{1178}{901} x^3 & x < 9 \\[2ex] -\dfrac{443407}{901} + \dfrac{707354}{4505} x - \dfrac{14556}{901} x^2 + \dfrac{2426}{4505} x^3 & otherwise \end{cases}$$

Since Release 4, spline supplies a piecewise function as a result (see also Chapter 8). Further processing of the result has thus been greatly facilitated.

```
f(2.5);
```

$$3.9455328$$

The illustration on the right again shows the 10 data points and the interpolation curve through these points. Please note that the curve deviates much less from the points than the one produced with interp in the previous section.

```
p1:=plot(f(x), x=1..10):
p2:=dotplot(dataxy, 0.1, 10/8):
with(plots): display([p1,p2]);
```

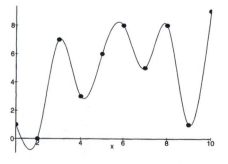

The function can be differentiated with `diff`. The first derivative is smooth, and the second derivative is at least still continuous.

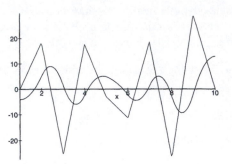

```
fd:=unapply(diff(f(x), x),x):
fd2:=unapply(diff(f(x),x,x),x):
plot({fd(x), fd2(x)}, x=1..10);
```

Approximation curves to given data points (regression)

In the `fit` subpackage, the `stats` package contains the `leastsqr` command which can be used to determine the coefficients of a linear combination of functions which describes the relation between two or more data lists.

For the following example, a data set of 50 points was generated. The x coordinates are randomly distributed between 0 and 100; the y coordinates were calculated with the sine function from the x data, which has been subjected to random deviations. They could be measurement data with randomly distributed measurement errors. $p1$ contains a point diagram of the data set which is shown in the following illustrations together with different approximation curves.

```
with(stats): with(fit): with(statplots): with(plots):
datax:=[seq(rand(100)(), i=1..50)]:
datay:=map(x->evalf(sin(x/100*Pi)+rand(30)()/100,4), datax):
p1:=scatter2d(datax, datay):
```

A quadratic function of the form $y = a0 + a1 * x + a2 * x^2$ is to be drawn though the data points. For this purpose, the `leastsqr` command must be passed a description of the required function in square brackets and a list of the two data sets in round parentheses. The description of the regression function consists of a list of all variables, a function with the function specification and a sequence of the coefficients sought.

```
leastsquare[[x,y], y=a0 + a1*x +a2*x^2, {a0,a1,a2}]([datax,datay]);
```

$$y = .08457467725 + .04016847076\,x - .0003995494686\,x^2$$

```
f:=rhs(");
```

$$f := .08457467725 + .04016847076\,x - .0003995494686\,x^2$$

The `display` command from the `plots` package combines the curve with the point diagram previously stored in *p1*.

```
p2:=plot(f, x=0..100):
display([p1,p2]);
```

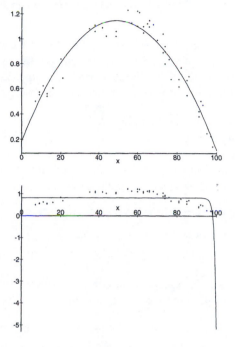

Because of the data distribution, the attempt to approach the data via an exponential function is destined to fail.

```
fy:=a0 + a1*exp(x):
f:=rhs(leastsquare[[x,y], y=fy,
    {a0,a1}]([datax,datay])):
p2:=plot(f, x=0..100):
display([p1,p2]);
```

The two illustrations above clearly show that the quality of the result strongly depends on the functions offered to `leastsqr` for combining. The command is not capable of determining parameters other than the coefficients of the function. Determination of $a0, a1$ and $a2$ for $f = a0 + a1 * \sin(a2 * x)$ is therefore not possible. Since Release 4, however, `leastsquare` also fails with simpler tasks: thus, it has not been possible to determine the coefficients $a0$ to $a3$ for the function $a0 + a1\sin(x/10) + a2\sin(x/20) + a3\sin(x/40)$. In Release 3, this still worked without problems, and also the `fit` command from the `share` library (see next page) promptly supplies the correct result.

`leastsqr` can also determine simple multi-dimensional compensating functions of the kind $y = a1 * x1 + a2 * x2 + ...$ The `seq` command determines the deviation between the nominal values in *datay* and the results of the regression function f.

```
datax1:=[1,2,3]: datax2:=[2,3,4]: datay:=[3,7,8]:
f:=rhs(leastsquare[[x1,x2,y], y=a1*x1+a2*x2, {a1,a2}]([datax1, datax2, datay]));
```

$$f := \frac{3}{2} x1 + x2$$

```
seq(subs(x1=datax1[i], x2=datax2[i], f-datay[i]), i=1..3);
```

$$\frac{1}{2}, -1, \frac{1}{2}$$

Multi-dimensional approximation functions with fit

In the share library, you can find the fit command which fulfils the same task as leastsqr, but has a slightly different syntax. The advantage of fit is that the code of this command is evidently better optimized. The command still supplies results when leastsquare throws in the towel after computing for what seems an endless time.

The following example once again calculates – starting with the *datax* and *datay* lists defined in the last section – a quadratic compensating curve. Apart from the last three decimal digits, the result is the same as that of leastsqr. Deviations can be found in the syntax, instead: fit expects the data in the first two parameters, a list of all functions whose linear combination is to be determined in the third parameter, and the variable in the fourth parameter.

```
with(share): readshare(fit,numerics):
f1:=fit(datax, datay, [1,x,x^2], x);
```

$$f1 := 0.08457467970 + 0.04016847061\,x - 0.0003995494671\,x^2$$

A graphic representation of the curve is not shown since there is no visual difference from the illustration in the previous section.

fit can also cope with non-linear functions. An approximation of the curve through three sine oscillations easily succeeds without problems.

```
f:=fit(datax,datay, a0 + a1*sin(x/10) +
a2*sin(x/20)+a3*sin(x/40), x);
p2:=plot(f, x=0..100):
display([p1,p2]);
```

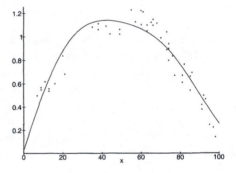

In the following example, the function $x1 + 2 * x2 + \cos(x1 * x2)$ was calculated for 50 random number pairs $(x1, x2)$ in the range between $(0, 0)$ and $(1, 1)$ and falsified with random numbers between 0 and 0.1. Subsequently, an attempt was made to reconstruct the original function by means of fit. fit was offered the three starting terms $x1$, $x2$ and $\cos(x1 * x2)$ plus an additional, previously non-existent term $x1 * x2$ for combination. fit succeeded in calculating the correct coefficients with only minimal deviations.

The syntax of fit becomes evident from the example: in the first parameter, a list of number pairs $([x1, x2], [x1, x2], [x1, x2], ...])$ is specified (*Caution*: error in the online help text); in the second parameter, the list of target values; in the third parameter, the target function; and in the fourth parameter, the list of variable names $[x1, x2]$.

```
datax1:=[seq(rand(100)()/100, i=1..50)]:
datax2:=[seq(rand(100)()/100, i=1..50)]:
datax12:=zip((x1,x2)->[x1,x2], datax1, datax2):
datay:=zip((x1,x2)->x1+2*x2+cos(x1*x2)+rand(100)()/1000, datax1, datax2):

f:=fit(datax12, datay, a1*x1+a2*x2+a3*cos(x1*x2)+a4*x1*x2, [x1,x2]);
```

$$f := 0.9886802218\,x1 + 1.994352600\,x2 + 1.043019133\,\cos(x1\,x2) + 0.05936779281\,x1\,x2$$

The illustration proves the small percentage deviation between the original function (not falsified with random numbers) and the approximation function calculated by `fit`.

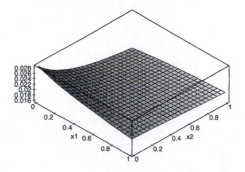

```
plot3d(1-(x1+2*x2+cos(x1*x2))/f,
    x1=0..1, x2=0..1,  axes=boxed,
    orientation=[-45,25]);
```

Syntax summary

```
interp([x0,x1 ... xn], [y0,y1 ... yn], x);
```
   calculates an interpolation polynomial of order $n - 1$ which leads through the specified data points.

```
readlib(spline);
spline([x0,x1 ... xn], [y0,y1 ... yn], x, n);
```
   supplies piecewise second- or third-order polynomials for the variable x through the specified data points.

```
piecewise(n, op(""));
```
   converts the result of `spline` – an If sequence – into an n-fold differentiatable `piecewise` function.

```
with(stats): with(fit):
leastsqr[[x1,x2..., y], y=a1*f1 + a2*f2 +..., {a1,a2...}]([datx1,datx2 ...
daty]);
```
   determines the coefficients a_i of the regression function y, where f_i are arbitrary functions of x_i.

```
with(share):    readshare(fit, numerics):
fit([x0,x1,x2 ...], [y0,y1,y2 ...], [f1,f2,f3 ...], x);
```
calculates the regression function $y = a1 * f1 + a2 * f2 + a3 * f3 + ...$, where arbitrary functions of the variable x may be specified for f_i.

```
fit([[x11,x21...],[x12,x22...],[...]...], [y1,y2...], [f1,f2...], [x1,x2...]);
```
calculates the multi-dimensional regression function $y = a1 * f1 + a2 * f2 + a3 * f3 + ...$. The functions f_i may be dependent on all variables x_i specified in the fourth parameter.

Chapter 23

Minima and maxima, linear optimization

This chapter describes several commands which are suitable for finding boundary values. `minimize`, `maximize` and `extrema` calculate extreme values of one-dimensional and multi-dimensional functions. Since these commands work purely symbolically, their field of application is restricted to trivial applications. More interesting are the commands provided by the `simplex` package. These are suitable for optimization of a target function which is restricted by a system of inequalities.

`minimize` and `maximize`
calculate the absolute minima and maxima of a function.

`extrema`
calculates extreme values of a function taking into account one or more conditions. `extrema` also specifies the location of the solution points.

`simplex`
denotes a package which contains several commands for carrying out linear optimizations. The two most important commands are again `minimize` and `maximize`.

Minima and maxima

The `minimize` and `maximize` commands try to determine the minimum or maximum of a function, assuming that only real numbers are inserted into the variables. As the following examples show, it is advisable not to trust the capabilities of these two commands too much. Prior to being used, `minimize` and `maximize` must be loaded with `readlib(minimize)`.

minimize shows that the function $(x + 1)/(x^2 + 1)$ never becomes smaller than $-\sqrt{2}/(4 + 2\sqrt{2})$.

```
readlib(minimize):
minimize((x+1)/(x^2+1));
```

$$-\frac{\sqrt{2}}{4 + 2\sqrt{2}}$$

minimize and maximize can also cope with simple multi-dimensional functions.

```
minimize(sin(x*y));
```

$$-1$$

```
maximize(sin(x*y));
```

$$1$$

Care must be taken with the absolute value function. Here, `minimize` yields an erroneous result (the correct result would be 0).

```
minimize(abs(sin(x)));
```
$$-1$$

Functions whose derivatives cannot be set to 0 without problems overstretch `minimize` (the command simply does not return a result).

```
f:=x^2+sin(x)+cos(2*x);
minimize(f);
```

The optional specification of the number range within which the function is to be minimized makes things even worse. In this case, Maple supplies an erroneous result.

```
minimize(f, x,-2..2);
```
$$4 + \cos(4) - \sin(2)$$

```
evalf(");
```
$$2.437058952$$

The illustration on the right shows the course of f in the critical range.

```
plot(f, x=-2..2);
```

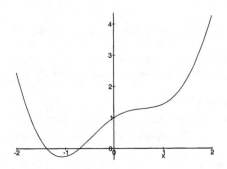

In order to determine the minimum manually, the function is derived. Subsequently, `fsolve` is used to determine the zero point in the range between -1.5 and -0.5. With this, not only is the amount of the minimum known (-0.2313), but also its location ($x = -1.075$).

```
diff(f, x);
```
$$2x + \cos(x) - 2\sin(2x)$$

```
fsolve(", x=-1.5..-0.5);
```
$$-1.074907239$$

```
evalf(subs(x=", f));
```
$$-0.2713228382$$

Extreme values with secondary conditions

More application possibilities are offered by the `extrema` command. It calculates extreme values of a function (thus, both minima and maxima) with the possibility of taking secondary conditions into account. When a variable name is specified in the fourth parameter, Maple writes a list of the solution locations into this variable. Complicated functions which would need numerical calculation of the extreme value overstretch `extrema` in the same way as the two commands in the previous section.

Prior to being used, the command must be read with `readlib`.

```
readlib(extrema):
extrema(x^2-x, {}, x);
```
$$\{-1/4\}$$

The command on the right searches for extrema in the function $x*y$, where the secondary condition $x + y = 1$ is taken into account. The function supplies the value of the minimum found. After the call of `extrema`, the variable sln contains a set giving the equations of the solution point.

```
extrema(x*y, x+y=1, {x,y}, 'sln');
```
$$\{1/4\}$$

```
sln;
```
$$\{\{x = 1/2, y = 1/2\}\}$$

Linear optimization

The `simplex` package contains several commands for carrying out linear optimizations. The two most important commands are `minimize` and `maximize` which are used to optimize a target function taking into account several restrictions. Both commands are passed the target function in the first parameter and the set of restrictions in the second parameter. The restrictions must be formulated with $\leq$ or $\geq$; the operators $<$ and $>$ are not allowed. Both the target function and the restrictions must be linear.

Note: As you will have noticed, the keywords `minimize` and `maximize` are used with two different meanings – for calculation of extrema of functions and for linear optimization. When you need both meanings of this command at the same time, you must not activate the `simplex` package with `with`. Instead, you must access the `simplex` variations of `minimize` and `maximize` under what have now become quite long names: `simplex[minimize]` and `simplex[maximize]`. Maple now loads the program code automatically when needed, so `with` is not necessary. The different names (one short and one long variation) allow a clear distinction between the otherwise homonymous commands.

In the following example, we want to calculate how the products P1 and P2 can be produced on the machines M1, M2 and M3, so that the sum of the profits (P1: £300, P2: £500) is as high as possible. To produce P1, machines M1 and M2 must be used for 2 hours each. To produce P2, machines M1, M2 and M3 must be used for 4, 2 and 6 hours, respectively. M1 can be used for a maximum of 170 hours per month, M2 for 150 hours and M3 for 180 hours.

```
with(simplex):
maximize(300*x1+500*x2, {2*x1+4*x2<=170, 2*x1+2*x2<=150, 6*x2<=180});
```
$$\{x1 = 65, x2 = 10\}$$

Thus, the maximum profit is reached by producing 65 pieces of P1 and 10 pieces of P2.

In the second example, `maximize` finds the optimum combination of four variables. The keyword `NONNEGATIVE` must be specified in the fourth parameter. This tells Maple that all four variables must be greater than or equal to 0. By specifying the variable name $eqsys$ in the fifth parameter, `maximize` writes the unsolved equation system of the optimization problem into that variable.

The example also shows a weakness of `maximize`: the command determines only one of the two possible solutions; $x1 = 0, x2 = 0, x3 = 0, x4 = 15$ would be a correct solution too.

```
maximize(6*x1+10*x2+8*x3+12*x4,
   {3*x1 + 2*x2 +           2*x4<=60,
      x1 +   x2 + 2*x3 +    x4<=45,
    2*x1 +                4*x4<=90,
    4*x1 +         4*x3 + 3*x4<=120,
      x1 + 2*x2 + 2*x3 + 2*x4<=30}, NONNEGATIVE, 'eqsys');
```

$$\{x2 = 0, x3 = 0, x1 = 15, x4 = 15/2\}$$

```
eqsys;
```

$$\{x1 = -\frac{\_SL5}{2} + 15 + \frac{\_SL3}{2} + x3, \_SL1 = \frac{45}{2} + \frac{\_SL5}{4} + \frac{\_SL3}{4} - \frac{3\,x3}{2},$$

$$\_SL2 = 30 + 2\,\_SL3 + 4\,x2 + 4\,x3, x4 = -x2 - \frac{3\,\_SL3}{4} + 15/2 + \frac{\_SL5}{4} - \frac{3\,x3}{2},$$

$$\_SL4 = \frac{75}{2} + \frac{5\,\_SL5}{4} + \frac{\_SL3}{4} + 3\,x2 - \frac{7\,x3}{2}\}$$

Transport problems

Besides linear optimization tasks, transport problems are the second most important problem area of operational research. (Operational research is that branch of science that is concerned with optimization tasks.) Maple does not provide a command for the immediate solution of transport problems, but by using some list commands, a given problem can be formulated in such a way that it is suitable for `minimize`. This is best shown by an example:

Three building sites need 160, 330 and 340 m^3 of gravel per week which is supplied by three gravel pits with a capacity of 220, 290 and 320 m^3. The transport costs between the gravel pits and the building sites look as follows (in £ per m^3):

	B1	B2	B3
P1	10	15	18
P2	10	17	19
P3	16	19	20

The problem can be formulated by means of a 3*3 matrix $x[1, 1]$ to $x[3, 3]$. The matrix element $x[i, j]$ indicates how much gravel is transported from a given gravel pit to a given building site. The target function to be minimized is $x[1, 1] * 21 + x[1, 2] * 15 + \ldots$

There are six restrictions for the problem: for each building site, the sum of all x in the corresponding column must match the required total quantity. For each gravel pit, the sum of all x in the corresponding row must not exceed the existing capacity. The expense of this relatively simple example might seem somewhat high, but it would not be any higher for an example with 20 sources and 14 target locations (apart from typing in the coefficients).

```
with(simplex):
gravel:=[220, 290, 320]:
building_site:=[160, 330, 340]:
cost:=array([[10,15,18],[10,17,19],[16,19,20]]);
```

$$cost := \begin{bmatrix} 10 & 15 & 18 \\ 10 & 17 & 19 \\ 16 & 19 & 20 \end{bmatrix}$$

```
x:=array(1..3,1..3):
restr:={seq(sum(x[i,'j'],'j'=1..3)=gravel[i], i=1..3)} union
        {seq(sum(x['i',j],'i'=1..3)=building_site[j], j=1..3)};
```

$$restr := \{x_{1,1} + x_{1,2} + x_{1,3} = 220, x_{2,1} + x_{2,2} + x_{2,3} = 290, x_{1,1} + x_{2,1} + x_{3,1} = 160,$$

$$x_{1,2} + x_{2,2} + x_{3,2} = 330, x_{1,3} + x_{2,3} + x_{3,3} = 340, x_{3,1} + x_{3,2} + x_{3,3} = 320\}$$

```
vars:={seq(seq(x[i,j], i=1..3), j=1..3)}:
```

Since the formulation of the target function through two embedded sum commands did not succeed, the set of summands was first generated by means of two loops. Subsequently, convert/'+' was used to convert this set into a sum. A detailed description of the loop command for can be found in Chapter 29.

```
target:={}:
for i from 1 to 3 do
  for j from 1 to 3 do
    target:=target union{x[i,j]*cost[i,j]}:
  od;
od;
target:=convert(target, '+');
```

$$target := 10\,x_{1,1} + 10\,x_{2,1} + 19\,x_{2,3} + 16\,x_{3,1} + 19\,x_{3,2} + 20\,x_{3,3} + 17\,x_{2,2} + 15\,x_{1,2} + 18\,x_{1,3}$$

The calculation of the solution is then surprisingly quick. With assign, the conditional equations of the solution are carried out as assignments.

```
minimize(target, restr, NONNEGATIVE);
```

$$\{x_{3,3} = 320, x_{3,2} = 0, x_{2,2} = 110, x_{2,3} = 20, x_{2,1} = 160, x_{1,2} = 220, x_{1,3} = 0, x_{3,1} = 0,$$

$$x_{1,1} = 0\}$$

```
assign("); eval(x);
```

$$\begin{bmatrix} 0 & 220 & 0 \\ 160 & 110 & 20 \\ 0 & 0 & 320 \end{bmatrix}$$

```
target;
```

```
  13550
```

The total result can subsequently be taken from the matrix x: building site 1 receives 160 m^3 from gravel pit 2; building site 2 receives 220 m^3 from gravel pit 1 and an additional 110 m^3 from gravel pit 2; building site 3 receives 20 m^3 from gravel pit 2 and 320 m^3 from gravel pit 3. The total cost is £13 550.

Syntax summary

```
readlib(minimize);
```
loads the program code for the `minimize` and `maximize` commands.

```
minimize(f);      minimize(f,x,x1..x2);
maximize(f);      maximize(f,x,x1..x2);
```
tries to determine the minima or maxima of the function in the entire number range or in the specified number range. The commands determine only the value of the extrema, not their location. The commands only work symbolically.

```
readlib(extrema);
```
loads the program code for the `extrema` command.

```
extrema(f, {second_cond}, {var}, 'loc');
```
determines extrema (minima and maxima) of the function f. Secondary conditions optionally specified in the second parameter are taken into account. The third parameter contains the variable or the set of variables. The location of extrema found is written in the form of equations into the variable specified in the fourth parameter. The command only works symbolically.

```
with(simplex);
```
activates the commands of the `simplex` package.

```
minimize(target_func, {restrict}, option);
maximize(target_func, {restrict}, option);
```
carries out a linear optimization of the target function, taking into account the restrictions specified with $\leq$ or $\geq$. In the third parameter, the option NONNEGATIVE can be specified – the additional condition $x_i \geq 0$ automatically applies to all variables.

Chapter 24

Series expansion

In many calculations, there are functions which can be mathematically processed only at very high expense (or cannot be processed at all). Especially in technical applications, such functions can often be substituted by a more manageable series expansion.

The biggest problem with the commands described in this chapter is that they are not homogeneous: some supply results of the data type `series`; others supply normal polynomials with an additional O term which specifies the order of the series expansion; the commands of the `powseries` package use yet another form of their own.

`series`
carries out a Taylor, Laurent or generalized power series expansion. A possible application of `series` is the solution of differential equations.

`mtaylor` and `poisson`
carry out multi-variable Taylor series expansions.

`FPS`
from the `share` library, contains the `FormalPowerSeries` command which determines general summation formulae of power series.

`powseries`
denotes a package that contains various commands for processing formal power series. The `share` package `PS` can be used to modify the functionality of the `powseries` commands.

`numapprox`
is a package that contains commands for numerical calculation of (usually rational) approximation functions.

Reference: The `eulermac` command, which generates an Euler-Maclaurin series for a general summation formula, has already been discussed in Chapter 15. Information on Fourier series expansion for periodic functions can be found in Chapter 25.

Taylor, Laurent and general power series expansion

The standard command for the generation of series expansions is `series`. Depending on the form of the function to be developed, it generates a Taylor, a Laurent or a general power series. In the first parameter, the command is passed the function to be expanded, in the second parameter the point of expansion. In the third parameter, the maximum order of the expansion can be specified. If this parameter is omitted, Maple uses the global variable `Order` (default setting 6).

```
series(sin(x), x=0,10);
```

$$x - \frac{1}{6}x^3 + \frac{1}{120}x^5 - \frac{1}{5040}x^7 + \frac{1}{362880}x^9 + O\left(x^{10}\right)$$

```
series(log(x), x=1);
```

$$x - 1 - \frac{1}{2}(x-1)^2 + \frac{1}{3}(x-1)^3 - \frac{1}{4}(x-1)^4 + \frac{1}{5}(x-1)^5 + O\left((x-1)^6\right)$$

`series` can also be used for the expansion of complex functions (around a complex expansion point). The example below shows an expansion around the point $z0 = I$.

```
series(1/(z^2+1), z=I);
```

$$-\frac{I}{2}(z-I)^{-1} + \frac{1}{4} + \frac{I}{8}(z-I) - \frac{1}{16}(z-I)^2 - \frac{I}{32}(z-I)^3 + \frac{1}{64}(z-I)^4 +$$

$$O\left((z-I)^5\right)$$

`series` also allows the expansion point ∞. In this special case, `series` calls the `asympt` command in order to carry out the series expansion. For this reason, the two commands `series(f,x=infinity)` and `asympt(f,x)` are equivalent.

```
series(arctan(x), x=infinity);
```

$$\frac{1}{2}\pi - \frac{1}{x} + \frac{1}{3}\frac{1}{x^3} - \frac{1}{5}\frac{1}{x^5} + O\left(\frac{1}{x^6}\right)$$

Further processing of series

`series` usually supplies its results in the data type `series`, making use of a fairly efficient storage of the series (in the form of the expansion point and the value of coefficients). For this reason, results generated by `series` cannot immediately be used for further processing.

```
f:=series(sin(x), x=Pi);
```

$$f := -x + \pi + \frac{1}{6}(x-\pi)^3 - \frac{1}{120}(x-\pi)^5 + O\left((x-\pi)^6\right)$$

```
evalf(subs(x=2, f));
```

$$0.9097898165 + O((2 - \pi)^6)$$

```
whattype(f);
```

series

The `convert/polynom` command can be used to convert the series into a normal polynomial. This polynomial can subsequently be used for calculation, simplification, differentiation, drawing, and so on.

```
p:=convert(f, polynom);
```

$$p := -x + \pi + \frac{(x - \pi)^3}{6} - \frac{(x - \pi)^5}{120}$$

The illustration shows the deviation of the series expansion of $\sin(x)$ around the point $x = \pi$ from the original function.

```
plot({p, sin(x)}, x=0..2*Pi);
```

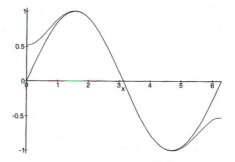

The assumption that each expression that ends in $O(...)$ is a series of the data type `series` is, however, misleading. The following series cannot be represented by the `series` data type, because x always occurs in the third root. In such cases, Maple uses a normal polynomial to which it adds the expression $O(...)$. For this reason, the `convert/polynom` command has no effect!

```
f:=series(tan(x)^(1/3), x=0);
```

$$f := \sqrt[3]{x} + \frac{x^{7/3}}{9} + \frac{13\, x^{13/3}}{405} + O(x^{16/3})$$

```
convert(f, polynom);
```

$$\sqrt[3]{x} + \frac{x^{7/3}}{9} + \frac{13\, x^{13/3}}{405} + O(x^{16/3})$$

```
whattype(f);
```

$+$

Even in the representation of series through normal sums, the order term is disturbing. The easiest way to remove it (no matter what the inside of $O(...)$ looks like) is by means of `select`. Since most of the commands presented in the further course of this chapter do not supply true series, but sums with an additional order term, this process is of great importance.

```
p:=f - select(has,f,O);
```

$$p := \sqrt[3]{x} + \frac{x^{7/3}}{9} + \frac{13\, x^{13/3}}{405}$$

Another special case occurs when, during a series expansion, `series` arrives at an exact result. This happens with the expansion of the elementary function x^2 around the point $x = 3$.

```
f:=series(x^2, x=3);
```

$$f := (9 + 6\,(x-3) + (x-3)^2)$$

```
simplify(f);
```

$$(9 + 6\,(x-3) + (x-3)^2)$$

Since the result is exact, the order term is dropped. Thus, the result looks like a normal polynomial. Nevertheless, it is internally represented through the `series` data type and must therefore be converted into a polynomial by means of `convert` before simplification into the original function x^2 succeeds.

```
whattype(f);
```

$$series$$

```
convert(f,polynom);
```

$$-9 + 6\,x + (x-3)^2$$

```
simplify(");
```

$$x^2$$

Within `series`, you can process series in the same way as other mathematical formulae: besides operations with scalar values (for example, multiplication of a series by a factor), you can also carry out combination operations with several series (addition, multiplication, and so on). In the following example, the series for $\sin(x)$ and $\cos(x)$ are multiplied by each other. The same result could be obtained with the command `series(sin(x)*cos(x), x=Pi/2)`.

```
s1:=series(sin(x),x=Pi/2);
```

$$s1 := 1 - \frac{1}{2}\left(x - \frac{1}{2}\pi\right)^2 + \frac{1}{24}\left(x - \frac{1}{2}\pi\right)^4 + O\left(\left(x - \frac{1}{2}\pi\right)^6\right)$$

```
s2:=series(cos(x), x=Pi/2);
```

$$s2 := -\left(x - \frac{1}{2}\pi\right) + \frac{1}{6}\left(x - \frac{1}{2}\pi\right)^3 - \frac{1}{120}\left(x - \frac{1}{2}\pi\right)^5 + O\left(\left(x - \frac{1}{2}\pi\right)^6\right)$$

```
series(1/s1, x=Pi/2);   #Series for 1/sin(x)
```

$$1 + \frac{1}{2}\left(x - \frac{1}{2}\pi\right)^2 + \frac{5}{24}\left(x - \frac{1}{2}\pi\right)^4 + O\left(\left(x - \frac{1}{2}\pi\right)^6\right)$$

```
series(s1+x^2, x=Pi/2);   #Series for sin(x)+x^2
```

$$\left(1 + \frac{1}{4}\pi^2\right) + \pi\left(x - \frac{1}{2}\pi\right) + \frac{1}{2}\left(x - \frac{1}{2}\pi\right)^2 + \frac{1}{24}\left(x - \frac{1}{2}\pi\right)^4 + O\left(\left(x - \frac{1}{2}\pi\right)^6\right)$$

```
series(s1*s2, x=Pi/2);   #Series for sin(x)*cos(x)
```

$$-\left(x - \frac{1}{2}\pi\right) + \frac{2}{3}\left(x - \frac{1}{2}\pi\right)^3 - \frac{2}{15}\left(x - \frac{1}{2}\pi\right)^5 + O\left(\left(x - \frac{1}{2}\pi\right)^6\right)$$

The use of functions in `series` does not always work without problems. In the example below, an attempt is made to determine the arc sine of the sinusoidal series. The result should be x; Maple, however, supplies a different result.

```
series(arcsin(s1), x=Pi/2);
```

$$\frac{1}{2}\pi - \left(x - \frac{1}{2}\pi\right) + O\left(\left(x - \frac{1}{2}\pi\right)^5\right)$$

```
simplify(convert(", polynom));
```

$$\pi - x$$

Solving differential equations via series expansions

One practical application of `series` is the manual solution of differential equations. This can be useful when `dsolve` with the `series` option fails (see Chapter 18). The centre of the following example is the differential equation $y - y' = \sin(\sqrt{x})$. This equation can be handled neither by the normal `dsolve` command nor by its `series` variation.

```
restart: dsolve(y(x)-diff(y(x),x)=sin(sqrt(x)), y(x));
```

$$y(x) = e^x \int -e^{-x} \sin(\sqrt{x})dx + e^x\_C1$$

```
dsolve({y(x)-diff(y(x),x)=sin(sqrt(x)), y(0)=0}, y(x), series);
```

In order to solve the differential equation manually, first a series expansion is carried out for $\sin(\sqrt{x})$. The result shows why `dsolve/series` cannot cope with this differential equation – it cannot handle the fractions in the powers.

```
siq:=series(sin(sqrt(x)), x, 8):
siq:=siq-select(has, siq, 0);
```

$$siq := \sqrt{x} - \frac{x^{3/2}}{6} + \frac{x^{5/2}}{120} - \frac{x^{7/2}}{5040} + \frac{x^{9/2}}{362880} - \frac{x^{11/2}}{39916800} + \frac{x^{13/2}}{6227020800} - \frac{x^{15/2}}{1307674368000}$$

Starting with the somewhat unusual series above, instead of the normal approach $y = a_0 + a_1 x + a_2 x^2 + a_3 x^3 + ...$, an alternative approach is chosen: $y = a_1 x^{3/2} + a_2 x^{5/2} + a_3 x^{7/2} + ...$ This approach implicitly contains the boundary condition $y(0) = 0$. The coefficients a_i are represented by an array.

```
a:=array(1..7):
fy:=sum(a[i]*x^(i+1/2), i=1..7);
```

$$fy := a_1 x^{3/2} + a_2 x^{5/2} + a_3 x^{7/2} + a_4 x^{9/2} + a_5 x^{11/2} + a_6 x^{13/2} + a_7 x^{15/2}$$

```
fyd:=diff(fy, x);
```

$$fyd := \frac{3 a_1 \sqrt{x}}{2} + \frac{5 a_2 x^{3/2}}{2} + \frac{7 a_3 x^{5/2}}{2} + \frac{9 a_4 x^{7/2}}{2} + \frac{11 a_5 x^{9/2}}{2} + \frac{13 a_6 x^{11/2}}{2} + \frac{15 a_7 x^{13/2}}{2}$$

With this, the differential equation can be written in the form $y - y' - \sin(\sqrt{x}) = 0$. The result is a rather complicated structure:

```
deqn:=fy-fyd-siq;
```

$$deqn := a_1 x^{3/2} + a_2 x^{5/2} + a_3 x^{7/2} + a_4 x^{9/2} + a_5 x^{11/2} + a_6 x^{13/2} + a_7 x^{15/2} - \frac{3 a_1 \sqrt{x}}{2} -$$

$$\frac{5 a_2 x^{3/2}}{2} - \frac{7 a_3 x^{5/2}}{2} - \frac{9 a_4 x^{7/2}}{2} - \frac{11 a_5 x^{9/2}}{2} - \frac{13 a_6 x^{11/2}}{2} - \frac{15 a_7 x^{13/2}}{2} - \sqrt{x} + \frac{x^{3/2}}{6} -$$

$$\frac{x^{5/2}}{120} + \frac{x^{7/2}}{5040} - \frac{x^{9/2}}{362880} + \frac{x^{11/2}}{39916800} - \frac{x^{13/2}}{6227020800} + \frac{x^{15/2}}{1307674368000}$$

The next step towards solving the differential equation is to order the equation by powers of x and set the resulting coefficients to 0. The resulting equations can then be used to determine a_i. For grouping the above expression by powers of x, the series command is used in a different way than originally intended – it fulfils the task with some flair, causing fewer problems than collect or sort.

```
coef:=series(deqn, x, 10);
```

$$coef := \left(-1 - \frac{3 a_1}{2}\right) \sqrt{x} + \left(a_1 + 1/6 - \frac{5 a_2}{2}\right) x^{3/2} + \left(-\frac{7 a_3}{2} + a_2 - \frac{1}{120}\right) x^{5/2} +$$

$$\left(\frac{1}{5040} - \frac{9 a_4}{2} + a_3\right) x^{7/2} + \left(-\frac{1}{362880} + a_4 - \frac{11 a_5}{2}\right) x^{9/2} +$$

$$\left(a_5 + \frac{1}{39916800} - \frac{13 a_6}{2}\right) x^{11/2} + \left(-\frac{15 a_7}{2} + a_6 - \frac{1}{6227020800}\right) x^{13/2} +$$

$$\left(a_7 + \frac{1}{1307674368000}\right) x^{15/2}$$

Since the expression contains 'crooked' powers, series supplies the result as a normal sum. The three following commands show how op can be used to access individual elements of the sum and, at a later stage, the factor in front of x^i.

```
whattype(coef);
```

$$+$$

```
op(1,coef);
```

$$\left(-1 - \frac{3 a_1}{2}\right) \sqrt{x}$$

```
op(1,op(1,coef));
```

$$-1 - \frac{3 a_1}{2}$$

With this knowledge, the conditional equations for a_i can be easily determined from the above polynomial. Since this would result in seven equations for six variables, the last term is not used (nops(coef)-1). Subsequently, the six unknowns a_1 to a_6 can be determined with solve without problems.

```
eq:=seq(op(1,op(i,coef)), i=1..nops(coef)-1);
```

$$eq := -1 - \frac{3\,a_1}{2}, a_1 + 1/6 - \frac{5\,a_2}{2}, -\frac{7\,a_3}{2} + a_2 - \frac{1}{120}, \frac{1}{5040} - \frac{9\,a_4}{2} + a_3,$$

$$-\frac{1}{362880} + a_4 - \frac{11\,a_5}{2}, a_5 + \frac{1}{39916800} - \frac{13\,a_6}{2}, -\frac{15\,a_7}{2} + a_6 - \frac{1}{6227020800}$$

```
solve({eq});
```

$$\{a_6 = -\frac{95699}{259459200}, a_5 = -\frac{29}{12096}, a_4 = -\frac{299}{22680}, a_3 = -\frac{5}{84}, a_2 = -1/5, a_1 = -2/3,$$

$$a_7 = -\frac{328111}{6671808000}\}$$

`assign` is used to assign the values to a_i permanently. Thus, the series for the required solution function y is completely determined:

```
assign(");
fy;
```

$$-\frac{2\,x^{3/2}}{3} - \frac{x^{5/2}}{5} - \frac{5\,x^{7/2}}{84} - \frac{299\,x^{9/2}}{22680} - \frac{29\,x^{11/2}}{12096} - \frac{95699\,x^{13/2}}{259459200} - \frac{328111\,x^{15/2}}{6671808000}$$

For safety, a check is carried out. As expected, all terms, except the one with the highest power, cancel themselves out. The remaining term corresponds to the order term $O(x^{15/2})$ of the series expansion.

```
simplify(fy-fyd-siq);
```

$$-\frac{4287317\,x^{15/2}}{87178291200}$$

The convergence of the result can be most easily shown graphically. As the illustration on the right shows, the result is usable for the value range up to about $x = 2$.

```
plot({fy-fyd, siq}, x=0..10,
    -1..1);
```

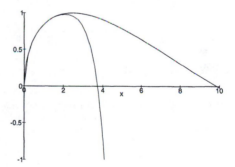

Multi-variable Taylor series expansion

The `mtaylor` command carries out Taylor expansions for multi-variable functions (whereas `series` can only cope with single-variable functions). The command call is in principle the same as for `series`; in the second parameter, however, a list of the expansion points of the variables in question must be specified. The optional third parameter is again used to specify the order of the series expansion. Please note that even with the default setting of 6 large series with up to 21 terms are generated. The command supplies the result as a normal polynomial without order terms. Prior to being used, the command must be loaded with readlib.

```
readlib(mtaylor):
mtaylor(log(x+y), [x=1, y=Pi], 3);
```

$$\ln(1+\pi) + \frac{x-1}{1+\pi} + \frac{y-\pi}{1+\pi} - \frac{(x-1)^2}{2(1+\pi)^2} - \frac{(y-\pi)(x-1)}{(1+\pi)^2} - \frac{(y-\pi)^2}{2(1+\pi)^2}$$

The poisson command is a variation of mtaylor. The main difference is that in trigonometric functions the coefficients are arranged in the canonical Fourier form. Unlike mtaylor, poisson is not capable of carrying out series expansions around an arbitrary point. Furthermore, compared with mtaylor, the choice of functions for which an expansion can be carried out at all is severely restricted.

The following example carries out a series expansion for the function $\sin(a+x) * \cos(b+y)$, both with poisson and with mtaylor. By means of combine/trig it can be shown that both results are identical.

```
readlib(poisson):
f:=sin(a+x)*cos(b+y);
f1:=poisson(f, [x,y], 3);
```

$$f1 := \frac{\sin(a+b)}{2} + \frac{\sin(a-b)}{2} + \left(-\frac{\cos(a-b)}{2} + \frac{\cos(a+b)}{2} \right) y$$

$$+ \left(-\frac{\sin(a+b)}{2} + \frac{\sin(a-b)}{2} \right) yx + \left(\frac{\cos(a-b)}{2} + \frac{\cos(a+b)}{2} \right) x$$

$$+ \left(-\frac{\sin(a+b)}{4} - \frac{\sin(a-b)}{4} \right) x^2 + \left(-\frac{\sin(a+b)}{4} - \frac{\sin(a-b)}{4} \right) y^2$$

```
f2:=mtaylor(f, [x,y], 3);
```

$$f2 := \sin(a)\cos(b) - \sin(a)\sin(b)y + \cos(a)x\cos(b) - \frac{\sin(a)\cos(b)y^2}{2} - \cos(a)x\sin(b)y -$$

$$\frac{\sin(a)x^2\cos(b)}{2}$$

```
combine(f1-f2,trig);
```

   0

General summation formula of a series

The series, mtaylor and poisson commands described up to this point supply series up to an initially specified order. In contrast to this, the FormalPowerSeries command from the share library is capable of determining the general representation of the series in the form of a summation formula.

```
with(share): readshare(FPS, analysis):
FormalPowerSeries(cos(x), x);
```

$$\sum_{k=0}^{\infty} \frac{(-1)^k x^{(2\,k)}}{(2\,k)!}$$

```
fps:=FormalPowerSeries(arcsinh(x), x=infinity);
```

$$fps := \ln(2) - \ln\left(\frac{1}{x}\right) + \frac{1}{2}\left(\sum_{k=0}^{\infty} \frac{(-1)^{(-k)}(1+2\,k)!\,4^{(-k)}\left(\frac{1}{x}\right)^{(2\,k+2)}}{(k!)^2(k+1)(2\,k+2)}\right)$$

In order to evaluate this sum, you must use `subs` to substitute the inert function `Sum` with the command `sum`. For $x > 1$, the resulting formula is identical to `arcsinh`.

```
f:=eval(subs(Sum=sum, fps));
```

$$f := \ln(2) - \ln\left(\frac{1}{x}\right) + \frac{1}{4}\frac{\mathrm{hypergeom}\left(\left[1,1,\frac{3}{2}\right],[2,2],-\frac{1}{x^2}\right)}{x^2}$$

You can also construct a power series from the general summation formula, by substituting not only `Sum` with `sum`, but at the same time `infinity` with an integer number n. Obviously, you can also obtain the same result with `series`.

```
eval(subs(Sum=sum, infinity=5, fps));
```

$$\ln(2) - \ln\left(\frac{1}{x}\right) + \frac{1}{4}\frac{1}{x^2} - \frac{3}{32}\frac{1}{x^4} + \frac{5}{96}\frac{1}{x^6} - \frac{35}{1024}\frac{1}{x^8} + \frac{63}{2560}\frac{1}{x^{10}} - \frac{77}{4096}\frac{1}{x^{12}}$$

```
series(arcsinh(x), x=infinity, 14);
```

$$\ln(2) + \ln(x) + \frac{1}{4}\frac{1}{x^2} - \frac{3}{32}\frac{1}{x^4} + \frac{5}{96}\frac{1}{x^6} - \frac{35}{1024}\frac{1}{x^8} + \frac{63}{2560}\frac{1}{x^{10}} - \frac{77}{4096}\frac{1}{x^{12}} + \mathrm{O}\left(\frac{1}{x^{14}}\right)$$

Formal series

The `powseries` package contains commands for processing formal series. This term is used to denote series which are defined by a general expansion formula. The `powseries` package allows calculation with such series. Some of the permitted operations are addition, subtraction, multiplication and division of two series, logarithmizing of series, construction of derivative and integral, and formation of the reverse series. The advantage of formal series is that, after calculation, they can be evaluated in arbitrary (!) order.

However, the package has some essential limitations:

- It is not suitable for calculations with normal series such as those supplied by the `series` command.

- In user-generated series, only the expansion point 0 is allowed; general series around an arbitrary point are not supported.

- Specification of coefficients for negative variable powers (that is, formulation of Laurent series) is not allowed.

The two most elementary commands of the package are `powcreate` and `tpsform`. With `powcreate`, a formula for the coefficients of the power series is defined. `tpsform` inserts the power series into a variable and writes the series up to order n as a series (data type `series`). In the second parameter of `tpsform` only one variable may be specified, but not $x - 1$ or a similar expression.

```
with(powseries):
powcreate(p(n)=1/n!); tpsform(p, x, 5);
```
$$(1 + x + \frac{1}{2}x^2 + \frac{1}{6}x^3 + \frac{1}{24}x^4 + O\left(x^5\right))$$

The command also allows construction of recursive formulae for coefficients. The variable p, however, must be previously deleted, otherwise Maple gets confused.

```
p:='p':
powcreate(p(n)=p(n-1)*p(n-2), p(0)=1, p(1)=1/2); tpsform(p, x, 5);
```
$$(1 + \frac{1}{2}x + \frac{1}{2}x^2 + \frac{1}{4}x^3 + \frac{1}{8}x^4 + O\left(x^5\right))$$

As soon as a reasonable series is to be constructed, the handling of `powcreate` becomes rather laborious. There is no simple way of differentiating between terms with even powers and terms with odd powers. In the next command, the sine series p is defined. The term $(1 + (-1)^{n+1})/2$ supplies the value 1 for even n and the value 0 for odd n, and thus eliminates all coefficients with even powers. $(-1)^{(n-1)/2}$ supplies alternate positive and negative signs for odd n. Subsequently, the series q for the cosine function is defined in the same way.

```
powcreate(p(n)=(1+(-1)^(n+1))/2 * (-1)^((n-1)/2)/n!); tpsform(p,x,9);
```
$$(x - \frac{1}{6}x^3 + \frac{1}{120}x^5 - \frac{1}{5040}x^7 + O\left(x^9\right))$$

```
powcreate(q(n)=(1+(-1)^(n))/2 * (-1)^(n/2)/n!); tpsform(q,x,9);
```
$$(1 - \frac{1}{2}x^2 + \frac{1}{24}x^4 - \frac{1}{720}x^6 + \frac{1}{40320}x^8 + O\left(x^9\right))$$

The `evalpow` command can be used to carry out various calculation operations with series. In the example below, the two series p and q are multiplied by each other. (Alternatively, the notation `multiply(p,q)` could have been used.) The result is compared with the series expansion for $\sin(x)\cos(x)$.

```
r:=evalpow(p*q);
    r:=proc(powparm) ... end
tpsform(r,x,9);
```

$$(x - \frac{2}{3}x^3 + \frac{2}{15}x^5 - \frac{4}{315}x^7 + O\left(x^9\right))$$

```
series(sin(x)*cos(x), x, 9);
```

$$(x - \frac{2}{3}x^3 + \frac{2}{15}x^5 - \frac{4}{315}x^7 + O\left(x^9\right))$$

reversion constructs the reversion of a series. The series for $\sin(x)$ thus becomes the series for $\arcsin(x)$.

```
r:=reversion(p);
    r:=proc(powparm) ... end
tpsform(r, x, 9);
```

$$(x + \frac{1}{6}x^3 + \frac{3}{40}x^5 + \frac{5}{112}x^7 + O\left(x^9\right))$$

```
series(arcsin(x), x, 9);
```

$$(x + \frac{1}{6}x^3 + \frac{3}{40}x^5 + \frac{5}{112}x^7 + O\left(x^9\right))$$

powdiff constructs the derivative of a series. As expected, the result – the derivative of the series for $\sin(x)$ – coincides with the series for $\cos(x)$.

```
r:=powdiff(p);
    r:=proc(powparm) ... end
tpsform(r,x,9);
```

$$(1 - \frac{1}{2}x^2 + \frac{1}{24}x^4 - \frac{1}{720}x^6 + \frac{1}{40320}x^8 + O\left(x^9\right))$$

A list of further calculation commands for series can be found in the syntax summary at the end of this chapter. Two more special commands are worth mentioning: **powpoly** generates formal series from polynomials, and **powsolve** is a very limited command for the solution of differential equations using the power series approach.

With **powpoly**, you have the possibility of further processing the results of the series commands of the previous sections with the **powseries** commands. The problem is that only a finite number of coefficients is present, but not a general formula for coefficients. This limits the precision of all further calculation steps and it means that some operations – such as differentiation – are not possible at all.

In the following example, **series** is used to carry out a series expansion for the tangent function up to order 10. The terms are converted into a polynomial with **convert/polynom** and stored in the series r. Subsequently, the series $p + r$ (that is, sine plus tangent function) is calculated and output up to order 15. In spite of the term $O(x^{15})$, the coefficients are only correct up to order 9, because the tangent series is only available up to that order.

```
s:=series(tan(x), x=0, 10);
```

$$s := (x + \frac{1}{3}x^3 + \frac{2}{15}x^5 + \frac{17}{315}x^7 + \frac{62}{2835}x^9 + O\left(x^{10}\right))$$

```
r:=powpoly(convert(s,polynom), x);
    r:=proc(powparm) ... end
```

```
t:=evalpow(p+r);
    t:=proc(powparm) ... end
```

```
tpsform(t,x,15);
```

$$(2\,x + \frac{1}{6}x^3 + \frac{17}{120}x^5 + \frac{271}{5040}x^7 + \frac{7937}{362880}x^9 - \frac{1}{39916800}x^{11} + \frac{1}{6227020800}x^{13} + O\left(x^{15}\right))$$

The `powsolve` command allows you to solve trivial differential equations (such as $y'' + y = 1$) via the power series approach. The result is again returned as a formal series. What is most irritating with this command is the fact that neither a special function (such as $\sin(x)$) nor a formal series may be specified in the differential equation. This makes the command completely unusable for any practical application.

The powseries extension PS

The PS package from the share library modifies the commands of the powseries package. The commands receive a new functionality which, at first sight, appears to allow easier handling. In practice, however, PS too reduces the formal power series to finite approximations, as does series. Thus, the general approach of the powseries commands is lost. In particular, it is no longer possible to determine the resulting series up to an arbitrary order at the end of a calculation operation.

```
restart:
with(powseries): with(share): readshare(PS, calculus): with(PS):
p1:=powcreate(sin(x),x);
```

$$p1 := x - \frac{1}{6}\,x^3 + \frac{1}{120}\,x^5 + O(\,x^6\,)$$

```
p2:=powcreate(cos(x),x);
```

$$p2 := 1 - \frac{1}{2}\,x^2 + \frac{1}{24}\,x^4 + O(\,x^6\,)$$

```
multiply(p1,p2);
```

$$x - \frac{2}{3}\,x^3 + \frac{2}{15}\,x^5 + O(\,x^6\,)$$

```
tpsform(p,x,10);
    Error, (in tpsform) wrong number (or type) of parameters
    in function series
```

Numeric calculation of approximation functions

The `numapprox` package collects together various functions for the calculation of approximation functions:

- `minimax` generates a rational approximation function which approaches the given function in a range $(x0..x1)$.

- `chebpade` also calculates a rational approximation function for the range $(x0..x1)$. The approximation function is composed of Chebyshev polynomials.

- `pade` is the third variation for calculating a rational approximation function. As in `series`, however, the approximation is only valid around a given point $x0$.

- `chebyshev` calculates a Chebyshev series for the specified function in the range $x0..x1$.

In addition, the package contains some other commands which, however, do not offer anything which is truly new: `taylor` and `laurent` are restricted variations of the `series` command. `hornerform` and `confracform` convert polynomials and rational functions into Horner's form or into a continued fraction – see `convert/horner` and `/confrac` in Chapter 10. `remez` is used by `minimax` for optimization of the rational function and is only in rare cases called directly by the user.

In the following examples, an attempt has been made to find an approximation function in the range 0 to 2 for the admittedly rather awkward function $\tan(x^2)$. The results are quite varied. Because of the discontinuity in the point $x^2 = \pi/2$, `series` would in any case have been overstretched in trying to generate a series that provides usable results on both sides of the discontinuity point. Through the use of rational approximation functions, however, such discontinuity points no longer constitute an insurmountable obstacle, because the discontinuity point can be reconstructed by way of a zero point in the denominator polynomial of the approximation function.

Notes: Depending on the case, the computing time of these commands can be very high. A decrease in `Digits` can lead to substantial improvements. Furthermore, the calculation algorithms are not completely stable. When the commands return an error message instead of a result, you can always try to make a small adjustment in the starting parameters (including the calculation precision). Additional examples of the use of the commands presented in this chapter can be found in the share file `numerics\approx.ms`.

The minimax command

First, the `minimax` command is used to calculate an approximation function for $\tan(x^2)$. The function to be approached is specified in the first parameter, the required x value range for the approximation function in the second parameter, and the list of required orders of the numerator and denominator polynomials in the third parameter. The first attempt is not very promising and, after about five minutes of computing time, ends with an error message. The meaning of the error message becomes clear when you look at the next but one illustration – the approximation function does indeed oscillate around the original function in a fairly uncontrolled way.

All further attempts to persuade `minimax` to cooperate, for example through different orders of polynomials, smaller or greater calculating precision, and so on, failed as well. Finally, the value range was restricted to 0 to 1, which caused `minimax` to supply a surprisingly good result (see the next illustration).

`minimax` shows a remarkable peculiarity: the results cannot be reproduced exactly. When the command is executed a second time with the same specifications, it yields (slightly) different results!

```
with(numapprox):
minimax(tan(x^2), x=0..2, [3,3]);
    Error, (in numapprox/remez) error curve fails to oscillate
    sufficiently; try different degrees

f1:=minimax(tan(x^2), x=0..1, [3,3]);
```

$$f1 := \frac{0.000010515300 + (-0.0004847052 + (1.002569588 - 0.4734972099x)\,x)\,x}{1 + (-0.4837870767 + (0.1033571051 - 0.2801586752x)\,x)\,x}$$

Although $f1$ was only calculated for the range between 0 and 1, it yields a good match with $\tan(x^2)$ even in a value range extended up to 2.

```
plot({tan(x^2), f1}, x=0..2,
    -10..10);
```

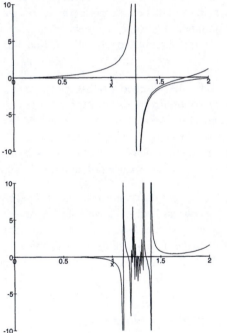

The illustration on the right shows the absolute deviation between $\tan(x^2)$ and the approximation function. It should, however, be noted that the relative deviation against the original function is not as high as it looks (because of the very high values of the $\tan$ function).

```
plot(tan(x^2-f1), x=0..2,
    -10..10);
```

The chebpade command

Next, an attempt was made to calculate a rational approximation function with `chebpade`. Calculation precision was significantly reduced in order to cut computing time. The usage of the command is the same as for `minimax`.

```
with(numapprox):
Digits:=5:
f2:=chebpade(tan(x^2), x=0..2, [4,4]);
```

$$f2 := \frac{0.293T(0,\%1) + 0.2321T(1,\%1) + 0.1603T(2,\%1) + 0.5141T(3,\%1) + 0.3003T(4,\%1)}{T(0,\%1) - 0.2488T(1,\%1) + 0.3306T(2,\%1) + 0.6395T(3,\%1) - 0.3925T(4,\%1)}$$

$$\%1 = 1.0x - 1.0$$

chebpade expresses the result in Chebyshev polynomials $T(n, x - x0)$. In order to be able to further simplify or evaluate the result, the orthopoly package must be loaded, in which the Chebyshev polynomial T is defined. The command with(orthopoly) must be repeated after each call of chebpade or chebyshev, since both commands delete the symbol T prior to starting calculation.

```
with(orthopoly):
normal(f2);
```

$$-\frac{0.0075000 - 0.58780x + 6.1648x^2 - 7.5540x^3 + 2.4026x^4}{-0.54740 - 10.465x + 22.715x^2 - 15.119x^3 + 3.1403x^4}$$

With the exception of the range immediately to the left of the discontinuity point, the coincidence with $\tan(x^2)$ is relatively high.

```
plot({f2, tan(x^2)}, x=0..2,
     -10..10);
```

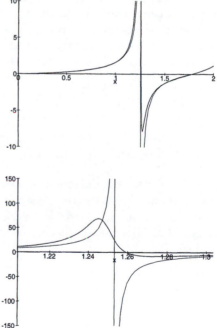

The illustration on the right shows a detailed view of the critical range around the discontinuity point $x0$.

```
x0:=solve(x^2=Pi/2)[1];
```

$$x0 := \frac{\sqrt{2}\sqrt{\pi}}{2}$$

```
plot({f2, tan(x^2)},
   x=x0-0.05..x0+0.05, -150..150);
```

The following two illustrations show the difference between absolute deviation (on the right) and relative deviation (on the left). While the absolute deviation is significant only around the discontinuity point $x0$, the relative deviation is also high where $\tan(x^2)$ tends towards 0.

```
plot(f2-tan(x^2), x=0..2, -10..10);        plot(1-f2/tan(x^2), x=0..2, -1..1);
```

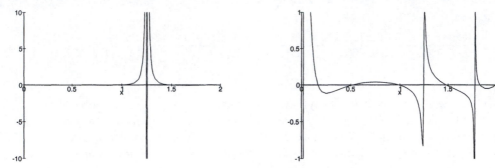

The pade command

For calculations with pade, the calculation precision was set back to the default value 10. The command differs from the other three commands of this section in that calculation of the approximation function is not carried out for a value range, but for a clearly defined point. In the example below, the location of the discontinuity point $x0$ calculated above is used. pade supplies a long formula which is symbolically exact (that is, it contains no floating point numbers). By means of a numerical evaluation with evalf, the formula can be reduced to a relatively short fraction.

```
with(numapprox): Digits:=10:
x0:=solve(x^2=Pi/2)[1]:
f3:=pade(tan(x^2), x=x0, [3,3]): evalf(normal(f3));
```

$$\frac{-2719774873.0x^2 + 632510616.6x^3 - 675187878.0 + 3212301282.0x}{(2.0x - 2.506628274)(-109716870.0x^2 + 895824869.0x - 1356288866.0)}$$

A true surprise is the coincidence of the Pade function with $\tan(x^2)$ in the critical range. In the illustration on the right, the functions can be distinguished from each other only for the marginal ranges.

```
plot({tan(x^2), f3}, x=0..2,
     -10..10);
```

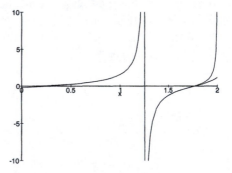

In practice, both the absolute deviation (on the right) and the relative deviation (on the left) of the functions are negligibly small around $x0$.

```
plot(tan(x^2)-f3, x=0..2, -10..10);        plot(1-f3/tan(x^2), x=0..2, -1..1);
```

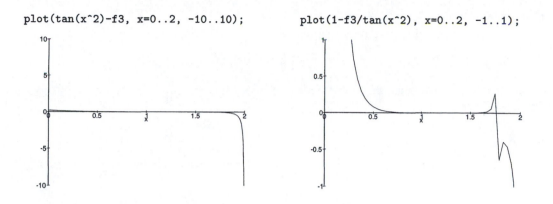

The chebyshev command

The chebyshev command does not generate a rational function, but a series of Chebyshev polynomials. In the first two parameters, the function to expand and the required value range are specified. The third parameter can (optionally) be used to specify the required maximum deviation. The attempt to assemble the sine function between 0 and 2 by means of Chebyshev polynomials succeeds without problems:

```
with(numapprox):
f:=chebyshev(sin(x), x=0..2, 0.001);
```

$$f := 0.3011446971 + 0.5402908908x - 0.4200961117\,(x-1)^2 - 0.08995878926\,(x-1)^3 +$$

$$0.03334431725\,(x-1)^4 + 0.004318229682\,(x-1)^5$$

```
with(orthopoly):
simplify(f);
```

$$0.00003346222800 + 0.9988206258x + 0.006663862760x^2 - 0.1801537614x^3 +$$

$$0.01175316884x^4 + 0.004318229682x^5$$

The approximation function oscillates relatively strongly around the original function, but no deviation is higher than the required 0.001.

```
plot(f-sin(x), x=0..2);
```

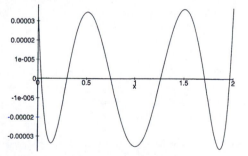

The attempt to reconstruct $\tan(x^2)$ with chebyshev is a total failure. The command supplies an endless row of Chebyshev polynomials up to order 162!

```
f:=chebyshev(tan(x^2), x=0..2, 0.001):
```

$$f := 0.7838211490 T(0, 1.0x - 1.0) + 0.3079994504 T(1, 1.0x - 1.0) -$$

$$1.027470638 T(2, 1.0x - 1.0) - ... + 1.366025105 T(162, 1.0x - 1.0)$$

As expected, this function has nothing at all in common with $\tan(x^2)$:

```
with(orthopoly):
plot(f, x=0..2, -100..100);
```

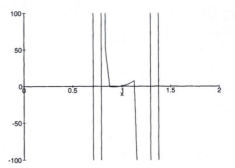

Syntax summary

```
series(f,x);      series(f,x=x0,n);
```
   carries out a Laurent, Taylor or general power series expansion for f around $x = 0$ or around $x = x0$ up to order `Order` or up to order n specified in the third parameter.

```
asympt(f,x);      asympt(f,x,n);
```
   carries out a series expansion for $x \to \infty$ up to order n.

```
whattype(");
```
   determines the data type of the last result. After the commands `series` and `asympt`, possible types are '+' or `series`.

```
convert(series, polynomial);
```
   converts a series of data type `series` into a generally usable polynomial.

```
ser:=ser-select(has, ser, O);
```
   removes the order term $O(x^n)$ from the series when the series is represented as a general sum.

```
Order:=n;
```
   defines the default setting for the order up to which the series are to be expanded.

```
readlib(mtaylor);      mtaylor(f,[x=x0,y=y0,...],n);
```
   carries out a multi-variable Taylor series expansion for $f = f(x, y, ...)$.

```
readlib(poisson);      poisson(f,[x=x0,y=y0,...],n);
```
   as above, with the exception that coefficients are arranged in the canonical Fourier form.

```
with(share): readshare(FPS, analysis):
FormalPowerSeries(f, x=x0);
```
    determines the general representation of the power series in the form of a summation formula.

Formal series

```
readlib(powseries);
```
    activates the commands described below.

```
powcreate(f(n)=...);
```
    defines the formal series f through a function for the coefficients of x^0, x, x^2, x^3....

```
powpoly(polynomial, x);
```
    converts the series specified as a polynomial into a formal series.

```
tpsform(f, x, n);
```
    returns the formal series f as series (data type `series`) of the variable x up to order n.

```
evalpow(f +-*/ g);      evalpow(f */^ s);      evalpow(f(g));
```
    carries out elementary calculations with the series f and g and the scalar s (addition, subtraction, multiplication, division, and so on).

```
powdiff(f);      powint(f);
```
    differentiates or integrates the series.

```
powlog(f);      powexp(f);
```
    create the logarithm and exponential function of the series.

```
reversion(f);
```
    generates the series for the inverse function.

```
with(share): readshare(PS, calculus): with(PS):
```
    modifies the commands of `powseries`. The commands are now easier to handle, but at the same time lose their general approach.

Numeric calculation of approximation functions

```
readlib(numapprox);
```
    activates the following four commands.

```
minimax(f, x=a..b, [z,n]);
```
    constructs a rational function of numerator order z and denominator order n which approaches the function f in the range between a and b.

`chebpade(f, x=a..b, [z,n]);`
   as above, with the exception that the function is assembled by using Chebyshev polynomials $T(n, x - x0)$.

`pade(f, x=x0, [z,n]);`
   constructs a rational approximation function which approaches f in the range around $x = x0$.

`chebyshev(f, x=a..b, eps);`
   calculates a series expansion of Chebyshev polynomials which approaches f in the range between a and b with a maximum deviation of eps.

`readlib(orthopoly):        T(n,x);`
   return the Chebyshev polynomial of order n. *Caution*: both `chebpade` and `chebyshev` delete T during execution, which means that `readlib` must be executed again!

Chapter 25

Fourier transformation

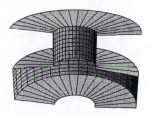

This chapter describes the commands provided by Maple for analytic and numeric Fourier transformation of non-periodic data. Furthermore, it is shown how Fourier series expansion for periodic signals can be carried out by means of a command that must be programmed first. The application areas for Fourier transformations and series expansions are manifold:

- The Fourier transformation for discrete data allows evaluation (spectral analysis) and further processing (smoothing) of measurement data affected by high transmission or measurement errors.

- The Fourier transformation for non-periodic functions can, amongst other things, be used for the solution of partial differential equations.

- With the Fourier series expansion, arbitrary periodic signals can be combined from sine (or cosine) functions of different frequencies. This allows you to analyze the behaviour of technical systems described by differential equations under the influence of periodic input values.

The following commands are the centre point of this chapter:

FFT, iFFT
carry out a Fourier transformation for discrete data and the inverse transformation.

fourier, invfourier
carry out a Fourier transformation for non-periodic functions and the inverse transformation.

fseries
generates a Fourier series for periodic functions. fseries is not a Maple command; the required program code (10 lines) is described in this chapter.

Fourier transformation for discrete data

The FFT command carries out a Fourier transformation for discrete data which reflects a non-periodic function course. The transformation corresponds to a transition from the time domain to the frequency domain. The data must be passed to the command in two separate arrays, one for the real part and one for the imaginary part. The number of data points must be an integer power of 2.

351

While the original data reflects the course in time of a function (over the time), the list of results specifies the corresponding frequency spectrum. The Fourier transformation of random numbers which essentially correspond to white noise results in a list of frequency values of approximately the same size, because in white noise all frequencies are equally represented. The Fourier transformation of a sine wave, in contrast, results in a frequency spectrum with a pronounced peak for the frequency of the wave; all the other values of the Fourier transformation should be 0. The frequency spectrum of a single rectangular pulse looks slightly more complicated (see the next two illustrations).

Prior to being used, the command must be loaded with `readlib`. In the following example, a rectangular pulse is Fourier transformed. In the real part, the starting data consist of 462 zeros, 100 ones and another 462 zeros (thus, a total of 1024 points). The imaginary part is zero throughout. For graphical representation of the starting data contained in *datar* and *datai*, these are combined into an embedded list in *dataxy*.

```
readlib(FFT):
datar:=array([0$462, 1$100, 0$462]):
datai:=array([0$1024]):
dataxy:=[seq([i, abs(datar[i]+I*datai[i])], i=1..1000)]:
```

The illustration shows the course in time of a rectangular pulse which is combined from discrete data points. With `plot`, these points are joined through a continuous line.

`plot(dataxy);`

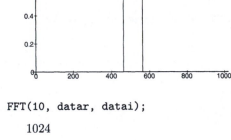

In the first parameter of FFT, the power of 2 is specified ($2^{10} = 1024$). FFT writes the result back into *datar* and *datai*, that is, the starting data is destroyed.

`FFT(10, datar, datai);`

    1024

The following loop shows the first five points of the Fourier transformed data set. The loop is formulated with the `for` command. If you have problems understanding this command, you should briefly consult the description given in Chapter 29 – loops will occur again in the present chapter.

```
for i from 1 to 5 do:
  evalf(datar[i]+I*datai[i],5), evalf(abs(datar[i]+I*datai[i]), 5);
od;
```

100., 100.

$-98.438 - .30201\,I, 98.438$

$93.841 + .57581\,I, 93.843$

$-86.465 - .79584\,I, 86.469$

$76.720 + .94154\,I, 76.726$

For graphical representation, the data must again be combined into a list of the form $[[x, y], [x, y], ...]$. The illustration on the right shows the value (!) of the complex data points.

```
dataxy:=[seq([i, abs(datar[i]+
                I*datai[i])],
        i=1..1000)]:
plot(dataxy, 1..50);
```

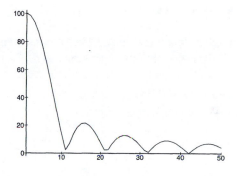

The commands FFT and iFFT for inverse transformation can be bracketed with evalhf. Then, evaluation is carried out making use of the computer's floating point arithmetic, which makes it much faster. In order to write the results back into the two original arrays, the names of these arrays must be bracketed with the keyword var.

```
evalhf(FFT(10, var(datar),
              var(datai)));
```

1024.

Analysis and processing of measurement data

The Fourier transformation is often used to analyze measurement data affected by measurement or transmission errors. In order to simulate such a situation, in the following example, a sine wave is overlaid with random numbers whose value is five times higher than the number range of the sine wave. In order to cut computing time, calculation precision is reduced to seven digits for the duration of this example.

```
Digits:=7: datar:=[seq(evalf(sin(50*2*Pi*t/1024)), t=1..1024)]:
```

The illustration on the right shows the first 100
points (1..100) of the still unfalsified sine wave.

```
dataxy:=[seq([i,datar[i]],
              i=1..1024)]:
plot(dataxy, 1..100);
```

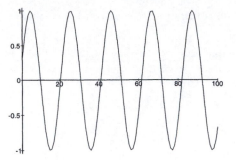

```
datar:=[seq(evalf(datar[i]+rand(1000)()/100), i=1..1024)]:
```

Through the above command, the data was overlaid with random numbers between 0 and 10. In
the illustration on the right, the sine wave is no
longer recognizable.

```
dataxy:=[seq([i,datar[i]],
              i=1..1024)]:
plot(dataxy, 1..100);
```

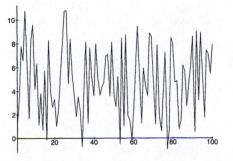

For the Fourier transformation, the data present
in the form of a list is converted into an array.
The result of the transformation is stored in the
variables $fdatar$ and $fdatai$. Please note that
with arrays, the copy command must be used!

```
datar:=array(datar):
datai:=array([0$1024]):
FFT(10, datar, datai):
fdatar:=copy(datar):
fdatai:=copy(datai):
```

The illustration on the right shows the critical
range of the frequency spectrum of the starting data. The frequency peak at frequency 50
is clearly distinguishable.

```
dataxy:=[seq(
  [i, abs(datar[i]+I*datai[i])],
  i=1..1024)]:
plot(dataxy, 30..70, 0..500);
```

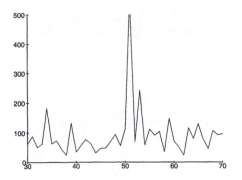

The commands on the right filter the frequencies between 0 and 100 out of the Fourier transformed data. A filter array is defined which contains 100 ones and then all zeros. The frequency spectrum cut in this way is subsequently transformed back into the time domain with iFFT.

```
filter:=array([1$100, 0$924]):
for i from 1 to 1024 do:
   datar[i]:=datar[i]*filter[i]:
   datai[i]:=datai[i]*filter[i]:
od:
iFFT(10, datar, datai):
```

The illustration shows the inverse transformed data after elimination of the higher frequencies. The curve is already much smoother, but still shows no great resemblance to the original sine wave.

```
dataxy:=[seq([i,datar[i]],
               i=1..1024)]:
plot(dataxy, 1..100);
```

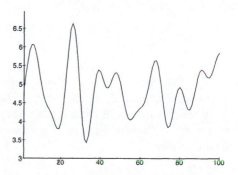

A farther-reaching reconstruction of the starting data can be achieved by improving the filter function. First, the spectrum is reduced to the frequency components between 40 and 60. Please do not forget to copy the original starting data back into *datar* and *datai*; it was temporarily stored above in *fdatar* and *fdatai*.

```
filter:=array([0$40, 1$20, 0$964]):
datar:=copy(fdatar):
datai:=copy(fdatai):
for i from 1 to 1024 do:
   datar[i]:=datar[i]*filter[i]:
   datai[i]:=datai[i]*filter[i]:
od:
iFFT(10, datar, datai):
```

The illustration shows the inverse transformed data where now all frequency components less than 40 and greater than 60 have been removed.

```
dataxy:=[seq([i,datar[i]],
               i=1..1024)]:
plot(dataxy, 1..100);
```

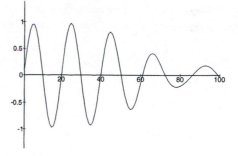

The result can be further improved by an even stronger filter function. The command on the right defines an exponential filter curve around the frequency 50.

```
filter:=array([0$40,
   seq(evalf(exp(-(i-10)^2/19)),
        i=1..19),
   0$965]):
```

The illustration on the right shows the course of
the above defined filter which lets the frequency
50 pass optimally, and the frequencies between
40 and 60 partially.

```
dataxy:=[seq([i,filter[i]],
              i=1..1024)]:
plot(dataxy, 30..70);
```

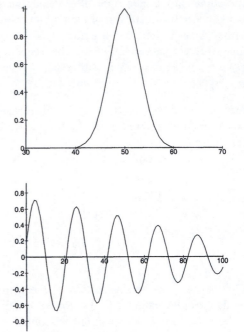

After repeating the execution of the already
twice listed commands (restore *datar* and
datai, filter and inverse transform with iFFT)
we obtain the following drawing of the reconstructed sine wave:

```
dataxy:=[seq([i,datar[i]],
              i=1..1024)]:
plot(dataxy, 1..100);
```

Fourier transformation of analytic functions

The commands `fourier` and `invfourier` carry out the Fourier transformation and the inverse transformation for analytic functions. The transformation from time function $f(t)$ into frequency function $F(w)$ is carried out according to the following formula:

$$F(w) = \int_{-\infty}^{\infty} f(t)e^{-Iwt}\,dt$$

Prior to using `fourier` and `invfourier`, the commands must be loaded by means of
`with(inttrans)`. In the first parameter, `fourier` is passed the function to be transformed; in the
second parameter, the time variable (t); and in the third parameter, the frequency variable (w).

In the following example, the unit-step function
Heaviside is used to define a rectangular pulse.
The function is abbreviated to the more widely
used and shorter name `sigma`.

```
with(inttrans):
alias(sigma=Heaviside):
f:=sigma(t+1)-sigma(t-1);
```

$$f := \sigma(t+1) - \sigma(t-1)$$

The illustration on the right shows the course of the rectangular pulse in the time domain. In order to draw the sides of the pulse sufficiently steeply, the `numpoints` option was set to 500.

```
plot(f, t=-2..2, numpoints=500);
```

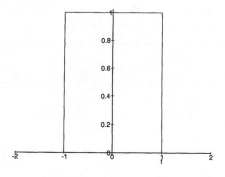

The Fourier transformation supplies complex powers of e. In Release 3 the simplification to the requested sine function succeeded immediately, but there are problems in Release 4.

```
g:=fourier(f, t, w);
```

$$g := e^{(I\,w)}\,(\pi\,\mathrm{Dirac}(w) - \frac{I}{w})$$

$$-e^{(-I\,w)}\,(\pi\,\mathrm{Dirac}(w) - \frac{I}{w})$$

```
g:=simplify(g);
```

$$g := 2\,\frac{I\,(\pi\,\mathrm{Dirac}(w)\,w - I)\sin(w)}{w}$$

`simplify` does recognize that $\mathrm{Dirac}(x)\,x$ can be simplified to 0, but the same simplification inside an (only slightly) more complex expression does not succeed. `Dirac` must be set to 0 with `subs` in order to arrive at the (mathematically correct) result.

```
simplify(Dirac(x)*x);
```

$$0$$

```
g:=simplify(subs(Dirac=0, g));
```

$$g := \frac{2\,\sin(w)}{w}$$

The illustration shows the frequency spectrum of the rectangular pulse, where only physically interesting frequencies greater than 0 have been drawn.

```
plot(g, w=0..4*Pi);
```

The inverse transformation into the time domain succeeds with `invfourier`:

```
invfourier(g, w, t);
```

$$\frac{-2\,\pi\,\sigma(-t-1) + 2\,\pi\,\sigma(-t+1)}{2\,\pi}$$

```
simplify(");
```

$$-\sigma(-t-1) + \sigma(-t+1)$$

The last example shows the transformation of the three Dirac pulses at the locations $t = -1$, $t = 0$ and $t = 1$ into the frequency domain:

```
f:=Dirac(t)+ Dirac(t-1)+Dirac(t+1):
g:=fourier(f, t, w);
```

$$\frac{-2\pi\,\sigma(-t-1) + 2\pi\,\sigma(-t+1)}{2\pi}$$

```
simplify(");
```

$$2\cos(w) + 1$$

Fourier series expansion for periodic functions

Fourier series can be used to represent given periodic functions (rectangular functions, sawtooth functions, and so on) by overlaying several sine and cosine waves of a different frequency. This is of great importance for practical applications as many differential equations can be solved for general sine or cosine waves (see next section).

At this moment, however, we must first write a command for Fourier series expansion which is currently missing from the Maple library. Fourier series for a periodic function $f(t)$ with a period length of $T0$ are defined as follows:

$$f(t) = \frac{a_0}{2} + \sum_{k=1}^{\infty}\left[a_k * \cos\left(\frac{2\pi k t}{T0}\right) + b_k * \sin\left(\frac{2\pi k t}{T0}\right)\right]$$

$$\text{with}\qquad a_k = \frac{2}{T0}\int_0^{T0} f(t) * \cos\left(\frac{2\pi k t}{T0}\right)dt$$

$$\text{and}\qquad b_k = \frac{2}{T0}\int_0^{T0} f(t) * \sin\left(\frac{2\pi k t}{T0}\right)dt$$

Thus, the decisive point is the calculation of the coefficients a_k and b_k from the given function f. Once these coefficients are known, the Fourier series can be put together as a simple sum. In Maple, the definition of a_k and b_k looks as follows:

```
ak:=2/T0_ * Int(f_ * cos(2*Pi*t_*k_/T0_), t_=0..T0_):
bk:=2/T0_ * Int(f_ * sin(2*Pi*t_*k_/T0_), t_=0..T0_):
```

The evaluation of the integrals is in most cases only possible in a purely numerical way, and for this reason the integral command is written directly in its inert form (upper case initial) (see Chapter 17). All variables occurring in the definitions are written with an underscore in order to avoid possible confusion with other variables.

Frequently, small rounding errors occur in the calculation of the coefficients. In order to avoid coefficients like 1.23410^{-16}, the chop function is defined. This function evaluates the parameter x numerically, multiplies it by 10^5, removes the digits after the decimal point, divides it again by 10^5 and thus supplies a result with a maximum of five digits after the decimal point.

```
chop:=x->evalf(round(evalf(x)*10^5)/10^5, 5):
chop(1/3), chop(1e-5), chop(1e-12);
```

$$0.33333, 0.000010000, 0$$

Building on `chop`, we can now define the new `fseries` command as a function:

```
fseries:=(f, t, T0, nmax) ->
      chop(subs(k_=0, f_=f, t_=t, T0_=T0, ak/2))  +
 sum('chop(subs(k_=n, f_=f, t_=t, T0_=T0, ak))' * cos(2*Pi*n*t/T0), n=1..nmax)+
 sum('chop(subs(k_=n, f_=f, t_=t, T0_=T0, bk))' * sin(2*Pi*n*t/T0), n=1..nmax):
```

The command uses the `sum` command twice to multiply the coefficients a_k and b_k by the corresponding sine and cosine functions. All the relevant parameters for the calculation of a_k and b_k are inserted with `subs`. The quotes around `chop` are needed to prevent Maple from evaluating the expression before `sum` inserts values for n.

The usage of the command is simple: in the first parameter, the function to be expanded is specified; in the second parameter, the variable contained in it; in the third parameter, the period $T0$; and in the fourth parameter, the number of terms to be calculated. Please note that the function specified in the first parameter does not have to be periodic. The command (see the definition of the integrals of a_k and b_k) evaluates the function only in the range between 0 and $T0$ and assumes that the function course repeats itself before and after this range. At least in its present form, the command is only suitable for numeric calculation of Fourier series.

In the first example, a Fourier series is expanded for a rectangular function of period 2. The function is defined as 1 between $t = 0$ and $t = 0.5$, otherwise as 0. The Fourier series is calculated up to the seventh order.

```
alias(sigma=Heaviside):
ff:=fseries(sigma(t) - sigma(t-1/2), t, 2, 7);
```

$$ff := 0.25000+$$

$$0.31831\cos(\pi t) - 0.10610\cos(3\pi t) + 0.063660\cos(5\pi t) - 0.045470\cos(7\pi t)+$$

$$0.31831\sin(\pi t) + 0.31831\sin(2\pi t) + 0.10610\sin(3\pi t) + 0.063660\sin(5\pi t)+$$

$$0.10610\sin(6\pi t) + 0.045470\sin(7\pi t)$$

The approximation of the rectangular function by a Fourier series of seventh order does not look particularly pretty, but is at least recognizable.

```
plot(ff, t=0..3);
```

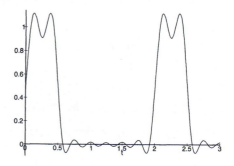

In the second example, a sawtooth function with a period of 1 is approximated by a Fourier series of order 15.

```
ff:=fseries(t, t, 1, 15):
plot(ff, t=0..3);
```

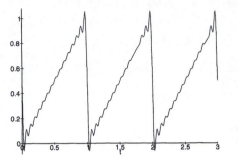

To conclude, a remark on the calculation of Fourier series with large numbers of terms: the chop function leads to clear results, but it entails a loss of precision. For an exact calculation, chop must therefore be redefined with evalf(x). In addition, in order to make the numeric calculation of the integrals succeed, the value of Digits must be increased in most cases. Because of the increasingly high frequency of sine and cosine terms in the definition of a_k and b_k, integration becomes extremely slow.

Solution of differential equations with Fourier series

A practical example concludes this chapter: the behaviour of an electrical serial oscillation circuit consisting of an ohmic resistor R, a coil L and a capacitor C is to be analyzed. Two sawtooth input voltages of different frequency are fed into the circuit one after the other. The task is to determine the voltage course at the resistor.

The two input voltages have a frequency of 10 and 2.5 hertz. During the period, the voltage rises from -0.5 to $+0.5$ volts and suddenly drops back to -0.5 volts. The specifications of the electrical components are: L = 2 henry, C = 100 μF, R = 100 Ω.

The idea for the calculation is simple: it is not possible to solve the system equation (a second-order differential equation) for a sawtooth function, but the solution of a sine function can be determined without too many problems. Via the Fourier series expansion, the sawtooth function is expanded into sine terms. These terms are inserted one after the other into the solution of the differential equation. The resulting individual solutions are summed to form the total solution.

First, the input voltage u is expanded into a Fourier series with fseries. It turns out that the series only contains sine terms (and no cosine terms) which slightly simplifies the further calculation.

```
i:='i': u:=(t-1/20)*10:
u1:=fseries(u, t, 1/10, 6);
```

$$u1 := -0.31830\sin(20\,\pi\,t) - 0.15915\sin(40\,\pi\,t) - 0.10610\sin(60\,\pi\,t) -$$

$$0.079580\sin(80\,\pi\,t) - 0.063660\sin(100\,\pi\,t) - 0.053050\sin(120\,\pi\,t)$$

The command below specifies the equation for the voltage $u(t)$ in the circuit, where $u(t)$ is expressed through the general term $b\sin(nt)$. At a later stage, the coefficients and frequencies of the Fourier expansion are inserted into b and n. When the Fourier expansion also contains cosine terms, the function $a\cos(nt) + b\sin(nt)$ must be used for specifying $u(t)$.

```
eq:=b*sin(n*t)=R*i(t)+L*diff(i(t),t)+1/C*int(i(t),t);
```

$$eq := b\sin(nt) = Ri(t) + L\frac{d}{dt}i(t) + \frac{\int i(t)dt}{C}$$

Since Maple certainly cannot solve the equation in this form, the whole equation is derived. This generates a second-order differential equation.

```
de:=diff(eq, t);
```

$$de := b\cos(nt)n = R\frac{d}{dt}i(t) + L\frac{d^2}{dt^2}i(t) + \frac{i(t)}{C}$$

After not much computing time, Maple finds a solution for this equation which extends over something like five pages. Simplification with `simplify` works wonders, but still supplies a result of about half a page which is not shown here. Please note the keyword `laplace` in `dsolve` which saves a lot of time. `dsolve` also finds the solution without this option, but only after intensive calculation.

```
dsolve({de, i(0)=0, D(i)(0)=0}, i(t), laplace):
sol:=simplify("):
```

In a manual calculation of this example, the exponential coefficients would certainly have been neglected. In this example, only the solution in the oscillating state is of interest. The result, however, is mathematically exact as is shown by inserting the solution into the differential equation.

```
subs(sol, de): simplify(");
```

$$b\cos(nt)n = b\cos(nt)n$$

Only the insertion of the component part specifications for R, L and C leads to a reasonably clear function for the current $i(t)$.

```
isol:=evalf(subs(sol, C=100*10^(-6), L=2, R=100, i(t)),5);
```

$$isol := (-1.0bne^{-25.0t}(-0.000007n\sin(nt)e^{25.0t} + 0.00000014n^2\cos(nt)e^{25.0t} +$$

$$0.0007\cos(66.145t) - 0.0007\cos(nt)e^{25.0t} - 0.00000014n^2\cos(66.145t) +$$

$$0.00026458\sin(66.145t) + 0.000000052916n^2\sin(66.145t)))\ \ /$$

$$(7.0 + 0.00000028n^4 - 0.0021n^2)$$

The last step in the calculation is to insert the terms n and b which result from the Fourier expansion of the sawtooth signal, and to sum the resulting currents $isol$. The coefficients b_i can be easily calculated from bk defined in the previous section. As expected, they match the coefficients of $u1$. The terms n clearly result from the Fourier series for $u(t)$ $(20\pi i)$.

```
bi:=seq(chop(subs(k_=i, f_=u, t_=t, T0_=1/10, bk)), i=1..15);
```

$$bi := -0.31830, -0.15915, -0.10610, -0.079580, ..., -0.021210$$

```
u1;
```

$$u1 := -0.31830\sin(20\,\pi\,t) - 0.15915\sin(40\,\pi\,t) - ... - 0.021210\sin(300\,\pi\,t)$$

```
sum(subs(b=bi[i], n=20*Pi*i, isol), i=1..15):
i1:=evalf(simplify("), 5);
```

$$i1 := -0.00040293\sin(125.66t) - 0.00059953e^{-25.0t}\cos(66.145t)+$$

$$0.00029903\cos(188.50t) - 0.000092312\sin(188.50t) + ...+$$

$$0.000025489\cos(628.32t) + 0.00069203\cos(125.66t)$$

The illustration on the right shows the input voltage $u1$ with a frequency of 10 hertz, represented by a Fourier series of order 15.

```
plot(u1, t=0..0.4);
```

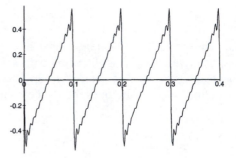

The resulting voltage at the resistor R results from the current multiplied by R = 100 Ω.

```
plot(i1*100, t=0..0.4);
```

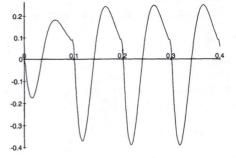

The following commands repeat the calculation for the second input voltage (with 2.5 hertz, that is, a period $T0 = 0.4$). The Fourier series was calculated up to order 25. For this, the chop function was redefined and Digits increased to 15. With the new $T0$, the formula for the voltage u and the term n (subs command) change as well compared to the previous example!

```
Digits:=15:
chop:=x->evalf(x):
u:=(t-1/5)*5/2:
bi:=seq(
    chop(subs(k_=i, f_=u, t_=t,
             T0_=4/10, bk)),
    i=1..25):
i:='i':
sum(subs(b=bi[i], n=5*Pi*i, isol),
    i=1..25):
i2:=simplify("):
```

The illustration on the right shows the voltage at R for a sawtooth input voltage with 2.5 hertz.

```
plot(i2*100, t=0..0.4);
```

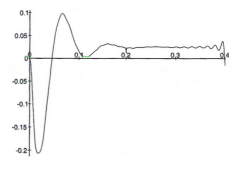

Syntax summary

```
readlib(FFT);    FFT(n, real, imag);    iFFT(n, real, imag);
```
carry out a fast Fourier transformation or the inverse transformation. *real* and *imag* are arrays containing the real and imaginary parts of 2^n data points. The result is written back into the same arrays.

```
evalhf(FFT(n, var(real), var(imag)));
evalhf(iFFT(n, var(real), var(imag)));
```
as above, but making use of the computer's floating point arithmetic.

```
with(inttrans);    fourier(f,t,w);    invfourier(f,w,t);
```
transforms the function $f = f(t)$ into the frequency domain w or carries out the inverse transformation into the time domain.

```
fseries(f,t,T0,n);
```
is not a Maple command, but has been defined in this chapter (Section 'Fourier series expansion for periodic functions'). It generates the Fourier series of the periodic function $f = f(t)$ with a period of $T0$ up to order n.

Chapter 26

Laplace, Mellin and Z transformations

Laplace, Mellin and Z transformations are usually employed for simplification of differential equations or difference equations. The solution process is similar for all transformations: in the first step, the starting equation is transformed – this normally leads to a simplification. The Laplace transformation, for example, converts a differential equation into a simple rational equation. The transformed equation is now solved, which usually succeeds with the relatively uncritical `solve` command. Finally, an attempt is made to transform the result back into the original system. This last step causes most of the problems, since the inverse transformation only succeeds under favourable conditions.

`laplace, invlaplace`
carry out the Laplace transformation of a real or complex function $f(t)$ to $F(s)$ and the inverse transformation. The Laplace transformation is mainly used for the solution of differential equations.

`mellin`
is a less widely used variation of the Laplace transformation. There is no possibility of an inverse transformation.

`ztrans, invztrans`
carry out a Z transformation for discrete functions $f(n)$ to $F(z)$ and the inverse transformation. The Z transformation is often used for the solution of difference equations.

Reference: The Fourier transformation, which thematically would also have fitted into this chapter, has been dealt with in the previous chapter in order to keep the chapters down to a reasonable length.

Laplace transformation

The Laplace transformation transforms the function $f(t)$, which is considered to be 0 for $t < 0$, into $F(s)$. The Laplace transformation is defined as follows:

$$F(s) = \int_0^\infty e^{-st} f(t) \, dt$$

The application of the `laplace` command is very simple: the function to be transformed is specified in the first parameter, its variable in the second parameter, and the variable of the transformed function in the third parameter.

```
laplace(cos(t), t, s);
```

$$\frac{s}{s^2 + 1}$$

`invlaplace` carries out the inverse transformation. The result must be transformed with `simplify`, `combine` or other commands in order to obtain the original form.

```
with(inttrans): laplace(cos(t-a), t, s);
```

$$\frac{s \cos(a) + \sin(a)}{s^2 + 1}$$

```
invlaplace(", s, t);
```

$$\cos(a)\cos(t) + \sin(a)\sin(t)$$

```
combine(",trig);
```

$$\cos(-t + a)$$

The commands `laplace` and `invlaplace` can also cope with the unit-step function `Heaviside`. This function is usually abbreviated as `sigma`.

```
alias(sigma=Heaviside):
laplace(sigma(t-1), t, s);
```

$$\frac{e^{-s}}{s}$$

```
invlaplace(",s,t);
```

$$\sigma(t - 1)$$

At first sight it looks as though `laplace` was unable to handle a step in the time value at an arbitrary moment a. Here, `assume` helps out: when the property $a > 0$ is defined for a, the transformation succeeds.

```
laplace(sigma(t-a),t,s);
```

$$laplace(\,\sigma(t - a), t, s\,)$$

```
assume(a>=0);
laplace(sigma(t-a),t,s);
```

$$\frac{e^{(-a^{\sim} s)}}{s}$$

```
invlaplace(", s, t);
```

$$\sigma(t - a^{\sim})$$

`laplace` also simplifies functions or equations in which derivatives and integrals occur. By abbreviating the expression `laplace(f(t),t,s)` with $F(s)$, the result is presented more clearly.

```
alias(F(s)=laplace(f(t),t,s)):
laplace(diff(f(t), t$2), t, s);
```

$$(F(s)s - f(0))\,s - D(f)(0)$$

```
laplace(int(f(T), T=0..t), t, s);
```

$$\frac{F(s)}{s}$$

laplace and invlaplace also master the convolution rule. In the example on the right, L is used as an abbreviation for the Laplace function in order to reduce typing effort and display the results more clearly.

```
alias(L=laplace):
L(int(f1(t-tau)*f2(tau),tau=0..t),t,s);
```

$$L(\, \text{f1}(\,t\,), t, s\,)\, L(\, \text{f2}(\,t\,), t, s\,)$$

```
F1:=L(f1(t),t,s);
```

$$\textit{F1} := L(\, \text{f1}(\,t\,), t, s\,)$$

```
F2:=L(f2(t),t,s);
```

$$\textit{F2} := L(\, \text{f2}(\,t\,), t, s\,)$$

```
invlaplace(F1*F2,s,t);
```

$$\int_0^t \text{f2}(\,\textit{\_U1}\,)\, \text{f1}(\,t - \textit{\_U1}\,)\, d\_\textit{U1}$$

Solving differential equations with the Laplace transformation

The most important application of the Laplace transformation is the solution of differential equations. Compared to the dsolve command already described in Chapter 18, the laplace command has the advantage that the calculation process can be controlled more precisely. For this reason, laplace often allows you to find a solution which dsolve (with the laplace option) refuses to give.

The principle of solving a differential equation with a Laplace transformation is quite simple: the differential equation of the function $y(t)$ is transformed. $y(t)$ becomes $Y(s)$; the differential equation becomes a normal equation. This equation is then solved for $Y(s)$ by means of solve. Finally, this solution is transformed back into the time domain.

The central point in the first example is the differential equation $y' + y = u$, where the function u represents a rectangular pulse between $t = 1$ and $t = 5$.

```
de:=diff(y(t),t)+y(t)=u;
```

$$de := \frac{d}{dt} y(t) + y(t) = u$$

```
u:=sigma(t-1)-sigma(t-5);
```

$$u := \sigma(t - 1) - \sigma(t - 5)$$

Prior to transforming the differential equation with laplace, the abbreviation $Y(s)$ is defined for $\mathcal{L}\{f(t)\}$.

```
alias(Y(s)=laplace(y(t),t,s)):
laplace(de, t, s);
```

$$Y(s)s - y(0) + Y(s) = \frac{e^{-s}}{s} - \frac{e^{-5s}}{s}$$

The resulting equation in s can be solved for $Y(s)$ without any problems. The boundary condition $y(0) = 0$ is inserted by means of subs.

```
sol:=solve(subs(y(0)=0,"), Y(s));
```

$$sol := -\left(-\frac{e^{-s}}{s} + \frac{e^{-5s}}{s} \right)(s+1)^{-1}$$

Problems occur with the inverse transformation: `invlaplace` cannot cope with the function for $Y(s)$ which is actually quite simple.

```
invlaplace(sol,s,t);
```

$$-\int_0^t e^{-\_U}(-\sigma(t-\_U-1)+$$

$$\sigma(t-\_U-5))\,d\_U$$

After simplification of the solution, the inverse transformation eventually succeeds.

```
simplify(sol);
```

$$\frac{e^{-s}-e^{-5s}}{s(s+1)}$$

```
invlaplace(", s, t);
```

$$\sigma(t-1)\left(1-e^{-t+1}\right)-$$

$$\sigma(t-5)\left(1-e^{-t+5}\right)$$

The illustration on the right shows the reaction of $y(t)$ to the rectangular input signal.

```
plot({",u}, t=0..9);
```

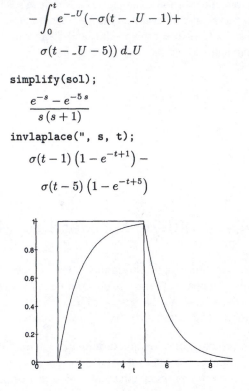

Analysis of an RLC oscillation circuit

The central point in the second example is once again the electrical circuit presented in the previous chapter in connection with Fourier series, which consists of a serial connection of a resistor R, a capacitor C and a coil L (L = 2 henry, C = 20 μF, R = 1 Ω). The task is to analyze the reaction of the circuit (that is, the current i) to different input signals (voltage u).

The circuit can be described by means of an integral differential equation which by way of differentiation is converted into a second-order differential equation.

```
u:='u':
sys:=u(t)=R*i(t) + L*diff(i(t),t) + 1/C*int(i(t),t):
de:=diff(sys,t);
```

$$de := \frac{d}{dt}u(t) = R\frac{d}{dt}i(t) + L\frac{d^2}{dt^2}i(t) + \frac{i(t)}{C}$$

Abbreviations are defined for the transformed functions $U(s)$ and $I(s)$. By the way, $I(s)$ does not cause conflicts with the imaginary unit I. The Laplace transformation of the differential equation again supplies a relatively simple equation in s. In contrast to the previous example, the input function $U(s)$ is still directly contained in it, because later on different functions are to be substituted for $U(s)$.

```
alias(U(s)=laplace(u(t), t, s), I(s)=laplace(i(t), t, s)):
laplace(de, t, s);
```

$$U(s)s - u(0) = R\left(I(s)s - i(0)\right) + L\left(\left(I(s)s - i(0)\right)s - D(i)(0)\right) + \frac{I(s)}{C}$$

With `solve`, the equation is resolved by $I(s)$. $u(0) = 0$, $i(0) = 0$ and $i'(0) = 0$ are substituted in the solution; the result is stored in the function iS. (`is` is a Maple keyword and therefore cannot be used as a variable.)

```
solve(", I(s));
```

$$-\left(U(s)s - u(0) + Ri(0) + Lsi(0) + LD(i)(0)\right)\left(-Rs - Ls^2 - C^{-1}\right)^{-1}$$

```
iS:=subs(u(0)=0, i(0)=0, D(i)(0)=0, ");
```

$$iS := -U(s)s\left(-Rs - Ls^2 - C^{-1}\right)^{-1}$$

The following steps are now repeated several times: different input signals $u(t)$ are assumed, transformed to $U(s)$ and inserted into the above solution for $I(s)$. Subsequently, $I(s)$ is transformed back to $i(t)$ and shown graphically.

First, the current i is to be calculated when (at the moment $t = 0$) a voltage of 300 volts is suddenly applied to the circuit. Subsequently, $U(s)$ is inserted into the solution for $I(s)$.

```
ut:=300: us:=laplace(ut, t, s);
```

$$us := \frac{300}{s}$$

```
subs(U(s)=us, iS);
```

$$-300\left(-Rs - Ls^2 - C^{-1}\right)^{-1}$$

After the inverse transformation, the result for $i(t)$ is simplified by inserting the component data.

```
it:=invlaplace(", s, t);
```

$$it := 600\sqrt{C}\, e^{-\frac{Rt}{2L}} \sinh\left(\frac{\sqrt{-4L + R^2C}\, t}{2L\sqrt{C}}\right)\frac{1}{\sqrt{-4L + R^2C}}$$

```
it:=simplify(subs(R=16, L=2, C=0.02, it));
```

$$it := 49.99999999e^{-4t}\sin(3.0t)$$

The illustration shows the input voltage and the voltage at the resistor R = 16 Ω. After a short transient effect (during which the capacitor loads and thus compensates the input voltage), the current again drops to 0.

```
plot({ut, it*16}, t=0..2);
```

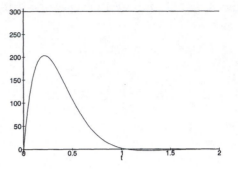

Next, we analyze how the circuit reacts to a sinusoidal input voltage of 50 hertz.

```
ut:=100*sin(2*Pi*50*t):
us:=laplace(ut, t, s);
```

$$us := \frac{10000\,\pi}{s^2 + 10000\,\pi^2}$$

```
invlaplace(subs(U(s)=us, iS), s, t):
it:=subs(R=16, L=2, C=0.02, "): simplify("): evalf(",5);
```

$$0.0040523\sin(314.16t) - 0.15909\cos(314.16t) - 0.21223e^{-4.0t}\sin(3.0t)+$$

$$0.15909e^{-4.0t}\cos(3.0t)$$

The current arrives at a stable oscillation only slowly. The illustration shows the voltage at the resistor R during the first second after switching on.

```
plot({it*16}, t=0..1,
     numpoints=2000);
```

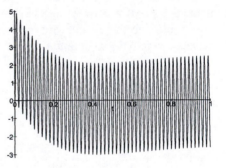

In the last example, the σ function is used to construct a trapezoidal input signal. The resulting transformed function becomes slightly more complicated:

```
ut:=t-(t-1)*sigma(t-1)-(t-4)*sigma(t-4)+(t-5)*sigma(t-5);
```

$$ut := t - (t - 1)\,\sigma(t - 1) - (t - 4)\,\sigma(t - 4) + (t - 5)\,\sigma(t - 5)$$

```
us:=laplace(ut, t, s);
```

$$us := s^{-2} - \frac{e^{-s}}{s^2} - \frac{e^{-4s}}{s^2} + \frac{e^{-5s}}{s^2}$$

In order to minimize the calculation effort, the component data this time is inserted prior to the inverse transformation of $I(s)$. Strangely enough, the substitution is only carried out correctly when the substitution rules are put into curly brackets. Furthermore, prior to the inverse transformation, the resulting expression must be simplified with `simplify` – otherwise `invlaplace` returns an unevaluated integral.

```
subs({R=16, L=2, C=0.02, U(s)=us}, iS): simplify(");
```

$$\frac{0.5 - 0.5e^{-1.0s} - 0.5e^{-4.0s} + 0.5e^{-5.0s}}{s\,(8.0s + s^2 + 25.0)}$$

```
invlaplace(",s,t): it:=evalf(",5);
```

$$it := 0.02 - 0.026667e^{-4.0t}\sin(3.0t) - 0.02e^{-4.0t}\cos(3.0t) -$$

$$0.5\sigma(t-1)\left(0.04 - 0.053333e^{-4.0t+4.0}\sin(3.0t - 3.0) - 0.04e^{-4.0t+4.0}\cos(3.0t - 3.0)\right) -$$

$$0.5\sigma(t-4)\left(0.04 - 0.053333e^{-4.0t+16.0}\sin(3.0t - 12.0) - 0.04e^{-4.0t+16.0}\cos(3.0t - 12.0)\right) +$$

$$0.5\sigma(t-5)\left(0.04 - 0.053333e^{-4.0t+20.0}\sin(3.0t - 15.0) - 0.04e^{-4.0t+20.0}\cos(3.0t - 15.0)\right)$$

The illustration shows the trapezoidal input voltage and the resulting output voltage at the resistor R.

```
plot({ut, it*16}, t=0..8);
```

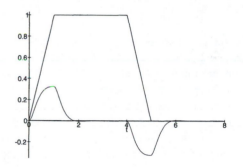

Mellin transformation

The Mellin transformation is defined as follows:

$$F(s) = \int_0^\infty t^{s-1} f(t)\, dt$$

The `mellin` command is called in the same way as `laplace` – in the first parameter, the function to be transformed; in the second parameter, its variable; in the third parameter, the variable of the transformed function.

The example shows the application of the `mellin` command. In some cases, the result can be further simplified with `simplify`.

```
with(inttrans): mellin(sin(t),t,s);
```

$$\Gamma(s)\sin(\frac{\pi s}{2})$$

```
mellin(t^a, t, s):
simplify(");
```

$$\frac{\sigma(s + a) - \sigma(-s - a)}{s + a}$$

Z transformation

The Z transformation transforms discrete functions $f(n)$ to $F(z)$. f is only defined for integer n greater than zero. The Z transformation is carried out according to the following formula:

$$F(z) = \sum_{n=0}^{\infty} \frac{f(n)}{z^n}$$

The commands ztrans and invztrans must be activated by means of with(inttrans). The call is the same as for laplace and mellin, with the same order of parameters.

```
with(inttrans):
ztrans(n^2,n,z);
```
$$\frac{z(z+1)}{(z-1)^3}$$
```
invztrans(",z,n);
```
$$n^2$$

A surprise occurs with the inverse transformation of $F(z) = 1$. invtrans formulates the result using the Delta function which, according to documentation and online help, does not exist. Mathematically, this function is defined in the same way as the Dirac pulse: it yields 1 for $n = 0$ and 0 for all other n. The function can also be used for the formulation of user-defined functions.

```
invztrans(1,z,n);
```
$$\Delta(n)$$
```
ztrans(n^2*Delta(n-3),n,z);
```
$$\frac{9}{z^3}$$

The evaluation of the Delta function, however, is not possible.

```
sol:=invztrans(
   (1-4*z^2) / (z^2-2*z+1), z, n);
```
$$sol := \Delta(n) - 3n - 5$$
```
seq(sol, n=0..3); n:='n':
```
$$\Delta(0) - 5, \Delta(1) - 8, \Delta(2) - 11,$$
$$\Delta(3) - 14$$

The Delta function must not be redefined, since this would cause ztrans not to function any more. Therefore, the lower case delta function is defined and used in the solution for substituting Delta. This detour now allows you to evaluate solutions containing the Delta function.

The definition of `delta` looks as follows: if x contains the value 0, the result is 1. If x is not 0, but it contains a numeric expression, the function yields 0. In all other cases, for example if x contains a symbol, such as n, the unevaluated function is returned. This must be enclosed in quotes in order to prevent a recursive call of `delta`.

```
delta:=x->
  if x=0 then 1;
  elif type(x,numeric) then 0;
  else 'delta(x)' fi:
sol:=subs(Delta=delta, sol);
```

$$delta := \delta(n) - 5 - 3n$$

```
seq(sol, n=0..3); n:='n':
```

$$-4, -8, -11, -14$$

Solving difference equations with the Z transformation

The Z transformation is used when the behaviour of discrete systems is to be calculated. Such systems occur in control engineering when a digital circuit periodically (that is, in discrete intervals and not continuously) measures input values and uses them to generate an output signal.

In the first example, the equation $f(k+2) - 4f(k+1) + 3f(k) = 1$ with $f(0) = 0$ and $f(1) = 1$ is to be solved. For this, the whole equation is Z transformed. In order to display the result more clearly, $F(z)$ is introduced as an abbreviation for `ztrans(f(k),k,z)`.

```
sys:=f(k+2)-4*f(k+1)+3*f(k)=1:
alias(F(z)=ztrans(f(k),k,z)):
ztrans(sys,k,z);
```

$$z^2 F(z) - f(0)z^2 - f(1)z - 4zF(z) + 4f(0)z + 3F(z) = \frac{z}{z-1}$$

$f(0) = 0$ and $f(1) = 1$ are inserted into the result; subsequently, the equation is solved for $F(z)$.

```
subs(f(0)=0, f(1)=1, ");
```

$$z^2 F(z) - z - 4zF(z) + 3F(z) = \frac{z}{z-1}$$

```
sol:=solve(", F(z));
```

$$sol := -\frac{\left(-z - \frac{z}{z-1}\right)}{(z^2 - 4z + 3)}$$

The required function $f(k)$ which satisfies the above formulated equation results from the inverse transformation to k.

```
fk:=invztrans(", z, k);
```

$$fk := \frac{3 \cdot 3^k}{4} - \frac{k}{2} - 3/4$$

```
seq(fk, k=0..5); k:='k':
```

$$0, 1, 5, 18, 58, 179$$

In the second example, $u(k)$ is to be calculated for the system $e(k) = u(k+2) - 3*u(k+1) + 2*u(k)$ when the `Delta` function is used as the input signal $e(k)$. With this, the pulse response of a discrete system is calculated.

```
alias(E(z)=ztrans(e(k),k,z), U(z)=ztrans(u(k),k,z)):
ztrans(e(k)=u(k+2)-3*u(k+1)+2*u(k), k, z);
```

$$E(z) = z^2 U(z) - u(0)z^2 - u(1)z - 3\,zU(z) + 3\,u(0)z + 2\,U(z)$$

```
uz:=solve(", U(z));
```

$$uz := -\frac{E(z) + u(0)z^2 + u(1)z - 3\,u(0)z}{-z^2 + 3\,z - 2}$$

Then, the Z transformed input signal $E(z)$ is inserted into the solution for $U(z)$.

```
ek:=Delta(k);
```

$$ek := \Delta(k)$$

```
ez:=ztrans(ek,k,z);
```

$$ez := 1$$

Prior to the inverse transformation, the initial state of the system, namely $u(0) = 0$ and $u(1) = -1$, and the input function $E(z)$ are substituted in uz.

```
subs(E(z)=ez, u(0)=0,
                u(1)=-1, uz);
```

$$-\frac{1 - z}{-z^2 + 3\,z - 2}$$

```
uk:=invztrans(", z, k);
```

$$uk := \frac{\Delta(k)}{2} - \frac{2^k}{2}$$

Since `invtrans` formulates the result with the `Delta` function, this function must be substituted with `delta` for evaluation. (`delta` has been defined in the previous section and yields 1 for $k = 0$ and 0 for all other k.)

```
uk:=subs(Delta=delta, uk);
```

$$uk := \frac{\delta(k)}{2} - \frac{2^k}{2}$$

```
seq(uk, k=0..5); k:='k':
```

$$0, -1, -2, -4, -8, -16$$

Syntax summary

```
with(inttrans);
```
activates the `laplace`, `mellin` and `ztrans` commands.

```
laplace(f,t,s);       invlaplace(F,s,t);
```
carries out the Laplace transformation of $f(t)$ to $F(s)$ and the inverse transformation.

```
mellin(f,t,s);
```
carries out the Mellin transformation of $f(t)$ to $F(s)$.

```
ztrans(f,k,z);        invztrans(F,z,k);
```
carries out the Z transformation of $f(k)$ to $F(z)$ and the inverse transformation.

Chapter 27

Vector analysis

This chapter describes the commands Maple provides for vector analysis, and their application for the simplification of complex integrals. The chapter also presents some examples of graphic representation of vector arrays.

`grad`
calculates the gradient of a scalar function.

`diverge, curl`
calculate divergence and rotation of vectorial functions. `grad, diverge` and `curl` can be employed in a large number of predefined coordinate systems.

`potential, vecpotent`
calculate a scalar or vectorial power function for a given vectorial function. All five commands are part of the `linalg` package.

`fieldplot[3d], gradplot[3d]`
graphically represent two-dimensional and three-dimensional vector arrays.

Gradient, divergence and rotation

The `linalg` package which has already been extensively dealt with in Chapter 14 (Vector and matrix calculus) contains several commands for vector analysis which have not yet been discussed. For better understanding of these commands it is necessary to clarify the distinction between scalar and vectorial functions: a scalar function (in the Cartesian coordinate system) is a function of three variables x, y and z which supplies a scalar (that is, a single value) as a result. Vectorial functions are the opposite: they supply a vector $(x1, y1, z1)$ as a result of three parameters x, y and z. Generally, scalar and vectorial functions can be defined as follows:

```
sf:=f(x,y,z):
vf:=[fx(x,y,z), fy(x,y,z), fz(x,y,z)]:
```

The `grad` command calculates the gradient of a scalar function. In the second parameter, the command is passed the list of variables of the function. The result is a vectorial function. For each arbitrary point, the resulting vector always points to the direction of the highest function increase (and thus stands normally on the level surfaces of the function).

```
with(linalg):
grad(sf, [x,y,z]);
```

$$[\frac{\partial}{\partial x} f(x,y,z), \frac{\partial}{\partial y} f(x,y,z), \frac{\partial}{\partial z} f(x,y,z)]$$

```
grad(x+x*y*z^2, [x,y,z]);
```

$$[1 + yz^2, xz^2, 2xyz]$$

`diverge` calculates the divergence of vector arrays. As a scalar function, divergence indicates the density of the sources of the vector array at any arbitrary coordinate point.

```
diverge(vf, [x,y,z]);
```

$$\frac{\partial}{\partial x} fx(x,y,z) + \frac{\partial}{\partial y} fy(x,y,z) + \frac{\partial}{\partial z} fz(x,y,z)$$

```
diverge([y*sin(x), x*cos(y), z], [x,y,z]);
```

$$y\cos(x) - x\sin(y) + 1$$

Rotation is calculated with the `curl` command. As a vectorial function, rotation indicates the strength and direction of the curls occurring in the vectorial array.

```
curl(vf, [x,y,z]);
```

$$[\frac{\partial}{\partial y} fz(x,y,z) - \frac{\partial}{\partial z} fy(x,y,z), \frac{\partial}{\partial z} fx(x,y,z) - \frac{\partial}{\partial x} fz(x,y,z), \frac{\partial}{\partial x} fy(x,y,z) - \frac{\partial}{\partial y} fx(x,y,z)]$$

The somewhat complicated result can be more clearly shown as a column vector by means of `convert(..., matrix)`.

```
convert(", matrix);
```

$$\begin{bmatrix} \frac{\partial}{\partial y} fz(x,y,z) - \frac{\partial}{\partial z} fy(x,y,z) \\ \frac{\partial}{\partial z} fx(x,y,z) - \frac{\partial}{\partial x} fz(x,y,z) \\ \frac{\partial}{\partial x} fy(x,y,z) - \frac{\partial}{\partial y} fx(x,y,z) \end{bmatrix}$$

The commands on the right show a further application of `curl`. Again, the result is transformed into a more readable form with `convert`.

```
curl([z*sin(x), z*sin(y),
      sqrt(x^2+y^2)], [x,y,z]):
convert(",matrix);
```

$$\begin{bmatrix} \frac{y}{\sqrt{x^2+y^2}} - \sin(y) \\ \sin(x) - \frac{x}{\sqrt{x^2+y^2}} \\ 0 \end{bmatrix}$$

`grad`, `diverge` and `curl` can be used in all coordinate systems defined in Maple. (Since Release 4, there are 31 three-dimensional coordinate systems at your disposal – see `?coords`. With `addcoords`, you can even define new coordinate systems.)

In order to calculate divergence in cylindrical coordinates, two additional parameters must be used to pass a list of the names of the three coordinates, and the name of the coordinate system.

```
vf:=[r*cos(phi),r*sin(phi),r]:
diverge(vf, [r,phi,z],
            coords=cylindrical);
```

$$3\cos(\phi)$$

In the second example, several `alias` abbreviations are introduced in order to represent the rotation of a generic function in spherical coordinates more clearly.

```
alias(R=R(r,theta,phi), Theta=Theta(r,theta,phi), Phi=Phi(r,theta,phi)):
curl([R, Theta, Phi], [r,theta,phi], coords=spherical):
convert(",matrix);
```

$$\left[\begin{array}{c} \dfrac{r\cos(\theta)\,\Phi + r\sin(\theta)\left(\frac{\partial}{\partial\theta}\,\Phi\right) - r\left(\frac{\partial}{\partial\phi}\,\Theta\right)}{r^2\sin(\theta)} \\[2ex] \dfrac{\left(\frac{\partial}{\partial\phi}\,R\right) - \sin(\theta)\,\Phi - r\sin(\theta)\left(\frac{\partial}{\partial r}\,\Phi\right)}{r\sin(\theta)} \\[2ex] \dfrac{\Theta + r\left(\frac{\partial}{\partial r}\,\Theta\right) - \left(\frac{\partial}{\partial\theta}\,R\right)}{r} \end{array} \right]$$

The last example shows the calculation of the gradient of a generic function in elliptical cylinder coordinates.

```
grad(f(u,v,z), [u,v,z], coords=ellcylindrical): convert(",matrix);
```

$$\left[\begin{array}{c} \dfrac{\frac{\partial}{\partial u}\,\mathrm{f}(u,v,z)}{a\,\sqrt{\sin(v)^2 + \sinh(u)^2}} \\[2ex] \dfrac{\frac{\partial}{\partial v}\,\mathrm{f}(u,v,z)}{a\,\sqrt{\sin(v)^2 + \sinh(u)^2}} \\[2ex] \frac{\partial}{\partial z}\,\mathrm{f}(u,v,z) \end{array} \right]$$

Note: Non-Cartesian coordinates can only be used with the `grad`, `diverge` and `curl` commands and with some `plot` commands. There is, however, no command to convert coordinate points between different coordinate systems.

Power functions

In complicated calculations it is often desirable to replace vector functions with simpler power functions. The commands `potential` and `vecpotent` help with the search for appropriate power functions.

potential checks whether there is a scalar power function for a given vector function vf. If so, the command writes the solution into the variable specified in quotes in the third parameter. The power function satisfies the condition $\operatorname{grad}(p) = vf$.

```
potential([x,y^2,z^3],
          [x,y,z], 'p');
```

$\qquad$ *true*

```
p;
```

$$\frac{x^2}{2} + \frac{z^4}{4} + \frac{y^3}{3}$$

```
grad(p, [x,y,z]);
```

$$[x, y^2, z^3]$$

vecpotent is a variation of potential and tries to find a vectorial (instead of a scalar) power function. The result satisfies the condition $\operatorname{rot}(p) = vf$.

```
vecpotent([y^2+z^2, x^2+z^2,
           x^2+y^2],
          [x,y,z], 'v');
```

$\qquad$ *true*

```
matrixform(map(simplify,v));
```

$$\begin{bmatrix} x^2z + \frac{z^3}{3} - x^2y - \frac{y^3}{3} \\ -y^2z - \frac{z^3}{3} \\ 0 \end{bmatrix}$$

```
curl(v, [x,y,z]);
```

$$[y^2 + z^2, x^2 + z^2, x^2 + y^2]$$

Gauss and Stokes integral theorems

The Gaussian integral theorem allows transformation between volume and surface integrals. With this transformation, the given integral can be simplified (where, depending on the given function and the form of the enveloping surface, one or the other form of the integral is easier to evaluate).

$$\iiint_V \operatorname{div} f \, dV = \iint_A f \cdot n \, dA$$

where n is the normal vector on the function f.

An example: we want to determine the surface integral over the function $f \cdot n$ along the surface of a cube between $(0,0,0)$ and (a,a,a), where $f = [e^x, \cosh(y), \sinh(z)]$. Already the construction of this integral is laborious. After all, we have to integrate over all six peripheral surfaces of the cube. By transforming it into a volume integral, we can also do without the calculation of the normal vector n.

```
f:=[E^x, cosh(y), sinh(z)];
```

$$f := [e^x, \cosh(y), \sinh(z)]$$

```
int(int(int(
    diverge(f,[x,y,z]),
  x=0..a), y=0..a), z=0..a):
simplify(");
```

$$2\,a^2\,(e^a - 1)$$

Stokes' theorem allows transformation between an integral over a three-dimensional surface and an integral along the boundary line of this integral. The formula is:

$$\iint_A (\mathrm{rot} f) \cdot n \, dA = \oint_C f \cdot r'(s) \, ds$$

where n is the normal vector on the integration surface A and $r'(s)$ the tangent unit vector along the integration curve s, with $r' = \frac{dr}{ds}$.

In the example of Stokes' theorem, we want to determine the line integral $f \cdot r'$ along the circle $x^2 + y^2 = 1$ for $z = 1$, where $f = [-3y, 3x, z]$. The double integral at the end of this example only shows the principle of the process; the result is evident anyway.

```
f:=[-3*y,3*x,z];
```

$$f := [-3\,y, 3\,x, z]$$

```
n:=[0,0,1];
```

$$n := [0, 0, 1]$$

```
dotprod(n,curl(f,[x,y,z]));
```

$$6$$

```
int(int(6,
  x=-sqrt(1-y^2)..sqrt(1-y^2)),
  y=-1..1);
```

$$6\,\pi$$

Graphic representation of vector functions

The `plots` package contains four commands for the representation of vectorial functions. The basic idea is the same for all four commands: a two-dimensional or three-dimensional grid is laid over the space to be represented. The value and direction of the vector occurring at that point are represented at each point of the grid by a small arrow.

`fieldplot` draws two-dimensional vector arrays. The two vector components are specified in a list; the next two parameters specify the drawing range.

```
with(plots):
fieldplot([x*y^2, y*x^2],
          x=-1..1, y=-1..1);
```

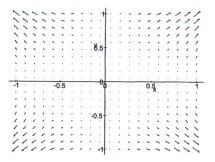

The command is also suitable for the representation of complex functions.

```
fieldplot([Re(sin(x+I*y)),
           Im(sin(x+I*y))],
  x=0..Pi, y=-1..1, axes=boxed);
```

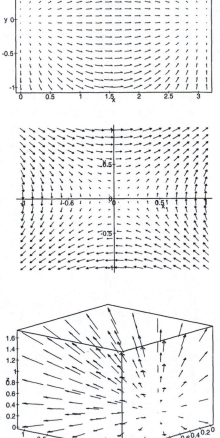

gradplot represents the partial derivatives of a scalar function (that is, the vectors $[\frac{\partial}{\partial x} f, \frac{\partial}{\partial y} f]$). The arrows option is used to set the required shape of the arrows. Please note that – unlike most other graphics options – upper case letters are compulsory.

```
gradplot(sin(x*y), x=-1..1,
         y=-1..1, arrows=SLIM);
```

fieldplot3d and gradplot3d are the three-dimensional variations of the above commands.

```
fieldplot3d([x,y,z],
   x=-1..1, y=0..Pi/2, z=0..Pi/2,
   orientation=[131,71],
   axes=boxed, grid=[5,5,5],
   arrows=SLIM, color=black);
```

The grid option is used to set the number of grid points for the three coordinate directions. With the color option, an arbitrary colour distribution can be specified. These and the command's other options are described in Chapter 20.

Syntax summary

```
with(linalg);
     activates the five commands described below.
```

`grad(f, [x,y,z]);      grad(f, [x,y,z], c);`
　　generates the gradient of a scalar function with three variables x, y and z. The result is a
　　vectorial function. The optional parameter c specifies a non-Cartesian coordinate system, for
　　example `coords=cylindrical`, `coords=spherical`, and so on. A list of available coordinate
　　systems can be obtained with `?coords`.

`diverge([fx, fy, fz], [x,y,z]);      diverge([fx, fy, fz], [x,y,z], c);`
　　calculates the divergence of a vectorial function. The result is a scalar function.

`curl([fx, fy, fz], [x,y,z]);        curl([fx, fy, fz], [x,y,z], c);`
　　generates the rotation of a vectorial function. The result is again a vectorial function.

`potential([fx, fy, fz], [x,y,z], 'p');`
　　tries to generate a scalar power function which satisfies the condition $\mathrm{grad}(p) = f$. The
　　command returns *true* or *false* and, if possible, writes the result into the variable p.

`vecpotent([fx, fy, fz], [x,y,z], 'p');`
　　writes (if possible) a vectorial power function into the variable p. The power function satisfies
　　the condition $\mathrm{rot}(p) = vf$.

Graphic representation of vector functions

`with(plots);`
　　activates the commands listed below.

`fieldplot([fx, fy], x=x0..x1, y=y0..y1);`
　　represents the two-dimensional vector function $[f_x, f_y]$ by means of small arrows.

`gradplot(f, x=x0..x1, y=y0..y1);`
　　represents the partial derivations of f using x and y with arrows.

`fieldplot3d([fx,fy,fz], x=x0..x1, y=y0..y1, z=z0..z1);`
　　as above, but for three-dimensional vector arrays.

`arrows=..`
　　specifies the arrow shape:
　　`THIN`: small, hook-shaped arrows.
　　`SLIM`: small arrows with a 'true' point.
　　`LINE`: lines without points.
　　`THICK`: thick arrows.

`grid=[nx, ny]      or      grid=[nx, ny, nz]`
　　sets the number of grid points in the two or three coordinate directions.

Chapter 28

Programming I: basics, internal structures

This is the first of three chapters which deal with programming in Maple. The subject has already occurred in the previous chapters – the first time in connection with user-defined functions in Chapter 8, then several times in connection with the formulation of simple `for` loops, and so on.

The three chapters are an introduction to Maple's programming language. However, you should be aware that they do not provide a complete and exhaustive treatment of the subject of programming. In particular, we would like to refer to the 'Programming Guide' which is included in the Maple distribution since Release 4. This manual explains Maple programming in over 400 pages and is very well structured from both the didactic and contents points of view (a veritable rare bird amongst original manuals!).

This chapter is above all intended to teach some fundamental knowledge. If you simply want to write a loop, you can skip this partly theoretical chapter for the moment. However, for advanced applications, the subjects dealt with in this chapter are an absolute must:

- code input
- rules for file name specification
- structure of Maple (kernel, library, packages)
- display of the Maple code used in commands
- structure and internal management of mathematical expressions
- storage of already calculated results (`remember` option)

Chapter 29 describes the procedural language elements of Maple. Procedural means those commands (keywords) which you use to construct loops and conditions, to define procedures, and so on. The chapter also discusses the handling of parameters (type check), local variables and the programming of options.

Chapter 30 then makes the big step from the single procedure to the development of new commands and whole packages including help texts. The chapter also describes how user-defined packages can be stored in the `share` library or in user libraries. The new command `seqn`, an improved variation of `seq`, will be used as an example.

Chapter 32 on graphics programming contains further examples of programming new commands.

The programming environment

Although Maple has been looked at up to now as a computer algebra program used primarily for accepting and processing mathematical commands, it can just as well be looked at as a programming language. Internally, Maple consists of a very small number of commands for the formulation of loops, branches, procedures, and so on. These commands constitute the programming language of Maple. All further commands (for example, `solve` for solving equations) are written in this programming language and are interpreted by the kernel. (See also the following section on the structure of Maple.)

You can use these commands to write your own programs or new commands. If you have some experience with a procedural programming language (Pascal, C, and so on), entering the realm of Maple programming will be very easy.

You are certainly going to carry out your first experiments via Maple's worksheet interface. Just enter the program code in the same way as a normal Maple command. If you need more than one line, (Shift)+(↵) takes you to the next line.

The example on the right shows the definition of a recursive function for the calculation of Fibonacci numbers. (A description of the most important keywords of Maple's programming language follows in the next chapter.)

```
f:=proc(x::nonnegint)
  option remember;
  if x=0 then 0
  elif x=1 then 1
  else f(x-1)+f(x-2) fi
end:

f(50);

    12586269025
```

You simply store the program code together with the worksheet file. When you load this file at a later stage and want to have the Fibonacci function available again, you must execute the command for the definition of f once again.

But soon the extremely restricted editing possibilities of the Maple interface will start annoying you. Of course, you can also use any other editor for writing your program code. With the `read` command, you can then read the text file into Maple (see also the following subsection on files and directories). The usual file name extension for Maple source code is `*.mpl`.

```
read 'test.mpl';
```

When your file contains syntax errors, `read` reacts with an error message and displays the faulty line. For longer procedures, it can make sense to set the `interface` variable `echo` to 2. This causes Maple to display all program lines previously read in and thus facilitates orientation in the code.

Note: In principle, you can also copy program code between Maple and your editor via the clipboard. In the current Windows version, however, this does not work satisfactorily: when pasting text into Maple, an empty line is inserted after each line. (The reason: internally, Maple uses a different end-of-line code than Windows.) Data transfer in the opposite direction causes problems too:

with each program line, Maple also copies the Maple input prompt > to the clipboard. Since this character does not belong to the program code, it must be painstakingly removed with the editor.

Maple also provides a simple debugger for finding faults in Maple programs. This debugger is described in Chapter 30.

Files and directories

The file naming conventions are a permanent source of frustration. The cause of these problems lies less in Maple itself than in the fact that Maple must cope with three quite different file systems (DOS/Windows, Apple, UNIX). This section gives some hints on the specification of file names.

- File names must be enclosed in left quotes '.

- In all Maple versions, the / character can be used as the directory separator. Under DOS/Windows, Maple automatically substitutes this character with \.

- Even when you work with the Windows version of Maple, specification of a single \ character in a file name is not allowed. \ is used (as in C or under UNIX) to identify special characters and acts as a qualifier for the following character. The special character \ itself can only be obtained by means of two \ characters, for example `directory\\name`.

A further problem with file access is the current directory. With the `read 'name'` command, the file `name` of the current directory is read. As a rule, however, the current directory is *not* the directory where the currently active worksheet is stored. There is no possibility, via program code, of storing or reading files in the directory in which the current worksheet is located. There is also no possibility of determining the current directory.

The directory which is considered as the current directory depends on the version of Maple and its configuration. In the Windows version, `maple\examples` is considered to be the standard current directory. You can redefine this setting in the Program Manager (Windows 3.1) or in the Explorer (Windows 95) (set new working directory).

Obviously, you can also specify the full file name for each file access (including the drive and all directories). However, if at a later stage you want to use your worksheet file on a different computer, all your path specifications will no longer be valid.

Reference: The subject 'Handling files' is not concluded with these few paragraphs. Chapter 29 describes Maple commands with which you can read and write files from within your program code (`fopen`, `fprintf`, and so on). Chapter 30 explains how you can store program code in binary format (both as an individual file and in the form of user-defined libraries).

The structure of Maple

Maple consists – to put it simply – of a program (the kernel) that defines the Maple programming language, and a mass of ASCII code in this programming language which defines the numerous commands. From this point of view, you could simply look at Maple as a programming language optimized for mathematical applications.

After starting Maple, you can use a large number of commands immediately. This is because some commands are built into Maple (such as seq) and the code of many additional commands is automatically loaded at the start of Maple or at the first call of the command in question.

From a user's point of view, Maple commands could be classified as follows:

- immediately available commands,
- commands that must be read with readlib prior to being used,
- commands in packages that must be activated by means of with, and
- commands in the share library (see next section).

Inside Maple, the breakdown looks slightly more sophisticated. With the immediately available commands, a distinction is made between commands and keywords that belong to the kernel and are present in compiled form and those commands that are automatically loaded at their first call. After the start of Maple, these commands are defined as follows:

```
command:='readlib('command')':
```

As soon as this command is called for the first time, Maple loads the corresponding code. In this way, many commands are available almost instantaneously, without cluttering the working memory with the code of countless commands which are currently not needed at all.

For all further library commands, you must execute the readlib command, as has often been described in the course of the previous chapters.

Prior to using commands from packages, you must usually execute the with command with the package name as parameter, for example with(linalg). (Alternatively, you can always enter the complete name of the command, for example linalg[vector] instead of vector.) With the with command, the commands occurring in the package are defined in the form already described above by means of readlib – thus, for the vector command:

```
vector:=readlib('linalg/vector'):
```

However, the code of this command is actually loaded only when it is used for the first time. By the way, the with command only works because the name of the package – for example *linalg* – already contains a table of these readlib instructions immediately after the start of Maple. You can view this table with op(linalg) (even prior to execution of with).

Apart from some internal commands which are present in the Maple kernel in compiled form, the encrypted code of all further commands (including the packages) is stored in the file lib\maple.lib. In order to allow Maple to find the required information sufficiently fast in this enormous file, `lib\maple.ind` contains an index for this file. The help texts for the commands are located in `lib\maple.hdb`. Together, these three files in their current version require more than 11 Mbytes of hard disk space.

With the auxiliary program `march`, you can generate a contents list of the library file, extract individual files or store additional files in the library. Details of this program follow in Chapter 30.

Via Maple's online help, you can obtain information on which commands belong to which group:

`?index`	overview of Maple keywords
`?keywords`	internal kernel commands (compiled)
`?index,statement`	keywords of the Maple programming language
`?index,procedure`	keywords plus tools for programming (debugger, and so on)
`?index,function`	list of all predefined functions
`?inifcn`	list of functions with short explanations
`?packages`	overview of the packages
`?ininame`	list of predefined variables, such as I and π
`?envvar`	list of environment variables, such as `Digits`
`?index,misc`	overview of help functions and external tools
`?operator`	overview of Maple operators
`?expressions`	operators and functions for the construction of mathematical expressions
`?share`	information on the structure of the `share` library
`?share,contents`	overview of the `share` library commands
	(first, `read(share)` must be executed)
`?updatesR4,language`	new issues in the Maple programming language in Release 4

The share library

The `share` library is a collection of additional commands and packages which are distributed together with Maple, but officially do not belong to the standard library and are not documented in the same way as other Maple commands. The commands of the `share` library come from Maple users who make their code available to other users. Additional or more up-to-date packages belonging to the `share` library can be obtained via the Internet – see the online help subject `?share,address`.

Prior to using commands from the `share` library, the library must be activated:

`with(share):`

Now, the code of individual commands can be read with `readshare`, for example:

`readshare(math,system);`

After loading commands from the `share` library, you can in most cases use `?command` to view a brief help text which explains how the command is handled.

As with the standard library, the `share` library commands are stored in a `maple.lib` file – but this time in the `share` directory. In addition, the `share` directory tree contains a large number of accompanying files: the program code in ASCII format (`*.mpl` files), help texts in ASCII format (`*.mph` files), worksheets which show the application of the library, and so on.

Furthermore, some commands come with TEX or LATEX files containing detailed information on the principles of operation and mathematical background of the commands. However, in order to be able to print these files or view them on screen, you need the TEX or LATEX typesetting program which as standard is only available on UNIX computers.

Please note that alteration of `*.mpl` or `*.mph` files in the `share` directory tree does not change the functioning of the library functions. Both the program code and the help texts are automatically read from the library files; the `share` directory tree serves only as additional documentation of the library. Information on how you can extend or modify the `share` library is given in Chapter 30. A contents list of the `share` library can be viewed with `march` – this command is also described in Chapter 30.

Inert commands

Inert commands, such as `Int` or `Diff`, have no meaning when used on their own. They only take effect in combination with other commands. Thus, `evalf(Int(...))` is not equivalent to `evalf(int(...))` – see Chapter 17.

The true function of inert commands is to prevent evaluation (at least temporarily). Most frequently, inert commands are used in combination with `evalf` in order to force a numeric evaluation. Since Release 3, `simplify` and `expand` are also capable of simplifying expressions containing inert commands. Inert commands can also be used to write mathematical expressions which are to be shown on screen exactly in this form (and not after evaluation):

```
Int(1/(1+x^3), x), Diff(x,y), Sum(n^2/n!, n=1..infinity),
  Product((1+1/n^5), n=a..b);
```

$$\int \frac{1}{1+x^3}\,dx, \frac{\partial}{\partial y}\,x, \sum_{n=1}^{\infty} \frac{n^2}{n!}, \prod_{n=a}^{b}\left(1+\frac{1}{n^5}\right)$$

There is no possibility of converting inert commands to their normal equivalents by means of `eval` or other commands. You can, however, use `subs` to force conversion to normal Maple commands:

```
f:=Int(1/(1+x^3), x): eval(subs(Int=int, f));
```

$$\frac{1}{3}\ln(x+1) - \frac{1}{6}\ln(x^2-x+1) + \frac{1}{3}\sqrt{3}\arctan\left(\frac{1}{3}(2x-1)\sqrt{3}\right)$$

Protection of commands

Keywords (see help text ?keywords) are internally integrated into Maple and cannot be altered. All other commands are stored in normal Maple variables. In order to protect these variables against accidental overwriting, they are protected with protect. An attempt to overwrite a variable protected in this way leads to an error message. However, this protection can be cancelled with unprotect. You can also use protect and unprotect to protect your own variables or the procedures stored in them.

Viewing Maple code

Investigating Maple code is certainly one of the most important sources of information for creating your own Maple procedures. Here you will find numerous examples – unfortunately without comments or other explanation – of how Maple itself (and therefore its commands) functions. With the exception of the commands belonging to the kernel and the compiled library commands, you can view the code of all Maple commands with print. The only thing you have to do is set the interface variable verboseproc to 2.

The abs command belongs to the commands integrated into the kernel and exists only in compiled form. Therefore, its code cannot be viewed.

```
interface(verboseproc=2):
print(abs);
    proc() options builtin; 49 end
```

The read command is one of the few kernel commands of Maple for which no information is available at all.

```
print(read);
  syntax error, reserved word
  'read' unexpected
```

cos is located in the standard library and is automatically loaded as soon as it is needed. The code consists of about 50 lines, of which only the first 10 are shown.

```
print(cos);
    proc(x)
    local n,t;
    options 'Copyright 1992 by the University of Waterloo';
        if nargs <> 1 then ERROR('expecting 1 argument, got '.nargs)
        elif type(x,'complex(float)') then evalf('cos'(x))
        elif type(x,'*') and member(I,{op(x)}) then cosh(-I*x)
        elif type(x,'complex(numeric)') then
            if csgn(x) < 0 then cos(-x) else 'cos'(x) fi
        ...
    end
```

The code of many commands is split into several procedures. Thus, there are a large number of convert/xxx procedures which carry out conversion of Maple expressions into various data types. In the online help of some Maple commands, this mechanism is mentioned as a simple means of extending them. For example, you can write a procedure evalf/constant/Name which returns the value of the new numerical constant Name.

The first attempt to view the procedure for `convert/listlist` fails because Maple has not yet loaded the code for this procedure. After a simple conversion has been carried out, the `print` command leads to the required result. Please note the correct notation: the partial names of the procedure are separated by / characters; the entire name is enclosed in right quotes.

```
print('convert/listlist');
```

>   *convert/listlist*

```
convert(array([[2],[1]]), listlist);
```

> $[[2], [1]]$

```
print('convert/listlist');
```

```
proc(a::{array, list})
local Seq, an, aa, ranges, names, b, n, i;
option
'Copyright (c) 1994 by Waterloo Maple Inc. All rights reserved.';
    if type(a, list) then an := 'unknown'; aa := array(a)
    elif type(a, name) then aa := eval(a); an := a
    else aa := a; an := 'unknown'
    fi;
    ...
end
```

Commands from packages must also be executed before the code can be viewed. Furthermore, the complete name of the procedure which results from the package name and the command name must be specified.

```
with(linalg): toeplitz([a,b,c]);
```

$$\begin{bmatrix} a & b & c \\ b & a & b \\ c & b & a \end{bmatrix}$$

```
print('linalg/toeplitz');
```

```
proc(L)
local i, j, n, A;
option 'Copyright (c) 1990 by the University of Waterloo. All \
rights reserved.';
    if args[nargs] = 'array' then
        _EnvLinalg95 := false;
        RETURN(procname(args[1 .. nargs - 1]))
    fi;
    ...
end
```

In many commands, the code is distributed across a number of further procedures. Thus, depending on the type of integral, the code of the integration command `int` branches into numerous other `int/integraltype` procedures. Such branching into further procedures occurs very frequently and makes analysis of complex commands a rather laborious and long-winded task.

When you want to find out how a command consisting of several procedures works, you can set the global variable infolevel[*command*] to a value between 2 and 5. The higher the value, the more information is displayed by Maple during processing of the command. However, this only functions when the procedures contain the userinfo command for output of information (as is the case with int, dsolve and simplify). infolevel[all]:=5 displays the maximum amount of information for all commands.

```
infolevel[all]:=5:
int(1/(1+x^3),x):
  int/indef:    first-stage indefinite integration
  int/ratpoly:    rational function integration
  parfrac/parfrac:    partial fraction decomposition
  factor/polynom:    polynomial factorization: number of terms    2
  parfrac/parfrac:    splitting    1/(1+_X)/(_X^2-_X+1)
  solve/linear:    # equations    2
  solve/linear/integer/sparse:    # equations    2
  solve/linear/integer/sparse:    c[1], -2+3*c[1], 3
  solve/linear/integer/sparse:    # equations    1
  solve/linear/integer/sparse:    c[2], 1+3*c[2], 3
  solve/linear/integer/sparse:    backsubstitution at:    2
  solve/linear/integer/sparse:    backsubstitution at:    1
  parfrac/parfrac:    exit partial fraction decomposition
  parfrac/parfrac:    split is    1/3/(1+_X)-1/3*(-2+_X)/(_X^2-_X+1)
```

```
print('int/indef');
    proc(f)
    local g, r;
    option remember, 'Copyright (c) 1992 by the University of
       Waterloo. All rights reserved.';
        userinfo(1, int, 'first-stage indefinite integration');
        if type(f, 'series') then RETURN('int/series'(f, _X))
        elif type(traperror(degree(f, _X)), 'integer') then
            RETURN('int/polynom'(f))
        elif type(f, '+') then RETURN(map('int/indef', f))
        ...
    end
```

Structure of mathematical expressions

Most Maple commands process mathematical expressions in some way or other. Some commands calculate with them (diff, int), other commands carry out equivalence conversions (simplify, solve) or evaluate the expression numerically (evalf). When you want to write commands yourself, you must know how mathematical expressions are structured and how they can be analyzed. Some basic information on this subject is also given in Chapter 10 which mainly deals with simplification of mathematical expressions.

In the following example, a typical mathematical expression is analyzed – the result of the integral over $1/(1 + x^3)$.

```
sol:=int(1/(1+x^3), x);
```

$$sol := \frac{\ln(1 + x)}{3} - \frac{\ln(x^2 - x + 1)}{6} + \frac{\sqrt{3}\,\arctan(\frac{(2\,x-1)\sqrt{3}}{3})}{3}$$

nops determines the number of terms of the expression; whattype gives information about the expression type. Thus, it is a sum composed of three summands. This indication, however, only refers to the highest level of the result.

```
nops(sol);
```
$$3$$

```
whattype(sol);
```
$$+$$

Alternatively to whattype, the type check can also be carried out with type. In some cases, type allows a finer differentiation. (For example, whattype yields series for all series, whereas type distinguishes between taylor and laurent.)

```
type(sol, '+');
```
$$true$$

The third term of the sum can be determined with op. For further analysis of this expression, the term is stored in the variable *op3*.

```
op3:=op(3,sol);
```
$$op3 := \frac{\sqrt{3}\,\arctan(\frac{(2\,x-1)\sqrt{3}}{3})}{3}$$

op3 is a product. op determines all factors of this product without specifying the position.

```
whattype(op3);
```
$$*$$

```
op(op3);
```
$$1/3, \sqrt{3}, \arctan(\frac{(2\,x - 1)\,\sqrt{3}}{3})$$

Now, the first factor of this product is stored in *op31* and is analyzed. It is the fraction $1/3$.

```
op31:=op(1,op3):
whattype(op31), op(op31);
```
$$fraction, 1, 3$$

The second factor contains $\sqrt{3}$. Maple represents roots by means of the exponent $1/2$.

```
op32:=op(2,op3):
whattype(op32), op(op32);
```
$$\hat{\ }, 3, 1/2$$

The third factor contains the arctan function. In this case, whattype only yields *function*. The name of the function can be determined with op(0,...). For most other data types, op(0,...) leads to an error message.

```
op33:=op(3,op3):
whattype(op33), op(op33);
```
$$function, \frac{(2\,x - 1)\,\sqrt{3}}{3}$$

```
op(0,op33);
```
$$arctan$$

Next, the contents of the function can be broken down:

```
op331:=op(1,op33):
whattype(op331), op(op331);
```

$$*, 1/3, 2x - 1, \sqrt{3}$$

You could also have determined *op331* directly from *sol* by means of an embedded op structure.

```
op(1,op(3,op(3,sol)));
```

$$\frac{(2x-1)\sqrt{3}}{3}$$

Analysis of mathematical expressions eventually leads – provided you have enough patience – to elementary mathematical expressions (numeric values, variables) which are joined by operators (such as +, *) or functions. This concept generally applies to other Maple data types as well – for example lists, arrays, series expansions, and so on.

The following command helps with the analysis of mathematical expressions. It breaks the expression passed as the parameter into ever smaller components and displays them with different indentation. The language elements occurring in this procedure will be explained in the next chapter. At this point, a rough outline of the conception of the procedure will suffice.

```
nestprint:=proc(x)
  local i,n;
  if nargs=2 then n:=args[2]; else n:=0; fi:
  for i from 0 to n do printf('   '); od:
  if type(x,function) then
    lprint(op(0,x));
    for i from 1 to nops(x) do: nestprint(op(i,x),n+1): od:
  elif nops(x)>1 then
    lprint(whattype(x));
    for i from 1 to nops(x) do: nestprint(op(i,x),n+1): od:
  else
    lprint(op(x));
  fi;
end:
```

The `if` condition in the third line checks whether a second parameter has been passed to the procedure. If so, it is assigned to n (this is the depth of indentation), otherwise n is assigned 0. The following loop uses `printf` to output n times 3 spaces.

The following `if` condition considers three cases: if the expression is a function, the function name is output with `lprint` and the contents of the function are recursively passed to `nestprint`. If it is any other type of expression with more than one term, the type of the term is determined with `whattype` and then output; the subterms are passed to `nestprint`. Otherwise, x already contains the smallest possible mathematical unit and is output directly.

Maple handles negative signs as multiplication by -1.

```
nestprint(-x);
   *
      -1
      x
```

Fractions are stored either with `fraction` or in the form of products with negative exponents. This means that the structure of mathematical expressions is not unique. There are two possible representations for the fraction $2/3$, both of which occur depending on the origin (calculation process) of the expression: $fraction(2, 3)$ or $' * '(2, ' \wedge '(3, -1))$.

```
nestprint(2/3);
   fraction
     2
     3
nestprint(2/x);
   *
     2
     ^
        x
       -1
```

On screen, you cannot recognize how the expression is stored internally. $2/3$ is in any case displayed as a fraction (and not in the form $2*3^{-1}$). The different representation variations do, however, affect the `latex` command which, instead of a compact fraction, suddenly comes up with a poorly arranged row of products with different powers.

Floating point numbers are stored in the form `float(a, b)`. a and b are integer numbers and describe the number $a * 10^b$.

```
nestprint(evalf(1/3));
   float
      3333333333
      -10
```

In the last example, the third summand of the integral is again analyzed. The example shows the number of individual components which make up seemingly simple mathematical expressions.

```
op3;
```

$$\frac{\sqrt{3} \, \arctan(\frac{(2\,x-1)\sqrt{3}}{3})}{3}$$

```
nestprint(op3);
   *
      fraction
        1
        3
      ^
        3
        fraction
           1
           2
      arctan
```

```
      *
         fraction
           1
           3
         +
            *
               2
               x
              -1
            ^
               3
               fraction
                 1
                 2
```

If you want to use the `nestprint` command again at a later stage, you should store it in a file with `save`. With `read`, you can then read the command at any time.

```
save nestprint, 'nestprt';
read('nestprt'):
```

Since Release 4, the `dismantle` command is available which in principle fulfils the same task as `nestprint`. The output format, however, is even more difficult to read than that of `nestprint`.

```
readlib(dismantle):                          PROD(5)
dismantle(op3);                                 SUM(5)
   SUM(3)                                           NAME(4): x
      PROD(5)                                       INTPOS(2): 2
          INTPOS(2): 3                              INTNEG(2): -1
          RATIONAL(3): 1/2                          INTPOS(2): 1
          FUNCTION(3)                            INTPOS(2): 1
             NAME(5): arctan                     INTPOS(2): 3
             EXPSEQ(2)                            RATIONAL(3): 1/2
                SUM(3)                        RATIONAL(3): 1/3
                                       INTPOS(2): 1
                                    RATIONAL(3): 1/3
```

Internals of management of mathematical expressions

In the previous section, some examples were used to describe how Maple assembles mathematical expressions. In this section, you will find information on how Maple manages these expressions.

Maple stores each mathematical expression only once. When the subterm $(1 + x)$ occurs twice in the formula $(1+x)^2 + (1+x)^3$, in the internal representation this subterm is referred to twice – once in the form $\hat{}(\to (1 + x^2), 2)$ and the second time in the form $\hat{}(\to (1 + x^2), 3)$. This mechanism applies both to elementary expressions (such as numbers or variables) and to arbitrarily complex compound expressions.

The `adrprint` command originates from a small change in the three `lprint` commands in `nestprint`. In addition to the operators and functions, it also outputs the corresponding complete expressions. Furthermore, for each mathematical (partial) expression, the address where it is stored is specified. To determine the address, `addressof` is used.

```
adrprint:=proc(x)
  local i,j,n;
  if nargs=2 then n:=args[2]; else n:=0; fi:
  for i from 0 to n do printf('    '); od:
  if type(x,function) then
    lprint(op(0,x), x, addressof(x));
    for i from 1 to nops(x) do: adrprint(op(i,x),n+1): od:
  elif nops(x)>1 then
    lprint(whattype(x), x, addressof(x));
    for i from 1 to nops(x) do: adrprint(op(i,x),n+1): od:
  else
    lprint(op(x), addressof(op(x)));
  fi;
end:
```

In the example on the right, you can see that the number 1, the variable x and the expression $(1 + x)$ are stored at the same address. Internally, mathematical expressions are thus mainly represented by means of pointers to elementary mathematical expressions or to already existing compound expressions.

```
adrprint((1+x)^2 + (1+x)^3);

   +    (1+x)^2+(1+x)^3    1551096
     ^     (1+x)^2    1593068
        +    1+x    1547444
              1    1554660
              x    1583824
           2    1554676
     ^     (1+x)^3    1593080
        +    1+x    1547444
              1    1554660
              x    1583824
           3    1554692
```

Internals of management of procedures

Procedures (and therefore commands too) are stored in completely normal variables. In principle, the instruction for defining a procedure looks as follows:

```
name:=proc(para1,para2,...) commands; end:
```

The variable *name* stores the code for the above defined procedure. When you now enter `name` (without parameters), Maple simply returns this character string. Thus, procedures – just like functions, tables and arrays – are excluded from automatic evaluation. The code of the procedure is only displayed when you enter `print(name)` or `op(name)` or `eval(name)`.

In addition, together with the procedure, six internal management information operands exist which you can access with `op(n,eval(name))`. For $n = 1$ to 6, Maple then supplies the parameters of the function, its local variables, its options (including the copyright notice), the remember table of already calculated results (see next section), a character string with a short description of the function, and finally the list of global variables.

In the following example, these six information operands are displayed for the `simplify` command. Because of the previously executed `restart` command, the remember table is empty; there is no short description, and the command does not use global variables.

```
restart;
seq([op(i,eval(simplify))], i=1..6);
```

$[s]$,

$[f, i, inds, r, rnormal, symb\_mode, cin, cout, v, prps]$,

$[remember, system, `Copyright 1992 by the University of Waterloo`]$,

$[], [], []$

Storage of already calculated results

One particular feature of Maple is that, for most commands, it stores the calculated results. When you calculate a complicated integral, it can be several seconds (or minutes) before Maple supplies the result. When you need the integral again, the result is presented almost instantaneously.

Internally, this apparent intelligence is achieved through a remember table which is stored in the fourth operand of the internal management information of a procedure.

```
simplify(sin(x)^2+cos(x)^2);
```

$$1$$

```
op(4, eval(simplify));
```

$$\text{table}([$$
$$\sin(x)^2 + \cos(x)^2 = 1,$$
$$(\sin(x)^2 + \cos(x)^2, power, trig) = 1$$
$$\sin = \sin$$
$$\cos = \cos$$
$$x = x$$
$$])$$

Since Release 4 the contents of the remember table for the function *name* can also be displayed with print(name) if the interface variable verboseproc is previously set to 3 (or a higher value).

The remember table of a procedure can be deleted with forget.

```
forget(simplify):
op(4, eval(simplify));
```

$$\text{table}([])$$

A special case is the int command. It does not possess a remember table. The command is so complex that it calls a large number of subprocedures, one of which is int/indef. This procedure comes already equipped with a table of predefined integrals which contains the integrals of the standard functions such as $\sin(x), \cos(x), \ln(x)$, and so on. Subsequently, this table is extended with the results of the integrals calculated by means of int.

The example on the right shows extracts from the remember table of the int command. Please note that it also contains the integral of $1/x$ which has only just been calculated.

```
restart;
int(1/x, x);
```

$$\ln(x)$$

```
op(4, eval('int/indef'));
```

$$\text{table}([$$
$$(ln(x)) = x * ln(x) - x$$
$$(abs(x)) = 1/2 * x * abs(x)$$
$$(1/x) = ln(x)$$
$$(sech(x)) = arctan(sinh(x))$$
$$...])$$

It has already been mentioned in Chapter 8 on user-defined functions that the remember option can also be used to equip user-defined functions with a remember table. Please refer to the fibonacci example used in that chapter to see a side effect of the remember table which may not be immediately obvious.

On the right, the `fibonacci` function of Chapter 8 is shown again. The function uses a recursive algorithm for the calculation of Fibonacci numbers.

```
f:=proc(x:nonnegint)
  option remember;
  if x=0 then 0
  elif x=1 then 1
  else f(x-1)+f(x-2) fi
end:
```

At first sight, the function shows a contradictory behaviour: in the Windows version, $f(1000)$ leads to a stack overflow because of the depth of recursion. However, the calculation succeeds without problems when $f(500)$ has been previously calculated. (Both results are only partially shown. $f(1000)$ yields a number of more than 200 digits.)

```
f(1000);
    Error, (in type/nonnegint)
    too many levels of recursion
```

```
f(500); f(1000);
    139423...125

    4346655768693...875
```

The reason for this curious behaviour lies in the remember table. During the calculation of $f(500)$, all Fibonacci numbers between 1 and 500 are stored in it. The recursion depth reaches 500 (in spite of the remember table). If $f(1000)$ is calculated before $f(500)$, the recursion depth reaches 1000, which (at least in the current Windows version) is too high. If, however, $f(1000)$ is calculated *after* $f(500)$, the calculation can be stopped halfway through the process – building on the already stored Fibonacci number for 500. Thus, the recursion depth only reaches 500.

To conclude, a final example that shows the implications of the remember table. The lines on the right define a recursive function which obviously lacks a termination condition – calling this function should therefore lead to a 'stack overflow error'.

```
test:=proc(x)
  option remember;
  test(x-1)+test(x-2):
end:
```

Before the function is executed for the first time, the function values `test(0)` and `test(1)` are defined by assignments. Maple enters these values into the remember table. For this reason, the calculation of $test(5)$ does not lead to an endless loop – when x has reached 2 after several recursive calls, immediate reference can be made to $test(1)$ and $test(0)$.

```
test(0):=0:
test(1):=1:
test(5);
    5
```

Now to the probably most surprising aspect of this example: calculation of $test(5)$ also succeeds when the `remember` option is omitted! Through the assignments $test(n) := m$, Maple now creates its own remember table and enters the function values for $x = n$. This remember table, however, is not automatically extended with the results of the execution of `test`.

Syntax summary

Libraries and packages

```
readlib(command);
```
reads the code of a command from the standard library.

```
with(package);
```
defines the names of the commands of the package by means of `readlib` instructions. When the command is used for the first time, Maple automatically loads its code.

```
with(share);
```
activates the `share` library.

```
readshare(command,directory);
```
reads the code of a command from the `share` library.

Management of mathematical expressions

```
op(expression);
```
supplies the operands of a mathematical expression as a sequence (for example a, b, c from $a + b + c$ or $\cos(a * b * c)$).

```
op(n, expression);
```
supplies the nth operand of an expression. For functions, $n = 0$ is allowed and yields the name of the function: thus, `op(0,sin(x))` yields `sin`.

```
nops(expression);
```
determines the number of operands of an expression.

```
whattype(expression);
```
determines the type of a mathematical expression (for example '+', '*', `function`).

```
type(expression, type);
```
checks whether the expression is of the specified data type.

```
readlib(dismantle):    dismantle(expression);
nestprint(expression);  adrprint(expression);
```
show the structure of mathematical expressions in the form of a hierarchical list. `dismantle` is a Maple command. `nestprint` and `adrprint` are defined in this chapter in the Section 'Structure of mathematical expressions'.

Internals of commands and procedures

```
op(n, eval(name));
```
displays management information on a command, a procedure or a function: for $n = 1$, the parameter names; for $n = 2$, the local variables; for $n = 3$, the command options; and for $n = 4$, the contents of the remember table.

```
interface(verboseproc=2):
print(name);    print('pack/name');    print(eval(name));
```
display the code of the specified command. For commands from packages, either the complete command name `'package/name'` or `eval(name)` must be used. The code can only be displayed after it has been loaded. For this, commands from packages must first be executed.

```
readlib(forget):    forget(command):
```
deletes the remember table of a command, a procedure or a function that uses the `remember` option.

```
protect(name);    unprotect(name);
```
`protect` protects a variable (or the procedure contained in it) against accidental assignments. `unprotect` cancels this protection.

Chapter 29

Programming II: procedural language elements

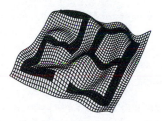

This chapter describes the most important commands for the creation of programs, that is, for the formulation of procedures, loops, conditions, and so on. Maple has a procedural programming language whose structure is similar to other programming languages such as C, Pascal or Fortran. The following list very briefly describes the most important commands discussed in this chapter:

`proc`
initiates a procedure. Procedures are used for programming functions, commands and operators.

`RETURN`
terminates a procedure and returns the contents of a variable as the result.

`for`
stands at the beginning of a loop.

`if`
is used for the formulation of conditions.

`readdata`, `readline`, `fopen`, `fscanf` and `fprintf`
are the most important commands for input and output of data.

In the context of describing these commands, different programming techniques are discussed – for example, type checking parameters, programming new operators or processing user-defined options which are passed by the program user in the form `option=setting`.

Reference: Introductory information on the definition of functions can be found in Chapter 8.

Procedures

Procedures begin with the keyword `proc`. Procedures are the basis for programming in Maple. They are used both for programming complicated commands and for formulating simple functions. The general structure of a procedure looks as follows:

```
name:=proc(x::type1, y::type2, ...)
  local 11,12,...;
  options ...;
  command; command; ...; command;
end:
```

We will now do a very brief survey of the elements of a procedure. Several subsections with more detailed information follow in this chapter.

After the keyword `proc`, the parameters of the procedure are specified. Parameters have the same effect as local variables; thus, a change in the parameter x does not affect the homonymous variable x of the Maple interface or of the calling procedure. Additional information on parameter lists and type checking follows later in this chapter.

After the parameter list, the list of local variables is defined. The scope of local variables is restricted to the procedure; interference with homonymous variables outside the procedure is not possible.

The keyword `options` can be used to specify several options which control the behaviour of the procedure. The most important of these options are `remember`, `operator`, `arrow`, `angle` and `trace`. These procedure options must not be confused with the options that the user of a command specifies in a parameter in the form `optname=setting`. The design of procedures which understand such options is discussed in a separate section later in this chapter.

We begin now with the actual code for the procedure. You can call an arbitrary number of commands, formulate conditions with `if`, construct loops with `for`, and so on. The results of the commands executed inside the procedure are not displayed on screen. You can, however, force screen output by means of `print` or `lprint` (without formatting). The definition of a procedure is terminated with the keyword `end`.

The return value

The return value of a procedure is the result of the last command. Alternatively, you can leave the procedure at any time with `RETURN` and also specify a return value for this case.

In the example on the right, the factorial function is programmed with `RETURN`. The recursive sample program is not protected against possible handling errors (for example, if a negative argument is specified). The subject of type checking is discussed later in this chapter.

```
test:=proc(x)
  if x=0 then RETURN(1): fi:
  x*test(x-1);
end:

test(4);
      24
```

Formalities

Whether you use colons or semicolons to separate commands in a procedure does not matter. The results of commands inside a procedure are not displayed on screen (provided that you do not change the value of the `interface` variable `printlevel`).

When `end` (that is, the last line of a procedure) is terminated with a semicolon, Maple displays the code of the procedure again after ⟨←⟩ has been pressed. For this reason, most procedure definitions in this book terminate with a colon which prevents the double display of the program code. The closing colon or semicolon does not affect the behaviour of the procedure.

As with functions, tables and arrays, procedures are not evaluated automatically. When you define the new procedure `name` and subsequently enter the command `name` without parameters, Maple simply answers by outputting the homonymous character string. In order to execute the code of a procedure, you must specify a parameter list in round parentheses. Procedures without parameters must be followed by an empty pair of parentheses.

The parameters of a procedure

The keyword `proc` is normally followed by a list of parameters of the procedure. At the call of the procedure, at least as many parameters must be specified as are specified in the procedure definition. More parameters are allowed and can be read via `nargs` and `args` (see below). Fewer parameters lead to a Maple error message.

`test` is defined with three parameters. In the procedure call, four parameters are specified, but the last parameter is ignored by the procedure. All data types (numeric values, lists, and so on) are allowed as parameters.

```
test:=proc(x,y,z)
  x,y,z:
end:
test(1,sqrt(2), [a,b,c], x);
```
$$1, \sqrt{2}, [4, b, c]$$

Maple complains that `test` was called with too few parameters.

```
test(1,2):
    Error, (in test) test uses a
    3rd argument, z, which is
    missing
```

Variable number of parameters

In many procedures, the number of parameters is variable. This applies especially to all procedures which can be passed an arbitrary number of options of the form `option=setting` (in an arbitrary order). In such cases, the two variables `nargs` and `args` can be evaluated inside the procedure. `nargs` contains the total number of parameters that have been passed. `args` contains these parameters as a set; individual parameters can be read with `args[n]`.

In the example on the right, a procedure is defined which must be passed at least two parameters. In the call, five parameters are specified. The first two are located in x and y, the remaining three are accessed via args[3] to args[5]. (Obviously – in spite of the parameters x and y – the first two parameters too are contained in args.)

```
test:=proc(x,y)
  local n;
  x, y, seq(args[n], n=3..nargs):
end:

test(a,b,c,d,e);

     a, b, c, d, e
```

Parameters in square brackets

In some Maple commands (in particular those from the stats package), some of the parameters are enclosed in square brackets. Although this does not lead to any recognizable advantage (and the user is only confused by an inconsistent syntax), you should at least know how you can implement this form of parameter passing.

When you call a procedure in the form command[x1,x2](x3), Maple considers the parameters in square brackets as still belonging to the command name. Inside the procedure, you can access the command name via the keyword procname. With op, you can then read the indices of the procedure name.

```
fn:=proc(x3)
  print(op(1,procname), op(2,procname), x3);
end:
fn[a,b](c);

     a, b, c
```

You can find a practical example of this form of parameter passing in Chapter 21, where the graphics commands of the statistical package are extended by the new commands yscale and yshift, still maintaining the syntax of the already existing commands xscale and xshift.

Type checking

Frequently, a procedure expects its parameters to be of specific data types – for example, integer numbers, lists, and so on – and only supplies correct results when the data types are correct. When a type check is to be carried out when the procedure is called, the data type of a parameter can be specified by means of the :: operator. (In Release 3, a simple colon was sufficient.)

In spite of the small programming effort, `test` supplies precise error messages.

```
test:=proc(x:nonnegint,
                   y:nonnegint)
  sqrt(x*y);
end:

test(1.5, 2):
  Error, test expects its 1st
  argument, x, to be of type
  nonnegint, but received 1.5
```

A complete list of data types supported by Maple can be found in the online help under `?type`. The following table shows some particularly important data types from the list of nearly 90 types:

`integer:`	integer numbers	`range:`	ranges in the form $a..b$
`float:`	floating point numbers	`set:`	sets $\{a, b, c\}$
`fraction:`	fractions	`list:`	lists $[a, b, c]$
`name:`	variable names	`table:`	tables
`algebraic:`	algebraic expressions	`array:`	arrays
`polynom:`	polynomials	`vector:`	vectors
`equation:`	equations	`matrix:`	matrices

The automatic type checking can also cope with quite complex expressions: by using curly brackets, several alternatives can be specified. For enumeration types (lists, sequences, and so on) the type of the list elements can be specified as well.

`x::constant..constant`	x must be a range of two constant numbers
`x::{list,set}`	x can be either a list or a set
`x::list('=')`	x must be passed a list of equations (for example $[x = 3, y = 4]$)
`x::anything`	x can be passed an arbitrary expression

When more types are admitted for one parameter or no type check is carried out at all, the data type can also be determined at a later stage by means of the `type` function.

The procedure `test` is to be passed two positive integer numbers. The type check is carried out via the `type` command. When types do not match, the procedure is terminated by `ERROR` with an error message.

```
test:=proc(x,y)
  if not type( [args],
    [nonnegint, nonnegint]) then
    ERROR('wrong parameter')
  fi:
  ...
end:
```

Peculiarities in handling variables and parameters

Local and global variables

Up to Release 2, all variables in a procedure which were not explicitly defined as local with `local` or included in the parameter list were considered to be global. In Release 3, the keyword `global` was introduced to label global variables. For undeclared variables, Maple decided whether the variables were local or global. In Release 4, things have changed: now, Maple sees as local all variables which are not explicitly declared as `global`. `local` has not become superfluous, however: it should still be used to declare all local variables in order to avoid warnings, such as *'i' is implicitly declared local*.

If you have no experience with other programming languages, here is a brief explanation of the terms 'local' and 'global'. Normally, it is not desirable for a procedure to modify variables which are used outside the procedure. When, for example, a loop for $i = 1$ to 10 is executed inside a procedure, an existing homonymous variable i outside the procedure should not be affected.

Local variables are not only local inside a procedure, but also in each call of the procedure. This is particularly important when a procedure recursively calls itself. In this call, memory is reserved for all local variables for each repeated call. A change in one level of the procedure does not affect the variables on the lower levels.

The procedure on the right generates a set containing the first n powers of the parameter x. Inside the `for` loop, the local variable i is used. Thus, a call of *test* does not affect the variable i outside the procedure.

```
test:=proc(x,n)
local i:
for i from 1 to n do
print(x^i);
od;
end:
i=0: test(x,2);
```

$$x, x^2$$

```
i;
```

$$i$$

In order to show the effect of global variables, the loop variable i is declared as global in the example on the right. Therefore, after calling the *test* procedure, i has a new value.

```
test:=proc(x,n)
  global i:
  for i from 1 to n do
    print(x^i);
  od;
  end:
i:=0: test(x,2);
```

$$x, x^2$$

```
i;
```

$$3$$

Global variables are employed when a procedure must change or read a variable with a specific name. For example, the options of a procedure can be controlled by global variables which are set prior to calling the procedure.

The example below defines the procedure fn which causes a floating point evaluation of the passed parameter. When the global variable _fn_digits has no value assigned to it, evaluation is carried out with the number of digits predefined in Digits, otherwise the number of digits is determined by _fn_digits. Information on if is given later in the chapter.

```
fn:=proc(x) global _fn_digits:
  if _fn_digits='_fn_digits' then evalf(x) else evalf(x,_fn_digits) fi:
end:

fn(1/3);

    .3333333333

_fn_digits:=20: fn(1/3);

    .33333333333333333333
```

One particular feature applies to environment variables such as Digits, which at first sight looks like a global variable: when such variables are modified inside a procedure, the change only applies within the procedure. Therefore, the calculating precision can be changed inside a procedure without having to fear consequences for further calculations in Maple.

Evaluation of variables

In general, Maple commands inside program code behave in the same way as during their interactive execution. Thus, it makes no difference whether you employ solve in a program or as a normal command.

The only difference between the interactive execution of a command and the execution of the same command inside a procedure occurs during variable evaluation: here, Maple has special rules which do not apply to any other programming language and which cause huge comprehension problems especially to experienced programmers (for whom such behaviour is not obvious at all). Even though the rules described below look very strange at first sight, they do make sense for a computer algebra system and allow efficient programming.

During interactive operation, Maple evaluates variables completely, even if chained assignments have to be taken into account. Thus, to nobody's surprise, $a + 1$ yields $c + 1$. (If c were assigned a value, Maple would obviously also calculate the result.)

```
restart:
a:=b:
b:=c:
a+1;

    c + 1
```

When the same variable assignments are carried out for local variables in a procedure, the result turns out to be $b + 1$! The result $c + 1$ can only be achieved when you write `eval(a)+1` instead of `a+1`.

```
test:=proc()
  local a,b,c:
  a:=b: b:=c: a+1;
end:
test();
```
$$b + 1$$

The reason: during interactive operation, Maple evaluates all variables as far as possible, but the automatic evaluation of local variables in procedures is limited to one level. (Therefore, the result is $b + 1$. Without any evaluation at all, the result would be $a + 1$.)

But it gets worse: while Maple evaluates local variables at least for one level, parameters are not evaluated at all. However, all mathematical expressions specified in a procedure call are evaluated completely (even if the procedure is called within a procedure). Within the procedure, however, parameters are completely passive and seem to be immune to assignments.

The third variation of *test* uses parameters for calculation, which is normally not what parameters are designed for. The result: $a + 1$! (However, even in this variation you arrive at the result $c + 1$ when you write `eval(x)+1` instead of `x+1`.) *test* modifies the variables a and b which both contain c after the call.

```
restart:
test:=proc(x,y,z)
  x:=y: y:=z: x+1;
end:
test(a,b,c);
```
$$a + 1$$

```
a,b,c;
```
$$c, c, c$$

Things look different again with global variables: these behave in exactly the same way inside the procedure as outside, that is, they are always fully evaluated.

```
test:=proc()
  global a,b,c:
  a:=b: b:=c: a+1;
end:
test();
```
$$c + 1$$

Summary: Inside procedures, global variables are evaluated completely, local variables only for one level and parameters not at all. Full evaluation can be forced at any time with `eval`.

Note 1: The operators ", "" and """ can also be used in procedures to access the last three results. As with global variables, these operators are fully evaluated. At the same time, however, they behave in the same way as local variables since they are locally available inside the procedure and do not affect the same operators outside the procedure. When entering the procedure, all three operators are empty.

The operators ", "" and """ are especially needed for calling procedures whose parameters are labelled with `uneval`. An example of the application of these operators can be found in the next chapter (description of the new `seqn` command).

Note 2: Even during 'full' automatic evaluation, procedures, tables and arrays are not evaluated. A procedure call is only carried out when brackets are specified; for tables and arrays, eval must be used (see Chapter 13, Section 'Assignment and copying of tables and arrays') in order to pass the contents (and not just the variable name). These too are peculiarities of Maple, but at least they apply both inside and outside procedures.

Reference: A practical example which shows the numerous implications of variable and parameter evaluation can be found in the next chapter, which describes the programming of the seqn command. seqn is a better alternative to seq (for some applications).

Modification of parameters

Modification of parameters inside the procedure is not common, but it is possible. In this case, however, specific rules must be observed both in the procedure call and in the procedure code.

Maple evaluates the parameters before they are passed to the procedure. When you pass $a + 3$ and a contains the value 4, the value 7 is passed to the procedure. In order to allow a variable to be changed by a procedure, two conditions must be satisfied: the variable must be passed alone (that is, a, not $a + 1$) and the evaluation of the variable must be prevented (that is, the procedure must be passed the name of the variable, not its contents).

Since Release 4, the second condition can be easily met by specifying uneval or evaln as the data type of the parameter. This has the effect that no evaluation at all is carried out at the parameter passing stage or that evaluation is only carried out up to the point where a variable name is present. (evaln, for example, evaluates z.3 to the name *z3*.)

The procedure *test* is passed the non-evaluated name of the variable a. After the call, a has the value 5.

```
restart:
test:=proc(x::evaln)
  x:=5;
end:
a:=3: test(a): a;

        5
```

In the second example, the value of the passed variable is to be incremented by 1. As a first attempt, you will probably formulate the procedure on the right. It is destined to fail because x is a parameter and as such is not evaluated inside the procedure (see previous section).

```
test:=proc(x::evaln)
  x:=x+1;
end:
a:=3: test(a): a;
  Error, too many levels of recursion
```

The corrected variation uses evaln in the first line to prevent evaluation when the parameter is passed, and eval in the second line to force evaluation inside the procedure.

```
test:=proc(x:evaln)
  x:=eval(x)+1;
end:
a:=3: test(a): a;

        4
```

test also works when a symbolic expression is passed in the parameter.

```
a:=sin(b): test(a): a;
```

$$\sin(b) + 1$$

Caution: In contrast to old procedures in which variables to be changed had to be specified in quotes (see next example), this is no longer allowed with the new code that uses `evaln`!

```
a:=3: test('a'):
  Error, Illegal use of an
  object as a name
```

Older Maple code (up to Release 3) operated without `evaln` labelling of parameters. Nothing else changes in the code of the procedure, except that the parameters to be modified must be enclosed in quotes (in order to prevent evaluation).

```
test:=proc(x:evaln)
  x:=eval(x)+1;
end:
a:=3: test(a): a;
```

$$4$$

Since arrays are excluded from automatic evaluation, modification of array elements is possible without labelling the parameter with `evaln`.

```
test:=proc(x::array)
  x[1]:=1:
end:
a:=array([0,0]): test(a):
print(a);
```

$$[1, 0]$$

Procedure options

The next command after `local` or `global` is `options`, which can be used to choose several options provided by Maple. These options control internal management and application of the procedure. Maple provides the following options:

`remember`: a remember table is managed for the procedure in which calculated results are stored. Especially with recursive procedures, this can lead to enormous savings in calculating time. The remember table can be directly manipulated via `op(4,op(name))` and deleted with `forget(name)`. See also Chapters 8 and 27.

`system`: when this option is used in combination with `remember`, the remember table is deleted during 'garbage collection'. A 'garbage collection' is a reorganization of memory during which information that is no longer needed is deleted. This process is automatically executed by Maple before it runs short of memory.

`builtin`: is used for procedures which are directly integrated into the kernel. This option cannot be used for programming user-defined commands.

`operator`: this option causes the function to be considered as a functional operator (this corresponds to the declaration `f:=x->y^2`). The option has no influence on the actual effect and functioning of the procedure.

arrow: this option is used in combination with operator and causes the function to be represented in arrow notation. arrow too does not change the functioning of the procedure.

```
test:=proc(x)
   options operator, arrow;
   x^2;
end:

print(test):
```
$$x \mapsto x^2$$

trace: this option causes each jump into the procedure and each return from the procedure to be documented. The option is particularly used for debugging recursive procedures. Further tips on this subject can be found in the debugging section in the next chapter.

Copyright: with this option, a copyright notice can be anchored in the procedure. Usually, a character string is specified which is enclosed in right quotes and begins with Copyright.

```
test:=proc(x)
   options 'Copyright mk 96';
   x^2;
end:

op(3, op(test));

   'Copyright mk 96'
```

Fast floating point evaluation of procedures

In principle, you can use evalhf(procedure(..)) to force a faster evaluation of a command in the floating point arithmetic of the computer. However, evalhf works only if the procedure resorts exclusively to commands and functions which could also be directly executed in the C programming language. Symbolic calculations are *a priori* excluded from evaluation by evalhf, together with many numeric processes (for example, for integration) and the commands for matrix calculus. Thus, evalhf can only be used in a sensible way when complex calculations without Maple special functions are to be carried out.

The procedure *test* calculates the sum of $1/x^2$ for $x = 1..n$. One peculiarity of the procedure is that the quote character " is used in the same way as a variable. The instruction 0: yields the result 0 and thus deletes ". "+1/i^2 refers to " and yields the result incremented by $1/i^2$. The last instruction in the procedure (":) supplies the return value of the procedure.

```
test:=proc(n)
   local i:   0:
   for i from 1 to n do:
      "+1/i^2:
   od:
   ":
end:
```

Normally the procedure is relatively slow because calculations are carried out symbolically. The command `test(2000)` therefore supplies a very large fraction which is numerically evaluated by `evalf`. When, in contrast, `test` is executed in `evalhf`, the result appears almost immediately in the precision of the hardware arithmetic (usually 16 digits). As a countercheck, the result is once more calculated with `add`.

```
test(2000): evalf(");
    1.644434192
evalhf(test(2000));
    1.644434191827396
Digits:=16:
evalf(add(1/n^2, n=1..2000));
    1.644434191827393
```

In procedures which are to be evaluated with `evalhf`, returning results in parameters is not allowed. But there is no rule without exceptions: arrays which are passed as parameters may be modified inside the procedure. However, this is only possible when the array variable is bracketed with `var`, and even in this special case only individual elements of the array may be modified (`x[1,2]:=..`), but not the array as a whole (`x:=..`).

The procedure `test` writes the value 0 into the first element of the array x. As a test, the procedure is passed the array $a := [1, 2]$. In order to allow floating point evaluation (which is only carried out for demonstration purposes), a must be bracketed with `var`.

```
test:=proc(x:array)
  x[1]:=0:
end:

a:=array([1,2]):
evalhf(test(var(a))): print(a);
    [0.0, 2.0]
```

User-defined operators

Normally, procedures are used to define new functions or commands. There is, however, also the possibility of defining new operators. User-defined operators always begin with the symbol '&'. The following three examples show the definition of operators for one, two or three operands. However, operators for more than two operands seldom make sense and, in their application, do not differ from normal functions.

When defining operators, the operator name starting with '&' must be enclosed in right quotes. The operator `&op1` squares the operand indicated after it.

```
'&op1':=proc(x)
  x^2;
end:

&op1 a;
    a^2
```

The second example shows an operator which builds the sum of the squares of both operands. As usual in Maple, the operator is placed between the two operands.

```
'&op2':=proc(x,y)
  x^2+y^2:
end:

a &op2 b;
    a^2 + b^2
```

Operators for three or more operands are called in the same way as normal functions, that is, the parameters are placed in parentheses after the operator.

```
'&op3':=proc(x,y,z)
  x+y+z;
end:

&op3(a, b, c);
```

$$a + b + c$$

Note: The `define` command can be used to define properties of operators – for example, whether the operator is associative, commutative, and so on. The command is, however, only of interest for formal operators, not for operators defined explicitly by a procedure. Formal operators are operators for which only the name exists. `define` deletes the definition of an operator by a procedure and only affects simplification of expressions containing formal operators.

Branches and loops

After having used `if` conditions in various examples in this book, we now supply their syntax (which is already known from other programming languages).

Branches, case distinctions and conditions are formulated in Maple with the keywords `if`, `then`, `elif`, `else` and `fi`.

```
if   condition1 then ...
elif condition2 then ...
elif condition3 then ...
else ...
fi;
```

Instead of the three dots, command sequences of arbitrary length may be inserted. The `elif` and `else` parts are optional, but each `if` condition must be terminated with `fi`.

Loops are formulated in Maple either with the known `seq` command (see Chapter 12) or with the keywords `do` and `od`. These keywords alone constitute an endless loop, and are therefore usually used in combination with `for` or `while`. Loops can be prematurely exited with `break`. `next` skips the remaining commands up to `od` and continues the loop from there. The following examples show some simple loops.

In the loop on the right, x cycles through the values 1, 2 and 3. It does not matter whether x has a value prior to the beginning of the loop – if this is the case, it is deleted. After the end of the loop, x has the value 4.

```
for x from 1 to 3 do
  print(x):
od:
     1
     2
     3
```

The example on the right is a variation of the previous example. The loop is cycled through in reverse direction and with a step width of -2. After the end of the loop, x has the value -1. The loop condition is tested at the beginning of the loop. If the condition is not met, none of the loop commands are executed. Therefore, loops of the form `for i from 1 to 3 by -1` are not executed at all.

```
for x from 5 to 1 by -2 do
  print(x):
od:
  5
  3
  1
```

A further `for` variation can be formulated with the keyword `in`. The loop variable is substituted one by one with all the elements of the list specified after `in`.

```
for i in [1,2,3] do
  print(i)
od:
  1
  2
  3
```

`while` can be used to formulate a loop that depends on a general condition. The loop is executed until the condition is no longer met. Please note the `eval` command in the increment of the control variable x by 1: without this command, Maple would build an endless loop for x. A particular feature of `while` loops is that the results of the commands contained in the loop are displayed. Therefore, the `print` command is omitted.

```
x:=0:
while(x<3) do
  x:=eval(x)+1:
od;
     x := 1
     x := 2
     x := 3
```

The `for` loop has an essential limitation: it cannot cope with symbolic start and end values and step widths. It is not possible to construct a `for` loop from 0 to π with a step width of $\pi/8$. In this case, Maple issues the error message 'unable to execute for'. Also, the formulation of a `while` loop following the above pattern causes problems. The expression `while(x<=Pi)` leads to the error message 'cannot evaluate boolean'. The following example shows a way to circumvent this problem.

In the loop on the right, x cycles through the values $0, \pi/8, \pi/4..., \pi$. (This time, no loop results are shown.) Please note the slightly more elaborate formulation of the `while` condition with `evalf`. This is used to avoid the error message 'cannot evaluate boolean'.

```
x:=0:
while(evalf(x)<=evalf(Pi)) do:
  print(x):
  x:=eval(x)+Pi/8:
od;
```

In the last example, do and od are used to formulate an endless loop which is prematurely exited
with break.

```
x:=0:
do
   x:=eval(x)+1:
   if x>3 then break; fi;
   print(x):
od:
   1
   2
   3
```

Commands with user-defined options

Many Maple commands are characterized by the fact that, after several rigidly predeter-
mined parameters, an arbitrary number of additional parameters may be specified in the form
option=setting. Most frequently, this situation occurs with graphics commands.

The following example presents a scheme which allows you to consider an arbitrary number of
options with default settings. In the first two parameters, the test command must be passed lists
(for example, for processing the coordinate points contained in them, or whatever; it makes no
difference for this example).

Furthermore, the three options optiona, optionb and optionc can be set, where for option A numeric values are allowed, for B character strings and for C a Boolean value (that is, *true* or *false*).
The default settings for the three options are 10, 'default' and *true*.

For evaluation of the option list, which is simply determined by means of args from all parameters
from the third position onward, the program makes use of the hasoption command. This command
accepts a list of options as the first parameter. In the second parameter, the name of the option
(and optionally the required data type) must be specified. The third parameter contains a variable in
which the setting of the option is stored. In the optional fourth parameter, a variable can be specified
which is passed the parameter list (minus the current option). If the variables for the third or fourth
parameter already have an assigned value, they must be passed in quotes.

hasfunction returns *true* or *false*, depending on whether the required option is found or not. This
is used in *test* in order to substitute default values for options that are not specified.

After determination of the three options, *opts* contains a list of all remaining options. This list could
now be passed on to other Maple commands, in case these are expecting options (for example, when
you program a new graphics command which builds on plot3d and want to pass that command's
option unchanged). In *test*, however, no further options are expected and an error message is
displayed.

The sample procedure terminates by displaying the settings of the three options. In a real application, this would be the point where the code proper of the procedure begins.

```
test:=proc(l1:list, l2:list)
  local opts, available, value, opta, optb, optc;
  opts:=[args[3..nargs]];
  if not hasoption(opts, optiona=posint, opta, 'opts') then
    opta:=10:
  fi:
  if not hasoption(opts, optionb=string, optb, 'opts') then
    optb:=abc:
  fi:
  if not hasoption(opts, optionc=boolean, optc, 'opts') then
    optc:=false:
  fi:
  if nops(opts)>0 then
    ERROR('invalid option', opts):
  fi:
  print(opta,optb,optc);
end:
```

The following four examples show the call of the `test` procedure. At the first call, two empty lists are passed; the procedure supplies the default settings of the options. At the second call, the options are specified. Examples three and four show the behaviour of the procedure when options are passed in the wrong format or when illegal options are passed.

```
test([],[]);
```

> $10, abc, false$

```
test([],[], optiona=5, optionb=xyz, optionc=false);
```

> $5, xyz, false$

```
test([],[], optiona=xy);
  Error, (in hasoption) The, optiona, option must be a, posint,
  but got, xy
```

```
test([],[], optiona=5, optionb=xyz, optionc=false, optiond=3);
  Error, (in test) invalid option, [optiond = 3]
```

Processing of files

It is often desirable to process data from other programs in Maple or to transfer the results from Maple to other programs. In such a case, the only reasonable means of data exchange is an ASCII file which contains the numbers (and sometimes also character strings) in a form understandable to both programs.

For this purpose, Maple provides an almost countless number of commands, and the number seems to increase with each new release. This section is limited to the most important commands. Further information on various file types, additional commands, and so on can be found in the file examples\lang.mws included with Release 4 and under the help subject ?file_types.

Note: The following examples assume that the three-line text file data.dat is located in the current directory. (Information on the specification of file names and directories can be found in the previous chapter under 'Files and directories' in the Section 'The programming environment'.)

File numbers

The specification of the file is a common feature for nearly all file processing commands. This can be carried out either directly by way of the file name or by way of a file number (file descriptor). In the second case, prior to the first access, the file number must be determined with fopen. After the last access, the file must be closed with fclose.

fopen must be passed the file name and the access mode (READ or WRITE). Optionally, the third parameter can be used to specify the data type (TEXT or BINARY) – in most cases, however, Maple recognizes the required type itself on the strength of the access mode.

The advantage of file numbers (new since Release 4) as opposed to direct specification of the file name lies in the possibility of accessing several files at the same time.

Reading text files

The readline command reads a line of text from a file. The program on the right opens the file data.dat, reads the text line by line into the string variable s and displays its contents on screen. Subsequently, the file is closed with fclose.

```
fn:=fopen('data.dat', READ):
s:=readline(fn):
while(s<>0) do:
  lprint(s):
  s:=readline(fn):
od:
fclose(fn):
  1 2 3
  4 5
  6.6 7 8e-8 9
```

readdata is suitable for reading pure number files. The numbers must be stored in the file line by line, separated by tabs or spaces. Other separators, such as commas or semicolons, are not allowed. In floating point numbers, a decimal point must be used (no comma). Exponents must be written in the form $123e456$. The alternative notation $123*10^{456}$ otherwise allowed in Maple is not permitted. The number range is limited to the double format used in the C programming language, that is, a maximum of 16 digits and exponents up to ± 310.

readdata is passed three parameters: the file name or file number, the number format (integer or float) and the number of columns. When the last two parameters are omitted, readdata only reads the first number of each text line and interprets the numbers as floating point numbers. As a result, readdata returns a (if need be, embedded) list.

readdata reads the first number of each line and returns the result as a list.

```
fn:=fopen('data.dat', READ):
readdata(fn);
fclose(fn):
    [1., 4., 6.6]
```

In the example on the right, the file name is specified directly. readdata expects integer numbers and builds lists of two numbers per line.

```
readdata('data.dat', integer, 2);
    [[1, 2], [4, 5], [6, 0]]
```

Another command suitable for reading text lines is fscanf. The command is passed the file number and a character string which describes the required data format. The syntax is the same as that of the homonymous C command. In particular, integer numbers are denoted by %d, floating point numbers by %f and character strings by %f. (An extensive description of the syntax is provided by the online help.) fscanf returns the result as a list.

In the example on the right, again the whole file is read, and all numbers are interpreted as floating point numbers. The end of the file is recognized with feof.

```
fn:=fopen('data.dat', READ):
while(not feof(fn)) do
  lst:=fscanf(fn, '%f %f %f'):
  lprint(lst):
od:
fclose(fn):
    [1., 2., 3.]
    [4., 5., 6.6]
    [7., .8e-7, 9.]
```

One more command for reading files is read. It can practically only be used in combination with save and is therefore described below together with that command.

Writing text files

Two suitable commands for writing text files are writeline and fprintf. Their application is very similar to readline and scanf.

The program on the right reads data.dat line by line and copies the character strings into the file datacopy.dat. writeline is passed the file number and the character string to be written.

```
f1:=fopen('data.dat',READ):
f2:=fopen('datacopy.dat', WRITE):
s:=readline(f1):
while(s<>0) do:
  writeline(f2,s):
  s:=readline(f1):
od:
fclose(f1): fclose(f2):
```

A second version of the same program can be formulated with `fprintf`. Here, you must not forget the special character \n for marking the end of line.

```
f1:=fopen('data.dat',READ):
f2:=fopen('datacopy.dat', WRITE):
while(not feof(f1)) do:
  s:=readline(f1):
  fprintf(f2, '%s\n', s):
od:
fclose(f1): fclose(f2):
```

Note: Depending on the version (UNIX, Windows, Apple), Maple considers the end-of-line characters of the corresponding operating system. See also the help text on `?file_types`.

Reading and storing binary files

Binary file access is normally carried out by means of the commands `readbytes` and `writebytes`. They can be used to read or write a given number of bytes. Data is passed either as a list of integer numbers or as a character string.

The most efficient way of copying a file in Maple looks as follows:

```
writebytes('datacopy.dat',
          readbytes('data.dat',infinity)):
```

During access, it is also possible to change the read or write position inside the file: `filepos` determines the current position or changes it. The `feof` function already employed several times checks whether the end of file has been reached.

The commands read and save

While the commands discussed up to now facilitate data exchange between Maple and other programs, the two commands `read` and `save` are of interest only inside Maple applications.

`save` stores the contents of Maple variables (thus, also lists, arrays, matrices, procedures, and so on) in a file, together with the names of the corresponding variables. Thus, when the file is loaded again at a later stage, the correspondence between data and variables is automatically restored.

When the file name ends in `.m`, Maple's internal binary format is used; otherwise, the file is stored as an ASCII text file. The variables stored in the file can be read back in with `read`.

The advantage of `read` and `save` over the commands described above is that even very large Maple expressions (for example, a matrix of 100 times 100 elements) can be stored very efficiently. The disadvantage is that the format (in particular the binary format) changes with practically each and every new release of Maple and is therefore not portable.

For this reason, the most important application of `read` is to read program code previously saved with `save` or `savelib`. More information on this subject can be found in the next chapter which describes how user-defined commands can be stored and managed in packages or libraries.

In the example on the right, the variable a which contains a 2*2 array is stored in the file `test.dat`. Subsequent to the `save` command, the resulting ASCII file is shown. The two line breaks have been inserted for reasons of space; `test.dat` itself consists of one single line.

```
a:=array([[1,2], [2.3, 1/3]]):
save a, 'test.dat';

a := array(1 .. 2, 1 .. 2,
[(2, 1)=2.3,(2, 2)=1/3,(1, 1)=1,
(1, 2)=2]);
```

By means of `read`, a can be easily read in again.

```
a:='a':
read 'test.dat':
print(a);
```

$$\begin{bmatrix} 1 & 2 \\ 2.3 & 1/3 \end{bmatrix}$$

Screen output, keyboard input

The two most widely used commands for output of information on screen have already been presented in this book more than once: `lprint` for output of unformatted character strings and `print` for output of formatted mathematical expressions. `printf` works similarly to `lprint`, but allows more precise control of the output (see `fprintf` under 'Writing text files' above). Besides these three commands which are specially designed for screen output, you can also use the `fprintf` and `writeline` commands described above for output on screen when `terminal` is specified instead of the file number. This is particularly useful for test purposes.

```
lprint(x^2, 1/3);
  x^2    1/3
```

```
print(x^2,1/3):
```

$$x^2, \frac{1}{3}$$

```
i:=3: f:=evalf(sqrt(3)):
printf('i has the value %d, f has the value % f', i, f);
  i has the value 3, f has the value   1.732050
```

```
writeline(terminal, 'abc', 'def'):
  abc
  def
```

If you wish to enter a character string via the keyboard, you can use a command which has already been introduced: when you specify `terminal` in `readline` instead of the file name, Maple expects your input from the keyboard. `readstat` can even accept and evaluate Maple commands. You can specify a character string as the parameter, and this is then displayed in front of the input cursor.

```
printf('Please enter a character string: '): s:=readline(terminal);
  Please enter a character string:
  > hallo
```

$$s := hallo$$

```
s:=readstat('Please enter a Maple command: ');
  Please enter a Maple command: > sqrt(x);
```

$$\sqrt{x}$$

Handling of character strings

In Maple, character strings are written enclosed in right quotes, for example 'abc'. Character strings can be stored in variables in the same way as all other Maple expressions. Since Release 3, the 512-character limit has been lifted. Character strings can now be of arbitrary length.

Several character strings are joined together into one character string with cat or with the concatenation operator '.'. length determines the length of a character string.

```
str:='abcde' . 'fghikl';
```

$$str := abcdefghikl$$

```
length(str);
```

    11

Maple expressions can be converted into character strings with convert, string. Immediate mathematical evaluation of character strings is not possible. evalf will function again only after reconversion into Maple expressions with parse.

```
convert(2/3, string);
```

$$2/3$$

```
evalf(");
```

$$2/3$$

```
parse(");
```

$$\frac{2}{3}$$

```
evalf(");
```

    0.666666667

substring determines a substring. In the range specification, the first and last characters must be specified. When only one character is to be read, the start and end characters must coincide (for example 3..3).

```
substring(str, 3..5);
```

$$cde$$

Since Release 4 negative indices too are allowed in substring, in order to provide easy access to the end of the character string. Please note, however, that the first character in the range must be specified first, followed by the last character. The range -1..-3 is illegal!

```
substring(str, -3..-1);
```

$$ikl$$

searchtext determines the position of a search pattern in a character string. The command yields 0 or the position of the first occurrence of a character string. The search range can be limited with an optional range specification. searchtext only supplies a result when the whole character string is contained in this area (and not just the first character!). Unlike searchtext, the command SearchText differentiates between upper case and lower case spelling.

```
searchtext('efg', str);
```

   5

```
searchtext('efg', str, 1..6);
```

   0

parse reads the passed character string and returns either an unevaluated Maple expression or the result of that expression. The character string can be passed with or without a terminating semicolon. Evaluation is only carried out when the keyword statement is specified in the second parameter.

```
parse('diff(sin(x),x)');
```

$$\frac{d}{dx}\sin(x)$$

```
parse('diff(sin(x),x)',statement);
```

  $\cos(x)$

sscanf works in a similar way to the fscanf command presented in the previous section. It reads data from the character string specified in the first parameter, taking into account the format specifications of the second parameter. The result is returned as a list.

```
sscanf('1 2.2 3.3', '%d %d %d');
```

  $[1, 2, 0]$

```
sscanf('1 2.2 3.3', '%f %f %f');
```

  $[1.0, 2.2, 3.3]$

```
sscanf('x=5,y=666', 'x=%d,y=%d');
```

  $[5, 666]$

sprintf works in a similar way to printf and fprintf, with the exception that output is not displayed on screen or written to a file; instead, the function returns a character string as a result.

```
sprintf('int %d, float %f', 3, 2.5);
```

  $int3, float2.5$

Syntax summary

Procedures

```
p:=proc(var1::type1, var2::type2 ...)
  local l1,l2 ...: global g1,g2 ...:
  options ...: description 'short description':
  command: ...: ...:
end:
```
    defines the procedure p. At the call of the procedure, an automatic type check of the parameters is carried out. If `evaln` or `uneval` is specified as the type, full evaluation of the parameters at call time is prevented (important for return parameters). $l1, l2...$ are considered as local, $g1, g2...$ as global variables. Possible procedure options are described below. Usually, the procedure returns the result of the last command as the return value. The procedure can, however, be prematurely terminated with RETURN; then the parameter specified with RETURN is considered as the return value. Procedure options:

    `remember`: all the results of the procedure are stored in a remember table.
    `system`: the remember table can be deleted during 'garbage collection'.
    `builtin`: the command is integrated into the Maple kernel.
    `operator`: `print` displays the procedure in bracket notation.
    `arrow`: `print` displays the procedure in arrow notation.
    `trace`: all jumps into and out of the procedure are displayed.

```
'&op':=proc(...)  ...  end:
```
    defines a new operator by means of the specified procedure.

```
nargs;
```
    contains the number of parameters passed to the procedure.

```
args;
```
    contains the passed parameters as a sequence.

```
evalhf(p);
```
    executes the procedure making use of the fast floating point arithmetic of the computer. Calculating precision is defined by the computer (usually 16 digits).

```
hasoptions(opts, name=type, 'setting', 'opts');
```
    helps evaluate user-defined options. The command checks whether *opts* contains an option of the specified name and type. If so, the setting is stored in the variable specified in the third parameter and `hasoptions` returns *true*. If another variable is specified in the optional fourth parameter, `hasoptions` uses it to store the option list minus the evaluated option.

Branches and loops

```
if   cond1 then ...
elif cond2 then ...
else ...  fi;
```
formulates an if condition. An arbitrary number of elif blocks is allowed. The elif and else blocks are optional; the condition must in any case be terminated with fi.

```
do ... od;
```
formulates an endless loop. Exit is only possible with break.

```
for var from start to end do ... od;
```
cycles the loop for integer values from *start* to *end*.

```
for var from start to end by step do ... od;
```
as above, except for an arbitrary step width for the control variable.

```
for var in list do ... od;
```
executes the loop body once for each element contained in the list.

```
while condition do ... od;
```
executes the loop as long as the condition specified after while is satisfied.

```
break;
```
exits the current loop and continues the program after od.

```
next;
```
skips the commands in the current loop and continues the loop with od.

Processing of files

```
fn:=fopen('file_name', type);
```
opens the specified file for reading (READ) or writing (WRITE).

```
fclose(fn);
```
terminates file access.

```
feof(fn);
```
checks whether the end of file has been reached.

```
pos:=filepos(fn);
filepos(fn, newpos);
```
determines or changes the current position inside the file.

```
fprintf(fn, format, data1, data2, data3 ...);
printf(format, data1, data2, data3 ...);
s:=sprintf(format, data1, data2, data3 ...);
```
formats the specified data in accordance with the format string and stores it in a file, displays it on screen, or supplies the character string as the return value. *format* codes are, amongst others, %d for integer numbers, %f for floating point numbers and %s for character strings. (A complete description of formatting options is provided by the online help.)

```
lst:=fscanf(fn, format);
lst:=sscanf(str, format);
```
reads data from a file or a character string and returns the elements found as a list. Similar to fprintf, *format* contains format specifications for the expected data.

```
readdata(fn, type, n);
```
reads the specified ASCII file line by line and returns an (embedded) list of number values. Either integer or float (default) can be selected as the data type. n specifies the maximum number of columns to be read.

```
readline(fn);
```
reads the next line from the specified file and returns the result as a character string. When the end of file is reached, the command returns the value 0.

```
writeline(fn, str1, str2 ...);
```
writes one or more character strings (separated by end-of-line characters) into the file.

```
readbytes(fn, n);
```
reads n bytes from the file and returns the data as a list of integer numbers. When the optional parameter TEXT is specified, the command returns a character string as the result. When the whole file is to be read, infinity can be specified instead of n.

```
writebytes(fn, data);
```
stores the specified data (a list of integer numbers or a character string) in the file.

```
save var,'datname';
```
stores the specified variable in a file in an internal Maple format. When the file name ends in .m, Maple uses a binary format; otherwise, the data is stored in ASCII format.

```
read 'datname';
```
reads the variables stored in the file back in.

```
print(a,b,c);
```
displays the expressions a, b and c on screen in formula format.

```
lprint(a,b,c);
```
displays the expressions a, b and c on screen as an ASCII character string.

```
s:=readline(terminal);
```
   allows you to enter a line of text via the keyboard.

```
s:=readstat('Explanation');
```
   allows input of a Maple instruction via the keyboard.

Handling of character strings

```
cat('abc', 'def');        'abc' .  'def';
```
   joins two character strings.

```
length(str);
```
   determines the length of a character string.

```
convert(expr, string);      parse(str);
```
   convert converts a Maple expression into a character string. parse carries out a conversion in
   the opposite direction.

```
substring(str, a..b);
```
   determines the substring of *str* that begins with the *a*th and ends with the *b*th character.

```
searchtext('pattern', str);      searchtext('pattern', str, a..b);
SearchText('pattern', str);      SearchText('pattern', str, a..b);
```
   determine the position of the specified pattern inside the character strings. When the search
   is unsuccessful, the commands return 0 as the result. The optional third parameter is used to
   limit the search range. SearchText differentiates between upper case and lower case spelling.

```
parse(s);      parse(s, statement);
```
   reads the character string *s* and returns the non-evaluated or the evaluated (second syntax
   variation) Maple expression.

Chapter 30

Programming III: user-defined commands and packages

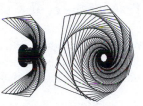

The sample programs shown up to now represent quickly programmable *ad hoc* solutions, which can be used once and then forgotten. When you program new commands which you want to use over and over again or distribute to other people, the requirements are higher. Such commands should be protected from operating errors. They should be equipped with reasonable online help, follow standard Maple conventions, and so on. This chapter deals with such conditions and contains information on the following subjects:

- error detection (debugger)
- analysis of time and memory requirements of procedures (profiler)
- assembly of user-defined packages
- use of march for creation of user libraries
- design of help texts for new commands

The central example of this chapter is the new command seqn which can be employed to generate embedded lists, allowing the use of loops of arbitrary step width. Several sections explain how this command is programmed, equipped with online help and finally integrated into a user-defined library or into the share library.

Error detection and protection

This section begins with a description of the tracelast and trace commands and the environment variables printlevel and infolevel which represent very simple tools for error detection. If these tools are not sufficient, you can use Maple's debugger which allows stepwise execution of a procedure. The auxiliary program mint is suitable for the analysis of text files containing program code. It gives information on variables and functions used, points out possible name conflicts, and so on. Finally, the traperror command is explained: this command allows you to catch possible errors and to prevent display of error messages on screen.

Tracing the course of a program with trace, printlevel and infolevel

When the procedure which you have just finished writing comes up with an error message instead of the required result, `tracelast` provides an easy way to determine the last instruction executed and the value of the variables at that moment.

In the following example, `seq` is to be executed for the values between a and b. Internally, the range is formulated by means of the variables $n1$ and $n2$. However, the code contains an error: the assignment to $n2$ uses the operator = instead of := . `tracelast` displays the local variables, so that the error can be found without problems.

```
test:=proc(a,b)
  local n1, n2, i:
  n1:=a: n2=b:
  seq(i,i=n1..n2);
end:
test(3,4);
  Error, (in test) unable to execute seq
tracelast;
  Error, (in test) unable to execute seq
    executing statement: seq(i,i = n1 .. n2)
    locals defined as: n1 = 3, n2 = n2, i = i
    test called with arguments: 3, 4
```

For a quick analysis of recursive functions, it is best to use the `trace` option. Maple then displays each jump into and out of the procedure, the result of each command and each assignment to a variable on screen.

```
test:=proc(x)
  option trace:
  if x>1 then x*test(x-1) else 1 fi:
end:
test(2);
    --> enter test, args = 2
    --> enter test, args = 1

  1

  <-- exit test (now in
      test) = 1}

  2

  <-- exit test (now at top
      level) = 2}

  2
```

The same effect as with the `trace` option can also be obtained by the homonymous command. Prior to executing a procedure without the `trace` option, `trace(procname)` is executed. During execution of the procedure, the same information as above is displayed. `untrace(procname)` cancels the effect of `trace`.

Hint: Using the two procedures `seq1` and `seqn` as an example, the file `chap32.mws` on the enclosed CD-ROM shows in quite an impressive way how `trace` can be used to follow the course of very complex procedures which even call each other.

A similar effect can also be obtained by changing the global variable `printlevel :=n`. This variable specifies up to which level n the evaluation of Maple commands is displayed. The following definition applies to the current evaluation level: commands which are immediately evaluated belong to the lowest level (0) and are always displayed. Each loop or `if` condition increases the level by 1, each procedure or each recursive procedure call increases the level by 5. Unlike `trace`, `printlevel` applies to all procedures and Maple commands.

The `userinfo` command only displays information when the global variable `infolevel` is set correspondingly. `userinfo` is suitable for showing the user of a procedure additional information on the internal processes within the procedure, if required. For example, `userinfo` is used in the `int`, `dsolve` and `simplify` commands to provide information on the selected integration method, type of differential equation, and so on.

The following example shows the application of `userinfo`: in the first parameter of the command, the information level is specified. The value range is 1 (important message) to 5 (rarely needed details). The second parameter specifies the name of the procedure for which information is to be displayed. The name does not have to be identical to the current procedure name. Also, several procedures that belong together may use the same `userinfo` name. From the third parameter onward, the information to be displayed is specified.

The sample procedure `test` squares the passed parameter and, depending on *infolevel[test]*, displays the message 'Hello world!'.

```
test:=proc(x)
   userinfo(3, 'test', 'Hello world!'):
   x^2:
end:
```

The procedure only displays the additional information when *infolevel[test]* is greater than or equal to 3.

```
test(3);
            9
infolevel[test]:=3:
test(3);
      test:    Hello world!
            9
```

Besides the above three methods of tracing the program course, you can obviously insert `print` or `lprint` instructions at different places in the program code. `print` formats mathematical expressions correctly (for example $\sqrt{x}$), `lprint` displays pure character strings (for example `x^(1/2)`).

The `ERROR` command displays the expressions and character strings specified as parameters on screen. However, after this, the procedure is aborted. This command is particularly useful for a controlled exit from a procedure after detection of an error (for example, incorrect use of a parameter). At the same time, the user can be presented with a clear error message.

The Maple debugger

Error detection in a user-defined procedure can be a very laborious process. Since Release 4, all Maple versions provide a simple debugger which helps with this task. The debugger is automatically activated when an interruption occurs inside a procedure. For this purpose, either a breakpoint must be set in the procedure to be analyzed, or a variable must be monitored. Subsequently, the procedure is started as normal. Program execution is interrupted in the previously specified line. Instead of its usual input prompt >, Maple now displays DBG> in order to show that the debugger is active. From now on, until the end of the procedure, Maple accepts various debugger commands which allow stepwise execution of the procedure.

The debugger can also be used to analyze most Maple commands, with the exception of those commands that for reasons of execution speed only exist in compiled form.

Unlike most other parts of this book, this section begins with a syntax summary of the commands for calling and controlling the debugger; examples follow afterwards. This facilitates the overview of the possibilities provided by the debugger. Further examples can be found in Chapter 6 of Maple's 'Programming Guide'.

Before you call the debugger

```
showstat(test);
```
displays the program code of the procedure *test* to be analyzed together with Maple's internal line numbers. These line numbers differ from the actual line numbers as they would be shown in a text editor, for example, because Maple internally splits lines that contain more than one command into several lines. Furthermore, some keywords (such as od or fi for terminating a loop or condition) are not considered as separate commands; thus, the corresponding line is not numbered.

```
stopat(test);
```
interrupts execution of *test* in the first line.

```
stopat(test,line_no);
```
interrupts execution of *test* in the specified line. (The line numbering of showstat applies.)

```
stopat(test,line_no,condition);
```
interrupts execution of *test* in the specified line provided that the condition is satisfied. In the condition, global and local variables of the procedure can be used.

```
stopwhen(globalvariable);
stopwhen([test,variable]);
```
interrupts execution of *test* when the contents of the specified variables changes. The second syntax variation is suitable for monitoring expressions containing local variables.

```
stoperror('error_text'); stoperror(all);
```
interrupts execution of the code when the specified error occurs. *error_text* must be specified using Maple's internal specification of the error, for example `division by zero`. When the keyword `all` is specified, the debugger is started at every error.

```
showstop();
```
displays a list of all breakpoints and monitoring expressions.

```
DEBUG();
DEBUG(condition)
```
When the `DEBUG` command is used at a given point in the program code of the procedure to be analyzed, execution of the code is interrupted at that point (in the second syntax variation only when the condition is satisfied).

```
test(parameter ...);
```
starts execution of the procedure *test*. The debugger is activated when program execution reaches a breakpoint or a monitored variable changes its value.

```
unstopat(...); unstopwhen(...); unstoperror(...);
```
cancels a breakpoint or a monitoring condition. The same syntax applies as with `stopat`, `stopwhen` and `stoperror`.

Controlling the debugger

Commands for controlling the debugger are written without the usual closing semicolon. While the debugger is active, normal Maple commands can be executed only to a very limited extent. In particular, it is possible to display and modify variables.

```
step
```
executes the next command.

```
next
```
executes the next command. If this is a control expression (loop, branching, and so on), the entire expression is executed in one go. Thus, `next` can lead to the execution of a number of commands.

```
outfrom
```
executes the commands in the current control expression and reinterrupts execution after terminating the expression.

```
return
```
executes the current procedure completely and interrupts execution after the return. `return` only makes sense when the procedure to be analyzed calls itself or calls other procedures.

`cont`
> continues program execution up to the next breakpoint or the next modification of a monitored variable.

`showstat`
`showstat procedure`
`showstat procedure lineFrom..lineTo`
`list`
> displays the entire program listing, parts of it, or (relative to the current line) the previous five lines and the next two lines. Breakpoints are marked with the characters ! or ? (with condition).

`where`
`where n`
> displays the call stack of a procedure. This is particularly useful for analysis of recursive procedures. In the second syntax variation, the stack display can be limited to the last n levels.

`stopat, stopwhen, stoperror`
`unstopat, unstopwhen, unstoperror`
> can be used in the same way as the homonymous Maple commands for setting and deleting breakpoints. Parameters are specified without parentheses and without commas.

`quit`
> terminates execution of both procedure and debugger.

Example

The following example shows the analysis of the recursive Fibonacci function f which does not work as expected for non-integer parameters. (The easiest way to remedy the problem would be to declare the parameter x as `x::nonnegint`. This would ensure that f can only be passed positive integer numbers.)

```
restart:
f:=proc(x)
  option remember;
  if x=0 then 0
  elif x=1 then 1
  else f(x-1)+f(x-2) fi
end:
f(2.5);
  Error, (in f) too many levels of
  recursion
```

`showstat` displays the code in a different format and with Maple's internal line numbers.

```
showstat(f);
  f := proc(x)
     1    if x = 0 then
     2       0
          elif x = 1 then
     3       1
          else
     4       f(x-1)+f(x-2)
          fi
  end
```

stopat is used to formulate a conditional breakpoint: the execution is to be interrupted in line 4 if at that point the variable x is less than 0.

```
stopat(f,4,x<0);
```

$$[f]$$

As expected, the execution of f is automatically interrupted. The debugger displays the value of x.

```
f(2.5);
  f:
      4 f(x-1)+f(x-2)?
DBG > x;
```

$$-0.5$$

where shows how this could happen. The parameter of the function is indicated in square brackets.

```
DBG > where
  TopLevel: f(2.5)
         [2.5]
  f: f(x-1)+f(x-2)
         [1.5]
  f: f(x-1)+f(x-2)
         [.5]
  f: f(x-1)+f(x-2)
         [-.5]
```

list once again shows the program code around the current line. A closer look should make it clear that the condition $x = 0$ is not suited for non-integer numbers. $x \leq 0$ would stop the endless recursion.

```
DBG > list
  f := proc(x)
    1     if x = 0 then
    2         0
          elif x = 1 then
    3         1
          else
    4?!     f(x-1)+f(x-2)
          fi
  end
```

With quit, the execution of the procedure is terminated and the debugger exited.

```
DBG > quit
  Warning, computation interrupted
```

Program code analysis with mint

As a last tool for detection of errors, there is the mint program which runs separately from Maple. At the start, this program is passed the name of a text file containing Maple code. mint analyzes the code and returns a list of errors and warnings as a result. mint can be made more informative by specifying values between 2 and 4 in the -i option. The following call of mint (for the DOS version of Maple) analyzes the file seqn.mpl described in the next but one section and writes the result into the file errors.lst.

```
mint -i 4 seqn.mpl > errors.lst
```

The file errors.lst does not contain error messages (because seqn – hopefully – is error-free by now), but provides information on the use of the symbols used. For example, you are told that the local variable *range* is also used in Maple (for example, as an option of `plot`). Calling a `plot` command inside the `seqn` procedure could thus lead to complications.

Since Release 4, a variation of `mint` is also available in the form of the built-in Maple command `maplemint`. The advantage of this command is that the program code need no longer be present in an external text file, but can also be defined directly in a worksheet. However, `maplemint` is less powerful than `mint` and, in its current version, still supplies rather dubious results.

Trapping of errors with traperror

While the previous subsections dealt with detection of errors, the task now is to call a procedure safely when errors might still be expected. (Even when the code is correct, errors can occur when wrong parameters are passed, available memory becomes insufficient, and so on.)

In Maple, there is no command of the `on error goto` type, with which several programming languages can react to errors without immediately terminating the procedure. Instead, Maple provides the `traperror` command which evaluates the expression passed as the parameter. If no error occurs during that evaluation, `traperror` simply returns the result of the expression; otherwise, it returns a character string containing the error message. The particular advantage of `traperror` is that, in spite of a detected error at the call of a function, the currently running program is not aborted.

Whether an error has occurred can be determined by means of the global variable `lasterror`. This variable is deleted by calling `traperror`. If an error occurs, the error text is stored in it.

The procedure `test` calculates the reciprocal value of the passed parameter. The evaluation of `test(3)` via `traperror` yields $1/3$; `lasterror` is not assigned a text.

```
test:=proc(x) 1/x: end:
traperror(test(3));
```
$$1/3$$
```
lasterror;
```
lasterror

`traperror` recognizes division by 0 and supplies the error message as a result. This error message is now also contained in `lasterror`.

```
traperror(test(0));
```
    `'division by zero'`
```
lasterror;
```
    `'division by zero'`

Analysis of time and memory requirements of procedures

The simplest way to measure the time and memory consumption of commands is provided by the `showtime` command. Once activated, after each executed command, it displays how much time and memory the calculation of the result required.

```
restart:
readlib(showtime):
showtime();

O1 :=
simplify(sin(x)^2+cos(x)^2);

            1

time = 0.12, bytes = 200690
```

In addition, the results are stored in running variables On which you can access. This provides a more practical mechanism than the symbols ", "" and """ for accessing the last three results.

```
O2 :=
int(1/(1+x^5),x):
time = 2.63, bytes = 2364518

O3 :=
O1;

            1

time = 0.01, bytes = 69042
```

`showtime` is switched off with the command `off`.

```
O4 :=
off;
```

More extensive information on the response time and memory requirements of procedures can be obtained by means of the `profile` command. This command was temporarily missing in Release 3, but it has been restored in the standard library in Release 4.

Prior to being used, `profile` must be loaded with `readlib`. All commands or procedures to be analyzed must be specified as parameters of `profile`. In the following example, the `nestprint` command defined in Chapter 28 is used to analyze the expression resulting from the integral $\int 1/(1 + x^5)dx$. `profile` is used to measure how much time and memory is taken up by the procedure `nestprint` and the commands `int` and `lprint`.

```
restart:
nestprint:=proc(x) ... end: # see Chapter 28
readlib(profile):
profile(nestprint,lprint,int):
nestprint(int(1/(1+x^5),x));
    +

        *

            fraction
    ...
```

```
showprofile();
function         depth     calls      time     time%           bytes    bytes%
-----------------------------------------------------------------------------
lprint               1       285     1.017     18.70         4808840     62.07
int                  1         1     2.540     46.71         2256736     29.13
nestprint           10       285     1.880     34.57          681372      8.79
-----------------------------------------------------------------------------
total:              12       571     5.437    100.00         7746948    100.00

unprofile(nestprint,lprint,int):
```

Some brief remarks concerning the interpretation of this table: during the analysis of the expression, nestprint has reached a recursion depth of 10 and has been (recursively) called nearly 300 times. Memory consumption, however, is relatively modest. Displaying the information on screen via lprint has taken up almost 20 per cent of the time. The huge memory consumption of lprint is peculiar.

Example: the new seqn command

The seq command has two basic disadvantages:

- The control variable is always incremented by 1; it is therefore impossible to construct loops with variable step width.

- Only simple sequences can be generated. Embedded lists must be constructed by using a very complicated nesting of seq commands.

Version 1

This section describes the gradual genesis of the new seqn command which avoids both pitfalls. In its function, the command basically corresponds to the Mathematica command Table. The first version of the new procedure looks as follows:

```
seq1:=proc(f, range)
  local i, data;
  data:=[]:
  for i from op(1,op(2,range[1])) to op(2,op(2,range[1])) by range[2] do
    data:=[op(data), eval(subs(op(1,range[1])=i, f))];
  od;
  op(data);
end:
```

Usage of the command can be recognized from the following example: in the second parameter, first the term $x = a..b$ known from the seq command and then the required step width are specified in the form of a list.

```
seq1(x^2, [x=1..2, 0.5]);
```

> $1, 2.25, 4.0$

Except for the op commands, the code of the program is easily understandable: for the local variable i, a loop from the start value to the end value is constructed. At each cycle through the loop, an additional list element is inserted into data. At the end of the procedure, the elements in this list are returned as a sequence.

Now to the op commands: range[1] contains the first list element, that is, $x = a..b$. The inner op command decomposes this expression into x and $a..b$. With the outer op command, a and b are determined.

Currently, the command differs in four essential points from the original:

- The command is in no way protected against operation errors.
- The command refuses to execute symbolic loops.
- The command only functions if the loop variable x was not previously occupied.
- The syntax variation seq(x, data) is missing. In the original, all elements of the list or set $data$ are inserted one after the other into x.

```
x:=3: seq1(x^2, [x=2..3,1]);   # is supposed to yield 4, 9
```

> $9, 9$

```
seq1(x^2, [x=0..Pi, Pi/2]);
     Error, (in seq1) unable to execute for statement
```

Three of the four problems are gradually eliminated in the course of this section. The greatest difficulties are caused by the third point, because in Maple it is sometimes difficult to state how far expressions are to be evaluated at a given moment. The last limitation could also be remedied in the code of seq1 without too much effort, but there is no need for it. (This variation of the seq command works well and does not need improving.)

Version 2: type check

The first modification of the procedure concerns the precise type checking of the second parameter: a list is required as the data type in the declaration of the parameter l. Subsequently, type is used to check the structure of l. If a step width of 0 is specified, the procedure is aborted. Now the procedure also recognizes the case $[x = a..b]$ with missing step width and sets a default step width of 1.

The second essential change to the program lies in the while loop which replaces the for loop of the first variation.

```
seq1:=proc(f, l::list)
  local i, data, range;
  range:=l:
  if not type(range[1],name='..') then
```

```
  ERROR('wrong parameter', range);
elif nops(range)>1 then
  if not type(range[2], algebraic) or evalf(range[2])=0 then
    ERROR('wrong parameter', range);
  fi;
else
  range:=[op(range), 1]:
fi;
data:=[]:
i:=op(1,op(2,range[1])):
while evalf(i)<=evalf(op(2,op(2,range[1]))) do
  data:=[op(data), eval(subs(op(1,range[1])=i, f))];
  i:=eval(i)+range[2];
od;
op(data);
end:
```

The first tests with the new command are quite positive. Now, the command also copes with a loop from 0 to π and, if needed, automatically generates loops of step width 1.

```
x:='x':
seq1(x^2, [x=0..Pi, Pi/2]);
```
$$0, \frac{\pi^2}{4}, \pi^2$$
```
seq1(x^2, [x=2..4]);
```
$$4, 9, 16$$

The attempt to formulate a loop with a negative step width, however, ends badly. The while condition is incorrectly formulated for this case and leads to an endless loop. (Click on the STOP button to terminate the program!)

```
seq1(x, [x=2..4,-1]); # endless loop
```

Version 3: considering negative step widths

In the third version, this special case is contemplated too. Depending on the sign, the operator $\leq$ or $\geq$ is stored in the local variable *comp*. The while condition is formulated using this operator. Please note the prefixed & character for labelling *comp* as an operator.

```
seq1:=proc(f, l:list)
  local i, data, range, '&comp';
  ... as above
  if evalf(range[2])>0 then '&comp':=(x,y)->(x<=y):
  else '&comp':=(x,y)->(x>=y): fi:
  while evalf(i) &comp evalf(op(2,op(2,range[1]))) do
    data:=[op(data), eval(subs(op(1,range[1])=i, f))];
    i:=eval(i)+range[2];
  od;
  op(data);
end:
```

Now, `seq1` also copes with descending loops. The command returns the empty set when the loop is formulated in such a way that x can never reach the target value.

```
seq1(x, [x=3..1, -1]);
```

$$3, 2, 1$$

```
seq1(x, [x=1..3, -1]);
```

Version 4: delayed parameter evaluation

The problem that `seq1` only works when x is unassigned is still not solved. In order to obtain a correct behaviour for this case, the parameter evaluation must be controlled very precisely: at the time of parameter passing, no immediate evaluation must be carried out – for this reason, the two parameters are labelled with `uneval` in the fourth variation of the program. The name of the loop variable is now explicitly stored in a separate variable *varname*. Substitution of this variable with i and evaluation of the resulting expression must now be carried out in two separate steps which require the use of an additional variable *tmp*.

```
seq1:=proc(f::uneval, l::uneval)
  local i, data, range, '&comp', varname, tmp;
  ... Type check as above
  varname:=lhs(range[1]):
  ... as above
  while evalf(i) &comp evalf(op(2,op(2,range[1]))) do
    tmp:=subs(varname=i, f):
    data:=[op(data), eval(tmp)];
    i:=eval(i)+range[2];
  od;
  op(data);
end:
```

Now, `seq1` behaves in the same way as `seq` and also works as required when the loop variable x is occupied prior to execution of the command.

```
x:=3;
```

$$x := 3$$

```
seq1(x,[x=1..3]);
```

$$1, 2, 3$$

Other possibly occupied variables are still handled correctly.

```
seq1(sin(n*x),[x=0..Pi, Pi/2]);
```

$$0, \sin(1/2\,n\,\pi), \sin(n\,\pi)$$

```
n:=1/8:
seq1(sin(n*x),[x=0..Pi, Pi/2]);
```

$$0, \sin(1/16\,\pi), 1/2\,\sqrt{2 - \sqrt{2}}$$

Version 5: seqn for embedded lists

In its present form, `seq1` still shares one limitation with the original: the command is suitable for simple sequences, but not for embedded lists. Such lists can be generated, but the call of `seq1` becomes far too complicated:

```
[seq1([seq1(x^y, [y=2..4])], [x=0..3])];
```

$$[[0, 0, 0], [1, 1, 1], [4, 8, 16], [9, 27, 81]]$$

It would be much more elegant if the same list could be generated with the following command:

```
seqn(x^y, [x=1..3], [y=1..3]);
```

We could now start writing a command `seq2` which supplies embedded lists as a result of two loops, and another command `seq3` for threefold embedded lists, and so on. More elegant is the following recursive solution which can be used to generate arbitrarily embedded lists. The basic idea is simple: when the new command `seqn` is called with more than two parameters, one parameter is passed on to `seq1` and `seqn` is recursively called with the remaining parameters. With each recursive call, the number of parameters is reduced by 1.

The code of `seqn` is surprisingly short, because the major part of the work is carried out by the existing procedure `seq1`. In `seqn`, a check is made as to whether more than two parameters were passed. If so, these parameters are stored in the variable *var*.

```
seqn:=proc(x::uneval, l::uneval)
  local remaininglist:
  if nargs>=3 then
    remaininglist:=args[3..nargs]:
    [seq1(seqn(x, "), l)];
  else
    [seq1(x,l)]:
  fi:
end:
```

The call of `seq1` is peculiar: probably, you would expect the following instruction:

```
[seq1(seqn(x, remaininglist), l)];
```

However, this instruction does not work because the second parameter of `seqn` is labelled with `uneval`. For this reason, Maple would pass the name `'remaininglist'` instead of its contents. The operator `"` is used to access the last expression and at the same time force its evaluation.

The examples on the right show two applications of `seqn`. In the first example, a simple embedded list of the function x^y is generated. The second example is slightly more tricky because the limit of the control variable is determined by the current value of x.

```
x:='x': y:='y':
seqn(x^y, [x=0..3], [y=2..4]);
```

$$[[0, 0, 0], [1, 1, 1], [4, 8, 16], [9, 27, 81]]$$

```
seqn(x^y, [x=0..3], [y=0..x]);
```

$$[[0], [1, 1], [1, 2, 4], [1, 3, 9, 27]]$$

Although at first sight it seems that everything is functioning well, `seqn` has a serious defect: the command does not work when the variables are occupied. The reason: in `seqn`, the first two parameters are labelled with `uneval` and therefore excluded from evaluation, but this does not apply to the further optional parameters.

seqn fails because [5 = 2..4], not [y = 2..4], is passed as the third parameter.

```
x:=3: y:=5:
seqn(x^y, [x=0..3], [y=2..4]);
Error, (in seq1) wrong
   parameter, [5 = 2 .. 4]
```

Version 6: the final version of seqn

Willy-nilly, we need yet another version of seqn. Since there is no way of excluding optional parameters from automatic evaluation, the syntax of the command must be changed. Instead of passing several lists of control variable ranges, we now pass one embedded list:

```
seqn(x^y, [x=1..3], [y=1..3]);     #previous
seqn(x^y, [[x=1..3], [y=1..3]]); #new
```

The embedded list is considered to be one parameter (no matter how many sublists it contains) and can therefore be excluded from evaluation without problems.

Owing to this change, the code of seqn becomes slightly more complicated. First, a check is made as to whether the parameter *ll* has been passed a list. If not, the procedure is immediately aborted with an error message. type(ll[1],list) is used to check whether the first list element of *ll* is itself a list. (Please note that type(ll, listlist) does not work. listlist assumes regularly constructed lists, for example with $4 * 4$ or $2 * 2 * 2$ elements.)

When the embedded list contains exactly one list element (for example [[x = 1..3]]), the outer bracket level is removed with op, and seq1 is called. Parameter passing is carried out, as in the previous version, with ". Surprisingly enough, Maple evaluates the intermediate result correctly, that is, only up to the inner sublist. If the contents of that sublist were evaluated too, the whole effort would have been in vain.

When there are further list elements, seqn is called recursively. seq1 is passed the first list element; seqn is passed the remaining ones. Now, for parameter passing, the last two results must be accessed with " and "".

```
seqn:=proc(x::uneval, ll::uneval)
  local firstlist, remaininglist:
  if type(ll,list) then        # check if list
    if type(ll[1],list) then   # check if embedded list
      if nops(ll)=1 then       # check if exactly one list element
        firstlist:=op(ll):
        [seq1(x,")];
      else                     # embedded list with several elements
        firstlist:=ll[1]:
        remaininglist:=ll[2..-1]:
        [seq1(seqn(x, "), "")];
      fi:
    else                       # simple list
      [seq1(x,ll)]:
    fi:
  else                         # no list, error
```

```
   ERROR('wrong parameter, expect list or listlist', 11):
  fi:
end:
```

The following examples show that seqn now functions as required, copes with occupied variables, inserts other variables as far as they are known, and so on. In particular, please note the third example in which the control variable x is used as the limit of the loop for y, the fourth example which generates a threefold embedded list, and the last example in which the variables m, x and y are occupied.

```
x:='x': y:='y':
seqn(x,[x=1..3]);
```

$$[1, 2, 3]$$

```
seqn(x^y, [[x=0..3], [y=2..4]]);
```

$$[[0, 0, 0], [1, 1, 1], [4, 8, 16], [9, 27, 81]]$$

```
seqn(x^y, [[x=0..3], [y=0..x]]);
```

$$[[0], [1, 1], [1, 2, 4], [1, 3, 9, 27]]$$

```
seqn(x+y+z,[[x=1..2],
             [y=10..20, 10],
             [z=100..200, 100]]);
```

$$[[[111, 211], [121, 221]], [[112, 212], [122, 222]]]$$

```
n:='n': m:=1/Pi: x:=3: y:=4:
seqn(n*m*x^y, [[x=0..3], [y=2..4]]);
```

$$[[0, 0, 0], [\frac{n}{\pi}, \frac{n}{\pi}, \frac{n}{\pi}], [4\frac{n}{\pi}, 8\frac{n}{\pi}, 16\frac{n}{\pi}], [9\frac{n}{\pi}, 27\frac{n}{\pi}, 81\frac{n}{\pi}]]$$

Reference: The complete program code of seq1 and seqn in a form which makes the commands usable as a package is shown later in this chapter ('Program code in text files').

Organization of user-defined packages and libraries

After you have invested much time in the development of commands, you will obviously want to store them in a form that makes usage under Maple as easy as possible and allows distribution to other Maple users. This section deals with different aspects of this subject: saving and loading commands with save and read, organizing your own packages with table and activating them by means of with, storing packages in the share library and finally creating your own libraries. User-defined libraries are necessary in any case if you want to equip your commands with their own online help (see next section).

Hint: The whole section is based on the two commands seq1 and seqn introduced in the previous section.

Saving and loading individual commands

The easiest way to store commands defined in a worksheet so that they can be easily loaded into another worksheet is provided by the `save` command mentioned in the previous chapter. It stores the names and contents of all specified variables. (*seq1* and *seqn* are variables as well, but they do not contain a numeric value, only the program code.) When no directory is specified with `save`, Maple stores the file in the current directory (see Chapter 28, 'Files and directories').

After a `restart`, the commands can be read again with `read` and subsequently used as before.

```
seq1:=proc ... end:          #see previous section
seqn:=proc ... end:

save seqn, seq1, 'seqn':
restart:
read 'seqn':
seqn(x^y, [[x=1..3], [y=1..3]]);
```

$$[[1, 1, 1], [2, 4, 8], [3, 9, 27]]$$

The file `seqn` contains the program code in ASCII format (however, without formatting; that is, comments, line breaks and indents are eliminated). Thus, `seqn` is only suitable for internal storage of the code. You must still store the original code in a worksheet or in a separate text file.

When the file name specified with `save` ends in `*.m`, Maple stores the contents of the variable in a binary format. (To be precise, even in this format only ASCII characters are used in order to allow the file to be sent via email. However, `seqn.m` is encrypted and, unlike `seqn`, cannot be read with an editor.) The advantage of the binary format is that the files are more compact and can be processed more efficiently.

```
save seqn, seq1, 'seqn.m':
restart:
read 'seqn':
seqn(x^y, [[x=1..3], [y=1..3]]);
```

$$[[1, 1, 1], [2, 4, 8], [3, 9, 27]]$$

Organizing commands in packages

Organizing a simple package is almost as easy as saving a command directly. For this purpose, the code must be stored in the elements of a table. This table is stored with `save`, loaded with `read` and activated by means of `with`. When the directory in which the package file is stored is inserted into the `libname` path, `read` can even be omitted (that is, `with` also takes care of loading the file).

The following commands assume that `seq1` and `seqn` are available. The name of the new package is `mypack`. The package is created by means of an empty table; subsequently, the two table elements `seqn` and `seq1` are created. Please note the `eval` commands: they are needed to ensure that the table elements contain not only the names of the commands but also their code.

```
mypack:=table():
mypack[seq1]:=eval(seq1):
mypack[seqn]:=eval(seqn):
```

If you know from the start that you want to create a package, you can obviously create the new commands seq1 and seqn directly with the names mypack[namexyz]:

```
mypack:=table():
mypack[seq1]:=proc ... end:
mypack[seqn]:=proc ... end:  # code as in the previous section
```

In any case, mypack now contains the new commands. The commands can be called under their full names:

```
mypack[seqn](x, [x=1..2, 0.5]);
```

$$[1, 1.5, 2.0]$$

Now, the whole package can be easily stored with save. For loading, you can again use read. In order to make the commands available not only under their (long-winded) full names but also in their short form, you must also execute with. Subsequently, the commands are available as usual.

```
save mypack, 'mypack.m';
restart:
read 'mypack.m';
with(mypack);
```

$$[seq1, seqn]$$

```
seqn(x, [x=0..Pi, Pi/6]);
```

$$[0, 1/6\,\pi, 1/3\,\pi, 1/2\,\pi, 2/3\,\pi, 5/6\,\pi, \pi]$$

What is still slightly irritating in comparison to 'true' standard library packages is the fact that prior to the with command read must be executed. This problem can be solved too: the global variable libname normally only contains the path leading to the standard library. When the share library is used as well, libname also contains the path to this library. When you extend libname with the path of the directories in which you store your package files, with takes care of loading the package files. This assumes, however, that the binary format with the file extension *.m is used for saving your files.

The following command extends libname with the path of the current directory, in which mypack.m was saved. (The . character always points to the current directory.) Subsequently, the package is easily activated with a single with command.

```
restart:
libname:=libname, '.';
```

$$libname := F : \text{``}MAPLEV4\text{``}lib,.$$

```
with(mypack);
```

$$[seq1, seqn]$$

```
seqn(x, [x=100..0, -10]);
```

$$[100, 90, 80, 70, 60, 50, 40, 30, 20, 10, 0]$$

Now, with functions as required, but the manual modification of libname is still irritating. This can be remedied too: one possibility is simply to store your package files in the directory of Maple's standard library. Particularly under UNIX, this variation is not really viable because you probably do not have write privilege for this directory and several users might wish to carry out different extensions.

Thus, it is better to store the new packages in a separate directory and to set libname accordingly in Maple's initialization file. In the Windows version of Maple, this file has the name maple.ini and is located in the current directory. For the location of initialization files in other Maple versions, please refer to the original documentation.

The initialization file can contain Maple commands which are automatically executed at the start of Maple. When you insert the following two lines into maple.ini, F:\mapleV4\mypacks is considered as the second library file. Now, with automatically looks for the required packages first in the standard library and then in the specified directory. When you work under UNIX, you will probably specify a directory inside your home directory and use / for separating the directories.

```
# maple.ini
print('Initialization file maple.ini'):
libname:=libname, 'f:\\mapleV4\\mypacks':
print('new libname', libname):
```

After a restart of Maple (or after the restart command), Maple displays two new screen outputs (as a sort of feedback to confirm that everything works). Provided that the file mypack.m has been moved from the current directory (where it was stored up to now by means of save) into the mypacks directory, with(mypack) can now be executed directly.

$$Initialization\ file\ maple.ini$$

$$new\ libname, F : \text{``}MAPLEV4/lib, f : \text{``}mapleV4\text{``}mypacks$$

```
with(mypack);
```

$$[seq1, seqn]$$

If, prior to the first use, initialization work has to be carried out in the package (definition of new data types, initialization of variables, and so on), you must define a procedure with the name mypack[init]. init is automatically executed by with.

The procedure chosen in this section is very easy, but it has some disadvantages:

- Generation and management of the program code for the new commands is carried out in a Maple worksheet, which is unsuitable for major projects.

- All new commands are available to the user. It would be better if individual commands were invisible on the outside and available only internally (for example, `seq1` which is only an auxiliary function for `seqn`).

- No online help can be linked.

All three disadvantages can be remedied with user-defined libraries.

Definition of user-defined libraries

Libraries are files which store a large number of definitions of new commands. Obviously, Maple's standard library could also be stored in hundreds of individual files (as was the case in earlier Maple releases), but this would be very inefficient. Therefore, all Maple commands which are not part of the kernel are stored in `lib\maple.lib`. The `share` library is located in a second file, `share\maple.lib`.

For library management, Maple provides the auxiliary program `march`. `march` can be used to determine all files contained in a library, to add or remove individual files, or to create new libraries from scratch.

`march` is controlled via several options, the most important of which are `-l` (display list of all files), `-a` (add file), `-u` (update file), `-x` (extract file) and `-d` (delete file). Any additional parameters depend on the option. In any case, the first parameter of `march` must specify the directory in which the library file is located. (See the syntax summary at the end of this chapter and the help text `?march`.)

Contents list of the standard library

With the following commands you can create a sorted contents list of the Maple standard library in a DOS window and store it in `libcontents.txt`. Under UNIX, the path specifications must be changed accordingly.

```
cd F:\mapleV4\bin.win
march -l ..\lib | sort > libcontents.txt
```

`libcontents.txt` contains the names of the `*.m` files, the date of the last modification, the position inside the file and an internal index number. The standard library contains about 4000 entries.

```
@.m                                                  95-12-14 14:01
1655318    888
@@.m                                                 95-12-14 14:01
2034612    485
about.m                                              95-12-14 14:04
240928     170
```

```
abs/abs.m                                    95-12-14 13:48
576718    121
abs/conjugate.m                              95-12-14 13:48
2755776   126
abs/csgn.m                                   95-12-14 13:48
1288883   201
abs/exp.m                                    95-12-14 13:48
1924135   128
...
```

You must never use the standard library for experimenting with libraries! If you destroy this library by mistake, you must reinstall Maple!

Creating a new library

The following paragraphs describe how to create a new library in the new directory `mylib`. First, you must create this directory, and then you must execute `march -c`. As the parameter, you must specify the name of the directory. In addition, `march` needs an indication of the estimated number of `*.m` files to be stored in the library. (The actual limit will be about twice that number; the online help does not provide more precise information.) With this, `march` creates the files `maple.lib` and `maple.ind` (which at the moment only contain management information) in the `mylib` directory.

```
cd F:\mapleV4\bin.win
march -c ..\mylib 10
```

Since Release 4, saving packages in this library can be carried out directly from within Maple by means of the `savelib` command. You no longer have to call `march`, as was the case in previous Maple releases. The precondition for a correct functioning of `savelib` is, however, that the global variables `libname` and `savelibname` contain the path to the new library directory. Please note that the spelling must match exactly (including upper case and lower case spelling which otherwise plays no role in Windows).

In order to automate the process as far as possible, you should set `libname` and `savelibname` directly in the initialization file `maple.ini`. (The `print` instructions are obviously optional.)

```
# maple.ini
savelibname:='f:\\mapleV4\\mylib':
libname:=libname, savelibname:
print('Initialization file maple.ini'):
printf('new libname: \n'):
print(libname):
printf('savelibname: \n'):
print(savelibname):
```

After a `restart`, `savelib` can immediately be used. With `read`, the definition of `seqn` and `seq1` is read again; the next three commands create the package `mypack`; and `savelib` stores the package in the library `maple.lib` in the `mylib` directory.

```
restart:
  init file maple.ini
  libname: F:\MAPLEV4/lib, f:\mapleV4\mylib
  savelibname: f:\mapleV4\mylib
read 'seqn':
mypack:=table():
mypack[seqn]:=eval(seqn):
mypack[seq1]:=eval(seq1):
savelib(mypack, 'mypack.m');
```

Now, usage of this package no longer differs from that of a standard library package:

```
restart:
  init file maple.ini
  libname: F:\MAPLEV4/lib, f:\mapleV4\mylib
  savelibname: f:\mapleV4\mylib
with(mypack);
```

$$[seq1, seqn]$$

```
seqn(x,[x=3..1,-1]);
```

$$[3, 2, 1]$$

Program code in text files

The examples used up to now assume that all commands for the definition of a package and its commands are carried out interactively in Maple. For more substantial packages, this is too laborious. A more practical solution is to store all commands for the definition of a package in a single text file which can then be processed with any available editor.

In principle, the text file mypack.mpl shown below contains the same commands that were up to now executed in Maple. There are, however, some subtle differences:

- seq1 is defined under the name 'mypack/seq1'. It is an internal command which can only be accessed via this long-winded name. This prevents the command from being used accidentally. seq1 is no longer part of the mypack table and is therefore no longer displayed during execution of with.

- seqn is defined directly as mypack[seqn]. seq1 is called under the new name 'mypack/seq1'.

- In savelib, 'mypack/seq1' must be specified explicitly. Since the command is no longer contained in the mypack table, it is also no longer automatically stored with mypack.

By means of the command read 'mypack.mpl', all commands of this file are executed, including the savelib command at the end of the file. In other words, you can easily edit and save mypack.mpl in the text editor of your choice. With read, you read the program code into Maple. Provided it does not contain syntax errors, it is immediately stored in its own library. In this way, the process of extending a library can be largely automated. (savelib automatically replaces the old version with the new version of the package.)

```
# file mypack.mpl for definition of the packages mypack with
# the internal command 'mypack/seq1' and the globally
# available command 'seqn'
mypack:=table():

'mypack/seq1':=proc(f::uneval, l::uneval)
  local i, data, range, '&comp', varname, tmp;
  if not type(l,list) then
    ERROR('wrong parameter, expected list', l);
  fi:
  range:=l:
  if not type(range[1],name='..') then
    ERROR('wrong parameter', range);
  elif nops(range)>1 then
    if not type(range[2], algebraic) or evalf(range[2])=0 then
      ERROR('wrong parameter', range);
    fi;
  else
    # default stepwidth 1
    range:=[op(range), 1]:
  fi;
  varname:=lhs(range[1]):
  data:=[]:
  if evalf(range[2])>0 then '&comp':=(x,y)->(x<=y):
  else '&comp':=(x,y)->(x>=y): fi:
  i:=op(1,op(2,range[1])):
  while evalf(i) &comp evalf(op(2,op(2,range[1]))) do
    tmp:=subs(varname=i,f):
    data:=[op(data), eval(tmp)];
    i:=eval(i)+range[2];
  od;
  op(data);
end:

mypack[seqn]:=proc(x::uneval, ll::uneval)
  local firstlist, remaininglist:
  if type(ll,list) then
    if type(ll[1],list) then
      if nops(ll)=1 then
        firstlist:=op(ll):
        ['mypack/seq1'(x,")];
      else
        firstlist:=ll[1]:
        remaininglist:=ll[2..-1]:
        ['mypack/seq1'(seqn(x, "), "")];
      fi:
    else
      ['mypack/seq1'(x,ll)]:
    fi:
  else
    ERROR('wrong parameter, expect list or listlist', ll):
  fi:
end:

savelib(mypack, 'mypack/seq1', 'mypack.m'):
```

Extension of the share library

Instead of defining your own library, you can also extend the `share` library. In principle, the `share` library is managed in the same way as a user-defined library. The difference is that the contents of the library are not read by means of `with`, but by means of `readshare`.

`readshare(name,dir)` first looks for the file `name.m` in the `dir` subdirectory of the `share` directory and then in the library file `maple.lib` in the `share` directory. Thus, you can carry out extensions both in the `share` library file itself and in the `share` directory tree. (During program development, the second variation is probably easier to handle.)

`readshare` works differently than `with`. While `with` expects a table and manages the entries itself, `readshare` is simply a variation of `read`. For this reason, the creation of package tables for the `share` library makes no sense (unless you also wish to execute `with` after the `readshare` command).

With the following commands, the program code for `seq1` and `seqn` is again read into memory. Subsequently, the commands are inserted into the `share\maple.lib` library under the name `myown/mypack.m`. `sharename` is initialized by means of `with(share)` and contains the `share` directory path.

```
restart:
with(share):
  See ?share and ?share,contents for information about the share library
read 'seqn':
savelibname:=sharename:
savelib(seq1, seqn, 'myown/mypack.m'):
```

The commands are used in the same way as all the other packages in the `share` library:

```
restart:
with(share):
  See ?share and ?share,contents for information about the share library
readshare(mypack,myown):
seqn(x, [x=1..3]);
```

$$[1, 2, 3]$$

Creating your own online help

With Release 4, the management of online help texts has been completely revised. This has both advantages and disadvantages.

First the advantages: the same layout possibilities are now available for help texts as for worksheet files. Any worksheet file can be used as a template for a help text. Thus, creating a help text is as easy as creating a worksheet. (This will be appreciated by those who have written their own help texts with Release 3.)

Now the disadvantages: the new format is incompatible with the one used in Release 3. Old help texts, often created with much labour, can no longer be used. Furthermore, the possibility no longer exists of formulating help texts as part of the program code, thus achieving a certain amount of automation. Also, help texts can only be created for libraries (but not for individual commands or packages stored in *.m files). And finally, the new help function is not documented. At least this problem can be remedied by the present section.

The idea of the new help function is that all help texts are stored in a small number of maple.hdb files. Normally, only two such files exist: one in the lib directory containing the help texts for the standard library and a second one in the share directory containing the help texts for the commands of the share library. In addition, new help files can be created in different directories by means of the worksheet command HELP|SAVE TO DATABASE (details on this command follow below).

When searching for a specific help text, Maple considers all help files whose directories are specified in the path of libname.

Creating a new help text

The creation of online help texts is the last stage in the development of packages. The preconditions are that the command to be described can already be used and that the directory in which the help file is to be stored is included in libname. It suggests that the help file be stored in the same directory as the new library.

In order to create a new help text, you must open a new worksheet. If there is already a command in Maple which works in the same way as your own command, you can open its help text and copy it into the new worksheet. This will save you much work and, at the same time, ensure a relatively uniform look for all help texts. (Look at the file part3\seqnhelp.mws on the enclosed CD-ROM. This file was used to create the help text for seqn.)

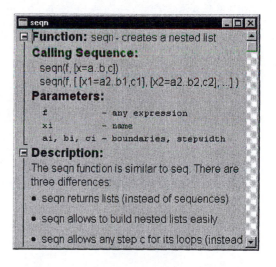

In order to store the worksheet as a help text, you execute the command HELP|SAVE TO DATABASE. You must enter two pieces of information into the dialog: the name of the help text (*topic*, thus, for example seqn) and the exact path of the directory in which the help file is to be stored (*database*). The path must match a path in libname. Optionally, you can specify additional names (*aliases*) for the help text and a main subject (*parent*, for example the package name). The *parent* subject is, however, ignored by the current Windows version.

Once a help file exists (that is, from the second subject onward), the process becomes easier: the dialog displays all existing help files pointed to by the variable *libname* (with the exception of the help files of the standard library and the share library, which cannot be modified). One of the help files can be selected with the mouse for storing the current worksheet.

When a help subject already exists, the old help text is overwritten by the new text without warning. With DATABASE|REMOVE, a subject can be deleted from the help file. (However, this does not reduce the size of the help file; the help text can simply no longer be displayed.)

Syntax summary

Error detection

```
tracelast;
```
displays information on the last error encountered (the program code of the line in which the error occurred, the contents of the parameters and local variables, and so on).

```
option trace;
```
displays information during evaluation of the current procedure. This option must be specified at the beginning of a procedure directly after the declaration of the local variables.

```
trace(procname);     untrace(procname);
```
has the same effect as the trace option, but can also be used at a later stage without having to modify the code.

```
printlevel:=n;
```
displays information on the evaluation of expressions up to level n. Conditions and loops increment the current level by 1, procedures by 5.

```
userinfo(n, 'name', x);
```
returns x as character string if $infolevel[name] \geq n$.

```
infolevel[name]:=n:        infolevel[all]:=n:
```
determines the amount of information to be displayed during processing of a given command or of all commands. n can assume values between 2 and 5. Information can only be displayed if this is provided for in the code of the command in question.

```
traperror(x);
```
evaluates x. When an error occurs, `traperror` returns a character string containing the error message, otherwise the result of x. The error message is also written in the global variable `lasterror`.

Reference: The commands for the Maple debugger are described under that heading earlier in this chapter.

Analysis of time and memory consumption

```
readlib(showtime);      showtime();      off;
```
displays calculating time and memory consumption during calculation after execution of each command. In addition, the results are stored in the running variables $O1, O2, O3, \ldots$. `off` terminates this mode.

```
readlib(profile)
profile(proc1, proc2, proc3 ...);
showprofile();
unprofile(proc1, proc2, proc3 ...);
```
`profile` specifies which procedures or commands are to be analyzed. After execution of the procedures, `showprofile` displays which procedures were (recursively) called and how many times, and how much calculating time and memory they used.

Loading and saving packages

```
save proc1, proc2, ..., 'name.m';
```
stores the procedures in a binary format in the file `name.m`.

```
read 'name.m';
```
reads the procedures into memory.

```
savelib(proc1, proc2, ..., 'name.m');
```
stores the procedures in the library file in the directory specified by *savelibname* (see below).

`with(name);`
> reads the file `name.m` from a directory specified in `libname` or from a library. `name.m` must contain the definition of a table `name`. After execution of `with`, the elements of this table are available as new commands.

`libname`
> contains the names of all directories that contain libraries and help files.

`savelibname`
> contains the name of the directory into which `savelib` is to write.

`sharename`
> contains the name of the directory of the `share` library (provided that prior execution of `with(share)` has been carried out).

Auxiliary program march

`march -l libdirectory`
> supplies an (unsorted) list of all individual files contained in `maple.lib`.

`march -x libdirectory libfile newfile`
> extracts a file from the library and copies it into a new file.

`march -a libdirectory newfile libfile`
`march -u libdirectory newfile libfile`
> inserts a new file into the library or updates the specified file.

`march -d libdirectory libfile`
> deletes the specified file from the library.

`march -p libdirectory`
> reduces the library to its minimum size by filling gaps created by modification of individual files in the library.

`march -c libdirectory n`
> creates a new library (`maple.lib` plus `maple.ind`) in the specified directory. n indicates the estimated number of individual files the library is to contain.

Chapter 31

Graphics III: special commands

This chapter deals with various special commands from the `plots` package which have not yet been described in the previous chapters on the subject of graphics.

`logplot, semilogplot, loglogplot`
draw functions with single-logarithmic or double-logarithmic axis scaling.

`densityplot, contourplot, filledcontourplot`
display two-parameter functions on a plane grid by means of shading or contour lines.

`complexplot[3d], conformal, rootlocus`
are used to visualize complex functions by separating the real and imaginary parts, by use of colours, by conformal representation or by representation of the zero points of a characteristic equation (root locus curves).

`coordplot, coordplot3d`
displays the structure of different coordinate systems. Since Release 4, Maple has more than 40 coordinate systems which in most commands can be set by means of the `coords` option.

`inequal, implicitplot3D, polyhedraplot`
are special commands for visualization of two-dimensional inequality systems, implicit three-parameter functions and polyhedra (dodecahedron, icosahedron, and so on).

`animate`
builds an animation from several graphics.

Reference: A general introduction to the subject of graphics is given in Chapters 19 (2D graphics) and 20 (3D graphics). These chapters describe numerous options which are also used in this chapter. Some graphics commands for special applications are discussed in Chapters 18 (Differential equations), 21 (Combinatorics, statistics, probability calculus) and 27 (Vector analysis). Information about graphics programming is given in the next chapter.

Graphics in logarithmic scale

Functions with exponential curves are often represented in a logarithmic scale for the y axis. The exponential relation between x and y is thus represented linearly.

The functions e^x and e^{2x} are represented by logplot as straight lines with different gradients. The function e^{x^2} maintains its exponential appearance.

```
with(plots):
logplot({exp(x), exp(x^2), exp(2*x)},
        x=0.1..10, 1..10^6);
```

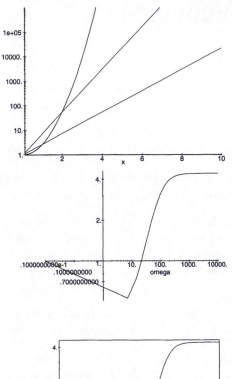

While logplot only changes the scale of the y axis, loglogplot uses logarithmic scaling for both axes. The illustration on the right shows the amplitude curve of a control function.

```
s:=I*omega:
f:=(1+s*2/5) * (1+s/9) /
   ((1+s) * (1+s/99)):

loglogplot( abs(f),
  omega=0.01..10000);
```

However, the above illustration is not really what one would expect. The logarithmic scaling is evidently not observed in the calculation of the supporting points of the curve. (In Release 3, this used to work better.) Therefore, the supporting points must now be specified with the sample option. Unfortunately, this does not change the idiosyncratic labelling of the coordinate axes.

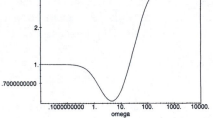

```
loglogplot(abs(f),
  omega=0.01..10000, axes=boxed,
  sample=[seq(10^(n/10), n=-20..50)]);
```

semilogplot is the counterpart to logplot: the x axis is represented in logarithmic scale, the y axis linearly. As with loglogplot, the sample option must be used to achieve a passable result.

```
semilogplot(argument(f)*180/Pi,
  omega=0.01..10000, axes=boxed,
  sample=[seq(10^(n/10), n=-20..50)]);
```

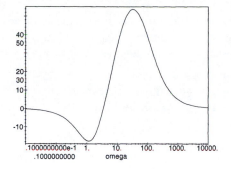

Two-dimensional grid graphics

In Chapter 20, we introduced the plot3d command which can be used to represent functions of the form $z = f(x, y)$ as three-dimensional surfaces. The two commands densityplot and contourplot presented in this section are suitable for two-dimensional representation of such functions.

densityplot is rather limited in its variations. It represents a two-parameter function in a grid of greyscales. The number of grid points can be set with grid=[n,m].

In the illustration on the right, the value range of the function f is represented by means of different shades of grey.

```
with(plots):
f:=(x-1)*(x+2)*(y-2)*(y+2):
densityplot(f, x=-3..3, y=-3..3,
           axes=boxed);
```

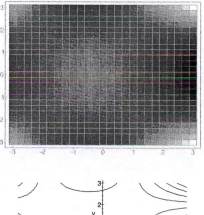

contourplot too represents functions of the form $z = f(x, y)$ in two dimensions. In the standard setting of this command, the value range of f is drawn by means of contour lines.

```
contourplot(f, x=-3..3, y=-3..3);
```

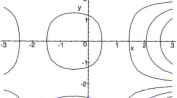

More precise results can be obtained by increasing both drawing precision (with `grid`) and the number of contour lines (with `contours`).

```
contourplot(f, x=-3..3, y=-3..3,
  grid=[30,30], contours=25,
  color=black, axes=boxed);
```

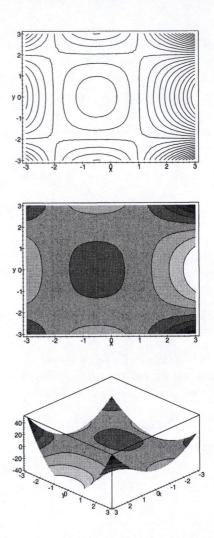

By means of the `filled` option, you can colour the equipotential areas as on a geographical map. With `coloring`, you can specify the required colour range.

```
contourplot(f, x=-3..3, y=-3..3,
  axes=boxed, filled=true,
  coloring=[white,black]);
```

Not very surprisingly, the three-dimensional variation of `contourplot` is `contourplot3d`. `shading=none` causes the contour lines to be drawn in black (not coloured).

```
contourplot3d(f, x=-3..3, y=-3..3,
  axes=boxed, filled=true,
  coloring=[white,black],
  shading=none);
```

`contourplot3d` can also cope with parametric functions $[fx, fy, fc]$. The function fc does not affect the form of the drawing but only its colouring. By means of an appropriate choice of the `orientation` option, `contourplot3d` can also be persuaded to show a two-dimensional representation of the result.

```
s:='s':
contourplot3d(
  [t*sin(s), t*cos(s), sin(s*t)],
  s=0..2*Pi, t=0..2,
  contours=20, filled=true,
  coloring=[white,grey],
  shading=none, orientation=[0,0]);
```

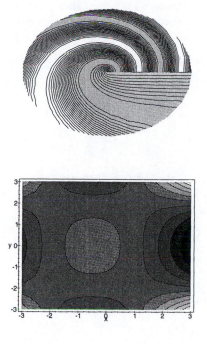

The `filledcontourplot` command from the share library is internally structured differently from `contourplot` and supplies very high quality drawings.

```
with(share): readshare(fconplot, plots):
filledcontourplot(f, x=-3..3, y=-3..3,
  coloring=[black, white], levels=10,
  axes=boxed);
```

Visualization of complex functions

The problem when drawing complex functions is that four variables (the real and imaginary parts of the function parameter plus the value and phase of the result) are to be shown in one drawing. A 'normal' three-dimensional drawing represents only three variables (for example, the z-values of a function drawn over the x and y coordinates).

One solution to this problem has already been introduced in Chapter 20: with `plot3d`, the value of the function can be represented as a three-dimensional surface, and the phase angle by means of colour distribution.

Easier alternatives are provided by the commands `complexplot` (two-dimensional representation of a function with one parameter), `complexplot3d` (three-dimensional representation of a function with two parameters), `conformal` (conformal representation of a grid distorted by the complex function) and `rootlocusplot` (representation of the zero point location of a characteristic function).

Two-dimensional representation of complex functions

`complexplot` represents single-parameter functions in two dimensions. Internally, `complexplot` essentially corresponds to the normal `plot` command for drawing a parametric function. The only difference is that `complexplot` generates the two partial functions for the x and y values (real and imaginary parts) automatically.

The illustration on the right shows the curve of
the tan function, when complex numbers between $-\pi - \pi I$ and $\pi + \pi I$ are inserted.

```
complexplot(tan(x*(1+I)), x=-Pi..Pi);
```

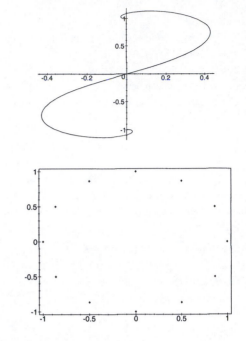

complexplot is also suitable for quickly drawing some complex points by simply using the
option style=point.

```
solve(z^12=1);
```

$$1, -\frac{1}{2} + \frac{1}{2} I \sqrt{3}, -\frac{1}{2} - \frac{1}{2} I \sqrt{3}, \cdots$$

```
complexplot(["], style=point,
  axes=boxed);
```

Three-dimensional representation of complex functions

Essentially, complexplot3d corresponds to plot3d with specification of a control function for the
color option. complexplot3d is, however, much easier to handle. As standard, the command draws
the value of a two-parameter function and uses the phase angle for colouring.

The illustration on the right shows the value
of the complex sine function. By setting the
orientation option, the drawing was rotated in
such a way that the real part goes from left to
right, the imaginary part from front to back.

```
complexplot3d(sin(z), z=-I..2*Pi+I,
  orientation=[-70,21], axes=boxed,
  style=patch, grid=[40,40]);
```

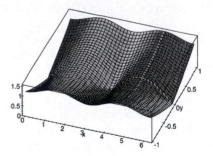

When two functions are passed to complexplot3d, the first function defines the z coordinate of the three-dimensional surface and the second function defines the colour. The illustration on the right shows the same function as above, with the exception that now the real part defines the z coordinate and the imaginary part defines the colour.

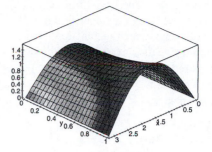

```
f:=sin(z):
complexplot3d([Re(f),abs(f)],
  z=0..Pi+I, style=patch,
  axes=boxed);
```

Some spectacular images (after spectacularly long computing times) can be obtained by visualizing Newton's algorithm for approximate determination of the zero points of complex functions ($N(z) = z - p(z)/(p'(z) + s\,I)$). An impressive colour representation can be found in the 'Learning Guide'; at this point, a black and white illustration must suffice.

```
p:=(z-1)*(z^2+z+5/4);
```

$$p := (z - 1)(z^2 + z + \frac{5}{4})$$

```
f:=unapply(z-p/(diff(p,z)-0.5*I), z);
```

$$f := z \rightarrow z - \frac{(z - 1)(z^2 + z + \frac{5}{4})}{z^2 + z + \frac{5}{4} + (z - 1)(2z + 1) - .5\,I}$$

f@@4 corresponds to $f(f(f(f(z))))$, that is, a fourfold embedding of a function. Maple evaluates f@@4 more efficiently than $f(f(f(f(z))))$.

```
complexplot3d(f@@4,-4-4*I..4+4*I,
  view=-1..2,style=patchnogrid,
  grid=[100,100]);
```

Conformal representation

The conformal command calculates the results of the complex function for a range of the complex number plane and draws the resulting distorted grid. In the first parameter, the command is passed the function to be represented; in the second parameter, a rectangular complex range. Maple covers the complex range with a grid, calculates the function values at the grid points and joins the resulting (complex) coordinate points.

The projection of the trivial function $f(z) = z$ immediately leads to the rectangular grid which `conformal` lays over the function. On screen, the drawing is displayed in two colours (vertical lines red, horizontal lines green). For printing your graphics, you should specify the option `color=black`.

```
with(plots):
conformal(z, z=-1-I..2+I,
        axes=boxed);
```

The first attempt to represent the function $1/z$ ends up with a fairly uninteresting drawing.

```
conformal(1/z, z=-1-I..2+I,
        axes=boxed);
```

The optional third parameter should allow you to limit the drawing range. In Release 3, this did work, whereas in Release 4, `display` must be used together with the `view` option. `grid` increases the precision of the grid.

```
display(conformal(1/z,
    z=-1-I..2+I, -4-3*I..4+3*I,
    grid=[50,50], axes=boxed),
  view=[-4..4, -3..3]);
```

The illustration on the right shows a slightly more interesting conformal representation. Please note that the drawing range only includes points of the right-hand complex half-plane.

```
conformal((z+1+I)^3, z=-I*2..2+2*I,
  grid=[40,40], axes=frame,
  scaling=constrained);
```

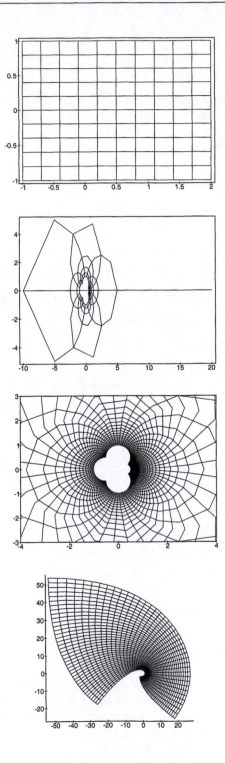

Root locus curves

Root locus curves display the zero points of the function $1 + k\,f = 0$ for the complex function f, with real numbers of a given value range being inserted in k. Thus, the `rootlocus` command solves the equation $1 + k\,f = 0$ one after the other for new values of k and joins zero points that belong together by continuous lines. Root locus curves are mainly used for judging the stability of control circuits.

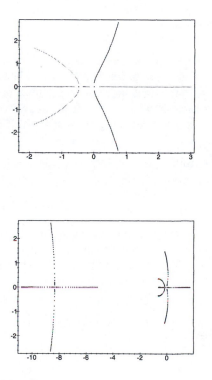

`rootlocus` displays the individual line curves in different colours. The `color` option has no influence on the colour of the curve, which reduces the quality of the representation in black and white print.

```
f:=(z*(z+0.5) - (z+2)*(2*z+0.5)) /
              (z^2*(z+0.5)^2);
```

$$f := \frac{z\,(z + .5) - (z + 2)\,(2\,z + .5)}{z^2\,(z + .5)^2}$$

```
rootlocus(f, z, -5..5, style=line,
          thickness=3);
```

When the option `style=point` is used, `rootlocus` draws only the points of the zero points without trying to join them with lines. This can be an advantage in complicated curves where under certain conditions `rootlocus` might be unable to recognize points that belong together.

```
f:=(1+s)^2 /
   (s^2*(1+4.5*s)*(1+0.12*s)^2);
```

$$f := \frac{(1 + s)^2}{s^2\,(1 + 4.5\,s)\,(1 + .12\,s)^2}$$

```
rootlocus(f, s, -5..5, style=point);
```

Graphics in different coordinate systems

Since Release 4, Maple can handle more than 40 predefined coordinate systems which in most `plot` or `plot3d` commands can be set by means of the `coords` option. A list of the predefined coordinate systems can be obtained with `?coords`.

The application of the coordinate systems is simple: in two-dimensional coordinate systems, the standard coordinates x and y are substituted with the coordinates of the system in question – in polar coordinate systems, for example, with r and ϕ. Obviously, you can continue to name the variables as you wish – including x and y.

```
plot(phi, phi=0..2*Pi,
  coords=polar);
```

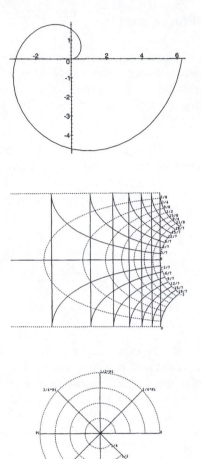

With the `coordplot` command, the structure of a coordinate system can be displayed. The illustration on the right shows a logarithmic coordinate system in which the lines of the two coordinates are differentiated by means of different line styles.

```
coordplot(logarithmic,labelling=true,
  linestyle=[1,2],
  scaling=constrained);
```

In the second parameter of `coordplot`, the range can be specified for which the coordinate system is drawn. The illustration on the right shows the grid for a polar coordinate system with $0 \leq r \leq 1$ and $0 \leq \phi \leq 7\pi/4$.

```
coordplot(polar, [0..1,0..7*Pi/4],
  labelling=true,
  grid=[5,8], linestyle=[1,2],
  scaling=constrained);
```

In the same way, three-dimensional coordinate systems can be used with `plot3d`. When `coords=spherical` is used to switch to spherical form, Maple expects the parameters in the form $r(\theta, \phi), \theta = \theta 0..\theta 1, \phi = \phi 0..\phi 1$. The commands below approximately draw the directional characteristics of an antenna. As with two-dimensional graphics, the `scaling` option prevents distortion of the axis scales.

```
r:=sin(phi) *
  cos(Pi/2 * sin(phi)*cos(theta));
```

$$r := \sin(\phi)\cos(\frac{\pi\,\sin(\phi)\,\cos(\theta)}{2})$$

```
plot3d(r, theta=0..2*Pi, phi=0..Pi,
       scaling=constrained,
       orientation=[-15,53],
       grid=[35,35],
       coords=spherical);
```

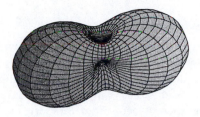

Cylindrical coordinates too are no problem. Now, the three parameters of plot3d are $r(\theta, z)$, $\theta = \theta 0..\theta 1$, $z = z0..z1$. This variation of plot3d is particularly suitable for representation of rotational solids.

```
plot3d(2+sin(z), theta=0..2*Pi,
   z=0..10, grid=[25,25],
   orientation=[45,71],
   coords=cylindrical);
```

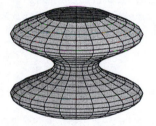

coordplot3d draws three surfaces for which two coordinates are varied and the third coordinate is kept constant (either 0 or 1). The optional second parameter can be used to set the value range of the coordinates. This has been used in the illustration on the right to allow a view of the inside of a cylindrical coordinate system.

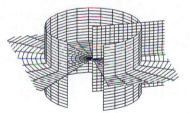

```
coordplot3d(cylindrical,
  [0..2, 0..7*Pi/4, -1..1],
  orientation=[-13,49]);
```

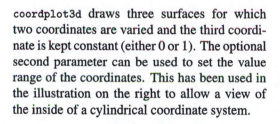

Special commands

Drawing inequality systems

Since Release 4, the `inequal` command is available which allows graphic display of a large number of two-dimensional inequalities. Handling the commands does not cause many difficulties; the unusual part is setting the options. `optionfeasible` defines how to represent the surface in a way that satisfies all inequalities. Similarly, `optionexcluded` is responsible for those surfaces that do not satisfy at least one inequality. `optionclosed` specifies the line format for border lines defined via $\leq$ or $\geq$ operators. `optionopen` is responsible for border lines defined via $<$ or $>$ operators.

```
inequal({x+y>=-1, x-y/2<=1, y-x/5<4},
  x=-5..4, y=-2..5,
  optionsfeasible=(color=grey),
  optionsexcluded=(color=white),
  optionsclosed=(thickness=3),
  optionsopen=(linestyle=3,thickness=1),
  axes=boxed);
```

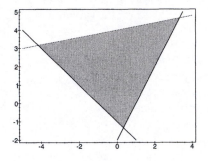

Implicit three-dimensional graphics

In Chapter 19 we introduced the `implicitplot` command which represents implicit functions graphically (for example, $x^2 + y^2 = 1$). This command has a three-dimensional variation which copes surprisingly well with three-parameter implicit functions.

The illustration on the right shows the spherical surface $x^2 + y^2 + z^2 = 1$. The surface is assembled in a slightly unusual manner from differently shaped, but easily recognizable, partial surfaces.

```
with(plots):
implicitplot3d(x^2+y^2+z^2=1,
  x=-1..1, y=-1..1, z=-1..1,
  grid=[10,10,10],
  scaling=constrained);
```

The formula $z + \sqrt{x^2 + y^2} - \sin(y^2 + z^3) = 0$ is admittedly a pure product of the imagination without any deeper mathematical or physical sense. The resulting drawing, however, looks quite pleasing.

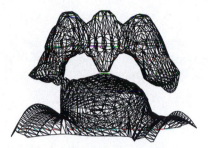

```
implicitplot3d(
  z+sqrt(x^2+y^2)-sin(y^2+z^3)=0,
  x=-2..2, y=-2..2, z=-2..2,
  grid=[20,20,10],
  orientation=[18,83],
  style=wireframe, color=black);
```

Polyhedraplot

The `polyhedraplot` command for drawing polyhedra (dodecahedron, icosahedron) is of little practical use, but the resulting graphics look very nice. The command is passed the coordinates of the centre point of the polyhedron. The options `polytype` and `polyscale` control the type and size of the polyhedron.

The illustration on the right shows the five polyhedra that can be drawn by `polyhedraplot`.

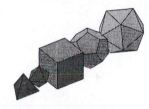

```
with(plots):
polys:=array([tetrahedron,octahedron,
    hexahedron,dodecahedron,
    icosahedron]):
seq(polyhedraplot([2.5*n^1.6,n,n/3],
    polytype=polys[n],
    polyscale=1.5+n*0.7), n=1..5):
display(["], scaling=constrained,
    orientation=[-126,56]);
```

Animation

The `animate` command calculates several two-dimensional graphics and subsequently shows them as a movie. `animate3d` is the three-dimensional variation of this command. In their handling, both commands are very similar to the `plot` and `plot3d` commands. When you want to assemble an animation from pictures that can only be drawn by special commands, such as `tubeplot`, you must use `display` for presentation of your movie.

The following command calculates 30 images in which a sine wave walks towards the left. `animate` differs from the normal `plot` command in its third parameter. This parameter specifies the variable which is to be varied in the individual images of the movie. The `frames` option is used to specify the required number of images.

```
with(plots):
animate(sin(x+phi), x=-1..8, phi=0..2*Pi, frames=30);
```

More computing time is used by the following command which represents a diverging three-dimensional sine wave. The range of ϕ has on purpose not been chosen from 0 to 2π – otherwise, one image of the movie would occur twice and the movie would show a perceptible jerk.

```
animate3d(sin(sqrt(x^2+y^2)+phi), x=-6..6, y=-6..6, phi=0..2*Pi-2*Pi/15,
  frames=15);
```

The commands below use a simple loop to calculate 10 images of a rotating spiral-shaped cochlea. The calculated drawings are stored in the list *data* and displayed by means of display. The option insequence=true must be used to ensure that display does not overlay the drawings but shows them as a sequence (as a movie).

```
data:=[]:
for i from 1 to 10 do
  phi:=2*Pi/10*i:
  data:=[op(data),
      tubeplot([-t^1.5/5,3*cos(t+phi),3*sin(t+phi)], t=0..8*Pi, radius=t/8,
          scaling=constrained,grid=[60,15])]:
od:
display(data, insequence=true,  orientation=[107,56]);
```

Syntax summary

```
with(plots);
```
    activates the commands described below.

Logarithmic curves

```
logplot(f, x=x0..x1);
semilogplot(f, x=x0..x1); loglogplot(f, x=x0..x1);
```
    represent the function $f = f(x)$ in a single-logarithmic or double-logarithmic coordinate
    system. In logplot, the y axis is scaled logarithmically, in semilogplot the x axis and in
    loglogplot both axes. The option samples=[x0,x1,x2,...] can be used to specify the supporting points in which the function f is evaluated.

Two-dimensional grid graphics

```
densityplot(f, x=x0..x1, y=y0..y1);
```
   represents the values of the function $f = f(x, y)$ in the specified range by means of different shades of grey.

```
contourplot(f, x=x0..x1, y=y0..y1);
```
   represents f by means of contour lines (lines of identical function values). The option `contours=n` specifies the number of contour lines. `filled=true` can be used to obtain a surface colouring of the equipotential surfaces. The option `coloring=[col1,col2]` specifies the colours between which the colouring is to vary. (A list of predefined colours can be obtained with `?color`.)

```
contourplot3d(f, x=x0..x1, y=y0..y1);
```
   is the three-dimensional variation of `contourplot`. In addition to the options listed above, all options of `plot3d` can be used.

```
with(share): readshare(fconplot, plots):
filledcontourplot(f, x=x0..x1, y=y0..y1);
```
   is an alternative to `contourplot(...,filled=true)`. The option `levels=n` specifies the number of contour lines; `coloring=[col1,col2]` specifies the colours between which the colour of the pattern is to be varied.

Visualization of complex functions

```
complexplot([z1,z2,z3,...], style=point);
complexplot(f, t=a..b);
```
   draws the complex points $z1, z2...$ or the complex function $f(z)$. Real and imaginary parts are converted into x and y values. a and b must be real numbers, whereas z may be a complex expression (for example, $t(1 + I)$).

```
complexplot3d(f, z=a..b));
```
   represents the function $f(z)$ in three dimensions. The complex numbers a and b define the value range on the complex number plane (corresponds to x and y). The z coordinate is determined by the value of f, the colour by the phase angle of f.

```
complexplot3d([f1,f2], z=a..b);
```
   as above, except that the real function $f1$ directly determines the z coordinate, and the real function $f2$ determines the colour.

```
conformal(f, z=z1..z2, z3..z4);
```
graphically represents the conformal projection of a rectangular grid by means of the complex function $f = f(z)$. The function's z values are chosen from the complex range $z1..z2$. The resulting lines are drawn in the complex range $z3..z4$. When this option is ignored (which is the case in Release 4), the drawing range must be limited with display(conformal(...), view=[r3..r4,i3..i4]). $r3$ and $r4$ are the real parts of $z3$ and $z4$, $i3$ and $i4$ the imaginary parts.

```
rootlocus(f,z,a..b);
```
draws the locus curve for $f(z)$. For this purpose, the equation $1 + k f = 0$ is solved several times, substituting k with values from the range $a..b$. The zero points of the equation that belong together are joined with lines in different colours.

Graphics in non-Cartesian coordinate systems

```
plot(v(u), u=u1..u2, coords=c);
plot3d(w(u,v), u=u1..u2, v=v1..v2, coords=c);
```
in nearly all plot commands, the coords option can be used to specify the required coordinate system. This causes a transformation of the two or three parameters u, v and w into the Cartesian coordinates x, y and z to be carried out. A list of all 45 predefined coordinate systems together with their transformation equations can be obtained with ?coords. Particularly important coordinate systems are polar (2D), spherical (3D) and cylindrical (again 3D). For some coordinate systems, additional optional parameters can be specified, such as ellipsoidal(2,4).

```
coordplot(c, [u1..u2, v1..v2]);
coordplot3d(c, [u1..u2, v1..v2, w1..w2]);
```
represents the coordinate system c graphically by projecting, for the optionally specified value range, a grid of points obtained through the corresponding coordinate transformation in the Cartesian system. With the option labelling=true, the individual coordinates can be labelled (functions satisfactorily only for two-dimensional coordinate systems).

Special commands

```
inequal({f1(x,y)>n1, f2(x,y)<n2, ...}, x=x1..x2, y=y1..y2);
```
represents the system of two-dimensional inequalities graphically. The options optionsfeasible and optionsexcluded specify how many surfaces are to be represented whose points satisfy or do not satisfy the inequality system. optionsclosed and optionsopen control drawing of the border lines for the operators $\geq$ and $\leq$, and for $<$ and $>$. The settings are specified in the form optionxy=(color=c, thickness=n1, linestyle=n2).

```
implicitplot3d(f, x=x0..x1, y=y0..y1, z=z0..z1);
```
   represents the implicit function $f = f(x, y, z)$ in the specified value range. The number of points to be calculated can be controlled via `grid=[nx,ny,nz]`.

```
polyhedraplot([x,y,z], polytype=name, polyscale=radius);
```
   represents one of the following polyhedra: `tetrahedron`, `octahedron`, `hexahedron`, `dodecahedron` or `icosahedron`.

Animation

```
animate(f, x=x0..x1, t=t0..t1);
```
   calculates several images of the function f, varying the variable t. Subsequently, the images are displayed as a movie. The `frames` option is used to specify the number of images to be calculated.

```
animate3d(f, x=x0..x1, y=y0..y1, t=t0..t1);
```
   as above, but for three-dimensional graphics.

```
display([g1,g2,g3..], insequence=true);
```
   displays the previously calculated graphics $g1, g2, \ldots$ in animated form (as a movie).

Chapter 32

Graphics IV: graphics programming

This chapter provides an introduction to graphics programming. The contents build on the previous chapters on graphics and programming. It starts with a general description of the most important data structures used for internal management of graphics (PLOT, PLOT3D, CURVES, POLYGONS, STYLE, COLOR, MESH, and so on).

It describes the commands of the plottools package which since Release 4 provides various basic graphic elements (arc, circle, and so on), together with commands for manipulation of existing graphics (rotate, stellate, cutout, and so on).

Subsequently, three specific sample programs are presented, namely:

- the new dotplot command for drawing dot diagrams,
- the new moebius command for drawing Möbius strips, and
- the new colorplot3d command in which colouring of three-dimensional graphics can be controlled more precisely than in plot3d.

The data structures PLOT and PLOT3D

The only official documentation of Maple's graphic data structures can be found in the help topic ?plot3d, structure. This help text contains the most important information in a very short form, but no examples. This information deficit is remedied in this chapter. The most important keywords are described using numerous examples. (A complete summary of all internal graphics commands is given in the syntax summary at the end of this chapter.)

473

The following command draws two lines from $(1,1)$ to $(2,2)$ and from $(1,2)$ to $(2,1)$. Maple automatically draws both lines in different colours: one green and the other red.

```
plot([[[1,1],[2,2]],
      [[1,2],[2,1]]]);
```

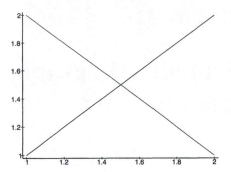

The easiest way to gain access to graphics programming is to look at the code of normal Maple diagrams. The internal structure of the diagram just calculated can simply be viewed with `lprint`:

```
lprint(");
  PLOT(CURVES([[1., 1.], [2., 2.]],COLOR(RGB,1.0,0,0)),
  CURVES([[1., 2.], [2., 1.]],COLOR(RGB,0,1.0,0)))
```

Graphics are stored by Maple in the `PLOT` and `PLOT3D` commands. During execution of these commands, the data contained in them is automatically displayed. Inside these commands, the elements of the graphics are in turn described by means of special commands, such as `CURVES` for specification of the coordinate points of a continuous line or `COLOR` for specification of colours. Many of these commands are homonymous with the options of the `plot` and `plot3d` graphics commands and differ from these only by their upper case spelling. The two following subsections discuss the most important graphics commands inside `PLOT` and `PLOT3D`.

Graphics commands in PLOT structures

The two most important graphics commands used inside `PLOT` are `CURVES` and `POLYGONS`. They can be used to draw lines and filled surfaces. Inside the commands, the coordinate points are specified in list form. For specification of several polygons in `POLYGONS`, the points of the individual polygons must be indicated in separate lists.

Colour setting is carried out via `COLOR(RGB, r, g, b)`, where r, g and b must each lie between 0 and 1. Alternatively, `COLOR(HUE, h)` is allowed. Colour specifications can either be set inside `CURVES` or `POLYGONS`, in which case they apply to the graphics elements described in the commands, or they can be set outside these commands, in which case they apply as the default setting for all graphics elements. In the graphics window, only those settings can be changed that have been carried out outside.

`STYLE` is used to specify how `CURVES` or `POLYGONS` data is to be displayed: `STYLE(POINT)` displays points, `STYLE(LINE)` displays lines, and `STYLE(PATCH)` displays colour-filled polygons. `STYLE(PATCH)` is only relevant inside `POLYGON` and even there only when a colour is specified at the same time.

The following examples illustrate the syntax of the graphics commands. Each example begins with the PLOT command. During execution of this command, the diagram is shown on screen in a separate window. For reasons of space, we omit printing these trivial drawings.

```
# draws a continuous line
PLOT(CURVES([[1,1],[2,2],[3,2],[4,2]], COLOR(RGB,0,0,0)));

# 4 points
PLOT(CURVES([[1,1],[2,2],[3,2],[4,2]], COLOR(RGB,0,0,0)),
    STYLE(POINT));

# line + 2 points
PLOT(CURVES([[1,1],[2,2],[3,2],[4,2]], COLOR(RGB,0,0,0), STYLE(LINE)),
    CURVES([[1,1.5],[2,2.5]], COLOR(RGB,1,0,0), STYLE(POINT)));

# two empty triangles
PLOT(POLYGONS([[1,1],[2,2],[1,3]], [[2,1],[2.5,2],[3,1]]));

# two empty triangles, STYLE does not change anything
PLOT(POLYGONS([[1,1],[2,2],[1,3]], [[2,1],[2.5,2],[3,1]],
              STYLE(PATCH)));

# two triangles filled with different colours (border colour 0),
# default option for STYLE is PATCH
PLOT(POLYGONS([[1,1],[2,2],[1,3]], COLOR(RGB,1,0,0)),
    POLYGONS([[2,1],[2.5,2],[3,1]], COLOR(RGB,0,1,0)));

# one triangle filled red, the other one outlined green
PLOT POLYGONS([[1,1],[2,2],[1,3]], COLOR(RGB,1,0,0), STYLE(PATCH)),
    POLYGONS([[0,1],[2.5,2],[3,1]], COLOR(RGB,0,1,0), STYLE(LINE)));
```

There is no possibility of drawing a polygon directly with a green fill and a red border. You can first draw a green filled polygon and subsequently a red continuous line (with CURVES). Please note, however, that with CURVES the common starting and ending point must be specified twice in order to close the line.

Maple provides no commands to draw sweeping curves or splines. In order to make a sine curve look smooth, a suitably high number of coordinate points must be specified in CURVES.

Besides the commands described above, there are others which are used to set coordinate axes, visual range, and so on. A summary of all these commands is given in the syntax summary at the end of this chapter.

Graphics commands in PLOT3D structures

The central data structures in PLOT3D are GRID and MESH. GRID contains the z coordinates of a rectangular three-dimensional surface rowwise in an embedded list. MESH is more flexible and allows description of arbitrarily shaped three-dimensional surfaces.

When you want to view the internal code of three-dimensional graphics previously generated by means of `plot3d` or related commands, you will be confronted with a problem: a three-dimensional drawing is composed of a huge mass of data whose display on screen results in many pages of dead numbers. In order to reduce the quantity of data to a reasonable size, you must use the `grid` option and drastically reduce the number of points to be drawn.

The illustration on the right shows the surface $z = x - y$. The number of corner points is reduced to only nine. (The default setting is $15 * 15 = 225$ points.) The drawing is stored in p and only subsequently displayed. Please note that the internal command terminates with a colon and thus prevents display of internal data.

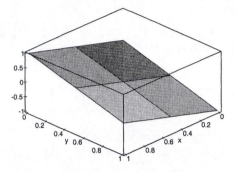

```
p:=plot3d(x-y, x=0..1, y=0..1,
     grid=[3,3], axes=boxed
     style=patch): p;
```

The internal representation of this drawing can be viewed with `lprint`:

```
lprint(p);
     PLOT3D(GRID(0 .. 1.,0 .. 1.,[[0, -.50000000000000, -1.],
       [.50000000000000, 0, -.50000000000000], [1., .50000000000000, 0]]),
       STYLE(PATCH), AXESSTYLE(BOX), AXESLABELS(x,y,))
```

The above lines clearly show the usage of the GRID command. The first two parameters define the range of the x and y coordinates. Since the coordinate points are equally distributed in this rectangle, the specification of the z coordinates in a (rowwise embedded) list is sufficient for a complete description of the drawing.

In the above example, the unnecessarily high precision of the number values renders clear display and interpretation of the data quite difficult. Since the `plot` commands internally make use of the (usually 16-digit) floating point arithmetic of the computer, the number of digits cannot be changed with `Digits`. `evalf(p,5)` does not help either, because `evalf` knows neither PLOT3D nor GRID and therefore does not change the parameters of these commands. In order to obtain a clear display of graphic data in spite of all this, we must program a new command.

`convertf` recursively searches a Maple expression for floating point values and reduces their number of digits to a reasonable size by means of `evalf`. The basic idea of this command corresponds to that of the `nestprint` procedure in Chapter 28. The command generates a new expression *result* and recursively substitutes all occurring floating point numbers by values of less precision. For changing individual terms inside the variable *result*, the `subsop` function is employed.

```
convertf:=proc(x,n)
  local i,result, new;
  result:=x;
  if type(result,float) then
```

```
      result:=evalf(result,n):
  elif nops(result)>1 or type(result, function) then
    for i from 1 to nops(result) do:
      new:=convertf(op(i,result), n);
      result:=subsop(i=new, result):
    od:
  fi;
  result:
end:
```

Now, the new command is used to view the code of two three-dimensional drawings with individual colour control. In the first example, the colour function is directly specified by means of the `color` option; in the second example, the `COLOR` command is used for definition of RGB values. In the resulting data structures, the `COLOR` command appears inside `GRID`, which contains either one or three colour values for each point of the drawing.

In the drawing process, the rectangular partial surfaces are represented by two small triangles. For the examples, it becomes evident why these triangles often show slightly different colours: Maple does not store a colour for each of the rectangular partial surfaces, but for each of the corner points of a partial surface.

```
p:=plot3d(x-y, x=0..1, y=0..1, grid=[3,3], axes=boxed,
          color=sqrt(2*x^2+y^2)):
lprint(convertf(p, 3));

    PLOT3D(GRID(0 .. 1.,0 .. 1.,
        [[0, -.500, -1.], [.500, 0, -.500], [1., .500, 0]],
      COLOR(HUE,0,.289,.577,.408,.500,.707,.816,.866,1.)),
      AXESLABELS(x,y,''),AXESSTYLE(BOX))

p:=plot3d(x-y, x=0..1, y=0..1, grid=[3,3], axes=boxed,
          color=COLOR(RGB, x, y, x*y)): lprint(convertf(p, 3));

    PLOT3D(GRID(0 .. 1.,0 .. 1.,
        [[0, -.500, -1.], [.500, 0, -.500], [1., .500, 0]],
      COLOR(RGB, 0,0,0, 0,.500,0, 0,1.,0, .500,0,0, .500,.500,.250,
        .500,1.,.500, 1.,0,0, 1.,.500,.500, 1.,1.,1.)),
      AXESLABELS(x,y,''),AXESSTYLE(BOX))
```

The `MESH` command appears more rarely. This command too defines a three-dimensional surface by way of the embedded specification of coordinate points. In contrast to `GRID`, x and y coordinates are specified as well. This allows the solid to be drawn with more flexibility. At the same time, however, the amount of data to be processed triples.

```
p:=plot3d([r*sin(phi), r*cos(phi), cos(r)], r=0..Pi, phi=0..2*Pi,
          grid=[4,4], style=patch):
lprint(convertf(p, 3));
```

```
PLOT3D(MESH([[[0, 0, 1.], [0, 0, 1.], [0, 0, 1.], [0, 0, 1.]],
    [[0, 1.05, .500], [.907, -.524, .500], [-.907, -.524, .500],
    [-.584e-14, 1.05, .500]],
    [[0, 2.09, -.500], [1.81, -1.05, -.500], [-1.81, -1.05, -.500],
    [-.117e-13, 2.09, -.500]],
    [[0, 3.14, -1.], [2.72, -1.57, -1.], [-2.72, -1.57, -1.],
    [-.175e-13, 3.14, -1.]]]),
  STYLE(PATCH))
```

As with GRID, explicit colours for individual points can be specified with COLOR. Instead of indicating a list of colour values, one of the following keywords can be used in COLOR to select one of Maple's predefined colour distribution algorithms: XYZSHADING, XYSHADING, ZSHADING, ZHUE, ZGREYSCALE and NONE (see Chapter 20).

The information on the remaining PLOT3D commands can be found in the syntax summary at the end of this chapter.

The plottools package

Since Release 4, graphics programming is supported by means of the plottools package. This package contains two types of command:

- Basic graphic elements, such as arc, from which drawings can be assembled. The result is a list of commands such as CURVES (see previous section). These commands can be displayed as graphics with display.

- Transformation commands such as rotate or cutout which can be used to modify existing drawings.

This section gives an introduction to the handling of these commands, but does not discuss each command in detail. A complete list of all two-dimensional and three-dimensional basic elements can be found in the syntax summary at the end of this chapter.

The construction of drawings from basic elements is very simple: as with the plot commands, besides their parameters, the plottools commands too can be passed additional options to control the look of the elements (colour, line style). Further options can be passed to display – however, these options then change the global result and not an individual element. Obviously, several elements can be combined into a list and then drawn together.

```
restart: with(plots): with(plottools):
display(arc([1,1], 1, 0..Pi/2,
        thickness=3),
    axes=boxed);
```

```
cseq:=seq(arc([1,1], n/100,
    n/100..2+n/100), n=1..100):
display([cseq], axes=none);
```

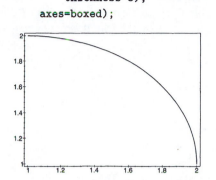

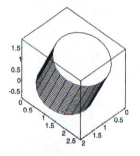

Transformation commands such as `rotate`, `translate` or `scale` can be applied both to basic elements and to finished drawings. The following four illustrations show the effect of `rotate`, once on a cylinder created with `cylinder` and once on a three-dimensional surface created with `plot3d`. Please note that in the second case, no `display` command is needed.

```
cyl:=cylinder([1,1,0], 1, 2):
display([cyl], axes=boxed);
```

```
c1:=rotate(cyl,Pi/8,0,0):
display(c1,axes=boxed,
    scaling=constrained);
```

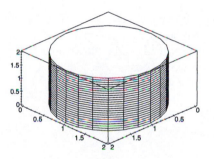

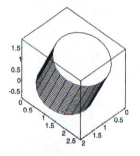

```
p:=plot3d(sin(x*y), x=0..3, y=0..3,
    axes=boxed, style=patch): p;
```

```
rotate(p, 0,Pi/2, 0);
```

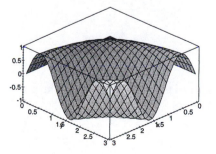

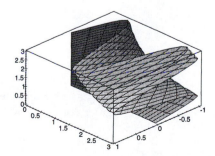

stellate determines the centre point of all passed polygons and, depending on the value of the second parameter n, shifts it outwards ($n > 1$) or inwards ($n < 1$). With this, several triangles are created from each polygon (which internally are obviously again represented as polygons). The following illustrations show this effect on a cube. The variable *opts* contains a set of options that are also used in the subsequent illustrations. The options are chosen in such a way that they guarantee the best possible quality in black and white printing.

```
cub:=cuboid([0,0,0],[1,1,1]):
opts:=style=patch, scaling=constrained, orientation=[45,66],
      color=grey, shading=none, lightmodel=light4:
```

```
display(cub, opts);
```
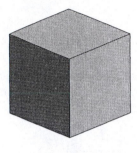

```
cs:=stellate(cub, 0.7):
display(cs, opts);
```
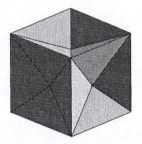

cutin reduces each polygon by the factor specified in the second parameter. cutout has the reverse effect: the inner part is cut out of the polygon. Both commands create transparent three-dimensional structures which are more recognizable, in particular with intertwined solids. Please note the square brackets around *cs* in the following two commands: these are needed because *cs* contains a sequence of POLYGON commands, whereas cutin and cutout expect a list.

```
display(cutin([cs], 3/4), opts);
```
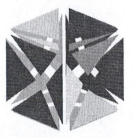

```
display(cutout([cs], 3/4), opts);
```
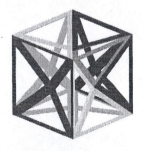

stellate, cutin and cutout assume that the data is present as POLYGON structures. The results of the plot3d command must be converted by means of convert(p, POLYGONS).

```
p:=plot3d(sin(x*y), x=0..2, y=0..2,
          grid=[15,15]):
pol:=convert(p,POLYGONS):
display(cutout(pol, 3/4), style=patch,
  color=grey, lightmodel=light4,
  axes=framed);
```

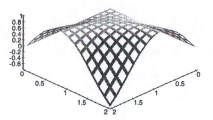

The dotplot command for the representation of point diagrams

When the option `style=point` is specified in the `plot` command, Maple does not join the data points with a continuous line, but represents each point with a small dot. These points, however, are relatively tiny and cannot be made substantially bigger with the option `symbolstyle`.

Here, the `dotplot` command affords relief. It draws the points as small regular polygons whose radius can be arbitrarily chosen. The command has already been employed in Chapter 22 where the task was to draw an interpolation curve through several given points.

The generation of the polygon lists is carried out with a separate procedure, namely by `polyg`. In five parameters, this command expects the x and y coordinates of the centre, the radii in the horizontal and vertical directions, plus the required number of corner points. As a result, the command supplies an embedded list containing the coordinates of the polygon. The calculating precision is limited to five digits.

```
polyg:=proc(x::numeric, y::numeric, rx::numeric, ry::numeric, n::numeric)
  local data, i;
  data:=[];
  for i from 0 to evalf(2*Pi-0.00001) by evalf(2*Pi/n) do
    data:=[op(data), [evalf(x+rx*sin(i),5), evalf(y+ry*cos(i),5)]];
  od;
  data;
end:
```

The two examples show the general usage of
polyg and the generation of a drawing using the
new command.

```
polyg(2, 2, 0.1, 0.1, 3);
```

$[[2.0, 2.1], [2.0866, 1.9500], [1.9134, 1.9500]]$

```
PLOT(POLYGONS(
    polyg(1,1,0.1, 0.1, 50),
    polyg(2,2,0.1,0.1,50),
    COLOR(RGB,0,0,0)),
  SCALING(CONSTRAINED));
```

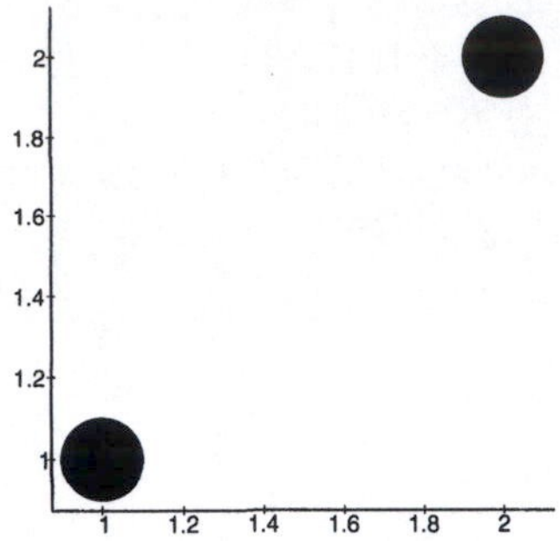

Now to the new `dotplot` command which uses `polyg`. The command is passed a list of coordinate points and the required radius. The required radius strongly depends on the coordinate ranges of the points. An optional third parameter can be used to set the proportion between horizontal and vertical radius. This becomes necessary when the x and y axes of the drawing are scaled differently (which is usually the case). The two examples below illustrate the effect of this parameter.

There is not much to be said about the code of the procedure: the list of polygon data is constructed in the local variable. It is assumed that the first parameter is of the form $[[x0, y0], [x1, y1], ...]$. The polygons are assembled from 25 points, which is largely sufficient for a round shape (at least for small radii). Subsequently, the coordinate points are placed into a POLYGON command and drawn with PLOT.

```
dotplot:=proc(data::list, rx::numeric)
  local i, pol, prop;
  if nargs>=3 then prop:=args[3]: else prop:=1: fi:
  pol:=[];
  pol:=seq(polyg(data[i][1], data[i][2], rx, rx*prop, 25),
           i=1..nops(data));
  pol:=POLYGONS(pol, COLOR(RGB,0,0,0));
  PLOT(pol):
end:
```

The following two commands illustrate the importance of the third parameter of `dotplot`: in the illustration on the left, the four points to be represented are drawn as circles of radius 0.1. Since the visible range of the x axis goes from 1 to 4, whereas the y axis range only goes from 1 to 2, the two axes are scaled differently, and the circles are distorted to ellipses. The second parameter can be used to prevent this distortion. Unfortunately, you will have to rely on trial and error, because the scaling of the axes depends not only on the coordinate range but also on the size of the graphics window or the paper you use for printing.

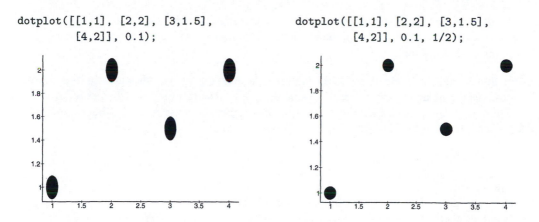

```
dotplot([[1,1], [2,2], [3,1.5],
        [4,2]], 0.1);
```

```
dotplot([[1,1], [2,2], [3,1.5],
        [4,2]], 0.1, 1/2);
```

Several other illustrations using `dotplot` can be found in Chapter 22, where point diagrams were combined with lines of interpolation curves.

The moebius command for representation of Möbius strips

Möbius strips are strips that are turned in on themselves by 180 degrees. Maple provides no command with which such strips can be directly drawn. A representation is therefore only possible by direct generation of a `PLOT3D(MESH(...))` structure.

The `moebius` command expects three parameters: a list of the coordinates of a frame lying in the z plane which after a z axis rotation by 180 degrees again shows its original form, the radius of the Möbius strip, and the required number of partial surfaces from which the strip is to be assembled. As the result, the command supplies an embedded list which can be displayed with `PLOT3D(MESH(...))`.

```
frame:=[[-1.5, 0.5, 0],
 [1.5, 0.5, 0],[1.5, -0.5, 0],
 [-1.5, -0.5, 0],[-1.5, 0.5, 0]];

PLOT3D(
  MESH(moebius(frame, 4.5, 40)),
  SCALING(CONSTRAINED),
  SHADING(XYZSHADING),
  STYLE(PATCH),
  ORIENTATION(-118,-104));
```

Now to the code of the new command which is split across a total of four procedures: `rotatex`, `rotatey` and `rotatez` rotate the points specified by their three-dimensional coordinate points by a given angle around the x, y or z axis. The coordinates must be specified in the form $[[x0, y0, z0], [x1, y1, z1], ...]$. The rotation angle is specified in degrees (not in radians). `translate` shifts the points by the vector $[dx, dy, dz]$.

Note: Unlike the `plottools` commands (described earlier in this chapter) the commands introduced in this section only process pure coordinate lists. The transformation of coordinates into `plot` expressions is not possible!

`moebius` first rotates the frame passed as the parameter around the z axis, subsequently shifts it from the coordinate centre and finally rotates it around the y axis. The resulting coordinates are stored in a list. These steps are repeated with increasing rotation angles until the frame has been completely rotated around the y axis and by 180 degrees around the z axis.

```
rotatex:=proc(pts::list, angle)
  local i,pi,y0,z0,sinus,cosinus,newlist;
  pi:=evalf(Pi);
  sinus:=sin(angle/180.*pi); cosinus:=cos(angle/180.*pi);
  newlist:=[];
  for i from 1 to nops(pts) do:
    y0:=cosinus*pts[i][2]-sinus*pts[i][3];
    z0:=cosinus*pts[i][3]+sinus*pts[i][2];
    newlist:=[op(newlist),[pts[i][1],y0,z0]];
  od;  newlist;
end:
rotatey:=proc(pts::list, angle)
  local i,pi,x0,z0,sinus,cosinus,newlist;
  pi:=evalf(Pi);
  sinus:=sin(angle/180.*pi); cosinus:=cos(angle/180.*pi);
  newlist:=[];
  for i from 1 to nops(pts) do:
    x0:=cosinus*pts[i][1]-sinus*pts[i][3];
    z0:=cosinus*pts[i][3]+sinus*pts[i][1];
    newlist:=[op(newlist),[x0,pts[i][2],z0]];
  od;
  newlist;
end:
rotatez:=proc(pts::list, angle)
  local i,pi,x0,y0,sinus,cosinus,newlist;
  pi:=evalf(Pi);
  sinus:=sin(angle/180.*pi); cosinus:=cos(angle/180.*pi);
  newlist:=[];
  for i from 1 to nops(pts) do:
    x0:=cosinus*pts[i][1]-sinus*pts[i][2];
    y0:=cosinus*pts[i][2]+sinus*pts[i][1];
    newlist:=[op(newlist),[x0,y0,pts[i][3]]];
  od;
  newlist;
end:
translate:=proc(pts::list, vec::list)
  local i,newlist;
  newlist:=[];
  for i from 1 to nops(pts) do:
    newlist:=[op(newlist),
```

```
                  [pts[i][1]+vec[1],pts[i][2]+vec[2],pts[i][3]+vec[3]]];
  od;
  newlist;
end:

moebius:=proc(pts::list, r, number)
  local i, newlist, newpts;
  newlist:=[];
  for i from 0 to number do:
    newpts:=rotatez(pts, 180./number*i);
    newpts:=translate(newpts, [r,0.,0.]);
    newlist:=[op(newlist), rotatey(newpts,360./number*i)];
  od:
  newlist;
end:
```

The concluding example shows two intertwined
Möbius strips.

```
mb1:=moebius(frame,4.5, 40):
mb2:=[]:
for i from 1 to nops(mb1) do:
  mb2:=[op(mb2),translate(
      rotatex(mb1[i],90), [4,0,0])]:
od:

PLOT3D(MESH(mb1),MESH(mb2),
  SCALING(CONSTRAINED),
  ORIENTATION(95,55));
```

The colorplot3d command for precise colouring of three-dimensional graphics

It has already been explained in Chapter 20 that Maple automatically scales the colour values speci-fied in the `color` option of `plot3d` to a range between 0 and 1. On the one hand, this makes life easy because you do not have to think about the formulation of the colour function. On the other hand, this has the disadvantage that you cannot precisely control colour distribution in a three-dimensional drawing. Therefore, you cannot colour several three-dimensional surfaces with different z ranges in such a way that points of equal height (that is, points with the same z value) have the same colour. It is equally impossible to use a general colour legend (for example, of the kind green for $z < 0$, yellow for $0 \leq z \leq 10$ and red for $10 \leq z$). The function of colour is thus reduced to the purely aesthetic aspect.

The `colorplot3d` command presented in the following paragraphs is a variation of the `plot3d` com-mand with restrictions concerning graphics variations. The particular feature of this command is that by means of the option `color=COLOR(RGB,fr,fg,fb)` a colour function can be specified that is *not* scaled by Maple. When individual colour components become less than 0 or greater than 1, the brightness of the component in question no longer changes. The restrictions of the command compared to `plot3d` are that no parametric diagrams can be drawn and that no other `color` options can be processed. However, with a more precise evaluation of the parameters, the command could be extended in that direction.

The following two diagrams show the application of the new command: in the first diagram, the function $z(x, y) = \sin(\sqrt{x^2 + y^2}) + \sin(x)$ is drawn; in the second diagram, the function value is generally increased by 1. In both diagrams, the same function is used to calculate the colour values: z values between -2 and 2 are represented by shades of grey between black and white. Since the lower diagram shows higher z values, the entire diagram appears brighter.

```
greyscale:=(x)->COLOR(RGB,x,x,x):
z:=sin(sqrt(x^2+y^2))+sin(x):
colorplot3d(z, x=-10..6, y=-10..5,
   color=greyscale(z*0.25+0.5),
   grid=[30,30], view=-2..3,
   axes=boxed, scaling=constrained);
```

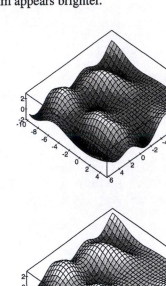

```
z:=1+sin(sqrt(x^2+y^2))+sin(x):
colorplot3d(z, x=-10..6, y=-10..5,
   color=greyscale(z*0.25+0.5),
   grid=[30,30], view=-2..3,
   axes=boxed, scaling=constrained);
```

Now to the code of the new procedure. The procedure expects four parameters. Three of them are listed in the parameter list; the fourth parameter of the form `color=COLOR(RGB,r,g,b)` must be specified as an option (at any point in the parameter list). During the evaluation of the options, only `grid=` and `color=` are taken into account directly. If the `grid` specification is omitted, 15*15 data points are calculated. From the `color` setting, the list of functions $[fr, fg, fb]$ is extracted and stored in the local variable c.

Both options are deleted from the option list by means of `subsop(i=NULL,opts)`. For this reason, incrementing the loop variable i is carried out in the `else` part of the loop. At the end of the procedure, the remaining options are passed to `display` and taken into consideration there.

The main task of the loop for calculation of graphic and colour data is to insert the two loop variables x and y into f and c. The names of the variables in f and c can be found in the local variables *varx* and *vary* and were taken from the two parameters *xrange* and *yrange*. The data lists for the diagram as such and its colour values differ in the sense that the first list is embedded, whereas the second list is linear. This is the reason why op is used quite a lot to turn lists into sequences when assembling the colour list.

Subsequently, the diagram is assembled with PLOT3D, GRID and COLOR and passed to display. This command is called in the long form plots[display] in order to avoid activation of the whole plots package.

```
colorplot3d:=proc(f::algebraic, xrange::'=', yrange::'=')
  local varx, vary, x, x0, x1, y, y0, y1, c, i, j, opts, gridopt,
        dataf1, dataf2, datac1, datac2:
  Digits:=6:
  #
  #     evaluate parameters
  #
  varx:=op(1,xrange): vary:=op(1,yrange):
  x0:=evalf(op(1, op(2,xrange))): x1:=evalf(op(2, op(2,xrange))):
  y0:=evalf(op(1, op(2,yrange))): y1:=evalf(op(2, op(2,yrange))):
  #
  #     evaluate options
  #
  gridopt:=[15, 15]:       # Default setting
  opts:=[args[4..nargs]]:
  i:=1:
  while i<=nops(opts) do:
    if type(opts[i], identical('grid')=list) then
      gridopt:=rhs(opts[i]):
      opts:=subsop(i=NULL, opts):  # delete from option list
    elif type(opts[i], identical('color')=function) or
         type(opts[i], identical('COLOR')=function) then
      c:=[op(2..4, rhs(opts[i]))]:
      opts:=subsop(i=NULL, opts):  # delete from option list
    else
      i:=eval(i)+1:
    fi:
  od:
  if c='c' then  # color option not found
    ERROR('incorrect or missing color function color=COLOR(RGB,r,g,b)'):
  fi:
  #     loop for calculation of graphic and color data
  #
  dataf1:=[]: datac1:=[]:
  for i from 1 to gridopt[1] do:
    x:=evalf(x0+(x1-x0)/(gridopt[1]-1)*(i-1)):
    dataf2:=[]: datac2:=[]:
    for j from 1 to gridopt[2] do:
      y:=evalf(y0+(y1-y0)/(gridopt[2]-1)*(j-1)):
      dataf2:=[op(dataf2), evalf(subs(varx=x, vary=y, f))]:
```

```
      datac2:=[op(datac2), op(evalf(subs(varx=x, vary=y, c)))]:
    od:
    dataf1:=[op(dataf1), dataf2]:
    datac1:=[op(datac1), op(datac2)]:
  od:
  #      display of drawing taking the remaining options into consideration
  #
  plots[display](PLOT3D (GRID(x0..x1, y0..y1, dataf1,
                               COLOR(RGB, op(datac1)))), op(opts));
end:
```

An application example to conclude: the illustration on the right shows the value of the complex function $\sin(x + Iy)$. The grey shades indicate the phase of the function: from dark grey for -180 degrees to white for 180 degrees.

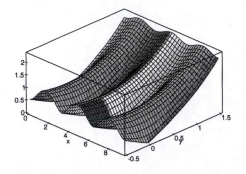

```
f:=sin(x+I*y):
colorplot3d(abs(f), x=-0..3*Pi,
  y=-0.5..1.5, color=greyscale(
    0.33+(Pi+argument(f))/(3*Pi)),
  orientation=[-45,45],
  grid=[40,40], axes=boxed,
  labels=['x', 'y', '']);
```

Syntax summary

```
PLOT(...);      PLOT3D(...);
```
  contain the graphics commands and options described below. The options COLOR and STYLE may be specified either inside or outside a graphics command and then apply either to that command alone or as a default setting. The remaining options must be specified outside a graphics command. The syntax of the options is specified for three-dimensional application. The parameter for the z component must be omitted for use with PLOT.

```
PLOT[3D](ANIMATE([...]), ...);
```
  contains a list of graphics commands for (three-dimensional) animations.

Graphics commands

```
CURVES([[x0,y0], [x1, y1]...], ...)
```
  contains the coordinates of a two-dimensional line or point diagram.

POLYGONS([[x0,y0], [x1,y1]...], ...)
    contains the coordinates of a two-dimensional polygon.

GRID(x0..x1, y0..y1, [[z00, z01, z02...],[z10,z11...]...], ...)
    contains the data of a rectangular three-dimensional surface.

MESH([[[x00,y00,z00], [x01,y01,z01],...],
      [[x10,y10,z10], [x11,y11,z11]...]...], ...)
    contains the data of a generic three-dimensional surface.

TEXT([x0,y0,z0], 'text', ...)
    defines the location and contents of a text. In the third parameter, horizontal and vertical
    text alignment can be specified by means of ALIGNABOVE or ALIGNBELOW and ALIGNLEFT or
    ALIGNRIGHT (the default is centred for both).

Options

AXESSTYLE(...)
    specifies the appearance of coordinate axes: possible settings are BOX, FRAME, NORMAL and NONE.

AXESLABELS(xt, yt, zt)
    specifies the location of axis labelling. For each of the three parameters a list of the form
    $[x0, x1, x2, ...]$ or $[x0 = $ 'text0', $x1 = $ 'text1', ...] or the keyword DEFAULT can be specified.

COLOR(HUE,h0, h1, h2, ...)
COLOR(RGB,r0,g0,b0, r1,g1,b1, ...)
    specifies the colour of a line/polygon or the colours of the partial surfaces of a three-
    dimensional surface.

COLOR(...)
    selects a standard algorithm for colouring three-dimensional graphics: XYZSHADING, XYSHADING,
    ZSHADING, ZHUE, ZGREYSCALE or NONE.

CONTOURS(n)   or   CONTOURS([c1,c2,c3,...])
    define number or location of contour lines. This option only makes sense in combination with
    STYLE(CONTOUR) or STYLE(PATCHCONTOUR).

LABELS('x', 'y', 'z')
    specifies the labelling texts for the coordinate axes.

LIGHT(phi, theta, r,g,b), AMBIENTLIGHT(r,g,b)
    define the illumination of a three-dimensional solid.

PROJECTION(n)
    specifies perspective distortion ($n = 0$ to 1).

```
SCALING(...)
```
   specifies axis scaling: CONSTRAINED or UNCONSTRAINED.

```
STYLE(...)
```
   specifies the graphic representation of data: POINTS, LINE, PATCH, CONTOUR, PATCHNOGRID, PATCHCONTOUR, HIDDEN.

```
TITLE('text')
```
   specifies the title of the drawing.

```
VIEW(x0..x1, y0..y1, z0..z1)
```
   defines the visible section of the drawing.

The plottools package

```
with(plottools);
```
   activates the commands of the plottools package. These commands allow you to generate and subsequently transform two-dimensional and three-dimensional basic graphic elements.

Two-dimensional basic graphic elements

```
arc([x,y], r, angle1..angle2)
arrow([x1,y1], [x2,y2], width, arrow_width, arrow_length)
circle([x,y], rad)
curve([[x1,y1], [x2,y2], ...])
disk([x,y], rad)
ellipse([x,y], rada, radb)
ellipticArc([x,y], rada, radb, angle1..angle2)
hyperbola([x,y], a, b, from..to)
line([x1,y1], [x2,y2])
pieslice([x,y], rad, angle1..angle2)
point([x,y])
polygon([[x1,y1], [x2,y2],...])
rectangle([x1,y1], [x2,y2])
```

Three-dimensional basic graphic elements

```
arrow([x1,y1,z1], [x2,y2,z1], [nx,ny,nz], width, arrow_width, arrow_length)
cone([x,y,z], rad, height)
cuboid([x1,y1,z1], [x2,y2,z2])
cylinder([x,y,z], rad, height)
```

```
dodecahedron([x,y,z], rad)
hemisphere([x,y,z], rad)
hexahedron([x,y,z], rad)
icosahedron([x,y,z], rad)
line([x1,y1,z1], [x2,y2,z2])
octahedron([x,y,z], rad)
point([x,y,z])
polygon([[x1,y1,z1], [x2,y2,z2],...])
semitorus([x,y,z], angle1..angle2, inner_rad, outer_rad)
sphere([x,y,z], rad)
tetrahedron([x,y,z], rad)
torus([x,y,z], inner_rad, outer_rad)
```

Transformation commands

```
convert(plot, POLYGONS);
cutin(poly, n);
cutout(poly, n);
rotate(plot2d, angle);
rotate(plot3d, anglex, angley, anglez);
scale(plot2d, sx, sy);
scale(plot3d, sx, sy, sz);
stellate(poly, n);
translate(plot2d, dx, dy);
translate(plot3d, dx, dy, dz);
f:=transform((u,v,w) -> [fx(u,v,w), fy(u,v,w), fz(u,v,w)]): f(plot3d);
```

The transformation commands are applied either to the result of a plot command or to a list of POLYGON commands. If needed, convert(plot, POLYGONS) can be used to convert MESH or GRID structures into polygons. transform carries out a coordinate transformation: for this purpose, a functional operator with two or three parameters (for two-dimensional or three-dimensional graphics) must be defined which returns a list of the new coordinates as its result. As its result, transform supplies a transformation function which is capable of processing Maple's internal graphics structures.

The new graphics commands of this section

```
dotplot([[x0,y0], [x1,y1]...], r, prop);
```

represents the specified data points by means of circles with radius r. The optional parameter *prop* specifies the elliptic distortion of the circles (default 1, that is, no distortion).

```
PLOT3D(MESH(moebius(frame, r, n)));
```
draws a Möbius strip. $frame$ contains the coordinate points of the cross-section in the form $[[x0, y0, 0], [x1, y1, 0], ...]$. The cross-section must show a 180-degree symmetry with regard to the z axis. r specifies the radius of the Möbius strip, n the number of partial surfaces.

```
colorplot3d(f, x=x0..x1, y=y0..y1, color=COLOR(RGB,fr,fg,fb), options);
```
draws the function $f = f(x, y)$, using the functions fr, fg and fb for colouring. Unlike plot3d, the colour values of these functions are not scaled and should therefore lie between 0 and 1.

Appendix A

Mathematica versus Maple

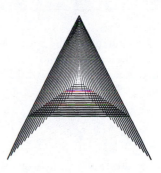

Besides Maple, Mathematica ranks among the most developed and the most widespread mathematical programs. Both programs have their advantages and disadvantages, and both have their faults. A decisive argument for the parallel use of both programs is their reliability. Since the programs originated independently of each other, two matching solutions for a mathematical problem give a very high probability that the solution is definitely correct.

It is obviously impossible to give a true introduction to Mathematica (and in a book on Maple, there is also no need), but nevertheless this appendix is intended to help you transfer the knowledge acquired in Maple as quickly as possible to Mathematica. The appendix gives specific tips on the different syntax conventions and describes commands for conversion of mathematical expressions between Mathematica and Maple.

Mathematica quick start

At first sight, Mathematica and Maple appear to be very similar. Many important commands – apart from some different syntax conventions – are handled in much the same way. The following Mathematica commands offer a first impression.

In the three commands on the right, the function f is defined, then its first derivative is constructed and subsequently simplified. Please note the different syntax: no terminating semicolon, assignments with =, square brackets, upper case and lower case spelling, access to the last result via %.

```
f=(x+1)/(x^2-3)
```
$$\frac{1+x}{-3+x^2}$$

```
D[f, x]
```
$$\frac{-2\,x\,(1+x)}{(-3+x^2)^2} + \frac{1}{-3+x^2}$$

```
fd=Simplify[%]
```
$$-\frac{3+2\,x+x^2}{(-3+x^2)^2}$$

Solve calculates the zero points of the derivative; the equation must be formulated with ==. Integrate essentially works in the same way as int.

Solve[fd==0, x]

$$\{\{x \to \frac{-2 - 2i\sqrt{2}}{2}\}, \{x \to \frac{-2 + 2i\sqrt{2}}{2}\}\}$$

fi=Integrate[f,x]

$$-\frac{\mathrm{ArcTanh}(\frac{x}{\sqrt{3}})}{\sqrt{3}} + \frac{\log(3 - x^2)}{2}$$

The illustration on the right shows the function f (double line thickness) and its first derivative. Plot is handled in the same way as plot, with the exception that ranges are specified in the form $\{x, x0, x1\}$ and options with ->.

```
Plot[{f, fd}, {x,0,5},
  PlotRange->{-10,10},
  PlotStyle->{Thickness[0.004],
              Thickness[0.002]}]
```

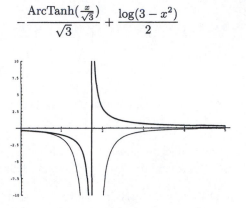

Since Version 3, Mathematica supports direct input and output of mathematical formulae.

$$\int \frac{1}{\pi + x^2} dx$$

$$\frac{\mathrm{ArcTan}\left[\frac{x}{\sqrt{\pi}}\right]}{\sqrt{\pi}}$$

The similarities between Maple and Mathematica resulting from the above examples conceal the fact that the two programs actually differ quite substantially.

The differences in syntax and handling between Mathematica and Maple can occasionally make you see red – often, very similar symbols have exactly the opposite meaning. Sometimes, this may make you think that this is all done on purpose and there is a system behind it, but that would probably be just a malicious supposition.

Input, notation

Malicious or not, input is terminated in Mathematica with (Shift)+(↵) and without a colon. In multi-line input, the line feed is obtained with (↵). When you want to write several commands on one line, you must separate them by semicolons – however, Mathematica will not display the results of these commands. Thus, the semicolon has the same meaning as the colon in Maple; (↵) and (Shift)+(↵) are inverted in their meaning.

In Mathematica, access to the last calculated results is obtained by means of %, %%, %%%, and so on. Alternatively, you can also specify %n to refer to the nth result. (In Mathematica, all input and output is automatically numbered sequentially.)

For multiplication of numbers, variables or functions, a space is sufficient in Mathematica – such as in x y. In unequivocal cases – for example 2x – you may even do without it.

In Mathematica, comments are initiated with (* and terminated with *).

Many commands can be specified in Mathematica in postfixed form with the operator //. This notation allows you to carry out easy modifications at a later stage and reduces the number of necessary bracket levels.

```
{{1,2},{3,4}}  // MatrixForm  (* displays the list as a matrix *)
Pi // N                       (* evaluates Pi numerically *)
D[x^2/(1+x^2)] // Simplify     (* simplifies the derivative *)
```

Brackets () {} []

Keywords in Mathematica always begin with upper case letters (thus, Pi, E, I); parameters are always placed in square brackets (thus, Sin[x], D[f,x]). Round parentheses are only used for grouping mathematical expressions (for example, $(a + b)c$).

The Maple data types for lists, sets, arrays, tables, vectors and matrices are all expressed in Mathematica with simple lists. Lists are placed in curly brackets. Thus, a 2*2 matrix has the form $\{\{1,2\}, \{3,4\}\}$. Mathematica's symbol pair {} is the closest to Maple's symbol pair [].

Access to individual elements of a list is carried out via the specification of the index in a double pair of [[]] brackets. Thus, {a,b,c}[[2]] yields the element b.

One of the most fundamental differences in using Mathematica lies in the completely different (and much more flexible) handling of lists. This subject is discussed in detail in a separate section below.

For ranges, which in Maple are specified in the form x=a..b, the Mathematica syntax is {x,a,b}. In the Table command (which is similar to the Maple command seq), ranges can also be specified in the form {x,a,b,s}, where s defines the step width.

Assignment and comparison symbols   = := − > ==

In Mathematica, assignments are generally made with a simple = character. The Mathematica instruction a:=b corresponds to the Maple instruction a:='b', whereas in Mathematica := is used for delayed assignments. Quotes as signs for blocking automatic evaluation do not exist in Mathematica (not even in a different syntactic form) and are not necessary because of the two different assignment operators. For the formulation of equations (for example, in Solve) or of conditions, the symbol pair == is used.

In Mathematica, options are set with the character combination -> (most frequently in the Plot commands). There is no similar command to subs. Temporary substitutions in Mathematica are initiated with /. and executed with ->. The easiest way to illustrate this is an example:

```
subs(x=0, y=1, z=3, f);    #  Maple
f /. {x->0, y->1, z->3}    (* Mathematica *)
```

The curly brackets are needed when several substitutions are to be carried out at the same time.

Definition of functions

In Mathematica, functions are generally defined by means of the operator :=. After terminating the input, Mathematica does not display any result, a fact that is due to the delayed effect of :=. Don't let this confuse you.

As in Maple, a difference is made between apparent functions and true functions. However, the syntax for functions with true parameters is easier to follow than in Maple:

```
f:=Sin[x] Cos[y]          (* apparent function *)
f[x_, y_]:=Sin[x] Cos[y]  (* function with true parameters*)
```

The function parameters are directly indicated in a parameter list and must end with the underscore character _. In Mathematica, this character must *not* be used in normal variable names! The character combination x_ represents a placeholder for a pattern (in this case, for an arbitrary parameter of the function f) with the name x.

Packages

Packages are activated in Mathematica with Needs["Group`Name`"], thus, for example, Needs["Graphics`Graphics3D`"]. One crucial point is *not* to use the name of a command contained in the package prior to being activated! If, by mistake, you have done this, you must first delete this name with Remove[command] before you activate the package with Needs.

Numeric calculations

Numeric calculations are carried out in Mathematica with the N command. In this command, the required number of digits can be specified in the second parameter – otherwise, the result is shown with a maximum of six digits after the decimal point. As in Maple, symbolic calculations are to be preferred as far as possible.

Unlike Maple, Mathematica remembers the precision of every numeric expression. 0.1 is only valid for six digits (minimum precision), whereas the value 0.100000000 is precise for nine digits. When two values of different precision are used in a calculation operation, Mathematica considers only the precision of the less precise number. Thus, you always have a guarantee that the result does not contain more digits than are really precise.

```
x=0.1; y=0.000000000000000000001; x+y
```

   0.1

```
x=0.100000000000000000000; y=0.000000000000000000001; x+y
```

   0.100000000000000000001

Mathematica even considers the loss of precision in longer calculations. When you invert a 20*20 matrix of 50-digit numbers, the number of digits in the result is reduced to 42 significant digits.

Lists

The biggest problems when switching between Mathematica and Maple (no matter in which direction) are certainly caused by the different conceptions of a list. While Maple has four different data types (lists, sets, arrays, tables) and some more types derived from them (vectors, matrices), Mathematica only has lists which are enclosed in curly brackets. And while Maple provides a large number of special commands for handling different list data types, list processing in Mathematica is mostly done automatically by means of operators. Here are some examples which would be unthinkable in this form in Maple:

Mathematica calculates with lists (and thus also with vectors and matrices) in the same way as with normal individual values. In Maple, you must work with map, zip or seq or evaluate the matrix commands with evalm. The operator . calculates the inner product.

```
{x,y,z}^{a,b,c}
```
$$\{x^a, y^b, z^c\}$$
```
Sin[{x,y,z}]
```
$$\{\sin(x), \sin(y), \sin(z)\}$$

The examples on the right show two special commands: Transpose transposes an embedded list, Flatten resolves one or more levels of brackets.

```
Transpose[{{x,y,z}, {a,b,c}}]
```
$$\{\{x,a\}, \{y,b\}, \{z,c\}\}$$
```
Flatten[%]
```
$$\{x, a, y, b, z, c\}$$

The automatic processing of lists in Mathematica strongly influences the formulation of complex tasks. Where in Maple you work with seq or even construct loops with for, in Mathematica you assemble multi-line expressions with countless levels of brackets. Once you have got used to it, you will find Mathematica's syntax more elegant and efficient. One cannot deny, however, that comparable Maple constructions, which must mostly be distributed across several commands, are easier to read and understand.

Mathematica's central command for the construction of lists is Table. It combines the features of the Maple command seq and the seqn extension presented in Chapter 30. Some examples of the application of this command conclude this section.

In its simplest form, `Table` works more or less in the same way as `seq` and supplies a simple list. However, `Table` can also be used with arbitrary step width or embedded. The Maple syntax variation `seq(x, x=list)` does not exist in Mathematica, but because of the automatic processing of lists, it is not needed.

```
Table[x^2, {x,1,3}]
```
$$\{1, 4, 9\}$$
```
Table[x, {x,1,2,0.2}]
```
$$\{1, 1.2, 1.4, 1.6, 1.8, 2.\}$$
```
Table[x^y, {x,3}, {y,3}]
```
$$\{\{1, 1, 1\}, \{2, 4, 8\}, \{3, 9, 27\}\}$$

Graphics

The handling of graphics commands in Mathematica is in principle the same as in Maple: the command is passed the function to be drawn and the drawing range; all further settings are made via options.

Two examples of Mathematica graphics can be found below and at the beginning of this appendix. Also, nearly all the chapter numbers in this book were produced with Mathematica. (Many of these illustrations would also have been possible in the same form or in similar form in Maple. The Mathematica illustrations, however, were already available from a book on Mathematica published in 1992; thus, they are a recycled product.)

With `FilledPlot` from the homonymous `Graphics` package, surface areas between two curves can be highlighted. The `GridLines` and `Frame` options control the appearance of the coordinate system.

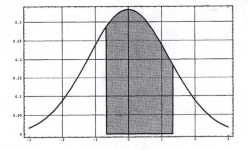

```
Needs["Graphics`FilledPlot`"]
f:=1/3/E^(x^2/3);
FilledPlot[
  {f, If[-2/3<x<4/3, 0, f]},
  {x,-3,3}, GridLines->Automatic,
  Frame->True]
```

Conversion between Maple and Mathematica expressions

Conversion from Maple to Mathematica

Since Release 3, the command `mathematica` is hidden in the `share` library. This command – which is not documented anywhere – converts Maple expressions into Mathematica syntax.

```
with(share): readshare(math,system):
mathematica(sin(sin(x^2*y^2)));
   Sin[Sin[x^2*y^2]]


mathematica(array([[a,b,c],[e,f,g]]));
   {{a, b, c}, {e, f, g}}

mathematica(Int(1/x, x=1..2));
   Integrate[1/x,{x, 1, 2}]
```

Conversion from Mathematica to Maple

For conversion of Mathematica expressions into Maple expressions, Jürgen Schmidt (Giessen University, www.uni-giessen.de/www-Mathematische-Physik) has programmed the command MapleForm and very commendably released it for distribution. In order to be able to use MapleForm, you must copy the file mathemat\maple.m from the enclosed CD-ROM into your Mathematica directory. In Mathematica, you execute the command <<maple.m to load the file.

Subsequently, you can use MapleForm in the same way as any other Mathematica command, that is, either as a function or with the // operator. When you want to prevent evaluation of a Mathematica command, you must additionally use the Hold command (see the third and fourth examples). Further information on MapleForm is given in the Mathematica Notebook math2mpl.ma which is also included on the CD-ROM.

```
Sin[Sin[x^2*y^2]] //MapleForm
   sin(sin(x^2*y^2));

MapleForm[{{a,b,c},{d,e,f}}]
   [[a, b, c], [d, e, f]];

Integrate[1/x, {x,1,2}] //MapleForm
   log(2);

Integrate[1/x, {x,1,2}] //Hold //MapleForm
   int('x^(-1)', 'x'=1..2);
```

Syntax conventions

Maple

```
command;
command:  command:  command:

command(expression);

command(expression, option=setting);

# comment

a*b;
2*Pi;
a:=b;
a:='b';
x:='x';
f:=x*y;
f:=(x,y)->sin(x)*cos(y);
gl:=2*x+3*y=1;

[[1,2],[3,4]];
list[2]; or:  op(2,list);
```

Mathematica

```
command
command; command; command;

command[expression] or:
expression //command
command[expression, option->setting]

(* comment *)

a b
2Pi
a=b
a:=b
Clear[x]
f=x*y
f[x_,y_]:=Sin[x] Cos[y]
eqn=2x+3y==1

{{1,2},{3,4}}
list[[2]]
```

Important commands

```
convert(f, parfrac, x);
diff(f,x);
dsolve({diff(y(x),x)+y(x)=1,
    y(0)=0}, y(x));
dsolve({diff(y(x),x)+y(x)=1,
    y(0)=0}, y(x), numeric);
evalf(f, n);
evalf(Int(f, x=a..b));
evalf(Limit(f, x=a));
expand(f);
factor(f);
int(f,x);
int(f,x=a..b);
limit(f, x=a);
normal(f);
plot(f, x=a..b, option=setting);
residue(f, x=a);
```

```
Apart[f,x]
D[f,x]
DSolve[{y'[x]+y[x]==1, y[0]==0},
    y[x], x]
NDSolve[{y'[x]+y[x]==1, y[0]==0},
    y[x], x]
N[f,n]
NIntegrate[f, {x,a,b}]
NLimit[f, x->a]
Expand[f]
Factor[f]
Integrate[f,x]
Integrate[f,{x,a,b}]
Limit[f, x->a]
Together[f] and:  Cancel[f]
Plot[f, {x,a,b}, Option->setting]
Residue[f, {x,a}]
```

```
seq(f,x=a..b);                    Table[f, x,a,b]
simplify(f);                      Simplify[f]
solve(f=a,x);                     Solve[f==a,x]
solvef(f=a,x);                    NSolve[f==a,x]
solvef(f=a, x, x0..x1, complex);  FindRoot[f==a, {x,xstart,x0,x1}]
subs(x=a, y=b, f);                f /. {x->a, y->b}
with(packagename);                Needs["Group`Name`"]
```

Elementary constants and functions

```
abs(x);          Abs[x]
argument(x);     Arg[x]
cos(x);          Cos[x]
exp(1);          E
I;               I
Im(z);           Im[z]
log(x);          Log[x]
Pi;              Pi
rand(a..b)();    Random[Integer, {a..b}]
Re(z);           Re[z]
sin(x);          Sin[x]
sqrt(x);         Sqrt[x]
tan(x);          Tan[x]
```

Appendix B

Contents of the CD-ROM

The CD-ROM contains all the examples in this book, the MaplePS program for processing Maple PostScript graphics (see Chapter 2), plus a Mathematica program for conversion of Mathematica expressions into Maple syntax. This appendix briefly describes the individual directories of the CD-ROM.

examples

This directory contains the example files for this book. It is divided into four subdirectories: `part1`, `part2`, `part3` and `etc`.

The directories `part1` to `part3` contain the files `chap01.mws` to `chap32.mws`. Not very surprisingly, `chap01.mws` contains the examples for Chapter 1, and so on. The worksheet files are divided into sections that match the structure of the chapters, so that individual examples can be easily found. For clarity, the examples for Chapter 4 are stored in 12 smaller files (`chap04a.mws` to `chap04k.mws`). `chap04.mws` only contains cross-references (hyperlinks) to these files.

examples\etc

`etc` contains various other files: `error.mws` contains examples with errors detected during work with Maple V Release 4. (The file has been sent to Waterloo Software by email.)

`styles.mws` is an empty Maple file containing the paragraph formats of the remaining sample files. `bwstyles.mws` is a variation which does without colours and is therefore particularly suitable for printing on black and white printers. Both files can be used via FORMAT|STYLE|MERGE EXISTING to redefine the paragraph formats of your own Maple worksheets.

mapleps

`mapleps` contains the Windows program `MaplePS.exe` in two versions: a 32-bit version for Windows 95/NT and a 16-bit version for Windows 3.1. This version should also run under OS/2. The directory also contains the source code for both versions (in Visual Basic 4.0 and 3.0). The program application is described in Chapter 2.

mathemat

`mathemat` contains two Mathematica files which allow conversion of Mathematica expressions into Maple format (see also Appendix A). In order to allow Mathematica to find the file `maple.m` with the new command `MapleForm`, `maple.m` must be copied into the Mathematica directory. The file can then be loaded with `<<maple.m`.

math2mpl.ma is a Mathematica workbook which illustrates the application of MapleForm. Similarly, the Maple file mpl2math.mws shows how Maple expressions can be converted into Mathematica syntax.

Note: The converter Mathematica → Maple has been made available by Jürgen Schmidt (Giessen University). The current version of this converter can be found on the Internet at the WWW address http://www.uni-giessen.de/www-Mathematische-Physik.

demo

demo contains demonstration versions of Maple: Release 4 for Windows and Macintosh systems, and Release 3 for UNIX systems. (You may find more up-to-date versions, bugfixes and patches on the WWW server of Waterloo Maple, Inc. at www.maplesoft.com.) The demonstration versions allow restricted use of Maple; that is, not all commands/extensions are supported. It is not possible to save or print worksheets.

References

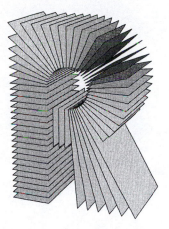

Bronstein I. N. and Semendjajew K. A. (1989). *Taschenbuch der Mathematik*, 24. Auflage. Teubner Verlagsgesellschaft

Char W., Geddes K. O., Gonnet G. H., Leong B., Monagan M. B. and Watt S. M. (1992). *Maple V First Leaves*. Springer

Char W., Geddes K. O., Gonnet G. H., Leong B., Monagan M. B. and Watt S. M. (1991). *Maple V Language Reference Manual*. Springer

Char W., Geddes K. O., Gonnet G. H., Leong B., Monagan M. B. and Watt S. M. (1991). *Maple V Library Reference Manual*. Springer

Gloggengießer H. (1993). *Maple V – Software für Mathematiker*. Markt & Technik

Heal K., Hansen M. and Rickard K. (1996). *Maple V Learning Guide*. Springer

Heck A. (1993). *Introduction to Maple*. Springer

Hörhager M. (1996). *Maple in Technik und Wissenschaft*. Addison-Wesley

Kofler M. (1995). *Mathematica – Einführung und Leitfaden für den Praktiker*. Addison-Wesley

Kopka H. (1992). LaTeX *– Eine Einführung*. Addison-Wesley

Kopka H. (1992). LaTeX *Erweiterungsmöglichkeiten*. Addison-Wesley

Kreyszig E. (1993). *Advanced Engineering Mathematics*, 7th edn. Wiley

Monagan M., Geddes K., Labahn G. and Vorkoetter S. (1996). *Programming Guide*. Springer

Peitgen H. and Richter P. (1986). *The Beauty of Fractals*. Springer

Redfern D. (1996). *The Maple Handbook*. Springer

Wolfram S. (1991). *Mathematica: A System for Doing Mathematics by Computer*. Addison-Wesley

The graduation examples in Chapter 4 have been taken (partly in a slightly modified form) from the annual reports of the Bundesrealgymnasium Adolf Pichler Platz, Innsbruck, years 1982 to 1988.

Index

Note: The page references given below refer to the beginning of the section of text in which a term is discussed and not necessarily to the page where it physically occurs.